Discovering World Religions at 24 Frames Per Second

JULIEN R. FIELDING

ATLA Publications Series, No. 4

THE SCARECROW PRESS, INC.
Lanham, Maryland • Toronto • Plymouth, UK
2008

SCARECROW PRESS, INC.

Published in the United States of America
by Scarecrow Press, Inc.
A wholly owned subsidary of
The Rowman & Littlefield Publishing Group, Inc.
4501 Forbes Boulevard, Suite 200, Lanham, Maryland 20706
www.scarecrowpress.com

Estover Road
Plymouth PL6 7PY
United Kingdom

British Library Cataloguing in Publication Information Available

Library of Congress Cataloging-in-Publication Data

Fielding, Julien R., 1969-
  Discovering world religions at 24 frames per second / Julien R. Fielding.
     p. cm. — (Atla publications series ; no. 4)
  ISBN-13: 978-0-8108-5996-8 (hardcover : alk. paper)
  ISBN-10: 0-8108-5996-3 (hardcover : alk. paper)
  eISBN-13: 978-0-8108-6266-1
  eISBN-10: 0-8108-6266-2
  1. Religion in motion pictures. 2. Asia—In motion pictures. I. Title. II. Title:
Discovering world religions at twenty-four frames per second.
  PN1995.9.R4F54 2008
  791.43'682—dc22
                                                            2008018837

∞™ The paper used in this publication meets the minimum requirements of American
National Standard for Information Sciences—Permanence of Paper for Printed Library
Materials, ANSI/NISO Z39.48-1992.

Contents

List of Films

Preface

Traditionally, university students have sat in a classroom, listened to a lecture, and read an accompanying textbook. Because of technology, times are changing. The average student checks and sends text messages through his phone, conducts research by using the Internet, watches movies on his iPod or on YouTube, and writes a blog—often all during the same sitting. This interactive environment has produced students who crave more stimulation; they want more than a dry regurgitation of facts. Because of this, educators need to make some changes to the classroom. And by that, I mean making learning more entertaining and interactive.

For my Introduction to World Religions class, I have always assigned a textbook. Not only is it portable but it also gives students something to read, highlight, and reread. They can use its dictionary, review its vocabulary lists, and answer provided questions. This said, a large number of students admit to having never read their texts. Their excuse is that they don't have either the time or the interest. Because of this, they rely on the educator for their information, and yet they complain that they have to endure another "boring old lecture." After one semester into teaching, I decided that I needed to enliven the learning environment. It was then that I hit upon the notion of screening, in class, a few feature films that contained obvious, and sometimes not so obvious, religious ideas.

To see if this would be an effective tool for learning, I asked for feedback. About 98% of the students were enthusiastic. One student explained that "the study of religion can be very difficult, and I think that films can tell stories that scripture and scholarly texts cannot." Another said, "I can read for days about [religion], and I will retain only about half of the information. Films help to paint a bigger picture." Finally, another student explained that seeing "the religion come alive on the screen helps me to remember the information better." A significant number of students admitted to being visual learners and that watching a film gave them a greater opportunity to succeed.

Before screening a film, I always give an overview of the material so that they aren't watching the film "cold." To make them active learners, I give them a list of questions to ponder while they watch the film. When we're done watching the film, we discuss every aspect, from story and characters to symbols. This gives them a chance to ask questions. Hook them with interesting characters and a good storyline, and they are sure to learn something—even if it's accidental.

This text was born from my in-class experiments, and it can be used in a variety of ways. Religious studies instructors can supplement traditional teaching techniques by screening a few films throughout the semester. I've found that this is the best way to see if students can take the ideas "off the page" and apply them. Any student can memorize dates and terms for a test, but chances are that once the test has passed, she won't have retained anything. Having her watch a film and then extricate the religious ideas makes her an active learner. She can't "wing" these exams.

This book is also intended for those who teach religion and film, which is an increasingly popular area of academic study. Unlike most of the texts on the market, which focus on Judaism and Christianity, this one covers the religions of East and Southeast Asia, specifically Hinduism, Sikhism, Zoroastrianism, Buddhism, Confucianism, Daoism, and Shinto. My initial plan was to cover all of the major religions—starting with an introduction and then covering every religion, from Hinduism to Islam—but I abandoned this for a number of reasons; I'll give a few of them. First, a quick search on Amazon.com revealed a glut of books on film and Christianity, in every imaginable form. I didn't feel the need to keep reinventing the wheel. As for Islam, there aren't any books, that I could find, specifically on religion and film, and the subject desperately needs to be covered. However, despite extensive research and viewings, I had a difficult time coming up with more than a few representative films. The problems are many. First of all, a significant number of recommended films, such as *Paradise Now* and even *Syriana*, tend to focus on the religion primarily in the context of Islamic fundamentalism, suicide bombings, and terrorism, which misrepresents the true spirit of Islam. Second, if you look to more mainstream Hollywood films, you find caricatures or worse. Little has changed in Hollywood since the embarrassing *True Lies* (1994), which features a maniacal, bomb-riding Muslim terrorist. In 2005 and again in 2007, the top-rated FOX TV series *24* cast Muslims as "nuke-detonating fanatics," prompting a backlash from Muslim-Americans.[1]

Short-listed for the chapter on Islam were *Robin Hood: Prince of Thieves* (1991), in which Morgan Freeman plays a Muslim, and *Kingdom of Heaven* (2005), which is set during the 12th century and focuses on the battle between the Crusaders and Saladin. But after more consideration, I decided that it was ridiculous to show a film about Robin Hood for a look at Islam, and the latter film, essentially an apologetic work by Ridley Scott, has been heavily criticized by scholars. Had I continued with this chapter, the only films that I might have included would have been *Le Grand Voyage* (2004), an exceptional French film about a young, liberal French-Moroccan who reluctantly drives his conservative father from the south of France to Mecca; and *Silent Waters* (2003), which I've included in the chapter on Religions in India. *Sabath: A Love Story* (2005) is a film that I found within the past few days and it looks to be promising, but I haven't had time to review it. It's an independent film from Canada about a Muslim woman who falls in love with a non-Muslim. The purpose of this text is to expose students to religious symbols, practices, and ideologies in an engaging manner. In the case of Islam, none of the films that I examined even came close to offering anything that wasn't better covered in any number of excellent documentaries.

When selecting the films that would be included in the chapters, I took several things into consideration: How easy is it to find the film? How intellectually accessible is it for a student who knows little to nothing about its religious context? How obvious is the religious tradition? How well and extensively does the film depict the religious tradition? Although students often groan when they have to watch a subtitled film, I think that showing a Confucian-themed film from China gives them a valuable window to another culture. And it's one they won't get by watching a mainstream Hollywood film.

Not everyone lives in a large and diverse metropolitan area, which means that if students can't be present during the in-class screening, they may have to rent the film and watch it outside of class. Before selecting my example films, I checked to see if they were generally available at a nationwide DVD store chain or through Netflix. (In some cases, the films can be purchased inexpensively through sources such as ebay.com or Amazon.com.) I also tried to avoid using too many obscure and hard-to-find titles for the educator's sake. Films were recommended to me, and yet I had a very difficult time getting ahold of them. Second, if a film is particularly difficult to understand, the beginner student won't stick with it. My objective is not to bore or utterly confuse the student but to open a window to a new way of seeing religion. Third, many films can be interpreted by using a religious tradition; however, you have to be very familiar with it to do this. Since, again, we're introducing students to religion and film; I wanted to keep things fairly obvious. Fourth, much academic ink has been spilled on too few films, so my objective was to unearth ones that haven't been "done to death." Finally, even though some films cover one aspect of a religion very well, they were deemed too specific for use. For instance, if you are studying Buddhism, at what do we look? Do we watch a film about Siddhartha, because he's the founder, or do we watch something about bhikkhus and bhikkhunis? Obviously, it was more difficult to come up with appropriate films for some religious traditions than others. Overall, my hope is that what I've included will prove helpful in your classroom and interesting to the students.

I absolutely love films and I love the fact that I get to share them with you. If you would like to share the experience you had while using this text, please contact me at www.jrfielding.com/contact.cfm.

On a final note, during my research I found various English translations for Sanskrit, Mandarin, and even Japanese words. Rather than research every word and figure out which method was used for that translation, I decided to use the English translations that I most commonly encountered. So it is possible that in the Chinese chapter you will encounter both Wade-Gilles and Pinyin translations. Also, you may find background material being repeated in several chapters. The reason for this is because I wrote each chapter as a standalone. You can read the book from cover to cover, and it's usually helpful to do this, but it isn't necessary.

ENDNOTE

1. For more, see "Muslims Rip '24' for Renewed Terror Role," *Associated Press*, 2007, www.msnbc.msn.com/id/16691306 (accessed 18 January 2008).

Acknowledgments

Since this book grew out of my in-class experiments, I want to thank the hundreds of students who have been my guinea pigs over the years and especially those who have provided feedback. A special thanks to the handful of students—Heather, Rachel, Matt W., Drew, Chris, Jenna, Tim, Matt F., and Emmanuel—who were so enthusiastic for this project during my fall 2007 Introduction to Religion class.

I want to thank my family for their support and encouragement, especially my mom, who read several chapters, and my husband, who not only read and commented on chapters but who also pitched in at the last minute, thus preventing this project from a complete derailment. A special thanks to Scott B. and Kristen for offering support and giving comments. It's important to have such enthusiastic cheerleaders. And much gratitude to William Blizek, PhD; the staff at the University of Nebraska at Omaha library, who renewed books again and again; Rebecca Stamberger and everyone at Allied Advertising for helping me with screenings; Reiko Take-Loukota, instructor of Japanese at the University of Nebraska at Omaha, for translations pertaining to *Spirited Away;* and the monks at the Gaden Shartse Monastery in Mundgod, Karnataka, India.

I also would like to extend my appreciation to the many filmmakers who crafted the motion pictures included in these pages, and all of the scholars whose research formed the backbone of my own. Without you, this book wouldn't exist. A special thanks to Clint Mansell, whose music from *The Fountain* provided mental stimulation during many, many long hours at a computer. To Jasper, Bodhisattva, and Fergus, thanks for reminding me, from time to time, to get out of my chair, stretch, and rejuvenate. My four-legged companions keep me sane. I also want to thank His Holiness the Dalai Lama and Thich Nhat Hanh for their tireless efforts in making the world a clearer thinking, more peaceful place.

And finally, thanks to April Snider, Andrew Yoder, Ann M. Beardsley, and everyone else at Scarecrow Press for your patience and confidence. I am eternally grateful.

1

What Is Religion?

DEFINING RELIGION

Before we begin a discussion of religion and film, we must first define "religion." A quick look at *Webster's New Collegiate* tells us that religion is "the service and adoration of God or a god as expressed in forms of worship." But do we need to have a god for religion to exist? If we say yes, this raises some problems when we look outside Western tradition. For instance, Theravada Buddhism is based on the teachings of its founder Siddhartha Gautama Shakyamuni, who, before his death, said, "You must be your own lamps; be your own refuges. Take refuge in nothing but yourselves." Buddhism doesn't deny the existence of gods or *devas*. In fact, they are believed to dwell in one of several heavens. The difference is that they, like all other beings, including humans, are also subject to *samsara*, the cycle of birth and death. Because of the accumulation of good deeds, the *devas* enjoy a very long and happy life; however, this joyful state doesn't last. Eventually they will "burn away" their good merit and will be reborn in lower realms of existence. Furthermore, their state of happiness blinds them to the realities of suffering, and thus they are hindered in their path to enlightenment.

Like Buddhism, Daoism and Confucianism, both religions of China, don't talk much about god or gods. The Dao, according to the Daodejing, isn't god per se, but a universal, impersonal force that gives rise to all things. To achieve harmony and long life, one must "exhibit the unadorned

and embrace the uncarved block, have little thought of self and as few desires as possible."[1] In the Confucian Analects, we learn that "the topics the
Master did not speak of were prodigies, force, disorder and gods" (7:21).
Confucius instead emphasized education as a way to create harmony and
order in society. So does the lack of a god or gods mean that we should reject these as religions?

It's important to realize that our traditional definition of religion is informed by a Western, monotheistic bias and by our ability to separate the sacred from the profane, the material from the spiritual. In the majority of
indigenous cultures, the line between the latter categories is blurred. They
"find the sacred within the landscape and the cycles of nature. They view
themselves as being entrusted by the Creator with the care of the earth."[2] For
them, too, the word *religion* doesn't even exist, and what we might label as religion is simply their "way of life." Judaism presents us with another interesting situation. To be Jewish is more a matter of birth than rearing, which means
a person could be culturally and socially Jewish but religiously follow something else. "This sense of kinship felt by the Jewish people may be more of a
'mystical' experience than a rationally definable one. Perhaps that is one of the
reasons why Jews have never quite been able to fit into the convenient categories used by historians or sociologists to define nations, races, religions, and
other social groupings. . . . The Jews are not just a religious faith, even though
they are that; and they are not just a nation, even though they are that too."[3]
This is why Judaism is referred to as a civilization.

So we ask again—just what makes something religious? This isn't easy to
answer. For centuries, scholars from different academic fields have grappled
with this very question and have come up with myriad answers.[4] For this text,
though, we will work with a definition posited by William A. Young in his text
The World's Religions: Worldviews and Contemporary Issues. He suggests that
"religion is human transformation in response to perceived ultimacy." To put
this into laymen's terms, when human beings perceive of "the ultimate," whatever that may be for them, they change their thoughts and outward behavior.
Let's break this definition into its basic components. From a Western perspective, the fact that human beings are the subject of our discussion may seem
obvious, but not from an Eastern or even an indigenous one. Buddhists, Jains,
and Hindus believe that being human is just one of many stages in the endless
rounds of rebirth. *Jatakas,* a compilation of more than 500 stories of the Bud-

dha's previous incarnations, show him exhibiting generosity, compassion, and sacrifice while he was a deer, a bird, an antelope, a dog, horse, monkey, bull, ox, rabbit, and even a tree-spirit. Aside from this, we can't know the experience of a rabbit or a tree, so we will focus on what we can observe—human beings. And we know that when they follow a religion, they alter or change their behavior to align with its principles; they transform themselves from one state to another.

One way a religion may ask us to change is to deny our so-called base desires. For instance, every religion that we will examine in this text tells us that we shouldn't commit murder or adultery, steal, or lie. On a very basic level, these prohibitions make sense, because by following them we avoid unnecessary societal disruption. Each religion has its own list of prohibitions. Buddhism, for example, asks its adherents to eschew drugs and intoxicating beverages. Judaism prohibits the consumption of pork and shellfish. Muslims are forbidden to convert to another religion, sometimes under the threat of death. All of these behaviors bring a person in line with other worshippers who assert a similar label. This way, if someone were to say, "I'm a Buddhist," people have a general idea of who that person is and where he or she stands on issues such as war and the consumption of meat.[5]

What makes these people transform themselves from one state to another? The ultimate can be God (monotheism), gods (polytheism), or even an impersonal force (nontheism). It can possess many different names, such as Krishna, Brahma, Great Mother, the Dao, Allah, Jehovah, and God. It can be immanent (being present in the world) or transcendent (existing beyond this world). Whatever the case, it is a force, a being, or "other" that gives meaning to life. It is, as the 20th-century theologian and philosopher Paul Tillich said, our "ultimate concern"—that which matters to us most in this world and beyond. It also helps us to make sense of who we are, where we came from, why we are here, how we should relate to others, and even where we are going after we die. Undoubtedly, religions haven't crumbled in the face of science or rational thought, because they can offer answers to these so-called answerable questions.

Religions take many forms and come in many varieties. So what makes scholars label them as religions and not philosophies? What qualities do they share? Again, this proves elusive. In their chapter on "The Nature of Religion,"[6] Alan F. Segal and Willard G. Oxtoby make several attempts at finding some unifying features. First, they take an inclusionary stance, examining those characteristics that religions seem to share. Their list includes a belief in a personal god or spirits, a path to personal experience of altered consciousness, a cohesive worshipping community, divinely sanctioned morality, and promise of life after death. After finding an exception to each one of these, they conclude that "it seems impossible to identify any feature that is absolutely essential in order for a tradition to qualify as a religion."[7] Next, they take an exclusionary stance, looking at ideologies that look like religions but are something quite different. In this category they include communism and philosophy. In the former, they conclude that while religion claims that "a power may exist above and beyond humankind," communism doesn't.[8] Communism, then, is "disqualified as a religion" because it lacks this element of transcendence.

The authors differentiate philosophy from religion in several ways. First, they explain that while philosophy is an "intellectual, rational pursuit; religion seeks a commitment of the will and the emotions." They then show that philosophical decisions are made by the individual, and decisions of a religious nature derive from the group. And finally, they state that ritual is more important to religion than it is to philosophy. In conclusion, they offer a "provisional definition" for religion, citing that it "is a sense of power beyond the human that is apprehended rationally and emotionally; appreciated corporately and individually; celebrated ritually, symbolically and discursively; and transmitted in conventionalized forms as a tradition that offers people an interpretation of experience, a view of life and death, a guide to conduct, and an orientation to meaning and purpose in the world."[9]

Ninian Smart, a 20th-century scholar, singled out about half of a dozen "shared" dimensions of religion.[10] Not all of these will be present for every religion, but they provide for us a language from which to work. The dimensions that we will look at are doctrine, myths, ethics, rituals, and symbols.

Doctrine

Doctrines are the officially sanctioned teachings of a religious institution. From this definition, we already recognize that for a doctrine to exist, it needs to have an official body behind it, a group or organization that must sanction the doctrine. In general, indigenous religions and most of the religions from Asia—Hinduism, Confucianism, Daoism, and Shinto—don't have a central authority that can serve this function. The only religions that stand out as having a definitive doctrine are Christianity, more specifically Catholicism, and Buddhism.

In the case of Catholicism, "before a teaching can be officially adopted and proposed for wider acceptance in the Church, a decision has to be made about its truth and the appropriateness of commending it to the larger community." This will be decided by an ecumenical council, a pope, or a body of bishops in union with the pope. Once a teaching becomes a doctrine, it is seen as consistent with the ecclesiastical tradition, from biblical messages to other pronouncements.[11] Drawing on the Bible, the Mass, the sacraments, church tradition and teaching, and the lives of the saints, the *Catechism of the Catholic Church*[12] is the official reference for teaching Catholic doctrine. Inside this text, one finds the Apostles' Creed and the Nicene Creed, two concise summaries of what the church teaches about God, Jesus, the Holy Spirit (in short, the Trinity), and the role of the church. "From the beginning, the apostolic church expressed and handed on her faith in brief formulae for all. But already early on, the church also wanted to gather the essential elements of its faith into organic and articulated summaries, intended especially for candidates for baptism." They are called "professions of faith," because they summarize that which Christians profess, as well as creeds, because the first word of each is usually *credo*, which in Latin means "I believe."[13] Although there are slight differences between the Nicene Creed and the Apostles' Creed, both teach that "God, the Father, . . . made heaven and Earth; [that] Jesus Christ is the son of God, was conceived of by the power of the Holy Spirit and was born of the Virgin Mary; [that] he was crucified, died, and . . . buried, [and then] in three days he rose again. He ascended into heaven and is seated at the right hand of the Father. And [that] he will come again to judge the living and the dead."[14]

Buddhism may not have a central authoritative body that makes official pronouncements for all adherents, but it does, at its core, have central teachings or doctrines on which all Buddhists agree. At its heart are the Four Noble Truths—that life is suffering, suffering comes from desire, suffering can be stopped by stopping desire, and that one must follow the Eightfold Path. Also central are the three characteristics of existence, which are suffering, impermanence, and *anatman* or "no self," and the concepts of karma, rebirth, and nirvana or enlightenment. Interestingly enough, all of these "doctrines" can be traced directly to the Buddha and his teachings. And how did the community decide this? Not long after the Buddha died, the monastic community needed to decide what the Buddha actually said and meant so that they could put these into a unified canon. They achieved this at the First Council, which lasted for seven months.[15] Discontented by the idea that to many people Buddhism is associated with "nothing beyond vegetarianism, nonviolence, peace and meditation," Dzongsar Jamyang Khyentse, a Buddhist monk and scholar, wrote *What Makes You Not a Buddhist.*[16] In the slim text, he boils everything down to four "seals," all of which were statements spoken by the Buddha: All compounded things are impermanent. All emotions are pain. All things have no inherent existence. Nirvana is beyond concepts.[17]

Although no official Jewish creed exists, Moses Maimonides, a 12th-century Jewish philosopher, formulated *13 Principles of Faith*, among which one finds: God is one, formless, all-knowing, and eternal; God gave the law to Moses; the words of the prophets are true; and Moses is chief of the prophets and it is to him that God gave Torah.[18] The fundamental Islamic objects of faith are mentioned in the Hadith of Gabriel, and they are "God, the angels, the scriptures, the prophets, the Last Day, and the measuring out. When theologians and philosophers undertook the classification and organization of religious knowledge, these six objects were divided up and placed into three broad categories known as *tawhid*, prophecy (*nubuwwa*), and eschatology or the Return (*ma'ad*). These came to be known as the three principles or roots (*asl*) of the religion." Shiites added to these justice (*'adl*) and (*imama*).[19] The foundation of Islam is acknowledging faith in Allah, who is the Absolute, transcendent yet immanent being who has existed throughout eternity. "He is the First and Last, the Visible and the Unseen. He has knowledge of all things" (Koran 57:3). To become a Muslim, one need only recite the *shahadah*, with sincerity before two Muslim witnesses: "There is no other god but God, and Muhammad is his messenger." Luminous beings incapable of disobeying God, angels are frequently mentioned in the Koran, and they serve various functions, most importantly to bring revelation (Gabriel) and to take a deceased person's soul (Azrael). The Koran mentions that God sent 3,000 angels to help in the Battle of Badr (624 C.E.)—even though outnumbered three to one, the Muslims won the day—and that "if you have patience and guard yourselves against evil, God will send to your aid 5,000 angels splendidly accoutered, if they suddenly attack you" (3:125).

The central scripture for Muslims is the Koran, which was revealed to Muhammad by the angel Gabriel. As the word of God, it is believed to be an infallible transcript of a tablet preserved in heaven. Since it was revealed in Arabic, adherents believe that "form is as essential as the meaning that the words convey. Hence only the Arabic Koran is the Koran, and translations are simply interpretations."[20] "According to Islamic understanding, God has made prophecy the central reality of human history; the cycle of prophecy began with Adam and was brought to a close with the [Koranic] revelation."[21] Some of the prophets mentioned in the Koran 21:1–21:112 include Abraham, Moses, Aaron, Isaac, Jacob, Lot, Noah, David, Solomon, and Job. Jesus, too, is considered a prophet, not a divine son of God. Muhammad is called the "seal of the Prophets" because no other prophet will come after him. Muslims believe in a Last Day or "end of times," when a person named the Mahdi will establish peace on Earth, and all humans will be resurrected to be judged, based on their actions on Earth. Those who obeyed God will enter paradise, those who didn't will go to hell. Finally, "faith in the measuring out means to understand that all good belongs to God. Everything other than God is lacking in good in some or many respects. People who have such faith will be grateful for the good they have, and they will trust God in respect of the good that they lack."[22] As one can see, doctrine is at the heart of several religions, and it represents the core ideas from which everything else develops.

Myth

Myth originally meant "sacred story," but today we frequently think of myths as untruths, fanciful exaggerated stories of ancient, bygone cultures. Ask for an example of a myth, and most people will recount a story from ancient Greece or Rome, or talk about King Arthur and his Knights of the Round Table. In the context of this book, however, myths are very real, and they serve several functions. First, they provide the worshipper with a cosmological map, explaining how everything began and where humans fit into the overall schema. Starting with the Book of Genesis, the Hebrew Bible reveals to Jews the chronological history of their people and their continued relationship with God. "The Jewish faith does not stop with 'And God created the heavens and the earth.' It starts there. It continues to acknowledge that 'I am the Lord your God who took you out of the land of Egypt.' He is a living

God, who continues to play a role in the universe He created. . . . The very essence of Judaism rests upon the acceptance of a spiritual-historical event in which our ancestors participated as a group, as well as upon acceptance of subsequent spiritual revelations to the Prophets of Israel."[23]

Until the end of World War II, the eighth-century C.E. texts, the *Kojiki* (Records of Ancient Matters) and the *Nihongi* (Chronicles of Japan from the Earliest Times to 697 C.E.) were taught in Japan as part of the educational curriculum. The *Kojiki* recounts the creation of Japan by Izanami and Izanagi, divine sister and brother; tales of Amaterasu, the Sun goddess, and myriad other *kami* or spirits; and the origin of Jimmu, the first emperor, and the Japanese people. The *Nihongi*, known as the *Nihonshoki*, also contains historical records, traditional myths, and stories relating to the imperial family and powerful clans. Furthermore, it depicts the growing influence of Indian and Chinese thought, especially Buddhism, on Japanese culture. Like the *Kojiki*, it begins in the "Age of the Gods," with the creation of Japan by the *kami*: "Izanagi-no-Mikoto and Izanami-no-Mikoto stood on the floating bridge of Heaven, and held counsel together, saying: 'Is there not a country beneath?' Therefore they thrust down the jewel-spear of Heaven, and groping about therewith found the ocean. The brine which dripped from the point of the spear coagulated and became an island which received the name of Ono-goro-jima. The two Divine thereupon descended and dwelt in this island."[24] Both of these texts contain the myths that form the basis of Shinto. Said to be composed by the sage Vyasa and dictated to Ganesha, the elephant-headed deity, the Indian epic *The Mahabharata* is presented as *itihasa-purana*, or history and myth.[25] It chronicles the struggles of the descendants of King Bharata, the legendary founder of India, while also providing its listeners or readers with "lessons on virtue, divine love . . . sacred duty and righteous practices, on character and training, on Brahma and the other gods."[26]

Second, myths contain examples of people who are worthy of emulation and those who aren't. Christians see Jesus of Nazareth, the founder of Christianity, as a role model. Today, many hold him up as the embodiment of self-sacrifice, humility, tolerance, and forgiveness, and when presented with a conflict in their own lives they ask themselves: What would Jesus do? Because it is said that Jesus and Siddhartha Gautama lived lives of chastity and poverty, Christians and Buddhists, respectively, have idealized these behaviors, thus developing a monastic dimension to these faiths.

Jews[27] look to the examples set by the prophets, especially Abraham and Moses. In Abraham, Jews see an obedient servant to God, a man who followed God's command to move to Canaan and who was willing to sacrifice his son, Isaac. He is additionally noted for his hospitality and kindness to guests. In Genesis 18:2–8, we read that "Looking up, [Abraham] saw three men standing near him. As soon as he saw them, he ran from the entrance of the tent to greet them and bowing to the ground he said, 'My lords, if it please you, do not go on past your servant. Let a little water be brought; bathe your feet and recline under a tree. Abraham hastened into the tent to Sarah, and said 'Quick, three *seahs* of choice flour. Knead and make cakes.'" After this, he finds a calf for his servant boy to prepare, and when it's ready, he sets it and curds and milk before the men.[28] Moses is revered by Jews, Muslims, and Christians because of his skills as a great visionary, leader, and redeemer. This biblical patriarch may even hold the key for businessmen—or so says Norman J. Cohen in his 2006 book, *Moses and the Journey to Leadership: Timeless Lessons of Effective Management from the Bible and Today's Leaders.* David, especially in Deuteronomistic history, is heralded as a model king who united the people of Israel, was an obedient servant to God,[29] and was a great military leader, leading his people to victory in battle as well as conquering the city of Jerusalem and bringing the Ark of the Covenant there. He also paved the way for his son, Solomon, to construct the Temple of Jerusalem. And he's credited as being the author of the Book of Psalms.[30]

Third, myths reinforce established social relationships, especially gender roles. Often these texts legitimize the woman's subordinate position. In the aforementioned *Nihongi*, Izanagi and Izanami decide that they will become husband and wife, so they make a pillar and begin walking around it. "When they met together on one side, the female deity spoke first. . . . The male deity was displeased, and said 'I am a man, and by right should have spoken first. How is it that on the contrary [you], a woman, should have been the first to speak? This was unlucky. Let us go round again." It is only when he speaks first that they get married and produce offspring.[31] Sita, the female protagonist in *The Ramayana*, is the "the model for all Indian women: pure affectionate, faithful."[32] Not only does she follow her exiled husband, Rama, into the forest for 14 years, but to prove her purity, she also agrees to a "trial by fire." Even after she is proven innocent of any sexual impropriety with the demon who abducted her, gossip gets the best of her husband and he exiles his now-pregnant woman into the forest. She remains there with her twin sons for 15 years. In *The Mahabharata*, Draupadi, wife to the five Pandava brothers, also emerges as a devoted wife who follows her husbands into exile. Interestingly enough, during the notorious dice game, one of her husbands, Yudhisthira, places her as a gambling wager. Although more a Hindu legal code than a source of mythology, *The Laws of Manu*, which is attributed to the mythical progenitor of humanity, further entrenches these views of a dependent female. It states that from girlhood to widowhood, a woman should never do anything on her own: "In childhood a female must be subject to her father, in youth to her husband, when her lord is dead to her sons. . . . Him to whom her father may give her, or her brother with the father's permission, she shall obey as long as he lives, and when he is dead, she must not insult [his memory]." And as for her personality, "She must always be cheerful, clever in [the management of her] household affairs, careful in cleaning her utensils, and economical in expenditure."[33] A similar picture of the "wife of noble character" can be found in the Book of Proverbs, from the Hebrew Bible: "She brings him good, not harm, all the days of her life. . . . She gets up while it is still dark; she provides food for her family and portions for her servant girls. . . . She watches over the affairs of her household; her husband also, and he praises her."[34]

So why is it that when we examine myths from different religious traditions we find so many similarities? Carl Jung, the 20th-century Swiss psychologist, believed that "myths are original revelations of the pre-conscious psyche, involuntary statements about unconscious psychic happenings and anything but allegories of physical processes."[35] These mythological archetypes are "manifestations of processes in the collective unconscious"[36] that "represent or personify certain instinctive data of the dark, primitive psyche, the real but invisible roots of consciousness."[37] This collective unconscious of which he speaks is a reservoir of our experiences as a species; it's our common matrix of psychic existence. Everyone is born with this reservoir and yet no one is conscious of it. Some examples of these archetypes are the hero, the maiden, the trickster, the wise old man, the shadow, and the animal.

Filmmaker George Lucas worked closely with Joseph Campbell, a Jungian, to incorporate these universal archetypes into his *Star Wars* saga,[38] and upon close inspection they are apparent. Luke Skywalker and perhaps Han Solo are the archetypal heroes on a journey who must rescue the maiden (Princess Leia) and fight against the shadow, which is often represented by a dragon, snake, or monster (Darth Vader[39] and Senator Palpatine). Our heroes in this story are aided in their quest by two wise old men (Obi-Wan Kenobi and Yoda). The trickster—a clown who causes problems for the hero—appears in the guise of Jar Jar Binks. And finally, the loyal animal archetypes can be found in Chewbacca and perhaps even C-3PO and R2-D2.[40] Campbell believed that myth served four functions: "realizing what a wonder the universe is, and what a wonder you are, and experiencing awe before this mystery" (mystical); "showing you what the shape of the universe is, but showing it in such a way that the mystery again comes through" (cosmological); "supporting and validating a certain social order" (sociological, and this includes ethics); and "how to live a human lifetime under any circumstances" (pedagogical).[41]

Ethics

With the exception of perhaps Shinto, most religions have an ethical dimension. The Decalogue, found in the Book of Exodus, provides Christians and Jews with prohibitions against worshipping more than one god and breaking the Sabbath.[42] In the Books of Leviticus and Deuteronomy, Jews find further rules, such as dietary laws, proscribed rituals, and taboos. Muslims, too, must follow dietary laws, as outlined in the Koran 5:3: "You are forbidden carrion, blood and the flesh of swine; also any flesh dedicated to any other than God. You are forbidden the flesh of strangled animals and those beaten or gored to death; of those killed by a fall or mangled by beasts of prey . . . also of animals sacrificed to idols." The two primary sources of Islamic ethics are the Koran and the Hadith, which are sayings of the prophet. Essentially, a Muslim must do what is good and refrain from what is evil, as is outlined in the aforementioned texts.

Since the sixth century B.C.E., Chinese scholars have studied the Analects to learn how to behave in society. From this text, they learn that they must be human-hearted, diligent, modest, and self sacrificing. Furthermore, they learn that they should respect their elders and cultivate virtues for "virtue never dwells alone; it always has neighbors" (chapter 25). As for Sikhs, they "must recall God constantly, work honestly and share what they earn. Self-centeredness [haumai] must give way to the Godward orientation of a gurmukh," which is a person who "shuns lust, anger, greed, attachment to things temporal, and pride. Sikhs must resist the temptation to renounce secular responsibilities, and must seek to live like a lotus, which is rooted in the mire, but unsullied by it."[43] Sikh ethics come from a number of sources, including the Guru Granth Sahib or Adi Granth, their sacred book; stories from the life of their religion's "founder," Guru Nanak; compositions of Guru Gobind Singh, the 10th-guru and founder of the Khalsa, a Sikh religious-military order; and the accounts of heroism and martyrdom of other Sikhs.

Rituals

Rituals are formalized, structured, repetitive, and stereotyped sequences of actions that are performed by adherents so as to bring myths and symbols to life and to connect or communicate with the ultimate.[44] For a Christian, baptism fulfills all of these functions. Essential to becoming a Christian, baptism is defined in the Roman Catechism as "regeneration by water in the word," and it involves the "sacramental washing by which the soul is cleansed from sin at the same time that water is poured upon the body."[45] For Catholics baptism is the first of the seven sacraments, and as an initiation rite, is "the door of the Church of Christ and the entrance to a new life." Although the specific details differ among Christian denominations, this ritual involves either the immersion of the person or the pouring of water, preferably consecrated, onto the person to be baptized. A priest then states, "I baptize you in the name of the Father, and of the Son, and of the Holy Ghost." Not only does baptism incorporate the worshipper to "Christ's mystical body," but it also connects the person to Jesus, whose baptism by John is directly referenced in the synoptic Gospels (Matthew 3:6–13, Mark 1:4–11, and Luke 3:16). Another central sacrament for Christians is the Eucharist or Lord's Supper. At this "meal" of bread and wine, worshippers commemorate the death and resurrection of Jesus. Furthermore, it serves as a memorial reenactment of Jesus' Last Supper, during which he handed bread to his disciples and said, "Take; this is my body." When he handed them a cup, he said, "This is my blood of the covenant, which is poured out for many" (Mark 14:22–24).

For Muslims, daily prayer or *salat* is a ritualistic act consisting of the recitation of various chapters of the Koran, while alternately standing, bowing, and prostrating oneself.[46] One of the five pillars of Islam, prayer must be performed five times a day at specific times: before dawn, at midday, three hours after midday, at sunset, and two hours after sunset. Before one can offer prayer, the worshipper must be dressed appropriately—in clean, respectful clothing—and have the intention to pray. Cleanliness extends to the rest of the body, and one must cleanse the entire face, hands, and feet either with water or sand. Once the person is ready, he or she lifts both hands up to the ears, says "Allah Akbar," and then recites the first chapter of the Koran, all the while facing Mecca. The recitation of additional chapters and the movement into various postures continues.[47] Prayer serves many functions for a Muslim: It brings him or her closer to Allah; is a lesson in discipline and willpower; is a seed of spiritual cultivation and moral soundness; is a safeguard against indecency and evil, against deviation and straying; teaches them humility; is a vigilant reminder of Allah and the constant revelation of his goodness; is a demonstration of true equality, solid unity, and brotherhood; is an expression of thankfulness to Allah and an appreciation of him; is a course of inner peace and stability; and is an abundant source of patience and courage.[48]

Shinto is largely concerned with impurity (*tsumi*) and its removal by purification (*oharai*) rituals. Impurity can be removed three ways: by a priest waving a *harai-gushi*, a wand of paper streamers, over the afflicted; by the loin-clothed or naked participant using water, either from a small bucket or under a waterfall; or by avoiding certain words or actions.[49] In the case of a Shinto wedding (*Shinzen Kekkon*), the "central act . . . is the purification of the couple and the families followed by the drinking of sake to commune with the *kami* [spirits] before whom the wedding is contracted."[50] Another distinguishing feature of a Shinto wedding is that the words *kiru* (cut) and *deru* (go out) must not be uttered during the ceremony, making the situation a bit difficult for the master of ceremonies. Another Shinto ceremony, the "ground-pacify festival" (*Jichin-sai*) involves having a priest "pacify" the *kami* by setting up sacred space (*himorogi*) that is circumscribed by a rope (*shimenawa*). The priest then purifies the area. This ritual is used to calm any *kami* in an area of new development—housing or roads—so that they don't bring about misfortune.[51]

Rituals are often performed at proscribed times, on certain "holy" days or dates. Jews, Christians, and Muslims all interpret God's injunction to "remember the Sabbath day and keep it holy" in different ways. Jews celebrate their Sabbath (*Shabbat* in Hebrew) from sunset on Friday until nightfall on Saturday. For many, this is "the high point of the week, around which all other days revolve. On the one hand it is a day in which we withdraw totally and completely from the demands of the world around us; on the other hand it is a day that we try to imbue with spiritual significance and meaning."[52] Not

only is it a time for "refreshing the body and the soul,"[53] it's also a "memorial
to the creation of the world" and to "the exodus from Egypt."[54] Preparations
must be made in advance, including cleaning the house and cooking the
meals, because work or *melakha* cannot be done on the Sabbath.[55] What's recommended is going to the synagogue, eating the Sabbath meal, and engaging
in a few other leisure-time activities, such as studying the Torah.[56] Catholics,
Eastern Orthodox, and traditional Protestants celebrate the Sabbath on Sunday with the Eucharist, which involves the eating of bread and drinking of
wine. For Muslims, Friday is their obligatory day of public prayer.[57] In the latter case, usually it is only men who go to the mosque, after noon, for prayer
and a service, which usually includes a sermon.

Finally, rituals may mark specific events, such as the birth of a child, the
coming of age of a child, a marriage, or a funeral. In keeping with Genesis
17:10–14, Jews circumcise their sons eight days after birth. When a boy
reaches his 13th birthday, he is known as a Bar-Mitzvah, which means "subject to the commandments." At this age he is considered an adult, and thus
obliged to observe the commandments. He can also be counted in a minyan,
the minimum number of adults needed to perform religious services. To commemorate this event, he is "called up to the reading of the Torah, there to recite the appropriate benedictions."[58] Girls are called Bat-Mitzvah at the age of
12. In many Sikh families, when a boy reaches 11 or 12 years old, he is taken
to a *gurdwara*, or Sikh temple, where his first turban is ceremonially tied on.
The purpose of this ritual is twofold: "It designates the respect with which the
turban is regarded" and "it demonstrates the significance of the male line in
Sikh families."[59] The Japanese consider the ages of 33 for women and 42 for
men to be particularly precarious. Therefore, in order to keep away any intended misfortune, many go to the local shrine where a Shinto priest can perform *yaku-barai*, a purification ritual.[60]

Finally, the Chinese lunar calendar is filled with auspicious and inauspicious times. One particularly dangerous and worrying time takes place on the
15th day of the seventh moon, when they observe *Yue Laan* or the Festival for
the Hungry Ghosts. It is believed that at this time the "gates to the underworld
are opened, and the ghosts [*kwai*] are free to roam wherever they like."[61] To
placate them, people offer gifts, such as food, paper clothing, and spirit
money, and entertain them with several days at the opera. The front-row seats
are always set aside for them. "No other festival in the year produces more

large scale community celebrations than this one." Huge incense sticks burn inside of the temporary temple, where constant streams of people come to offer prayers.[62]

As one can see, rituals can be performed by the laity or by the religious elite. And they can be employed in worship services, as a means of purification, or to atone for some transgression. This simply means that the nature of rituals is complex; however, no matter which religion we look at, we will always find that they are a way of communicating with whatever or whomever adherents consider to be the "ultimate."[63]

Symbols

Symbols represent or suggest abstract ideas or concepts, and they do this by reason of association or relationships. This simply means that a symbol has to have context. If we walk into a mathematics class and see a cross written on the board, we probably wouldn't assign to it any religious meaning. In this setting and within this context, we would think of it as a plus sign. But place that same symbol on the top of a church, and most Westerners will associate it with Jesus' method of execution. Christians will take the meaning even further, because for them this symbol is personal; it represents to them Jesus' sacrifice for all of humanity. The same goes for colors, which to some degree are culturally relative. Take the color white. Ask someone in the West what it signifies and he or she will typically reply, "Purity, virginity, and innocence." How do they make that connection? Primarily because of its association with weddings; typically, the bride wears a white dress.[64] In a Christian context, white is the color of the Resurrection—during Easter, church altars are covered with white lilies—and it is associated with the Virgin Mary, who wears this color during the Assumption. "White is prescribed for Christmas, Easter, the feast of the Ascension, and other joyous celebrations in the Church, as well as for services related to the Blessed Sacrament, feasts of Mary, of angels, confessors, virgins and women who were not martyred."[65]

Now ask someone from India, and that person will counter that white is the color of death and mourning. Why? Possibly because the dead are usually wrapped in white shrouds. Chinese opera, many of which are based on historical drama, classical stories, and folk and religious tales, has its own color symbolism. A character who has a predominantly white face indicates treachery and craftiness; a black face, impartiality, uprightness, and honorability; a red one, courage and generosity.[66] As in the Hindu tradition, in China, white also is the color of mourning, and it is considered unlucky to wear "anything white in one's hair."[67] In China, red was the traditional color of marriage, as women wore it at their wedding day. Contrast these color associations with those found in the Western tradition, where black usually signifies evil, death, and mourning, and red means passion and love. "Red and black are also the colors of purgatory and the devil."[68]

Learning what symbols mean to a religion is integral to getting an insider's view. One of the central symbols of Daoism is the yin-yang. With its mirrored black and white shapes, it reminds Daoists that harmony comes from the balance of opposites. To know wet, we must know dry; for light, dark; for male, female. For a Daoist, problems in the world arise when one side is not balanced by the other. Images of a wheel have special significance for a Buddhist. Not only does it represent the Wheel of Life, but it also represents the Buddha's teachings. After all, the Buddha's first sermon is often called the Turning of the Wheel of the Dharma or Law. In Hinduism, the wheel has traditionally been seen as a symbol of the sun. In Hindu myth, Shiva gave Vishnu a *chakra* (wheel) to use as a weapon.[69]

The lotus flower is significant in many Asian cultures. In India, the white lotus "became a symbol of purity and lucidity and finally the symbol of the earth itself as it floats on the primeval ocean. The god Brahma himself was first seen seated on a lotus afloat in this ocean." Additionally, this flower is associated with the goddesses Lakshmi and Sarasvati.[70] As Buddhism spread from India to the rest of East Asia, it brought with it the symbol of the lotus. Like this flower that has its roots in the mud but blooms, unsullied and beautiful, the human being, too, must try to remain pure while living in an impure world. The Buddha is frequently depicted as sitting on a lotus flower. Today, in China, the lotus represents "the wish for the continuity of luck, wealth, promotion or children."[71] Finally, the *torii*, a pi-shaped Shinto structure, indicates to a Japanese person this he or she is about to enter sacred space and that the *kami* are present.

Animal symbols are important to many religions. Monkeys are largely revered throughout Asia, primarily because of religious stories. Hanuman, a monkey king from *The Ramayana*, is, for many Hindus, a model of self-sacrifice and devotion to God. Not only did he assist in the rescue of Sita from the evil Ravana, but he also retrieved life-giving medicinal herbs when Lakshmana, Rama's brother, was wounded. Known as a great scholar and the author of a grammar, he is worshipped as a god. In China, the best-known monkey is Sun Wu-kong, who appears in Wu Ch-eng-en's 16th-century novel *Journey to the West*, which continues to be popular today. In the story, Monkey travels with Hsuan-tsang, also known as Tripitaka, a Buddhist pilgrim, and his other disciples—Pigsy and Sandy—to India. Not only does Monkey prove to be the best of the accompanying disciples, but he's also deemed worthy of receiving sacred Daoist teachings. Furthermore, in South China, the monkey is worshipped as *Qi-tia da-sheng*, which means "the great saint equal to heaven."[72] Finally, since the word for monkey and "high-ranking official" are pronounced the same way in Chinese, *hou* "represents a wish for advancement and prosperity."[73] According to one Tibetan myth, the Tibetan people are said to have descended from a monkey.

Usually viewed in the West as a beneficent animal, the dog is seen differently depending on the country and even the region. In China, the dog is the 11th creature in the zodiac, and it is said that during its year, one will find both happiness and dissent. In Taiwan, it is believed that dogs, when they die, should be thrown into the water. If they are buried, they will turn into a demon. "If you dream that a dog has bitten you, it means that your ancestors want to eat . . . if someone is suspected of being a spirit, it is enough to sprinkle him with dog's blood—he will then appear in his real form." Furthermore, the dog is thought to be the companion of Er-lang, the god who rids the world of demons.[74] In South and West China, the dog is revered for its contributions to society and its faithfulness. Folk stories explain it brought either rice and/or millet to humans. The Yao, a minority group in China, venerate the dog as its forefather. The Bhutanese believe that "from among all sentient beings, dogs have the best opportunity to be reborn as humans." Their folk stories even tell us that long ago, the gods were angry with humans and were about to punish them, when the dog interceded. "It is said that the food left behind for the dogs is what we survive on today. Dogs are also said to be helpful in the afterlife: when we're lost in the darkness of the hereafter, dogs are believed to lead us with a light glowing on their tails to a better place. Many of the Himalayan Buddhist saints . . . had dogs as their closest companions." A popular Bhutanese aphorism is: "If merit is to be earned, be good and kind to dogs."[75]

During the Middle Ages, bestiaries, which are moralizing natural histories, became incredibly popular with Christians, and the symbolism contained within greatly influenced the artistic tradition. Monkeys symbolized sin, lust, and the devil in disguise. The dog represented fidelity in marriage and, because it guards a flock, came to symbolize the priest. The dove is associated with the Holy Spirit, while the raven is associated with evil, the devil, and death. This is largely due to its black color and habit of scavenging. The fish and lamb were associated with Jesus.[76] It is said in myths that the female pelican "pierces her breast to revive her children with her own blood. Not surprisingly, because of this the pelican was associated with the Eucharist."[77] Mythological animals also were included in Christian bestiaries. For instance, the phoenix, which is said to be reborn from its ashes, became a popular symbol of the Resurrection.[78]

Shinto practitioners believe that several animals can bear sacred energy. Foxes are thought to possess supernatural powers and can bewitch people by changing their form. They are believed to be messengers of Inari Myojin, the *kami* of rice cultivation and grain cereals. Statues of foxes, usually wearing red bibs, are found at shrines dedicated to Inari.[79] At the large and historically famous shrine Mitsumine Jinja in Saitama Prefecture, wolves are revered as "sacred guardians of the mountain." Here, too, the souls of wild dogs are enshrined.[80] The giant black crow (*yatagarasu*) who guided the grandson of Amaterasu in his travels is revered in the Kumano cult.[81]

To some degree, symbols can become so entrenched in a culture that we may have a difficult time transcending them. Consider the case of the swastika. If someone from the West sees a man who has a shaved head and sports a tattoo of this symbol, he or she would assume that the person is a hatemonger. Why? Because most of us have been taught to associate the swastika with Adolph Hitler, who, for the West, conjures up images of fanaticism, anti-Semitism, and evil. This association, again, is conditioned by our cultural experience. Even glancing at the definitions listed in *Webster's Dictionary* indicates this bias. Both our culture and the dictionary describe its formation; the second definition elaborates with "adopted as the official emblem of the Nazis and the Third Reich."

The fact is that the swastika is an ancient and ubiquitous symbol, representing life, the sun,[82] good luck, and immortality. It has been and, in many cases, still is used in China, Japan, India, and southern Europe. "Swastika" derives from the Sanskrit word *svasti*, which means "happiness, well-being,"[83] and to Hindus it is an auspicious and sacred symbol. It isn't uncommon for Hindus, particularly Bengalis, to give their children this as a personal name, for example, Bollywood actress Swastika Mukherjee. In Buddhism, "the swastika can be angled clockwise or counter-clockwise. The former is the 'seal of the heart of the Buddha' and often to be seen on the breast of statues of the Buddha." In China, it is a "very old form of the character *fang*, meaning the four regions of the world." In decoration, it can be used to depict 10,000 years of luck; when five swastikas are placed in a configuration with the same number of bats and the symbol for longevity, it means fivefold fortune and happiness and long life.[84] The swastika has been used by American Indians, especially the Navajo and Hopi.

Sacred Space

Finally, when we look at the various religions, we notice that each has a concept of sacred space. What makes a place sacred? Jews, Christians, and Muslims all consider Jerusalem to be their sacred city but for different reasons. For Jews, Jerusalem is home to the Wailing Wall, the last remaining piece of King Solomon's temple. It is also the site of Mount Zion, which Jews and Muslims believe contains the burial site of King David, and for Christians it is the site of Jesus' Last Supper. Other holy places for Christians are the Church of the Holy Sepulchre, which marks the site of the Resurrection; Bethlehem, where Jesus was born; Golgatha, where Jesus died; and the Mount of Olives, where Jesus is said to have ascended to heaven. Muslims believe that Muhammad took a celestial journey from whence today sits the Dome of the Rock. Buddhists consider Bodh Gaya, which is the site of Siddhartha's nirvana, to be sacred. Also sacred to Buddhists are Lumbini, Siddhartha's birthplace; Sarnath, where he gave his first sermon; Kushinagar, where he died; and Sanchi, where one finds many Buddhist stupas, monasteries, temples, and pillars. Hindus believe that bathing in the River Ganges, which is considered a goddess, will remove all sin and cure all ills. Because this many devotees congregate on the banks of this river during various festivals, and the dying want to spend their last minutes there. The Grand Shrine at Ise is Japan's most sacred shrine because of its association with Amaterasu Omikami, who is believed to be the ancestor of the emperor and his family. Because these sites are imbued with power, adherents often visit them at least once in their lives.

EASTERN AND WESTERN ORIENTATIONS

It may not hold true in every case, but, in general, we can see marked differences between Eastern and Western religions, especially when we look at them in terms of the nature of the universe, the role of humans, attitudes toward the natural world, and the exclusivity of belief.

The Nature of the Universe

Many Eastern religions claim that the universe is cyclical and eternal, thus having no beginning and no end. Hinduism teaches that the universe goes through an endless cycle of creation and destruction. Each universe lasts about 4,320,000 years, and during that period it passes through four *kalpas* or eons, which are the Krita, Treta, Dvapara, and Kali Yugas. "In the Krita age dharma is four-footed and complete; and so is truth, nor does any gain accrue to men by unrighteousness. In the other three ages, dharma is successively deprived of one foot, and through theft, falsehood and fraud the merit is diminished by one-fourth." As the universe moves from the first *yuga* to the last, human life gets shorter, natural calamities worsen, and human societies, which begin as moral and upright, forget dharma and become overwhelmed by avarice, lust, ignorance, animosity, and covetousness.[85] (Currently we are in the Kali Yuga, which is the age of strife.) Once the universe is destroyed, another one will begin, and the process will start all over again.[86]

When it comes to the nature of the universe, Buddhism is largely silent. After all, Buddhism wasn't intended to provide "theoretical answers to philosophical questions," and we can find evidence of this in the *Shorter Discourse to Malunkyaputta*. In this text, a monk poses a number of questions about the nature of the universe to the Buddha, such as is the world eternal? Is it infinite? And is the soul the same as the body? The monk says that if he doesn't get answers to these, he will leave the practice. The Buddha replies not with an answer but with a story about a man who is wounded by an arrow and is brought to a surgeon for treatment. Before accepting treatment, though, the man asks a series of questions about the person who shot him: To which caste did he belong? How tall was he? What color of skin? What kind of bow did he use? And on and on. "All this would still not be known to that man, and meanwhile, he would die."[87] The point of this story is that these sorts of speculative questions are "unbeneficial and don't lead to disenchantment, to dispassion, to cessation, to peace, to direct knowledge, to enlightenment, to nirvana."[88]

Even if the Buddha wouldn't talk about the nature of the universe, one can still find full systematic accounts of Buddhist cosmology in the *Abhidharma*, which are commentaries on the Buddha's teachings. In his *Visuddhimagga* (Path of Purification), Buddhaghosa, a fourth-century B.C.E. Buddhist scholar, explains that the universe goes through cycles of births, deaths, and rebirths. While being destroyed by the elements fire, water, and wind, the morality of human beings will deteriorate.[89] As the Dalai Lama explains, "We have been going through the cycle of life and death for far longer than our planet existed. Our past lives are therefore infinite, as are the beings who have given birth to us."[90] Rather than embrace this concept, though, Buddhists such as Thich Nhat Hanh, who is echoing the Buddha, suggest that we need to move beyond these concepts. "We think that we exist only from this point in time until this point in time, and we suffer because of that notion. If we look deeply, we will know that we have never been born and we will never die."[91]

The Daodejing (The Way and Its Power) suggests that the Dao existed before the universe ever came into being: "The nameless was the beginning of heaven and earth; the named was the mother of the myriad creatures" (chapter 1) and "There is a thing confusedly formed. Born before heaven and earth. Silent and void" (chapter 25). Daoism also suggests that the universe is "constantly recreating itself in a continuing evolution," and it is in a "constant process of genesis and development from a single component, the primordial breath or energy, which is known as *chi* or *qi*.[92] In the Daodejing we read, "The way begets one; one begets two; two begets three; three begets the myriad creatures. The myriad creatures carry on their backs the yin and embrace in their arms the yang and the blending of the generative forces of the two" (chapter 42). Even American Indians see the concept of linear time as "foreign and unnatural. To them, the true nature of time is like the rhythms of the natural world."[93]

By contrast, religions originating in the Middle East—Zoroastrianism, Judaism, Christianity, and Islam—teach that the universe has a beginning and an end. The Hebrew Bible or *Tanakh* begins with the Book of Genesis and the story of creation: "In the beginning, God created the heavens and the earth" (1:1), every living creature, and finally, man (Adam), whom God created in his image, and woman (Eve). From this event, the whole history of humanity evolves. "The narrative in some sense purports to be history. This we assume from its concern for chronology, its inclusion of archival material, its interest in political and military events, its preoccupation with etiology and long-range causality."[94] The Bible "anticipates the modern genre of documentary history."[95] Despite the seemingly comprehensive scope of the text, the authors have been highly subjective in their choice of material, presenting a "very partisan and polemic perspective in relation to the culture of its milieu."[96] This is the story of the Jewish people, their covenant with God, and the latter's continuing relationship with the Jewish people throughout history.

The focus of the Bible, then, is primarily "this worldly" rather than "other worldly." In fact, the Hebrew Bible terminates with 2 Chronicles 36:12,[97] and a proclamation by King Cyrus of Persia that says, "The Lord God of Heaven has given me all the kingdoms of the earth and has charged me with building him a house in Jerusalem, which is in Judah. Any one of you of all his people, the Lord his God be with him and let him go up." By ending this way, "The author of the books of Chronicles . . . was setting out to give to his contemporaries an understanding of their current position as a small subject people under alien rule, in the light of his interpretation of the past. This involved seeing that small community in the light of the whole story from creation to the restoration under Cyrus. . . . It also involved offering an understanding of the contemporary significance of the two major institutions of that history: kingship and Temple."

Furthermore, the Books of Chronicles provides an "idealized picture of the true people, loyal to their God and to the law of Moses" but whom, through a final disobedience, are exiled to Babylon, "leaving an empty land to recover by observing the forgotten Sabbaths."[98] The Hebrew Bible doesn't end on a "supernatural" note, but on a very real and human one. And we can see, this "human" focus in Jewish spirituality, which is the "experience of the transcendent dimension of life as an individual and as a member of a people. This spirituality, however, is not otherworldly but rather emphasizes the belief that the truest path to God does not involve leaving the concerns of this world. . . . The sacred Jewish myth does not draw the Jew up to heaven; it draws heaven down to the Jew."[99]

As far as discussion of an "end" to the universe and human life is concerned, a few later biblical books, such as Isaiah, Ezekiel, and Jeremiah, are eschatological, meaning that they focus on the "end of days." Some themes therein include: the Messiah, Judgment Day, the messianic era, the time-to-come, retribution, resurrection of the dead,[100] and the afterlife.[101] Again, since

Judaism tends to focus more on actions than beliefs, it hasn't spent a lot of time speculating about the world to come. The Torah and Talmud focus on the purpose of one's life on Earth, which is to fulfill one's duties to God and one's fellow human beings. Moses Maimonides demonstrates this tendency to focus on the here and now in his attempt to strip Jewish messianism of its supernatural elements. He believed that the true Messiah wouldn't be someone who performed miracles and revived the dead but would "be a king descended from the house of David, a scholar knowledgeable in the Torah, occupied himself with the commandments, and observed the precepts of the Written and Oral Law."[102] Even when talking about the afterlife, Jews aren't in accordance. Mystical branches of Judaism, especially Kabbalah, talk at length about "heaven and hell, consuming fires, vicious snakes and threatening demons," and the kinds of horrors that await the sinner after death.[103] Some Jewish mystics even believe in the transmigration of the soul.[104] Contrast this with Jews who have interpreted these ideas figuratively or metaphorically. Maimonides, for example, denied the existence of *Gehinnom* or hell, explaining that it was a metaphor and not an actual place.[105]

Because the followers of Jesus were Jews, their identity was tied to the Hebrew Bible but they reinterpreted it in a new way. They saw themselves as representing the "true Israel" and Jesus of Nazareth was seen as the long-awaited Messiah. The Christian Bible also begins with the Jewish creation story, but it is no longer bookended by a story about a people living under a foreign ruler. Instead, the last book of the Christian Bible is the Apocalypse of John or Book of Revelation, which tells about the end of the world, when the Earth will be visited by any manner of calamities, including earthquakes, hail, fire, and the sea turning to blood, and by the return of Jesus of Nazareth, the embodiment of "goodness," who will engage in a battle against the anti-Christ, the embodiment of "evil." Christians see the Bible as a series of unfolding events that are heading toward a cataclysmic end; everything leads up to that moment. "The Book of Revelation . . . is a fitting close to the Holy Scriptures, for its final chapters depict the consummation toward which the whole biblical message of redemption is focused."[106] Furthermore, the Book of Revelation "affirms Christianity's original hope for an immediate transformation of the world and assures the faithful of God's prearranged plan, including the destruction of Evil and the advent of Christ's universal reign, is about to be accomplished."[107] Rather than focus on this world, as the Jews tend to do, Christians look with trepidation and anticipation for the end of the world as humans know it.

Role of Humans

Eastern religions, such as Hinduism and Buddhism, acknowledge that being born a human being is an incredibly rare occurrence so when it happens, one should make good use of it. For Hindus a human being is unlike other beings in that it has freedom of choice and the opportunity to learn about the world: "The concern and quest for meaning, as far as we know, is unique to the human species." A human birth also affords him or her the opportunity to be liberated from the cycle of birth and death. As Shankara wrote, "What fool is there than the person who having obtained a human body, neglects to achieve the real end of this life?"[108] Buddhism echoes these sentiments. "Imagine a blind turtle, roaming the depths of the ocean the size of the universe. Up above floats a wooden ring, tossed to and fro on the waves. Every 100 years the turtle comes, once, to the surface. To be born a human . . . is more difficult than that turtle [surfacing] accidentally with its head poking through the wooden ring."[109] Because of this difficulty, and because "life is short, limited and brief," and full of suffering and tribulation, "one should do good [things] and live a pure life; for none who is born can escape death."[110] Being born a human is rare and affords one the opportunity to achieve enlightenment—only humans can do this—but this doesn't mean that they are better or worse than any other being. As Thich Nhat Hanh says, a human being is made up of nonhuman elements—air, water, the forest, the river, the mountains, and the animals—and when "we look deeply into living beings, we find that they are also made of non-living-being elements. So-called inanimate things are alive also. Our notions about living beings and inanimate things should be removed for us to touch reality."[111] The interconnection between humans and the natural world, too, can be found in American Indian traditions. In his speech to his people, when they were preparing to move across Puget Sound, Chief Seattle said, "Every part of this earth is sacred to my people. Every shining pine needle, every sandy shore, every mist in the dark woods. . . . All are holy in the memory and experience of my people. We know the sap which courses through the trees as we know the blood that courses through our veins." He continues, reminding them that the Earth is their mother, and the bear, deer, and great eagle, their brothers.[112]

The three world monotheisms may differ on several points, but for the most part they concur that humans are the pinnacle of and reason for creation. Genesis 1:27 explains that at the end of the sixth day, God "created man in his own image, in the image of God he created him; male and female he created them." And in Genesis 2:7, "the Lord formed man of dust from the ground and breathed into his nostrils the breath of life; and man became a living being." Jews interpret "made in his image" to mean that human beings are special, and that their purpose is to "refine the image of God within."[113] Being made in God's image doesn't mean that humans physically resemble God for "he" doesn't have form. What humans do possess are God's qualities, such as love, intelligence, and goodness. Finally, many believe that the creation of human beings is the purpose of creation. After all, only humans can perfect or destroy the world.[114]

From the Catholic perspective, "The human person is an individual creature, distinguished from all others by the gift of freedom, bodily incarnated as male and female and animated by the spiritual principle . . . human persons are, in a sense, co-creators with God of both the world and its history . . . Only when the human person is understood in this larger context—not only as an individual, but also as social being, as historical being, and as being-in-this-world—can our theology of human existence hope to be comprehensive and catholic."[115] And as for Muslims, they believe that humans are created in the "form" of God, which means "the reflection of God's names and qualities, for otherwise God is formless and imageless." To be human is to carry God's spirit at "the depth of one's being." Furthermore, they believe that humans didn't ascend from "lower forms of life, but descended from on high, from a Divine prototype. Therefore, humanity has always been humanity and it has always had religion."[116]

Attitudes toward Nature

Eastern religions tend to see human beings as a part of nature rather than apart from it. An important Mahayana Buddhist scripture, the Flower Garland Sutra (*Huayan jing*), talks about the interdependence and interpenetration of the universe, referring to this web of relationships as Indra's net or the jeweled net of Shakra. "This one jewel consists of the connections of many jewels to form the net. . . . Without the existence of one, all cannot exist."[117] According to Buddhist scholar Rita M. Gross, "Interdependence is the most commonly invoked concept in Buddhist environmental ethics to date. Most often, it is celebrated as a view of our relationships with our world that invites and requires ecological concern."[118] As Thich Nhat Hanh explains, "We have to remove the notion of human as something that can survive by itself alone. Humans can survive only with the survival of other species. This is exactly the teaching of the Buddha, and also the teaching of deep ecology."[119] In animistic religions such as Shinto, nature is seen to be alive, inhabited by myriad *kami* who dwell in mountains, waterways, trees, and rocks. Throughout Japanese history, especially during the Edo period (1600–1868), there has been a push for the conservation of natural resources, such as water and forests. During the aforementioned period, a person caught stealing a twig had his finger amputated; for tree theft, he lost his head.[120]

Both Confucianism and Daoism advocated living in accordance with the Dao, which represents the natural law and order of things. "As Heaven has a dimension of Nature or Natural Law, harmony between Heaven and humans is understood to be a cooperative relationship between humans and their natural environment, in which natural laws should be followed and the natural environment protected. From this, a kind of Confucian eco-ethics develops, aiming at establishing a state of harmony between humans and Nature. Confucian eco-ethics is based on the perceived agreement between the Way of Heaven and the way of humans."[121] Acting in accordance to the Dao is so important to the Chinese that Chinese medicine, including acupuncture; martial arts, especially T'ai Chi Chuan; and even geomancy or feng shui have developed as a way to accomplish this. Those who believe in feng shui, for example, believe that humans and their environment are linked, so if someone interferes in any way with the landscape, the human being will feel its effects. "As in a large organism, everything is interdependent and pulsating with energy, penetrating and embracing every single part. In this thinking, the environment should be utilized thoughtfully, since harmful interference hits back like a boomerang. . . . The basic logic of feng shui is straightforward—when the landscape is rich and healthy, humans may prosper; when the landscape deteriorates, people suffer."[122]

As for Jews and Christians, their understanding of the relationship between humans and nature has been shaped by Genesis 1:26–29, which includes the lines "and let [humans] have dominion over the fish of the seas, and over the birds of the air, and over the cattle, and over all the earth, and over every creeping thing that creeps upon the earth" and "Be fruitful and multiply, and fill the earth and subdue it." Many environmental activists have strongly criticized these religions for these ideas and have even credited them with creating our current environmental crisis. In his 1967 essay, Lynn White Jr. was particularly condemnatory toward Western Christianity, calling it "the most anthropocentric religion the world has seen," and stating that it is this focus that "leads to the exploitation of the Earth."[123] Nearly 40 years later, this sentiment continues.[124]

Many acknowledge that a polarity exists in the Jewish worldview, between the holy and profane, good and evil, and even God and nature: "God is generally regarded in rabbinic Judaism as different from and above the world, on one hand, and closely involved and concerned with the world and its inhabitants, on the other." Furthermore, God is seen as both immanent and transcendent.[125] Scholars, though, are responding to critics by showing how Judaism is consistent with environmentalism. Aloys Hutterman claims that this oft-referenced passage from the Hebrew Bible is "the most misunderstood part."[126] He then points to several biblical passages that counter this "dominion of the world" theory, including the story of Noah (Genesis 9:8–17). God doesn't command Noah to save just his human life, but he is told to construct the ark to save "the whole animal life of the world."[127] Manfred Gerstenfeld has stressed the need for the development of Jewish environmental studies as an academic field: "Systematic study in this field will thus yield many additional important insights for better understanding of the Jewish tradition, in general, and its environmental aspects in particular."[128] And Rabbi Lawrence Troster suggested in 2004 that "Judaism needs a comprehensive, contemporary, environmental theology—one that can serve as a foundation for a thorough code of ethics. Beyond that, Judaism must provide guidelines for day-to-day living by creating a body of environmental law, or *halakhah*, and by infusing Jewish ritual and liturgy with an ecological awareness."[129]

Christians, too, have responded to their detractors, and "since the 1980s, virtually every major Christian denomination has issued some kind of formal declaration on environmental stewardship." In addition, in 1979, Pope John Paul II declared St. Francis of Assisi to be the patron saint of ecologists.[130] Some scholars have even refuted criticism by "stressing the immanence of God, and particularly the Holy Spirit, in creation, thereby undercutting the dualism of God and nature that characterized the Western

Christian tradition."[131] Others, such as John Chryssavgis, find a more ecological theology in Orthodox Christianity, which, unlike the West, "never separated humans from nature" nor did it "glorify the rationality of the individual."[132]

Muslims have much in common with Judaism and Christianity because in the Koran one also finds the idea that "God created Adam in his own image" and that "God taught Adam the names, of all of them" (2:31). Muslims understand that the role of humans is to be a vicegerent or representative on the Earth, and since only they were taught all of the divine names and were created in God's form, "everything in the universe exists to be ruled by human beings."[133] However, this doesn't mean one should misuse the Earth's resources. As is pointed out, "the ecological and social [crises] of modern times are nothing but signs of misused vicegerency"[134] and that "the ecological and environmental disasters in many parts of the Islamic world today . . . must not be seen as the result of Islamic teachings."[135] Unlike Jews and Christians, Muslims have only recently begun articulating "an explicitly Islamic environmental ethic . . . largely in response to the critique of Christianity."[136]

Exclusivity

Another difference between the Eastern and Western traditions pertains to exclusivity. If we were to go to Japan, it wouldn't be uncommon to find someone who supports Shinto on the local and national levels, prays to Amida Buddha for a positive future birth in the Pure Land, and uses feng shui to achieve harmony in his or her home or workplace. Elements of Confucianism may also be seen in the way that the person interacts with members of the community. "In Japanese religion exclusive affiliation to one religious tradition is rare; the general rule is a plurality of religions, with the same person participating in several religions simultaneously."[137] For the most part, Confucianism, Buddhism, Daoism, and even popular and folk traditions coexist in East Asian countries such as China and Korea.

This wouldn't be the case with Christianity, Judaism, or Islam, though, because these religions stress absolute adherence to "one god." The *Catechism of the Catholic Church* explains that "The ruptures that wound the unity of Christ's Body—here we do distinguish heresy, apostasy and schism—do not occur without human sin."[138] Later it states that "St. Paul speaks of the 'obedience of faith' as our first obligation. He shows that 'ignorance of God' is the principle and explanation of all moral deviations. Our duty toward God is to believe in him and to bear witness to him."[139] The first commandment requires us to nourish and protect our faith . . . and to reject everything that is opposed to it."[140] One of the various ways of sinning against the faith includes "apostasy," which is "the total repudiation of the Christian faith."[141] Paul writes in Thessalonians 5:7–9 that the angels will inflict vengeance on those who "do not know God and upon those who do not obey the gospel of Lord Jesus. They shall suffer the punishment of eternal destruction and exclusion from the presence of the Lord and from the glory of his might." Hebrews 6:4–8 reminds believers that "it is impossible to restore again to repentance those who have once been enlightened . . . if they commit apostasy, since they crucify the Son of God on their own account and hold him up to contempt. . . . [For land that] bears thorns and thistles . . . is worthless and near to being cursed; its end is to be burned." During the fourth, fifth, and sixth centuries C.E., "canonical penance was reserved for serious sins, e.g., apostasy, murder, heresy, and adultery. These were matters of common public knowledge. The offender would receive a form of liturgical excommunication and was forced to leave the celebration of the Eucharist at the Offertory, along with the catechumens."[142]

Although a controversial and debated issue, apostasy in Islam can lead to dire consequences: "If you renounced the Faith you would surely do evil in the land and violate the ties of blood. Such are those on whom God has laid His curse, leaving them deaf and sightless" (Koran 47:21) and "Those that disbelieve and debar others from God's path and in the end die unbelievers shall not be shown forgiveness by God" (47:34). Unbelievers are said to go to hell, where they will suffer torment: "Those who have denied the Book and the message we sent through our apostles shall realize the truth hereafter: when, with chains and shackles round their necks, they shall be dragged through scalding water and burnt in the fire of Hell" (Koran 40:67–73). Today, about a half a dozen or so Muslim countries stipulate capital punishment for apostates. The most sensational example of this involved Abdul Rahman, an Afghan citizen who was arrested in early 2006 and threatened with the death penalty for converting from Islam to Christianity.

Oral and Written Traditions

Religions can also differ as to how much they rely on the written word and rational thought. Zen Buddhism, particularly the Rinzai tradition, employs koans, absurd unsolvable questions, to help the practitioner cut through intellectual, rational thought and "leap to another level of comprehension." One of the more famous Zen sayings comes from Lin Chi, Zen Master, who said, "If you meet the Buddha, kill him." This can be explained by the second Kalama Sutra, in which the Buddha tells his disciples not to follow something simply because it is tradition, it is socially acceptable, or comes from authority. Rather, he said, to observe it firsthand, and if these things are good, blameless, praised by the wise, and when adopted lead to benefit and happiness, then accept and practice them.[143] Experience is the key. The Daodejing explains that the "Dao that can be named is not the Dao" (chapter 1) and that "What cannot be seen is called evanescent; what cannot be heard is called rarefied; what cannot be touched is called minute. These three cannot be fathomed" (chapter 14). As in these examples, many religious traditions find words to be too limiting to be of any use. Others believe that their sacred texts come directly from God, and so must be treated with reverence and strict adherence. Jewish traditionalists believe, as Rabbi Hayim Halevy Donin says, "that God's will was also made manifest in the Oral Tradition or Oral Torah which also had its source at Sinai, revealed to Moses and then orally taught to the religious heads of Israel."[144] He continues, "Torah is the embodiment of the Jewish faith. It contains the terms of his Covenant with God. It is what makes a Jew a Jew."[145] On this issue, one can essentially separate adherents into two camps—those who examine religion and those who "experience" religion. In the first group are the traditionalists who read and ruminate on their sacred scriptures; in the second group are the mystics who try to go beyond the text so that they can touch the divine. Mysticism is a "highly sophisticated form of religious belief, often very cerebral and almost always elitist in nature, but it also posits a level of direct and intuitive spirituality that transcends the intellect." In general it also tends to involve "a highly ritualized set of practices, often ascetic in nature, designed to bring the mystic closer to the Divine."[146]

Before we end our discussion of religion, it's important to remember that studying religions presents its own set of challenges. As they enter a geographical region or culture, religions adapt to whatever existed before them. Thus, if we were to look at Christianity as it is practiced in Africa, Japan, Italy, and the United States, we would find myriad differences. Thus, it's probably better to say that there are Christianities as well as Buddhisms. We also find a spectrum of adherence. Some people take a liberal approach to their religion, believing that religion must adapt and change to the times; while others take a more orthodox approach, tending to resist change, by holding to established laws, practices, and dogma. Furthermore, we often find disparity between what the religion says about itself and how it is interpreted by the laity. Sometimes the two are very different. What we will find in this book are the basic concepts as outlined in the religious traditions themselves; these are the ideals. How individuals choose to interpret these ideas is another subject entirely.

On one last note, we might wonder why anyone practices religion at all. Throughout the centuries, various pundits have predicted the death of religion, either because it goes against reason, is infantile, or is a tool of control. Voltaire, the 18th-century French writer, said that "Nothing can be more contrary to religion and the clergy than reason and common sense." Karl Marx, the 19th-century economist, said, "Religion is the sigh of the oppressed creature, the heart of a heartless world . . . it is the opium of the people." And Sigmund Freud, the 20th-century psychologist, explained that "Religion is an illusion and it derives its strength from the fact that it falls in with our instinctual desires." So why, after several centuries, in our increasingly "rational" and scientific world, does religion persist? As Émile Durkheim, the 19th-century sociologist, explains, religion is "an eminently collective thing"; it is, in essence, that which holds us together. Religion provides a great number of people not only with a sense of identity but also with a sense of belonging. It serves a psychological purpose, providing people with hope and giving their lives meaning. It gives comfort to those who are anxious, fearful, or facing death. As the old adage goes, "There aren't any atheists in a foxhole." And, perhaps most importantly, it provides answers to the tough questions—Who am I? From whence did I come? Where am I going?

Science and religion have been said to be at odds; however, this isn't always believed to be the case. Charles Darwin's studies on natural selection and evolution may have undermined the literal interpretation of the Bible, but "even the highly conservative papacy" failed to include his works in the Index of Forbidden Books. The Catholic Church has basically also said that "so long as Darwin's theory was not used to explain the nature and origin of the human soul, the theory [would be] regarded as a reasonable, albeit unproven, hypothesis."[147] Furthermore, Pope John Paul II has even been quoted as saying that "Science can purify religion from error and superstition; religion can purify science from idolatry and false absolutes. Each can draw the other into a

wider world, a world in which both can flourish."[148] The Dalai Lama, especially, is trying to bring science and religion together, and he has encouraged
neuroscientists to investigate the connection between Tibetan Buddhism and
cognitive science.[149] Interestingly enough, during a conversation between as-
tronomer and astrobiologist Carl Sagan and the Dalai Lama, the former
asked what would happen if science could disprove a fundamental tenet of
Buddhism, such as reincarnation. The Dali Lama replied, "If science can disprove reincarnation, Tibetan Buddhism would abandon the idea."[150] The
20th-century physicist Albert Einstein himself said of Buddhism that "if
there is any religion that would cope with modern scientific needs, it would
be Buddhism. . . . Buddhism is a combination of both speculative and scientific philosophy. It advocates the scientific method and pursues that to a fi-
nality that may be called rationalistic. In it are to be found answers to such
questions of interest as: What is mind and matter? Of them, which is of
greater importance? Is the universe moving toward our goal? What is man's
position? Is there living that is noble? It takes up where science cannot lead
because of the limitations of the latter's instruments. Its conquests are those
of the mind."[151] Finally, Baha'i, one of the world's youngest religions, teaches
that "science and religion are two complementary systems of knowledge" and
that the "harmonious interaction of science and religion, each operating
within its proper sphere, [is] one of the prerequisites for the establishment of
a peaceful and just society."[152] Baha'ullah, the founder of Bahá'i, actually declared that religion must be in accord with science and reason, and if it isn't
then it is superstition. "For God has endowed us with faculties by which we
may comprehend the realities of things. . . . If religion is opposed to reason
and science, faith is impossible."[153]

THE JUNCTION OF RELIGION AND FILMS

Now that we've discussed religion, how exactly does film play a part? Religion
permeates our lives, so it's not surprising that it spills into our literature, our
music, our TV shows, our video games, and our films. In fact, news magazines
are full of stories about the intersection of religion and the arts. When they
aren't gossiping about Tom Cruise's Scientology or Madonna's Kabbalism,
they are writing features on "How *The DaVinci Code* Undermines Faith" or
"How Mel Gibson's controversial *Passion of the Christ* promotes anti-Semitism."
The academic study of religion in film began in earnest in the late 1960s; how-

ever, it didn't really gain momentum until the 1990s. In those 40 or so years, scholars have found religious meaning in everything from *One Flew over the Cuckoo's Nest* to *The Lord of the Rings*. There are overt examples such as in *Kundun*, which is a biopic on the Dalai Lama, and in the *Ten Commandments*, and some not so overt ones such as *Superman* and *The Machinist*.

In this book, we will use film as a way to examine religion in practice. For the sake of example, let's look at *Daredevil*, the 2003 film based on a Marvel Comics character and starring Ben Affleck. On the surface, the film is an action-adventure that promises fight sequences, cool gadgets, and maybe even a love story. Dig deeper and we find something much more. By using the lens of Christianity, we find a crime-fighting character who literally resembles the devil—he sports a red leather suit complete with horns. Like most super-heroes, he uses violence against his foes. But in this instance, Daredevil is morally ambivalent about doing this because his surrogate father figure, Father Everett, tells him "Vengeance is a sin. Violence begets violence." Because of his upbringing, the man behind the Daredevil persona grapples with a very real religious question: Is it right to use violence in defense of the innocents? Should he be a physical embodiment of "eye for an eye" or should he "turn the other cheek"? He wonders, is he an angel of mercy or a devil? In terms of symbolism, throughout the film, we see religious iconography, such as a statue of Mary, a cross, and a confessional booth. Bullseye, the villain, even crosses himself before entering a church.

Most people go to the movies for entertainment. They want to laugh or maybe cry, nothing more. They are passive viewers, which means that they don't critically analyze what they have watched. They don't want to leave the cinema and discuss such elements as characters, themes, and symbolism. And yet, this is exactly what we will be asking the student to do. Without a doubt, it can be challenging. As Joe Boggs says in his book *The Art of Watching Films*, "We must somehow remain almost immersed in the experience of the film while we maintain a high degree of objectivity and critical detachment. Difficult though it may seem, this skill can be developed, and we must consciously cultivate it if we desire to become truly 'cineliterate.'"[154]

To get the most out of the cinematic experience, a person should be familiar with each religious tradition before sitting in front of the screen. Then, while watching the film, it's a good idea to take notes. Pay close attention to the presence of doctrine, myths, ethics, rituals, and symbols. Listen to what the characters are saying and notice what they are doing or how they are be-having. What might they represent? Does this film's story have wider implica-tions? Is color significant to the film? Do we see any symbols that might be religious in nature? Obviously, to extract every religious detail, every nuance, from a film on one screening is impossible. In fact, it's advisable to watch a film several times before an in-depth analysis can be made. But, as Boggs states, "Film analysis does not end when the film is over. In a sense, this is when it really begins."[155]

ENDNOTES

1. Lao Tzu, *Tao Te Ching*, book 1:19, trans. D. C. Lau (London: Penguin Classics, 1963), 23.

2. Ann Marie B. Bahr, *Religions of the World: Indigenous Religions* (Philadelphia: Chelsea House, 2005), 6.

3. Rabbi Hayim Halevy Donin, *To Be a Jew: A Guide to Jewish Observance in Contemporary Life* (New York: Basic Books 1972), 9.

4. Daniel L. Pals, *Eight Theories of Religion* (New York: Oxford University Press, 2006), pre-sents the theories of eight men who have "exercised a shaping influence not only on religion but on the whole intellectual culture of the 20th century." These men include E. B. Taylor and James Frazer, Sigmund Freud, Émile Durkheim, Karl Marx, Max Weber, Mircea Eliade, E. E. Evans-Pritchard, and Clifford Geertz.

5. For a religion to "exist," it needs to have more than one adherent. For instance, say that you meet someone who says that he or she follows the "religion of DaDa." You might inquire as to what followers of this religion believe, what they do. If you asked how many other people follow this religion, and the person said, "No one else does. It's just me," then we would concur that DaDa is more a personal philosophy than a religion.

6. Willard G. Oxtoby and Alan F. Segal, eds., *A Concise Introduction to World Religions* (New York: Oxford University Press, 2007), 540–66.

7. Oxtoby and Segal, eds., *A Concise Introduction to World Religions*, 557.

8. Oxtoby and Segal, eds., *A Concise Introduction to World Religions*, 559. The authors look at the cult of Chairman Mao in terms of communism and then discount it as a form of religion.

9. Oxtoby and Segal, eds., *A Concise Introduction to World Religions*, 559.

10. Ninian Smart, *Worldviews: Cross-cultural Explorations of Human Beliefs* (New York: Charles Scribner's Sons, 1983).

11. Richard P. McBrien, *Catholicism* (New York: HarperCollins, 1994), 42–43.

12. U.S. Catholic Church, *Catechism of the Catholic Church with Modification from the Editio Typica* (New York: Doubleday, 1995). This edition is the first new catechism in more than 400 years.

13. U.S. Catholic Church, *Catechism of the Catholic Church*, 58.

14. U.S. Catholic Church, *Catechism of the Catholic Church*, 56–57.

15. The next two councils dealt primarily with issues that concerned the monastic community. The Second Council, ca. 380 B.C.E., resulted in a schism between the Theravada and Mahayana Buddhists. The former was more orthodox in their adherence to the Buddha's words; the latter was more liberal. The purpose of the Third Council, under Emperor Ashoka, was to draft statutes for monks.

16. Dzongsar Jamyang Khyentse, *What Makes You Not A Buddhist* (Boston, MA: Shambhala, 2007).

17. Khyentse, *What Makes You Not A Buddhist*, 3. For more from this book, see the chapter on Buddhism.

18. Although many attempts have been made at fixing a Jewish "Articles of Faith," it lacks authoritative sanction on the part of a supreme ecclesiastical body. Therefore, Maimonides' *13 Principles of Faith* has not been recognized as final or as a universally binding force. Typically Orthodox Jews are more likely to accept these than Reform Jews. In his book *What Do Jews Believe*, David S. Ariel expounds on many of these ideas under his section on God.

19. Sachiko Murata and William C. Chittick, *The Vision of Islam* (New York: Paragon House, 1994), 43.

20. Murata and Chittick, *The Vision of Islam*, xv.

21. Seyyed Hossein Nasr, *Islam: Religion, History, and Civilization* (San Francisco: Harper San Francisco, 2003), 62.

22. Murata and Chittick, *The Vision of Islam*, 113.

23. Donin, *To Be a Jew*, 24.

24. *Nihongi*, trans. W. G. Aston (Rutland, VT: Tuttle, 1972), 10–12.

25. Since the text works on different levels, Jacqueline Suthren Hirst suggests that "it would . . . be incorrect to say that the *Mahabharata* has been understood simply as history. On the other hand, to deny that it is in some sense 'historical' ignores one of its most vital dimensions." For more on this discussion, see chapter 5, "Myth and History," in *Themes and Issues in Hinduism*, ed. Paul Bowen (London: Cassell, 1998), 105–16.

26. *Themes and Issues in Hinduism*, 111.

27. Jews, Christians, and Muslims revere many of the same prophets of the Hebrew Bible, so many of the noted examples apply to all three monotheistic faiths.

28. Jaroslav Pelikan, ed., *Sacred Writings*, vol. 1, *Judaism: The Tanakh* (Philadelphia: Jewish Publication Society, 1985).

29. King Saul had only ruled for two years when God selected David to take his place. Saul was the model of disobedience.

30. David is a controversial historical figure who also engaged in some unsavory activities, such as committing adultery and murder. For more on this side of King David, see Baruch Halpern, *David's Secret Demons: Messiah, Murderer, Traitor, King (Bible in Its World)* (Grand Rapids, MI: Wm. B. Eerdmans, 2003).

31. *Nihongi*, trans. W. G. Aston, 12–13.

32. Jan Knappert, *An Encyclopedia of Myth and Legend: Indian Mythology* (London: Diamond Books, 1995), 234.

33. Terry D. Bilhartz, *Sacred Words: A Source Book on the Great Religions of the World* (New York: McGraw Hill, 2006), 187.

34. Bilhartz, *Sacred Words*, 40–41.

35. C. G. Jung, "The Psychology of the Child Archetype," in *Psyche & Symbol: A Selection from the Writings of C. G. Jung*, ed. Violet S. de Laszlo (New York: Anchor, 1958), 117.

36. Jung, "The Psychology of the Child Archetype," 118.

37. Jung, "The Psychology of the Child Archetype," 123.

38. George Lucas is interviewed on *Joseph Campbell—The Hero's Journey* (1997) and *Joseph Campbell and the Power of Myth* (1988), both of which are available on DVD.

39. The shadow represents the dark side of the ego and is a repository for all of the qualities that we shun, including cruelty, lust for power, greed, and thoughts of murder. The shadow is the alter ego of the hero, his doppelgänger. The goal of the hero is to recognize and face the shadow, thus diminishing its power. Interestingly enough, in *The Empire Strikes Back*, as part of his Jedi training, Luke must enter a cave. There he encounters what appears to be Darth Vader. When Luke "defeats" the dark Sith, the front part of the helmet falls away, revealing that Luke has confronted and overcome himself. As Jung said in *Archetypes of the Collective Unconscious*, "whoever looks into the mirror of the water will see first of all his own face. Whoever goes to himself, risks a confrontation with himself. The mirror does not flatter, it faithfully shows whatever looks into it; namely the face we never show to the world. . . . But if we are able to see our own shadow and can bear knowing about it, then a small part of the problem has already been solved." Taken from C. G. Jung, *The Basic Writings of C. G. Jung*, ed. Violet Staub de Laszlo (New York: Modern Library, 1959), 304.

40. As of this writing, if you do a survey of the Top 10 highest grossing Hollywood films of all time, they are *Titanic*, *Star Wars*, *Shrek 2*, *E.T: The Extra-Terrestrial*, *Star Wars: Episode I—The Phantom Menace*, *Pirates of the Caribbean: Dead Man's Chest*, *Spider-Man*, *Star Wars Episode III—Revenge of the Sith*, *The Lord of the Rings: The Return of the King*, and *Spider-Man 2*—and you discover that Lucas was certainly onto something. Most of these films conform to Jung's theory of universal archetypes, and are about a hero on a journey who must confront and defeat the shadow. (Of the *Spider-Man* films, the third one contains the most blatant example of a hero battling his "dark side.") The film that has most in common with the *Star Wars* saga is *The Lord of the Rings* trilogy, which also has a number of heroes (Frodo, Sam, various Hobbits, Legolas, and Aragorn), a wise old man (Gandalf), the shadow (Saruman, Sauron, and the Orcs), various maidens (Arwen and Galadriel), and a trickster (Gollum). Also conforming to this formula are the Harry Potter films, *The Chronicles of Narnia: The Lion, the Witch and the Wardrobe*, and the *Matrix* films, which all rank in the Top 40. A number of screenwriting books have drawn upon Campbell's ideas, including the very popular *The Writer's Journey: Mythic Structure for Writers* by Christopher Vogler. Another text, *Myth & the Movies: Discovering the Myth Structure of 50 Unforgettable Films*, by Stuart Voytilla, shows concrete examples of how these films have used Campbell's myth structure

41. Joseph Campbell and Bill Moyers, *The Power of Myth*, ed. Betty Sue Flowers (New York: Anchor, 1991), 31.

42. For Jews this day is Saturday; for Christians, Sunday.

43. Eleanor Nesbitt, "Sikhism," in *Ethical Issues in Six Religious Traditions*, ed. Peggy Morgan and Clive Lawton (Edinburgh, Scotland: Edinburgh University Press, 1996), 100.

44. For an anthropological definition of what constitutes "ritual," see Kristin Norget, *Religion and Culture: An Anthropological Focus* (Upper Saddle River, NJ: Prentice Hall, 2007), 97–127.

45. "Baptism," *New Advent Catholic Encyclopedia*, www.newadvent.org/cathen/02258b.htm#III (accessed 10 February 2008).

46. "Religion and Ethics—Islam," *British Broadcasting Corporation*, 2006, www.bbc.co.uk/religion/religions/islam/practices/salat.shtml (accessed 10 February 2008).

47. "How to Perform the Daily Prayers," *Al-Islam.org*, al-islam.org/nutshell/files/prayers.pdf (accessed 10 February 2008). A much longer, more detailed version at "Salah. The Muslim Prayer," *University of Buffalo Muslim Student Association*, is wings.buffalo.edu/sa/muslim/library/salah/index.html (accessed 10 February 2008).

48. "Position and purpose of prayer in Islam," *Kingdom of Saudi Arabia's Ministry of Islamic Affairs, Endowments, Da'wah and Guidance*, www.al-islam.com/articles/articles-e.asp?fname =alislam_R30_E (accessed 10 February 2008).

49. Stuart D. B. Picken, *Essentials of Shinto: An Analytical Guide to Principal Teachings* (Westport, CT: Greenwood Press 1994), 172.

50. Picken, *Essentials of Shinto*, 173.

51. Picken, *Essentials of Shinto*, 172.

52. Donin, *To Be a Jew*, 64.

53. Donin, *To Be a Jew*, 64.

54. Donin, *To Be a Jew*, 65, 67.

55. Some of the forbidden activities, as outlined in Torah, include cooking and baking; grinding, fine chopping, straining; washing clothes; doing any handicrafts, such as knitting or embroidering; constructing or repairing; writing or erasing, drawing, painting, coloring, typing; hair cutting, shaving or cutting nails; kindling or extinguishing a fire (this includes lighting a candle or smoking); cutting or tearing; fishing and trapping; garden care or lawn maintenance; and carrying, pushing, or moving an object more than six feet. Thirty-nine categories of activities regarded as work are mentioned in the Mishnah. Rabbis and sages have also compiled an additional list, on which one finds switching on and off electric lights and journeying on the Sabbath, even on foot, beyond the "Sabbath boundary," which is roughly three-quarters of a mile from the place where the worshipper is staying. Donin, *To Be a Jew*, 90–92.

56. Donin, *To Be a Jew*, 82. Some of the other approved activities are discussing and reviewing with children what they have been studying and doing all week; taking a leisurely stroll, socializing with friends and family, attending synagogue-organized lectures, sleeping, playing games with the family, and other "activities in the Sabbath spirit."

57. The reason stated for this is that on a Friday Adam was created, he entered paradise, and he was expelled from paradise. It is further believed that the hour of Judgment Day will arrive on a Friday.

58. Donin, *To Be a Jew*, 285.

59. Hew McLeod, *Sikhism* (New York: Penguin Books, 1997), 143.

60. Picken, *Essentials of Shinto*, 173.

61. Joan Law and Barbara E. Ward, *Chinese Festivals* (Hong Kong: South China Morning Post, 1982), 67.

62. Law and Ward, *Chinese Festivals*, 68.

63. Smart, *Worldviews: Cross-cultural Explorations of Human Beliefs*, 125.

64. Gertrude Grace Sill, *A Handbook of Symbols in Christian Art* (New York: Collier Books, 1975), 30. According to the author, the wearing of white for brides is an "outgrowth of the Roman custom of white robes for Vestal Virgins."

65. Sill, *A Handbook of Symbols in Christian Art*, 30.

66. Wang-Ngai Siu and Peter Lovrick, *Chinese Opera: Images and Stories* (Seattle: University of Washington Press, 1997), 36.

67. Wolfram Eberhard, *A Dictionary of Chinese Symbols: Hidden Symbols in Chinese Life and Thought* (New York: Routledge, 1988), 313.

68. Sill, *A Handbook of Symbols in Christian Art*, 29–30.

69. Knappert, *An Encyclopedia of Myth and Legend: Indian Mythology*, 65.

70. Knappert, *An Encyclopedia of Myth and Legend: Indian Mythology*, 187.

71. Vivien Sung, *Five-Fold Happiness: Chinese Concepts of Luck, Prosperity, Longevity, Happiness and Wealth* (San Francisco: Chronicle Books, 2002), 194.

72. Eberhard, *A Dictionary of Chinese Symbols*, 192.

73. Sung, *Five-Fold Happiness*, 86.

74. Wolfram Eberhard, *A Dictionary of Chinese Symbols: Hidden Symbols in Chinese Life and Thought* (New York: Routledge & Kegan Paul, 1986), 81.

75. Kunzang Dorji, "A (Bhutanese) Dog's Life," in *Lonely Planet: Bhutan* (Oakland, Calif.: Lonely Planet Publications, 1998), 69.

76. Sill, *A Handbook of Symbols in Christian Art*, 16–27.

77. Sill, *A Handbook of Symbols in Christian Art*, 24.

78. Sill, *A Handbook of Symbols in Christian Art*, 25.

79. Stuart D. B. Picken, *The A to Z of Shinto* (Lanham, MD: Scarecrow Press, 2006), 62. For more information on Inari, see Picken's entry on pages 85–86.

80. Picken, *The A to Z of Shinto*, 145.

81. Picken, *The A to Z of Shinto*, 30.

82. According to the *Encyclopedia of Myth and Legend: Indian Mythology*, the swastika is a "sign of the sun-god Surya, as a symbol of his generosity" (240).

83. Michael H. Kohn, trans., *The Shambhala Dictionary of Buddhism and Zen* (Boston, MA: Shambhala, 1991), 214.

84. Eberhard, *A Dictionary of Chinese Symbols*, 280–81.

85. Klaus K. Klostermaier, *A Survey of Hinduism* (New York: State University of New York Press, 1994), 117. He quotes her from the *Code of Manu* or *Manusmrti*.

86. According to some Hindus, the deity Brahma creates the universe, Vishnu maintains it, and Shiva, in his fiery dance, destroys it.

87. Bhikku Bodhi, ed., *In the Buddha's Words: An Anthology of Discourses from the Pali Canon* (Boston: Wisdom, 2005), 232.

88. Bodhi, ed., *In the Buddha's Words*, 233.

89. Roger J. Corless, *The Vision of Buddhism: The Space under the Tree* (New York: Paragon House, 1989), 248.

90. Nicholas Vreeland, ed., *An Open Heart: Practicing Compassion in Everyday Life* (New York: Little Brown, 2001), 120.

91. Thich Nhat Hanh, *The Heart of the Buddha's Teaching* (New York: Broadway Books, 1998), 127.

92. Isabelle Robinet, *Taoism: Growth of a Religion*, trans. Phyllis Brooks (Palo Alto, CA: Stanford University Press, 1997), 7.

93. Bilhartz, *Sacred Words*, 325.

94. Joel Rosenberg, "Bible: Biblical Narrative," in *Back to the Sources: Reading the Classic Jewish Texts*, ed. Barry W. Holtz (New York: Simon & Schuster, 1984), 63–64.

95. Rosenberg, "Bible: Biblical Narrative," 63–64.

96. Rosenberg, "Bible: Biblical Narrative," 64.

97. The Hebrew Bible or *Tanakh* is arranged by the Torah, which are thought to be the Five Books of Moses—Genesis, Exodus, Leviticus, Numbers, and Deuteronomy; the *Nevi'im*, which includes several of the historical books, the three major prophets, and the 12 minor prophets; and the *Kethuvim*, which includes Psalms, Proverbs, Job, the Song of Songs, Ruth, Lamentations, Ecclesiastes, Ester, Daniel, Ezra, Nehemiah, and I and II Chronicles. With the exception of the first five books of the Bible, the arrangement of these books differs considerably in the New Testament. In fact, I and II Chronicles are the 13th and 14th books, and the last book is Malachi, which "point so clearly to the New Covenant, conclude the books of the prophets and precede, in our English Bibles, the New Testament" (Introduction to the Book of Malachi in the New Oxford Annotated Bible). The arrangement of the New Testament was, in fact, approved at various church councils in 393 C.E., 397 C.E., and 419 C.E.

98. *The Oxford Companion to the Bible*, ed. Bruce M. Metzger and Michael D. Coogan (New York: Oxford University Press, 1993), 116.

99. David S. Ariel, *What Do Jews Believe? The Spiritual Foundations of Judaism* (New York: Schocken Books, 1995), 126–27.

100. "There is a strong belief, shared by many Jews, that when the Messiah appears there will be a resurrection of the dead and that those who lived a pious life will roll underground to the Holy Land to be resurrected." To prepare for this trip, sometimes earth from Israel is put into the wooden coffin. Alfred J. Kolatch, *The Jewish Book of Why* (New York: Penguin Compass, 2000), 53.

101. Kolatch, *The Jewish Book of Why*, 218.

102. Kolatch, *The Jewish Book of Why*, 230.

103. Kolatch, *The Jewish Book of Why*, 79.

104. Kolatch, *The Jewish Book of Why*, 80.

105. Kolatch, *The Jewish Book of Why*, 76.

106. Introduction, "The Revelation to John," in *The New Oxford Annotated Bible*, Revised Standard Version (New York: Oxford University Press, 1973), 1493.

107. Stephen L. Harris, *Understanding the Bible*, 3rd ed. (London: Mayfield, 1992), 394.

108. Anantanand Rambachan, "Human Nature and Destiny," in *Themes and Issues in Hinduism*, 1998, 11–12.

109. Sogyal Rinpoche, *The Tibetan Book of Living and Dying*, ed. Patrick Gaffney and Andrew Harvey (San Francisco: Harper San Francisco, 1992), 114.

110. Bodhi, ed., *In the Buddha's Words*, 206.

111. Hanh, *The Heart of the Buddha's Teaching*, 126–27.

112. Bilhartz, *Sacred Words*, 350

113. Ariel, *What Do Jews Believe*, 50.

114. Ariel, *What Do Jews Believe*, 53.

115. McBrien, *Catholicism*, 158.

116. Nasr, *Islam: Religion, History and Civilization*, 35.

117. *Sources of Chinese Tradition: From Earliest Times to 1600*, vol. 1, compiled by Wm. Theodore De Bary, and Irene Bloom (New York: Columbia University Press, 1999), 471–73.

118. From "Toward a Buddhist Environmental Ethic," in *Worldviews, Religion, and the Environment: A Global Anthology*, ed. Richard C. Foltz (Belmont, CA: Wadsworth/Thomson, 2003), 165.

119. Hanh, *The Heart of the Buddha's Teaching*, 126–27.

120. Brian Bocking, "Japanese Religions," in *Worldviews, Religion, and the Environment*, 247.

121. Xinzhong Yao, *An Introduction to Confucianism* (New York: Cambridge University Press, 2000), 175.

122. Ole Brun, "Feng shui and the Chinese Perception of Nature," in *Worldviews, Religion and the Environment*, 237.

123. The article was titled "The Historical Roots of Our Ecologic Crisis" and it appeared in *Science* magazine. For more about White and the impact of his article, see "Introduction: Beyond Lynn White, Jr.," *Counterbalance.net*, www.counterbalance.net/enviro/intro-frame.html (accessed 10 February 2008).

124. Al Gore, *Earth in the Balance: Ecology and the Human Spirit* (Boston, MA: Houghton Mifflin, 1992). Gore discusses the domination of nature theme in the Judeo-Christian tradition.

125. Ariel, *What Do Jews Believe*, 23.

126. The article, "Genesis 1—The Most Misunderstood Part of the Bible," can be found in *Worldviews, Religion, and the Environment*, 280–89. Other articles in chapter 8 (Judaism) are Tikva Frymer-Kensky's "Ecology in a Biblical Perspective," 290–96; Steven S. Schwarzschild's "The Unnatural Jew," 296–306; and Arthur Waskow's "And the Earth Is Filled with the Breath of Life," 306–17.

127. "Genesis 1," in *Worldviews, Religion, and the Environment*, 283.

128. Manfred Gersenfeld, "Jewish Environmental Studies: A New Field," Jerusalem Center for Public Affairs (April 2001). Found online at http://www.jcpa.org/art/jep1.htm. (accessed 11 February 2008).

129. Rabbi Lawrence Troster, "From Apologetics to New Spirituality: Trends in Jewish Environmental Theology," *Coalition on the Environment and Jewish Life*, 2004, www.coejl.org/scholarship/jetheology.pdf (accessed 11 February 2008).

130. Introduction to chapter 9, "Christianity," in *Worldviews, Religion, and the Environment*, 318.

131. McBrien, *Catholicism*, 258. The author gives Jurgen Moltmann, *God in Creation: A New Theology of Creation and the Spirit of God* (New York: Harper & Row, 1985), as one example.

132. The article is titled "The World of the Icon and Creation: An Orthodox Perspective on Ecology and Pneumatology," in *Worldviews, Religion, and the Environment*, 342–49.

133. Murata and Chittick, *The Vision of Islam*, 122.

134. Murata and Chittick, *The Vision of Islam*, 124.

135. Nasr, *Islam: Religion, History and Civilization*, 72.

136. Introduction to chapter 10, "Islam," in *Worldviews, Religion, and the Environment*, 357.

137. H. Byron Earhart, ed., "Introduction: The Nature of Japanese Religion," in *Religion in the Japanese Experience: Sources and Interpretations*, 2nd ed. (Belmont, CA: Wadsworth, 1997), 3.

138. U.S. Catholic Church, *Catechism of the Catholic Church*, 817.

139. U.S. Catholic Church, *Catechism of the Catholic Church*, 2087.

140. U.S. Catholic Church, *Catechism of the Catholic Church*, 2088.

141. U.S. Catholic Church, *Catechism of the Catholic Church*, 2089.

142. McBrien, *Catholicism*, 838.

143. "The Instruction to the Kalamas," *Buddhistinformation.com*, www.buddhistinformation .com/the_kalama_sutra.htm (accessed 10 January 2008).

144. Donin, *To Be a Jew*, 24.

145. Donin, *To Be a Jew*, 27.

146. George Robinson, *Essential Judaism: A Complete Guide to Beliefs, Customs and Rituals* (New York: Pocket Books, 2000), 362.

147. McBrien, *Catholicism*, 104.

148. "Our knowledge of God and nature: physics, philosophy and theology," *L'Osservatore Romano*, 1988, clavius.as.arizona.edu/vo/R1024/ppt-Message.html (accessed 11 February 2008).

149. In addition to the Dalai Lama's book *The Universe in a Single Atom*, other books on the subject include B. Alan Wallace's *Contemplative Science: Where Buddhism and Neuroscience Converge* and *The Dalai Lama at MIT*.

150. Lynda Obst, "Valentine to Science—Interview with Carl Sagan," *Interview Magazine*, 1996, findarticles.com/p/articles/mi_m1285/is_n2_v26/ai_18082728/pg_1 (accessed 11 February 2008).

151. Martin J. Verhoeven, "Buddhism and Science: Probing the Boundaries of Faith and Reason," *Religion East and West* 1 (June 2001): 77–97.

152. "What Is the Bahá'í Attitude towards Science and Technological Progress?" *Bahá'í International Community*, www.bahai.org/faq/social_action/science (accessed 11 February 2008).

153. "'Abdu'l-Bahá on Science and Religion," *Bahá'í International Community*, info.bahai .org/article-1-5-3-1.html (accessed 11 February 2008).

154. Joseph M. Boggs and Dennis W. Petrie, *The Art of Watching Films* (New York: McGraw-Hill, 2008), 4.

155. Boggs and Petrie, *The Art of Watching Films*, 5.

2

Religions in India

India is comprised of several ethnic groups, including Indo-Aryan 72%, Dravidian 25%, Mongoloid, and other 3% (2000). More than two-thirds of the population still lives in a rural area. The predominant religion is Hinduism, with 80.5% of the population following this faith. Making up the rest are Muslims 13.4%, Christians 2.3%, Sikhs 1.9%, other 1.8% (2001 census). It is estimated that more than 700 million people in the world consider themselves to be Hindu, with growing numbers also living in Guyana (35% of the population), Nepal (80%), Bhutan (25% Indian and Nepalese-influenced), Mauritius (48%), Bangladesh (16%), Malaysia (1%), and the United Kingdom (1%).[1]

THE BASICS
The religion commonly referred to as Hinduism poses a number of problems with respect to a definition of religion. First of all, the term *Hinduism* itself is a foreign one, initially designating primarily those people living in a specific geographical region[2] and later referring to members of the priestly caste or simply those who were not Muslims, Christians, or Jains.[3] A more appropriate indigenous term is *Sanatana Dharma*, which means "eternal duty"; however, the term has far-reaching implications, encompassing everything from ethics to human responsibility and interaction. What is commonly known as Hinduism is very much a "way of life," permeating every stage from birth to death and beyond.

43

Second, the religion has neither a centralized authority, someone who makes religious decisions for Hindus, nor a unified system of belief. This means that religious beliefs can vary from one region to another, making it difficult for one to say that "this is Hinduism." Furthermore, India is a land inhabited by a plethora of gods—by some scholars' estimates, 330 million. With all of these deities, one assumes that Hindus are polytheists, but even that isn't a given. A number of Hindus consider themselves to be monotheists, asserting that God is one, he just appears in different guises to different people. Other followers are more pantheistic, believing that God manifests itself in the physical world around them. If anything can be said of Hinduism, it is that it is rich in its diversity.

Why does Hinduism have so many variations? Some of this stems from its history, which itself is undergoing reassessment and debate. Traditionally, scholars have cited the Dravidians as India's earliest known inhabitants. They lived in the Indus River Valley, in modern Pakistan, where an urban civilization flourished between ca. 3000 and 1000 B.C.E. Two important sites are Harappa and Mohenjo-daro, where archaeologists have uncovered detailed town planning and drainage systems, including a "great bath." This bitumen-lined tank with steps leading in and out of it indicates that the culture used water for ritual purposes. Furthermore, scientists have found evidence of a proto-Siva (or Lord of the Animals) in a yogic posture, phallic symbols, and a large number of goddess figurines. Because the only surviving written records, steatite seals, have yet to be translated, much is not known about these people.

Around 1500 B.C.E., another group of people, the Aryans ("noble ones"), moved into the Indian subcontinent.[4] These nomadic people are the authors of the Vedas (Sanskrit for "knowledge"), the most venerated of Hindu writings. The Aryans had a stratified social system with Brahmins, or priests, at the top. Their sacred duty was to perform sacrifices to myriad gods. Among the most popular of these deities were Indra, the creator and ruler of the universe, who slays demons and preserves humans and gods; Agni, the god of fire; Varuna, god of the sky and protector of truth; and Soma, the lord of plants. For the most part, these Aryan gods represented forces of nature that humans could manipulate through sacrifice, thus ensuring fertility, good crops, wealth, and peace.

The Vedas were composed between ca. 1500 B.C.E. and 600 B.C.E. and are still transmitted orally by priests. In contrast to Hindu literature that is considered to be *smriti* ("what is remembered"), the Vedas are considered to be *shruti* ("that which is heard") or that which was directly revealed to ancient seers or *rishis*, who heard and then translated these primordial sounds into human language. Considered canonical, these texts are thought to be free from human imperfections; their truth is considered eternal. Written in Sanskrit, the Vedas are divided into four collections: the Rig-Veda, the Sama-Veda, the Yajur-Veda, and the Artharva-Veda. The Rig-Veda is the oldest and probably best known of the four. It is divided into 10 books (*mandalas* or circles) and contains 1,028 hymns, one of which is the *Gayatri* mantra,[5] which every Brahmin should recite daily. Also contained within it is the *Purusha Shukta* or story of the primordial man. In this, one learns that by sacrificing *Purusha* (Man), everything in the universe—including the moon, the sun, even the gods themselves—is formed. "His mouth became the Brahmin [priest]; his arms were made into the warrior [*kshatriya*], his thighs the people [*vaishya*] and from his feet the servants [*shudra*]."[6] As for the other texts, the Sama-Veda repeats some of the hymns found in the Rig-Veda and sets them to melodies or *saman*. The Yajur-Veda is a collection of ritual prayers (*yajus*) that were used by priests during the fire sacrifice. The Artharva-Veda, named after the sage Atharvan, preserves many pre-Aryan traditions and contains spells, charms, and magical formulae that could be used for healing, warding off evil forces, and harming one's enemies.

In about the ninth century B.C.E., the *Brahmanas* or prose commentaries on the Vedas began to appear. The purpose of these books was to guide priests through the sacrifices, explaining the finer points of ritual, including the proper time and place for ceremonies. Since the world was created and upheld through sacred sounds, it was paramount that the priests intoned the syllables without error. It was believed that performing the ritual animal sacrifice exactly and intoning the sacred words precisely kept the universe in order and intact and brought blessings to those making the offerings. Because priests performed the sacrifices, they enjoyed an increasingly important social role during the Vedic period. Since they were expected to remain ritually pure— the gods would be insulted if given impure offerings—priests were prohibited from "polluting" occupations, such as performing manual labor, engaging in trade or agriculture, or other activities. Their primary activity was to study the Vedas and perform the rituals.

Over time additional societal divisions based on birth or occupation also developed. Included in these are the *kshatriyas* or warriors and leaders;

vaishyas or commoners and includes merchants, landowners, and money-lenders; and *shudras* or those who engage in manual labor. This caste system, as it is commonly called, was hierarchical and, in many ways, based on levels of "purity."[7] In fact, the first three castes—*brahmins, kshatriyas,* and *vaishyas*—are called the "twice born" because males between the ages of 8 and 12 years old undergo the *upanayana,* or sacred thread ceremony. As time went on, more and more occupational-based subdivisions or *jati* formed. Those who didn't really fit into a caste were referred to as untouchables or outcastes, and they were made to perform the most ritually impure jobs, including cleaning toilets, working with corpses, and tanning animal skins.[8]

It has been speculated that by the seventh century B.C.E., people were becoming increasingly dissatisfied with a religion that placed an overemphasis on priests and sacrifice. Appearing at the end of the *Brahmanas,* the *Aranyakas* or forest treatises were intended for those who left behind their everyday lives so that they could retire to the forests and engage in ascetic practices, such as fasting, abstaining from sleep and sexual activity, and meditating. These texts indicate that people were becoming more introspective and that the spiritual path was becoming more egalitarian. Some of the *Aranyakas* are referred to as the Upanishads, 100 or so texts that get their name from the notion of students "sitting near by" their gurus to learn cosmic truths. Most of the Upanishads are short and are written in dialogue form. Only about a dozen are popular today.

Emerging from these writings are many of the basic concepts of Hinduism, including *samsara,* the endless cycle of existence; karma, the moral law of cause and effect, which states that every action has a consequence in this life and the next; atman, the pure, unchanging eternal soul that is at the source of everyone; and Brahman, the eternal, infinite "ultimate" that lies behind all reality and is unknowable to the rational mind. *Moksha* or liberation from the cycle of birth and death is possible, the Upanishads claim; one must simply see that which lies behind *maya* or illusion. It was, in essence, "waking up" to the way things truly were, seeing one's true nature. To do this, one must bring one's thoughts and body under control through self-denial and discipline (yoga), eventually turning one's attention from the sensory world toward the within. As it is stated in the *Brihadaranyaka* Upanishad IV:4: "When all the desires that surge in the heart are renounced, the mortal becomes immortal . . . here in this very life . . . but the Self; freed from the body, merges in Brahman, infinite light, eternal life."[9] *Moksha* wasn't an option for everyone, though. It was only available to those who were born into one of the twice-born castes. Because the caste system was so rigidly enforced, some consolation was given to those born into lower castes. They were instructed to follow their dharma, or duty, as dictated by their caste, gender, and stage of life uncomplainingly, so that in their next life, they might be rewarded by being reborn into a higher caste. If one didn't adhere to dharma and caste obligations, then one could be reborn as an animal, an insect, or even in one of the hell realms.

In addition to *shruti* texts, Hindus hold to a second collection of texts called *smriti*, a word that means tradition, referring to the fact that these are of human, not divine, origin. At the end of the Upanishad era, around the third century B.C.E., there arose in India a legalistic tradition, culminating in the *Dharma Shastras*. Of these law books, the most important is *The Laws of Manu*, also known as *Manusmriti*. Attributed to Manu, the mythical progenitor of humanity, it deals with codes of conduct, civil and criminal law, and punishment. The diverse topics covered include marriage, the preparation of food,[10] sex, politics, and gender issues. It also upholds the caste system and outlines what each person must and must not do. The *Laws of Manu* stresses that everyone has a responsibility to one's dharma and that if people ignore these eternal rules, which are dictated by caste and gender, then society will fall into chaos. For example, (4:97) states, "It is better [to discharge] one's own [appointed] duty incompletely than to perform completely that of another; for he who lives according to the law of another is instantly excluded from his own."[11] Furthermore, it outlines what duties one must perform at each stage of life. For the twice-born male, life begins as a student (*brahmacarin*), when one finds a teacher (guru) and studies the Vedas. After studying, the male, at about 25 years old, enters the householder stage (*grihastha*), when he must "marry a wife of equal caste who is endowed with auspicious [bodily] marks."[12] His duty is to earn a living, produce heirs (preferably male), and support his parents. "When a householder sees his [skin] wrinkled, and [his hair] white, and the sons of his sons, then he may resort to the forest," thus entering the forest-dweller stage (*vanaprastha*).[13] It is during this time that he turns away from the material world, abandoning all attachment to worldly objects: "Having studied the Vedas in accordance with the rule, having begat sons in accordance with the sacred law, and having offered sacrifices according to his ability, he may direct his mind to the [attainment] of final liberation"

(6:36). During the final stage of life one becomes a *sannyasin*, a wandering ascetic who may spend his last days on the banks of the Ganges, waiting for his death. As many scholars have pointed out, only a few men undertake the last two stages, and women generally only observe the first three. *Moksha* is just one of the four goals that Hindus are permitted to pursue in their lifetimes. Other legitimate goals are *kama* or pleasure, sexual or intellectual; *artha* or materialism; and *dharma* or duty. All are expected to follow the latter.

The remaining *smriti* texts are epic tales of great heroes and heroines, the most popular being the *Mahabharata* and the *Ramayana*. Both were written ca. 400 B.C.E. and 300 C.E. Four times the size of the Christian Bible, the *Mahabharata* is the longest poem ever written. The title actually translates to the great story of the Bharatas, referring to King Bharata, the legendary founder of India. Its central story is the conflict between the five sons of Pandu (the Pandavas) and their cousins, the Kauravas, for the throne. And although the story contains many plots and subplots, highlights include a rigged dice game during which Yudhisthira, the eldest of the Pandavas, loses everything, sending him, his four brothers, and their wife Draupadi into the forest for 13 years; a scene during which the Kauravas try to strip Draupadi naked but she is protected by Krishna, who supplies her with an endless length of sari; and, of course, the "famous" battlefield scene. This section of the *Mahabharata* is titled the Bhagavad-Gita, the most popular Hindu text in the world. Of it, Gandhi said, "The book struck me as one of priceless worth. The impression has ever since been growing on me with the result that I regard it today as the book *par excellence* for the knowledge of the Truth. It has afforded me invaluable help in my moments of gloom."[14] He also took to memorizing one to two verses daily in the morning, during his ablutions: "I remember having thus committed to memory 13 chapters."[15] For Gandhi, the Bhagavad-Gita was an "infallible guide of conduct . . . a dictionary of daily reference."[16] Thinkers as diverse as Einstein, Thoreau, and Jung each praised the 700-stanza poem whose title means "Song of God."

Essentially a dialogue between Arjuna, the supreme Pandava archer, and Lord Krishna, the Bhagavad-Gita[17] takes place on a battlefield just prior to the eruption of a great civil war between these two related families. Looking across at the faces of his foes, Arjuna suffers a crisis of conscience, realizing that he cannot kill his friends and relatives, and he drops his bow. Krishna, who acts as Arjuna's charioteer, gives the warrior some valuable lessons on life and death: "He who thinks this self a killer and he who thinks it is killed, both fail to understand; it does not kill nor is it killed" (stanza 19). "Look to your own duty; do not tremble before it; nothing is better for a warrior than a battle of sacred duty" (stanza 33). "Be intent on action, not on the fruits of action; avoid attraction to the fruits and attachment to inaction!" (stanza 47).[18] In these excerpts, Krishna reinforces several important concepts. First, he reminds Arjuna that everyone has an eternal and indestructible atman. You cannot kill that which cannot be killed. Next, he talks about dharma. Since Arjuna is a *kshatriya*, he must perform his duty as a warrior. He was born to fight. "Having regard to your own duty also, you ought not to falter, for there is nothing better for a *kshatriya* than a righteous battle. Happy those *kshatriyas* . . . who can find such a battle to fight—an open door to heaven. But if you will not fight this righteous battle, then you will have abandoned your own duty and your fame, and you will incur sin."[19] Finally, he explains that if Arjuna approaches his task with complete detachment, meaning that he is unmotivated and unaffected by the possible outcome, he can avoid acquiring negative karma.

The Bhagavad-Gita reveals four "ways to god," including *karma yoga, jnana yoga, raja yoga*, and *bhakti yoga*. The first discipline is performing selfless action, performing one's dharma without expecting anything in return. The second means taking the intellectual path, the way of studying and internalizing the sacred texts. The third is disciplining the body and mind by using breathing techniques and correct postures. The fourth, which is presented as the highest goal of living, is today the most common way to god. Having ecstatic love for a personal deity is the ultimate goal for these worshippers, and the end result is union with god. "Whoever bears me in mind at the moment of death accedes to my own mode of being. Then muse on me always, for if you fix your mind and soul on me you will come to me set free from doubt" (8:5).

The subject of Valmiki's *Ramayana* is the righteous king Rama (believed to be the seventh avatar of Vishnu) and his beloved wife, Sita. The story begins with Rama's miraculous birth, and by the end of the first book, he has married Sita. Shortly after their wedding, Rama is exiled to the forest for 14 years, and Sita joins him. During this time, she is abducted by Ravana, a 10-headed demon from Lanka. Rescue is possible because of Rama's brother, Lakshmana, and Hanuman, the monkey king, and his army. Since their creation, both the *Mahabharata* and *Ramayana* have been incredibly popular, influencing "the thought, imagination, and outlook of the vast mass of Indian people. . . . The very first Indian film, *Raja Harischandra* (1913), was based on the *Ramayana*, and since then scores of filmmakers have mined this and the *Mahabharata* for plots and themes. In addition, certain topics associated with motherhood, patrimony and revenge, for example, articulated in films such as *Mother India* (1957), *Awaara* (1951) and *Zanjeer* (*Chains*, 1947) are directly traceable to these epics."[20] The depiction of these epics has extended beyond film, for they are regularly performed in stage productions and are the source of comic books, books, and more.[21] In his autobiography, Gandhi explains that he and his father used to listen to the *Ramayana* being read every evening by a man, who apparently cured himself of leprosy by "regular repetition" of this text. "Today, I regard the *Ramayana* of Tulsidas as the greatest book in all devotional literature."[22] Gandhi said that in his youth, he was terribly afraid of ghosts and spirits. The remedy, as recommended by his nurse, was repetition of the name of Rama.[23]

For the most part, Vedic literature was inaccessible to the average person; therefore, the *Puranas* ("ancient story") emerged between ca. fourth to eighth century C.E. to accommodate their needs. These stories of the gods can be found in 18 major and 18 minor texts. Each book features not only narratives about the deities' lives but also hymns, an outline of history, and discussion of cosmology. Furthermore, they emphasize bhakti and dharma. For the most part, the various texts focus on Brahma, Vishnu, and Shiva. When worshiped together, these three deities form the *Trimurti*, representing respectively, creation, preservation, and destruction.[24]

As was previously mentioned, deities are ubiquitous in India; however, Vishnu, Shiva, and Shakti prove to be the most popular. Their exploits can be found in the *Vishnu Purana*, *Shiva Purana*, and *Markandeya Purana*. Followers of Krishna look to the *Bhagavata Purana*, which discusses the 10 avatars of Vishnu, who is the protector and preserver of the world and life. When depicted, Vishnu, a blue deity reclines on or stands near a giant many-hooded serpent named Shesha, and wears a garland of flowers around his neck and a tall crown on his head. In his four hands he holds a conch, a disc, a mace, and the lotus flower. This benevolent and merciful being "descends" to Earth in time of need, assuming one of many avatars or physical forms. These range from a tortoise to a dwarf;[25] however, his best-known forms are Krishna, Rama, Siddhartha Gautama or the Buddha, and Kalki, the soon-to-come savior who will bring an end to evil. Like the other deities, he has a consort. When he is Vishnu, his wife is Lakshmi, goddess of wealth and beauty; when Krishna, she is Radha, the most beloved of the cowherds; when Rama, she is Sita, his faithful wife. Garuda, which has the head, wings, talons, and beak of a bird but the body and limbs of a man, is his vehicle. Followers of Vishnu, about 580 million people or 60% of all Hindus, are called Vaishnavites and they can be identified by the V-shaped mark that they may put on their forehead, between their eyebrows. Also associated with Vishnu is Hanuman, the monkey deity renowned for his selfless devotion to Lord Rama in the *Ramayana*.

Like Vishnu, Shiva dates to the Rig-Veda. But in Shiva's case, he possessed a different name—Rudra, the howler. Seen as the god of truth, asceticism, death, and justice, Shiva is also lord of the mountains and of animals. Shiva actually has two sides—the ascetic and the erotic, the benevolent and the malevolent. His destructive side can be seen when he's depicted as Shiva Nataraja. His dancing form is encircled by flames, and his typically matted hair flows out at the sides. One of his four arms plays a drum, another points to his outstretched leg, another holds a flame, and the final one is extended in blessing. His only stationary leg stands on and crushes the dwarf-demon of ignorance. In his more peaceful yogic guise, Shiva can be found seated in the lotus position, on a tiger skin, meditating on top of Mount Kailasa in the Himalayas. His body is often white, his throat blue. Around his neck, he wears prayer beads and a cobra. On his forehead are three horizontal lines that flank his third eye.[26] His matted hair is typically piled on top of his head, and a crescent-shaped moon hangs from it like an ornament. The story goes that he caught the River Ganges in his hair so that it wouldn't flood the Earth. Now it flows from his locks. Siva carries a trident and rides Nandi, the white bull. His consort is Parvati, the "mountain goddess" who assumes other guises. His son is Ganesha, the elephant-headed god who is the "remover of obstacles" and is said to have broken his tusk so that he could act as Vyasa's scribe on the *Mahabharata*. Prayers are offered to Ganesha at the beginning of worship, before a wedding, and before embarking on a journey or new task.[27] Shiva and his consort also can be worshipped as the phallic lingam and the cup-shaped yoni.

Shakti or Devi is the powerful and active energy of the goddess; she is the universal mother. She plays many roles and takes many forms; however, the ones that concern us here are Kali and Durga, for both are the feminine element in their most ferocious aspect. Kali is known as the "black mother"; however, her name also means time. She has a fearful appearance. She is typically naked, except for a "skirt" of severed human arms. Her eyes are wide, her tongue sticks out, and from her mouth drips blood. Around her neck is a garland of bleached skulls; in two of her four hands she holds a bloody sword and a severed head, which may have been given to her by her devotees.[28] Another hand offers a gesture of fearlessness—at least for her worshippers. One story tells of her ecstatic dance that nearly left her husband, Shiva, dead. When she is portrayed in this manner, Kali stands over her spouse's prostrate body. Kali is the goddess of death, disease, and destruction; however, she also liberates people from these same aspects of life. Kalighat, her temple, is in Kolkata (formerly Calcutta), a city that is named after her. She is regarded as one of the principal deities of Bengal. In India about 50 million worship Devi.

Durga means "inaccessible," "fort," and "invincible," and that's certainly what she is. According to the *Durga Mahatmya*, Mahishasura, a buffalo demon, was threatening the very existence of the gods, so together they formed this formidable goddess to defeat him. Although it is said that she has 1,000 arms, Durga is typically only depicted with 10. In each, she holds a weapon, given to her by the various deities. Some of these include Vayu's (god of the wind) bow and arrow, Vishnu's discus, Shiva's trident, Agni's sword, Varuna's conch and noose, Indra's thunderbolt, Yama's (god of death) sword and shield, and Vishwakarma's (god of architecture) axe and armor. She sometimes can be seen with a lion; at other times she is riding a tiger. Unlike Kali, Durga has a serene countenance. On her head, she wears a tall crown that is encircled by a nimbus. The Durga *puja* is celebrated every year, particularly in Bengal. During this festival the nine different forms of the goddess are worshipped over nine days.

The practice of *puja*, which is the act of revering or worshipping one or more deities, dates to the early centuries of the Common Era; however, it became characteristic of Hindu worship. Ideally *puja* is performed in the early morning. Upon rising, one washes oneself and rinses one's mouth. The image or images of the deity, usually in the form of a sculpture or portrait, will be located on a shelf or altar. To this image, the worshipper will offer food (fruit, yoghurt, ghee, and honey), drink (water or milk), and perhaps flowers while chanting mantras or singing songs. The person may also light a lamp before the deity, or she or he may burn incense. The image of the deity, in general, is not believed to be inhabited by the god. Instead, it is seen as a focal point for honoring and communicating with the god. During *puja*, the deity is treated with great reverence and devotion. He or she is treated as a guest, as a lover, or as a child.

Worshipping the deity can also take place in a temple, particularly during the various festivals that dot the Hindu calendar. Each region has its own particularities; however, most Hindus celebrate Holi and Diwali. Referred to as "The Festival of Colors," Holi takes place in March or April, thus heralding the arrival of spring. During this holiday, young and old, male and female, pepper each other with colored water and powder. It is a joyous occasion that allows participants to break down social taboos. The holiday has its origins in a story about a young Krishna, who playfully threw colored powder on Radha and all of the other *gopis*. Diwali, too, comes from a story about Vishnu. An abbreviation of the Sanskrit word *Deepavali*, which means rows of lights, this holiday commemorates the return of Rama and Sita after their 14-year exile as was mentioned in the *Ramayana*. Hindus prepare for Diwali for weeks, cleaning and decorating their homes. During the main festival, people decorate their roofs and windowsills with lamps, dress in new clothes, and set off fireworks. Not only does this festival herald the beginning of the financial year but it is also a celebration of good over evil. Ganesha and Lakshmi are venerated at this time.

A large number of Hindus follow the path of devotional worship of a deity as a means for achieving *moksha*. Others engage in philosophical or intellectual discourse. Probably one of the best-known philosophical systems is Advaita Vedanta, which is a nondual or monistic system that is credited to Shankara who lived from 788 to 829 C.E. He claimed that the world we see is not real, and it is our ignorance of reality that keeps us from Brahman. Believing in an independent atman is also ignorant, he said. To cut through this *maya*, we must worship a personal god and then move onto a higher experience of oneness, realizing that atman equals Brahman. Advaita Vedanta is just one position. Others are *dvaita* or dualistic.

Hinduism isn't the only religion in India. During the fifth and sixth centuries B.C.E., two *kshatriyas*—Vardhamana Mahavira and Siddhartha Gautama—became founders of their own religions, Jainism and Buddhism, respectively. Although they shared the Hindu concepts of karma, reincarnation, and *samsara*, these religious systems differed in that they rejected the importance of sacrifice, gods, and caste; the infallibility of the Vedas; and the role of the Brahmins. They claimed that anyone could achieve release from *samsara* by performing austerities. Hinduism reacted by becoming more philosophical, and, in some cases, reabsorbing these new leaders into their pantheon. In the *Vishnu Purana*, it explains that Vishnu took the form of the Buddha and a Jain mendicant so as to dissuade people from making sacrifices. Apparently the demons were becoming too powerful, and this was Vishnu's way of defeating them.[29] Buddhism reached its zenith in India during the third century B.C.E., when Ashoka converted to the religion and made its concepts of tolerance and nonviolence the guiding principles of his empire. This influence was short-lived, though. By the seventh century C.E., Buddhism was disappearing from the landscape, and by the 13th century, it was all but gone. A minor revival occurred in 1956, when B. R. Ambedkar, an untouchable, not only converted to Buddhism, which makes no caste distinctions, but he also advocated that others do the same. Today, Buddhism is the fifth-largest religion in India, with about 6 million followers in Maharashtra (Ambedkar's state), nearly 400,000 in Karnataka; 300,000 in Uttar Pradesh, which borders Nepal; 240,000 in West Bengal; and 209,000 in Madhya Pradesh.[30] As in the case of Buddhism, Jainism maintains a presence in Maharashtra (1.3 million), Madhya Pradesh (545,000), Karnataka (410,000), and Uttar Pradesh (207,000). It also has considerable numbers in Rajasthan (650,000) and Gujarat (525,000).[31]

Arab merchants brought Islam to India in the seventh century C.E., and over the centuries the religion has met with considerable success. By the 11th century it was widespread in the north, hitting its zenith under the Mughals, who ruled between 1526 and 1857. This meeting of Islam and Hinduism gave rise to a new religion in the 15th century—Sikhism, which is the fourth-largest religion in India. Today, Islam is the second largest. Christianity also has a presence in India. It was brought to the country by Syrians in the fourth century C.E. Interestingly enough, the Acts of Thomas, ca. 200 C.E., claims that Thomas, one of the apostles, "evangelized India, and to this day there are Thomas Christians in India who call Thomas the founder of their faith."[32] All of these religions forced Hindus to reexamine and in some cases reform their own beliefs. At no time was this more evident than during the 19th and 20th centuries. Ram Mohan Roy (1772–1833) was an important early reformer, who drew upon his own Hindu tradition, particularly the Upanishads, but also embraced the monotheism of Christianity. Roy rejected "meaningless" rituals and the infallibility of the Vedas. He also tried to purify Hinduism of its social evils, such as the caste system and especially sati, the practice of burning widows with their deceased husbands. The result of this Hindu and Christian blend was the Brahmo Samaj. Paramahamsa Ramakrishna (1836–1886) and his disciple Swami Vivekananda (1863–1902) packaged and delivered a nonsectarian Hinduism to the West. In fact, the former stressed that "all religions-are-the-same."[33]

The most instrumental reformer during this period was Mohandas K. Gandhi (1869–1948), who was also known as "the Mahatma" or Great Soul. Gandhi himself was born a Hindu, a Vaishnava, and he "read books by Vivekananda and Tagore, and memorized the Bhagavad Gita."[34] When he was a youth, he was exposed to a variety of religious traditions. His parents visited temples dedicated to Shiva and Rama, and his father was friends with Jains, Muslims, and Parsis. (The concept that he's best known for, *ahimsa* or absolute nonviolence, comes from Jainism.) This diverse background gave him, he said, an "early grounding in tolerance for all branches of Hinduism and sister religions."[35] Gandhi said that he believed "in the fundamental truth of all great religions of the world. And I believe that if only we could, all of us, read the scriptures of the different faiths from the stand-point of the followers of those faiths, we should find that they were at the bottom, all one and were all helpful to one another."[36] In addition to texts from his own religious tradition—he especially revered the Ramayana and the Bhagavad-Gita—Gandhi also read the New Testament. The Sermon on the Mount, in particular, went "straight to his heart."[37] Furthermore, a friend, Abdulla Sheth, gave Gandhi "a fair amount of practical knowledge of Islam."[38] Although he remained a Hindu, Gandhi challenged the "social evils" that came from it, such as the caste system and the ill treatment of untouchables, and he questioned the treatment of widows. His ideas, especially about giving Muslims more political power, proved too challenging, and in 1948 he was assassinated by a Hindu fundamentalist.[39]

When India gained independence from Great Britain on August 15, 1947, its people were guaranteed, under the Constitution, "liberty of thought, expression, belief, faith and worship" and the right to freedom of religion. What's more, the country was deemed a secular republic. This, of course, doesn't mean that everyone supports this. The past 60 years have witnessed

Hinduism merging with intense nationalism, creating such political arms as the Rashtriya Swayamsevak Sangh (RSS; National Volunteers Corps). The goal of this organization is to "have an organized Hindu society in which all its constituents and institutions function in harmony and coordination." Furthermore, members "consider the Hindu society itself as 'Janata Janardana'— god incarnate. Any service rendered to this society, accepting nothing in return, is for him the worship of his god, the 'Samajaroopee Parameshwar' [the god in the form of society]."[40]

The organization further explains that since the "weaker sections in society become easy prey for exploitation and conversion to other faiths," they are doing what they can to meet these groups' social needs. They want to "activise [sic] the dormant Hindu society" against the Muslims and Christian "missions" who threaten Hindu identity. The RSS isn't alone in its mission. Other groups attempting to achieve similar aims are the Vishva Hindu Parishad (VHP; World Hindu Council) and the Bharatiya Janata Party (BJP; "Indian People's Party"). Of the latter group, Ziauddin Sardar explains that "Its ideology of *Hindutva*, or Hindu nationalism, is based on the idea that all Hindus are one and that India, therefore, is an exclusively Hindu nation and should be ruled by a Hindu government." He claims that the party is promoted by the middle class, who believe that Islam and Christianity are an imposition on "Hindu India." And they do more than just talk about taking back Hindu India. He states that they have actively promoted violence, leading to the 1992 destruction of the Babri Mosque in Ayodhya, and the BJP has a list of 3,000 mosques that the group plans on converting to temples.[41] Between 1998 and 2001, the BBC reported on a number of violent attacks against Christian nuns and priests, particularly in Kerala, where Christians number about 20% of the population. A report issued by the Human Rights Watch found that "between January 1998 and February 1999, the Indian Parliament reported a total of 116 incidents of attacks on Christians across the country" with numbers highest in Gujarat. Attacks have ranged from the destruction of institutions to the raping of nuns.[42]

For the most part, these are isolated incidents. As was previously mentioned, the Indian Constitution promises freedom of religion; however, for this to exist, it needs to be safeguarded. As K. R. Narayanan, then president of India, said during his outgoing speech in 2002, "It is important for us today to introspect and realize that what makes India's unity and democracy credible and enduring is this precious tradition of tolerance. . . . My parting appeal to you . . . is to guard our tradition of tolerance, for that is the soul of our culture and civilization, that is the spirit of our Constitution, and that is also the secret of the successful working of our democracy and the secret of the coherence of this vast country as a united nation."[43]

THE FILMS

As is mentioned in *Indian Popular Cinema,* there is a real distinction between popular and artistic cinema in India. Popular films, as the authors state, are "largely melodramatic, often musicals, conveying simple clear moral messages; they represent a distinctly Indian approach to cinema as a form of mass entertainment."[44] The other types of films are directed by internationally recognized auteurs, such as Satyajit Ray, and "constitute only about 10 percent of the total output." These tend to be realistic, without the typical song-and-dance routines. Although there are certainly exceptions, the films that have been chosen for exploration in this and subsequent chapters will draw primarily from the artistic tradition because filmmakers working within this milieu tend to focus on deeper issues, offering perhaps a more reliable snapshot of society and its problems.

American Desi (2001)—Written and directed by Piyush Dinker Pandya. Running time: 100 min. English. USA: Unrated. Genre: Comedy

Summary: Krishnagopal Reddy (Deep Katdare) is an ABCD, an American-Born Confused Desi; essentially he is Indian only by birth. As he and his friend Eric (Eric Axen), a blonde, blue-eyed all-American guy, get into the car and leave for the university, Kris can't wait to leave his culture behind. But as soon as he arrives on campus, he learns that this won't be so easy. After all, his roommates are all Indian—Ajay Pandya (Kal Penn), a "gangsta" wannabe; Jagjit Singh (Ronobir Lahiri), a Sikh; and Salim Ali Khan (Rizwan Manji), a Muslim. It also doesn't help that the woman he's interested in, Nina Shah (Purva Bedi), is a culturally proud Indian. Hoping to woo and win the girl, Kris sets out to rediscover his roots.

American Desi is one of several films that has been written and directed by American-raised Indians who are translating their identity crisis onto the big screen. Although they "feel" American, they just can't seem to "escape" their

Indian heritage, from which they have become alienated. In most cases, their cultural estrangement rears its head either when they go away to the university or when they are expected to get married. As if to prove how American Kris (as he prefers to be called) is, *American Desi* begins with scenes of him packing in his typical, middle-class bedroom. As the camera pans, we see that it is filled with trophies and photos of him playing various sports; he even has a poster of a rock band and a scantily clad blonde on his wall. In his closet, we see a pornographic magazine. The only object that might divulge Kris's heritage is a small framed photo of him and his parents in front of the Taj Mahal.

Contrasting with Kris is his mother, a devout, traditionally dressed Vaishnavite. While classical Indian music plays in the background, she performs *puja*, by lighting a lamp, burning incense, and offering flowers to various images of Krishna and Ganesha that sit on an altar dedicated to this purpose. As Kris and his friend, Eric, prepare to leave the house, Kris's mother appears, holding in front of her a metal tray, on which she has flowers, a lit lamp, and red *kumkum*. Despite her son's protests, she then performs *aarti* (also written *arati*), which is "worship of an image or honored person by moving lighted camphor or oil lamps in a circular way on a plate in front of that image"[45] During this ritual, she dots Kris's and Eric's foreheads with the red substance, circles her son's frame with the tray, and then offers him *prasad* or food that has been blessed by the gods.[46] The purpose of this act is to keep him safe from harm and bless him before he embarks on his journey. Even though Kris rolls his eyes during the ritual, Eric is a bit more open-minded, remarking that "I need all the help I can get." At the conclusion of the act, Kris must bend down to honor his mother and father. Just as the young men leave the house, every Reddy family member rushes over to bid them good luck and farewell. Kris's father reminds him to call home when he gets to the university, because his mother will be fasting until she hears from him.[47] This sentiment echoes what Gandhi wrote in *The Story of My Experiments with Truth*: "The outstanding impression my mother has left on my memory is that of saintliness." He explains that she was deeply religious, never taking her meals without her daily prayers. "To keep two or three consecutive fasts was nothing to her. Living on one meal a day during Chaturmas [a period of four months] was a habit with her." He recalls one time during the rainy season, when the sun rarely makes an appearance, that she said she would refrain from food until she saw the sun.[48]

Just in case the audience hadn't figured out that Kris doesn't respect his traditions, the conversation that takes place in the car should drive this point home. Wondering what had just taken place, Eric says, "Kris, you know that ceremony that your mom performed . . ." Cutting him off, Kris replies, "Don't ask me anything about it. I just wait there until she finishes." "She was blessing us, right?" Eric continues. "We're not married or anything? I saw this documentary on the Discovery Channel that said how the dot was a symbol of marriage." Kris replies, "Whatever it means, I'd wipe that shit off your forehead before you start attracting Hare Krishnas." With their saffron robes, shaved heads, and drum playing, Hare Krishnas have a relatively negative image in the West and have been lampooned in American comedies such as *Airplane.*

Kris's situation doesn't improve when he gets to the university. To his horror, his roommates aren't White Anglo-Saxon Protestants, but they are three Indians—a Muslim, a Sikh, and an Afro-centric Hindu. And in contrast to Kris, his roommates embody their faiths. For instance, Ajay frequently wears Hindu-related clothing. In one scene, he sports a Krishna decorated T-shirt. In other scenes, his clothes are decorated with the *aum* symbol. According to Klostermaier, this mystical symbol, also called the "*pranava,* contains the universe. It consists of the first and the last vowel and the last consonant of the Sanskrit alphabet, therefore encompassing all words."[49] Every religious work begins and ends with *aum,* because it is supposed to be auspicious, and the sound is purported to have created the universe. Finally, as Kris walks through the dorm room, we see that the walls are decorated with various religious images of deities.

The irony of Kris's anti-Indian bias lies in his birth name—Krishnagopal, which indicates his parents' affiliation with the blue, flute-playing deity. In Sanskrit, "Gopal" means "the cowherd," and it refers to the Puranic stories of his childhood pastimes in Vrindavan, where he was raised by cowherds. As if to visually drive home the connection between the deity and this character, at the beginning of the film, when Kris's mom is performing her *puja,* the camera stops on an image of the young deity and then dissolves into a shot of Kris in the exact same posture. At another time, Kris rejects his name and the viewer sees a close up of Ajay's shirt, which features a cherubim-faced Krishna.

Because most of the characters in the film are Hindu, references to the religion abound. During an Indian group's planning meeting, the students talk about celebrating Diwali, Holi, and the Navratri (Ganga), which is the nine-day festival during which nine forms of Shakti/Devi are worshipped. Performed during Navratri are the *garba* and *rass* dances, both of which are shown at the end of *American Desi*. Rass participants, who wear traditional clothing and hold a *dandias* or wooden stick in each hand, stand in a circular configuration. As they move to the drumbeat, they whirl and strike their brightly colored sticks against those held by other dancers. "This Dance of Swords" represents the Puranic fight that occurred between Durga and the defeated buffalo demon. In the film, as the characters arrive at the Navratri celebration, they enter through a papier-mâché image of Ganesha. In the middle of the room is a giant animated Durga, who stands next to a tiger. In honor of the dance's theme, at the end of the film, Kris fights with Rakesh Patel (Anil Kumar), Nina's insanely jealous friend, and he emerges triumphantly. As Jagjit says, "It's just like in a Hindi film where the hero defeats the villain." One can't help but notice that this sequence takes on religious overtones. Just as Durga vanquished the demon so too does Kris.

Several comments made in the film remind the viewer of another Hindu belief—that of rebirth. For example, someone tells the very artistically talented Jagjit that he must be "Van Gogh's reincarnation" and Kris says that Ajay is a "reincarnation of M. C. Hammer." Another offhand comment made to Gautam Rao, a teacher's assistant, when he is drunk is that he should take some Ayurvedic medicine for his condition. From the Sanskrit words meaning "life knowledge," Ayurveda is a system of traditional Indian medicine. The underlying assumption of this practice is that "sickness is due to an imbalance of the three bodily humors and by changing the patient's diet, habits and thoughts; the proper balance can be reestablished."[50] Some Ayurvedic personalities believe that this form of medicine comes from Brahma himself.

Although no one gets married in the film, many characters talk about marriage. Salim says several times that he doesn't want to marry an American-born Desi. When the time is right he will tell his parents, and they will get the process moving along. He is, of course, talking about arranged marriages, which are still common among Indians. When Farah Saaed's (Sunita Param) parents drop in unexpectedly, they meet Salim who is dressed in a full *burqua* to avoid detection. Thinking he's a nice Muslim girl from Lucknow,[51] Farah's mother tries to fix her (him) up with a nice boy back home. After all, she doesn't want to wait until her late 20s to get married or she'll end up with an old man who advertises in the newspaper. In another scene, Jagjit acts as a go-between to patch up problems between Kris and Nina. No one really talks specifically about caste in the film; however, Jagjit sends an e-mail to Nina, trying to convince her to give Kris another chance. He ends his "ad" with "caste is no bar." Hinduism allows followers to pursue wealth (*artha*), pleasure (*kama*), duty (dharma), and release from the cycle of birth and death (*moksha*). This second pursuit is in evidence when Ajay picks up a copy of the Kama Sutra in the university bookstore. Known in the West as a notorious lovemaking manual, the text, which was written in the fourth century C.E. by a Brahmin named Vatsyayana, addresses a variety of social issues, including education for men and women, and marriage and caste. It even offers magic practices for good luck, invisibility, and virility.[52]

In addition to Hinduism, those watching *American Desi* can learn more about Islam and Sikhism. For example, when Kris is moving into the dorm room, we see that Salim has his Koran on a pedestal next to his bed. This reminds the viewer that Muslims treat the Koran with the utmost respect. "For Muslims, everything about the [*Koran*] is sacred—its sounds, the very words of the Arabic language chosen by God to express His message, the letters in which it is written, and even the parchment or paper that constitutes the physical aspect of the sacred text." Furthermore, Muslims "usually do not touch it unless they have made their ablutions and are ritually clean."[53] On two occasions we see Salim praying—once in the dorm room, seated on a prayer rug, and once at a mosque, where men and women are separated. Each time, Salim bows and mutters, "Allah Akbar," which is Arabic for "God is Great." Finally, when Farah's parents arrive at their daughter's dorm room, they greet each other with "*Eid Mubarak*," which means "Blessed Festival" and is a greeting used during the holidays.

The film's representations of Sikhism aren't quite as obvious. For instance, we never see Jagjit pray or engage in any other religious behavior; however, the fact that his last name is Singh, which means lion, and the way that he's dressed do reveal a few things about him: He's probably a member of the *khalsa* (Pure Ones), a community vowing total dedication to Sikhism.[54] We get a verbal hint that Jagjit is a monotheist, when he says to Kris, "Have faith in God, yaar." Jagjit usually wears a brightly colored turban or a *dastar*, which, for Sikhs, is a symbol of "royalty and dignity."[55] When he doesn't wear a turban, we see that his hair is unshorn and kept in a top knot. Members of the *khalsa* cannot cut any hair on their bodies. Jagjit also wears a *kara* or steel bracelet, which reminds the wearer of restraint in his actions and remembrance of God at all times. Finally, at one point, he talks about his father's sword, another one of the five k-named items that signify a member of the *khalsa*. In this case, the *kirpan* is a ceremonial sword and it is a "symbol of dignity and the Sikh struggle against injustice."[56]

Water (2005)—Written and directed by Deepa Mehta, with dialogue by Anurag Kashyap. Running time: 117 min. Hindi. Rated PG-13 for mature thematic material involving sexual situations and for brief drug use. Genre: Drama/Romance. Oscar-nominated for Best Foreign Language Film.

Summary: Set in 1938, *Water* depicts the plight of widows who are living in an ashram in the holy city of Varanasi. Shown through the eyes of the prepubescent Chuyia (Sarala), the film shows the ill treatment that they must endure, and it demonstrates to what lengths these poverty-stricken women must go in order to survive.[57] Additional characters include Madhumati (Manorama), a strong-willed, overweight "madam"; Shakuntala (Seema Biswas), a Brahmin who befriends the newest arrival; Kalyani (Lisa Ray), the beautiful, long-haired "jewel" of the ashram; and Narayan (John Abraham), an idealistic and romantic follower of Gandhi.

The film begins with a quote that is gleaned from *The Laws of Manu* (5:156–164). It reads, "A widow should be long suffering until death, self-restrained and chaste. A virtuous wife who remains chaste when her husband has died goes to heaven. A woman who is unfaithful to her husband is reborn in the womb of a jackal." As the credits appear, we see a young, long-haired prepubescent girl blissfully eating. Oblivious to what's going on around her, she playfully pokes the feet of the man lying next to her. She is chastised. This is the audience's introduction to Chuyia, a girl who doesn't even remember being married to her middle-aged husband and who then faces the bewildering prospects of being a widow for the rest of her life. Stripped of her jewelry, Chuyia, who now must only dress in white, gets her hair cut and her head shaved before being dropped off at the doorstep of an ashram for widows. Like most of the women inside, Madhumati has accepted her fate, and tells

Chuyia, "In grief, we are all sisters here, and this house is our refuge. Our Holy Books say that a wife is part of her husband, while he's alive. And when husbands die, God help us, wives also half die, so how can she feel pain?" Chuyia, who never accepts societal expectations, replies, "Because she's half alive." Throughout the film, Chuyia will serve as a revolutionary force that will transform the hearts and minds of those around her.

Mehta sets the film during Gandhi's life, because he, too, tried to change long-standing attitudes not only toward those who lived outside of the caste system but also toward widows. In the film, the eunuch pimp claims that Gandhi said, "Widows are strangers to love and nobody should be a stranger to love."[58] Even though these events "happened" seven decades ago, widows still face tremendous difficulties in India. In Deborah Hastings's 2005 article *India's Unwanted: 30 Million Widows*, she explains that being a widow is "one of the worst stigmas a woman can endure. . . . Excluded from family gatherings, for fear the mere fall of her shadow will bring bad luck and tragedy . . . many journey to the holy cities of Vrindavan and Varanasi, where they beg, and are paid a pittance to recite prayers in the temple."[59] Mehta, herself, explained in her "director's statement" that she was inspired to make the film after seeing a widow in Varanasi. The image of her "bent like a shrimp . . . sitting on her haunches, arms outstretched on her knees, head bowed down in defeat" remained with the director for 10 years.[60]

After Shakuntala spreads turmeric on Chuyia's head, to soothe her razor burn, the girl remarks that Shakuntala is a savior, just like the goddess Durga. It isn't a coincidence that Mehta gives her characters the names that she does. In most of her films, names serve a religio-symbolic purpose. Chuyia, which means mouse, reminds us of Ganesha's vehicle. Because this small animal can chew through anything, it also is instrumental in "removing obstacles." When the *ladoo*-loving widow learns Chuyia's name, she says, "the mouse with sharp teeth." On the surface, the child seems to be harmless; however, as the film progresses, we learn how much of a catalyst she will be to change, especially for Shakuntala, whose name in Sanskrit means "bird." She shares her name with a character in the *Mahabharata*,[61] a kind, beautiful woman who was raised in an ashram. Symbolically, Shakuntala does represent a Durga-like figure who rescues the young girl and Kalyani from a life of servitude and prostitution. At the beginning of the film, she is the most accepting of her lot in life; however, as events unfold she undergoes dramatic changes.[62]

The name Kalyani also appears in the *Mahabharata*, and is listed among a large number of "illustrious mothers" and "auspicious ones." According to the Matsya Purana, this is one of Sati's—Shiva's first wife—108 names. "Having recited these names, Sati immolated herself. She was later reborn as Parvati or Uma."[63] Associating Kalyani with such a tragic figure foreshadows her own ending. Because she is so beautiful, Madhumati prostitutes Kalyani out to various men. Even though viewers might think that this practice is rooted in fiction, it's actually a very real phenomenon. "For the younger widows—some barely teen-agers, despite laws that forbid child marriages—there is the additional threat of being forced into sex with landlords, rickshaw drivers, policemen, even Hindu holy men. . . . The tradition of their being forced to have sex with other men in their husbands' families, or to sell sex, was once so widespread that the Hindi word 'randi,' or widow, became a synonym for prostitute."[64] With the exception of her "unchaste" behavior, Kalyani conforms to the depiction of women in traditional Indian cinema in that they generally uphold "traditional virtues of virginity, devotion to God and family, and service to men."[65]

Hope for this character comes in the guise of Narayan, who despite disapproval from his mother and society, wants to marry Kalyani. However, it isn't to be. After Kalyani learns that Narayan's father was one of her clients, she drowns herself, fulfilling this association between her and the self-sacrificing goddess.[66] Narayan or Narayana comes from the Sanskrit for "refuge of man." More importantly, this is also "one of the most exalted titles of Vishnu or Krishna.[67] Even when Chuyia first meets the tall, spectacles-wearing man and he tells her his name, she immediately recognizes that he shares a name with Vishnu. The association between this character and Krishna doesn't stop at his name. When he is with Kalyani, the two form a symbolic lover-beloved pair reminiscent of Krishna and Radha. Kalyani herself is a devotee of the blue god, and in her room we see a small altar on which several statues of Krishna sit. After praying to him, she tells Chuyia to say "*Jai shree Krishna* 108 times and soon you'll fly away." She then takes off her *mala* beads and gives them to Chuyia for prayer. Her devotion to Krishna is crystallized in Narayana, who like Krishna, plays the flute. While being ferried across the Ganges to a client, Kalyani asks her pimp if Krishna takes on human form, obviously in response to her earlier meeting with Narayan. The pimp confirms her beliefs. Toward the end of the film, Narayan asks Kalyani what color she will wear first, and she replies blue, because it's the color of Lord Krishna. He furthers the reference by saying that if she wears a blue sari bordered by gold, she'll be as beautiful as a peacock feather. Klostermaier states that peacocks are often associated with "Krishna and his dalliance with the *gopis*."[68]

While Narayan is waiting for Kalyani to meet him, he's playing the flute, almost beckoning her to him. When she arrives, he recites from Kalidas' poem *Meghdoot*. The Sanskrit words "megh" and "doot," he explains, mean cloud and messenger, and that the poem is about the separation of two lovers. The cloud, he tells her, resembles Lord Vishnu, in Krishna's guise. Furthermore, the place where the widows live has a special connection to the god. "Vrindavan's appeal to widows over the centuries has rested on the belief that Krishna . . . played along the banks of the Jumna River here as a boy and teased young girls as they bathed in it. Krishna's appeal to the widows is said to lie partly in his boyhood waywardness, and partly, in his adult incarnation, as the ideal lover."[69] How has Kalyani endured all of these years as a widow? She tells Narayan that the Bhagavad-Gita has told her to learn to live like a lotus untouched by the filthy water in which it grows. Being practical, he tells her that "Krishna was a god. Not everyone can live like a lotus flower." She counters with yes, they can. The line that Kalyani is referring to can be found in chapter 5, part 10, and it reads: "The man who acts, having rendered his actions to Brahman and abandoned attachment, is untainted by evil, in the same way that a lotus leaf is untainted by water."[70]

The focus of *Water* is society's negative attitude toward widows, and this can be seen in a number of scenes. For instance, after getting a bath, Kalyani's puppy runs away. Chuyia chases it, pursued by Kalyani, who accidentally bumps into a woman. This person indigently tells Kalyani that widows shouldn't run around like unmarried girls. And since she's now polluted her, she will have to bathe again. During a wedding scene that takes place near the river, Shakuntala goes to draw water and is warned not to let her shadow touch the bride. Even Narayan's Anglophile friend tells him that there's a famous saying, "Widows, bulls, slippery steps, and holy men. Avoid these, and liberation awaits." There are a number of reasons why widows are considered inauspicious. For one thing, it is commonly believed that the Hindu wife protects her husband from death, and she does this by "serving him, providing him with food, care and children; by performing religious rituals, including fasts, on his behalf; and by remaining devoted and loyal."[71] This power or *sat* is thought to be so great that it can literally save his life. Therefore, when the husband dies, she is blamed. His illness or death is proof that she did something wrong in a past life or that she has failed to fulfill her duties as a wife. As a widow, she became "an ogress that ate her husband with her karmic jaws."[72]

Because of her "complicity" in his death, a widow endures all kinds of physical and psychological torture. Not only is she subjected to violence, poor nutritional health, homelessness, and ostracism, but she is also treated as a bad omen. "According to the Skanda Purana, widows are to be avoided: 'The widow is more inauspicious than all other inauspicious things. At the sight of a widow, no success can be had in any undertaking, excepting one's mother; all widows are void of auspiciousness. A wise man should avoid even her blessings like the poison of a snake.'"[73] Furthermore, to see a widow in the morning or to face her while going on a journey could bring misfortune. Because of this, she is supposed to keep herself separate from others.[74] Following Auntie's death, Shakuntala says, "God willing, she'll be reborn as a man," again reminding us that women are typically thought of as second-class citizens. What's perhaps the strongest indictment against this treatment of widows in *Water* is that, like Chuyia, several characters came to the ashram as children. During her conversation with Narayan, Kalyani explains that she was about nine when she was widowed, and she had never even met her husband.

Narayan doesn't believe that widows deserve to be treated like untouchables. Like Gandhi, he believes that they should be liberated. Even when he discovers that Kalyani has been made a prostitute, he opposes his mother and society, insisting that he will marry her. The Brahmin priest, too, seems sympathetic to the widows. Shakuntala even approaches and asks him if it is really written in the Holy Books that widows should be treated badly? He replies that widows have three options: They can burn with their husbands, lead a life of self-denial, or if the family permits, marry her husband's younger brother. He adds that a law was recently passed that favors widow remarriage. Shocked at this, she asks why she's never heard of it. "We ignore the laws that don't benefit us," he replies. Later on in the film, Narayan supports this sentiment. When Shakuntala asks him why widows have been sent to the ashram, he says that for their families, it means "one less mouth to feed, four saris saved, one bed, and a corner is saved in the family home. There is no other reason. Disguised as religion, it's just about money." Despite this economic truth, because feelings of impurity and inferiority are so entrenched in many women, they simply never question what they are being asked to do. To demonstrate this quiescent attitude, the fresh-faced Chuyia innocently asks where she might find the house for men widows. Outraged, the other widows exclaim how horrible it is for her to say that: "God protect our men from such a fate. May your tongue burn. Pull out her tongue and throw it in the river."

As for Hindu rituals, on many occasions the widows are shown praying, using *mala* beads, or sitting in front of a sculpture of Krishna. Since the ashram is just steps away from the Ganges River, we see pilgrims bathing in the water, washing away their sins. In one scene, a follower of Siva (on his forehead he has three horizontal white lines) walks by as Chuyia and Shakuntala pray: "O Sacred River, Radiant like the moon, Home of the Eminent . . ." Chuyia, who is bored, cuts her off. As they leave the river, they join the other widows from the ashram who are sitting around a Brahmin priest. They listen as he recites passages from the sacred texts. During a wedding scene we see a Saivite priest performing *puja* in front of a sculptural representation of Nandi. In the background, cremations are taking place. Madhumati is a devotee of Shiva, and she can be seen praying to him. After Auntie dies, there is a short funerary scene, during which her shrouded body is placed in the water. The women in the ashram then perform a fast, forgoing food and water. As it says in *The Laws of Manu* (5:157), "When her husband is dead she may fast as much as she likes, [living] on auspicious flowers, roots, and fruits, but she should not even mention the name of another man."[75] During Kalyani's "funeral," the Brahmin priest describes the nature of the atman or soul, saying that it is something that cannot be cleaved by weapons, cannot be burned by fire, eternal and all pervading. Near the end of the film, the women celebrate Holi, a festival that allows them to break out of their all-white existence, allowing them to "wear color" and celebrate life.

While sitting on the banks of the Ganges, Shakuntala remarks that the Hindu texts say that life is an illusion, referring to the concept of *maya*. The word *maya* itself is related to "measure," "create," and "display," and it refers to an illusory image or deception of sight. Vishnu, in particular, uses his power to assume diverse shapes and, on a larger level, create the universe itself. "Enthralled by ourselves and the effects of our environment, regarding the bafflements of *maya* as utterly real, we endure an endless ordeal of blandishment, desire and death. . . . *Maya*—the world, the life, the ego, to which we cling—is as fugitive and as evanescent as cloud and mist." The goal for Hindus is to cut through the illusion and see the world as it really is.[76] In one well-known story, Narada, a sage, asks Vishnu to reveal to him the secret of *maya*. Reluctantly the deity agrees, telling him to plunge into a nearby lake. When the sage comes back out, he has been transformed into a beautiful woman. She soon marries and, with her husband, has children and grandchildren. Over time, bad feelings erupt between her husband and her father and this leads to a war, during which many of her family members are slain. Distraught, she visits the battle-field, builds a giant funeral pyre, and throws herself into the flames. Just as she does, Narada finds himself in the lake. "Who is this son whose death you are bewailing?" Vishnu asks. "This is the semblance of my *maya*, woeful, somber, and accursed. Not the lotus-born Brahma, nor any other of the gods . . . can fathom its depthless depth. Why or how should you know this inscrutable?"[77] In another story starring Narada, when he asked Vishnu to show him his *maya*, he was told to go and fetch water, which he did. On the first door he knocked, he came face-to-face with a beautiful woman. Transfixed by her, he immediately forgot why he had come. Over time, he married the woman, and they had children. After 12 years, the rainy season was particularly brutal. The waters quickly rose and flooded his village. Narada fled with his family, but tragedy struck. First, he lost his youngest child to the rushing waters, then his second, and finally, his wife. When the unconscious Narada awoke, he could only weep. It was then that a familiar voice called out to him, asking where the water was. It was Vishnu, who said, "Now do you comprehend my *maya?*"[78]

The film hints that Narayan is going through the four stages of life. He has just finished his exams, thus ending the student stage, and now his mother is frantic for him to start a family, thus entering the householder stage. She is even trying to arrange a marriage for him. But Narayan rejects this "tradition" and tells her that he has selected his own bride-to-be. When Narayan tells her she's a widow, though, his mother counters that Gandhi has turned him into a lunatic and that Narayan can't do it, because it's a sin. Her concern might be that if Narayan marries a widow, and they have a son, according to *The Laws of Manu* (3:156), as the son of a widow, at his death one would be forbidden from "feeding him."[79] If one feeds and honors the dead, it is said that the "host's ancestors going back seven generations will be perpetually satisfied."[80] Madhumati supports this sentiment by saying that widows "must live in purity and die in purity." Furthermore, she states that if a widow remarries she will send all of the other widows to hell and curse them. Again, as it says in

The Laws of Manu (9:64–66), "twice-born men should not appoint a widow woman to (have a child with) another man, for when they appoint her to another man they destroy the eternal religion. The appointment of widows is never sanctioned in the Vedic verses about marriage, nor is the remarriage of widows mentioned in the marriage rules. For learned twice-born men despise this as the way of animals, which was prescribed for humans as well when Vena was ruling the kingdom."[81]

Caste isn't discussed much in the film; however, Narayan's father explains the privileges of being a Brahmin, telling his son that they can "sleep with whomever they want and the women they sleep with are blessed." A crestfallen Narayan replies that "Lord Ram told his brother never to honor those Brahmins who interpret the holy texts for their benefit." Narayan is probably referring to the *Ramayana,* and possibly to Javali, a "learned Brahmin and a Sophist," who questioned Rama's values of faith, law, and duty and told him that there could be no afterlife. Rama repudiates him for his impiety. Chapter 3 of *The Laws of Manu* outlines which caste should marry which, and what happens when intercaste marriage occurs.

Finally, it's fitting that the film ends with Gandhi remarking that he used to believe that God is Truth and now knows that Truth is God. Since meeting Chuyia, Shakuntala has felt pulled between her conscience and her faith. She even asks the Brahmin priest what happens when these seem to be at odds. Gandhi provides us and Shakuntala with the answer: "The pursuit of truth is invaluable for me, I trust it will be the same for you." In essence, the film queries: Is this unfair treatment of women and widows under Hinduism God-given or is it simply distorted thinking used by those in power so as to control the weak and powerless?[82]

White Rainbow (2005)—Written and directed by Dharan Mandrayar. Running time: 94 min. English and Hindi. Rated PG-13 for some thematic elements and violent content.

On a final note, in 2005 another film was released that deals with the subject of widows in India. *White Rainbow* tells the story of four women—Priya (Sonali Kulkarni), Roop (Amardeep Jha), Mala (Shameem Shaikh), and Deepti (Amruta Subhash)—and "their journey to overcome the societal stigma and grim reality of widowhood." The story begins with the sudden death of Priya's husband and the miscarriage of their child. The affluent woman makes a pil-grimage to Vrindavan, where she befriends the three aforementioned widows. Roop is an elderly woman, who after being rejected by her children, is forced to make her way on the streets; Mala was disfigured when her mother-in-law poured kerosene over her and ignited it; and Deepti was widowed at 15, phys-ically and sexually abused by her brothers-in-law, and then forced into pros-titution. Writer and director Dharan Mandrayar said that he was inspired to write the script while his son was reading a novel about a 13-year-old widow banished to Vrindavan. Initially, he didn't believe the story. After all, his mother hadn't suffered this fate. But after conducting research on the subject, he heard many worse stories, four of which he chose to fictionalize. "My film is about four . . . widows who start challenging the myths and tradition that surround the widows. In the process they undergo a transformation. From a world of no colours, they see the rainbow at the end of the tunnel," he said in one interview.[83] For more on the film, go to its official site at www.whiterain-bow.com.

Additional Films That Contain Some Hindu References

The Legend of Bagger Vance (2000)—Based on the book by Steven Pressfield; directed by Robert Redford. Running time: 126 min. English. Rated PG-13 for some sexual content. Genre: Drama/Romance.

Summary: A disillusioned World War I veteran and former golf champion, Rannulph Junah (Matt Damon) reluctantly agrees to play in an exhibition against golf greats Bobby Jones and Walter Hagen. Before the war, Junah was a golfer to be reckoned with; now he's a down-and-out alcoholic. As one char-acter says, he's "confused, broken." But things are about to change. A mysteri-ous caddy appears, named Bagger Vance (Will Smith), who helps Junah get back his "authentic swing."

On the surface, *The Legend of Bagger Vance* is a sports film with supernat-ural elements, a *Field of Dreams* for golf enthusiasts. But underneath, it's a retelling of the Bhagavad-Gita, only instead of taking place on the battlefield, this one occurs on a golf course. Shorten Rannulph Junuh's name to a first ini-tial and last name and you have R. Junuh (Arjuna), the Pandava archer who lost his resolve once he saw all of the faces of his friends and relatives on the enemy's side. As for Bagger Vance, his name is a "variation on Bhagavan, a name for Lord Krishna," who in the Hindu text serves as Arjuna's charioteer and moral teacher.[84] The film isn't a simple cut-and-paste copy of the Gita, though. The two sources differ considerably; however, one can find some shared concepts. For instance, R. Junuh's search for the "authentic swing" is like Arjuna's discovery of the true self or atman; Junuh's reluctance to play golf is similar to Arjuna's reluctance to fight; and Bagger's advice to stop worrying about where the ball goes but just hit it, is similar to Krishna's explanation of performing one's dharma. In the Bhagavad-Gita, he explains that one must perform an action without being attached to the result:[85] "That action which is prescribed, unaccompanied by attachment, undertaken without desire or aversion by one who is not interested in the result, is said to be purely constituted."[86]

ABCD (1999)—Written by Krutin Patel and James McManus; directed by Patel. Running time: 105 min. English. Unrated. Genre: Drama.

This small indie film's title tells it all. It's about American-Born Confused Desi siblings Raj (Faran Tahir) and Nina (Sheetal Sheth) and their struggles with identity. On the surface, at least, Raj seems to conform to his mother's (Madhur Jaffrey) expectations—he's an accountant with an impressive firm and he's engaged to a traditional Indian woman. Nina is more openly hostile to her cultural roots. She is promiscuous and often disrespectful to her mother. Even when love comes knocking in the guise of India-born Ashok (Aasif Mandvi), she rejects him, instead choosing to reconnect with and eventually marry Sam (Rex Young), an all-American guy who represents everything she isn't.

Like *American Desi*, *ABCD* deals with the questions facing children of Indian immigrants. How do they identify themselves? How do they assimilate without losing their cultural roots?[87] Unlike *American Desi*, this film presents characters who aren't easy to warm up to, and based on the responses found on various online boards a fair number of real life ABCD's tend to vehemently dislike the film. Critical reviews, however, have been largely laudatory. For the purposes of this book, *ABCD* contains some useful scenes that show Hindu ritual and culture. For instance, in the beginning Raj and Nina visit a Hindu temple where one sees statues of Krishna and Ganesha, among others.[88] Raj even says that when he was a child the story of Ganesha losing his head scared him.

It is generally acknowledged that during the Vedic period worshippers ate meat and performed animal sacrifices. Over time, though, this changed, undoubtedly because of the influence of Buddhism and Jainism, both of which extol the virtues of vegetarianism. Today, not all Hindus are vegetarian, but the majority is. *ABCD* acknowledges this fact with a scene in which Nina goes on a date with Ashok to a fast-food restaurant. Looking over the menu, he realizes that as a vegetarian all he can eat are the French fries. Nina, who explains that she's a "lapsed Hindu," orders a hamburger.[89] The inclusion of this scene demonstrates how "modern" and Americanized Nina has become.

As was previously mentioned, widows are supposed to wear a white or ochre sari, give up all ornaments, including earrings and bangles, and eat the barest of foods. Since Anju is a widow, she follows this tradition, saying that she only wears widow's white. She also maintains a connection to her deceased husband, whom the audience sees in a portrait decorated with flower garlands, by talking to him. Anju is a typical mother, who believes that her children should get married and, themselves, have children. Traditionally, a "wife's primary duty is to bear children, especially sons . . . [because they] continue to contribute to the family economy even after they are married, whereas daughters go to their husbands' homes."[90] Anju spends much of the film worrying about her children's marital futures, particularly her daughter's. Afraid that Nina will never find a suitable husband, Anju consults an astrologist and a palm reader. So that they can ensure the best results, Hindus believe that it's critical to know auspicious and inauspicious dates, and they do this by consulting an astrologer or *jyotisi*. "In many families the competent *pandit* will draw a child's horoscope immediately after birth; and all the important occasions in the child's life will be determined according to it. There will be very few Hindu weddings for which the astrologer has not selected the *muhurta*, the auspicious hours, when the marriage is being solemnized."[91] Anju also believes that if her daughter would only "learn to make *samosas*," she'd meet someone nice.

The film actually deals a lot with Indian attitudes toward dating and marriage. For most of the film, Raj plays the dutiful son. He's agreed to an arranged marriage with Tejal (Adriane Forlana Erdos), a very traditional girl who cooks for him and studies Indian dance. Even when Raj says he's going away for a while, she claims that she will wait for him. Nina is the complete opposite. She is a veritable pariah for her promiscuity and open sexuality. In one scene, she gets picked up by a guy at the bar and within a few minutes, she's kissing him. The film explains that Hindus aren't supposed to show affection in public, and in Bollywood films the actors very rarely kiss.[92] On the subject of love and marriage, this film echoes what many of the others say, "what do the two have to do with each other?" "Love comes after marriage," says Anju, who knew her husband just two weeks before marrying him. Like many Indian cinematic mothers, Anju wants to set Nina up on a date with a fleet of eligible Indian males whose educational degrees, professional status, and annual incomes she knows by heart. Nina protests, but ends up going out with her childhood friend Ashok to appease her mother. At first, they seem to get along well, until Ashok proposes on the second date. This act only leads Nina back to her former boyfriend. In the end, Nina remains defiant and marries Sam, not in a traditional Indian wedding, but dressed in white, in a church.

Mr. and Mrs. Iyer (2002)—Written and directed by Aparna Sen. Running time: 120 min. English, Tamil, Bengali, Hindi, Punjabi, Urdu. Unrated. Genre: Drama.

Hearing that her mother-in-law is ill, Mrs. Meenakshi Iyer (Konkona Sen Sharma), a devout South Indian Brahmin, and her infant son, Santanam, board a bus bound for Calcutta.[93] But before their long journey begins, she is introduced to a wildlife photographer named Raja Chowdhury (Rahul Bose), who promises to "look after" the young mother. As the bus traverses the scenic countryside, the audience meets the other passengers, a veritable microcosm of India that includes an elderly Muslim couple, a Jew, several Sikhs, and many Hindus. The trip isn't without its conflicts. Some passengers are outright hostile to each other, and the bus eventually comes to a roadblock. Not wanting to lose any time, the driver takes a shortcut, which eventually leads them into an even tenser situation. Traffic is backed up and stalled because, as they learn from the police, Muslims and Hindus have been fighting in the area. To prevent further deaths, the police impose a curfew and passengers are ordered back to their vehicles. Darkness falls. The silence is broken by a group of men carrying torches. Threatening violence, they demand entrance to the bus. Once inside, they begin asking the passengers to offer their names, and eventually to reveal their religions. These men are looking for Muslims. They find them, thanks to the Jewish man, who fears that his circumcised penis will get him killed. To protect Raja, Mrs. Iyer lies, saying that he is her husband. After the men have gone, Raja reveals to her that he, too, is a Muslim. (His real name is Jehangir.) Having grown up with prejudice against Muslims, she is very upset at this seemingly blatant act of betrayal. But the two aren't about to go their separate ways. Because they are stranded and she desperately wants to get "home," the two end up working together to overcome their obstacles.

Mrs. Iyer is a Brahmin and, therefore, must adhere to strict dietary rules. As its says in *The Laws of Manu*, "The Brahmin eats but his own food, wears but his own apparel, bestows but his own alms; other mortals subsist through the benevolence of the *brahmana*."[94] Because ritual purity is so important for this caste, Mrs. Iyer's mother makes her daughter's food. Later in the film, when she and Raja must stay at a guest house in the forest, she refuses to eat anything that the owner might prepare. Brahmins won't eat cooked food that is prepared by others, but uncooked food is acceptable. Furthermore, they won't accept water across caste lines, because it is easily defiled. In the film, she does borrow Raja's water but never lets the bottle touch her lips. *The Laws of Manu* also states that twice-born men should avoid eating garlic, onions, and fish. Brahmins eat only those foods prepared with clarified butter or ghee. Called *pakka*, these foods can be offered to the gods and guests of high status. Alcohol is prohibited.[95] Although, Meenakshi is very educated—she has a master's degree in physics—she is blinded by her deeply ingrained traditional, and prejudicial, attitudes. In fact, when she explains these dietary restrictions to Raja, he reacts with incredulity, remarking that this is the 21st century.

In addition to discussion of dietary rules and restrictions, *Mr. & Mrs. Iyer* demonstrates other religious symbols and practices. The two main characters talk briefly about the *bindi* that Meenakshi wears on her forehead, saying that not only is it a sign of being married but that it also represents the "all-seeing third eye."[96] When the "terrorists" are asking the passengers questions, one man exclaims that he's a Brahmin and he pulls out his *jenoi* or "sacred thread," which he would have received during the *Upanayana* ceremony. The audience also catches a glimpse of Muslim practice. Before the older Muslim is taken off the bus and shot, he takes out his rug and performs his prayers, facing Mecca.

As well as being a film about caste, *Mr. & Mrs. Iyer* also shines a light on Hindu-Muslim relations in India, which are increasingly tumultuous in many areas. As director Aparna Sen said in an interview, "I have been deeply concerned about the ugly head of fundamentalism that has been ravaging the country continuously. . . . It pains me to see that the secularism that Jawaharlal Nehru and Mahatma Gandhi stood up for is almost extinct. Even among the urban middle class and the upper middle class, the so-called educated, enlightened class, secularism is absent."[97] Watching the film, in some ways, is like seeing history enacted. Fighting between the two religions has been particularly prevalent in Ayodhya, a site considered holy by both groups. The worst violence occurred in 1992, when "2,000 people died in clashes after Hindu nationalists tore down the 16th-century Babri mosque."[98] Hindus believe that the site originally had a temple marking the birthplace of Rama, and they were incensed that it was now a Muslim site. A decade later, the retaliatory violence was still so intense that, as we see in the film, the military moved in and imposed a curfew.[99] Conflicts between Hinduism and Islam are nothing new. Tremendous violence and the death or displacement of millions of people followed the 1947 partition of the South Asian country into India and the Muslim countries of Bangladesh and Pakistan.[100]

The Guru (2002)—Written by Tracey Jackson; directed by Daisy von Scherler Mayer. Running time: 94 min. English, Hindi. Rated R for strong sexual content, including dialogue and for language. Genre: Comedy.

Ram[101] Gupta (Jimi Mistry) makes his living by giving dance lessons to middle-aged and elderly Indian women, but he's not satisfied. He wants to go to America and become a star. His friend Vijay (Emil Marwa) encourages him to come to New York, where he claims to live in a penthouse and drive a Mercedes-Benz. Ram uproots himself and makes the transatlantic move, but to his surprise, upon his arrival he learns the truth. Vijay is a waiter in an Indian restaurant; he drives a cab and lives in a small apartment with three other Indians. Ram moves in and begins work at the restaurant but is fired after he gets into a fight with a customer. Still hoping to become famous, he begins going to auditions. But little does he know, he is auditioning for a part in a pornographic film. It is during one audition that Ram meets Sharonna (Heather Graham), a sweet porn star who's leading a double life. Ram is smitten with the woman, and he asks her to give him some advice on how to "perform." The turning point in the film comes when a hired "guru" passes out at a socialite's house, and Ram, who is a waiter at the party, must assume the guru's place. Donning a turban, he takes on the guise of Swami Bu and dispenses Sharonna's sex lessons. An instant hit, Ram eventually gains notoriety as the "Sex Guru," and he gains the "stardom" that he so desperately seeks. But does fame come at too high of a price?

The Guru satirizes Westerners and their penchant for Eastern thought, even when it's far from authentic.[102] Lexi (Marisa Tomei), a neurotic wreck of a woman, embodies everything that's shallow about the West, especially its quest for easy-to-understand "wisdom" that has come from a distant shore. The scene where Gupta performs the Macarena for his clueless audience is indicative of this. Although his Indian friends immediately recognize the popular dance, Lexi proclaims, "I think it's one of those dervish, spiritual transient things," and she joins the conga line. This romantic comedy plays on myriad stereotypes, especially that all East Indians wear turbans, have a "third eye" in the middle of their forehead, and dispense great mystical wisdom. Poking fun at this, the filmmakers depict the "real" guru as a drunk who simply transforms himself by donning a costume. Not knowing the difference, his American audience is easily taken in.

The Love Guru (2008)—Written by Mike Myers and Graham Gordy; directed by Marco Schnabel. English, Hindi. Rated PG-13 for crude and sexual content throughout, language, some comic violence and drug references. Genre: Comedy.

A similar film is *The Love Guru*, which is set for release in June 2008. Co-written by and starring Mike Myers, the comedy is about Pitka, an American who, as a child, was left at the gates of an ashram in the mythical city of Harenmahkeester, India, and raised by gurus. One of them is named Guru Tugginmypuddha (a cross-eyed Ben Kingsley). Pitak returns to the United States to seek fame and fortune in the world of self-help and spirituality. His unorthodox methods are put to the test when he must settle a rift between a hockey player and his estranged wife.

According to the film's official site (www.lovegurumovie.com), the character Guru Pitka first popped into Myers' head after his father had died and, in his grief, he had begun a "serious personal spiritual quest that led him to gurus and ashrams and then, unexpectedly, full circle back to comedy again." Myers explained that "What struck me as I began meeting gurus like Gary Zukav and

Deepak Chopra is how actually really funny they are. I started to realize that the whole idea of enlightenment is really, at heart, to just lighten up." Hindu organizations in India and the United States have both attacked the film, calling for a boycott. Lila D. Sharma, president of the India Heritage Panel in Chandigarh, India, issued a statement, claiming that "Hollywood is trying to make money by laughing at our holy men and in the process creating a stereotype." In the United States, Raja Zed, president of the Universal Society of Hinduism, said that the trailer of the film "appears to be lampooning Hinduism," and that because "people are not very well-versed in Hinduism . . . this might be their only exposure. They will have an image in their minds of stereotypes. They will think most of us are like that." In an effort to quell detractors, Paramount promised to screen *The Love Guru* for a group of Hindu leaders. Best-selling self-help "guru" Deepak Chopra, who has been a friend of Myers for 15 years, also came to the comedian's defense, saying that "the premature outcry against the film is itself religious propaganda. As viewers will find out when the movie is released . . . no one is more thoroughly skewered in it than I am—you could even say that I am made to seem preposterous." Before making his film, Myers consulted Chopra to get his blessing. Chopra consented, because, as he said, the comedian "has the most profound understanding of Eastern wisdom, traditions and spirituality. . . . In the end, the movie is about self-esteem and love. It is about, in fact, love being the ultimate truth. He goes about it in a very silly, humorous way, but that's his style."[103] Not only does Chopra have a cameo in *The Love Guru*—he and Guru Pitka play rivals—but Myers also wrote the forward to Chopra's latest book, *Why Is God Laughing?* In it, he calls Chopra one of his most recent heroes. *The Love Guru* debuted at number four at the U.S. box office, taking just $14 million on opening weekend. Hindu leaders have credited their organized boycott and campaign against the film as contributing factors to the film's failure.

The Mystic Masseur (2001)—Directed by Ismail Merchant; based on the book by V. S. Naipaul. Running time: 117 min. English. Rated PG for mild language. Genre: Drama.

Director Ismail Merchant presents a sort of flip side to this "fake guru" theme with his film *The Mystic Masseur* (2001). Set in Trinidad during the 1940s, it follows the exploits of Ganesh Ramsumair (Aasif Mandvi), a failed schoolteacher and village masseur who in time becomes a revered mystic and eventually a politician. Just some of the people he "cures" are a man who has an amorous fascination with bicycles and a boy pursued by a malicious cloud.

A Little Princess (1995)—Based on the Frances Hodgson Burnett novel; di-
    rected by Alfonso Cuaron. Running time: 97 min. English. Rated G. Genre:
    Family.

As the film opens, it is 1914, India. A seven-year-old girl named Sara Crewe (Liesel Matthews) is entertaining a woman named Maya and her son with the story of a beautiful princess who lived in a mystical land. As she continues, the audience sees the heroine of her story, a richly adorned, sari-wearing woman named Sita (Alison Moir). Banished to the forest, she is joined by her blue-hued, flute-playing husband named Prince Rama (Liam Cunningham). We immediately recognize this as the story of the *Ramayana*.

Even though *A Little Princess* is about the motherless Crewe, who is sent to an all-girl's school in New York while her father, Captain Crewe (also Cunningham), serves during World War I, short scenes from the Indian epic are shown throughout. The purpose is to underline the film's overall theme of "the power of imagination" and to parallel the events in Sara's own, increasingly horrible, life. Sara begins telling the story in India, but her move to the United States cuts the narrative short. She starts all over again in New York as a way to liven up the boring old "classics" that are recited nightly to her schoolmates.

She explains to the other girls that Sita saw a wounded deer and asked her husband to go and help it. To keep her safe, Rama drew a circle around her, telling her that as long as she remained inside of it, she would remain unharmed. Her compassion proved her undoing. The 10-headed demon, Ravana, disguised himself as an "old beggar man," and, even though she didn't have any money to give him, she stepped outside of her protective circle to give him her bracelets. At this moment, the demon stole her away and locked her in a tower. As Rama approaches the palace, the demon fires 10 poison arrows at him. Once they land, they release a thick, yellow smoke that renders him unconscious. (At this point, we see Sara's own father being overwhelmed by a cloud of mustard gas.) Eventually the smoke lifts, and Rama is saved by a gazelle that offers its life in exchange. In the end, Rama faces Ravana, killing him with what appears to be lightning.

It's true that the *Ramayana* exists in many forms; however, the one re-counted in *A Little Princess* deviates considerably from most standard versions. For instance, in R. K. Narayan's shortened version of the tale, the demon Mareecha promises to help Ravana lure Sita away by transforming himself into a golden deer. Seeing it at her gate, Sita asks her husband to catch it for her so she can keep it as a pet. Rama agrees and is about to leave when Lakshmana stops him. "I would not go near it. It may be just an illusion presented before us. It's not safe. Who has ever heard of an animal made of gold and gems? It's a trick."[104] But Rama pursued it nonetheless. After a while, he realized the truth of his brother's remark, and he shot the deer. Upon being struck, Mareecha disguised his voice as Rama's and called out to Sita and Lakshmana for help. Fearing for her husband's life, Sita insists on following the voice. Knowing that his brother will be safe, Lakshmana tries to comfort her. When she still insists, he leaves, telling her that dharma alone will protect her.

We have to turn to William Buck's version to learn that the angry Lakshmana, who chides Sita for sending Rama after the deer and now sending him to obey "a false voice," draws a circle around her with the tip of his bow. "Do not step out of this circle and do not cross this line. Let these trees witness that I have done right!" In this version, Sita is presented as petulant and not very wise, for as soon as Lakshmana leaves, she exits the circle to tend to the *brahmana*.[105] It is at this time that she is snatched by the demon and whisked away to Sri Lanka. On their way to rescuing Sita, Vishnu and Lakshmana are joined by many other beings, including Jambavan, a bear; Jatayu, an eagle; and Hanuman, the ruler of the monkey clan. During the siege of Sri Lanka, Lakshmana and Rama are fighting Indrajit, one of Ravana's sons, and his "serpent darts" make the heroes swoon on the battlefield. They are saved by the arrival of Garuda, the mighty eagle, who scatters the darts, thus allowing the men to get to their feet. This might be the scene that takes place in *A Little Princess*, but, again, it's very different.

In the end, battles are fought between the various demons (who are the relatives of Ravana) and Hanuman and his forces. Rama and Ravana do face each other on the battlefield. The former invokes a weapon called the *Gnana*, which means wisdom, and causes the enemy to evaporate into thin air. Ravana counters with an *asthra* called *Thama*, which creates total darkness in all worlds as well as hail, rain, and tornadoes. Rama counters with another weapon called the *Shivasthra*. When Rama gets close enough, he begins cutting off Ravana's heads, but another one grows in each place and the decapitated heads turn into more demons. At wits' end, Rama pulls out his "last chance" weapon called the *Brahmasthra*, which was used by Brahma himself. Hurling it into Ravana's heart, which the demon forgot to make invincible, Rama finally slays his foe.

As was mentioned, Hanuman, the monkey king, plays a tremendous role in the *Ramayana*, so it's odd that he's left out of Sara's stories. The scriptwriter of *A Little Princess* doesn't forget him, though. While Sara and her father are sailing to New York, we see a mysterious Indian man, dressed in a turban, and carrying a monkey on board. He shows up later in the film as the curiously named Ram Dass[106] (Errol Sitahal), a sort of guru to a man who lives next door to the all-girl's school and who also has lost his son in the war. The Indian man, who may be Rama himself, orchestrates the film's happy ending. His monkey, by the way, is named Hanuman. Finally, whether or not it was intentional, *A Little Princess* seems to teach its audience about *maya*—the illusionary world created by the mind of god. In this case, it's Sara who weaves one magical tale after another.

Shadow Kill (Nizhalkkuthu) (2002)—Written and directed by Adoor Gopalakrishnan. Running time: 90 min. Malayalam. Unrated. Genre: Drama.

Set in the state of Kerala during the early 1940s, the film focuses on Kaliyappan (Oduvil Unnikrishnan), a hangman who has become increasingly disturbed by the way he earns his living. "My hands are stained with sin," he says. Although his position affords him and his family special privileges, such as free food and clothing and a tax-free house and farmland, it also brings with it misery. After passing the executioner on a dirt path, two of the villagers engage in a philosophical debate: "Who bears the sin of a hanging? The one who executes or the one who orders?" says one. "Depends on who makes the final decision," says the other man, then explains that the Maharaja absolves himself of all blame by granting pardon to the condemned in the form of a clemency order, which deliberately arrives a few minutes after the man has been killed. "Then who bears the sin?" the other man asks. No one answers this question.

Kaliyappan is caught between a veritable rock and a hard place. He can't challenge his orders and he really has no means of absolution, so he increasingly seeks comfort at the bottom of a glass of alcohol. To some degree, he also takes a measure of solace in the thought that he's just carrying out Kali's wishes. He keeps the hangman's noose in his prayer room, which features a picture of the divine goddess on a low shelf. When the villagers find themselves feeling ill, they visit him for a "cure." He then cuts off a small piece of the noose and burns it, creating holy ash. "It's a riddle, if you think about it," he says, "someone's life ends on the hangman's rope. When you burn that rope, its ash gives life to others. I don't understand." A man sitting in the bar with him responds, "It's all Mother's blessings. One rope ends, another begins." Those who are helped by this miracle cure are a woman with a feverish child and another woman who is having an epileptic fit. When she stops seizing, he says, "The evil spirit is gone." At the local bath, three village women praise the executioner's healing powers, saying that "now there's a halo around him" and that it is during these times that "the goddess reveals herself through him."

The hangman hasn't had to perform his job in a while, but that doesn't last. Much to his horror, orders arrive, telling him that in the next few days he must hang another man. He makes the usual preparations, such as praying to the goddess, performing *aarti* before her image, being ritually bathed by his wife, and undergoing penance, but he becomes increasingly agitated, requiring more alcohol. It helps him to pull the rope, he explains. As the execution nears, he becomes tired from all of the alcohol, so to keep him awake, some local men begin by telling him a tale about Saint Nandanar, "who went straight to heaven without changing his earthly form." Nandanar, it is explained, was an untouchable who became a faithful follower of Shiva. Because he was an outcaste, he couldn't go inside the deity's temple, but because his devotion was so pure, the stone Nandi, which was blocking his view, moved aside to let him look in. When this story fails to keep the executioner awake, the men try another story, which fails to be of interest. Finally, they begin an "inappropriate" tale about a 13-year-old girl who was raped and murdered. Imagining his youngest daughter as the story's protagonist,[107] the emotionally wrecked hangman breaks down and simply cannot perform his job. Sadly, his son, a follower of Gandhi, must eschew his vows of nonviolence and take his father's place.

The award-winning *Shadow Kill*[108] is a morality tale that poses some universally challenging questions, such as: Does justice exist when it is "the poor who go to the gallows"?[109] What responsibility do we have for our actions? On the former issue, several characters remark that money and influence can buy anything, and that no one cares about truth and righteousness these days. On the latter issue, the main character vacillates. On the one hand, he says that "It's all in God's hands" and "Kali, I am a tool. You are sin and sinner." But on the other, we learn that he has suffered "karmically" for what he's done. One villager states that after Kaliyappan hanged an innocent man, "within 10 days, his first wife died in childbirth." What's even worse is the fact that since the hangman's youngest daughter has entered puberty, her much older brother-in-law has started lusting after her. Because the girl is naïve, the audience knows that she won't meet with a happy end, and she doesn't. Perhaps foreshadowing the horrible events to come, at the beginning of the film, a schoolteacher recites a poem: "Time should not be wasted without seeking the truth. Death is a certainty. Accept it as a reality. People keep planning and plotting. Never a thought that they will die one day. Should the thought occur, they don't see it happening in the next 100 years." Then he follows with "In our short life span, we don't think about our own death, which strikes unexpectedly. We imagine that a tragic end is for others. It is only when you make the pain of others your own that you become human."

As *Shadow Kill* takes place during the 1940s, Kaliyappan's son, Muthu, is depicted as a follower of Gandhi and one engaged in the struggle for independence from Britain. Evidence of the Mahatma's influence can be seen when Muthu returns home, bringing with him a spinning wheel. Gandhi spun every day and encouraged everyone in India to follow suit. "My idea is to get these women to spin yarn, and to clothe the people of India with *khadi* woven out of it."[110] The spinning wheel became, for him, a symbol of sacrifice, of overcoming poverty, and of nonviolence; he called it the country's salvation. For Muthu, another way of practicing nonviolence is to renounce the eating of meat. So when his mother tells him that she will make him a nice lamb soup, he tells her "fruits, tubers, leaves . . . there are other things to eat." To this his mother responds, "What's wrong with my son? Are you going to put on your holy robes and renounce this world?" Muthu's words echo Gandhi's own and could have come directly from the Mahatma's autobiography, in which he writes that man's "diet should consist of nothing but sunbaked fruits and nuts He can secure enough nourishment both for the tissues and the nerves from fruits like grapes and nuts like almonds."[111] As for the "nice lamb soup,"

Gandhi would have replied, "To my mind the life of a lamb is no less precious than that of a human being. I should be unwilling to take the life of a lamb for the sake of the human body. I hold that, the more helpless a creature, the more entitled it is to protection by man from the cruelty of man."[112]

Finally, the film touches briefly on the inequities of gender. At the beginning of the film, Kaliyappan's youngest daughter is shown in school. While she is listening to her teacher recite a poem, we see a trickle of blood run down her leg; she has "attained womanhood." To celebrate this event, she must undergo a ritual, during which she is washed, a garland is placed around her neck, and she and her family must feed the other women in the village. All the while, a Shaivite priest officiates. The "joy" of such an event is shattered when the teen learns that "she can't go to school anymore." According to Ishrat Jahan, from childhood, a Hindu girl "is expected to perceive herself as a little woman, incorporating into her character the womanly traits."[113] Even while she attends school, the girl must learn domestic skills from her mother. When she attains puberty, her physical movements are much more restricted. "This sudden constricture of movement indeed creates in her a distinct 'self' which differentiates her from the boys. It is in this period that she is given a clear definition of her future role as a good wife and mother by the family and by society at large. Such a task is hence done by direct verbal communication from the women often associated with them, by exposing her to the characters of ideal women that have been read and talked about for generations, by exposing her to religious and household activities that women are properly engaged in, and by an attempt to restrict her association with the male world."[114]

Outsourced (2006)—Written by George Wing and John Jeffcoat; directed by John Jeffcoat. Running time: 103 min. English, Hindi. Rated PG-13 for some sexual content. Genre: Comedy/Romance.

Before we leave Hinduism, it is worth mentioning the 2006 indie *Outsourced*. Cowritten and directed by John Jeffcoat, this comedy-romance focuses on Todd (Josh Hamilton), an American call center manager who discovers that his department is being outsourced. If that isn't bad enough, he also learns that he has to go to India so he can train his replacement, Puro (Asif Basra). As a fish-out-of-water story, *Outsourced* demonstrates some of the particulars of Indian culture, such as the taboo against eating with the left hand, and the rules against public displays of affection. Social obligations are also high-lighted. Todd meets his hostess and she immediately asks him if he's married. When he replies no, she remarks that he's old enough to be a grandfather. As far as religion is concerned, we see people bathing in the Ganges, and cele-brating Holi. There is even a short discussion of Kali, who early in the film can be seen on the wall in Todd's guest room, and later on the dashboard. Todd asks, "Why would you want a goddess of destruction in your car?" Asha (Ayesha Dharker), an emerging love interest, replies: "Sometimes destruction is a good thing. She ends one cycle so that a new one can begin." Furthermore, reverence of cows is highlighted in the film. For example, Todd goes to a Mc-Donald's type restaurant in India, and yet no beef burgers are on the menu. And when he nonchalantly talks about how Americans brand their cattle so they can keep track of them, one woman asks, "With a red hot iron?" Unfazed, Todd says "Yeah." "But wouldn't the cow run away," a man asks. "Oh no, we only do it to baby cows, when they are small enough to hold them down . . ." Todd's voice trails off. A woman responds by covering her mouth in horror. "A suggestion, Mr. Todd," Asha says. "You need to learn about India." *Outsourced* debuted at the Toronto Film Festival and had considerable success at various other film festivals. The official site is www.outsourcedthemovie.com, where one can buy copies of the DVD and soundtrack.

OTHER RELIGIONS IN INDIA

Zoroastrianism

Such a Long Journey (1998)—Based on the book by Rohinton Mistry; directed by Sturla Gunnarsson. Running time: 113 min. English. Unrated. Genre: Drama.

Summary: Set against the turbulence of the 1971 war over Bangladesh, the film centers on Gustad Noble (Roshan Seth), a Parsi bank clerk, and his wife, son, and daughter. His peaceful routine is thrown into chaos when an old friend, Jimmy (Naseeruddin Shah), contacts him, asking him to deposit a large sum of money in the bank. Matters worsen when his rebellious son leaves home, his daughter gets malaria, and his wife falls under the influence of an eccentric woman in the apartment upstairs.

Today, there are only about 100,000 followers of Zoroastrianism, and their numbers are declining. Some of the reasons for this decline are that Parsis often marry late in life, thus having few, if any, children. They also don't believe in conversion or marriage outside of the religion. If a Parsi and a non-Parsi have a child, in general, he or she is not considered a Parsi. The situation is so dire that it is predicted that by 2020, Parsis—Indian Zoroastrians, which in 2001 numbered about 70,000—will be reduced to just 23,000 persons.[115] This monotheistic religion developed in Iran and southern Russia ca. 1200 B.C.E, under the vision of Zarathushtra (Zoroaster), who was reacting against the polytheism and rituals of the Aryan religion. He claimed to have had a series of visions during which he received messages from Ahura Mazda (Ohrmazd in Pahlavi), the supreme and "Wise Lord" who demands ethical purity and who judges people after their death, based on their deeds. One of the key ideas that he learns from these visions is that the cosmos is torn between two opposing forces. Ahura Mazda is goodness, while Angra Mainyu (Ahriman in Pahlavi) is his evil rival. Humans have a role in the world—they must choose between good and evil.

After Zarathushtra died, his ideas continued to spread, becoming the state religion of Iran between the third and seventh centuries C.E. Gradually the religion declined because of the rise of Islam. After a period of tolerance, Zoroastrians began to be persecuted in Iran. To escape this situation, in the 10th century C.E., many Zoroastrians fled to India, specifically Mumbai (formerly known as Bombay), where today most Parsis reside. Although their numbers have been small in India, they have had a great impact on the country. Because they tend to be hardworking, highly educated professionals, with literacy rates at about 98%, they have been very successful. Impressed by their entrepreneurial acumen, especially in the areas of banking and shipping, the British dubbed them "the Jews of India." By the 19th century, they dominated Mumbai's commercial sector.[116]

Such a Long Journey begins with a short history lesson, saying that 1,200 years ago, the Persian Empire was conquered by Arabs. A small band of Zoroastrians fled to India, where they "became the architects and administrators of Bombay." Amid its political themes, the film also shines light on Parsi religious practice. For example, it begins with a scene of Gustad performing the *Kusti* prayer. Facing east and standing in front of a lit candle, he recites sacred verses while untying and tying the *kusti*, which is a sacred thread girdle.[117] Prayer is, as Gustad says, "a very powerful thing. It can put a smile on your face and a light in your eyes." Several characters make reference to the *dakhma* or

Tower of Silence. For instance, at the dinner table, Dinshawji (Sam Dastor), Gustad's guest and coworker, remarks that the chicken they are eating would "make the corpses in the Tower of Silence sit up." After he dies later on in the film, the audience catches a brief glance at Parsi death rituals. For instance, a short time after death, the corpse is washed and dressed in a clean suit of white cotton clothes, and then placed on a white sheet on the ground. Gustad views the body in this state. Later, the corpse will be taken to the Tower of Silence, cylindrical walled structures that are open at the top so that the corpse can be devoured by birds of prey. The reason for this is threefold: first, when one dies, it is believed that a corpse demon comes into the body and contaminates it. Second, it is against their faith to bury, burn, or submerge the dead, which are contaminating, because the sacred elements—fire, water, and earth—cannot be defiled. And third, it is considered an act of charity to feed the birds with our bodies.[118] At the end of the film, Jimmy also dies and is taken to the Tower of Silence. His good friend Ghulam Mohamed (Om Puri) notes that since he isn't a Parsi, he is forbidden from entering the sacred structure.

About 18 million people call Mumbai home, and in this metropolis live people who practice a variety of faiths. In addition to exploring Zoroastrianism, *Such a Long Journey* displays religious iconography from some of these other religions, particularly Christianity and Hinduism. Gustad lives in a filthy neighborhood where people come in droves to urinate on a wall outside his apartment complex. Trying to bring change to his neighborhood, he encourages a sidewalk artist to use this wall as his canvas. After some reluctance, he takes Gustad's advice. As the camera pans across the wall, we see images of Brahma, the Pietà with Mary holding Jesus, Ganesha, Shiva Nataraja, and Saraswati. Over time, the wall becomes a veritable temple. People from all religious backgrounds come to place flowers, burn incense, and light candles in front of the images. When the artist hears of a miracle involving a statue of the Virgin Mary that cries real tears, he adds it to his wall. By this point in the film, Gustad's world is unraveling, so the desperate man travels to the Christian shrine where he offers a sacrifice—a wax figural sculpture—and prays for help. As the artist says, "a miracle, magic or religion . . . what's the difference as long as it works."

Being Cyrus (2005)—Story by Kersi Khambatta; directed by Homi Adajania. Running time: 90 min. English. Unrated. Genre: Comedy/Drama/Thriller.

Being Cyrus (2005) offers a rather different take on Parsi family life. Dinshaw Sethna (Naseeruddin Shah) is a dope-smoking retired sculptor who opens his arms to a stranger named Cyrus (Saif Ali Khan). The story revolves around the dysfunctional Sethna family and an old dilapidated building in Mumbai where Dinshaw's father, his brother, and brother's wife live. Coined an "intriguing, psychological drama," the film has been popular with critics and audiences alike.

Sikhism

Sikhism dates to the 15th century in the Punjab region of northern India. Its founder, Guru Nanak, apparently went to the river to perform his daily rituals and disappeared. When he returned, he revealed that he had seen God and that his mission was to teach that "there is neither Hindu nor Muslim, so whose path should I follow? I will follow God's path, and God is neither Hindu nor Muslim."[119] Nanak died in 1539, after founding and guiding a group of students or Sikhs. Following him were a series of 10 gurus[120] who continued to build the faith. Before the last guru, Gobind Singh, died in 1708, he announced that from now on the sacred text called the Adi Granth or Guru Granth Sahib would henceforth be the last and final teacher. Like Islam, Sikhism teaches that there is only one transcendent God, who doesn't take physical form. Like Hinduism, it affirms the validity of *samsara*, karma, and *moksha*. However, of the latter term, this release from the cycle of birth and rebirth comes through God's grace, not by personal effort. Sikhism does reject certain components of Hinduism, such as the importance of ritual and pilgrimage.

Several films contain Sikh characters. As previously mentioned, one of the key characters in *American Desi* is a Sikh. Main characters who happen to be Sikhs occur in *Bend It Like Beckham* (2002) and *Bride & Prejudice* (2004).

Bend It Like Beckham (2002)—Written by Gurinder Chadha and Guljit Bindra; directed by Chadha. Running time: 112 min. English. Rated PG-13 for language and sexual content. Genre: Comedy/Drama/Romance/Sport.

The first film tells the story of Jessminder Kaur Bhamra (Parminder Nagra), the daughter of orthodox Sikhs, who defies her parents' wishes to play football. One knows that they are Sikh, because, among other things, Jess's name

Kaur, which means "princess," is taken by Sikh women as their second name, and there is a painting of Guru Nanak on her parents' wall.[121]

As with so many other films, *Bend It Like Beckham* deals with the issues facing the children of immigrants. In Jess's case, her parents believe that she should be learning how to make a full Punjabi meal instead of playing a boy's sport. The opposite of Jess is her sister, Pinky (Archie Panjabi), who is shown getting married in a traditional wedding.

Bride and Prejudice (2004)—Directed by Gurinder Chadha. Running time: 107 min. English, Hindi. Rated PG-13 for some sexual references. Genre: Musical/Comedy/Romance.

Bride and Prejudice isn't as overtly religious, probably because it's loosely based on the Jane Austen novel, *Pride and Prejudice*; however, it is set in the holy city of Amritsar. Located in the northwest part of India, in the state of Punjab, Amritsar is home to the Golden Temple (Harimandir Sahib), which is the spiritual center of Sikhism. The fifth guru, Arjan, initiated the construction of this shrine in 1588. Kenyan-born, British-raised filmmaker Gurinder Chadha is a Sikh.

Bollywood/Hollywood (2002)—Directed and written by Deepa Mehta. Running time: 105 min. English. Rated PG-13 for sensuality/partial nudity, some crude language and drug references. Genre: Romance/Comedy/Drama.

Bollywood/Hollywood has a main character who is Sikh. Her name is Sunita Singh (Lisa Ray). Her parents are more devout than she, and they have an image of the *Khanda* on their refrigerator. Represented on the *Nishan Sahib* or holy flag, the symbol is comprised of the double-edged sword or *khanda* in the middle, a *chakkar* or circular weapon, and two single-edged swords or *kirpans*. Separately, the *khanda* is "a metaphor of Divine Knowledge; its sharp edges cleaving Truth from Falsehood"; the *chakkar*, "being a circle without beginning or end symbolizes the perfection of God who is eternal"; and the *kirpans*, which represent *meeri* and *peeri*, symbolize temporal and spiritual authority.[122]

Silent Waters (*Khamosh Pani*) (2004)—Directed by Sahiba Sumar. Running time: 99 min. Punjabi, Urdu. Unrated. Genre: Drama.

Silent Waters looks at historical tensions between Sikhs and Muslims in Pakistan. Set in 1979, when General Zia-ul-Haq took control of the country and stoked the fires of Islamic nationalism, the film focuses on Ayesha (Kirron Kher), a Muslim woman who gets by on her late husband's pension and by teaching young girls about the Koran. Her hopes lie with her son, Saleem (Aamir Malik), but he soon gets caught up with a group of Islamic fundamentalists who are upset that Sikh pilgrims want to pray at a holy site. The increasing tensions between the two groups causes Ayesha's past to resurface, and this leads to tragic consequences.

The film is based on actual events that transpired when the Indian subcontinent was partitioned in 1947 into India and Pakistan. Before this happened, in the Punjab, Muslims and Sikhs lived a relatively peaceful coexistence. But when the partition occurred, they turned against each other. Women were caught in the middle: Muslim men grabbed Sikh women; Sikh men abducted Muslim women. The consequences for the women were dire. They were raped, bought, sold, and murdered. Sometimes the abductees married their abductors. To "save" their women from this horrible fate, male family members on both sides forced mothers, daughters, and sisters to commit suicide. In the film, some women are ordered to leap into a well while the men prayed. In another scene, a Sikh man says that the men shot all 22 women in the village. This not only preserved their chastity but it also protected the family's honor. The estimated number of abducted women has been placed at about 50,000 Muslims in India and 33,000 Hindus and Sikhs in Pakistan. It is feared that this number is much lower than the actual one.[123] The film suggests that even if the women survived being abducted and tried to make their way back to their original villages, "no one wanted them."

In the director's notes, she explains that after researching "the idea of violence against women during the Partition of the Indian subcontinent" she "found a reference to abducted women along the borders of Punjab and Bengal." When she tried interviewing the residents about it, she was met with silence. Ayesha, then, "represents a woman caught in a conflict and as such she represents a universal dilemma. . . . [She] is portrayed with Sufi characteristics—an open and giving personality—whose philosophy of life is 'There is no God but the sum of all Gods.'" This sentiment also reflects the director's Sufi worldview, she said. *Silent Waters* is primarily about Muslims—fundamentalist and Sufi; however, about 50 minutes in, it gives its audience a glimpse at

Sikh religious practices. The men, wearing multicolored turbans and uncut beards, arrive off the train and immediately make their way to their shrine, where they bathe in its surrounding pool. They then share in a communal meal or *langar*. In another scene, pilgrims are seen combing their long hair and then tying it into a top knot. When another man arrives, they greet him with "Hail the Guru! Hail the Victor!" At the end, when Saleem goes through his mother's trousseau, he finds a book in which there is an image of Guru Nanak and a Sikh holy book, emblazoned with the *khanda*.

Minor Sikh characters can be found in *Where's the Party, Yaar* (2003), a Sikh character owns a convenient store, and in Spike Lee's *The Inside Man* (2006), in which the police investigating a bank robbery pull a turban-wearing man aside for questioning. Indignant at being "profiled," he asks, "Why can't I go anywhere without being harassed?" and then demands his turban back. This role is played by Waris Singh Ahluwalia, a Sikh model-cum-actor who also costars in *The Life Aquatic with Steve Zissou* (2004).[124] Another cinematic Sikh occurs in *The League of Extraordinary Gentlemen* (2003). Being faithful to Alan Moore's graphic novel, the film's creators have made Captain Nemo (Naseeruddin Shah) a Sikh, sporting a blue turban and a long beard, and carrying a curved sword.[125] Since Nemo is a scientist, a mechanic, an engineer, an inventor, and a freedom fighter, Sikh-related message boards were all abuzz with this positive depiction of a Sikh. It's no wonder. Even though Jules Verne stated that Nemo hailed from India, he had never before been played by an Indian actor. Actors who have stepped into the role are Lionel Barrymore, Thomas Mitchell, Herbert Lom, Robert Ryan, Omar Sharif, Jose Ferrer, Ben Cross, and Michael Caine.[126] As some have pointed out, though, the "triumph" has been marred by ignorance. Based undoubtedly on misconceptions about Sikh religious practices, the production team has him mistakenly worshipping Kali and having a statue of Ganesha on the Nautilus.[127]

The Fall (2006)—Written by Dan Gilroy, Nico Soultanakis and Tarsem Singh; directed by Tarsem Singh. Running time: 117 min. English. Rated R. Genre: Adventure/Drama.

Finally, Tarsem Singh's *The Fall* includes an "Indian" (Jeetu Verma) among the four, later five, heroes seeking revenge against Count Odious. Based on the character's dress, we can assume that he's a Sikh. Not only does he fight with a long, curved sword, but he also has a small dagger tucked into his belt. Furthermore, he always sports a colorful turban, under which we find long cascading hair, and he has a beard and mustache. As a side note, another of the "heroes," called simply the Mystic (Julian Bleach), with his long dreadlocks and loin cloth, looks very much like a follower of Shiva. And finally, during one scene, a group of men appear to perform the Kecak dance, also known as the Balinese monkey chant. Taken from the *Ramayana*, the dance is typically performed by about 100 bare-chested men, who sway, wave their hands, and make a "chak-chak-chak" sound.

NOTABLE DIRECTORS

Mira Nair

Mira Nair was born in 1957 in Bhubaneswar, India, and educated at Delhi University and Harvard University. She began her career as an actress but soon made the transition from documentary filmmaker to feature film director with the Academy Award–nominated *Salaam Bombay!* The 1988 film follows the very hard lives of several street children who are trying to survive in Mumbai, a city of drug-pushers, prostitutes, and pimps.[128] *Salaam Bombay!* was nominated for an Oscar. Her next film was *Mississippi Masala* (1991), an interracial love story between an Indian woman (Sarita Choudhury) and a black man (Denzel Washington) set in the American South. Using the 1972 expulsion of Indians from Uganda, Africa, under the repressive regime of Idi Amin, as a backdrop, the film explores racism and cultural prejudices within Indian culture.[129] Her next Indian-themed film was *Kama Sutra: A Tale of Love* (1996). Of it, Nair said, "I was inspired to make this film, in a way, to counter the sexist spectacle of these film industries. The kind of emotionless way that sexuality is presented . . . so I wanted to go back to a time when love was something to be taken very seriously and was believed to have a philosophical and sacred dimension to it."[130]

Two years later, Nair made *My Own Country* for television. Based on Abraham Verghese's autobiography, the film tells the story of an East Indian doctor specializing in infectious diseases who starts a crusade against AIDS. In 2001 Nair returned to Indian themes for her film *Monsoon Wedding*, which "interweaves stories taking place in the four days leading up to a middle-class Punjabi wedding."[131] Although it draws on Bollywood conventions—there's the arranged marriage and ostentatious wedding—it's very much a Western film, dealing with a variety of social issues, including rape, infidelity, and homosexuality. "For me, the film is also a meditation on the different aspects of love, the magic blinding love that hits you, as well as misplaced love, and what I call old-shoe love."[132]

Her latest film, released 2006, is *The Namesake*, which is based on Pulitzer Prize–winning writer Jhumpa Lahiri's eponymous novel. The film begins in India with Ashoke Ganguli (Irfan Khan) meeting his soon-to-be bride Ashima (Tabu), a classically trained singer. They don't stay in India long, though. When he is offered a fellowship at MIT, they move to New York, where they try to make a life for themselves. They eventually expand their family by a son, Gogol (Kal Penn), and a daughter, Sonia (Sahira Nair). Because their children grow up in the United States, they are more American than Indian. Gogol is the most rebellious. Not knowing the story behind his name, he decides to change it to Nikhil. And rather than date a nice Bengali girl, he chooses Maxine (Jacinda Barrett), a rich, white girl who clearly doesn't understand or respect Gogol's culture.[133] Gogol eventually comes around and marries Moushumi (Zuleikha Robinson), a British-raised Francophile, but their relationship collapses. In the end, the film, like several others already mentioned, throws light on the tightrope that many children of immigrants must try to walk. As Nair said, "*The Namesake* is the story of the sacrifices our parents made for their children and which we now cannot perhaps think of. It is a deep human way of telling the story of millions of us who left one home for another, who have known what it means to combine old with the new."[134]

As of this writing, Nair is in preproduction on *Shantaram*, which is based on Gregory David Roberts's semiautobiographical debut novel. The story is narrated by Lin (later Lindsay), an escaped convict who flees a maximum security prison in Australia and lands in Mumbai. He and his friend and guide, Prabaker, enter Mumbai's underworld, where Lin reinvents himself as a doctor. Attached to the film are Johnny Depp and Bollywood legend Amitabh Bachchan. The Warner Bros. picture is slated for a 2009 release date. (It was delayed because of the Writers Guild of America strike.) Of the 16 films—short and feature-length—listed in her filmography, the vast majority feature Indian characters. She addressed the reason for this in an interview from 1988, saying, "It's [India] what makes my heartbeat faster, and I just follow my heartbeat. Also, the fact that I feel my roots are very much there."[135]

Deepa Mehta

Deepa Mehta was born in Amritsar in 1950. Her father was a film distributor who owned a number of movie theaters, so she spent a lot of her youth watching hundreds of films. At that time, though, she didn't think about being a filmmaker. Instead, when she attended the University of New Delhi, she majored in philosophy. While working in New Delhi, Mehta met Paul Salzman, a Canadian filmmaker. They eventually married and in 1973 she immigrated to Canada, where she still lives.

In 1974, she made her Canadian directorial debut with the 24-minute documentary *At 99: A Portrait of Louise Tandy*. Throughout the 1970s and early 1980s, she continued to work on various documentaries. In 1987, she made the transition to feature films, producing and codirecting *Martha, Ruth and Edie*. Next came another feature-length film, *Sam & Me*, which tells the story of an Indian who moves to Canada to seek his fortune. The 1991 film won an honorable mention at the Cannes Film Festival. Mehta gained more experience behind the camera, directing several episodes for *The Young Indiana Jones Chronicles* TV series, and another feature film, *Camilla*. Everything changed for the director in 1995. Now divorced, she began work on *Fire*, the first part of her controversial trilogy. By training her magnifying glass on one family, Mehta reveals the downside to arranged and loveless marriages and the cultural and social straightjackets that women are forced to wear.

In *Fire*, Ashok (Kulbhushan Kharbana) is a successful businessman who works alongside and lives with his extended family that includes his wife Radha (Shabana Azmi), his brother Jatin (Javed Jaffrey), their elderly mother (Kushal Rekhi), and their servant (Ranji Chowdhry). Since Radha and Ashok have no children, and no one approves of Jatin's choice for a wife, he is more or less forced into marrying Sita (Nandita Das), who joins the household. Ashok, who is middle aged, has become a follower of a religious guru named Swamiji, and thus spends all of his free time with him. He's also taken a vow of celibacy, leaving the childless Radha even lonelier and unfulfilled. She and Sita, whose adulterous husband spends little time with her, have a lot in common, and the women become friends . . . and eventually much more.

Of the film Mehta said that ultimately it is "about loneliness. It is about the hypocrisy of our society today. It is a film about how women don't have choices in a patriarchal setup. . . . *Fire* is about a lack of choices. . . . Every character in the film, whether male or female, is a victim of society's rules and regulations."[136] *Fire* won accolades for the director and at the Vancouver International Film Festival was named Most Popular Canadian Film. But the response in India wasn't quite as positive. In New Delhi and Mumbai, Hindu nationalists, particularly the militant Shiv Sena party, and right-wing activists vandalized cinemas, pressured cinemas to suspend showing the film, and even called for Azmi to be "stripped of her membership of the federal parliament," saying that "she has insulted Indian women." One prominent Hindu leader said that "attacks would cease if the two women were shown to be Moslem instead of Hindu." He also said that he was "enraged because the two women . . . were named Sita and Radha, leading Hindu goddesses worshipped all over the country."[137]

As was previously mentioned, Radha is Krishna's most beloved *gopi* or cowherd. Popular stories abound of their romantic interplay: he watches her bathing in the water and steals her sari; she begs him for it back. As when Krishna and Radha embrace they create the world, so too do a young married couple. "Krishna is a million men; Radha a million women."[138] Mehta is underlining the tragedy of her loveless, barren character by giving her the same name as the free-spirited, sexually playful Radha. Sita, who is also an incarnation of Lakshmi, is "the model for all Indian women: pure, affectionate and faithful."[139] Not only does she dutifully follow her husband into the forest, but when she is rescued from Ravana and her fidelity is questioned, she never hesitates to prove her purity and she vows to undergo a test by fire. The story doesn't end there, though. Even after she demonstrates her purity, charges are still raised, and Rama exiles the pregnant queen to the forest.[140]

At the end of the film, it is Radha, not Sita, who must undergo an *agnipariksha* or trial by fire. At the end of the film, Ashok has learned of the women's relationship. Angered, he tries to embrace his wife, but she rebuffs him. She then accidentally catches her sari on fire. As she tries to extinguish the flames, her husband rushes to his mother's aid, leaving her to "save herself." In the end, the women run away together. The title of the film takes on various meanings, but primarily it seems to be what's missing from the women's marriages. It takes a kiss from the rebellious Sita to ignite something that's been long dead inside of Radha.

Two years later, *Earth*, the second film in the trilogy, was released. This time Mehta's subject was much larger, focusing on the political vacuum left after the British vacated India in 1947. Based on Bapsi Sidhwa's novel *Cracking In-*

dia, the film is set in Lahore. At the center of the story is a young, wealthy Parsi girl named Lenny (Maia Sethna), her much-desired Hindu nanny Shanta (Nandita Das), and two potential Muslim suitors, Hassan (Rahul Khanna), a masseur, and Dil (Aamir Khan), also known as "the ice candy man." As the film progresses, Shanta falls in love with Hassan. This relationship deeply wounds Dil, who will eventually exact his revenge. As in so many films, we see that civility and friendship among those of different faiths—Hindu, Sikh, Parsi, and Muslim—are only a veneer that falls away under the right circumstances. In this case, the catalyst is a train full of dead Muslims that arrives in the local depot. By the end of the film, chaos and anarchy threaten to destroy everyone. As Mehta said of the event, "The partition of India was like a Holocaust for us, and I grew up hearing many stories about this terrible event. Naturally I was attracted to this subject. . . . Film is a powerful medium and my hope is that *Earth* will produce a dialogue and force people to think more deeply about the cost of such divisions. If people want to separate they should understand what it would really mean. . . . I hope that *Earth* will put this into perspective. I think I have made a film that shows the futility of sectarian war, a film that is anti-war."[141]

For various reasons, Mehta took a break from the trilogy to make *Bollywood/Hollywood* (2002), which as its title suggests, means it's a veritable blending of Hollywood and Bollywood formulae. Set in Canada, the film centers on the Seth family, which consists of the widow matriarch (Moushumi Chatterjee), the grandmother (Dina Pathak), son Rahul (Rahul Khanna) and daughter Twinky (Rishma Malik). Both children are of marriageable age; however, as tradition dictates, the already-engaged Twinky can't get married until her brother does. Not yet ready to settle down, Rahul hatches a plan. After he meets Sue (Lisa Ray) at a bar, he decides to hire her to act as his fiancée. She agrees. But Rahul is in for a surprise. Although she doesn't look it, Sue is actually Sunita, an Indian who is so convincing that Rahul's entire family falls in love with her. And by the end, so does Rahul.

For the Hollywood side of the title, Mehta chooses elements from *Pretty Woman*, and for the Bollywood side, she pokes fun at stereotypical elements in these films and throws in several musical numbers for good measure. Just about anything is up for ridicule, including Westerners and Indian culture. For example, Rahul's first girlfriend, Kimberly (Jessica Pare), sees Indian culture through New Age eyes, particularly Deepak Chopra. She even dies while trying to levitate. Another jab is at Westerners who believe that Hindus are ecumenical, preferring no deity over the others or as one of the characters states, "All Gods are equal." As a counter to this, the Shakespeare-quoting grandma retorts, "Hindu gods are number one." In the film Mehta again questions how Indian females are viewed. During Sunita's "interview" with Killer Khalsa (Mike Deol), the wrestler that her parent's would like her to marry, he asks her, "What is your favorite subject [at the university]? Cooking? Home science?" He can't fathom that she might be more than a housewife. Finally, the film does contain a number of religious symbols, including images of Krishna, Lakshmi, Ganesha, and Hanuman. The Seths' gate even sports a giant *aum* symbol.

   Water, the final part of the trilogy, was released in 2005, but like *Fire*, this film wasn't without controversy. Mehta actually began work on it five years earlier; however, she was forced to abandon shooting when a "rioting mob of 2,000 attacked and burned the sets of the production . . . and issued death threats against the director" and her actresses, then Shabana Asmi and Nandita Das. Even though the government stepped in, the problems continued. Mehta's effigy was being burnt in cities across the country, and a protestor threatened to commit suicide by jumping into the Ganges. For "public safety" reasons, the production was shut down. To get her film completed, Mehta moved production to Sri Lanka. Lisa Ray replaced Das; Biswas replaced Azmi.[142] In her director's notes, Mehta explained that "in retrospect, *Water* reflected what was taking place in India in some form or other; the rise of Hindu fundamentalism and high intolerance for anything that viewed it with skepticism." Well received in the West, *Water* failed to attract much of an audience in India. Although greeted with good reviews, the film was said to cater largely to a niche audience. As of April 5, 2007, it had grossed only $704,501; compare this to its domestic lifetime gross of almost $3.3 million. In Canada, it was $2.25 million.[143] The irony of the situation is that those who were so vehement against the film didn't resume protests when it was released in India because "nobody is watching the film. It has met a quiet death."

   As of this writing, Mehta is in production on *Exclusion*, a drama that focuses on a little-known Canadian incident from 1914. An entrepreneur hired a ship, "the *Kamagata Maru*, to transport 375 Indian men, most of them political dissidents, to Canada. They are eventually sent home after the port of Vancouver denies them entry." Of the film, Mehta said, "*Exclusion* explores racism and the basis of all racism—which is economics."[144] John Abraham, the actor who played Narayan in *Water*, Manisha Koirala, and Mahima Chaudhry are set to star in the project. Another source lists Amitabh Bachchan in the cast.[145] According to the CBC.ca site, Mehta will go "Hollywood" with her subsequent film, *The Julia Project*, which is "about an American woman who marries into the Korean royal family."

ENDNOTES

1. "World Factbook," *Central Intelligence Agency*, 2008, www.cia.gov/library/publications/the-world-factbook/ (accessed 14 February 2008).

2. The Persian term means "those who live beyond the Indus River."

3. Richard H. Davis, "Religions of India in Practice," in *Asian Religions in Practice: An Introduction*, ed. Donald S. Lopez Jr. (Princeton, NJ: Princeton University Press, 1999), 8–55.

4. Western scholarship contends that the Aryans invaded India, thus subjugating the native Dravidians. This Aryan Invasion Theory, as it is called, has come under fire by Indian scholars as being paternalistic and imperialistic. For discussion of this debate, read chapter 3 in Klaus K. Klostermaier, *Hinduism: A Short History* (Oxford: One World, 2000), 34–46.

5. In Sanskrit, it is *Om Bhur Bhuvah Svaha. Tat Savitu Varenyam. Bharga Devasya Dhimahi. Dhiyo Yo Nah Prachodyaat.* Jan Knappert, *An Encyclopedia of Myth and Legend: Indian Mythology* (London: Diamond Books, 1995).

6. James Fieser and John Powers, *Scriptures of the World's Religions* (Boston, MA: McGraw-Hill, 2004), 8.

7. Caste actually comes from the Portuguese word *casta*, which means race. The Sanskrit term is *varna*, meaning color.

8. Over the centuries, outcastes have been the target of abuse and violence, prompting Gandhi to call them *harijan* or "Children of God." In his autobiography, he said that "If untouchability could be a part of Hinduism, it could but be a rotten part of an excrescence." The caste system was officially abolished by Indian law; however, old traditions die hard. "As early as the 1930s, just two decades after the first Indian film was made, caste became a central issue of cinematic exploration in films like *The Untouchable Girl* (*Achut Kanya*). A more sophisticated approach to caste can be seen in *Sujata* (of high caste), produced in 1959." See K. Moti Gokulsing and Wimal Dissanayake, *Indian Popular Cinema: A Narrative of Cultural Change* (Stoke on Trent, UK: Trentham Books, 1998), 8–9. A more recent look at the subject is Roland Joffe's 1992 film, *City of Joy*, which is set in Calcutta and depicts some of the ill treatment and ostracism faced by outcastes—in this situation, lepers.

9. *The Upanishads*, trans. Eknath Easwaran (Tomales, CA: Nilgiri Press, 2000), 48–49.

10. In Mohandas K. Gandhi's autobiography, he mentions *Manusmriti* several times. On page 30, he mentions that "the story of the creation and similar things in it did not impress me very much, but on the contrary made me incline somewhat towards atheism." Chapters about diet and the like, he explains, seem to run counter to daily practices. He mentions the text at least

twice with regard to its exhortation of "eating meat," a practice that he felt was wrong. For more about Gandhi's commitment to vegetarianism, read Mohandas K. Gandhi, *The Story of My Experiments with Truth* (New York: Dover, 1983), 235–36.

11. Fieser and Powers, *Scriptures of the World's Religions*, 44.

12. Fieser and Powers, *Scriptures of the World's Religions*, 46.

13. Fieser and Powers, *Scriptures of the World's Religions*, 47.

14. Gandhi, *The Story of My Experiments with Truth*, 59.

15. Gandhi, *The Story of My Experiments with Truth*, 232.

16. Gandhi, *The Story of My Experiments with Truth*, 233.

17. A film version of this text, titled *Bhagwat Geeta*, was made in 1993 by G. V. Iyer; however, it is not available in the United States. In India, it won the Golden Lotus Award at the National Film Awards.

18. Film version titled *Bhagwat Geeta*, made in 1993 by G. V. Iyer.

19. Richard Hooker, "Bhagavad Gita Krishna's Answer," 1996, www.wsu.edu/~dee/ancindia/gita2.htm (accessed 10 February 2008).

20. Gokulsing and Dissanayake, *Indian Popular Cinema*, 17.

21. From 1986 to 1988, *The Ramayana* was a TV series in India. In 1989, the British theater director Peter Brook made *The Mahabharata* into a miniseries. By using a multinational and multiracial cast, the production was intended to demonstrate that the story is universal.

22. Gandhi, *The Story of My Experiments with Truth*, 28–29.

23. Gandhi, *The Story of My Experiments with Truth*, 28. See also pages 282 and 307.

24. Brahma, who no longer enjoys popularity on his own, is represented as having four faces, each looking in a different direction. His consort is Saraswati, the goddess of learning and wisdom. His vehicle is Hansa, a swan or white goose.

25. The 10 avatars are as follows: Matsya the fish, Kurma the turtle, Varaha the boar, Narasingha the half-man, half-lion; Vamana the dwarf; Parasurama, the axe-wielding Rama; Rama, the hero of the *Ramayana*; Krishna the flute-playing, *gopi*-loving man; Buddha, the founder of Buddhism; and Kalki, the white-horse-riding man who will come at the end of the Kaliyuga. The first two avatars serve a salvific function—Matsya saves Saint Vaivaswata from a great flood and Kurma becomes the pivot on which Mount Mandara rests; the next six all kill a different demon (Parasurama protects the Brahmins from the tyrannical *kshatriyas*), Buddha removes suffering from the world, and Kalki ushers in the end of time.

26. His followers, Shaivites, about 220 million Hindus, also wear this marking on their foreheads.

27. The stories of how he got an elephant head vary. One states that Parvati fashioned a boy from the dirt of her body and then breathed life into him. Because she was going to bathe, she told him to guard the entrance. Shiva appeared. When forbidden from seeing his wife, he cut off the boy's head. Parvati reappeared, and once she saw what her husband had done, was distraught. To make amends, Shiva told his attendants to bring him the head of anyone sleeping with his head pointing north. A baby elephant was found doing just this, so its head was brought back and placed on the dead child. This elephant-headed deity is celebrated on *Ganesh Chaturthi*.

28. *Thuggees*, the origin of the word *thug*, were groups of robbers and murderers who claimed to worship Kali. Their preferred method of killing was strangulation. They were stamped out by the British in the 19th century. Thuggees have been depicted in such films as *The Deceivers*, starring Pierce Brosnan, and *Indiana Jones and the Temple of Doom*, starring Harrison Ford. One of the most recent books on the subject is Kim A. Wagner, *Thuggee: Banditry and the British in Early Nineteenth-Century India* (New York: Palgrave Macmillan, 2007).

29. Davis, "Religions of India in Practice," 29.

30. Office of the Registrar General, Census of India, 2001, www.censusindiamaps.net/page/Religion_WhizMap1/housemap.htm (accessed 10 February 2008).

31. For more on Buddhism, go to chapter 3.

32. Elaine Pagels, *Beyond Belief: The Secret Gospel of Thomas* (New York: Vintage, 2004), 39. To read the Acts of Thomas online, go to www.gnosis.org/library/actthom.htm.

33. Klaus K. Klostermaier, *A Survey of Hinduism* (New York: State University of New York Press, 1994), 438.

34. Klostermaier, *A Survey of Hinduism*, 450.

35. Gandhi, *The Story of My Experiments with Truth*, 29.

36. Bombay Sarvodaya Mandal, www.mkgandhi.org/religionmk.htm (accessed 10 February 2008).

37. Gandhi would vacillate on Christianity. In his early years, he developed a "sort of dislike" for it, primarily because missionaries "abused Hindus and their gods." His attitude softened somewhat over time to the faith, and he found much to like in the sayings of Jesus. He also compared Jesus with the Buddha. Gandhi, however, didn't like the Old Testament. He found it difficult to read and it held for him little interest or understanding. He said that the Book of Genesis "sent him to sleep." For more on his reactions to Christianity, read pages 29–30, 106–8, and 118–20 in Gandhi, *The Story of My Experiments with Truth*.

38. Gandhi, *The Story of My Experiments with Truth*, 93.

39. Richard Attenborough's 1982 cinematic biography *Gandhi* is truly epic in scale, beginning with his years in South Africa and ending with his assassination. The critically acclaimed film won eight Oscars. Controversy has surrounded the 2007 film, *Gandhi, My Father*, now available on DVD, which focuses on the turbulent relationship between Gandhi and his oldest son, Harilal. Prominent figures in India called for the film to be banned because it "attempts to tarnish the image of a national hero." Despite the protests, critics across the globe have praised it, calling it, as *Newsweek* did, an "emotionally charged, compelling film." The official site is www.gandhimyfather.erosentertainment.com. As a side note, *Gandhi, My Father* is instructional from a religious studies perspective. It contains various overtly Hindu scenes, including a partial marriage ceremony, discussion of Holi, a procession of performers calling people to see their performance of the *Mahabharata*, a partial *Durga puja*, and a funeral. Furthermore, we hear about Gandhi's ecumenical stance on religion and his distaste of untouchability. Briefly, Harilal converts to Islam and then converts back to Hinduism, more specifically the Arya Samaj.

40. Rashtriya Swayamsevak Sangh, 2003, www.rss.org/New_RSS/Mission_Vision/Why_RSS.jsp (accessed 10 February 2008).

41. Ziauddin Sardar, "Haunted by the Politics of Hate," *New Statesman*, 2006, www.new statesman.com/200601300022 (accessed 10 February 2008).

42. *Human Rights Watch* 11, no. 6(C), www.hrw.org/reports/pdfs/i/india/india999.pdf (accessed 10 February 2008).

43. "Uphold tradition of tolerance, says Narayanan," *The Hindu*, 2002, www.hinduonnet.com/thehindu/2002/07/25/stories/2002072504370100.htm (accessed 10 February 2008).

44. Gokulsing and Dissanayake, *Indian Popular Cinema*, 23.

45. Klostermaier, *A Concise Encyclopedia of Hinduism*, 24.

46. Kris initially offers his left hand to take the offering, but his mother rebuffs him until he gives the right hand. In Northern India, only the right hand is used for eating; the left hand is considered impure.

47. According to Sharada Sugirtharajah, "It is a common belief among devout Hindu women that their fasts and vows will protect their husbands and children." "Women in Hinduism," in *Themes and Issues in Hinduism*, ed. Paul Bowen (London: Cassell, 1998), 63.

48. Gandhi, *The Story of My Experiments with Truth*, 2.

49. Klostermaier, *A Concise Encyclopedia of Hinduism*, 32.

50. Klostermaier, *A Concise Encyclopedia of Hinduism*, 33.

51. Uttar Pradesh has a considerable Muslim population.

52. Mira Nair cowrote and directed the 1996 film *Kama Sutra: A Tale of Love*, a story about two women—one, a low-caste servant and the other, a high-caste princess—who become sexual rivals when they reach maturity.

53. Seyyed Hossein Nasr, *Islam: Religion, History and Civilization* (San Francisco: Harper, 2003), 42.

54. For more about Sikhism, go to the end of the chapter.

55. In many families, when a boy reaches the age of 11 or 12, he is taken to a Sikh temple and there, in the presence of the holy text, "his first turban is ceremonially tied on." Hew McLeod, *Sikhism* (New York: Penguin, 1997), 143.

56. The other k's are the *kachha* or short breeches, and the *kangha* or comb. For more information on the *khalsa*, go to www.sikhs.org/khalsa.htm. Once one undergoes the *Khalsa* initiation, one must "avoid the four cardinal prohibitions, including cutting one's hair, consuming meat that has been slaughtered according to the Muslim rite (halal meat, or kuttha), engaging in extramarital sex, and using tobacco. Taking drugs or intoxicants is also eschewed. McLeod, *Sikhism*, 145.

57. Interestingly, the 1983 film *Phaniyamma*, which is unavailable in the United States, tells a very similar story of a child bride whose husband dies not long after their marriage. Based on the novel by M. K. Indira, the film follows Phani over 70 years, beginning with her as a girl who suffers in silence to a woman who defies tradition. Gokulsing and Dissanayake, *Indian Popular Cinema*, 82–83.

58. Other Gandhian ideas are mentioned, including his wanting to call the untouchables *harijan*, and his adherence to freedom and *satya* or truth.

59. "India's unwanted: 30 million widows," International Herald Tribune, 2005, www.iht.com/articles/2005/01/30/news/India.php (accessed 10 February 2008).

60. "Water," *Fox*, 2006 , http://www.foxsearchlight.com/water (accessed 10 February 2008).

61. The authors of *Indian Popular Cinema* remind the reader that Indian cinema maintains the status quo, which is why these epics occur time and again. They have served as "ideological instruments employed for the expansion of values and beliefs, endorsed by the ruling classes. There is also a significant way in which the Indian popular cinema legitimizes its own existence through a reinscription of its values onto those of the two epics." Gokulsing and Dissanayake, *Indian Popular Cinema*, 18.

62. One could also say that the director draws an analogy between Mitthu, the parrot, and the women in the ashram. Just as the bird is kept confined by Madhumati, so are the women, particularly Kalyani after it's announced that she will be marrying Narayan. Instead of accepting this, Madhumati locks Kalyani in her room. In a fit of anger, Chuyia tries to free the bird, but in fact kills it, just as her announcement seals Kalyani's fate. Shakuntala, now armed with the knowledge that by law, widows can remarry, is the one who sets Kalyani free.

63. "The Matsya Purana," *Dharma Kshetra*, www.dharmakshetra.com/avatars/Matsya%20 Purans.html (accessed 10 February 2008).

64. John F. Burns, "Once Widowed in India, Twice Scorned," *New York Times*, 1998, www2 .soe.umd.umich.edu/rpkettel/NY_Times_article.pdf (accessed 10 February 2008).

65. Gokulsing and Dissanayake, *Indian Popular Cinema*, 10.

66. Historically, a number of women opted for, or were forced into, "voluntary suicide." The most commonly known form of is known as suttee or sati ("virtuous woman"). Rather than endure the miserable lives ahead of them, they immolated themselves on their dead husband's funeral pyre. Even though this practice was prohibited in 1829 by the British, it re-emerged in 1987 when Roop Kanwar, an 18-year-old widow, was burned with her husband. Andrea Major, ed., *Sati: A Historical Anthology* (New Delhi: Oxford University Press, 2007).

67. Klostermaier, *A Concise Encyclopedia of Hinduism*, 126.

68. Klostermaier, *A Concise Encyclopedia of Hinduism*, 138.

69. Burns, "Once Widowed in India, Twice Scorned."

70. *The Bhagavad Gita*, trans. W. J. Johnson (New York: Oxford University Press, 1994), 24–25.

71. Major, ed., *Sati: A Historical Anthology*, xxvii

72. Major, ed., *Sati: A Historical Anthology*, xxviii.

73. Burns, "Once Widowed in India, Twice Scorned."

74. Sushma Sood, "Domestic Violence: Towards a New Theoretical Approach," 1994, www.aic .gov.au/publications/proceedings/27/sood.pdf (accessed 10 February 2008).

75. *The Laws of Manu*, trans. Wendy Doniger and Brian K. Smith (New York: Penguin Books, 1991), 115.

76. Heinrich Zimmer, *Myths and Symbols in Indian Art and Civilization*, ed. Joseph Campbell (Princeton, NJ: Princeton University Press, 1974), 26.

77. Zimmer, *Myths and Symbols in Indian Art and Civilization*, 29–31.

78. Zimmer, *Myths and Symbols in Indian Art and Civilization*, 31–35.

79. *The Laws of Manu*, 59.

80. *The Laws of Manu*, 58.

81. *The Laws of Manu*, 204–5.

82. In 1994, Seema Biswas starred in *Bandit Queen*, which is based on the true story of Phoolan Devi, a low-caste woman who was sold into marriage at 11 years old and then repeatedly victimized throughout much of her early life. "Liberated" by a bandit, she soon joins them and rises to lead the group, exacting revenge on anyone who has wronged her. Devi became a sort of Indian version of Robin Hood, because she stole from the rich and gave to the poor. She also was seen as the physical embodiment of *shakti*, particularly Durga—violent and bloodthirsty but also benevolent to those whom society had wronged. She was assassinated in 2001. For more about her, go to news.bbc.co.uk/2/hi/south_asia/1456441.stm.

83. "White Rainbow, Emancipation of Widows," Screen India, 2004, www.screenindia.com/fullstory.php?content_id=7398 (accessed 10 February 2008).

84. "Legend of Bagger Vance," *Hinduism Today*, 2001, www.hinduismtoday.com/archives/2001/3-4/16_bagger_vance.shtml (accessed 10 February 2008).

85. To fully explore all of the parallels between the film and the Bhagavad-Gita, one can read Steven J. Rosen, *Gita on the Green: The Mystical Tradition Behind Bagger Vance* (New York: Continuum International, 2000).

86. *The Bhagavad Gita*, trans. W. J. Johnson, 77.

87. A significant number of novels have emerged in the past decade in which the main Indian-American character struggles with the fact that he or she is not quite Indian and not quite American. Just a few of these authors are Tanuja Desai Hidier, Amulya Malladi, Anjali Banerjee, Kavita Daswani, and Kirin Narayan.

88. According to the director's commentary on the DVD, the scene was filmed in an actual temple.

89. A class action suit, filed by Harish Bharti, a Seattle lawyer who is a Hindu, was brought against McDonald's in 2001. He claimed that the fast-food giant mislead vegetarians, many who were vegetarian for religious reasons, making them believe that the fries were cooked in 100% vegetable oil. It was revealed that the company used beef extract. For more on this, read "McDonald's Supersizes Hindu Endowment," *Hinduism Today*, www.hinduismtoday.com/press_releases/mcdonalds (accessed 10 February 2008). The International Society for Krishna Consciousness also maintains a large number of vegetarian restaurants throughout the world.

90. Robin Rinehart, ed., *Contemporary Hinduism: Ritual, Culture and Practice* (Santa Barbara, CA: ABC-CLIO, 2004), 25.

91. Klostermaier, *A Survey of Hinduism*, 326.

92. In early 2007, an arrest warrant was issued for American actor Richard Gere after he publicly kissed Bollywood actress Shilpa Shetty. A judge claimed that this behavior contravened India's strict public obscenity laws.

93. For more information on the Iyer Brahmins, go to http://www.keralaiyers.com/manthram.

94. Klostermaier, *A Survey of Hinduism*, 338.

95. "Dietary Law," *Encyclopedia Brittanica*, www.britannica.com/eb/article-66416/dietarylaw#538310.hook (accessed 10 February 2008).

96. In the mid- to late 1990s, several non-Hindu celebrities "popularized" the wearing of a sari and a *bindi*, most notably singers Gwen Stefani and Madonna who, along with a slew of

other Hollywood types—everyone from Prince to Mira Sorvino—also took to adorning themselves with henna or *Mehndi*. This ancient form of body "art" has been used primarily by Middle Eastern and East Indian women on their wedding day. Some Indians were outraged at this trend, calling it just another form of "cultural appropriation." It's OK and even fashionable for white women to dress in Indian clothes, they complained, but when Indian women dress traditionally, they are told to "go home." One of the most articulate blog rants on the subject was penned by Ananya Mukherjea, a teacher and sociology student at CUNY. Available at Ananya Mukherjea, "indo-chic," www.makezine.org/indo.html (accessed 10 February 2008).

97. "Aparna Sen Makes a Statement Again," *India Today*, 2002, www.rediff.com/entertai/2002/jul/27aparna.htm (accessed 10 February 2008).

98. "Hindus-Muslim Violence Imperials India," *Time Magazine*, 2002, www.time.com/time/world/article/0,8599,213670,00.html (accessed 10 February 2008).

99. A highly regarded Bollywood film dealing specifically with this intense period is *Bumbai* or *Bombay* (1995), which depicts the conflict on a very personal level. Going against tradition, a Hindu man marries a Muslim woman, and they have children. Not long afterward, the mosque is torn down and India is thrown into chaos. The rest of the film depicts how the violence and prejudicial attitudes affect this one family.

100. For a more in-depth discussion of the situation, see K. Jaishankar and Debarati Haldar, "Religious Identity of the Perpetrators and Victims of Communal Violence in Post-Independence India," *ERCES Online Quarterly*, 2004, www.erces.com/journal/articles/archives/v02/v_02_04 .htm (accessed 17 February 2008).

101. Ram is short for Rama, the seventh avatar of Vishnu.

102. For a much rawer look at Westerners and their penchant for Eastern religions, see Jane Campion's 1999 film *Hideous Kinky*. In it, Kate Winslet plays an Australian woman who follows a charismatic guru to India. Worried about the changes occurring in their daughter, her parents hire an American expert (Harvey Keitel) to deprogram her. An interview with director Jane Campion can be found online at "Holy Smoke: A Conversation with Jane Campion," Australian Broadcasting Corporation, 1999, www.abc.net.au/rn/talks/8.30/relrpt/stories/s75034.htm (accessed 10 February 2008).

103. For more on Chopra's responses to the film, see "Chopra: 'Guru' Film Not Insulting," *Time*, 2008, http://www.time.com/time/arts/article/0,8599,1811275,00.html (accessed 11 June 2008).

104. R. K. Narayan, *The Ramayana: A Shortened Modern Prose Version of the Indian Epic* (New York: Penguin Books, 1972), 82.

105. William Buck, *Ramayana* (Berkeley: University of California Press, 2000), 169.

106. There is a real Ram Dass who is a contemporary spiritual teacher. In the 1960s, he was friends with Timothy Leary. He also wrote the 1971 best seller titled *Be Here Now*.

107. Since it is revealed that the executioner's son-in-law is lusting after his youngest daughter, it is difficult to know if the hangman is simply inserting his family members into the story or the events are actually taking place.

108. It won the FIPRESCI Prize at the Bombay International Film Festival and the Silver Lotus Award at the National Film Awards in India.

109. Sister Helen Prejean, a Catholic nun, asks the same question in her books *Dead Man Walking* and *The Death of Innocents: An Eyewitness Account of Wrongful Executions.*

110. Gandhi, *The Story of My Experiments with Truth*, 447.

111. Gandhi, *The Story of My Experiments with Truth*, 239.

112. Gandhi, *The Story of My Experiments with Truth*, 208.

113. "The Social Construction of 'Self' and Womanhood in a Hindu Village of Bangladesh," *Journal of World Anthropology*, 2007, www.wings.buffalo.edu/research/anthrogis/JWA/V3N1/Jahan-art.pdf (accessed 10 February 2008).

114. "The Social Construction of 'Self,'" *Journal of World Anthropology.*

115. Sooni Taraporevala, "Parsis: The Zoroastrians of India: A Photographic Journey," *Overlook*, 2004. Also, for more in-depth discussion of demographics, see the UNESCO Parsi Zoroastrian Project, "Demographics," www.unescoparzor.com/project/demographics.htm (accessed 10 February 2008).

116. For more information on their business acumen, see "The World's Successful Diasporas," *World Business*, 2007, www.worldbusinesslive.com/Entrepreneurship/Article/648273/the-worlds-successful-diasporas (accessed 10 February 2008). For more about religious practices, see Mary Boyce, *Zoroastrians: Their Religious Beliefs and Practices* (New York: Routledge, 2001), and S. A. Nigosian, *The Zoroastrian Faith: Tradition and Modern Research* (Montréal: McGill-Queen's University Press, 1993).

117. For fuller explanation, see Avesta-Zoroastrian Archives, "The Kusti Ritual," www.avesta.org/ritual/ritualk.htm (accessed 10 February 2008).

118. For the textual basis for this, read Fieser and Powers, *Scriptures of the World's Religions*, 237–39. See also "The Zoroastrian Dakhma-nashini Mode of Disposal of the Dead," *World of Traditional Zoroastrianism*, tenets.zoroastrianism.com/dakhma33.html (accessed 10 February 2008).

119. McLeod, *Sikhism*, xxviii; the author explains that the teachings of Nanak "cannot reasonably be regarded as a syncretism of Hindu teachings and Islam as so many popular books have suggested." Although the Sant movement, of which Nanak was a part, included some Muslim elements, and certainly Sikhism is also monotheistic, "The burden of their teachings was weighted heavily toward concepts found in Hindu ideals."

120. The 10 Gurus are Nanak (1469–1539), Angad (1504–1552), Amar Das (1479–1574), Ram Das (1534–1581), Arjan (1563–1606), Hargobind (1595–1644), Hari Rai (1630–1661), Hari Krishan (1656–1664), Tegh Bahadur (1621–1675), and Gobind Singh (1666–1708).

121. After a child is born, the Sikh parent chooses his or her name in the following manner: "The Guru Granth Sahib is opened at random and a name for the child is chosen, beginning with the same letter as the first composition on the left-hand page. No distinction marks boys' and girls' first names." McLeod, *Sikhism*, 143.

122. "Religious Emblems," *Sikhism Home Page*, www.sikhs.org/khanda.htm (accessed 10 February 2008).

123. "Silent Waters Press Kit," *First Run Features*, 2003, www.firstrunfeatures.com/shopsite_sc/store/html/presskits/silent_waters_press_kit/silent_waters_press_kit.pdf (accessed 10 February 2008).

124. In a blog from January 1, 2005, the author of Vij.com states that even though he has high praise for director Wes Anderson for treating Ahluwalia as something more than a "token" Sikh, he criticizes the studio's marketing campaign for "cropping" the minority actors out of the shots. For more, see http://www.vij.com/archive/waris_star_turn.html.

125. In a 2001 interview with Brad Stone, Moore said of the character, "Nemo is a sort of Sikh fanatic, which you tend to forget when you see him being played by James Mason or someone like that." Brad Stone, "Alan Moore Interview," *The Comic Wire*, 2001, www.comicbookresources .com/news/newsitem.cgi?id=554 (accessed 10 February 2008).

126. Andy Seiler, "You'll Soon Know Mo' about Nemo," *USA Today*, 2003, www.usatoday .com/life/movies/news/2003-06-03-mo-dvd_x.htm (accessed 10 February 2008).

127. "Indian in Western Hearts," *buzzle.com*, 2005, www.buzzle.com/editorials/3-31-2005-67849 .asp (accessed 10 February 2008).

128. A more recent documentary that turns its attention to poverty, prostitution, and children of the streets is *Born into Brothels: Calcutta's Red Light Kids* (2004). The film won an Academy Award. For an older look at prostitution in Mumbai, look for *The Courtesans of Bombay* (1983).

129. To read excerpts from interviews with Nair and her husband, Columbia University professor Mahmood Mamdani—he was expelled from Uganda in 1972—go to "Uganda: The Return," *pbs.org*, 2007, www.pbs.org/frontlineworld/rough/2007/05/uganda_the_retuint.html (accessed 10 February 2008).

130. Sheila Benson, "Eroticism of Kama Sutra Goes beyond Mere Titillation," *Orlando Sentinel*, 1992, www.mirabaifilms.com/wordpress/?page_id=22 (accessed 10 February 2008).

131. Peter Bowan, "Standing on Ceremony: Mira Nair Returns to India for Monsoon Wedding," *Filmmaker Magazine*, 2001, www.mirabaifilms.com/wordpress/?page_id=26 (accessed 10 February 2008).

132. Joan Dupont, "Mira Nair Peels Back Layers of Punjabi Society," *International Herald Tribune*, 2001, www.mirabaifilms.com/wordpress/?page_id=32 (accessed 10 February 2008).

133. Before she meets his parents, he tells her that public displays of affection are discouraged. Disregarding what he says, she holds his hand and kisses him. Later in the movie, she shows up at a funeral dressed like a Westerner, in black and in a sleeveless dress, while everyone else is dressed in traditional white.

134. Rajesh Kumar, "Mira Nair Returns to Her Kolkata Chromosomes with 'Namesake'," *KolkataScoop*, 2005, www.mirabaifilms.com/wordpress/?page_id=48 (accessed 10 February 2008).

135. "Many Stories in India Are Just Crying Out to Be Made," *Cinema India-International*, 1988, www.mirabaifilms.com/wordpress/?page_id=17 (accessed 10 February 2008).

136. Deepa Mehta, "What's Wrong with My Film? Why Are People Making Such a Big Fuss: Deepa Mehta Defends Her Film *Fire*," *Rediff.com*, 1998, www.rediff.com/entertai/1998/dec/10fire .htm (accessed 10 February 2008).

137. "Hindu Leader Says Lesbian Film Should Be about Moslem Family," *South Asian Woman's Network*,1999, www.sawnet.org/news/fire.html#2 (accessed 10 February 2008).

138. Knappert, *An Encyclopedia of Myth and Legend*, 203.

139. Knappert, *An Encyclopedia of Myth and Legend*, 234.

140. Knappert, *An Encyclopedia of Myth and Legend*, 234.

141. Richard Phillips, "If People Want to Separate, They Should Understand What It Would Really Mean," *The World Socialist Web Site*, 1999, www.wsws.org/articles/1999/aug1999/meh-a06 .shtml (accessed 10 February 2008).

142. "Production Notes," *Mongrel Media*, 2005, water.mahiram.com/production.html (accessed 10 February 2008).

143. "Water," *Box Office Mojo*, 2006, www.boxofficemojo.com/movies/?id=water06.htm (accessed 10 February 2008).

144. "New Mehta Film about Kamagata Maru Incident," *Canadian Broadcasting Corporation*, 2006, www.cbc.ca/news/story/2006/10/24/exclusion-mehta.html (accessed 10 February 2008).

145. "Deepa Mehta's Signs Big B for Exclusion," *Indiafm.com*, 2007, www.indiafm.com/ news/2007/02/19/8920/index.html (accessed 10 February 2008), and "Deepa Mehta Inks Deal with Amitabh," *Hindustan Times*, 2007, www.hindustantimes.com/StoryPage/StoryPage.aspx?id =15bc1940-da4b-4400-808d-607b9a04a9a9&&Headline=Big+B+signs+Deepa+Mehta+film (accessed 10 February 2008).

3

Buddhism

STATISTICS

Theravada and Mahayana Buddhism exert a tremendous influence on the lives of those people living in East and Southeast Asia. The countries with the most significant number of followers include Bhutan (75% are "lamaistic"), Burma (89%), Cambodia (95%), Japan (84% mixed with Shinto), South Korea (23.2%), Laos (65%), Macau (50%), Malaysia (19.2%), Nepal (10.7%), Mongolia (50% are "lamaistic"), Sri Lanka (69%), Taiwan (93% mixed with Daoism), Thailand (95%), and Vietnam (9.3%).

India, where Buddhism began, has only a negligible number of followers. Current estimates indicate that there are somewhere between 200 and 500 million adherents worldwide, making Buddhism the fourth-largest world religion.[1] According to a 2001 American Religious Identification Survey, conducted by the doctorate-granting institution of the City University of New York, there are slightly more than 1 million Buddhists in the United States.[2]

THE BASICS

The period between 900 B.C.E. and 200 B.C.E. has been coined the Axial Age,[3] and kingdoms stretching from Greece to China experienced violence, religious intolerance, and political instability during this time. India, too, witnessed great changes, particularly in areas along the Ganges Rivers. The seventh and sixth centuries B.C.E. saw tremendous economic activity that resulted in social, religious, and political upheaval, and people reacted to these changes in various ways. Those working within the Hindu/Brahmanic orthodoxy retained Vedic concepts and practices but expanded them. The result was the Upanishads, also known as *Vedanta* or end of the Vedas. Those coming from a non-Brahmanic, ascetic tradition rejected the Vedas, the caste system, the superiority of the priests, sacrifice and rituals, and even the centrality of the gods. The result was the rise of such heterodox systems as Buddhism and Jainism. This chapter will take a closer look at Buddhism.

To become a Buddhist, one doesn't need to engage in rituals or ceremonies, make a formal declaration of faith, pray to a god or goddess, or attend a temple. One isn't born a Buddhist and there isn't an elaborate process of conversion. In fact, what Buddhism offers its adherents isn't a sense that this knowledge was "handed down from previous teachers" but that it was a product of the direct experience and insight of its founder.[4] Anyone who has an interest in Buddhism is invited to "verify" its basic principles through his or her own experience, because "even faith should be rooted in instigation and inquiry and not based solely upon emotional leanings and blind belief."[5] So what makes a person a Buddhist? Regardless of whether one is a lay person or a monk or nun, all Buddhists are encouraged to take refuge in the Buddha, the dharma, and the *sangha*—or as we might say in common parlance, the teacher, the teachings, and the community of believers. Because these are seen as having great value, they are referred to as the Triple Gem or Three Jewels.

The Teacher

The founder of Buddhism wasn't a celestial being. Rather he was born a *kshatriya* near Lumbini, in modern-day Nepal, during the fifth century B.C.E.[6] His full name was Siddhartha ("wish-fulfiller") Gautama, and his father, Suddhodana, belonged to the Shakya clan.[7] In Siddhartha's "biography," we find fantastical elements combining easily with more "realistic" ones.[8] For instance, it's said that before he was conceived his mother, Mayadevi, dreamed that a white elephant entered her side and went into her womb. It is also said that after carrying her child for 10 months, she gave birth in a grove while standing up; a tree bent down to assist her. When she died seven days later, Mayadevi's sister, who was also married to Suddhodana, raised the boy as her own.

Shortly after Siddhartha's birth, a sage visited the palace and predicted that the child would follow one of two paths: He would either be a *chakravartin*[9] ("world ruling" monarch) or a Buddha ("awakened" being). Not wanting his son to renounce the world, Suddhodana raised Siddhartha in extreme luxury, free from every form of suffering. Accounts say that the young man divided his time between three palaces (one for the hot season, one for the cold season, and one for the rainy season), wore only the finest clothes, and was surrounded by the most beautiful women and objects. Despite his father's best efforts to keep his son contented, Siddhartha still wanted to see the world beyond the palace gates. Acceding to his son's wishes, Suddhodana set the stage for these visits, removing anything unpleasant or ugly. Siddhartha happened upon some "unpleasantries," though, and these are known as the "four sights." The first three—old age, sickness, and death—demonstrate that youth, good health, and permanence are just an illusion. The fourth sight, which was a saffron-robed ascetic, showed Siddhartha the path of renunciation. At 29 years old, the prince left behind his wife of 13 years, Yashodhara, and his son, Rahula,[10] and set out to free the world from suffering. He became a bodhisattva or "one who is awaiting enlightenment."

As a wandering exiled monk or *shramana*, Siddhartha immediately sought out spiritual teachers to guide him. During this period, he gained knowledge and achieved advanced meditative states of consciousness, but he still hadn't attained enlightenment. For the next six years, he followed the path of extreme asceticism. While sitting in the lotus position, he suffered exposure to the heat and the cold, slept on an uncomfortable bed, survived on only a grain of rice a day, and drank only rain water. Because he ate so little, his hair fell out, and when he placed his hand on his stomach, he could feel his spine. Near death, he realized that self-mortification wasn't getting him any closer to his goal. Having lived a life of hedonism in the palace and now one of extreme renunciation, Siddhartha vowed to follow the Middle Way, the path between the extremes. He resumed eating and drinking.

Siddhartha next ventured to the town of Bodh Gaya, where he began a period of reflection under a fig tree (*ficus religiosa*), also known as the Bodhi tree.[11] He vowed that he would attain enlightenment or he would die trying. It was at this time that Mara, the god of death, showed up, determined to thwart Siddhartha's plans. The demon began by tempting the young man with his voluptuous daughters. When this didn't work, Mara promised to grant Siddhartha anything he desired, but the prince turned down his offer. At this rejection, Mara became furious and conjured up images of demons and warfare. But neither of these dissuaded the young prince from his task, and he remained serene and steadfast. Mara tried again, saying that it was he, Mara, who should sit on the throne of enlightenment. Siddhartha countered this statement by referring to the great merit that he, Siddhartha, had accumulated during his past lives, and he called upon the Earth to support his claim. It did, by quaking and driving away Mara.[12] With the demon gone, Siddhartha sat in deep contemplation. He passed through three watches of the night, during which he saw his past lives, witnessed the rebirth of others in one of five (later, six) realms of being according to their deeds; and finally, came to understand the cause of suffering. Then, after 49 days of meditation, Siddhartha, at 35 years old, attained complete enlightenment. The bodhisattva became a Buddha, an awakened being for which there would be no more rebirths; he had attained nirvana, a state of bliss beyond suffering.

The Buddha, as he will be known henceforth, knew that what he had learned would be difficult to convey to others, yet he was moved by compassion for all sentient beings, knowing that those who had only a "little dust in their eyes" would benefit from his experience.[13] The *Tathagata* or "Truth-attained One" delivered his first sermon in the Deer Park at Sarnath, near Varanasi, thus setting into "motion the wheel of his teaching." To his five disciples, he explained that one should follow the Middle Path, because it "gives vision, which gives knowledge, and which leads to calm, to insight, to enlightenment, to Nibbána [nirvana]."[14] He also outlined for them the Four Noble Truths. But more on that later.

For the next 45 years, the Buddha wandered throughout northern India, spreading his message to the masses and ordaining many into his *sangha*. When the Buddha entered his 80th year, his health began to fail. Although others lamented the impending loss, the Buddha explained how "this body is not me. Unlimited by the body, unlimited by the mind, a Buddha is infinite and measureless."[15] Before he died and realized *parinirvana*, or his final release, he and his disciples shared a meal that was prepared for them by Chunda, a goldsmith. Scholars debate over whether this was a dish made from pork or mushrooms,[16] but whatever it was, it made the Buddha deathly ill, and he died soon after. Before he did, though, he told his disciples that they should be a refuge unto themselves; rely on themselves and nothing else. "Hold fast to the dharma as your lamp, hold fast to the dharma as your refuge, and you shall surely reach nirvana, the highest good and the highest goal."[17] Furthermore, he reminded them that "all things that come into being must pass away. Strive earnestly."[18] After the Buddha died, his body, as was the custom, was cremated. The bones that remained once the funeral pyre was extinguished were divided and placed under commemorative stupas, which are bell-shaped memorial monuments.[19]

Dharma

The second refuge for Buddhists is the dharma or *dhamma*, which are the "teachings," and many of them can be traced to the historical Buddha and his disciples. One of the most important lessons that Buddha taught was that the three marks or characteristics of all conditioned phenomena are suffering (*duhkha* or *dukkha*), nonself (*anatman* or *anatta*), and impermanence (*anitya* or *anicca*). He discussed the first mark at length during his Deer Park sermon. In fact, suffering is the cornerstone of the dharma and can be found in his discussion of the Four Noble Truths.

The First Noble Truth states that life, in all realms of rebirth, is characterized by suffering. The Buddha explained that it can be found in birth, old age, death, sorrow, grieving, dejection, and despair. "Contact with unpleasant things is suffering; not getting what you want is also suffering. In short, the five aggregates of grasping are suffering."[20] Suffering is more than just unhappiness, pain, disappointment, and misery, though, as it also contains the ideas of "imperfection" and "unsatisfactoriness." It's also that vague floating sense that our lives aren't quite what they could be—that we could have more money, a better job, a prettier or more handsome face, a trimmer waistline . . . a better life. When some people hear that "life is suffering," they counter with "but don't we also experience moments of happiness?" Buddhism never denies that life contains joy, friendship, and love; in fact, the Buddha said that the spiritual life is "good friendship, good companionship and good comradeship," because they help us to develop and cultivate the Noble Eightfold Path.[21] What Buddhism says is that none of these "conditions" can last. According to the Buddha, everything is impermanent and bound to perish. For instance, when a person first falls in love, he is intoxicated, walking on air. He can't wait to hear his beloved's voice or see her face. But flash forward to one month, one year, or 10 years after that initial meeting, and we discover that our feelings have changed. As much as we try to convince ourselves otherwise, nothing stays the same.

The Second Noble Truth concerns the source of our suffering, and the Buddha found this to be thirst (also known as *tanha*) for sense-pleasures, for existence and becoming, and for nonexistence. Rather than realizing that joyful moments can't last, we cling to them as if they can. And instead of realizing that pain and disappointment are momentary, we flee from them. This craving can result in lust for money and sensual pleasure, for a long life and eternal youth, and, if we are infirm or depressed, the desire for death. Few of us want to hear that our first breath contains the seeds of our own death and that every minute brings us closer to that inevitable end. Another misconception that we hold on to is that we will all live to a "ripe old age." Many of us prepare and plan for a future that may not exist. Car crashes, accidental poisonings, fatal falls, and bad health can kill us at any time. Many people grasp at tangible objects, believing that a new car, home, wardrobe, spouse, or cell phone will make them happy. Others grasp at ideas or viewpoints, believing that these, too, are enduring. And still, most cling to the idea of an "I," which we believe is eternal and unchanging. The Buddha often refers to these people as "the immature," and he reminds us that "all created things are transitory; those who realize this are freed from suffering"[22] and that "death comes and carries off a man absorbed in his family and possessions as the monsoon flood sweeps away a sleeping village."[23] During his "Fire Sermon," the Buddha said that everything was burning, including the eye, the ear, the nose, the tongue, the body, and more. And what makes them burn? Lust, fire, delusion, birth, aging and death, sorrow, lamentations, pain, grief, and despair.[24]

To see how craving leads to suffering, let's examine the life of a woman who works a stressful 50-hour-a-week job. At some point, she will begin pining for a vacation and some much-needed rest and relaxation. Let's say that she schedules her two-week holiday. Almost immediately, she will become excited by the thought of getting away, imagining what she will do and what she will see. When the day of her vacation finally arrives, she is exhilarated. That feeling will undoubtedly be hampered by the long lines at the airport, the baggage checks, delayed flights, cramped seating on the airplane, her snoring or overly talkative neighbor, and unappetizing airplane food. Once she arrives at her destination, she might breathe a sigh of relief: finally, the vacation is underway. Depending on her expectations, the vacation could still prove to be a disappointment—her hotel room might be noisy, dirty, or hot/cold, and the location might not resemble the travel brochure—or it may be very satisfying.

Either way, when her two weeks come to a close, she will become sad and frustrated, knowing that she has to return to work. Even if she could quit her job and be on permanent vacation, she, like most people, would become "bored" by the day-in-day-out sameness and would long for something new.

The reality is that no matter who we are or what our situation, we are never satisfied. We are always chasing that permanent state of excitement and happiness, when in fact existence is ever-changing and unstable; life is always in flux. Many of us want to be like the celebrities we see in the magazines. We want their fame, beauty, charisma, and money. But few realize that celebrities also suffer. And, sadly, none of the qualities for which we admire them last. Not realizing this, some people engage in criminal behavior to ensure an "easy and carefree life" with all of its amenities. They end up killing their spouses, robbing banks, embezzling from their employers, or selling narcotics. As the Buddha said, "All of the troubles and strife in the world, from little personal quarrels in families to great wars between nations and countries, arise out of this selfish 'thirst.'"[25]

The Third Noble Truth tells us simply that suffering can end; we just have to stop grasping and craving. We might compare the Buddha to a physician who "diagnosed" the human condition. Not only did he tell us that everyone suffers but he also explained that this ailment has an origin: it comes from desire, which in turn gives rise to rebirth. Then he gave us hope, telling us that there was a cure from this affliction. His "prescription" can be found in the Fourth Noble Truth, which says to follow the Eightfold Path, and this entails having right understanding (view), right thought (intention), right speech, right action, right livelihood, right effort, right mindfulness, and right concentration.

The Eightfold Path is usually broken into three categories; with the first two listed as wisdom, the next three as ethical conduct, and the last three as mental discipline. Right understanding means that we see things as they truly are. We can do that by fully comprehending the Four Noble Truths and letting them penetrate our being. We understand that life is characterized by suffering, and that its source lies within ourselves. We don't pray for someone else to "fix" it but realize that we have the ability within ourselves to change our perceptions. Right thought means that we think in ways that are altruistic, benign, and beyond selfishness. Instead of feeling ill will, hatred, and violence toward others for perceived "wrongs" against us, we detach ourselves from these thoughts and extend love and nonviolence to all beings. As scholar and monk Dzongsar Jamyang Khyentse says, being nonviolent doesn't mean smiling and being meek. "The fundamental cause of violence is when one is fixated on an extreme idea, such as justice or morality. When you have no ego, no clinging to the self, there is never a reason to be violent. When one understands that one's enemies are held under a powerful influence of their own ignorance and aggression, that they are trapped by their habits, it is easier to forgive them. . . . When we transcend believing in the extremes of dualistic phenomena, we have transcended the causes of violence."[26]

Ethical conduct means having right speech, right action, and right livelihood. The first of these means that when we talk, we have a purpose and we are polite. We don't lie, we don't slander or gossip about others, we avoid malicious or impolite words, and we say only what is necessary. Idle talk is discouraged. Right action means abstaining from the destruction of life, from taking what isn't ours, from engaging in sexual misconduct, and from misusing the senses—moderation in all things is the key. We don't engage in criminal behavior, nor do we take drugs or drink alcohol. What we should do is provide a model for others to follow. Right livelihood means choosing a profession that doesn't violate the Eightfold Path. Naturally, we shouldn't kill, steal, cheat, lie, or engage in sexual misconduct, nor should we engage in professions that lead others to engage in these behaviors. Laypersons are discouraged from professions that involve the use of or sale of weapons, animals for slaughter or human beings for slavery, intoxicants, and poison. Also discouraged are jobs that involve making predictions, such as astrology, geomancy, or palmistry, and those involving magic, such as making charms or placing spells. Based on these, some unsuitable professions would be a fisherman, a butcher, a gambler, a prostitute, a bar owner, a drug dealer, an arms dealer, a fortune teller, and a soldier.

The last three categories are right effort, right mindfulness, and right concentration, and they are considered to be critical to facilitating mental discipline. Right effort tells us that we must never be lazy minded. We should actively prevent unwholesome states of mind from arising, and if and when they do arise, we should get rid of them. We must strive to develop and cultivate wholesome states of mind. As the Buddha said, the person "makes an effort, arouses energy, applies his mind and strives."[27] Right mindfulness means to live in the present, paying particular attention to the activities of the body, particularly the breath; to sensations or feelings; to the activities of the mind, especially the appearance and dissolution of lust, hatred, and delusion; and to ideas, thoughts, and conceptions.[28] By being aware, one develops insight and vanquishes fear, desire, and languor.

Finally, right concentration is sometimes called right meditation, because while following this path the adherent goes through four stages of *dhyana* or meditation to attain nirvana. One can meditate on any number of objects, from a light to a corpse, with the purpose of shifting one's attention away from the sensory world. During the first stage, one relinquishes desires and unwholesome states of mind, such as lust, restlessness, and skeptical doubt; joy and happiness remain. During the second stage, one suppresses all intellectual activity so as to develop tranquility and "one-pointed absorption," which means that one abides in the here and now. In the third stage, joy passes away, but happiness remains as does mindful equanimity. The Buddha explained this stage as "becoming conscious in the very depths of the unconscious. Even my body was flooded with that joy of which the nobles say, 'They live in abiding joy who have stilled the mind and are fully awake.'"[29] And finally, the last stage sees the disappearance of all sensations; only equanimity and awareness remain.[30] As the Buddha said, at this stage one "goes beyond the duality of pleasure and pain and the whole field of memory-making forces in the mind." Furthermore, one is beyond "the reach of thought, in that realm of complete purity which can be reached only through detachment and contemplation."[31] Zen monk and scholar Thich Nhat Hanh said that meditation consists of two parts. The first is to stop: stop running after ideas, the past, the future, and happiness, and instead focus on the present, where "life is available." This is the practice of "calming our body and emotions through mindful breathing, mindful walking, and mindful sitting." The idea is to live each moment at the deepest level possible. The second aspect is "looking deeply to see the true nature of things. . . . Doing everything mindfully is the practice of meditation, as mindfulness always nourishes concentration and understanding."[32] As the Buddha said, "Meditation brings wisdom; lack of meditation leaves ignorance. Know well what leads you forward and what holds you back, and chose the path that leads to wisdom."[33]

Other teachings of the Buddha

As we have seen, suffering is the first mark of conditioned existence. However, it doesn't exist in a vacuum. In fact, none of the three marks do; they are interdependent. Suffering is caused by our thirst for permanence, and yet the

Buddha had discovered that "all karmically constituted things are impermanent; they are not fixed, not comforting, and are characterized by constant
change. . . . For all beings, all creatures, all living things, life is limited by
death."[34] As Dzongsar Jamyang Khyentse explains, impermanence doesn't
mean "death, as we usually think, it means change."[35] Furthermore, if we accept that change is inevitable and that death is a part of the cycle, we no
longer grasp, and if this happens, then we don't think about what we do or
don't have, and that gives us the freedom to live "freely." "By realizing that all
things are assembled, that deconstruction is infinite, and that not one of the
components in all creation exists in an autonomous, permanent, pure state,
he was liberated. . . . Seeing things in this way, they begin to dissolve all
around us."[36]

Another foundational Buddhist concept is interdependent co-arising,
which states that "everything is a result of multiple causes and conditions";
nothing in the cosmos is independent.[37] To put this into perspective, look at a
simple cup of tea. It is made up of a cup, water, and tea leaves. Look a bit
deeper, and you realize that you needed someone to actually make the tea. You
also needed a water company, an electric company, a tea manufacturer, and a
tea distributor. Go before that, and you find that someone had to pick those
leaves, purify that water, burn that carbon or those fuel rods. Even further
back, you had to have the right growing conditions, including sunlight, water,
and soil, and someone needed to put those plants in the ground. A cup of tea
is also dependent on all of those people who, centuries ago, figured out that
by adding hot water to some leaves you produced a very refreshing beverage.
A cup of tea is a process of events that stretches into the past, takes place in the
present, and reaches into the future.

The 12 links in the chain of interdependent co-arising (also known as the
chain of causation and/or dependent origination) are ignorance (*avidya*), volitional action (*samskara*), consciousness, mind-body, or name and form; six
sense organs, contact, feelings, craving (*trishna*) or desire, becoming, birth, aging, and death. Ignorance conditions volitional actions, which condition consciousness, and so on. "As soon as ignorance is present, all the other links . . .
are already there. Each link contains the other links."[38] To show how these
links lead a person through endless rounds of birth and death, artists have depicted them in the outermost edge of the Wheel of Life. If we look at it as we
would a clock, at 1 o'clock, we see ignorance illustrated by an old and sight-

less man with a stick; at 2 o'clock we find a potter whose pots symbolize his karmic deeds; at 3 o'clock a monkey is jumping from one branch to another, symbolizing the major consciousness that in the ignorant springs uncontrolled from object to object; at 4 o'clock we find two people sitting in a boat, symbolizing the inseparable nature of name and form; at 5 o'clock we see a house with five windows and a door, representing the six senses; at 6 o'clock we see a man and woman embracing, the consequence of which is sensual perceptions; at 7 o'clock we find a man who is pierced by arrow, thus representing our emotions; at 8 o'clock a woman offers a man a drink, thus representing desire and "thirst for life"; at 9 o'clock we see either a man and woman engaging in sexual union or a man picking fruit from a tree, thus representing attachment and grasping; at 10 o'clock a pregnant woman represents the coming of new life; at 11 o'clock a woman gives birth; and at 12 o'clock we see an old person leaning on a stick or a man carrying a corpse, thus showing us the inevitable end for us all.[39] Interdependent co-arising is so critical to Buddhist thought that of it the Buddha said whoever sees it also sees the dharma, and whoever sees dharma also sees interdependent co-arising.[40]

During his second sermon, the Buddha spoke about something else that we cling to, and that is the idea of a fixed and permanent self, usually referred to as the ego or the "I." Scholar Peter Harvey explained that believing in an "ego" means that "however much one changes in life from childhood onwards, some part remains unchanged as the 'real me.'" It also causes us to act as if death happens to others but not to us. Furthermore, it means that we take ownership of our bodies and our mental states, saying that "I am tired, angry, happy or depressed."[41] The Buddha stated that the "ego," the unchanging "I," is a fallacy. We are not what the Hindus call atman, which is an eternal, unchanging self, but *anatman* or nonself. We aren't a permanent, eternal, integral, and independent substance within an individual; we are a transitory and changeable coming together of five interdependent aggregates: matter, sensations, perceptions, mental formations, and consciousness.[42] Each of these depends on the other to exist; however, none are the same for two consecutive moments. Just like everything else in existence, we are a process. We find a useful explanation on the "composite nature of the individual" in the *Questions of King Menander*, which dates to the middle of the second century B.C.E. In the "Simile of the Chariot," Milinda (Menander) queries Venerable Nagasena about the nature of the individual. He asks, "What is Nagasena . . . his hair, nails, teeth, skin or any other part of the body?" To these, the monk repeatedly says, "No." The monk then asks the king about the nature of a chariot? Is it its parts? Is it something other than its separate parts? To both of these, the king replies, "No." "Then," the monk says, "I can find no chariot. The chariot is mere sound. What then is the chariot? . . . There is no chariot." To this the king says that it's on account of all these components that the vehicle is called a chariot. To this Nagasena replies, "It's just the same with me. It's on account of the various components of my being that I'm known by the generally understood term, the practical designation Nagasena."[43]

The best way to recognize this ever-changing self is to look at photos of someone from various stages of his or her life. Compare images captured at six months old, 5 years, 18 years, 38 years, 55 years, and 80 years, and ask: What remains constant? When asked who "we" are, we usually list our names, ages, occupations, educational levels, socioeconomic standing, hobbies, personality traits, household income, gender, height, weight, hair color, eye color, marital status, and more. But do those really mean that we are an "us"? Over time, our faces wrinkle, our weight fluctuates, our bones shrink, we become richer or poorer, we may move, change occupations, change our hair color, we may forget facts that we learned . . . nothing stays the same. Every minute we are different. As Dzongsar Jamyang Khyentse said, "Siddhartha realized that there is no independent entity that qualifies as the self to be found anywhere, either inside or outside of the body. Like the optical illusion of a fire ring, the self is illusionary. . . . Clinging to the fallacy of the self is a ridiculous act of ignorance; it perpetuates ignorance; and it leads to all kinds of pain and disappointment."[44] Furthermore, he states that "one way or another, directly or indirectly, all emotions are born from selfishness in the sense that they involve clinging to the self . . . [they] arise when particular causes and conditions come together. . . . The moment we accept those emotions, the moment we buy into them, we have lost awareness and sanity."[45]

Like Hindus, Buddhists also believe in *samsara*, which means "wandering" and indicates that all beings go through innumerable rounds of birth and death. When life ends in one place, the being's "mental continuum" arises in another body, and *samsara* continues. At this point, some wonder, if we don't have a "soul," how is it that we can be reborn? Again, we can turn to the *Questions of King Menander* for answers. To the question of "Is it true that nothing transmigrates, and yet there is rebirth?" Nagasena responds, "Suppose a man lights one lamp from another—does the one lamp transmigrate to the other? So there is rebirth without anything transmigrating."[46] When he talks about death, Thich Nhat Hanh frequently uses the example of a cloud. A cloud was water in an ocean, in a lake, and in a river. Heat from the sun gave it birth, but it couldn't come from nothing. Scientifically this isn't possible. It is impossible for a cloud to die. It can become water and snow but it cannot become nothing. "When I drink tea, it's very pleasant to be aware that I am drinking cloud."[47]

So why, if all beings transmigrate, do we find differences among them? Why are some people attractive while others are ugly? Why are some rich while others are destitute? Why are some people sickly while others are in perfect health? These questions, too, were asked of Nagasena, and his reply was karma: "They are born through karma, they become members of tribes and families through karma, each is ruled by karma, it is karma that divides them into high and low."[48] The law of karma (*kamma*), which translates to "action" or "deed," is generally understood to be a universal law of cause and effect. Actions can be wholesome (morally commendable and likely to produce fortunate births) or unwholesome (morally blameworthy and likely to produce unfortunate births), but for Buddhists the key to generating karma is the intention behind those actions. If a person willfully kills another being, bad karma will be the result. If a person accidentally or unknowingly kills another, bad karma won't result. Furthermore, our words, thoughts and deeds can all bring forth bad or good karma, but the result doesn't have to be immediate. It can take thousands of lifetimes for it to bear fruit. Only deeds free from desire, hatred, and ignorance have a neutral karmic effect. Buddhist scholar and monk Walpola Rahula explained that "The theory of karma should not be confused with so-called 'moral justice' or 'reward and punishment.'" Whereas the former idea relies on a supreme being who makes laws and then judges and punishes or rewards his followers accordingly, the latter is "ambiguous and dangerous, and in its name more harm than good is done to humanity."[49] Essentially, karma emphasizes human responsibility, for people make their own futures based on what they do. As it is said, "Beings reap the fruit of actions—good or bad—which they themselves have done (there is no other doer) with their body, speech and mind."[50] In fact, even though other beings exist in various realms, for the most part only humans have the freedom to make choices.

Karma also plays a significant role in rebirth. As it is said, "Beings are own-ers of their karma, heirs of their karma; they originate from their karma, are bound to their karma, have their karma as their refuge."[51] Depending on one's deeds, a being will be reborn into one of six realms or *gati* ("mode of exis-tence"), and then when the "generative karma has spent its force, they pass away to take rebirth elsewhere as determined by still another karma that has found the opportunity to ripen."[52] These realms are also depicted in the Wheel of Life. The top three, which include the gods, the titans or demigods, and hu-mans, are seen as the higher realms; the bottom three, which include animals, hells, and hungry ghosts, are the lower realms.

On the Wheel of Life, the highest Buddhist realm is that of the gods or *devas* ("shining ones"), and it is subdivided into 26 heavens. Those who are born into one of these paradisiacal levels have performed good deeds, such as revering their mother, father, and family elders; being generous, peacekeepers, and virtuous, and upholding the dharma.[53] Although most Westerners would see being born into a heavenly realm as positive, Buddhists see it differently. Since *devas* enjoy immense happiness, they can't recognize the truth of suffer-ing, and thus can become hindered in their path to nirvana.[54] Furthermore, this and every other realm comes to an end; it is just an illusion that they will continue in eternity.

The next realm is that of the titans or *asuras* (demons). Depending on the tradition, these beings are seen either as enemies of the gods, always practicing guile and deception but who do no injury, or as the lower gods who dwell on the summit of the world mountain Sumeru. Directly across from the titans is the human realm. Even though humans are driven by egotism and ignorance, and have lives characterized by suffering, this realm is thought to be the best one in which to be born, because only humans can attain nirvana. As was pre-viously mentioned, one's past actions will determine how one lives as a human. For instance, "the woman who is of good morals and little passion, who abhors her femaleness and constantly aspires to masculinity, will be reborn as a man. . . . All karmic rewards resemble the acts of which they are the natural outcome: suffering from sin, happiness from good deeds, and a mixture of two from a mixed deed."[55] In the lower half of the Wheel of Life, directly under the human realm, is the animal realm. Evil deeds of the body, speech, and mind re-sult in one being born here, which is characterized by fear and oppression. For example, those who are attached to sensual pleasures are reborn as geese, pigeons, and donkeys; those who are hostile and selfish become tigers, cats, jack-als, bears, vultures, wolves, or other carnivores.[56] Because animals are thought to act primarily on instinct, only in rare cases can they generate good karma. Directly across from the animal realm is the one inhabited by the hungry ghosts or *pretas* ("departed ones"). Excessive attachment to human life as well as greed, envy, and jealousy cause rebirth in this realm. *Pretas* suffer horrible torments. For instance, someone who hinders the practice of almsgiving and who gives nothing of himself will become an emaciated *preta*. Even though these beings suffer from excessive thirst and hunger, they are unable to quench these because they have large stomachs and mouths the size of a needle. Those who deprive others of their wealth and who give only to regret it afterwards be-comes a *preta* who consumes excrement, phlegm, and vomit.[57] Finally, at the very bottom of the Wheel one finds the hell realms, which consist of eight hot and eight cold hells. Those destined for birth in this realm have engaged in murder, deceit, slander, robbery, and more. Torments include being piled in a heap and slaughtered; being killed, revived, and killed again; being cut by hot saws; and being continuously burned. The worst hell, called *avici* "because be-ings there are burned by such a horrible fire that even their bones are melted, and because, in the midst of their suffering, there is no interval allowing them any respite," is endured by those who have angered beings of great virtue, who have killed a disciple of the Buddha, or their mother or father or teacher.[58]

The three "poisons" (*kleshas*)—greed, hatred, and delusion (sometimes called ignorance)—keep us tethered to the Wheel of Life, and they are de-picted in the center of this wheel as a rooster, a snake, and pig, respectively. Sometimes these poisons are referred to as the "three roots," because from them other defilements grow, including pride, envy, anger, laziness, and anger. Although there is no "first cause," as it were, because the world is eternal and without beginning, ignorance causes us to be reborn and suffer. In this situa-tion, ignorance means that we have a veil over our eyes that prevents us from seeing the world clearly. Not seeing impermanence, we build and protect our egos while grasping for material goods. When we or our possessions are threatened, we squabble and fight. The way to prevent this from occurring is to cultivate wisdom, which corrects ignorance. And how do we cultivate wis-dom? By following the Eightfold Path.

As was previously mentioned, the "goal" of Buddhism is nirvana, which in Sanskrit means "to cool by blowing" and "extinction." But what is nirvana? As

Nagasena tells King Milinda, just as you cannot measure the water or count the creatures in the ocean, you would not be able to explain the form, makeup, age, or size of nirvana. However, when pressed, he does say that it is "peaceful, blissful and exalted."[59] Scholar and monk Walpole Rahula explains that nirvana is absolute freedom from all evil, craving, hatred, ignorance, duality, relativity, time, and space.[60] "One lives the holy life with Nirvana as its final plunge (into the Absolute Truth) as its goal, as its ultimate end." Rahula explained that nirvana is "not a state or a realm or a position in which there is some sort of existence. . . . There is no such thing as 'entering into Nirvana after death.'"[61] One doesn't die and then attain nirvana; it can be attained right now. Those who realize nirvana live fully in the present, and enjoy and appreciate life as it is. "He is free from selfish desire, hatred, ignorance, conceit, pride, and all such 'defilements.' He is pure and gentle, full of universal love, compassion, kindness, sympathy, understanding and tolerance."[62] How does one attain nirvana? The Buddha explained that one can contemplate the "unattractiveness of the body, perceive repulsiveness in food, perceive discontent with the entire world, and contemplate impermanence in all formations." When one does this, "the perception of death is well established within him." Another way is to be "secluded from sensual pleasures and unwholesome states."[63] In a nutshell, nirvana means to see oneself and the world through eyes unclouded by dust.

During his lifetime, the Buddha encountered people who wanted answers to myriad metaphysical questions, such as is the world eternal? Is the world finite? Is the soul the same as the body? And does the *Tathagata* exist after death? The Buddha refused to respond to these, because whether or not one learned these answers, the person would still die. Demanding answers before getting on the path is like a man who has been shot by a poisoned arrow and, before he will let the surgeon treat him, demands to know to which caste the shooter belonged, what the shooter's name and clan was, what the shooter looked like, where he lived, and what the composition of the bow and arrow was. The Buddha said that he left certain questions "undeclared," because they weren't "beneficial"; they didn't belong to "the fundamentals of the spiritual life, didn't lead to disenchantment, to dispassion, to cessation, to peace, to direct knowledge, to enlightenment, to nirvana."[64] When asked, "Is there a self?" the Buddha refused to respond. His reason, he said, was that if he said there was a self, he would be associating himself "with the renouncers and Brahmins who are eternalists." If he said there wasn't a self, then he would be associating with those who are "annihilationists." If he asserted there was a self, "would that be in accord with the knowledge that all elements in reality are without self?" And if he asserted that there is no self, the confused questioner would have been even more confused, saying, "Formerly, I had a self, but now it does not exist."[65] In yet another story, the Buddha refused to address a question about the nature of nirvana.

We've talked a lot about what the Buddha and his disciples said, but we haven't said much about where these teachings can be found. The Buddha spread his message orally—he didn't leave behind any writings—and the oral tradition continues to be important. What was remembered by his disciples was eventually written down in two Indian dialects, Sanskrit and Pali, which is a simplified form of the former. Today, the authorized canon for Theravadin Buddhists is the Pali Canon or the Tripitaka (in Pali, *Tipitika*), which is divided into three "baskets." The first of these is the *Vinaya-pitaka*, which contains the 227 rules for monks and the 311 rules for nuns. These comprehensive rules address everything from how to dress to the appropriate punishments for breaking the rules. The second basket is the *Sutra-pitaka*, and it consists of more than 10,000 sermons and sayings of the Buddha and his disciples. They are grouped into five sections. Of these, the last group, called *The Division of Little Books*, contains the most popular stories, including the *Jataka* (547 "birth stories" of the Buddha) and the *Dhammapada*, 423 verses that purportedly came directly from the Buddha. The third basket is the *Abhidharama-pitaka*, and within these seven books one finds scholarly discourses on philosophy and psychology. Theravadan Buddhists also rely on commentaries, particularly those composed by Buddhaghosa, a Sri Lankan monk who lived during the fourth century C.E. Of his 19 commentaries, his most famous is the *Visuddhimagga* (*Path of Purity*).

Mahayana Buddhists don't reject the Tripitika; however, over time, they have expanded their canon to include additional sutras, such as the massive Perfection of Wisdom Sutras (*Prajnaparamita*), which focuses on the 10 perfections found in the bodhisattva. It also contains the Heart Sutra and the Diamond Cutter Sutra; the Lotus Sutra, which focuses on devotion to the eternal cosmic Buddha; the Three Pure Land Sutras, which are central texts for Pure Land adherents; and the Garland Sutra. Many of these were originally written in Sanskrit but have been translated into East Asian languages. Tantric texts also exist, such as the widely translated *Bardo Thodol Chenmo*, which is known in English as the *Tibetan Book of the Dead*, and the *Songs of Milarepa*.

Sangha

The Buddha converted many people during his life. They, in turn, became members of his *sangha*, and they spread his teachings to others. It is reported that among his disciples were many members of his own family, including his wife, his cousin Ananda, and his son. The Buddha's stepmother, Mahajapati, the woman who had raised him, asked to join the *sangha* but was denied. Rather than accept this decision, she organized a group of women who dressed as ascetics and entreated him again. He relented. The reason cited for his initial response was that the Buddha didn't want to upset family life.[66] Remember, that the predominant religion at the time, Hinduism, taught that women should never be independent. Buddhism would prove to be more egalitarian, giving women and those from low castes a way "out" of their situations.

Monks and nuns, *bhikshus* and *bhikshunis* respectively, follow the example of the Buddha by shaving their heads, donning monastic robes, living communally during the rainy season, and following the 10 Precepts, which include not taking life; not stealing; being chaste; not telling falsehoods; not taking intoxicants; eating moderately and not after noon; avoiding entertainment, such as music and drama; not using flowers, perfumes, or jewelry; eschewing high or comfortable beds; and not using gold or silver.[67] In the *Dhammapada*, which are the sayings of the Buddha as collected by his followers, the Buddha admonishes those who take the vows but don't practice them: "Shaving one's head cannot make a monk if one is undisciplined, untruthful, and driven by selfish desires. He is a real monk who has extinguished all selfish desires, large and small. Begging alms does not make a *bhikshu*; one must follow the *dharma* completely. He is a true *bhikshu* who is chaste and beyond the reach of good and evil. . . . Observing silence cannot make a sage of one who is ignorant and immature. . . . Not by rituals and resolutions, nor by learning, nor by celibacy, nor even by meditation can you find the supreme, immortal joy of nirvana until you have extinguished your self-will."[68] Because monks and nuns couldn't work, they had to rely on nature or the laity to provide them with sustenance. This isn't a one-way relationship, though. By feeding the monks, the laity receives dharma lessons and spiritual services, particularly after a person has died, and they earn "good merit" for their actions. The laity must follow the first five of the aforementioned precepts. While the conservative schools teach that only fully ordained renunciants can attain *arhatship*, the more liberal branches of Buddhism stress the potential in everyone. In a discussion with King Milinda, the monk Nagasena gives his rationale for becoming a monk. He says it is true that laypersons and monks can attain the same path; however, the layperson will have a much harder time. He demonstrates this by comparing a layperson to an old man riding a decrepit horse without any provisions, and a monk to a young, strong man on horseback with all of the equipment he needs. If you send them both on a journey of 3,000 leagues away, who will most likely arrive at the destination?[69]

Since the Buddha didn't leave behind a spiritual successor, any writings, or an organized central authority, within the first few centuries after his death, several councils had to be convened. At the First Council, held at Rajagaha, 500 senior monks gathered to recite the Buddha's teachings, making sure that they were remembered accurately. This council lasted seven months. About 70 years later, a Second Council was held at Vesali with the purpose of addressing laxity that had arisen with regard to monks following the 10 Precepts. Eventually, disagreements over monastic discipline and doctrine resulted in a schism between the more orthodox and conservative "branch" of Buddhism known as Theravada ("Way of the Elders") and the reformist and liberal branch known as Mahasanghikas ("Members of the Great Order").

The emperor Ashoka (ca. 268–239 B.C.E.) was instrumental in spreading Buddhism beyond the Indian subcontinent. In the early years of his political life, he had relied on violent means to consolidate India, and it is said that he grew remorseful over the bloodshed. To atone for his actions, he converted to Buddhism and ruled with a policy of tolerance and nonviolence. Pillar Edict VII details some of his kindhearted measures: "I have had banyan trees planted along the roads in order to provide shade for beasts and people, and I have had mango groves planted. And, I have had wells dug and rest areas built every mile, and here and there I have had watering holes made for the enjoyment of beasts and humans. . . . I am doing this so that people may follow the path of Dharma."[70] It is said that he went on pilgrimage to places where the Buddha had lived and, when there, unearthed various relics and redistributed them throughout his empire. Under his patronage missionaries were sent to Syria, Egypt, Burma, Sri Lanka, and Greece; stupas were erected, and new

monasteries were endowed. It is also said that he called the Third Council at
Pataliputra, during which the *sangha* was reorganized and reformed.

Even though Ashoka discouraged schisms within the Buddhist community,
they were inevitable, and over the centuries two divisions have emerged: Theravada ("The Way of the Elders") and Mahayana ("The Great Vehicle"). Theravada is the oldest and most conservative form of Buddhism, dating to the
first centuries after the death of the Buddha. Followers look to the Buddha
and his disciples as models for their behavior; therefore, like the Buddha, they
strive to become *arhats*, celibate monks or nuns who achieve liberation. They
also adhere to the Pali canon as authoritative. In general, there still exists a
sharp distinction between the monks and the laity. With about 125 million
followers, Theravada is the predominant form of Buddhism in Southeast Asia,
including Sri Lanka, Cambodia, Laos, Burma (Myanmar), Thailand, and
South Vietnam.

During the first century C.E., Mahayana Buddhism arose in opposition to
its more traditional form, which was referred to derogatorily as *Hinayana*.
This term means the "lesser or smaller vehicle," implying that because adherents emphasized the taking of monastic vows, they offered only a small raft to
those seeking nirvana. Mahayanists saw this emphasis on self-liberation as
selfish. What they advocated was for lay and monastic adherents to strive for
buddhahood via the bodhisattva ("enlightenment being") path. As the Dalai
Lama explains it, "a bodhisattva is a person who cultivates the aspiration to
achieve complete enlightenment for the benefit of all living beings and who
has also pledged to engage in the deeds that are the most beneficial in fulfilling this aim for working for others."[71] Those on the path are encouraged to
develop six *paramitas* ("perfect realization"): giving, mindfulness trainings,
inclusiveness, diligence, meditation, and understanding.[72] Mahayanists claim
to offer a large raft to the other side, essentially promising "salvation" for all.

So, where did these ideas originate? Mahayana Buddhists claim that they,
too, are following the teachings of the Buddha. Their canon draws upon the
Tripitaka, but it is organized differently, and they include other previously
"undiscovered" teachings of the Buddha. In these, one finds new philosophical and theological ideas, such as *shunyata* (emptiness)—as it says in the Heart
Sutra: "form is emptiness, emptiness is form"—and the existence of three
bodies of the Buddha, which are essence, bliss, and transformation. Another
Mahayana concept is *upaya* or skillful means, which means that "there are no

particular fixed means of awakening. One need not be limited by Buddhist practices taught previously, which were, after all, only provisional and limited in scope. In reality, everything is potentially a means to awakening."[73]

Being more devotional in nature, Mahayanists look to an expanded "pantheon" of transcendent Buddhas and bodhisattvas, including Maitreya ("Loving One"), Amitabha ("Boundless Light"), the Medicine Buddha, Avalokitesvara ("the Lord Who Looks Down"), and Manjushri ("He Who Is Noble and Gentle"). Devotees pray, worship, and call on these various beings for assistance. Mahayanists were found predominantly in northern India; therefore, their teachings spread into East Asia, specifically China, Taiwan, Korea, and Japan. One could say that Mahayana is an umbrella term, because as it adapted to local cultures and extant religious traditions, it produced a wide variety of beliefs and practices. The most popular include Ch'an, T'ien T'ai, Pure Land, Zen (Soto and Rinzai sects), Tendai, Shingon, Jodo, Joho Shinshu, and Nichiren. Mahayana Buddhism is the largest of the three traditions, with about 185 million followers worldwide.

Mahayana Buddhism, in its tantric form, is called Vajrayana ("The Diamond Vehicle" or "Adamantine Vehicle"),[74] is also known as Tantrayana ("Tantra Vehicle"), Mantrayana ("Mantra Vehicle"), Tibetan[75] Buddhism, and Tantric Buddhism. As the Dalai Lama explains, it is "considered by the Tibetan tradition to be the highest vehicle . . . in addition to meditative practices for enhancing one's realization of emptiness and bodhicitta ('the genuine altruistic aspiration to attain full enlightenment for the sake of all beings'), this system also includes certain advanced techniques for utilizing the various elements of the physical body in one's meditative practice."[76] Tantric Buddhism arose in northeast and northwest India sometime between the sixth and seventh century C.E., and eventually spread to Tibet, Nepal, Ladakh, Sikkim, Bhutan, and Mongolia. This esoteric tradition teaches that one can rapidly attain buddhahood in this lifetime by using certain rituals, reciting mantras (powerful sounds), such as *Om Mani Padme Hum*,[77] and using *mudras* (symbolic hand gestures) and visualization exercises. Two of the most popular visualization exercises are the creation and contemplation of sand *mandalas*, which are a kind of two-dimensional map of the universe, and the use of meditational deities, known as *yidam*. Based on an individual's psychological makeup, he or she will be given a particular buddha or deity to invoke during practice. But rather than seeing it as external to oneself, the adherent will "unite and merge with it." "The deities are understood as metaphors, which personalize and capture the infinite energies and qualities of the wisdom mind of the buddhas. Personifying them in the form of deities enables the practitioner to recognize and relate to them. Through training in creating and reabsorbing the deities in the practice of visualization, he or she realizes that the mind that perceives the deity and the deity itself are not separate."[78] In general, Tibetans meditate on five transcendent buddhas: Amitabha, Amoghasiddhi, Akshobhya, Ratnasambhava, and Vairochana. Each is associated with a cardinal direction, and each is paired with a wife or consort. If one reads the *Tibetan Book of the Dead*, these buddhas actually "appear" to the deceased or dying in either wrathful or benign forms. For instance, on the third day of the *bardo* (the intermediate state between life and death), the yellow Lord Ratnasambhava appears seated on a horse and carrying a wish-granting gem; and on the fourth day, the red Lord Amitabha appears seated on a peacock throne and carrying a lotus. Many of those living in East Asia, particularly Japan, China, and the Himalayas, are devoted to Amitabha, who "is the primordial Buddha of the Lotus or Padma family; he represents pure nature, and symbolizes the transmutation of desire, the predominant emotion of the human realm." Furthermore, he is "the limitless, luminous nature of our mind."[79]

Tantra is concerned with the integration of ideas that might seem unconventional, and some adherents have purportedly engaged in taboo practices, such as the eating of meat, drinking of alcohol, and engaging in sexual practices. Although, as scholar William Theodore de Bary explained, "Many Tantric circles practiced such rites only symbolically."[80] The belief is that passion can only be exhausted by passion. In Vajrayana, we see the development of a philosophy that admits "the emptiness of all things, but maintains that, once the emptiness was fully recognized, the phenomenal world was not to be disparaged, for it was fundamentally identical with the universal Emptiness itself."[81] As it says in one text, "Those who do not see things as they are think in terms of *samsara* and *nirvana*. Those who see things as they are think of neither *samsara* nor *nirvana*. . . . By nature, the jewel of the mind is free from the colorations of false imaginings; it is originally pure, unproduced, without inherent self-existence, immaculate. Therefore, because of this fundamental purity of the mind, one should strive to do everything that fools condemn, by means of union with one's own tutelary deity."[82] Scholars say that the uniqueness of Tibetan Buddhism comes from the fact that when the religion took root in Tibet, it blended with the already present animistic and shamanistic elements and practices found in the native religion Bon. The result has been an integration of pre-Buddhist deities and demons with the Four Noble Truths.

What also makes Vajrayana unique is its emphasis on the personal transmission of secret wisdom from a master to a disciple in an unbroken, continuous lineage; the existence of spiritual teachers/authorities (*lamas*); and the religio-political role of the Dalai Lama, who is not only thought to be the incarnation of Avalokiteshvara, the bodhisattva of compassion, but also the reincarnation of all previous Dalai Lamas. Unlike Theravadin Buddhism, Vajrayana places considerable emphasis on rituals. In fact, there is often a religio-magic dimension to this branch. Probably the best known Vajrayana text is the *Bardo Thodol* ("Liberation through Hearing in the Intermediate State") or more commonly known in the West as *The Tibetan Book of the Dead*. It is believed that after a person dies, he or she exists in an in-between state (*bardo*) for 49 days. Therefore, when someone is dying or someone has died, a monk is called to recite the text during that period, because it teaches the deceased about the six worlds that one person will encounter before being reborn. Even though the 42 peaceful beings and 58 angry divinities that one encounters appear to be real, the truth is that they are just emanations of the mind.

FILMS

Little Buddha (1993)—Directed and cowritten by Bernardo Bertolucci. Running time: 123 min. English. USA. Rated PG. Genre: Drama.

Summary: Lama Norbu (Yin Ruocheng) flies from Bhutan to Seattle to search for the reincarnation of his long-deceased teacher Lama Dorje (Venerable Geshe Tsultim Gyelsen). A tip leads him to a blonde American boy named Jesse (Alex Wiesendanger), whose parents, Lisa (Bridget Fonda) and Dean (Chris Isaak), are initially incredulous at the prospect. To help Jesse and his family learn more about Buddhism, the lama gives them a book about the Buddha's life. As the film unfolds, we find out that it is essentially two stories in one: the search for the reincarnated lama and the search for Siddhartha's enlightenment.

Despite any flaws that it might have, *Little Buddha* is laudable for the sheer fact that it accomplishes what no other film has—it acts as a veritable primer on the religion. It begins with Lama Norbu telling the story of a goat and a high priest. The priest wanted to sacrifice the goat to the gods, he says, so the priest raised a knife to the goat's throat. The goat suddenly began to laugh. This shocked the priest, who said, "Why do you laugh? Don't you know I'm about to cut your throat?" The goat replied, "Yes. After 499 times of dying and being reborn as a goat, I will be reborn as a human being." Then the goat began to cry. The priest asked, "Why now are you crying?" The goat replied, "For you, poor priest. Five hundred lives ago, I, too, was a high priest, and I sacrificed goats to the gods." The priest dropped to his knees, saying, "Forgive me. From now on, I will be the protector of every goat in the land." "Now," Lama Norbu asks his classroom of child monks, "What does this ancient story teach us?" And, in unison, the children reply, "That no living creature must ever be sacrificed." One child moves forward and asks Norbu what happened to the goat. He responds that it had many rebirths as a human being until, one day, he turned into someone very strange indeed—Champa (Jigme Kunsang). At this, the monk sitting beside him begins to "baa," much to the delight of the children. This story comes from the *Matakabhatta Jataka*,[83] also known as *The Goat That Laughed and Wept*, and it conveys several messages. First, as the children said, it reminds the reader or listener of the Buddhist prohibition on killing any being; secondly, it illustrates the concept of rebirth in the various realms, in this case the animal and human realms; and thirdly, it demonstrates that the Buddhist path of nonviolence is karmically preferable to the Hindu or Vedic way of animal sacrifice; our actions have consequences in this life and beyond.

Assuming that most Westerners don't know much about Buddhism, let alone the story of Siddhartha, the film reveals to us his biography through an "illustrated" story. After their first encounter, Lama Norbu leaves behind a book titled *Little Buddha: The Story of Siddhartha*, and throughout the film it is read to or by Jesse. This narrative begins with Siddhartha's mother, Queen Maya, traveling to her parents' home. The caravan stops for a rest, and the very pregnant woman remembers "a very strange dream" that she had in which a baby elephant appeared at her side and blessed her with its trunk. Next her birth pains begin, and a tree bends down to protect her, offering her its branches for support. Once the baby is born, he is fully conscious, his eyes are wide open, and he is strong enough to stand on his own legs. The baby speaks, "I have been born to reach enlightenment and free all creatures from suffering." "And, it has been said," Jesse's mom continues, "that lotus blossoms grew in his footsteps."

Lisa begins the next installment of the story before putting Jesse to bed. In this segment, Suddhodana has named his child Siddhartha, which means "he who brings good." He is presenting his son to the villagers, when an unexpected guest arrives—a revered hermit and astrologer Asita, whom nobody had seen for years. Upon looking at the child, the man announces that "he'll be master of the world or its redeemer." Wanting to hear nothing of this, Suddhodana announces that his son can be a great teacher when he's older, but when he's young, he will become a king. To this, Asita says, "The gods often betray the wishes of mortal men." It is then said that Queen Maya died a week later of an illness that "no doctor could cure."

Returning to the narrative, Jesse asks Lama Norbu if the Buddha was a god. To this the lama replies, "No, he was a real person." "Like Jesus?" Jesse asks. "Yes, quite a bit like Jesus, though he was born long before." At this point, we see Prince Siddhartha as a young man, married to the Princess Yashodhara, and already "a great horseman and a great archer." Siddhartha is truly living an "enchanted life." Siddhartha becomes interested in the outside world only after hearing a woman singing about her childhood home "which she can never forget." Siddhartha asks his wife if such beautiful places really do exist. His wife responds, "I've heard that only suffering lies beyond these walls." To show his naïveté, he asks what suffering is. Perhaps knowing of Suddhodana's plans, Yashodhara reminds Siddhartha that they have everything they could possibly want; everything is perfect. He agrees, and then says, "So, what is this feeling I have? If the world is so beautiful, why have I never seen it? I've not even seen my own city. I must see the world . . . with my own eyes." At this, Yashodhara cries.

Siddhartha gets his wish to venture outside the palace; however, his father has made sure that nothing upsets him or reminds him of the realities of life. Once the palace doors open, the smiling and cheering villagers throw flower petals in his path. Everything has been sanitized. Then, two old beggar men make their way down a long alleyway, offering Siddhartha his First Sight. When Siddhartha asks Channa what "old" means, his servant responds, "Old age destroys memory, beauty, and strength. In the end, it happens to us all."

Amazed by this, Siddhartha asks, "To everyone? To you and to me?" "It is better not to concern yourself with these things," Channa replies, just as two palace guards arrive to carry away the old men. At this, Siddhartha leaps from his shimmering gold chariot and follows. As he winds his way through the village, he encounters two more sights. When he encounters illness, it is represented by a groaning leprous woman and several other similarly afflicted beggars who are huddled inside a hut. For death, he witnesses an enshrouded corpse being washed and attended to by a Shaivite priest on the banks of a river. As tears roll down his cheeks, he watches a body being burned on a funeral pyre. The camera lingers on the sizzling fat and the charred bones emerging from beneath the flames. It is at this moment that Siddhartha learns about suffering and discovers compassion; "they were him and he was them."

The next installment of the story begins with an image of Suddhodhana having makeup applied to his face, undoubtedly to get rid of any sign of wrinkles, and dye being applied to his hair to cover the gray. Siddhartha comes in and asks his father why he has hidden the truth from him for so long, why he has lied to him about old age, sickness, death, and poverty. His father replies that it was out of love. But this love has become a "prison," Siddhartha says, and he now knows that he must find an answer to suffering. When the young prince says he's leaving, his father tells him that he is now a father; a husband, and that he has a "duty."[84] Siddhartha isn't persuaded for he knows that staying with his family will only allow them to suffer, die, and be reborn over and over again. He then vows to "lift this curse." After placing the ashes from the dead in his father's hands, Siddhartha prepares to leave the palace. In response, his father calls out to his guards, telling them to lock the gates and not to let him leave. As he shouts these commands, he frantically washes the ashes off of his hands.[85]

Before leaving the palace for good, Siddhartha visits his family one last time. As he looks for Channa, a "magic mist" has descended, putting everyone into a deep sleep.[86] Siddhartha finally finds his loyal servant, awakens him, and tells him to get his horse. Together, they leave the palace, only to realize that "the whole world is dreaming." Jesse, who is now reading the story by himself, says, "For Siddhartha, the dream was ending. His long journey of awakening had begun." Siddhartha and Channa eventually arrive at a forest, where emaciated ascetics are walking around and chanting. With this fourth sight, Siddhartha descends from his horse, cuts off his hair, removes his jewelry and fine clothes, and sits in meditation. The half-naked men—some who have finger-nails growing through their hands, and others who have pierced tongues—sit down and watch Siddhartha as the thunder rolls overhead. To shield him from the storm, a giant cobra emerges and acts as an umbrella. This miracle alone encourages the five ascetics to become his first disciples. For six years, Siddhartha and his followers lived in silence and never left the forest. For drink, they had rain; for food, they ate a grain of rice, a broth of mud, or the drop-pings of a passing bird. "They were trying to master suffering by making their minds so strong they would forget about their bodies," Lama Norbu says.

At this point, an emaciated and heavily bearded Siddhartha hears an old musician talking to his pupil, saying, "If you tighten the string too much, it will snap; if you leave it too slack, it won't play." From this simple statement, Siddhartha realizes the truth of the Middle Way. He takes a drink and eats some food, but he is soon rejected by his own disciples, who think that he has turned his back on the path. "To learn is to change," Siddhartha calls to them, but they ignore him. Seeking confirmation that he's on the right path, Siddhartha puts his food bowl in the river and says, "If I can reach Enlighten-ment, may this bowl float upstream." Naturally, it goes against the current.

The story of Siddhartha concludes near the end of the film, when Jesse, Gita, and Raju—all candidates for the reincarnated Lama Dorje—are walking around a large tree in Gita's yard. This immense banyan reminds them of the tree under which Siddhartha sat at Bodh Gaya. While he's deep in meditation, five girls appear to him; all are the daughters of Mara, Lord of Darkness: "They were the spirits of pride, greed, fear, ignorance, and desire, and they were sent to tempt Siddhartha from his search," Lama Norbu says. Even though the women sing, dance, and play on a swing, Siddhartha isn't dis-tracted and he continues to smile serenely. "Siddhartha was looking beyond form, beyond the present, and now Mara was enraged," Lama Norbu contin-ues. With a mighty growl, Mara conjures up a storm, and the girls turn to dust. In his anger, Mara hurls fireballs at Siddhartha, then crashing waves. Next, he sends a giant army that marches toward him, shooting fire-tinged arrows, but the arrows transform into flower petals. "It seemed as if Mara had been de-feated, but in fact, he had not yet given up the battle," Lama Norbu says. "He attacked again." This time Siddhartha faces himself: "You who go where no one else will dare, will you be my god?" "Architect, finally I have met you. You will not rebuild your house again." "But I am your house, and you live in me."

"Oh Lord of my own ego, you are pure illusion. You do not exist. The earth is my witness." At this point, it is revealed that the other Siddhartha was Mara in disguise, and he vanishes. The enlightened Siddhartha begins to glow. Siddhartha had "achieved the great calm that precedes detachment from illusions. He had reached beyond himself; he was beyond joy or pain, separate from judgment, able to remember all that he had been . . . a girl, a dolphin, a tree, a monkey. He could see beyond the universe. He had seen the ultimate reality of all things. He understood that every movement in the universe is an effect provoked by a cause. He knew that there was no salvation without compassion for every other being. From that moment on, he was called the Buddha, the Awakened One." And here, the narrative ends. The story of the Buddha's life has been retold countless times and in many texts; however, the screenwriters of *Little Buddha* seem to have been culled theirs from the *Buddhacaritakavya Sutra* (*Poetic Discourse on the Acts of the Buddha*), which is a poetic narrative attributed to Asvaghosa, who lived in northern India in the first and second century C.E.[87] For the most part, their account is faithful to the Buddhist texts.

In addition to recounting the story of the Buddha, the film also touches on several key Buddhist concepts, such as reincarnation, impermanence, and emptiness. The benefit of watching this film is that the audience is exposed to these concepts in two ways—through the traditional story of the Buddha and through the more modern story involving the search for a reincarnated teacher. In this "second part" of the film, audiences get to encounter the teachings as distilled through a Vajrayana lens. For instance, Tibetan Buddhists believe that after death ordinary beings and incarnate lamas undergo a different process. For the former, "Rebirth is a harrowing process, a frightful journey into the unknown, a process over which one has no control. One is blown by the winds of karma into an intermediate state (*bardo*) and then into a new lifetime."[88] It's very likely that rebirth, which must occur 49 days later, would take place in one of the lower realms, because beings in those realms are as numerous as the "stars in the sky on a clear night." Furthermore, as in traditional Buddhist thought, one can only escape the endless cycle of births by being on the path and attaining nirvana.

The rebirth of a lama differs considerably. "As 'emanation bodies,' incarnate lamas are technically buddhas, free from the bonds of karma. Their rebirth is thus entirely voluntary." None of them have to be reborn, but out of their compassion, they choose to return. Another major difference is that they are in control of their rebirth; they determine where they will be born, to whom, the form that their bodies will take, and the capacity of their minds.[89] This practice of "identifying the successive rebirths of a great teacher" has been practiced by all Vajrayana sects since the 14th century, and it continues to be a central component of their society.[90]

Reflecting this aspect of Tibetan belief, in *Little Buddha*, Lama Norbu explains that "We believe that everyone is reborn again and again, but there are a few very special beings who come back as spiritual guides, particular people who we can identify." In *The Tibetan Book of Living and Dying*, Sogyal Rinpoche[91] writes that when these people die, they may leave precise indications of where they can be found once they are reborn; "one of his closest disciples or spiritual friends may then have a vision or dream foretelling his imminent rebirth."[92] Dreams and omens are important to Tibetan Buddhists. In fact, Lama Norbu comes to Seattle because of a dream. Kenpo Tenzin[93] (Sogyal Rinpoche), a monk in Seattle, tells Lama Norbu that in his reoccurring dream Lama Dorje (his name, we are told means "thunderbolt" in Tibetan) was pointing to an empty site, which became the future site of Jesse and his family's home. Jesse, it is explained, was born one year after Lama Dorje died, thus alluding to the fact that Tibetans believe there is a short period in between (*bardo*) incarnations. By the time Lama Norbu arrives, Jesse is, in fact, nine years old, which is the same amount of time that has passed since Lama Dorje died. Furthermore, when Lama Norbu is talking with the mother of Gita, the third candidate, she tells him of a time when Lama Dorje showed up at their home, unannounced, and before he left, he put his hand on her stomach. After he died, she became pregnant, something she didn't think was possible.

According to the 14th Dalai Lama's biography, a number of signs and visions led a search party to him when he was just a three-year-old boy named Lhamo Thondup. Looking into the waters of the sacred lake, a senior lama saw the Tibetan letters *Ah*, *Ka*, and *Ma* float into view. "These were followed by the image of a three-storied monastery with a turquoise and gold roof and a path running from it to a hill. Finally, he saw a small house with strangely shaped guttering." Believing that the letter *Ah* referred to a northeastern province, this was where the search party went. The remaining letters led them to areas that brought them closer and closer to the child.[94]

When a reincarnated master is located, he must undergo an authentication process. "It is common for small children . . . to remember objects and people from their previous lives."[95] As we see in the movie, Jesse recognizes a photo of Lama Dorje and his bowl. In the case of the Dalai Lama, he immediately recognized the leader of the search party as well as several objects belonging to the 13th Dalai Lama. As he pointed to each object, he said, "It's mine. It's mine." It is also said that he could speak in the 13th Dalai Lama's dialect, even though it was unknown in his area. In *Little Buddha*, Lama Norbu tells Dean that if Jesse is found to be the reincarnation of Lama Dorje, he will "receive a special education. He could become a very powerful leader in our society, a spiritual leader." This, too, is accurate. "Great care is taken in the upbringing of *tulkus*. Even before their training begins, their parents are instructed to take special care of them."[96] Because they are believed to possess the "wisdom memory of realized masters," many undergo a more rigorous and intensive training than other monks. When in the monastery all monks must study logic, Tibetan art and culture, Sanskrit, medicine, and Buddhist philosophy, which means studying the *Prajnaparamita*, the *Madhyamika* (philosophy of the Middle Way), the *Vinaya-Pitaka*, the *Abidharma-pitaka*, logic, and epistemology.[97]

In the film, to determine which of the three children is Lama Dorje, the monks "consult with the abbot of the monastery and all of the experts." In the end, they call upon an oracle, who falls into an ecstatic trance. While the monks chant and drum, the oracle moans and thrashes around. When he finally speaks in Tibetan, a monk hurriedly writes down what he says. Shamanism and animism continue to exist in Tibet, and, as in other indigenous traditions, the shaman communicates with the spirit world while in an altered state of consciousness. Tibetans rely on these oracles or mediums (*kuten*) to foretell the future and to serve as protectors and healers. "However, their primary function is to protect the Buddha Dharma and its practitioners."[98] When in a formal setting, the oracle will be dressed in an elaborate outfit that weighs more than 70 pounds. As seen in the film, "The ceremony begins with chanted invocations and prayers, accompanied by the urgings of horns, cymbals and drums." As time progresses, the oracle enters his trance, which continues to deepen throughout. "His breathing begins to shorten and he starts to hiss violently. Then, momentarily, his respiration stops." Once the possession is complete, the lamas can ask their questions of him.[99]

In *Little Buddha*, Lama Norbu and Dean are in the monk's quarters and the topic of reincarnation comes up. Realizing that Dean is skeptical about the process, the lama begins preparing a cup of tea. "In Tibet, we think of the mind and the body as the contents and the container," he says, and then he breaks the cup. "Now the cup is no longer a cup. But what is the tea?" "Still tea," says Jesse's father. "Exactly. In the cup, on the table, or on the floor, it moves from one container to another but it's still tea. Like the mind after death, it moves from one body to another but it is still mind. Even in the towel, it's still tea. The same tea." This example recalls those that were provided to King Milinda by Nagasena, who said that rebirth was like a flame passing from one candle to another. He also said that it is like milk that can be made into curds, butter, or ghee; they are all made from milk but aren't the same as the milk. Instead, "they depend on it entirely for their production."[100]

When Dean, Jesse, and Lama Norbu arrive in Kathmandu, the subject turns to impermanence. Jesse asks what it is. Lama Norbu replies, "You see these people? All of us? And all the people alive in the world today. A hundred years from now, we'll all be dead. That is impermanence." This also ties into the idea of emptiness. As Sogyal Rinpoche says, "Everything is what we call 'empty' . . . lacking in any lasting, stable, and inherent existence; and all things, when seen and understood in their true relation, are not independent but interdependent." Examples he gives are waves in the sea, which although they seem to be unique, are "empty of separate identity but 'full' of water." Another example is a tree, which again seems solitary, but in fact it is a series of interconnections: rain, soil, wind, seasons, moonlight, starlight, and sunlight—all form part of this tree.[101]

Tibetan Buddhists have a unique way of dealing with death, and we see this at the end of *Little Buddha*. While the three children are undergoing an initiation ceremony, Lama Norbu goes into the prayer room. Sitting in front of myriad *bodhisattvas* and butter lamps, he places a finger on one side of his nostril and exhales. He repeats this with the other side. Finally, he centers his eyes on his nose and begins to meditate.[102] "He's dying," Dean whispers to another monk. "We're dying with every minute," comes the reply. "Death is a big part of life. Every breath that we breathe . . . we die." Once it is announced that Lama Norbu has died, the monks begin chanting the Heart Sutra, while several other monks wave incense. Lama Norbu makes one last appearance to chant, in English: "Form is empty, emptiness is form. No eye, ear, nose,

tongue, body, mind, no color, sound, smell, taste, touch, existing thing." Jesse
finishes with "No Jesse, no you, no death, no fear." Lama Norbu's voice continues, "No old age in death. No end to old age in death. No suffering. No
cause of or end to of suffering. No path. No wisdom. And no gain. No gain.
Thus bodhisattvas live in perfect understanding with no hindrance of mind.
No hindrance, therefore, no fear. Far beyond deluded thoughts. This is nirvana." With this recitation ended, Lama Norbu's head is covered with a white
cloth.

It's not surprising that the monks would recite the Heart Sutra, because
it is perhaps the most famous of all Buddhist texts. Comprised of only 276
words, it is recited, and has been recited for 1,600 years, in Japan, China,
Korea, and Vietnam. It is "renowned for its terse expression of the perfection of wisdom, the knowledge whereby buddhahood is achieved. In part
because of its brevity . . . in part because of its potency . . . the Heart Sutra
has been put to a wide variety of ritual uses."[103] Interestingly enough, Lama
Norbu is told that one night Gita was chanting prayers in Tibetan in her
sleep. In reality, she was chanting in Sanskrit, the Heart Sutra, which
Champa then recites.

At the conclusion of the film, we return to Seattle, where a very pregnant
Lisa[104] and Jesse are waiting for Dean to show up in a boat, so that they can
distribute Lama Norbu's ashes. In fact, all three of the children are given some
of Lama Norbu's ashes. As he learned in the story of Siddhartha, Jesse puts the
ashes in a bowl and sets it on the water. Raju, now a monk, attaches the ashes
to balloons and lets them fly over the Himalayas. At Gita's house, a Tibetan
nun chants *Om Mani Padme Hum*, while Gita releases the ashes over her
banyan tree. As Sogyal Rinpoche explains, *Om Mani Padme Hum* "embodies
the compassion and blessing of all the buddhas and bodhisattvas, and invokes
the blessing of Avalokiteshvara, the Buddha of Compassion."[105] It is explained
that each syllable has a specific and potent effect in bringing about transformation. By purifying the six poisonous emotions—pride, jealousy, desire, ignorance, greed, and anger—their corresponding six realms of *samsara* are also
purified, thus preventing rebirth in these realms and dispelling the suffering
inherent in each. As it says in the *Tibetan Book of the Dead*, "when the sound
of *dharmata* roars like a thousand thunders, may it all become the sound of
six-syllables."[106] Reciting these six syllables is an expression of compassion and
of the longing for liberation "for the sake of all sentient beings."[107] Further-

more, they are so ubiquitous that one finds them inscribed on everything from bracelets to prayer wheels.

In just a little over two hours, *Little Buddha* manages to paint a portrait of its founder; explains in visual terms various Buddhist concepts, such as reincarnation, impermanence, and emptiness; and, perhaps more importantly, exposes the viewer to the colorful world of Tibetan Buddhism, from its imagery to its rituals. From the beginning, we see shaved-headed monks dressed in their characteristic saffron and burgundy robes. On the walls of the monastery hang *thangkas*, colorful pictures or paintings that can be used in several ways: as visual reminders of general Buddhist teachings, to serve a ritual function, or, most importantly, to "function as support for memory in the process of visualization."[108] When Lama Norbu leaves the monastery in Bhutan, he offers a white silk scarf (known as a *khata*) to his elder, who then puts it around Lama Norbu's neck as a blessing, and in the traditional Tibetan fashion, they press their foreheads together. "This exchange lends a positive note to the start of any enterprise or relationship and indicates the good intentions of the person offering it."[109] As Lama Norbu goes out the door, several monks are in the early stages of constructing a sand *mandala*. When Lama Norbu returns, it is almost completed. As he explains, as soon as they finish, the monks will destroy it with one gesture, thus signifying the impermanence of all things. *Mandala* literally means "circle," and its purpose is to symbolize the cosmos in a two- or three-dimensional form.[110] Each *mandala* is also a "sacred mansion, the home of a particular meditational deity who represents and embodies enlightened qualities, ranging from compassion to heightened consciousness and bliss." Typically, these objects are created for rituals of initiation and for meditation purposes.[111] Speaking of meditation, on the plane ride to Bhutan, Jesse goes over to Lama Norbu, who is still and serene. Jesse asks him what he's doing. "I'm meditating," the lama says, then he explains that meditation means "being totally quiet and relaxed, separating yourself from everything around you, setting your mind free like a bird. And seeing your thoughts, as if they were passing clouds. If we can all learn to meditate in the right way, we can all reach Enlightenment." At the end of the film, it is explained that Lama Norbu can meditate for 10 or more days straight, and if he wishes, enter the state of death at his own will. In his book *The Tibetan Book of Living and Dying*, Sogyal Rinpoche relates the story of a retreat master who had perfected yoga practice to the point that he could choose a day to die, and when it arrived, three days later, he did. "And that day, without any visible illness or difficulty, the master passed away in his meditation."[112]

Throughout *Little Buddha*, we see a variety of ritual objects. For instance, when Jesse and his mother arrive at the Dharma Center in Seattle, we see monks painting *thangkas* and murals on the wall. When Jesse meets Champa, he is performing various *mudras* or ritual hand gestures. Around his wrist he wears *mala* beads, which are used by Buddhists in much the same way that Catholics use the rosary. These strings of 108 beads are used to count repetitions in the recitation of various mantras. When Jesse enters Lama Norbu's room, one can see a prayer wheel sitting on a chest. Larger ones are seen when Lama Norbu, Jesse, his dad, and Champa arrive in Kathmandu, Nepal. While Jesse walks near the Boudhanath stupa, which Tibetans call Chorten Chempo, "the Great Stupa," we see pilgrims spinning them. Handheld prayer wheels consist of a hollow metal cylinder, typically ornamented with sutras, that is mounted on a rod handle. Inside the cylinder, one finds a tightly wound scroll on which a sacred mantra is printed. A weight usually hangs from the top so as to facilitate spinning. By rotating the wheel, one "recites" the prayer innumerable times. The same principle applies with the larger prayer wheels. Many Buddhists go on pilgrimage to sacred stupas or temples, and while there they spin giant wheels on which one finds auspicious symbols and mantras, especially *Om Mani Padme Hum.*

The film also touches on the political situation of Tibet with Lama Norbu explaining that since the Chinese occupation in 1959, they have been in exile in Bhutan, Nepal, and India. Jesse's father remarks that he "knows about the invasion of Tibet and the tragedies that happened." What they are referring to is the fact that before the Chinese invasion in 1949–1950, Tibet was the only country with a Buddhist theocracy. Monasteries, temples, and hermitages were founded in every village and town, and it is estimated that by 1959, there existed more than 6,259 monasteries with nearly 600,000 resident monks and nuns. Inside these religious centers, one found tens of thousands of statues and other religious artifacts, as well as Buddhist texts on subjects ranging from astrology to medicine. "Tibetan national identity became indistinguishable from its religion."[113] All of that changed once the communists took control. Since religion was seen as "the opiate of the masses" and Chairman Mao saw Buddhism as one of the "Four Olds," a systematic destruction of monasteries, scriptures, and religious artifacts began in earnest. For instance, during the summer of 1966, the Red Guards were allowed to release their "revolutionary energies by invading ancient Tibetan temples and monasteries, destroying religious paintings, books, printing blocks, statues, and treasures that the Communists considered to be 'feudal relics.'"[114] By 1980, only about eight Tibetan monasteries remained intact. The monks and nuns, too, came under fire. Of the 600,000, more than 110,000 were tortured and killed; more than 250,000 were forcibly disrobed.

The general population hasn't fared much better. "Tibetans have been deprived of their most basic human rights, including the right to life, movement, speech and worship. More than one sixth of Tibet's population of six million died as a direct result of the Chinese invasion and occupation." Today, China continues to rebuild Tibet, but without Tibetan support and involvement. Furthermore, since 1983, an unprecedented number of Chinese have been relocated to Tibet, reducing the native population to almost minority status.[115] Over the past several decades, hundreds of thousands of Tibetans have fled the country; many of them have joined the Dalai Lama in exile in Dharamsala, India.

Other Films on Tibetan Religion and Culture

The political situation in Tibet and the rising profile of the Dalai Lama, who was awarded the Nobel Peace Prize in 1989, seem to have captured the imagination of Western filmmakers, and in 1997 at least two films on these subjects were released. Directed by Martin Scorsese and based on a script by Melissa Mathison, *Kundun* chronicles the life of Tibet's 14th Dalai Lama, from his childhood to his exile in India. Nominated for four Oscars, it is rated PG-13 for violent images and has a running time of 134 minutes. *Seven Years in Tibet*, which is a remake of a 1956 film, is based on the story of Austrian mountain climber Heinrich Harrer (Brad Pitt). After being taken as a prisoner of war, he escapes to Tibet, where he becomes friends with a 14-year-old Dalai Lama. Directed by Jean-Jacques Annaud and based on Harrer's book, the film is rated PG-13 for some violent sequences and has a running time of 139 minutes.

For the non-Hollywood treatment of Tibet, *Mountain Patrol: Kekexili* (2004) is based on the true story of a team of volunteer rangers who cross unforgiving terrain in the Kekexili wildlife reserve to capture a band of ruthless poachers. The mountain patrol's objective is to try to save the endangered

Tibetan antelope. Although not about Buddhism per se, the film contains some Buddhist iconography and rituals. In the beginning, one sees a man using a *mala* while he chants. And in another scene, we watch monks performing a "sky burial." During this process, monks chant while they ritually cut up his body and feed his remains to vultures. Tibetans practice several types of burial, but, despite protests from the Chinese government, this is still the most popular, primarily because the ground on the Tibetan plateau is difficult to dig and fuel is scarce. Furthermore, Tibetans believe that once the person dies, the body is simply an empty vessel.[116] Sometimes, the skullcap and the thigh-bone are retained to be used later in rituals.[117] The skull can serve as a container for sacred food and drink, as a receptacle for prayers, and as a drum. Thighbones are sometimes turned into trumpets.[118] Using human remains in this way is yet another reminder of the impermanence of life and of one's own mortality. People in the film also use prayer wheels and chant *Om Mani Padme Hum.*

Dreaming Lhasa (2006)—Written by Tenzing Sonam; directed by Ritu Sarin and Tenzing Sonam. Running time: 90 min. English, Tibetan. Unrated. Genre: Adventure/Drama.

Dreaming Lhasa is probably the best film on the subject of Tibet. This independent feature focuses on Karma (Tenzin Chokyi Gyatso), a Tibetan filmmaker from New York who journeys to Dharamsala, India, to make a documentary about political prisoners. Dhondup (Jampa Kalsang), a former monk, is one of her subjects. He eventually explains to Karma and her assistant Jigme (Tenzin Jigme) that his mother's dying wish was for him to venture to India, find a man named Loga, and return to him a silver charm box. Karma is drawn into the search for the enigmatic Loga, and along the way falls in love. Written by Tenzing Sonam and co-directed by Sonam and Ritu Sarin, *Dreaming Lhasa* is the first dramatic feature by these documentary filmmakers, and it is the first internationally recognized feature film by a Tibetan to explore the contemporary reality of Tibet. As it says on the film's official site, www.dreaminglhasa.com, "Ritu and Tenzing have been making documentaries on Tibetan subjects for many years but their longtime desire was to make a feature film that would tackle comprehensively the issues closest to their heart—the political and cultural reality of Tibet under Chinese occupation, the in-between world of the younger generation of refugees who have never seen their homeland, and the gradual dying out of the older generation whose memories of a free Tibet are the only living link to the past."

Because the filmmakers are themselves documentarians, their film feels "authentic" and with the exception of Jampa Kalsang, who has acted in *Windhorse* and *Himalaya*, all of the actors are nonactors. In fact, three of the older actors—Phuntsok Namgyal Dhumkhang, Tsering Topgyal Phurpatsang, and Tenzin Wangdrak—were in the resistance movement against the Chinese. Phuntsok Namgyal Dhumkhang was an official in the Tibetan government before following the Dalai Lama into exile. Furthermore, the monks, nuns, and lay people who tell their stories of torture and imprisonment to Karma, are, in fact, portraying themselves.

By watching this film, not only does the viewer learn of the political situation facing Tibetans in exile and in their homeland, but he also gets to experience Tibetan culture and religion. For instance, oracles and dreams are taken very seriously by Tibetans, and Dhondup speaks several times of a dream he had that he took as a sign. Together, Dhondup and Karma even visit an oracle, who goes into a trance. We see characters turning prayer wheels, talking about *Om Mani Padme Hum* and karma, using mala beads, and more. There is even a candlelight vigil held for the Panchen Lama, with one man going on a 49-day hunger strike for the youth's release. Few, if any films, touch on the situation of the Panchen Lama ("Great Scholar" Lama), also known as His Holiness the 11th Panchen Lama of Tibet who is believed to be the reincarnation of Amitabha, the Buddha of Infinite Light. Furthermore, he is a divine leader who either identifies or is identified by the Dalai Lama, and one typically tutors the other. In May 1985, Gedhun Choeyki Nyima, the six-year-old identified by the Dalai Lama as the 11th Panchen Lama, and his family disappeared. One year later, suspicions were confirmed that the Chinese government had taken him. To make matters worse, Chinese officials nominated and installed its own Panchen Lama, named Gyaltsen Norbu, saying that the identification of this person was an internal affair of China and that the Dalai Lama was forbidden to perform a function he had done since the 17th century. To this day, the teen and his family remain in detention.[119]

Another aspect rarely, if ever, discussed in a film about Tibet is the role of the CIA in training Tibetan resistance fighters. As it says on the film's official site, "the older characters . . . are drawn from the many former resistance fighters that Ritu and Tenzing interviewed by making their film on the CIA's involvement in Tibet. As the Tibetan struggle increasingly takes on a non-violent character, references to Tibet's armed struggle are gradually sidelined and the sacrifices made by these men are in danger of being forgotten, even by Tibetans themselves." Not surprisingly, Ritu and Tenzing, in 1998, made a documentary on the subject, available through White Crane Films, called *The Shadow Circus: The CIA in Tibet.*

MAHAYANA ON FILM: ZEN

During the mid-first century C.E., Buddhism traveled from India to China, and over time the religion was reshaped to become characteristically Chinese. Several schools developed, especially T'ien T'ai, Pure Land, and Ch'an,[120] and were exported to Korea and Japan. Of these, Ch'an, which in Japan is called Zen, is probably the best known to Westerners, because of the 1960s counterculture.[121] The focus of this tradition is meditation with the goal of discovering a "reality in the innermost recesses of the soul; a reality that is the fundamental unity which pervades all the differences and particulars of the world. This reality is the mind, or the Buddha-nature that is present in all sentient beings."[122] Furthermore, reality is seen to be empty (*shunyata*) and beyond words and concepts. In fact, one branch of Zen, called Rinzai, uses koans (literally "public notice") to take the student beyond intellectual thought.

A koan "is a problem or a subject for study, often, at first sight, of a totally intractable, insoluble kind, to which the student has to find an answer."[123] The answer isn't attained through intellectual thought, though. After disciples receive their koan from their master, they let it infiltrate their minds, their being. "It will be as if you swallow a red-hot iron ball, which you cannot spit out even if you try. All the illusory ideas and delusive thoughts accumulated up to the present will be exterminated, and when the time comes, internal and external will be spontaneously united. . . . Then all of a sudden an explosive conversion will occur, and you will astonish the heavens and shake the earth."[124] Koans can be worked on in whole or in part. Sometimes the entire koan may be studied, together with the commentaries, or individual parts may be singled out by the teacher. As we've seen, the key is to immerse oneself patiently and wholeheartedly in the koan.[125] It may take anywhere from an instant to several years, but eventually the student will come to a solution. If it is acceptable to the teacher, the student will receive another and so on. Of the 1,700 koans, several are well known in the West, including "What is the sound of one hand clapping?" "What was your original face before your parents were born?" and "Has a dog the Buddha nature?"[126]

As in Tibetan Buddhism, Zen stresses the importance of the master-disciple relationship, and emphasis is placed on the authenticity of the teacher, for example, making sure that he or she comes from the right lineage. Transmission of the teachings is "mind to mind" and many koans emphasize this wordless practice. For instance, in one koan whenever the teacher, who is named Gutei Osho, was asked about Zen, he simply raised his finger. The Buddha, too, often responded with silence. In one of the best-known examples, "Shakyamuni Buddha was at Mount Grdhrakuta, [when] he held out a flower to his listeners. Everyone was silent. Only Mahakashyapa broke into a broad smile. The Buddha said, 'I have the True Dharma Eye, the Marvelous Mind of Nirvana, the True Form of the Formless, and the Subtle Dharma Gate, independent of words and transmitted beyond doctrine. This I have entrusted to Mahakashyapa."[127] Zen practice may seem different from the other forms of Buddhism, but the goal is the same—enlightenment or *satori*.

Two Western films deal specifically with the Zen tradition: *Erleuchtung Garantiert*, a German film that in English means *Enlightenment Guaranteed*; and *Zen Noir* (2004), which is an independent American film.

Enlightenment Guaranteed (2000)—Written and directed by Doris Dorrie. Running time: 109 min. German. Unrated. Genre: Drama/Comedy.

Enlightenment Guaranteed is about two brothers who travel to Japan for a temporary stay in a Zen monastery. Gustav (Gustav-Peter Wohler), a feng shui expert, has been planning this trip for some time, but complications ensue when his brother, Uwe (Uwe Ochsenknecht), suffers a crisis. His wife has left him and has taken the children, and now he's an inconsolable wreck. Reluctantly, Gustav takes Uwe with him to Sojiji Soin Father Temple in Monzen. Once they get to Tokyo, the men check into their hotel and then set out for dinner. Because neither of them speaks the language, they get lost and can't find their way back to their hotel. The situation becomes increasingly worse—they can't get access to any money, they get separated, and both end up homeless. Eventually, they find each other and journey to the monastery where they spend their days sitting in meditation, chanting, and cleaning the *zendo.* Although not very much of the 109-minute film is spent in actual Zen practice, the overall message of the film is clearly Buddhist. After Uwe's wife leaves him, he gets a lesson in impermanence. He also sees, as Gustav points out, that "to live is to suffer. Buddha's First Noble Truth." When the men are lost in Tokyo and are essentially stripped of everything—their money, basic comforts, food, and ability to communicate—they are thrown into an emotional abyss. Their situation is a kind of living koan: it forces them to see the world and everything in it with clearer eyes. In fact, they come away from the experience seeing what really matters, and they learn to live in the present.

Zen Noir (2004)—Written and directed by Marc Rosenbush. Running time: 71 min. English. Unrated. Genre: Drama/Comedy/Mystery.

Zen Noir is a murder mystery that takes place at a Zen temple. A nameless detective (Duane Sharp), still mourning the loss of his wife, arrives to investigate, but his investigation is stalled by questions that are met with even more questions. For example, he asks one monk, "Where were you at the time of the murder?" and the response is "What exactly do you mean by time?" Increasingly confused and unnerved by his inability to solve the crime through logic and rationality, the detective finds himself draw into a deeper, darker, more personal mystery, the answer to which may be the mystery of death itself. As the producers of the film note, "*Zen Noir* is a murder mystery in which the murder is a koan for the detective and the movie is a koan for the audience."[128] In an interview, the filmmaker, who said he came up with the idea for *Zen Noir* while "sitting in a temple in Chicago at 4:30 a.m. in the morning," admits that this isn't an easy film.[129] And he's right. Unless the audience member has an overview of Zen practice and koans, he or she can become as confused as the detective, especially once the mysterious oranges start appearing. However, in the end, the film deals with something everyone can understand—the fragility of life and the inevitability of death. *Zen Noir* has a running time of 71 minutes, and although unrated, contains some nudity.

Why Has Bodhi-Dharma Left for the East? (1989)—Written and directed by Yong-Kyun Bae. Running time: 137 min. Korean. Unrated. Genre: Drama.

Many scholars have already discussed the South Korean film *Why Has Bodhi-Dharma*[130] *Left for the East?* (1989), which focuses on three monks—an old master, a young man, and an orphan—who live in a remote monastery near Mount Chonan. And although it has been hailed as a masterpiece, it contains little dialogue, which may make it difficult for those encountering Zen Buddhism for the first time.

Spring, Summer, Fall, Winter . . . and Spring (2003)—Written and directed by Ki-duk Kim. Running time: 103 min. South Korean. Rated R for strong sexuality. Genre: Drama.

A newer but equally poetic film, Kim Ki-duk's *Spring, Summer, Fall, Winter . . . and Spring,* has been referred to by one critic as "an elegantly simple, profound Buddhist fable." This film takes place on a remote lake, where an elderly master (Oh Young-soo) lives with his young novice (Kim Jong-ho) on a floating monastery. Seasons pass and the boy is now 17 years old (Seo Jae-kyung). A young woman (Hayeo-jin) is brought to the monastery to be healed, and while she's convalescing she and the young monk become romantically and then sexually involved. Ensnared by his lust, he follows her, leaving the monastery behind. More seasons pass, and the former monk (Kim Young-Min) is now a 30-year-old fugitive from justice; jealousy has caused him to commit a violent crime. He returns to the monastery, and the old master punishes him by making him carve sutras from the *Prajnaparamita* onto the deck of the monastery. He collapses from exhaustion, and when he awakes he is arrested and taken away by police. The old monk prepares a ritual funeral pyre for himself. The now mature adult monk (Kim Ki-duk) returns to the floating monastery for spiritual training. A woman arrives and leaves behind an infant for the monk to raise. The cycle is complete or is it just beginning? *Spring, Summer* contains many Buddhist themes, such as the law of karma and the cyclical nature of existence. It also demonstrates the emotions that tie us to the Wheel of Life. As the old monk says, "Lust awakens the desire to possess. And that awakens the intent to murder." Because of its picturesque setting, the film allows us to contemplate nature and witness impermanence and interconnectedness.

Temptation of a Monk (1993)—Directed by Clara Law. Running time: 118 min. Hong Kong. Mandarin. Unrated. Genre: Adventure/Drama/Romance.

One final film that deserves mention is Clara Law's theatrical film *Temptation of a Monk.* Set in seventh-century China during the Tang Dynasty, the film centers on General Shi (Wu Hsin-Kuo), the crown prince's guard. During a chess game with his rival, the man is convinced to remain "neutral" during a "peaceful coup." But that decision will come back to haunt him, for in the end, he is betrayed, and the crown prince and his entire family are slaughtered at the Xuan Wu Gate. For his complicity in this deed, the general isn't punished; he is rewarded—his father's name is restored, his mother is made a noble, he is given a handsome reward, and he and his mother are served a banquet of fine food and drink. But none of this sits well with the general. Even though he is "innocent" in this matter of fratricide, he vows to his mother that he will remove himself from royal service, won't seek vengeance, and won't commit suicide. Instead, he will wander the countryside, maintaining the honor of his family.[131]

The general keeps his promise and, with his soldiers, seeks refuge, quite literally, in a Buddhist monastery. Sporting freshly shaven heads, green robes, and prayer beads, the men await their teacher, who arrives in the guise of a 10-year-old boy. His first lesson is that "a monk must observe the 10 Prohibitions: No killing, no stealing, no adultery, no wild talk, no drinking, no wearing of perfumed oils . . ." He is interrupted at No. 7, when one of the men ask, "Little Brother, what's your name?" He responds, "Elder Brother," and continues with "no listening to or watching song and dance, no sitting on tall and wide beds, no eating at wrong hours, and no hoarding treasures. He who violates any of these will be expelled from the monastery." The child also explains that because the men's "sins" are serious, it's unlikely that, in this life, they will attain the highest wisdom. However, if they follow the young monk's example, observe the prohibitions, be ascetic, and work hard, they may "see the light of Buddha after centuries." The incredulous men ask the child how old he is, and if his parents sent him to the monastery. To the last question, the child simply responds, "No parents. Empty of all burden." One of the heavier soldiers complains that he's hungry, and the child tells him he's already had his meal for the day; no eating after midday. In all, this scene is accurate in its depiction of the monastic rules and the reality of monastic seniority being not based on age but on the number of one's years of practice.

After this brief introduction to what's expected of them, the men walk, single file, to the temple, where other monks are already chanting. On the altar are burning candles and statues of buddhas and bodhisattvas. The child instructs the men to sit and bow before the images. A bell can be heard clanging in the background. Even though the men have become monks, they continue to act like laymen, plotting and planning inside of their dormitory. All of them laugh at their growling stomachs. In the morning, as part of their monastic chores, the men sweep the courtyard. One of their fellow soldiers left in the middle of the night, using the excuse that he's going to kill a wolf, presumably for food. But when he doesn't return, the other men imagine that he's deserted, gone to the enemy, is feasting, or is engaging in relations with women. Several talk about going after him and beheading him. Others begin fighting. The contrast between how the men look—like monks—and how they think— like men ensnared by greed, anger, and ignorance—is startling. The only one who seems to be affected by his spiritual surroundings is the general, who cuts up his military map and lets it fly away in the wind. (This foreshadows the end of the film, when he will reject his life as a soldier for the path of the monk.)

In the next scene, the child monk instructs the general that ringing the giant bell that sits in the courtyard "wakens all creatures imbided in *samsara*. Morning and night, it tolls 108 times, in three rounds of 36 times." The general begins striking the bell but doesn't do as he is instructed. The number 108 is important in Buddhism, and prayer *malas* also contain this number of beads. As writer Clark Strand explains, King Vaidunya once asked the Buddha to teach him the main point of the dharma so that he could practice it and teach it to others. To this the Buddha replied that if the king wanted to eliminate earthly desires, he needed to make a circular string of 108 *bodhi* seeds, and with each bead, recite the three refuges.[132] How did Buddhists come up with this specific number? Strand says that it boils down to simple mathematics. Everyone has six varieties of delusion, multiply that by past, present, and future perceptions, then multiply this again times the two conditions of the heart (pure and impure), and by the three possible sentiments toward sense objects (like, dislike, and indifference). The end result is 108.[133]

In the film, the general is soon led to the abbot of the monastery, and he is rebuked for his previous behavior. The abbot tells him that he must obey the monastic rules, practice charity, and strictly observe the 10 Prohibitions. "Moreover," he said, "in this world there are 13 mortal and 16 venial sins.[134] Repent each one. If you breach the prohibitions again . . . 40 lashes. Your personal effects will be burned, and you'll be expelled." When asked to repent, the general remains silent. "Before Buddha, who are you to be so proud? Go. Kneel for 100 joss-sticks, say Buddha's name 100,000 times," the abbot says.

The general does as he's told, and we see him kneeling before a colossal Buddha (who has a swastika carved into his chest). The child monk stands behind him, counting the recitations on his *mala*. When the general stops, the child hits him with a "stick of encouragement,"[135] telling him to continue: "Follow the Buddha, the dharma, and the monks." But the stubborn general ignores him, saying that heaven and earth are merciless. The child continues, "Make the wish to attain *sukhavati*.[136] To find the world of supreme bliss." The general is too proud, though, and will not sublimate his ego or his will. So he grabs the stick from the child and threatens to beat him with it: "What use are the 10 Prohibitions? Buddha? Where is he? I'm going to kill you. Will you still talk of mercy?" He laughs and continues swinging the stick, smashing it into everything he sees. The cowering child monk eventually straightens up and tells the general that he won't report him, then he adds, "Say Buddha's name."

Later in the courtyard, we see the general sweeping. The arrival of Princess Scarlet (Joan Chen), who has brought with her fowl and wine, interrupts his practice. When the men reply that breaking the 10 Prohibitions gets a monk expelled, she tells them that they didn't kill the bird and the prohibitions don't forbid the consumption of meat. The men begin fighting over the food, and break the fifth prohibition against the consumption of alcohol. "This isn't wine," she says, "This is medicine to cure sober minds." Laughing, the men prepare to leave the monastery. In the outside world, they break more of the prohibitions, gorging themselves on food, watching a puppetry show and other entertainers, and enjoying the company of beautifully attired women. (One man is tempted by a transvestite.) This descent into the sensual world shows how enticing it can be. One could even liken this scene to Siddhartha's temptation by Mara. At this point, the viewer might remember one of the twin verses from the *Dhammapada*: "As a strong wind blows down a weak tree, Mara the Tempter overwhelms weak people who, eating too much and working too little, are caught in the frantic pursuit of pleasure."[137]

The child monk, who has followed them, is unfazed by these temptations and shouts, "Monster, monster," when several prostitutes embrace him. For the most part, the general also acts as an uninterested observer, but this changes when the princess informs him of the latest political developments. The brother who murdered the crown prince is now emperor. Peace reigns and everyone considers him to be a good monarch, she says. And what of the crown prince's followers, the general inquires. They have either been beheaded or, if they sang the praises of the new emperor, were made into generals, she says. At this, General Shi laughs, saying, "This is not the world I still long for in my dreams." The princess ignores him, saying that she's come a long way to see him, and he isn't even paying attention to her. "Beauty is transient," she says. "Remember how I look now. Remember well." Finally, he gives into this spirit of hedonism, and together they dance, and plan a future together.

In the story of the Buddha, Siddhartha Gautama discovers the transience of beauty right after his son is born. To celebrate the birth, Suddhodana arranges a night of feasting and entertainment. After the party, everyone falls asleep. When Siddhartha wakes up, he sees that the once-beautiful dancing girls have disheveled clothing, their bodies are in awkward and shameful postures, and their makeup is smeared. Some are snoring, grinding their teeth, and drooling. The spell is broken, and Siddhartha prepares to leave the palace for good. "Thinking that someone is beautiful is a concept. Clinging to that concept confines you, ties you in a knot, and imprisons you. But if you think that someone is ugly, that is also a concept, and that will also bind you."[138] The truth of the matter is that all women are empty of both ugliness and beauty.[139] The *Dhammapada* also proves useful when contemplating this scene from *Temptation of a Monk*: "Look on the world as a bubble, look on it as a mirage, then the King of Death cannot even see you. Come look at this world! Is it not like a painted royal chariot? The wise see through it, but not the foolish."[140]

Discovering that he's a wanted man, the general orders his soldiers back to the monastery. One of the men says that he would rather hide in the brothel; another wants more wine. But none get to enjoy transient pleasures for much longer, because the emperor's guards corner them in a passage. The princess, who comes to their aid, is slain as are many of the soldiers-turned-monks. In short, it's a veritable bloodbath. In the aftermath, the general no longer admits his "innocence" but recognizes that he too is a traitor.[141]

Finally, the broken and devastated general ventures to a dilapidated monastery, and finding an elderly man there, begs to be accepted. He collapses on the stone steps. When he awakes, he begs again, saying that he's looking for a place of peace. The old man, revealed to be the abbot, allows him entrance. The general immediately begins shaving the heads of several very elderly monks. He also sweeps the monastery clean, and when he's tidied up, he places a piece of wood on the altar. Using a stick, he beats the woods and starts chanting. The old abbot comes and chastises him, "Didn't you want peace?" he asks.

"I want to say the evening prayers," the general replies. The old monk grabs the wood, and instructs his younger novice to go to his room and sleep. "I can't sleep, my heart's not at peace," says the general. "Go find something to eat." "Not hungry." "You don't eat, stomach is empty . . . heart is not. . . . Go, dig in the fields at the foothills." "A lot of wild desires. Why is it like this?" "It's meant to be like this . . . go, go, go knock out there." "I try to forget but I can't." "Who wants to forget?" "I do." "Who," the abbot asks. "Jing Yi." "Who is Jing Yi? Starved to death, who'll remain? Who'll be there? Who? Stop the shit, get this clear first. The shit makes even the Buddha rage." Then the old man laughs. Why does the abbot attempt to dissuade the general from Buddhist practice? Ch'an Buddhism stresses that this reality is *shunyata* or empty; it is also inexpressible in words and inconceivable in thought. This reality can only be understood through intuition, which could be attained by calming the mind. Therefore, "such conscious efforts such as heeding the teachings of the Buddha, reciting the sutras, worshiping Buddha images, or performing the rituals are really of no avail and should be abandoned."[142]

In the *Dhammapada*, the Buddha explains that those who are on the path realize that all created things are transitory, and that all states are without self. However, leaving the body and the ego behind is difficult. This is why the Buddhist tradition is replete with stories about the truth of *anatman* or no-self. One particularly gruesome tale was translated into Chinese in the early fifth century C.E., and it concerns a man who, while spending the night in a deserted house, encounters two demons. The first one arrives carrying a corpse. The second one demands the body, and when he doesn't get it, he fights with the first demon. Looking for some verification on the matter, the demons turn to the hiding man. No matter what he says, he knows he's going to anger one of the demons, and he's right. The second demon tears off the man's arm and throws it down. The first demon replaces it with the arm from the corpse, and so on. Finally, the demons eat what was once the living man's body, and leave. In amazement, the man contemplates his situation. Who is he, if he no longer has his former body? The man eventually comes upon some monks, and he tells them his story. From it the monks conclude that "not just now, but from its beginning up until the present, your body has all along been devoid of Self. It was only because of the coming together of the five basic elements that you thought, 'This is my body.' But there is no difference between your former body and that which you have today."[143] The same could be said of the self or ego. It is empty of permanence; instead, it is a coming together and dissolution of the five aggregates. And this is what the abbot is trying to teach the general.

After contemplating what the monk said, the general comes knocking at the abbot's door, claiming that he has the answer. At first, he seems to understand what the old man meant: "Starved to death. I'm the same as the others. Fundamentally all the same. Fighting in battles, killing countless people. Did I have innate mercy? Xuan Wu Gate, was it for righteousness? He'd thought about titles and fame! He wanted to be a grade-one generalissimo. Leading armies of millions. Acquiring great fame, betraying his lord. This heart, same as those curs'. Base, black, filthy, cold-blooded. This vile skin-bag of a body, what use is it?" He then begins violently slamming his body against the wall. His true epiphany doesn't come, though. As we can see from his rant, he is moving beyond ego and realizing that his actions were motivated by greed, hatred, and ignorance. However, as he admits, he can't let go of the past. "When you are 100 years old like me, you will forget even if you don't want to," the old man says. "When you're deaf with age, isn't there peace? Trouble-seeker." The old man dismisses the general, telling him to contemplate. He finishes by saying, "Here is here, there is there. Why use your heart to think?" The old man laughs.

At the end of the film, a woman named Violet (also played by Joan Chen) shows up at the monastery. She claims that her deceased husband was connected to this monastery, and she hopes that the abbot will let him be cremated there. "It was my late husband's last wish," she says tearfully. The old man explains that the monastery is in great disrepair with no extra hands to help with the funeral. What's more, he's forgotten the "Great Deliverance Chant." The woman will not be denied, though, and the monks fulfill her wishes, burning the body and chanting at his funeral. While she watches the flames devour her husband's corpse, she sings, "Dew on the grass. How easily it dries in the sun. Dew evaporates. Tomorrow it reappears. Man dies and goes. When will he return?" She passes out. The general and the abbot prepare a remedy for the woman, and then apply lighted cones to her acupressure points. (This demonstrates that in addition to studying sutras, monks also study medicine.) Since the general has not yet conquered his emotions, desire surfaces, and he is drawn to the widow. He caresses her.

The next day, instead of leaving the monastery, Violet begs the general to talk to the abbot about letting her shave her head and become a nun. Undoubtedly driven by lust, he entreats the abbot, saying, "She has a devoted heart." At first the abbot resists, "How do you know her heart? Do you know your heart?" Finally, the abbot relents and tells the general to shave her. The general admits that he doesn't know how to shave a woman. "Saving a life, what does it matter if a man or a woman? Fat or lean, meat is meat. Stomach not hungry, peace in the world." Before the woman has her long hair shaved off, the abbot reminds her that she can no longer have worldly thoughts. The same reminder is appropriate for the general, who after shaving the woman, caresses her ear.

Later, while he's meditating, facing a wall, she comes up from behind him and begins to seduce him. She caresses him, telling him that he's not a monk but a general who has cut off thousands of heads. They make love, during which she ties his hands behind his back. She then tells him that she is arresting him and taking him back to the capital. The general has, once again, been deceived. Despite his monastic training, the general continues to be seduced by beautiful women because he hasn't learned detachment. No matter who we are, our desires are powerful and can overtake even the most devout human. A Japanese Zen fable tells how an older and younger monk were about to cross a river when a beautiful young woman came upon them. When she asked them to ferry her across, the younger monk hesitated. After all, he had taken vows and wasn't supposed to touch women. By contrast, the older monk didn't give it a second thought. He lifted her, carried her across, and set her down. Several hours later, the still-surprised younger monk queried his walking partner: "Aren't we monks? Why did you carry her?" The older monk replied, "I put her down a long time ago. Why are you still carrying her?"[144]

Once Violet has the general where she wants him, she bites him on the neck, drawing blood. In pain, the general screams. Hearing the commotion, the abbot arrives and hits the woman on the back of the head with his walking stick. She falls over dead. "Dead. It's a wild wolf," he says, "Not sleeping at the time to sleep. Not eating at the time to eat." The abbot leaves the room. The next day, the general and the abbot are eating. The general asks about the temple and the story of the rock behind them. The abbot simply replies, "Forgotten." The general continues, telling him that he knows the story. The rock, he says, was once on the mountain, but it got thirsty one day, so it jumped down to the river and drank its fill, but then it couldn't get back up. The abbot corrects him, "No, it was the river rising up to the hilltop. It drank half the river and then lay here." "Is there a difference," the general asks, then smiles.

Looking at him sideways, the abbot, says "Eat your rice at the time to eat rice."
"This is congee, not rice." "Is there a difference?" Both men laugh.

All of this talk about "eat when it's time to eat; sleep when it's time to sleep"
comes straight out of Zen lore. In one story a disciple asks his master how to
put enlightenment into action, how to practice it every day. His master replies,
"By eating and sleeping." Confused, the disciple explained that everyone eats
and sleeps. Yes, but "not everyone eats when they eat, and not everybody sleeps
when they sleep." This story illustrates the idea of being present, no matter
what we are doing, no matter how mundane the activity.[145] The abbot's attitude and actions are very much in line with Ch'an Buddhism, particularly
with the ninth-century Chinese master Hsuan-chien, who "called upon his
followers to do just the ordinary things in life—to drink when thirsty, to eat
when hungry, to pass water and move the bowels, and when tired, to take a
rest." Furthermore, he said that "nirvana and *bodhi* are dead stumps to tie your
donkeys," and the 12 divisions of sacred teachings are "only lists of ghosts,
sheets of paper fit only for wiping the pus from your boils."[146]

After the abbot dies, the emperor's soldiers arrive, telling the general that
he must return to the palace. To this he states, "This armor doesn't keep you
warm. It hampers farm work. It's useless." His arch-nemesis, General Huo,
presents himself in full armor, and shoots an arrow at the general-turned-
monk. Unfazed he replies, "When will your arrow not rip things?" General
Huo taunts him about the Xuan Wu Gate incident and about Scarlet, the murdered princess, but the general continues walking into the monastery. The soldiers shoot burning arrows after him and wait. When he doesn't come out,
General Huo goes inside the monastery, where he finds General Shi stroking
a bird, "It's hurt," he says. General Huo tries to get Shi to fight him, telling him
that in every dream he has he cuts off Shi's head. Finally, the two struggle in
the burning building. "Be you Buddha, I'll cut off your head,"[147] Huo says,
then charges at him. An axe that Shi holds breaks off into Huo's neck and he
dies.[148] "Eat at the time to eat. Sleep at the time to sleep. Die at the time to die,"
General Shi says, as the building continues to burn. At the very end of the film,
General Shi, now very much a monk, rides away on a white horse.

Throughout most of the film, we see the general encounter the three
poisons—greed, anger, and ignorance—and repeatedly be defeated by them.
In the end, though, he sees clearly. He knows that the dream he had about life
was just that—a dream. He learns to see beyond anger and beyond pleasure.

And he begins to live in the moment, eating when he should eat, sleeping when he should sleep. This is right mindfulness. During his speech to the abbot, we also see that he understands that everyone is "fundamentally the same." By the end of the film, we get the sense that the general is becoming what the Buddha describes as a "true Brahmin." He has conquered his passions, has let go of fear, has trained his mind to be still, and isn't angry or causes harm to others even when they attack him; he is fearless, unshakable, and has conquered death.[149] Furthermore, the "true Brahmin" sees beyond duality, which General Shi seems to do. In the beginning of the film, he thought he was an innocent victim, by the middle, he thinks he's a traitor, and by the end, he suggests that he's both and neither. Everyone performs good and bad deeds, has good and bad thoughts; the key is to remain detached, to not cling to anything in the world.

BUDDHIST THEMES

Because Buddhism has a strong philosophical[150] foundation, we can draw upon its concepts to understand non-Buddhist films. And by this, we mean that these films don't take place in a monastery, don't have monks or nuns as characters, and probably wouldn't even be thought of as Buddhist by their creators.[151]

The Lookout (2007)—Written and directed by Scott Frank. Running time: 99
    min. English. USA. Rated R for language, some violence and sexual content.
    Genre: Crime/Drama/Thriller.

Summary: Chris Pratt (Joseph Gordon-Levitt) seems to have everything. He's a good-looking young man from a wealthy and prominent family. He is a champion hockey player, is popular with other students, and has a beautiful girlfriend, Kelly (Laura Vandervoort). That changes on prom night when Chris is driving on Route 24, a seemingly deserted highway with his girlfriend and two friends in tow. He wants to show Kelly the fireflies, so he switches off the convertible's headlamps. Worried that they are going too fast and can't see the oncoming traffic, his friends convince him to turn the lights back on. He does so just seconds before slamming into the back of a stalled combine harvester. This accident changes Chris's life forever. Not only does he have to deal with the deaths of his two friends and the injury of his girlfriend, but now he also must cope with his own psychological transformation. His traumatic head injury leaves him with alternating moments of rage and sadness, and creates in him a socially awkward sense of disinhibition. What's most troubling to him, however, is his difficulty in "sequencing" information; in short, he can't always remember events in order. To help him, he carries a pocket-size notebook in which he jots down daily reminders. Because of these problems, his only job prospect has been working nights in a small town bank as a janitor. Chris tries to grapple with his disability but he can't. He just wants to be who he was.

Gary Spargo (Matthew Goode), an asthmatic whom Chris meets in a local bar, promises to fix everything for him. First, he deals with Chris's relationship problems by pairing him with Luvlee Lemons (Isla Fisher), a sweet and bubbly stripper who is only too happy to sleep with her "high school hero." Next, Gary promises him something much more enticing—a way to get his life back. But there's a catch: Chris must be the lookout while Gary and his friends rob Chris's employer. When Chris has the money, Gary promises, he will have the power. And why not commit the crime? After all, doesn't Chris deserve to take back that life that, in Gary's words, was "ripped out from underneath him"?

The Lookout reminds us of the first two Noble Truths: that life is characterized by suffering and that it is caused by grasping. Throughout the film, Chris is suffering. Even though he believes it's his disability that's to blame, the real source of his suffering is his desire for a permanence that doesn't exist. He wants to be who he used to be, but he can't. Gary is selling him a lie, and because of his "ignorance," Chris takes the bait. Why? Because Gary reminded him of how envied he was. He also absolved him of any responsibility for his current state, saying that something "out there" took his life away. And if that happened to him, Gary says, "I don't think I'd give even half a rat's ass about what was right or wrong." Gary is clouding Chris's eyes with illusion or *maya*. Moments from Chris's past probably do look great, especially when he's only focusing on the happiest of snapshots. The reality is that life is characterized by moments of happiness and sadness, success and defeat. It's also characterized by change; nothing stays the same. Chris's desire to return to the past simply prevents him from living in the present.

Letting go of desire isn't easy. It takes mindfulness, and initially Chris lacks that. He believes that being rich, in control, independent, and in love are the key to happiness, because he believes they will last. Buddhism would say, again, that Chris is being ignorant. Not only will his belief in permanence result in criminal behavior, but it will also turn him against the very people who really care about him. He is failing to see his interdependence and the emptiness of all things. "He who maintains the doctrine of emptiness is not allured by the things of the world, because they have no basis. He is not excited by gain or dejected by loss. Fame does not dazzle him and infamy does not shame him. Scorn does not repel him, praise does not attract him. Pleasure does not please him, pain does not trouble him. He who is not allured by the things of the world knows emptiness, and one who maintains the doctrine of emptiness has neither likes nor dislikes. What he likes he knows to be only emptiness and sees it as such."[152] Interestingly, the only character who "sees" through Gary's scheme is Chris's roommate, Lewis (Jeff Daniels), a blind man[153] who dreams of opening a restaurant. Even when Chris mocks his roommate for hitting on a waitress, Lewis doesn't respond with anger but honesty. He knows who he is, and he's accepted it. What does it hurt to try?

If we look at the film with regard to the Eightfold Path, we can see that Chris's wrong understanding sets off a chain reaction of other wrongs. He violates right speech by lying and using harsh words against Lewis and "Deputy Donut." He then takes wrong action, by stealing, overindulging in alcohol, and eventually taking a life. Obviously being a thief means assuming wrong livelihood. When it comes to right effort, Chris again fails. The saddest moment in the film comes when Chris's boss tells him that he will give him a chance as a teller, "because he's shown hard work and dedication." This occurs right before the bank robbery. Had Chris only devoted as much time to convincing his boss that he could be a teller as he did drinking beer, falling in with the wrong crowd, and dreaming of "getting his life back," things might have worked out differently for him.

Again, Chris should have been more mindful in his life. And this goes all the way back to that drive on Route 24, the catalyst for the film. No one told him to turn off the lights on the car or to speed. He made that choice, because he wanted to impress his girlfriend. And now he has to live with the consequences. Furthermore, instead of feeling sorry for himself, he should have made more of an effort to let go of his past and live in the present, thus leading to a more "hopeful" future. He even has the opportunity for growth, but because of pride, he doesn't take advantage of it. For instance, when his case manager (Carla Gugino) asks him if he's having any problems, he lies, saying that "he's great."

The Buddhist laity must adhere to five precepts, which include not destroying life, not stealing, not committing sexual misconduct, not lying, and not taking intoxicating substances. If we look at Chris's behavior in *The Lookout*, he violates every one of these. Furthermore, the Buddha talked about five hindrances; emotions that prevent a person from achieving nirvana. These are doubt, lust, hatred, worry, and languor. Again, all of these hold Chris back from moving on with his life and from rejecting Gary's criminal plan. Just to single out two of these, Chris hates what he's become, and he despises his father for keeping him dependent on him. But hatred or anger wasn't enough to ensnare Chris. Just as he was leaving Gary's farmhouse, Luvlee shows up on the stairs, dressed only in a T-shirt and underwear, asking him if he's leaving. Lust was all it took to make Chris a willing accomplice. With right concentration, Chris might have noticed that we aren't a fixed and unchanging "I" but that we are a process. Chris should also stop worrying about not being who he thinks he should be but accept and embrace transformation. As Thich Nhat Hanh reminds us, "Impermanence is what makes transformation possible."[154]

Chris isn't the only one having difficulty adjusting to who he has become. His father, in particular, is blinded by the past. He still engages his son in a game of chess, even though Chris can no longer play. And he won't support his son's plans of opening a restaurant, thus helping him to move on. Lewis, again, is the only one who can "see" clearly. After a disastrous Thanksgiving dinner at Chris's family's mansion, Lewis tells Chris that maybe he shouldn't go home anymore. Many of the characters in *The Lookout* view Chris as disabled and treat him as such. Chris has to learn to overcome his embarrassment at not having lived up to society's expectations, which include having a girlfriend or wife, having a "respectable" job, being able to smooth talk the ladies, and being strong and masculine. Chris has to realize that he's just fine the way he is.

The end of the film brings some hope, because Chris is finally seeing clearly. As painful as it might be, he realizes that Luvlee didn't actually care about him and that Gary was only manipulating him. He also realizes that robbing the bank was wrong. Chris's revelation comes after he has a dream about his girlfriend Kelly. In this dream, Chris follows her into a building, where she lifts up her skirt to reveal a prosthetic leg. "It's part of me now," she says. Eventually, Chris realizes that his disability is also who he is, and that's OK. It's time to "let go" and move forward. As he says, "What happened that night on old Route 24 is a part of me now. I just hope that one day Kelly will be ready to see me again, and I can finally tell her what I've only been able to say in my dreams. Until then, all I can do is wake up, take a shower with soap, and try to forgive myself. And if I can do that, then maybe others will forgive me, too."

The Brave One (2007)—Directed by Neil Jordan. Running time: 119 min. English. USA. Rated R for strong violence, language, and some sexuality. Genre: Crime/Drama/Thriller.

Summary: Erica Bain (Jodie Foster), a radio host, walks the streets of New York, so that she can share its sounds and stories with her audience. She loves the city because it houses all of her memories. But it's also changing, mutating into something ugly and dangerous. She discovers this late one night, while she's out walking through the park with her fiancé, David (Naveen Andrews), and their German shepherd. Inside a tunnel, they are brutally attacked by a trio of thugs. Her fiancé is killed; she's barely alive in a comatose state. When she wakes up three weeks later, she's a changed woman. As she confesses on the air: "I always believed that fear belonged to other people . . . weaker people. . . . It never touched me. And then it did. And when it touches you, you know that it's been there all along, waiting beneath the surface of everything you loved. And your skin crawls, and your heart sickens, and you look at that person you once were, walking down that street, and you wonder will you, will you ever be her again?" Erica is left with a hole in her heart, one that she thinks can only be filled by her obtaining a gun. Initially, she uses it for protection, but as the film progresses she uses it to bring about the kind of justice that only exists in storybooks—swift and absolute.

Erica Bain is a lot like Chris Pratt. Her perceived idyllic life comes to a shattering end one night, and after she emerges from a coma three weeks later, she finds herself disappearing; a frightening but compelling stranger is taking her place. Where she was fearless before her violent confrontation, she is now terrified of the streets she once loved. Rather than accept that life is unpredictable, and that nothing lasts, Erica allows fear to overpower her. Not believing that she can survive another day without a gun, she goes to a pawn shop to procure one. The employee tells her that she must fill out the necessary paperwork and wait. Not willing to do this, she leaves the store. A stranger quickly approaches her, offering to sell her a gun "under the table" for $1,000. She doesn't hesitate, even though by doing this, she is contributing to the criminal element that she wants to combat. Like Chris Pratt, she lacks true understanding.

Erica begins carrying her loaded gun with her whenever she leaves her apartment, probably without the intention of using it. She just feels safer having it next to her. All of that will change, though. One night she's in a local convenience store, looking for a soft drink, when the female employee's ex-husband comes in. Angry about custody over their children, the man pulls out a gun and shoots the woman several times. Not believing what she's witnessed, Erica tries to avoid detection. When she accidentally causes a noise, the man comes after her. During the confrontation, Erica shoots and kills him. At this point, her actions stem from self-defense; there exists no intention to kill. Once outside the store, the visibly shaken woman sheds her jacket, throwing it into a trash can, and she lights up a cigarette. When she gets home, she takes a shower with her clothes on. Finding that she is capable of killing someone rattles Erica, but it doesn't make her get rid of the gun. In fact, she continues to carry it in her purse.

The next time Erica resorts to violence, she is riding the subway when two black males begin harassing her fellow commuters. They start by stealing a young man's iPod, and when an older man tries to "interfere," they turn on him. Everyone but Erica decides to avoid any further conflict by exiting the subway. With only Erica on board, naturally, the men come over to her, brandishing a knife and threatening to rape her. Again, without hesitation, she pulls out her gun, shoots them both, and then leaves her subway car. This act could also be deemed self-defense, but as the film progresses we find that the line between what's morally acceptable and what's morally unacceptable begins to blur. Couldn't Erica have removed herself from harm's way? Clearly, others did. At this point, we might say that her intention was to kill. As she herself asks, "Why didn't my hands shake? Why doesn't anyone stop me?" we wonder why she doesn't simply turn herself into the police. At one point in the movie she tries, but she can't bring herself to do it. Erica is trying "to live," and to do this she's transforming into someone else.

It isn't long before the media catches wind of the story, and soon everyone, including the police, is wondering who this vigilante might be. Feeling more emboldened by her power—she swaps her trademark hoodie for a leather jacket—Erica begins walking the streets late into the night. On a desolate street, a man in a town car calls her over. Even though most people would ignore him, she walks over and even gets into the backseat of the car. Seeing that the woman next to her is drug-addled and probably being kept against her will, Erica makes an attempt to save her. Before exiting the car, she pulls her gun on the driver and tells him to give the woman the money that he owes her. The women get a few yards from the car before he tries to run them over. In "self-defense," Erica shoots and kills him. Is Erica finding the criminals or are they finding her?

This question is in the back of one's mind when Erica commits her next violent act. While talking with Detective Mercer (Terrence Howard), the lead police officer on this vigilante murder case, Erica learns that for years he's been trying to put away a ruthless criminal but thus far he hasn't found a "legal" way to do it. For whatever reason, Erica goes to the man's office building, follows him to his car and, after a struggle, plants a crowbar into his skull. Those watching the film should question her actions. Is she morally justified in becoming judge, jury, and executioner? Is she merely doing a job that the police seem incapable of doing? Is she motivated by helping others or is she fulfilling a revenge-driven bloodlust? Does killing make her "feel good" and powerful?

Finally, even though the police have found the man who is responsible for killing her fiancé and attacking her in the park, Erica denies "seeing" her assailant in the lineup. She would rather take care of him herself. And she does. Having learned his address, she ventures into his neighborhood and, after locating him and his accomplices, guns them down one by one. For his own reasons, Detective Mercer, who has arrived on the scene, helps her to avoid capture, telling her to shoot him so that he can claim he shot the victims out of self-defense. Even though this emotional ending tends to bring cheers from the audience, it should instead generate more questions, especially if we view the film through a Buddhist lens.

In an interview for the film, Jodie Foster said that "I think we all have these ideas that there are lines that we would never cross and people we could never be. And yet, you don't know who you would become in a certain circumstance. You might assume, intellectually, what your ethics might be, but until you are forced into a situation that challenges you, that changes you, you can't know who you would be." Director Neil Jordan agreed with her, saying that "I think when we are wronged, a part of us would love to react with a kind of primitive brutality so we could right it immediately. But we don't because civilization teaches us not to do that. So the spectacle of seeing someone descending into a morally questionable area is both horrifying and fascinating at the same time."[155] The Buddha knew that people are poisoned by hatred, greed, and ignorance, so he stressed the importance of being mindful, something we can achieve by meditating. If we haven't trained ourselves to see the world as it is, and we haven't learned to conquer our senses by cultivating a sense of detachment, then Foster and Jordan are right, people do act compulsively out of fear, anger, lust, and greed. Erica Bain certainly does. She believes that the only way to achieve closure is to adhere to the Judeo-Christian law code of an "eye for eye, tooth for a tooth" (Exodus 21:23–25). If she took some time to truly reflect on her assailants, she would see that they are no different than she is. They also wake up, eat breakfast, get dressed, have families, and experience love and hatred. On a deeper level, they are also a coming together of five aggregates; they were born, they live, and they will die. As it says in the *Dhammapada*, "Everyone fears punishment; everyone fears death, just as you do. Therefore, do not kill or cause to kill. Everyone fears punishment; everyone loves life as you do. Therefore do not kill or cause to kill."[156] The Dalai Lama explains this even further, saying that we should feel gratitude toward those who inflict harm on us, because "such situations provide us with a rare opportunity to put to test our own practice of patience. It is a precious occasion to practice not only patience but the other bodhisattva ideals as well. . . . The poor enemy, on the other hand, because of his negative action of inflicting harm on someone out of anger and hatred, must eventually face the consequences of his or her own actions. It is almost as if the perpetrator of the harm sacrifices himself or herself for the sake of our benefit."[157]

Even though Erica had seen New York City, she never really saw it as it truly was. And that's because, metaphorically, she was living in the realm of the gods, where she lived a blissful, carefree existence. The violent incident in the tunnel propelled her into a kind of hell realm, where fear and anger were the norm. Neither state is real, though. They are simply emanations of her mind, which has never been controlled. As it says in the *Dhammapada*, "The disciples of Gautama are wide awake and vigilant," with their thoughts focused on the Buddha, the dharma, the *sangha*, sense-training, compassion, and meditation day and night.[158] Living in the world isn't easy. It's painful and complex. Buddhism acknowledges this, but it never advocates violence. Instead, it instructs us to set our minds free and go beyond birth and death: "If you want to reach the other shore, don't let doubts, passions and cravings strengthen your fetters. Meditate deeply, discriminate between the pleasant and the permanent, and break the fetters of Mara."[159] It also says that "one who conquers himself is greater than another who conquers a thousand times a thousand men on the battlefield. Be victorious over yourself and not over others. When you attain victory over yourself, not even the gods can turn it into defeat."[160]

Furthermore, Buddhism reminds us that we become what we think. So if we dwell on thoughts of hatred—thinking about how someone attacked us or robbed us—we will never be free from hatred. "For hatred can never put an end to hatred; love alone can. This is an unalterable law."[161] And just as rich merchants who are traveling alone avoid dangerous roads, the *Dhammapada* says, so should everyone avoid dangerous deeds. Like those "rich merchants," Erica knows that if she ventures into a crime-ridden area of town, she's going to encounter problems, but she doesn't care. She is looking for trouble, and more often than not, she finds it. This is why we can't say that she's truly acting in self-defense when she kills the men on the subway or the man in the town car. She's courting danger because she's motivated by revenge.

The film suggests that with her dog in hand and the "bad" guys finally brought to justice, Erica can now achieve closure. However, if we examine her actions in terms of karma, it's highly unlikely that she is going to escape punishment. As was said earlier in the chapter, to create good or bad karma, one must perform an action with intention. Scholar Peter Harvey explains that "as the force of will behind an action increases" so does the amount of karmic "demerit." Not only does premeditation increase the seriousness of an action, but so does performing a wrong action while not thinking it's wrong. "Thus killing a human or animal without compunction is worse than doing so with trepidation."[162] When we look at Erica's actions, several of her killings involved premeditation, especially in the case of her last four victims, and as her killings escalate, she finds that her hands no longer shake. This suggests that she feels justified in what she's doing.[163] Buddhism reminds us that "beings reap the fruit of actions—good or bad—which they themselves have done (there is no other doer) with their body, speech and mind."[164] Because Erica has slain living beings out of delusion, fear, and anger, according to Buddhist texts, once she dies she is destined for *samjiva* hell. It is called this, because "beings there, during many thousands of years, are killed only to be revived (*samjivanti*) and killed again and again."[165] According to the *Abhidharmakosa*, the life span of *samjiva* hell lasts 500 years.[166]

As it has been said, after a being dies, he or she is reborn into one of six realms. But before rebirth can take place, according to Tibetan Buddhists, that being exists in a kind of limbo, an intermediate state that has "an average duration of 49 days, and a minimum length of one week. But it varies. . . . Some can even get stuck in the *bardo*, to become spirits or ghosts . . . during the first 21-days of the *bardo*, you still have a strong impression of your previous life, and this is therefore the most important period for the living to be able to help a dead person."[167] What happens in the *bardo?* During the first few weeks, we don't realize that we are dead, and we have the sense that we are just as we were in life. People often return home to meet their families and loved ones, but when they try to communicate with them, they are met with silence because the living don't know that they are there.[168] In the *bardo* of becoming, a person relives every experience from his or her life, and then every seven days, he or she relives the experience of death once again, with all of its suffering. What makes it worse is that if one was tormented in death, that state will be repeated at seven times the intensity. Furthermore, "all of the negative karma of previous lives [returns] in a fiercely concentrated and deranging way. Our restless, solitary wandering through the *bardo* world is as frantic as a nightmare, and just as in a dream, we believe we have a physical body and that we really exist. Yet all the experiences of this *bardo* arise only from our mind, created by our karma and habits returning."[169]

Stay (2005)—Directed by Marc Forster. Running time 99 min. English. USA. Rated R for language and some disturbing images. Genre: Drama/Mystery/ Thriller.

To encounter the confusion and fear experienced before and during the *bardo*, one can watch the film *Stay*. Based on a script by David Benioff, the film centers on a disturbed university art student, Henry Letham[170] (Ryan Gosling), who tells his "substitute shrink," Dr. Sam Foster (Ewan McGregor), that, unless someone can save him, he's going to kill himself in three days. After this first encounter, Sam finds that he's losing his own grip on reality, as he, too, is thrust into a nightmarish place between life and death. With the assistance of his girlfriend, Lila (Naomi Watts), Sam races to unlock the dark secrets of Henry's tortured psyche.

The film begins with what seems to be a car crash on the Brooklyn Bridge. Henry sits next to the burning wreckage for a few minutes, and then gets up and walks away. Henry's face quickly morphs into Sam's as Sam wakes up and cycles to work. These first five minutes should give viewers the sense that something isn't quite right. What we thought was a car crash is explained during a psychiatric session as pyromania; Henry has set his car on fire, but he doesn't know why. On Henry's second trip to Dr. Foster's office, he divulges that he's now hearing voices. In fact, he's having difficulty differentiating the "real voices" from those in his head, which say: "I didn't move him. I know you're not supposed to move 'em. I can't watch anymore. Stay with me, Henry. Stay with me."

As the film progresses, the linearity of the narrative becomes increasingly convoluted. We see events from different perspectives and from different angles. Often sequences are repeated, images are doubled or tripled, and flashbacks of that mysterious car ride are replayed many times. The audience is, for the most part, as confused as the characters. Adding another element of strangeness to the film is the fact that Henry seems to possess supernatural abilities. For instance, not only can he make accurate predictions—he forecasts hail and reveals the message in a fortune cookie long before anyone has received it—but he also restores his blind father's sight. Everything is made clear by the end of the film, though, and we realize that what we've just watched are emanations of Henry's dying mind. He was in a car crash, and although he survived, he's barely alive. Everything we've witnessed in the film are his fears projected onto the spectators who are standing over his dying body.

Since the film is about the near-death experience (NDE)—the featurette on the DVD, *Departing Visions*, features interviews with those who have had NDEs—*Stay* probably could be seen through the lens of other religious traditions. What makes it seem particularly Buddhist, though, is its insistence that "all is mind." For instance, during an early scene, Sam asks Henry what the marks are on his arm. Henry replies, "Oh, I burned myself." When asked why he would do this, Henry says, quite matter-of-factly, "I'm practicing for hell." "Why do you think you're going to hell?" "'Um, cause of what I did. What I'm going to do." Henry then puts his fingers, which are fashioned into a gun, to his head, indicating that he's going to commit suicide. We have to keep in mind that these are the thoughts of a dying man. He isn't going to kill himself, and yet that's how he interprets what's happening or has happened to him. Later in the film, the guilt-ridden[171] Henry believes that he's killed his parents. He's even written "Forgive me" all over his apartment walls. Again, nothing that he says is true, but because he believes these things to be so, they are so to him. Interestingly enough, as it says in Henry's psychiatric file, "Henry Letham has a fertile, powerful imagination. If he maintains his concentration, he will create new worlds with his art."

Another reminder that "all is mind" comes about 30 minutes into the film. Sam and his blind mentor, Dr. Leon Patterson (Bob Hoskins), are playing chess. After some discussion about Sam's relationship with Lila, Leon begins talking about one of Sigmund Freud's cases in which a patient's child is dying. In the story the father keeps a nightly vigil next to his son's bed. Once the boy has died, he is given a wake. Not long after his family sets up a circle of candles around the boy's body, the exhausted father falls asleep. He dreams that his son is standing beside him, holding his arm, and whispering, "Father, can't you see that I'm burning?" This story of the "burning child" is featured in Freud's 1900 work, *Interpreting Dreams*, and it can be understood as the fulfillment of the father's wish that the child were still alive. Undoubtedly, the father feels helpless in the face of the child's death, and this dream gives him another chance, at least in his mind, to do what he couldn't in life: "save" his son. It isn't surprising that this story is included in *Stay*, because even though Henry[172] is fatally wounded, he doesn't know it. In this intermediate state, he sees himself as he would like to be—walking around and finding someone who can save him.

In Buddhism, we find at least two instances where the Buddha mentions something being on fire, and both are applicable to *Stay*. In the *Dhammapada*, the Buddha asks, "Why is there laughter, why merriment, when this world is on fire? When you are living in darkness, why don't you look for light? This body is a painted image, subject to disease, decay and death, activated by thoughts that come and go. What joy can there be for him who sees that his white bones will be cast away like gourds in the autumn?"[173] A similar message can be found in the Parable of the Burning House, which is in the Mahayana text, the Lotus Sutra. In it, a householder lives in a great mansion that has only one door. One day, his house bursts into flames. He manages to get out, but his children are still inside, playing with their toys. "They do not know, do not realize, do not understand that the house is on fire, and are not upset. Even caught in that inferno, being burned by those flames, in fact, suffering a great deal, they are oblivious to their suffering, and the thought of them getting out does not occur to them."[174] The father's first thought is to gather the children in his arms and carry them out, but because there is only one door this is quickly dismissed. Next, he calls out to the children, but they don't pay him any attention. Knowing that children enjoy toys, he tells them that outside of the house he has all sorts of carts for them to play with; all they have to do is come out and get them. Naturally, the children come running. Even though the father only had one type of cart for them, the important thing was that they were saved from the dangers of the burning house.

In both the section from the *Dhammapada* and in the parable, these stories illustrate that even though suffering, ignorance, old age, illness, and death surround us, human beings fritter away their days by chasing after transitory enjoyments. The Buddha, like the father in the story, uses his skillful means to draw the ignorant masses out to the safety of nirvana.[175] If we look at Henry's situation in a Buddhist context, during his life he acted as most of us do. He was born, grew up, found a girlfriend, bought a wedding ring for her, went to university, and before his accident, he was driving with his parents to an event. He didn't think about death; he wasn't prepared for it, because he probably thought he was going to live into his golden years with his wife at his side. But death can and does strike at any time. Henry is frightened and confused in death, because during his life, he didn't meditate on death; he wasn't prepared for it.

As soon as Leon finishes telling the story of the "burning child," Henry walks in, and seeing the blind man, recoils in fear because he believes Leon should be dead. "I watched you die," he says. Several images quickly flash across the screen. If we slow the film down, we can see images of Leon, dead in a car, and then we see a family portrait of Henry, Leon, and a woman. Leon is Henry's father. This is when guilt sets in, and an agonized Henry claims that "I did it. It's my fault." When Sam tries to comfort Henry, the young man explodes, shoving over the chess table and yelling, "Everything you know is a lie." (Of course, he's talking to himself.) Unfortunately, Henry himself is so confused that he can't see the truth; he doesn't know that he's dying. "According to tantric physiology, the sign of actual death is not the cessation of inhalation or circulation of blood, but the appearance of the mind of clear light. People remain in this state of lucidity for *three days* [my emphasis], but most are so frightened by the strangeness of the experience that they lapse into unconsciousness and pass through the period of the arising of the mind of clear light unaware of what is happening."[176] At the end of the three days, that being dies and enters the *bardo.*

About 40 minutes into the film, Sam visits Henry's psychiatrist, Dr. Levy (Janeane Garofalo), and finds her in a terrible state. She's been drinking alcohol and taking prescription medication. Sam wants to "sober her up" by putting her in the shower. While he's lifting her, she says, "Bathe the corpse. We won't really be corpses though, will we? It will be more like a memory of nothing." As was already mentioned, during his life the Buddha was asked the same questions about the afterlife. People wanted to know if, after we die, we are eternal or if we become essentially nothing. Because he felt that metaphysical questions were pointless, he refused to respond.

The strangest sequence in the film occurs when Sam meets Henry's mother, Maureen. She's sitting on the porch when he arrives, and together they walk into the house, which is empty. Lying on the floor is Olive, a mastiff. Mrs. Letham says that she and Olive keep each other company, "We've been alone in this house for a thousand years. Most days I don't say a single word. Sometimes I'm silent so long, I forget how to speak." Maureen then asks Sam if he hates her, and if so, maybe that's why he did it. Confused, Sam asks her who she thinks he is. "Henry," is her response. While the two continue to speak, we can hear voices in the background. If we listen closely, we discover that they are conversations from the past. During one, Maureen is telling her son that dogs are a big responsibility. Suddenly, blood begins pouring from Mrs. Letham's head, and Olive bites Sam. (Henry later reveals that Olive has been dead since he was 12. She had a tumor in her liver and was put to sleep.)

After the attack, Sam is talking to a police officer, and he learns that Maureen and her husband have been dead for months. They were killed in a car wreck, and their house is still empty. Sam says, "I just spoke to Maureen Letham an hour ago" to which the officer replies, "It's probably just someone's confused." Immediately following this scene, we watch Henry walk into a 25-cent stripper club. While the women dance, scenes from Henry's life flash on a movie screen in the background. Henry cries, while the words "forgive me" play over and over again. A bit later, Sam tries to counsel Henry, telling him "to open your eyes a little wider." But Henry still can't see, because he's attached to the idea that he killed his parents and that he's going to hell. "Or maybe I'm already there. I don't know." By inserting an excerpt from *Hamlet*—that Denmark, like life, is a prison because "thinking makes it so"—into the film, the screenwriter sharpens the concept that all is mind. As the Buddha said, "Our life is shaped by our mind."[177]

At nearly 70 minutes into the film, Sam is following Athena, Henry's girlfriend, down a spiral staircase that goes on and on. At one point, they hear indistinct voices, and Sam loses Athena. Panic-stricken he calls out to her and begins running down the stairs. He slips and falls, causing the engagement ring he bought for Lila to slip out of his pocket and hit the ground. It lands, creating a flash of light, which then freezes. And suddenly we see images from Henry's life again, and we hear a voice saying, "I'm just trying to figure out if I'm the king or the farmer." Next we see and hear a slowly beating heart. The sound of someone saying "Still there" wakes Sam up.

As the film nears the end of its 99 minutes, Henry visits his father, asking him if he's lonely and why Henry's mom isn't with him. Leon tells Henry that he has the wrong man and that he has to leave. To this, Henry replies, "I don't want to go. I don't wanna die." Henry then heals his father, who still doesn't recognize him. Before he leaves, Henry asks his father, "Remember that time we found all those dead sparrows in the yard? Do you remember that? They were in that tree that got hit by lightning." Later Leon confronts Sam at a pay phone, and Sam is surprised that Leon can see. "I can see everything," he replies. "For the first time, I can see everything." Sam asks him, "What's happening to us?" Leon replies, "The Buddhists had it right all along. The world is an illusion."

The end of the film takes place on the Brooklyn Bridge. Sam tells Henry that he no longer knows what's real anymore. Henry replies, "You are. You're real. And you're trying to save me. You're just too late. 'Cause I gotta wake up." "You are awake. Look around you. If this is a dream then the whole world is inside it." Not long after this, Henry "shoots himself in the head," and we move outside of his "dream world" into the "real world" where we see Henry, who has been in a car crash, being tended to by Lila and Sam. But it's too late, and he dies. According to Buddhism, Henry—whether he's speaking as Leon or as Sam—is correct: the world is an illusion and dream. As the Buddha explained,

"The senses are as though illusions and their objects as dreams. For instance, a sleeping man might dream that he had made love to a beautiful country girl, and he might remember her when he awoke. What do you think—does the beautiful girl he dreamed of really exist? . . . In just the same way a foolish and ignorant man of the world sees pleasant forms and believes in their existence."[178]

Jacob's Ladder (1990)—Directed by Adrian Lyne, written by Bruce Joel Rubin. Running time: 116 min. English. USA. Rated R. Genre: Drama/Fantasy/ Horror.

Another film set within the *bardo* is *Jacob's Ladder* (1990), which focuses on a traumatized Vietnam War veteran (Tim Robbins) who is now a postman in New York City. Even though he's no longer at war, his life is far from idyllic. During his waking life, he sees and is attacked by demons, is visited by his dead son (Macaulay Culkin), has flashbacks, and uncovers a conspiracy plot within the government. Like *Stay*, the film hints at what's going on from the beginning. In one scene, Jacob goes to a palm reader who tells him that his life line has ended; he's already dead. He brushes off her comment with a smile and it's "just my luck." In an earlier scene, Jacob's wife leaves some photos for him at his apartment. While looking through them with his girlfriend, Jezebel, she says, "It's amazing, huh, Jake? Your whole life . . . right in front of you." And indeed this is what's happening to him; his life is flashing before him, because he died at the beginning of the film. Everything that follows is a construct of his mind in the intermediate state. However, the unsuspecting viewer fails to "figure out" the film until the credits roll, undoubtedly prompting another viewing.

How *Jacob's Ladder* differs from *Stay* is that while *Stay* contains no overt religious ideology or symbolism, *Jacob's Ladder* blatantly lays Judeo-Christian ideas over Buddhist ones. The title[179] itself comes straight from the Book of Genesis in the Hebrew Bible, and it refers to a dream that Jacob had during which divine messengers ascended and descended a stairway between heaven and earth.[180] All of the main characters in the film have biblical names, including Jacob, Sarah, Jezebel, Michael, Paul, Eli (short for Elijah), and Gabe (short for Gabriel), and in the aforementioned scene, during which Jezebel and Jacob are looking at photos, she tells him that his children have weird names. His response is that "they're biblical. They were prophets." In a slightly later scene, Jacob has had his neck adjusted by his chiropractor, Louis, and he sees a strange flash. When his eyes refocus, Jacob tells Louis that he "looks like an angel . . . an overgrown cherub." During a scene in the middle of the film, Jezebel asks Jacob if she's still an angel. He responds, "with wings. You transport me, you know that? You carry me away." What she says next demonstrates how Rubin combines Eastern thought—it's all mind—with Western symbolism, "We're all angels, you know . . . and devils. It's just what you choose to see." Another scene that contains Western ideology (but one that also sounds very Buddhist) occurs after Jacob has hurt his back and has been rushed to the hospital. Terrified by the horrors he must confront, such as an eyeless doctor, Jacob is eventually rescued by Louis, who asks his patient if he's ever read Meister Eckhart, the medieval German theologian. "He saw hell, too," Louis says. "You know what he said? The only thing that burns in hell is the part of you that won't let go of your life—your memories, your attachments. They burn 'em all away, but they're not punishing you, he said. They're freeing your soul. So the way he sees it, if you're frightened of dying and holding on, you'll see devils tearing your life away. But if you've made your peace then the devils are really angels freeing you from the earth. It's just a matter of how you look at it, that's all." In his memoir, Rubin explains how Eastern religions concur with Eckhart on this matter. For them, the body doesn't die, he said, only the illusion of the body does. And if one isn't prepared to be stripped of these illusions, death will be painful. "If you have spent a lifetime angrily fighting with the world around you, you may not enjoy discovering that you have, in fact, been doing battle with yourself. You will fight this knowledge. You will see terrifying visions. Hell will become a real place." The opposite perspective yields the opposite result—death is seen as liberation. These, he said, are the underlying themes of *Jacob's Ladder*.[181] One final, overtly Judeo-Christian moment in *Jacob's Ladder* occurs when a chemist named Michael recites Psalm 23:4: "Yea, though I walk through the valley of the shadow of death, I shall fear no evil," before giving Jacob a demon-dispelling drug that "sends him to Paradise."

Rubin, himself, is Jewish by birth, but admits to having "an inner life that transcends religious form."[182] His interest in Tibetan Buddhism is well documented, and in the late 1960s he even ventured to Nepal, where he had a three-hour conversation with the Dalai Lama, who "volunteered to adopt Rubin as his first non-Tibetan student."[183] The story behind *Jacob's Ladder*, as recounted by writer Jeffrey Paine, is that "Rubin had been reading the *Tibetan Book of the Dead* for six months when he decided to sample" some LSD from his refrigerator. "During the next 24 hours he felt he lived a billion years and a million lives. He was subsequently seen not back at work at NBC but living among the Tibetans in Nepal and northern India."[184] According to Rubin, *Jacob's Ladder* began as a dream, one that saw him traversing the bowels of New York City. "The more I examined the dream, the more the movie emerged. This would not be the story of a man going to hell, but of a man already there. It would be the story of a man who had already died, but did not know it. . . . The horror of the movie would be in the revelation that hope is hell's final torment, that life is a dream that ends over and over with the final truth, that life is never real, that we are all creatures trapped in eternal suffering and damnation. The only problem that I had with this idea was that I did not believe it."[185] As he explains, many Eastern religions talk about the various after-life realms, including heaven and hell, not as actual places but as projections of the mind with the goal of going beyond mind. "Ultimately it is believed that all human beings will awake to the entrapment of these illusions, that they will step off the endless wheel of life and death, and find nirvana, peace, the cessation of suffering. The trick for me was how do I write a movie about this?"[186] Inspired by Robert Enrico's *Occurrence at Owl Creek Bridge* and *The Tibetan Book of the Dead*, Rubin wrote and rewrote his script.

As we read his account, we learn that Rubin struggled to present Eastern themes to a Western audience that hadn't "transcended the principal of duality, of good and evil."[187] "I wanted to see the spirit of a man escape the duality of human existence," he writes, "the complexity of good and evil, the enthrallment of light and dark. That's why I had written the film. It was the whole reason for its existence."[188] Furthermore, having been raised in a Judeo-Christian culture, he admitted to having had a difficult time transcending his own classical images of heaven and hell. For example, for Jacob's demons, he was inspired by the hybrid creatures found in Hieronymus Bosch's paintings, and for his treatment of heaven, he drew upon engravings by Gustave Dore, because he said that they "are probably the best realizations of angelic space I have seen."[189] It was British director Adrian Lyne who balked at using this imagery, because "he despised the image of devils with horns and pointed tails," Rubin writes in his memoir. "He felt that people are too familiar with the classical renderings of the demonic soul."[190] Further-more, the Dore images didn't "enthuse him. Hell has been tamed by familiar-ity. He wanted something contemporary that would burn itself into the audience's consciousness."[191] Unconventionally, Lyne chose to use a hospital as a manifestation of the underworld.

Rubin had considerable difficulty getting studio executives to green-light a movie version of *Jacob's Ladder*. Even though many loved his script, it went unproduced for nearly a decade. In fact, a writer for the *American Film* mag-azine had included it in his list of the 10 best unproduced screenplays in Hol-lywood. Rubin, at one time, was even dropped by his agent because his work was deemed "too metaphysical."[192] *Jacob's Ladder* is often seen as simply a hor-ror film or a thriller with audience's missing its Eastern vocabulary com-pletely, probably because it is still largely unknown to them. And judging by feedback and reviews, it's a film that cinemagoers either love or hate.

REINCARNATION

In general, most Hindus and Buddhists believe in reincarnation or rebirth. Even though this concept doesn't belong to the monotheistic tradition,[193] the number of Westerners who believe in it is on the rise. For instance, in 1950 a survey was conducted in England, and 5% of the responders said they believed in reincarnation. In 1990, the number was between 12 and 24%.[194] For the past 30 years, Hollywood has increasingly used reincarnation as a plot device. A short list of films that deal with reincarnation, although typically envisioned from a Judeo-Christian[195] perspective are *Audrey Rose* (1977), a man (An-thony Hopkins) attempts to convince a family that their 11-year-old girl is ac-tually his reincarnated daughter; *Heaven Can Wait* (1978), a Los Angeles Rams quarterback (Warren Beatty) comes back as a recently murdered millionaire (James Mason); *Oh Heavenly Dog* (1980), a private investigator (Chevy Chase) comes back as a dog (Benji) and must solve his murder; *All of Me* (1984), the soul of a dying millionaire (Lily Tomlin) is transferred, accidentally, into her lawyer's body (Steve Martin); *Switch* (1991), a womanizing male chauvinist (Perry King) is murdered only to come back as a sexy blonde (Ellen Barkin); *Prelude to a Kiss* (1992), while a young couple is walking down the aisle, an old man comes up and kisses the bride, resulting in a strange transference; *The Dark* (2005), a couple (Maria Bello and Sean Bean) who recently lost their daughter, Sarah, is visited by a young girl who claims to have died 60 years ago and who bears an uncanny resemblance to Sarah; and *The Return* (2006), a traveling businesswoman (Sarah Michelle Gellar) begins having nightmares of a murder that took place nearly two decades ago.

Rinne (2005)—Directed by Takashi Shimizu, written by Takashi Shimizu and Masonari Adachi. Running time: 96 min. Japanese. Japan. Rated R for violent and disturbing content. Genre: Horror.

A recent film that deals with reincarnation from a Buddhist perspective is the Japanese horror film *Rinne*, known in English as *Reincarnation* (2005). *Rinne* is essentially a film within a film within a film. A famed Japanese director, Matsumura (Kippei Shiina), is making *Memories*, a movie based on one of the "most brutal indiscriminating murders in Showa's history." The perpetrator was Professor Omori (Shun Oguri), who, for whatever reason, went on a murderous rampage in a hotel that left 11 dead, including all of the employees, hotel guests, and his 10-year-old son and 6-year-old daughter. His wife, although wounded, survived. After the murders, the professor killed himself. The most disturbing part of the 35-year-old case is that Omori filmed the entire event. Matsumura bases his screenplay on the murders; however, his focus isn't on the offender but on the victims, because, as he explains, "It's regretful that they died. They endured to live and feared to die. That's what I wanted to express. By doing so, I think I can let them rest in peace." Aspiring actress Nagisa Sugiura (Yuka) is handpicked to play the part of the murdered daughter, and even before she is cast, she has visions of a long-haired girl who is dressed in a yellow dress and carries an oversize doll. Her costars, too, have strange visions and nightmares about the decades-old crime. When shooting begins, the cast members begin to suffer very familiar fates—the same ones that they are to act out in the film.

To establish the concept of reincarnation, the film begins with three young women discussing what they were in their past lives. One was supposedly a penguin; another was a fleeing soldier. Even though the penguin is "cute," it is rationalized that being a fleeing soldier is better because it is human. In Buddhism, human births, because of their rarity and for the opportunity they present for getting out of *samsara*, are preferable. During an audition, an aspiring actress named Yuka Morita (Marika Matsumoto) says that although she doesn't like horror films, she would love to play the role of a murder victim.

When pressed further she responds, "I was killed once in a previous life. Therefore, I could use that experience in my acting." She continues, "It seems like I still have memories from it. Since I was a child, I sometimes remember things I'm not supposed to know. It's probably because I had experienced those before I was reincarnated. It was a woman. She was probably strangled to death." What makes this scene particularly interesting, from an American perspective, is that no one seems surprised by what she says. If this same script had been used in a Hollywood production, this scene would have been played for comic relief, with everyone around her either rolling their eyes or laughing. As Takashi Shimizu explained in *Memories of Reincarnation*, a DVD bonus feature, in Japan the concept of reincarnation is a well established, because of Buddhism and Shinto. In fact, "Shinri-kyo claims that people are reincarnations of their ancestors and that if there is unhappiness or misery, the essential cause lies with the ancestors."[196] Because Americans don't draw from the same religious traditions, Shimizu didn't believe that *Rinne* would be popular in America, where it was shown as part of the After Dark Horrorfest 2006. When asked about his personal beliefs on reincarnation, the director replied that "A part of me wants to believe it, but I won't know until I die . . . I don't know what to say. If I say I believe it, people may think I'm a weird guy that believes in reincarnation and makes horror movies."

To offer a balanced view of "recalled memories," *Rinne* includes a scene during which a psychology professor lectures on "cryptomnesia phenomenon." As he explains, "This particular symptom is often linked to the term 'past life,' or the concepts of 'reincarnation' and 'transmigration.' As for the religious and the moralists, they use it as convenient material to prove their own religious beliefs." This is immediately followed by a discussion between two students. The woman, Yayoi Kinoshita (Karina), explains that she has a reoccurring dream about a hotel that she had never seen before. Laughing, the male student says, "Didn't you listen to the lecture? Isn't it, what . . . crypto. . ." The woman interrupts him, "There is a triangle-shaped red roof like this. The walls and the hallways felt so real." He counters with, "I bet you've been there. You just don't remember. Maybe when you were a child?" She says no, "When I looked at my old album, I didn't see any photos like that. I asked my parents but they didn't know where it was." She continues, saying that when she asked her mother about it, her mother was surprised, because when the woman was a child she "really wanted to go to the hotel in my dream."

Obviously, a horror film titled *Reincarnation* will support the traditional religious belief over a psychological theory coined by Theodore Flournoy (1854–1921). And it does. Still intrigued by her dreams, Yayoi Kinoshita asks her male friend to introduce her to Yuka Morita. During a shared drink in the university cafeteria, Yukia asks Yayoi if they've met before. When Yayoi says no, Yuka replies, "I'm sorry. That might be from my previous life." Yayoi asks her if this sort of thing happens to her frequently. "You know, sometimes you seem to know a place even though you've never been there before." Yayoi replies, "It's déjà vu, isn't it?" "That happens to everybody, but you just can't remember." So how does one tell the difference between past-life memory and forgotten memories, Yayoi asks. "It's easy. Do some research." And together, the women go to the library, where Yuka finds a newspaper article about the 35-year-old massacre. Pointing to one of the victims' photos, she says, "This person was me in a previous life. It says she was strangled." To prove her point, the woman removes her purple scarf and reveals a very noticeable purple "birthmark" under her chin that stretches from ear to ear, which looks as if a ligature had just been removed. The correspondence between a person's birthmark or birth defect and a remembered wound that usually resulted in one's previous death is not unusual. Accounts have been found all over the globe. Intrigued by this, Ian Stevenson, M.D., has spent more than three decades researching this subject, and in 1997, Praeger published his exhaustive sourcebook titled *Reincarnation and Biology: A Contribution to the Etiology of Birthmarks and Birth Defects*.

Wanting to learn more about the murders, Yayoi seeks out the only survivor—Ayumi (Miki Sanjo), the wife of the killer. When she arrives at the el-derly woman's house, she prays at the *butsudan* or household Buddhist altar, where we see lit candles, photos of the deceased, and two *ihai* or memorial tablets. Typically made of black lacquer embossed in gold, the *ihai* is often considered to be "the place of abode of the ancestors."[197] "I'm praying for them every day," the mother says. "However, those children have not found peace yet. That's what I feel." Yayoi presents to Ayumi a drawing of two children standing in front of the fateful hotel then she relates that she drew the image as a child. "Have you been there?" the old woman asks. "I have never been there before," she replies, "but I used to have dreams about his house over and over." The old woman retrieves a scrapbook, and gives it to Yayoi. Inside, she finds photographs, scribbled notes, and newspaper clippings. Even though everyone believed Professor Omori to be crazy, his widow said that after rereading his notes, she found something much different. In the scrapbook we see the words, "the human body is just a vessel." "Somehow, he got off the track from his specialty field. Where do humans come from? Where do they go? Will our memories and thoughts disappear when our bodies are dead? He was studying that subject very seriously." At this moment, we watch another flashback, during which Omori is filming his children in the bathroom. He stops, tells them, "I'll see you again," and raises a knife to kill them. "I wonder if he was experimenting with them," the widow says.

As in most Asian horror films,[198] ghosts are ever present in *Rinne*. As Shimizu explains in *Memories of Reincarnation*, unlike American horror films, which rely on external forces such as monsters and psychopaths wearing masks for scares, the Japanese tend to prefer psychological horror; where the scares come from within. Another difference is that the Japanese typically don't draw a line between the everyday world and the spirit world. "Nearly every festival, every ritual, every custom is bound up in some way with relationships between the living and the dead, between the present family and its ancestors, between the present occupation and its forebears."[199] Although this doesn't stem from Buddhism, many Japanese believe that when a person dies, he or she may stay in spectral form, especially in the case of "unfulfilled obligations, a need for vengeance, feelings of jealousy, the desire for proper burial or more ritual,"[200] and interact with the living.

Japanese ideas regarding death and the afterlife are quite complex, primarily because they stem from several different religious traditions, including Buddhism, Shinto, and folk religion. From Buddhism, they get the idea of rebirth into various heavens and hells as rewards and punishments. From Shinto comes the concept that after death people go to the Land of Yomi, a dark underworld. And from folk beliefs, they learn of a spirit world with which shamans can communicate. Furthermore, "Folk belief holds that there is a ghostly realm interlaced with the world of humans. Under certain conditions, the spirits (called *tamashii* or simply *tama*) present themselves to the living."[201] This is certainly the case in *Rinne*. The professor's deceased daughter is frequently seen, playing with a red ball or clutching her doll and staring menacingly. Ghosts of the murdered employees also appear throughout the film, peering into Nagisa's peephole, standing in a forest, and appearing in reflective images. Once the cast and crew return to the "scene of the crime," we see the spirits of the deceased walking and standing around, just as they did in life. And at the end, their reincarnated selves must relive their previous deaths.

Buddhism isn't the only religious tradition in Japan, and *Rinne* reflects that. Before shooting on the film begins, a Shinto priest performs an *oharai* (purification) ceremony. The purpose of it is to ensure the safety and success of the film, by ridding the place, person, or object of "impurities that could be causes of misfortune."[202] In a dream sequence about 50 minutes into *Rinne*, Nagisa stands in the middle of the street, a large white *torii* or gateway to a Shinto shrine appears in the background.

Karma is the driving force in *Rinne*. The professor has committed heinous acts, and for those acts there will be consequences. Early in the film, we believe—as Nagisa does—that she has a connection to the murdered girl, because she is that girl reincarnated. And why wouldn't we? After all, Nagisa is timid, quiet voiced, and seemingly innocent. She also re-experiences the murders through the eyes of a victim not the perpetrator. This is why the ending of the film packs such a tremendous punch. All of the reincarnated victims are drawn to the hotel, where they all die again. We learn that Yuka was indeed who she thought she was—the strangled maid. The director, Matsumura, was the 10-year-old son of Omori. Yayoi was the 6-year-old daughter, and she dies in the closet, still clutching the creepy animated doll that says, "We'll stay together forever." And Nagisa, who earlier in the film has mysteriously "found" the 8-mm movie projector, is revealed to be Omori himself. Her karmic "fate" is the worst of all, because she is unable to escape her "undead" victims who keep coming for her.

If we consult with the Wheel of Life and examine the eight hell realms, we find that those who kill other beings are reborn into *samjiva* or hell of repetition. This overarching hell has 16 subdivisions, including the "Hell of Many Pains," which is "reserved for those who torment or torture others. Those who crush, burn, smoke or hang other beings by various methods, who torment *children* [my emphasis] or enemies are tortured in this hell exactly as they caused others to suffer." [203] Based on this description alone, we might conclude that Nagisa has been consigned to this hell realm, either mentally or physically. By being cast as the girl in the film, Nagisa must relive the murders, experiencing the fear, pain, and suffering that she inflicted on her victims. In one particularly poignant scene, the director pulls out the murdered girl's doll from a box, and tells his lead actress that it "must have a soul of regret." He then makes her "think deeply of that girl when she was killed as she held this doll." We can only surmise that none of the events in the end of the film actually "happened," they were simply mental afflictions, as seen in the last scene, where Nagisa is in a full body restraining device in a mental ward. As her last act of "vengeance," Omori's widow opens a slot in the door and throws in her daughter's doll and her son's red ball. The children appear in the cell, saying "We'll stay together forever." Omori's punishment continues.

Just as the hell realms dissuade people from performing unwholesome acts, they also act as "the dark labyrinths of the mind encumbered by the obstacles of ignorance and self-deceit. The purpose of this grotesque portrayal of human torment is to initiate the individual seeking enlightenment into the horror chambers existing within himself where he can identify with the faceless anonymous sinners suffering immeasurable torments." The idea is that those who reflect on these, in light of the dharma, will be freed from the bonds of ignorance and attain nirvana.[204]

Groundhog Day (1993)—Directed by Harold Ramis, written by Danny Rubin and Harold Ramis. Running time: 101 min. English. USA. Rated PG for some thematic elements. Genre: Comedy/Fantasy/Romance.

Karma is also behind the events in *Groundhog Day* (1993). This comedy focuses on a self-centered, sarcastic, callous, and sometimes cruel weatherman, Phil Connors (Bill Murray), who reluctantly travels to Punxsutawney, Pennsylvania, to cover the annual Groundhog Festival. With six more weeks of winter predicted, a blizzard begins, stranding Connors, his cameraman, Larry (Chris Elliott), and his producer, Rita (Andie MacDowell). For an undisclosed reason, Phil wakes up the next day and discovers that it's February 2, Groundhog Day, all over again. The next day is the same, and the next and the next. He must repeat the same day until he can learn that what he does affects the outcome.

About 30 minutes into the film, Phil says that "You make choices and you live with them." Unfortunately, most of his choices have been driven by ego. He loathes other people, and when he does talk to them, it's so he can manipulate them. For example, he asks one woman details about her past so that the next day he can pretend to know her, with the objective of getting her into bed. At another time, he memorizes an armored car's routine so that he can steal from it. And so on. Believing that he's immortal, he goes on a reckless car ride across some railroad tracks, takes up smoking, and eats a table full of cakes and doughnuts. His typically happy and optimistic producer is disgusted by what she sees, and she recites from Sir Walter Scott: "the wretch, concentered all in self. Living, shall forfeit fair renown. And, doubly dying, shall go down. To the vile dust, from whence he sprung. Unwept, unhonor'd, and unsung." He laughs at her suggestion that he's egocentric, because he fails to see things as they truly are.

As his days in Punxsutawney turn into months and possibly decades,[205] Phil becomes embittered and depressed. What was once fun has become an indeterminable hell, and, thinking that the groundhog is the key to his situation, he kidnaps it and with it on the steering wheel, he drives off a cliff. Not dying in the subsequent explosion, Phil tries killing himself in other ways—electrocuting himself, standing in front of a truck, and jumping from a tower. But he cannot die even though he's also been stabbed, shot, poisoned, frozen, and hung. "I'm a god," he tells Rita. "I'm not the God, I don't think . . . I am an immortal." To prove his divine status, he goes around the diner and tells her what he knows about its customers. Incredulous at his accuracy, she asks him if it's a trick. "Maybe the real God uses tricks. Maybe he's not omnipotent. He's just been around so long He knows everything."

Whereas Phil is unfeeling, self-absorbed, and impatient, Rita is, as Harold Ramis described her, pure of soul and spirit, she's kind, generous, forgiving, and honest.[206] At first, Phil thinks he can manipulate her as he's done with the other women. But the minute she smells a rat, she responds with a slap to the face. Over time, as he starts listening to her and responding to her, his interest goes beyond the superficial. He develops a genuine interest in her and eventually he falls in love. As he says to her while she's sleeping, "I think you're the kindest, sweetest, prettiest person I've ever met in my life. I've never seen anyone who's nicer to people than you are." Rita exhibits many characteristics of a bodhisattva. She is full of joy and faith, and concentrates on developing the perfection of generosity to a high degree. She prays for world peace, and even though Phil is a "jerk" she spends time with him, maybe because she looks beyond his nasty exterior and realizes that he's suffering and in pain. Furthermore, she avoids being immoral—she won't sleep with Phil—and is patient and compassionate. She uses her insight to see into Phil's character so that she can guide and teach him in "the most precisely appropriate ways."[207] She is the person that Phil needs to become.

In what could be seen as the turning point in the film, Rita spends the day with Phil, and while they are sitting on his bed and tossing cards into a hat, he tells her that the worst thing about his eternity in Punxsutawney is that tomorrow she will have forgotten all about this, and she will treat him like a jerk again. She denies this. "It's all right. I am a jerk," he says, indicating that for the first time he's developing mindfulness. Why the change of heart? "I've killed myself so many times," he says, "I don't even exist anymore." "Sometimes I wish I had 1,000 lifetimes," Rita counters. "I don't know, Phil. Maybe it's not a curse. It just depends on how you look at it." Again, *Groundhog Day* echoes the idea that "all is mind." If Phil thinks that he's living in hell, it will be a hell. If he thinks positively and tries to use the time to change, it can be a kind of heaven.

After this scene, Phil meets the homeless man—the same one he's passed by countless of times—and he finally stops and hands over a wad of money. Smiling and carrying coffee and pastry, Phil walks up to his coworkers and, for once, he doesn't tell them what to do; he asks them what they think they should do about setting up the camera. He then lends a hand in carrying the equipment and he even strikes up a conversation with his cameraman. Phil is becoming a changed man. Rather than complaining about his situation, he takes up piano lessons and learns how to create ice sculptures. He also gives love to the world rather than sarcasm. On another day, Phil meets the homeless man in an alley. He is out of breath, so Phil takes him to the hospital, but it's too late. The man dies. Realizing that he can do something about it, the next day, he takes him to the diner and feeds him. But the man dies again, even after Phil tries to resuscitate him. From this moment on, Phil begins doing good deeds—saving a child who falls from a tree, helping three women who have a flat tire, and saving a man who's choking. But he's no longer performing actions for himself (wrong intention), he wants to improve the lives of others (right intention). Rather than trying to *be* a good person, he *is* a good person. And that's what makes Rita fall in love with him.

As Thich Nhat Hanh writes, "Love, compassion, joy and equanimity are the very nature of an enlightened person. They are the four aspects of true love within ourselves and within everyone and everything." He continues, saying that to develop the first aspect of true love, we have to "practice look-ing and listening deeply so that we know what to do and what not to do to make others happy." We also have to understand them and their needs oth-erwise the love isn't true.[208] As the film progresses, Phil starts listening to what others have to say, not so he can get the upper hand but because he de-velops a genuine interest in them. When he first arrives in Punxsutawney, he calls the locals "hicks" because he only sees them from the outside. Once he knows them, deeply, he wants to settle down there, realizing that they are friendly and kind.

The second aspect of true love is *karuna*, which is the "intention and ca-pacity to relieve and transform suffering and lighten sorrow." Also known as compassion, *karuna* means that a person feels genuine concern for others and tries to relieve their suffering.[209] In the beginning, Phil doesn't care about any-one but himself. He sees the homeless man on the corner and just walks on by. Eventually, he comes to see him as a human being, and even takes to calling him "Pop" and "Dad." He also realizes that this man must be cold, hungry, and lonely. Wanting to ease his suffering, Phil gives him money, food, and medical services, and he also spends time with him. The homeless man isn't the only recipient of this kindness; Phil extends it to the entire town. As is said during the DVD documentary, *Weight of Time*, for him, "It isn't about being the hero of the town, it's about doing what you can do in the moment to make things better instead of making things worse. If other people interpret that as you be-ing the god of the town, which in a way he becomes, so be it, but that isn't his aim." As Harold Ramis adds, "When he stops worrying about himself all the time and starts living a life of service to others then his life gets very full and rich, indeed. And when he embraces where he is and what he can do."

The third aspect of love is joy, which a person brings to himself or herself and then extends to others. Joy comes from living in the present and being thankful for the small things in life,[210] such as the snow on the ground, the fact that we are able-bodied, and that we have friends. In the beginning, Phil sees his job as a stepping stone; he would rather be a bigger star at a larger network. He doesn't appreciate Punxsutawney—the place or its people—and he can't wait to do his newscast so he can leave it behind. Rita, on the other hand, ex-hibits true joy. She thinks the Groundhog Day story is sweet, and she enjoys watching the excitement of the townspeople. Not only does she feel joy for herself, but she delights in the joy of others.

The fourth element is probably the most difficult to attain, and that's "equanimity, nonattachment, nondiscrimination, even-mindedness, or letting go . . . we shed all discrimination and prejudice, and remove all boundaries between ourselves and others."[211] Whether the characters achieve this or not is difficult to say; however, Phil has certainly grown from his initial encounters with Rita. In the beginning when she mentions her love of French poetry or her prayers for world peace, he is flippant, almost condescending to her. But once he tries "stepping into her shoes," his judgmental attitude falls away. In the end, he comes to appreciate her for who she is not for what she can do for him. As Ramis says during *The Weight of Time*, Phil goes from "looking like a man who is in love to actually being in love." As someone says in the documentary, "The greatest gift for [Phil] is becoming finite again, he's going to die, he's going to age, and time will go on. But now he has the keys to use that time well, and to begin that journey of time he wakes up and is with his beloved."

Of the film, Ramis explained that it contains a "Nietzchean/Buddhist premise of eternal repetition and what we could learn from it. And the response from the spiritual community was unbelievable. I literally got letters from every known religious organization and discipline . . . all claiming the movie, all saying you must be one of us because this movie so perfectly expresses our philosophy." Ramis, however, claims that the concept of a man who no longer thinks about himself but starts performing service is "what Mahayana Buddhism is all about."[212] The writer, Danny Rubin, explained in the documentary, *The Weight of Time*, that the film allows us to experience what Phil does; therefore, we, too, go through the catharsis of realizing that our lives are pointless and then, after emptying out completely, we get to rebuild and realize that our lives do have a point.

NOTABLE DIRECTORS

Khyentse Norbu

Khyentse Norbu, also known as His Eminence Dzongsar Jamyang Khyentse Rinpoche, was born in 1961 in a remote area of eastern Bhutan. At seven years old, he was recognized as the third incarnation of Jamyang Khyentse Wangpo, a 19th-century saint, scholar, and principal lama of Tibet's Dzongsar Monastery. Until 12 years old, he pursued his studies at the Palace Monastery of Gangtok, Sikkum. He continued his education in Bhutan, and later India, studying Buddhist philosophy. He had his first encounter with film when he was 19 years old. While traveling from his home to college, he caught a glimpse of a Bollywood epic on TV in an Indian railway station. Not long after this, filmmaker Raymond Steiner gave him his first lesson in photography. Eventually the monk made his way to London's School of Oriental and African Studies. In the early 1990s, he enrolled in a four-week course at the New York Film Academy, and he was hired to be a consultant on Bernardo Bertolucci's *Little Buddha*, in which he has a minor role at the end. It was under this Italian master that he acquired an apprenticeship of sorts. He continued his education by watching the films of Ozu, Tarkovsky, and Satyajit Ray, and he parlayed what he learned into his 1995 short, *Ette Metto*, which focuses on village life in Bhutan. The 24-minute film was inspired by Tagore. He followed this one year later with *The Big Smoke*, a six-minute short about "life as a storyteller's story." Neither film has been released.

In 1999, he wrote and directed his first feature *Phorpa*, in English known as *The Cup*. Inspired by a true story, the film focuses on two young boys Palden (Kunsang Nyima) and Nylma (Pema Tshundup) who have fled Tibet for the monastery-in-exile in the Himalayan foothills of northern India. After they are ordained as monks, they get swept up in soccer fever. Palden's roommate, Orygen (Jamyang Lodro), and the latter's friend, Lodo (Neten Choklin), are soccer crazy and will do anything to see the World Cup soccer final match on TV. The film is notable for a variety of reasons. Not only was the cast and crew made up of nonactors—they were mostly monks and novices at the Chokling Monastery—but the film was also the first feature-length film to be made in Bhutan. About the film, Norbu said, "I see *The Cup* as an insider look at the touchstones of Tibetan culture and society, especially now, when they face the insecurities of exile and the challenges of a modern world. But this isn't just a Tibetan issue. It's something faced by traditional cultures everywhere. That's why I identify so much with the character of Geko. He's torn, isn't he? On the one hand, he knows there's no way to preserve the essence of the Buddhist teachings without some basic discipline. On the other hand, he understands just how important this business of winning a football cup is. What should he do?"[213] Furthermore, the director explains that the film dispels the myth that all monks are pious and disciplined. People "forget that monks are human too. The monastic code is an ideal, a goal to be hit."[214] *The Cup* is rated G and has a running time of 93 minutes.

Four years would pass before Norbu would again venture behind the camera. His sophomore effort, *Travellers and Magicians*, is once again set in Bhutan, and it focuses on Dondup[215] (Tsewang Dandup), an impatient government officer who, after living one month in a small village, is so bored that he decides to seek his opportunity in "the land of his dreams," the United States, a place where he believes he can make a lot of money. On his journey out of town, Dondup meets an old apple seller (Ap Dochu), a monk (Sonam Kinga), a rice papermaker (Dasho Adab Sangye), and his 19-year-old daughter, Sonam (Sonam Lhamo). To pass the time while they are waiting for a ride, the monk tells his own story[216] about a "dreamland." The lead character in his tale is Tashi (Lhakpa Dorji), the eldest son of a farmer who is sent to study magic. His flaw is that he is lazy and only thinks of girls. His younger brother, Karma (Namgay Dorjee), is smarter but no one realizes this, so he is kept at home to work. Like Dondup, neither brother is satisfied with his life. Tashi isn't interested in school, he only dreams of faraway places; and Karma thinks that life would be better if he were in school.

One day during lunch, Karma tricks his brother into thinking that he's drinking wine, when he's actually drugged him. Seeing a horse instead of their donkey, Tashi climbs on and goes for a wild ride into a remote part of the forest. A storm erupts and Tashi, who is injured and has lost his horse,[217] is forced to take refuge with Agay (Gomchen Penjore), an old man, and Deki (Deki Yangzom), his young, very beautiful wife. During his extended stay, Tashi becomes infatuated with the man's wife, falling under her spell. His unwholesome thoughts soon lead to lust, adultery, and murder. As the monk says, "We human beings can be savages when driven by passion." As is often the case, once the "lovers" have poisoned the old man, and he hasn't yet died, they begin fighting. Tashi runs away to escape his situation, and she follows. When he turns back to find her, it's too late; she's fallen into the river and has drowned. Thus the illusion of beauty, love, and permanence evaporates. The same goes for Dondup. In the beginning of the film he can't wait to leave Bhutan, but once he meets Sonam he changes his mind. To this the monk says, "A peach blossom is beautiful. But you see a blossom is only beautiful because it is temporary."

What's particularly Buddhist about the film is its message of living in the present. As the monk says, "The minds of human beings are so convoluted. What we hoped for yesterday, we dread today." The film also cautions the viewer that "the grass isn't always greener on the other side of the fence." When asked why he's leaving Bhutan, Dondup says that he can make a lot of money in the United States, even by washing dishes or picking apples. To this the monk replies, "So, you're giving up an officer's job to pick apples? Just don't get lost there like Tashi." And, he cautions, "You should be careful with dreamlands, because when you wake up, it may not be very pleasant." In Tashi's story, we see that no one is happy with his or her situation in life. Tashi envies the old man for having such a beautiful wife, but he fails to see the treachery in her heart. Having spent so many years with the same woman, the old man no longer sees her beauty but sees her as a thing to possess. Because his wife is so much younger than he, they must live in a very isolated place— otherwise, "some young man would have taken her long ago." "We men may grow old," he continues, "but our minds don't age. Our jealousy stays young." The film also subtly stresses the value of living not for oneself but for others. For instance, Sonam has good enough scores to go to university but she de- cides to return to the village to help her father. After all, her mother is dead and he's all alone. "Isn't it our duty to look after our parents when they're old?" she asks Dondup. He, on the other hand, doesn't care that the village could benefit from a young man such as himself; he only wants excitement and money. Even when he seems to do a good act—letting the apple seller take the only seat on a bus—he has an ulterior motive: to stay with Sonam. Finally, the film suggests that living a simpler, rural life is best. When Sonam and her father leave the traveling party, the monk tells her to stay in the village because "urban life is depressing."

As in the case of *The Cup*, no professional actors were used in making *Trav- ellers and Magicians*. In keeping with the ways of the country, many major production decisions were determined by *mo*, an ancient method of divina- tion performed by specially skilled lamas. Also in line with Norbu's Buddhist beliefs, special religious ceremonies known as *pujas* were performed through- out production to remove obstacles, quell local demons, and increase auspi- ciousness.[218] Shot entirely in the Dzongkha dialect, the official language of Bhutan, *Travellers and Magicians* is rated PG and has a running time of 108 minutes.

Some people might find it odd that Norbu is a Buddhist monk who is mak- ing films, and he has addressed this in interviews. "Film is a medium and Bud- dhism is a science. You can be a scientist and at the same time, you can be a filmmaker," he said. Furthermore, he has said that "film could be seen as a modern-day *thangka*. Having said that, I am not claiming that either of my films are spiritual, though, because of my obvious background, you might find a little of Buddhist influence in both works."[219]

Byambasuren Davaa

Born in 1971 in Mongolia, Byambasuren Davaa worked as a speaker and assistant director for Mongolia's Public TV before attending the Film Academy in Ulaanbaatar, the country's capital. In 2000, she moved to Munich, where she began studying documentary film at the Academy of Television and Film. Two projects that are of particular interest to us are *The Story of the Weeping Camel* (2003), for which she and Luigi Falorni received an Academy Award in the best documentary category, and *The Cave of the Yellow Dog* (2005). The 2003 docudrama[220] is set in South Mongolia, in the Gobi Desert, and it centers on an eight-person, multigenerational nomadic family of shepherds. During the film's 93 minutes, we witness their often harsh way of life and their close kinship with their sheep and camels. The story behind the documentary is that after a difficult pregnancy, one of their camels gives birth to a white colt and then rejects it. The family does everything in its power to reconcile the mother and infant, including sending their two sons across the desert to find a healing musician so that they can perform a "Hoos ritual." When the man finally arrives, he hangs a violin over the mother camel's hump and lets the wind blow through it. This seems to calm the mother. The young mother of the family sings to the camel while stroking her side. The musician begins playing. The colt is brought over to its mother, and, after more singing and playing, the mother camel finally allows her colt to suckle. The reconciliation complete, the mother camel weeps.

At the beginning of the film, the grandfather tells us the legend of the camel, saying that many years ago, God gave antlers to the camel as a reward for the goodness of its heart. One day a rogue deer came and asked to borrow them. The camel trusted him, so he lent them to the deer. This was a mistake, as the deer never brought them back. Since then camels keep gazing at the horizon, awaiting the deer's return. A bit later, he tells another story about the camel. When God created the zodiac, he says, the camel wanted to be one of the signs. Unfortunately, God couldn't grant his wish. Instead, he gave the animal some of the traits of the other 12 animals of the zodiac, such as the tail of the snake, ears of the pig, and eyes of the ox. In addition to hearing myth, we see religious ritual. At the beginning of the film, one of the grandmothers throws a milk-like substance to the four cardinal directions and prays. About 40 minutes into the film, most of the family members get dressed up and gather food for a ritual. They arrive at a wooden pole, wrapped in a blue cloth, where several lamas are accepting the offerings. A conch shell is blown, a bell rung, and the ceremony begins. "We, the Mongolian people, honor nature and its spirits," one lama says. "Nowadays, mankind plunders the earth more and more in search of her treasures. This drives the spirits away. [The ceremony] should protect us from bad weather and from diseases. We have to remember that we are not the last generation on Earth. Now we'll pray for forgiveness, so that the spirits may come back." Another bell is rung, and chanting begins. On a makeshift altar, we see small candles burning in front of clay effigies of humans and a camel. Inside the nomadic family's yurt, which is a temporary round house, we also see a laughing Buddha, images of a bodhisattva, and photos of the ancestors.

The traditional ways of life in Mongolia are being changed through modernization. So, as the director said in an interview, within this climate, for her next film she wanted to explore "which values and beliefs . . . the children [are] growing up with. Can tradition and modernization exist side by side in harmony?"[221] Thus begins *The Cave of the Yellow Dog*, a story about a five-member family of herders living in northwest Mongolia, an area to which Davaa has ancestral links. The docudrama begins with a father and his daughter burying a dog under some stones. The six-year-old girl, Nansal, asks him what he's doing with the dog's tail. He replies that he's putting it under its head, so that he'll be reborn as a person with a ponytail and not as a dog with a tail. Incredulous, the girl asks, "Oh, really?" The father then says that "Everyone dies, but no one is ever truly dead." Although what develops over the next 93 minutes is a story of the age-old bond between humans and animals, this one also has a Buddhist twist.

While out collecting dung for fuel, Nansal chances upon a cave-dwelling puppy. She brings it home, naming it Zochor, which means "colorful." Because of the dog's "uncertain origin," her father, Batchulum, fears that he might have been living with wolves and he tells her to get rid of it. She refuses. Nansal's mother offers a different take on the situation, saying that maybe it was "fate" that brought the dog into their lives. The mother ends up being "correct" because, at the end of the film when the family moves on to a new location, the father decides to leave the dog behind. He ties it to a stake, and they set off. After a short distance, they discover that they've "lost" their youngest. When the father goes back for his son, he finds that Zochor is protecting the boy from the gathering vultures. Having a change of heart, Nansal's father brings the dog back with him, and they continue their journey, dog in tow.

The "characters" in *The Cave of the Yellow Dog* talk a lot about reincarnation. For instance, about halfway through the film, Nansal ends up at her grandmother's yurt. During a conversation, the older woman says that Nansal is "lucky the dog didn't end up in the Cave of the Yellow Dog." When pressed as to what that is, the old woman begins a story: Long ago, a rich family lived in these lands. They had a daughter who became very ill. No medicine could cure her, so they turned to a wise man for advice. He told them that "your yellow dog is angry. You must send him away." "Why?" the father asked. "He protects our herd." The wise man offered no explanation. Since the father couldn't bear to kill the dog, he hid it in a cave from which it was impossible to escape. Every day he brought it food, until the one day when he found it missing. Because her parents had followed the wise man's advice, their daughter got better. She eventually fell in love with a young man, and they got married and had a child. Nansal asks what happened to the dog. To which her grandmother replies, "Perhaps the dog was reborn with a ponytail." Nansal asks if she will be reborn as a person in her next life. The grandmother takes a handful of rice and pours it over a needle that she's holding in her other hand. "Tell me when a grain of rice balances on the tip of the needle," she says. Nansal tries over and over again, then says, "That's impossible." "See . . . that's how hard it is to be born again as a person. That's why a human life is so valuable." In an interview, Davaa said that in this yurt, "Nansal gets to know her cultural and spiritual roots. The fable shows the viewer a new appreciation of life. . . . My grandmother told me the fable of the yellow dog many years ago and with it she communicated to me one of the greatest worldly wisdoms. With my film, I would like to make this story available to other people from other cultural backgrounds."[222] When the girl finally returns home, she queries her mother if she remembers her past lives. Her mother's reply is, "I don't think so." "Why not?" "Only little children can do that. They often tell colorful stories. People say they're talking about previous lives." "Did I talk about those things? What kinds of stories did I tell?" Nansa asks before her mother finally puts her to bed.

Several scenes in the film depict religious symbols and rituals. For instance, about 20 minutes into the film, we see the mother sitting in front of a mirrored dresser, on which there is a photo of the Dalai Lama, the Laughing Buddha covered with children, which is supposed to promote fertility, and an image of the Medicine Buddha. She lights a butter lamp and some incense, and it sounds as if she's whispering *Om Mani Padme Hum*. She also overturns a small metal container and pours a milk-like substance into it. At one point, Nansal's younger brother is playing with the ceramic Laughing Buddha, and the middle sister chastises him, saying, "You can't play with Buddha." Inside the grandmother's yurt, we see a *mala*, and butter lamps burning before a devotional image. And after the family has dismantled their yurt and are preparing to leave, they thank the "beautiful country of Khangai" for letting them spend the summer there. The husband puts a few rocks on top of each other in the center of where the yurt stood, and his wife pours milk over it and sings. She pours the remaining milk over the wheels of their cart. Both of Davaa's films are in Mongolian and are rated G.

On a final note, *Story of the Weeping Camel* and *Cave of the Yellow Dog* are perhaps the best known films about Mongolia and its people; however, within the last few years, a number of other films have been released that shed light on this vanishing culture, including *Mongolian Ping Pong* (*Lu Cao Di*), *Khadak.*

Mongolian Ping Pong (2005)—Written and directed by Hao Ning. Running
    time: 102 min. Mongolian. Unrated. Genre: Comedy/Drama.

The former comedy/drama is written and directed by Hao Ning. It has been referred to as a Mongolian version of *The Gods Must Be Crazy*, because both films demonstrate a collision of cultures with the introduction of a random object from modern culture into traditional life. In *Mongolian Ping Pong*, a ping pong ball is found floating in a stream on the Mongolian steppe. The prepubescent Bilike (Hurichabilike) finds it. At first he assumes it's a bird's egg, but his grandmother tells him that it's a magic glowing pearl sent by the gods. Unconvinced he and his friends, Erguotou (Geliban) and Dawa (Dawa), venture to a distant monastery, where they query the lamas. They, too, are stumped. Then, the answer arrives—on TV. Knowing now that this is the "national ball of China," the boys prepare for a very long trip to the country's capital, Beijing, so that they can return it. This award-winning film is in Mongolian with English subtitles. It has a running time of 102 minutes and is not rated.

Khadak (2006)—Written and directed by Peter Brosens and Jessica Hope Woodworth. Running time: 104 min. Mongolian. Unrated. Genre: Drama.

The award-winning *Khadak* isn't as straightforward, narratively, as *Mongolian Ping Pong*, because it draws upon the people's shamanic tradition. Set in the frozen steppes, the film centers on Bagi (Batzul Khayankhyarvaa), a teen-aged nomadic herder and his family. One day, while he is out retrieving a lost sheep, he suffers an epileptic fit. His concerned family members consult with a shamaness (Dashnyam Tserendarizav), who revives him and announces that he is destined to become a shaman. When he rejects his "calling," his grandmother tells him that denying such a destiny brings misfortune. Not long after, government officials arrive at Bagi's yurt, announcing that a plague affecting livestock is spreading through the land. To keep the people "safe," they must be relocated to a mining town. Their animals are then quarantined and killed. In this desolate and bleak mining town, Bagi meets Zolzaya (Tsetsegee Byamba), a rebellious coal thief whose life he saves. After he suffers another fit, he is hospitalized, and told by the physician that he can be treated with modern medicine. Not long after this, he has his first true shamanic journey, during which the shamaness from his village gives him a mirror. His soul struggles back through waterways and ruins but he cannot relocate his body. Zolzaya, who has a sort of psychic link to him, helps. As the film's official site (www.khadak.com) says, "with his mirror he causes blue sacred scarves to fall by the hundreds from the sky. A breathtaking revolution ensues."

Khadak is about a "community in transition in which external market forces are impacting the traditional lifestyle of the herdsmen." Politics play a part in the film; however, its real focus is, as the official site says, the "Mongolian worldview, which is a fusion of Tibetan Buddhism and Siberian shamanism. Most Mongolians believe that every individual has his or her own personal connection with *tengger*,' which can be translated as sky or heaven. The sky is considered the measurer of truth and is the ultimate judge of mans' actions. If ill is done by the hand of man then the sky will show its displeasure by inflicting a natural disaster upon the land. Symbolizing the sky is the sacred blue ceremonial scarf, one of the key visual motifs in the film. (*Khadak*) is about the human condition seen through a Mongolian prism with its ongoing movements and tensions between past and future, between growth and decay, between creation and destruction, between the search for meaning and the encounter with the absurd. But the most essential conversation the film should inspire is about man's fundamental need to rethink his relationship with nature." When *Khadak* was screened in Mongolia, 25 shamans attended. Afterward, they "expressed their deep respect and gratitude to the team, saying that the film is an incredibly accurate portrayal of their beliefs." The filmmakers, although not Mongolian, have spent much of their careers making films about the Mongolian landscape and its people. Between 1993 and 1999, Brosens directed and produced his so-called "Mongolian Trilogy," which consists of the documentaries *City of the Steppes*, *State of Dogs*, and *Poets of Mongolia*. Wentworth's first film, *Urga Song* (1999), was shot in Mongolia.

ENDNOTES

1. "World Factbook," *Central Intelligence Agency*, 2008, www.cia.gov/library/publications/the-world-factbook/ (accessed 14 February 2008).

2. American Religious Identification Survey, City University of New York, 2001, www.gc.cuny.edu/faculty/research_briefs/aris/key_findings.htm (accessed 14 February 2008). Some scholars estimate that there may be several million Buddhists in the United States, and have suggested that it is the country's fastest growing religion. See, for example, Charles S. Prebish and Kenneth K. Tanaka, eds., *The Faces of Buddhism in America* (Berkeley: University of California Press, 1998).

3. The term *Achsenzeit*, which translates to Axial Age or Axis Age, was coined by German philosopher Karl Jaspers in his book *Vom Ursprung und Ziel der Geschicte* (1949). In his discussion, he mentions Confucius and Lao-Tse of China, the Buddha in India, Zoroaster of Persia, the prophets in Palestine, and various philosophers in Greece. Karen Armstrong reinvigorated the term in her 2007 book *The Great Transformation: The Beginning of Our Religious Traditions*.

4. John S. Strong, *The Experience of Buddhism: Sources and Interpretations* (Belmont, CA: Wadsworth/Thomson Learning, 2002), 32–34.

5. Bhikkhu Bodhi, ed., *In the Buddha's Words: An Anthology of Discourses from the Pali Canon* (Somerville, MA: Wisdom, 2005), 87.

6. Scholars debate the actual dates of Siddhartha's birth and death. As Peter Harvey writes in his *Introduction to Buddhism: Teachings, History and Practices* (Cambridge: Cambridge University Press, 2002), 9: "Buddhist sources say that Gotama died either 218 or 100 years before the consecration of emperor Ashoka. From references in Asokan edicts to certain Greek kings, this

can be dated to c. 268 BCE." He continues saying that these accounts were generally accepted by scholars who listed his dates as ca. 566 to 486 BCE or 448 to 368 BCE. Modern scholars have listed his dates as ca. 480 to 400 BCE.

7. Siddhartha is often referred to as Shakyamuni, which means sage of the Shakya clan.

8. The details of Siddhartha Gautama's life must be gleaned from a number of texts, including "the Sarvastivadins' *Lalitavistara*, the Theravadins' *Nidanakatha*, and Asvaghosa's poem, the *Buddhacarita*." Stories of Siddhartha's past lives as animals, humans, and even gods, are known as Jataka Tales. It is also believed that Siddhartha was the fourth reincarnate of five earthly buddhas. For more about this, see Harvey, *Introduction to Buddhism: Teachings, History and Practices*, 14–31.

9. A *chakravartin* or *mahapurusha* (a great man) bears the 32 marks of perfection on his body, including "level feet; sign of a 1,000-spoked wheel on the soles of his feet; long, slender fingers; broad heels; curved toes and fingers; soft, smooth hands and feet; arched feet; lower body like an antelope's; arms reaching to the knee; virile member without narrowing in the foreskin; powerful body; hairy body; thick, curly body hair; golden-hued body; a body that gives off rays ten feet in every direction; soft skin; rounded hands, shoulders and head; well-formed shoulders; upper body like a lion's; erect body; powerful, muscular shoulders; 40 teeth; even teeth; white teeth; gum's like a lion's; saliva that improves the taste of all foods; broad tongue; voice like Brahma's; clear blue eyes; eyelashes like a bull's; a lock of hair between the eyebrows; a cone-shaped elevation on the crown of the head." Michael H. Kohn, *The Shambhala Dictionary of Buddhism and Zen* (Boston: Shambhala, 1991), 61. Many of these marks are used when depicting the Buddha in art.

10. *Rahula* means "fetter" or "anchor."

11. This took place in Bodh Gaya, which is in the state of Bihar, India.

12. One can look at Siddhartha's temptation in a figurative way. Mara represents all of the psychological turmoil that might confront a person in his situation, including greed, lust, and fear.

13. Harvey, *Introduction to Buddhism*, 22.

14. Walpola Rahula, *What the Buddha Taught* (New York: Grove Press, 1974), 93.

15. *The Dhammapada,* trans. Eknath Easwaran (Tomales, CA: Nilgiri Press, 1999), 44.

16. For discussion of this, see Arthur Waley, "Did Buddha Die of Eating Pork? With a Note on a Buddha's Image," *Melanges Chinois et Bouddhiques,* 1932, www.ccbs.ntu.edu.tw/fulltext/jr-mel/waley.htm (accessed 15 February 2008); and R. Gordon Wasson and Wendy Doniger O'Flaherty, "The Last Meal of the Buddha," *Journal of the American Oriental Society* 102, no. 4 (October 1982).

17. *The Dhammapada,* trans. Easwaran, 44.

18. *The Dhammapada,* trans. Easwaran, 46.

19. Veneration of these relics began in the early period of Buddhism and continues today. For a short overview, see Vicki Mackenzie, "Jeweled Demise," *Tricycle* (Spring 2007): 74–77, 118–19. For a 13th-century primary source, see *The History of the Buddha's Relic Shrine*, a translation of the *Sinhala Thupavamsa*, Stephen C. Berkwitz, trans. (Oxford: Oxford University Press, 2007). For a comprehensive overview, see John S. Strong, *Relics of the Buddha* (Princeton, NJ: Princeton University Press, 2004).

20. James Fieser and John Powers, eds., *Scriptures of the World's Religions* (New York: McGraw Hill, 2004), 83.

21. Bodhi, ed., *In the Buddha's Words*, 240.

22. *The Dhammapada*, trans. Easwaran, 162.

23. *The Dhammapada*, trans. Easwaran,164.

24. Ñanamoli Thera, trans., "Adittapariyaya Sutta," *accesstoinsight.org*, 1993, www.accesstoinsight .org/tipitaka/sn/sn35/sn35.028.nymo.html (accessed 15 February 2008).

25. Rahula, *What the Buddha Taught*, 30.

26. Dzongsar Jamyang Khyentse, *What Makes You Not a Buddhist* (Boston: Shambhala, 2007), 113–14.

27. Bodhi, ed., *In the Buddha's Words*, 239.

28. Rahula, *What the Buddha Taught*, 48.

29. *The Dhammapada*, trans. Easwaran, 47.

30. Rahula, *What the Buddha Taught*, 48–49.

31. *The Dhammapada*, trans. Easwaran, 47.

32. Thich Nhat Hanh, *The Heart of the Buddha's Teaching: Transforming Suffering into Peace, Joy and Liberation* (New York: Broadway Books, 1999), 210.

33. *The Dhammapada*, trans. Easwaran, 163.

34. Strong, *The Experience of Buddhism: Sources and Interpretations*, 100.

35. Khyentse, *What Makes You Not a Buddhist*, 16.

36. Khyentse, *What Makes You Not a Buddhist*, 16–17.

37. Hanh, *The Heart of the Buddha's Teaching*, 221.

38. Hanh, *The Heart of the Buddha's Teaching*, 229.

39. Hanh, *The Heart of the Buddha's Teaching*, 230. For an interactive tour of the Wheel of Life, courtesy of the Buddha Dharma Education Association, go to www.buddhanet.net/wheel2.htm.

40. Bodhi, ed., *In the Buddha's Words*, 312.

41. Peter Harvey, *An Introduction to Buddhism: Teachings, History and Practices* (Cambridge: Cambridge University Press, 2002), 51.

42. As explained in *The Shambhala Dictionary of Buddhism and Zen*, in Theravada Buddhism "this analysis is limited to the personality; in Mahayana, it is applied to all conditionally arising *dharmas*. This freedom from self-nature is called *shunyata* (emptiness)." Kohn, *The Shambhala Dictionary of Buddhism and Zen*, 8.

43. William Theodore de Bary, *The Buddhist Tradition in India, China and Japan* (New York: Vintage, 1972), 22–23.

44. Khyentse, *What Makes You Not a Buddhist*, 44–45.

45. Khyentse, *What Makes You Not a Buddhist*, 41.

46. De Bary, *The Buddhist Tradition in India, China and Japan*, 24–25.

47. Thich Nhat Hanh, "What Happens When You Die?" *plumvillage.org*, 2007, www.plumvillage .org/dharmatalks/html/whathappenswhenyoudie.html (accessed 15 February 2008).

48. De Bary, *The Buddhist Tradition in India, China and Japan*, 25.

49. Rahula, *What the Buddha Taught*, 32.

50. Strong, *The Experience of Buddhism*, 38.

51. Bodhi, ed., *In the Buddha's Words*, 150–51.

52. Bodhi, ed., *In the Buddha's Words*, 150.

53. Strong, *The Experience of Buddhism*, 41.

54. See the entry *deva* in Kohn, *The Shambhala Dictionary of Buddhism and Zen*, as it explains all of the various heavenly realms.

55. Strong, *The Experience of Buddhism*, 41.

56. Strong, *The Experience of Buddhism*, 39–40.

57. Strong, *The Experience of Buddhism*, 40.

58. Strong, *The Experience of Buddhism*, 39.

59. Strong, *The Experience of Buddhism*, 117.

60. Rahula, *What the Buddha Taught*, 38.

61. Rahula, *What the Buddha Taught*, 41.

62. Rahula, *What the Buddha Taught*, 43.

63. Bodhi, ed., *In the Buddha's Words*, 399.

64. Bodhi, ed., *In the Buddha's Words*, 232–33.

65. Strong, *The Experience of Buddhism*, 104–5.

66. One version of the account can be found in Strong, *The Experience of Buddhism*, 51–55. Even though women were allowed to be nuns, they had to follow the eight cardinal rules, as outlined on pages 54–55. A recent account of the continuing inequalities among monks and nuns is in the 2005 Sharon Stephens Book Award winner, Kim Gutschow, *Being a Buddhist Nun: The Struggle for Enlightenment in the Himalayas* (Cambridge, MA: Harvard University Press, 2004).

67. Women have to follow an additional eight (in Thailand and Burma) or ten (in Sri Lanka) vows, which include (1) even if a nun has 100 years' seniority, she must worship, welcome with raised clasped hands, and pay respects to a monk though he may only be a monk for a day. (2) A nun must not keep her rains-residence at a place that is not close to the one occupied by monks. (3) Every two weeks a nun must ask the monks the day of Uposatha (days when they renew their dedication to the dharma through mediation and intensive reflection) and to approach the monks for instruction and admonition. (4) When the rains-residence has ended, a nun must attend the Pavarana ceremony at both the monks' and nuns' assembly. At each she must invite criticism. (5) A nun who has committed a *sanghadisesa* offense must undergo penance for a half-month in each assembly of monks and nuns. (6) A nun must arrange for ordination by the assemblies of monks and nuns for a female novice only after two years' probationary training under her in the observance of six training practices. (7) A nun should not revile a monk for any reason. (8) Nuns are prohibited from exhorting or admonishing monks. Monks should exhort nuns when and where necessary. All of these rules must be strictly adhered to for life. Venerable Karuna Dharma, "Daughters of the Buddha," *Tricycle* (Winter 2006): 51.

68. *The Dhammapada*, trans. Easwaran, 158–59.

69. Strong, *The Experience of Buddhism*, 124.

70. Strong, *The Experience of Buddhism*, 95–96.

71. Dalai Lama, *The World of Tibetan Buddhism: An Overview of its Philosophy and Practice* (Boston: Wisdom Publications, 1995), 89.

72. For further explanation on these, see chapter 25 in Hanh, *The Heart of the Buddha's Teaching.*

73. Norman Fischer, "Revealing a World of Bliss," *Tricycle: The Buddhist Review* (Winter 2006): 72.

74. In Hinduism, the *vajra* is Indra's thunderbolt. In Buddhism, this object, also called the *dorje* in Tibetan, is "not a weapon but a symbol of the indestructible." As it says in the *Shambhala Dictionary of Buddhism* and Zen, "here it stands for true reality, emptiness, the being or essence of everything existing." Kohn, *The Shambhala Dictionary of Buddhism and Zen*, 241.

75. To some degree, "Tibetan" is also an umbrella term, referring to traditions found in countries that have been deeply influenced by Tibetan culture and religion, such as Nepal, Bhutan, and Mongolia.

76. Dalai Lama, *The World of Tibetan Buddhism*, 11.

77. The translation is "Ah! The jewel is in the lotus."

78. Sogyal Rinpoche, *The Tibetan Book of Living and Dying* (San Francisco: Harper San Francisco, 1997), 285.

79. Rinpoche, *The Tibetan Book of Living and Dying*, 232.

80. De Bary, *Buddhist Tradition in India, China and Japan*, 114.

81. De Bary, *Buddhist Tradition in India, China and Japan*, 114.

82. Strong, *The Experience of Buddhism*, 194.

83. "Matakabhatta Jataka," *accesstoinsight.org*, www.accesstoinsight.org/lib/authors/kawasaki/bl135.html#jat018 (accessed 15 February 2008).

84. This hints at Siddhartha's Hinduism, which informs its followers that based on one's caste, gender, and stage of life, everyone has a dharma to follow.

85. Interestingly enough, at this point the Buddha's story stops, and we learn that Evan, Dean's friend whom we never see on camera, has had a fatal "accident." Instead of being honest with Jesse about the incident, he pulls the car over to the side of the road and gets out so he can cry without letting Jesse see him "suffering." Like Suddhodana, Dean tries to shelter Jesse from the harsh realities of life and from the world "outside the palace." The film does a fine job of weaving in the Four Noble Truths, especially the first two that "life is suffering" and that "we suffer because of attachment." And the best way of doing this is through Evan, who before his "accident" has gone bankrupt. It is his death that makes Dean reassess his attitude toward reincarnation. Even though, for teaching purposes, it can seem annoying that Siddhartha's story is chopped up and inserted throughout the film, the purpose is to show that as Jesse encounters the story of Siddhartha, he too is transforming, going from a state of "sleep" to one of "awakening."

86. None of the palace guests are shown to be particularly disheveled; however, in many accounts, it is said that the once-enticing dancing girls, who had performed for Siddhartha earlier in the evening, looked hideous, with their hair messed up, their makeup smeared about their faces, and drool coming from their mouths. This was yet another reminder to Siddhartha that nothing—not even beauty—lasts.

87. Excerpts can be found in de Bary, *Buddhist Tradition in India, China and Japan*, 57–72.

88. Donald S. Lopez Jr., ed., *Religions of Tibet in Practice* (Princeton, NJ: Princeton University Press, 1997), 22–23.

89. Lopez, ed., *Religions of Tibet in Practice,* 23.

90. Lopez, ed., *Religions of Tibet in Practice,* 23.

91. He is the same person who played Kenpo Tenzin in *Little Buddha.*

92. Rinpoche, *The Tibetan Book of Living and Dying,* 99.

93. During the exchange between Jesse's mother and Kenpo, he explains that he is a teacher of astrology, and then adds that the Tibetans have a very advanced system of astrology. What's interesting about the juxtaposition between Jesse's mother's profession as a math teacher and the monk's "profession" as an astrologer is that while Westerners accept math as a hard science, few would say that astrology is anything more than superstitious. The entire film includes situations like this so as to challenge the viewer's dependence on a rational and "realistic" approach to the world. In the beginning of the film, Jesse's parents, especially his father, take a somewhat condescending and dismissive attitude toward the lama's claim that Jesse is the reincarnation of Lama Dorje. However, at one point Jesse's mother, Lisa, mentions that it was just like having the Three Wise Men coming to their house. Jesse's dad laughs, saying at least they didn't say that Jesse was immaculately conceived. This scene demonstrates that although people often accept the stories of their own religious tradition without question—even when they might seem equally incredulous to outsiders—they may "mock" those of other traditions. To read more about Tibetan Buddhism and astrology, see Tsering Choezom, "Outline of the Tibetan horoscope," *tibet.com,* 1996, www.tibet.com/Med_Astro/astro2.html (accessed 15 February 2008).

94. "From Birth to Exile," *dalailama.com,* www.dalailama.com/page.4.htm (accessed 15 February 2008).

95. Rinpoche, *The Tibetan Book of Living and Dying,* 99.

96. Rinpoche, *The Tibetan Book of Living and Dying,* 99.

97. "From Birth to Exile," *dalailama.com.*

98. "Nechung—The State Oracle of Tibet," *tibet.com,* 1997, www.tibet.com/Buddhism/nechung_hh.html (accessed 15 February 2008).

99. "Nechung—The State Oracle of Tibet," *tibet.com.*

100. Rinpoche, *The Tibetan Book of Living and Dying,* 91.

101. Rinpoche, *The Tibetan Book of Living and Dying,* 37.

102. Sogyal Rinpoche said that some masters do pass away while sitting in meditation, with the body supporting itself. The example he gives is Kalu Rinpoche who died in 1989. For more on this, see Rinpoche, *The Tibetan Book of Living and Dying,* 266–73.

103. Donald S. Lopez, "Exorcising Demons with a Buddhist Sutra," in *Religions of Tibet in Practice,* 511. For an elaboration on the Heart Sutra, see *Essence of the Heart Sutra: The Dalai Lama's Heart of Wisdom Teachings,* Thich Nhat Hanh's *The Heart of Understanding: Commentaries on the Prajnaparamita Heart Sutra,* and two books by Donald S. Lopez, *The Heart Sutra Explained* and *Elaborations on Emptiness.*

104. We can only assume that Lisa is pregnant with Lama Norbu, because once he knew that Jesse was the incarnation of his teacher, he told Jesse that once he died Jesse would have to find him.

105. Rinpoche, *Tibetan Book of Living and Dying*, 389.

106. Rinpoche, *Tibetan Book of Living and Dying*, 390–91.

107. Kohn, *The Shambhala Dictionary of Buddhism and Zen*, 163.

108. Kohn, *The Shambhala Dictionary of Buddhism and Zen*, 223–24.

109. This short article also discusses the eight types of *khatas* as well as the inauspicious occasions for *khata* use. "Katas or Silk Scarves," *tibet.com*, 1998, www.tibet.com/Buddhism/katas .html (accessed 17 February 2008).

110. Kohn, *The Shambhala Dictionary of Buddhism and Zen*, 138.

111. "The Kalachakra Mandala," *tibet.com*, 1997, www.tibet.com/Buddhism/kala1.html. (accessed 17 February 2008).

112. Rinpoche, *The Tibetan Book of Living and Dying*, 249.

113. "Religion and National Identity," *tibet.com*, 1996, www.tibet.com/WhitePaper/white7 .html (accessed 17 February 2008).

114. Stanley Karnow, *Mao and China: A Legacy of Turmoil* (New York: Penguin Books, 1990), 281.

115. R. Keith Schoppa, *Twentieth-Century China: A History in Documents* (New York: Oxford University Press, 2004), 200–201.

116. For more detail, see Pamela Logan, "Witness to a Tibetan Sky-Burial: A Field Report for the China Exploration and Research Society," *caltech.edu*, 1997, www.alumnus.caltech.edu/ ~pamlogan/skybury.htm. (accessed 17 February 2008).

117. Other common ritual elements used by Tibetan Buddhists are the bell (*ghanta*); the *vajra*, or scepter with four pronged ends; and the *phurpa*, a ritual dagger used to exorcise demons. For more on this, see Elizabeth Lyons, Heather Peters, Ch'eng-mei Chang, and Gregory L. Possehl, *Buddhism: History and Diversity of a Great Tradition* (Philadelphia: University of Pennsylvania Museum, 1985), 37–39.

118. In *Little Buddha*, Jesse picks up a trumpet made from a human femur in Lama Dorje's quarters.

119. For full information on this situation, visit www.savetibet.org/news/positionpapers/ panchenlama.php (accessed 12 June 2008).

120. The word Ch'an is a translation of the Sanskrit term *dhyana*, which means meditation.

121. Several of the Beat writers, including Gary Snyder, Jack Kerouac, Philip Whelan, and Allen Ginsberg, became interested in Zen, thus giving the religion widespread exposure. British writer Alan Watts, too, exposed Americans to Eastern religions.

122. Kenneth Ch'en, *Buddhism in China: A Historical Survey* (Princeton, NJ: Princeton University Press, 1973), 357.

123. Katsuki Sekida, trans., *Two Zen Classics: The Gateless Gate and The Blue Cliff Records* (Boston: Shambhala, 2005), 14. Saying that there is an "answer" to a koan isn't really correct, because none have universally recognized "answers." It is up to the master to decide whether or not the student has correctly answered the koan.

124. From the commentary on the *Mumonkan*. Sekida, trans., *Two Zen Classics*, 28.

125. Sekida, trans., *Two Zen Classics*, 17.

126. In Mumon's Comment, we read "When you meet the Buddha, you kill him; when you meet the patriarchs, you kill them." Mark Salzman sets this koan at the center of his 1994 novel, *The Soloist*. The main character, Renne Sundheimer, is serving as a juror on a murder trial involving the brutal killing of a Zen Buddhist master. The killer in this case is a Buddhist acolyte, who interpreted this koan literally. By the end of the novel, Renne himself solves the riddle.

127. Sekida, trans., *Two Zen Classics*, 41.

128. Marc Rosenbush, "Profound Questions," *zenmovie.com*, www.zenmovie.com/questions .html (accessed 17 February 2008). The DVD is only available for purchase through this website.

129. Michael Wenger, "The Making of a Zen Mystery," *Buddhadharma: The Practitioner's Quarterly* (Winter 2006): 94.

130. Bodhidharma was a fifth-century Indian Buddhist monk who is considered to be the 28th patriarch of Buddhism, in a direct line from Shakyamuni Buddha, and first patriarch of Ch'an. Accounts say that he sat immovable, staring at a wall, for nine years. Others state that he cut off his eyelids so that he didn't fall asleep during meditation. Popular stories credit him for the Shaolin style of kung fu, saying that he taught the monks the 18 boxing techniques as a way to condition their bodies. It is said that all of the long hours of sitting meditation had made their bodies weak.

131. Many Confucian ideas can be found in the film, from honoring one's parents to rulers gaining the Mandate of Heaven.

132. Clark Strand, "Worry Beads," *Tricycle: The Buddhist Review* (Winter 2006): 38.

133. Strand, "Worry Beads," 39. The article also explains the proper way to use the *mala* and how to say the *nembutsu*, which means "to think of Buddha." A commonly recited *nembutsu* is *Namu Amida Butsu*, which is supposed to help a person be reborn in the Pure Land.

134. Undoubtedly, the translator was coming from a Roman Catholic background or tradition, because Buddhism doesn't speak about transgressions as mortal or venial sins.

135. During Zen practice, a monk walks around the *zendo* with this stick. It is used to keep monks awake, to help them correct their posture, and more importantly to relax tense muscles.

136. According to *The Shambhala Dictionary of Buddhism and Zen*, the literal translation of this is "the Blissful," and it is the Pure Land that is reigned over by Amitabha, who created it by his karmic merit. Faithful devotion to this Buddha and the recitation of his name will cause the adherent to be reborn in this western paradise, where he or she will live out his or her remaining days until entering nirvana. This concept comes from the *Sukhavati-vyuha* or *Sutra of the Land of Bliss*. Kohn, *The Shambhala Dictionary of Buddhism and Zen*.

137. *The Dhammapada*, trans. Easwaran, 79.

138. Khyentse, *What Makes You Not a Buddhist*, 64.

139. Khyentse, *What Makes You Not a Buddhist*, 65.

140. *The Dhammapada*, trans. Easwaran, 125.

141. Like the general, most people see themselves and the world in dualistic terms—good and evil, sin and sinner—but Buddhism claims that this is illusion. The goal of meditation is to go beyond dualism and subjective perceptions of the subject and the object.

142. Ch'en, *Buddhism in China*, 358.

143. Strong, *The Experience of Buddhism*, 108.

144. Khyentse, *What Makes You Not a Buddhist*, 69.

145. Rinpoche, *The Tibetan Book of Living and Dying*, 79.

146. Ch'en, *Buddhism in China*, 358.

147. "Be you Buddha, I'll cut off your head" sounds a lot like what the Ch'an master I-hsuan said to his disciples: "Kill everything that stands in your way. If you should meet the Buddha, kill the Buddha. If you should meet the Patriarchs, kill the Patriarchs. If you should meet the *arhats* on your way, kill them too." Even though this indicates that the screenwriter might have known the koan, it's unlikely that its usage here indicates that Huo possesses any Buddhist insight. He is driven by greed, anger, and ignorance.

148. Having watched the scene multiple times, it's difficult to know if General Huo falls into the axe or runs into the axe. It seems unlikely that General Shi swings it into his adversary's neck, as that wouldn't go along with the Buddhist ideal of renouncing violence and anger, particularly because up until this point, he's been a violent man. One could also say that this scene clearly demonstrates how enslaved General Huo is by his anger, whereas General Shi simply wants peace.

149. *The Dhammapada*, trans. Easwaran, 195–98.

150. Many Westerners even debate whether or not Buddhism should be considered a religion at all, instead claiming that since it doesn't contain many of the usual "trappings" of religion—specifically, worship of a god or gods—it should be labeled a philosophical system.

151. Author Dean Sluyter agrees. In his book, he's found Buddhist "lessons" in such non-Buddhist fare as *Snow White and the Seven Dwarves* and *The Truman Show*. Dean Sluyter, *Cinema Nirvana: Enlightenment Lessons from the Movies* (New York: Three Rivers Press, 2005).

152. De Bary, *The Buddhist Tradition in India, China and Japan*, 97.

153. Interestingly enough, Asian films typically feature a blind person who knows more or who can see better than the sighted characters.

154. Hanh, *The Heart of the Buddha's Teaching*, 133.

155. From the official production notes, courtesy of Warner Bros. Pictures.

156. *The Dhammapada*, trans. Easwaran, 111.

157. Dalai Lama, *The World of Tibetan Buddhism*, 81.

158. *The Dhammapada*, trans. Easwaran, 168.

159. *The Dhammapada*, trans. Easwaran, 186.

160. *The Dhammapada*, trans. Easwaran, 104.

161. *The Dhammapada*, trans. Easwaran, 78.

162. Harvey, *Introduction to Buddhism*, 201.

163. As Harvey explains, nothing is cut and dried in Buddhism. Although the first precept is regarded as the most important one for Buddhists, most lay Buddhists have been prepared to break it in self-defense, and many have helped to defend the community. See chapter 9 for more on Buddhist ethics. Harvey, *Introduction to Buddhism*.

164. Strong, *The Experience of Buddhism*, 38.

165. Strong, *The Experience of Buddhism*, 39.

166. Daigan Matsunaga and Alicia Matsunaga, *The Buddhist Concept of Hell* (New York: Philosophical Library, 1972), 45. As the authors explain in their conclusion, the Buddhist

concept of hell serves two purposes. For those who are more "enlightened" they were intended to "induce self-reflection," causing the person to break through the "pitfalls of self-deception." For those who weren't as reflective, they were intended to instill morality. "The concept of Buddhist hells serves as such a means (*upaya*), pointing the way to enlightenment and the purpose of the hells is to transform the nature of the human mind."

167. Rinpoche, *The Tibetan Book of Living and Dying*, 291.

168. Rinpoche, *The Tibetan Book of Living and Dying*, 289.

169. Rinpoche, *The Tibetan Book of Living and Dying*, 290.

170. His last name is an anagram of Hamlet, Shakespeare's brooding Danish prince. When Sam encounters Athena for the first time, she is reciting lines from this tragedy.

171. Harvey explains that Buddhism does not encourage the development of strong guilt feelings. "Guilt is seen as part of the natural karmic result of unskillful action, and may therefore act as a deterrent. It should not be further indulged in, though, to produce self-dislike and mental turbulence, a spiritual hindrance. Regretting misdeeds is skillful, but only if this does not unnecessarily harp on past failings." Buddhism doesn't encourage us to focus on past faults but strive for future successes. Harvey, *Introduction to Buddhism*, 200.

172. If we return to the first image of *Stay*, Henry is sitting near a burning car, even though by the end of the film we see that that car was never on fire; it suffered a blowout.

173. *The Dhammapada*, trans. Easwaran, 116.

174. Strong, *The Experience of Buddhism*, 148.

175. Strong, *The Experience of Buddhism*. As explained in the introduction to the passage, this parable also was used to illustrate the superiority of the Mahayana path over other Buddhist traditions.

176. John Powers, *Introduction to Tibetan Buddhism* (Ithaca, NY: Snow Lion, 1995), 299.

177. *The Dhammapada*, trans. Easwaran, 78.

178. De Bary, *The Buddhist Tradition in India, China and Japan*, 98.

179. According to the Internet Movie Database, the title in Norway and Sweden is *Jacob's Inferno*, obviously referring to *Dante's Inferno*, which also discussed, in detail, Dante's trip through hell. "Jacob's Ladder," *Internet Movie Database*, www.imdb.com/title/tt0099871/ (accessed 17 February 2008).

180. Several scenes containing metaphysical discussions of demons and angels, as well as images of these creatures, were deleted from the screenplay. For example, during the antidote sequence, Michael transforms into a glowing being that floats above Jacob. The ending as envisioned by Rubin also differs considerably from the cinematic version. After some fierce battles with demons, a celestial stairway appears before him. On it are angelic forms who are moving up and down. The script is available in print form from Applause Books (2000) and online from Bruce Joel Rubin, "Jacob's Ladder," *dailyscript.com*, www.dailyscript.com/scripts/JacobsLadder.html (accessed 17 February 2008).

181. Bruce Joel Rubin, *Jacob's Ladder* (New York: Applause Theatre Book, 1990), 191.

182. Dan Epstien, "The Mouse That Roared," *ugo.com*, www.ugo.com/channels/filmTv/features/brucejoelrubin (accessed 17 February 2008).

183. Jeffrey Paine, *Re-enchantment: Tibetan Buddhism Comes to the West* (New York: W. W. Norton, 2004), 175–76.

184. Paine, *Re-enchantment*, 175.

185. Rubin, *Jacob's Ladder*, 150.

186. Rubin, *Jacob's Ladder*, 151.

187. Rubin, *Jacob's Ladder*, 155.

188. Rubin, *Jacob's Ladder*, 190.

189. Rubin, *Jacob's Ladder*, 195. It's interesting to note that the same source imagery was used by director Vincent Ward for *What Dreams May Come*.

190. Rubin, *Jacob's Ladder*, 180–81.

191. Rubin, *Jacob's Ladder*, 189.

192. Rubin, *Jacob's Ladder*, 164. Screenplays written prior to *Jacob's Ladder* include *Brainstorm* (1983), which is about researchers who discover how to record and play back people's experiences; and the Oscar-winning *Ghost* (1990), which is a love story about a murdered man and his partner. *My Life*, which came out in 1983, is about Bob Jones (Michael Keaton) who has terminal cancer and must confront his own mortality. When "modern" medicine fails to offer him any hope, he visits an Asian "healer" named Mr. Ho (Haing S. Ngor) who, after he examines him, tells him that he holds on to too much anger and that it is poisoning him. "Do you want to carry so much pain into your next life?" "My next life?" Jones replies. "The last second of your life is the most important moment of all. It's everything you are, ever said, ever thought, all rolled into one. That is the seed of your next life. Until that last moment, you still have time. You can change everything. You can let go of your fear, let go of your anger." The ideas he conveys here are very Buddhist, particularly that "anger" really is one of the three poisons, tying the person to the cycle of birth and rebirth, and the concept of reincarnation. Rather than embrace what Mr. Ho says, Jones storms out, referring to him as a quack. Later, he returns to Mr. Ho's clinic and sees considerable results. Whereas his medical doctor gave him about three months to live, after his holistic treatments—they are reminiscent of Reiki—he lives long enough to see the birth of his son. As in *Jacob's Ladder*, *My Life* contains Eastern and Western religions. For example, Jones's estranged brother is shown getting married in an Eastern Orthodox church.

193. George Robinson says in his book that during the medieval period Jewish mystics included the notion of reincarnation through the transmigration of souls. George Robinson, *Essential Judaism: A Complete Guide to Beliefs, Customs and Rituals* (New York: Pocket Books, 2000), 193.

194. Tony Walter and Helen Waterhouse, "A Very Private Belief: Reincarnation in Contemporary England," *Sociology of Religion* (Summer 1999), www.findarticles.com/p/articles/mi_m0SOR/is_2_60/ai_55208520 (accessed 17 February 2008).

195. Although there are thought to be "hints" at reincarnation in the book of Deuteronomy 25:5–10, one has to look to the oral Jewish tradition for more on the subject. For instance, Rabbi Isaac Luria, in his book *The Gates of Reincarnation*, explains how various biblical personalities lived, died, and were reborn as different individuals. The 17th-century Rabbi Menachem Azarya of Fano covers similar material in *Reincarnation of Souls*. According to *The Complete Idiot's*

Guide to the Talmud by Rabbi Aaron Parry, a source aimed at the general public, "The dead can come back to Earth in a couple of different ways." The first is by temporarily entering the body of a living human being. This is known as *ibbur neshama*. Another, called *dybbuk*, is when an unhappy or vengeful soul inhabits another person's body so that it can "rectify some part of its past." The only way to get rid of this "spirit" is for a religious person to perform an exorcism. Interestingly enough, for most of the films listed, from *All of Me* to *The Return*, this scenario applies more often than does the one from an Eastern tradition.

196. Stuart D. B. Picken, *Essentials of Shinto: An Analytical Guide to Principal Teachings* (Westport, CT: Greenwood Press, 1994), 218.

197. Ian Reader, *Religion in Contemporary Japan* (Honolulu: University of Hawaii Press, 1991), 91.

198. Japanese horror films are referred to as J-Horror, and some of the better known ones are *Ringu* (The Ring), *Ju-On* (*The Grudge*), *Honogurai Mizu No Soko Kara* (*Dark Water*), *Kairo* (*Pulse*), all of which were remade by Hollywood; *Shibuya Kaidan* (*The Locker*), *Yogen* (*Premonition*), and *Kansen* (*Infection*). Korean horror films, well regarded in their own right, have earned themselves the moniker K-Horror, and include such films as *Yeogo Goedam* (*Whispering Corridors*), *Sorum*, *Pon* (*Phone*), and *Janghwa, Hongryeon* (*The Tale of Two Sisters*).

199. Michiko Iwasaka and Barre Toelken, *Ghosts and the Japanese: Cultural Experience in Japanese Death Legends* (Logan: Utah University Press, 1994), 6.

200. Iwasaka and Toelken, *Ghosts and the Japanese*, 16.

201. Thomas P. Kasulis, *Shinto: The Way Home* (Honolulu: University of Hawaii Press, 2004), 76-7.

202. Picken, *Essentials of Shinto*, 172–73.

203. Matsunaga and Matsunaga, *The Buddhist Concept of Hell*, 108.

204. Matsunaga and Matsunaga, *The Buddhist Concept of Hell*, 78.

205. It is never said implicitly in the film how long Phil relives the same day. Based on the skills that he acquires, one can surmise that it's a very long time. Cowriter Danny Rubin said that his original script began in the middle of events, not even showing the onset of the "time warp." In fact, he said that it didn't even matter why the repeated day started.

206. From the liner notes inside of the special edition DVD.

207. See the perfections and stages of the bodhisattva. Harvey, *Introduction to Buddhism*, 122–24.

208. Hanh, *The Heart of the Buddha's Teaching*, 170–71.

209. Hanh, *The Heart of the Buddha's Teaching*, 172.

210. Hanh, *The Heart of the Buddha's Teaching*, 173.

211. Hanh, *The Heart of the Buddha's Teaching*, 174.

212. Michael Sragow, "King of Comedy," *Salon.com*, 2000. www.dir.salon.com/story/ent/col/srag/2000/11/02/ramis/index2.html (accessed 17 February 2008).

213. "Production Notes," *the-cup.com*, www.the-cup.com/cup_aboutproduction.html (accessed 17 February 2008).

214. "Production Notes," *the-cup.com*.

215. Dondup turns his back not only on traditional village life but also on everything Bhutanese. He wears an I Love New York shirt, even though he's never been there; he smokes, has long hair, decorates his room with posters of Western-looking Asian women, and he listens to rock 'n' roll on a boombox. At one point, he's even working out to pass the time.

216. Norbu explained that "A big part of *Travellers and Magicians* is actually adapted from a Buddhist fable about two brothers, one aspiring to become a magician." Khyentse Norbu, "Comments from Writer-Director Khyentse Norbu," *zeitgeistfilms.com*, 2003, www.zeitgeistfilms.com/films/travellersandmagicians/presskit.pdf (accessed 17 February 2008).

217. One might say that the horse and Tashi's ensuing wild ride serves as a metaphor for Deki and the emotional roller coaster ride she takes Tashi on. In the beginning both the horse and Deki seem like beautiful and captivating creatures. But neither are what they seem. As Tashi says, he couldn't control the horse and it dropped him in the middle of nowhere. The emotions he has for Deki, too, spiral out of control, leading him from unwholesome thoughts to unwholesome acts. It isn't a coincidence that the "force" that put the events into motion was his aptly named brother, Karma.

218. "About the production," *zeitgeistfilms.com*, 2003, www.zeitgeistfilms.com/films/travellers andmagicians/presskit.pdf (accessed 17 February 2008).

219. Khyentse Norbu, "Comments from Writer-Director Khyentse Norbu," *zeitgeistfilms.com*, 2003, www.zeitgeistfilms.com/films/travellersandmagicians/presskit.pdf (accessed 17 February 2008).

220. Although Davaa shoots on location and uses real people, she always follows a storyline in her films. In an interview for *The Story of Weeping Camel*, her partner, Luigi Falorni, explained that "we looked at each shot as a window, therefore keeping it simple and quiet, to maintain a linear, peaceful storyline. This doesn't imply strict documentary observation, however. Some action important to the structure of the story, which did not occur while the camera was running, was re-shot with the family's cooperation." "The Story of the Weeping Camel," *german-cinema.de*, www.german-cinema.de/app/filmarchive/film_view.php?film_id=1035 (accessed 17 February 2008).

221. Byambasuren Davaa, "Director's Notes," *caveoftheyellowdog.co.uk*, www.caveoftheyellow dog.co.uk (accessed 17 February 2008).

222. Byambasuren Davaa, "Director's Notes."

4

Religions of China

STATISTICS

As of July 2007, China has an estimated population of about 1.3 billion people, of which almost 92% are Han Chinese. Although China is officially atheist, its main religions are Daoism (Taoism) and Buddhism. According to many recent news reports, Confucianism is gaining in popularity. Of the total population, between 3% and 4% are said to be Christian; 1% to 2% are Muslim.

Taiwan has an estimated population of 23 million, of which 84% are Taiwanese. About 93% of the population practices a mixture of Buddhism and Daoism.[1]

THE BASICS

Over the centuries, China's religious landscape has been characterized by the interplay of Daoism and Confucianism, both of which are of Chinese origin; Buddhism, which arrived from India and became established in China during the first century C.E.; and popular or folk tradition.[2] Since none of these religions demand exclusivity, the Chinese typically practice all four. They can do this because each religion operates within its own sphere: Confucianism structures social interactions; Daoism helps one to gain harmony with nature and the spirit world; Buddhism deals with death and the afterlife; and popular religion covers everything in between. As scholar Julia Ching explains, popular religion "crosses the lines of demarcation between Confucianism, Taoism and Buddhism. . . . Its basic ideas and values coincide with those that pervade the culture as a whole, with particular relevance to human concerns for personal and communal survival in a sometimes harsh world."[3] Of the three teachings (*san jiao*)—Buddhism, Daoism, and Confucianism—Daoism is the one most closely tied to popular religion.

Officially, China has been an atheist country since 1949, when the Communists gained control. And even though the Constitution of 1954 guarantees citizens the freedom of religion, the Marxist Party line is that religion is the "sigh of the oppressed creature, the heart of a heartless world, and the soul of soulless conditions. It is the opium of the people."[4] The belief is that in a classless society, religion will eventually wither away. When this wasn't forthcoming in China, Mao Zedong (1893–1976), in 1966, launched the Cultural Revolution with the intention of destroying everything that seemed "backward," especially Confucianism and liberal thinking. As it says in the *Sixteen Points: Guidelines for the Great Proletarian Cultural Revolution*, the objective was, among other things, "to criticize and repudiate the reactionary bourgeois academic 'authorities' and the ideology of the bourgeoisie and all other exploiting classes, and transform education, literature, and art and all other parts of the superstructure."[5]

Religion was far from destroyed, though. During the Chairman's life, a "cult of Mao" developed, elevating him to demigod status. After he died, and especially since the early 1980s, "China has witnessed an explosion of activities commonly called religious, including church attendance, pilgrimage, geomancy, temple building, *qi gong* practice, and so on."[6] To find evidence of the aforementioned religions, one needs only to look at Chinese films[7] that have been produced since the 1980s. Confucianism, Daoism, Buddhism, popular religion, Christianity, and even evidence of a Maoist cult can be seen in films by directors as diverse as Zhang Yimou, Ang Lee, Fruit Chan, Ronny Yu, Clara Law, Tian-Ming Wu, and Yang Zhang.

Daoism and Confucianism[8] are indigenous to China,[9] and when examined side-by-side, they appear to contradict one another. Whereas Daoism advocates passivity, "unlearning," and harmony with the natural world, the more conservative Confucianism stresses social responsibility, education, and the cultivation of virtues. Daoism emphasizes individual freedom; Confucianism stresses social roles and one's conformity to them. Despite their contradictory natures, Daoism and Confucianism are seen as complementary and are usually followed by the same practitioners.

Daoism

Daoism gets its name from the Dao, which means "the Way" or "the path," and as it is stated in one of its principal texts, the Daodejing (*The Way and Its Power*), the Dao is nameless, eternal, the origin of heaven and earth, the mother of all things, infinite and boundless; "it subsists in nothingness" and is "shape without shape, form without form." The Dao itself is composed of two opposing yet complementary forces, referred to as the yin and the yang. The former is described as feminine, dark, wet, yielding, and passive; the latter is masculine, light, dry, aggressive, and active. Not to be understood as good and bad, or good and evil, the yin and yang are simply different sides to the same coin; one cannot exist without the other. Furthermore, they contain aspects of each other as can be seen in the T'ai Chi symbol, which is a circle divided by a curved line into equal sections; with white on the left, and black on the right. If we look closely at the white side, we see inside of it a circle of black, and on the black side, we find a circle of white. This indicates that yin contains the seed of yang and vice versa; one follows the other. At certain times *yin* will wax but eventually it will wane, giving rise to *yang*, which also goes through a process of waxing and waning; such is the continuous cycle.

Traditionally scholars have divided Daoism into two categories: philosophical and religious.[10] Philosophical Daoism describes the earliest type, which arose during the Late Warring States Period (479–221 B.C.E.), and religious Daoism describes a later development, which appeared at the end of the Han Dynasty (206 B.C.E.–220 C.E.). The figure most associated with philosophical Daoism is Lao-tzu, who is also known as Laozi and Lao-tse,[11] the reputed author of the Daodejing whose life dates to the sixth century B.C.E. According to Sima Qian's *Shih-chi* (*Records of the Grand Historian*), which dates to the second and first century B.C.E., this philosopher's surname was Li, his personal name was Erh, and he lived in Chou. "Lao-tzu cultivated the Dao and its virtue. He taught that one should efface oneself and be without fame in the world. After he lived in Chou for a long time, he perceived that [it] was in decline, so [he] departed."[12] Before Lao-tzu could leave, riding on the back of a water buffalo, the keeper of the pass asked him to write down his teachings. The old master agreed, and produced for him the Daodejing, which consists of 81 chapters and 5,000 characters. Not much is known about what happened to Lao-tzu after this; however, it is reported that he lived for anywhere between 160 and 200 years. His long life was "a result of cultivating the Way and nurturing longevity."[13] As we see from this "biography," Lao-tzu was not the philosopher's real name, instead it was an honorific title given to him with *Lao* meaning elder and *tzu* is a suffix, showing respect.

The focus of Lao-tzu's teaching was the sage, who transcends all human weaknesses and self-centeredness. He was a person who lived for the benefit of others. As it says in chapter 49 of the Daodejing: "The sage has no fixed mind of his own; he immerses his own mind in the mind of all people." The sage is the embodiment of the Dao and *de* or virtue. For Lao-tzu the image of the paradigmatic individual was an infant because, without exerting any effort, it realized the characteristics of the highest virtue, which were being spontaneous, innocent, simple, original, generous, and selfless.[14] When born, humans are like an uncarved block (*pu*), and Lao-tzu encourages us to return to that original state. Lao-tzu also stresses living in accordance with the natural way, which means practicing nonaction (*wu-wei*), having no fixed opinions, being spontaneous, and seeing everything as one.

Although little is actually known about Zhuangzi (Chuang-tzu), the second primary figure of philosophical Daoism, it is speculated that he lived from about 375 B.C.E. to 300 B.C.E. From the *Records of the Grand Historian*, we learn that his personal name was Chou, he was a native of Meng, and he once served as an official in a lacquer garden. He also "inherited the basic philosophy of Lao-tzu, had very broad learning and was said to have written works amounting to some 100,000 words."[15] In his mystical writings, which bear his name, his overall message is to be free. We can do this by freeing our minds from logic and empirical levels of meaning. Zhuangzi, himself, used "fables— a kind of metaphorical discourse—to wake the human mind to the realm of possibilities and to sever it from all realistic attachments."[16] Like Lao-tzu, Zhuangzi was concerned with the idea of a superior man. But whereas Lao-tzu's message was more political, Zhuangzi's was more personal, and he advised the would-be "sage" to remove from his mind anything that was contrary to the Dao. The sage should also act without acting (*wu-wei*), love others, see beyond distinctions, and not be guided by money or property. "His glory is in enlightenment [for he knows that] the 10,000 things belong to one storehouse, that life and death share the same body."[17]

Zhuangzi said that once we see beyond distinctions—such as good or bad, beautiful or ugly—we would start accepting life as it is. Humans, he said, are the masters of their own suffering, and by seeing beyond distinctions we could free ourselves from our self-created bondage. In his view, "the man who has freed himself from conventional standards of judgment can no longer be made to suffer, for he refuses to recognize poverty as any less desirable than affluence, to recognize death as any less desirable than life." There was no reason for the sage to withdraw from society, because to do so indicated that he still saw distinctions. The sage remains in society but acts without motives of gain or striving. "In such a state, all human actions become as spontaneous and mindless as those of the natural world. Man becomes one with Nature, or Heaven, as [he] calls it, and merges himself with the Dao."[18]

The establishment of Daoism as distinctly religious, referred to as *Daojiao*, occurred during the mid-second century C.E., when "Zhang Daoling[19] received the first of a series of revelations from Taishang Laojun, the Lord Lao the Most on High. . . . [He] began to spread the teachings he had received and established the first organized Daoist system, named True Unity of Celestial Masters." Eventually this movement divided itself into a number of parishes, to which membership required the payment of five pecks of rice. The Celestial Master and his associates stressed the importance of repenting for one's mistakes, performing good works, and cultivating one's character. They also incorporated folk traditions and practices, thus ensuring its acceptance throughout China. As scholar Stephen F. Teiser explains, "Nearly all types of rituals performed by Daoist masters through the ages are evident in the early years of the Way of the Celestial Masters. Surviving sources describe the curing of illness through confession, the exorcism of malevolent spirits, rite of passage in the life of the individual, and the holding of regular communal feasts."[20] Over the centuries, Daoism has come into contact with other religious systems and has been changed by them. Buddhism, in particular, has had a considerable effect on Daoism, which adopted aspects of its worldview, including such concepts as "karma, rebirth and hell; ethics, including precepts and monastic vows; and philosophical speculation, such as notions of emptiness and the logic of enlightened states."[21] During the Period of Disunity (265–589 C.E.), the cross-pollination of Buddhism and Daoism resulted in the creation of Ch'an Buddhism. From popular religion, Daoism borrowed a number of rituals and protective practices as well as a variety of deities.

Throughout China's history, Buddhism, Confucianism, and Daoism have each experienced the favor and patronage of the ruler. For Daoism its apex of favor occurred during the Tang Dynasty (618–907 C.E.). Because the imperial family shared Lao-tzu's surname, they elevated his status, referring to him as the "Sage Ancestor-Emperor of the Abstruse Origin," and made his birthday a national holiday.[22] They also ordered the construction of thousands of Daoist monasteries and nunneries to which a dozen princesses devoted their lives. Whereas the Confucian Classics had previously formed the core curriculum of the civil service exams, during this period, the Daodejing was elevated to a superior position over them, and a new examination system was created, whereby scholars learned in Daoism could be qualified for civil service.[23] Late imperial China was characterized by unity and integration, and it was during this period—the Ming (1368–1644) and Qing (1644–1911)—that the teachings of Daoism, Confucianism, and Buddhism were integrated, resulting in what is known as Neo-Confucianism. During the modern period, especially during the mid-20th century, Daoism hasn't fared as well with the ruling party. The Communists have attacked it for being "superstitious," and many of its temples and texts were destroyed during the Cultural Revolution (1966–1976). Acceptance of Daoism is increasing on the mainland, but it's a long way from being as popular as it is in Taiwan, where the True Unity of Celestial Masters continues, or in Hong Kong. Religious Daoism also exists in Malaysia, Thailand, Singapore, and wherever large Chinese communities exist, such as San Francisco and Honolulu.

How can we characterize Daoist beliefs? The core principles are following the Dao and cultivating virtue. Essentially, a sage should model himself or herself on the Dao. When this happens the result is harmony, balance, and *de*. When the sage doesn't, disharmony will result. In the case of a ruler, because the Daodejing has been thought of as a political manual, if this person rules with force or is motivated by riches and power, ways contrary to the Dao, he will eventually be overthrown. "When something reaches an extreme, the opposite will emerge, and it will emerge not only from the outside, but also from the inside."[24] These concepts provide the foundation of Daoism, but it would be incorrect to say that Daoists sit around all day philosophizing about the nature of the universe. There is also a very public side to this religion, and it can be witnessed at any Daoist temple, where practitioners burn incense and spirit money; and pray to myriad deities, asking for guidance and protection.

Contemporary Daoist rituals can be performed by one specialist or by a troupe of people who provide a veritable theatrical experience with singing, dancing, chanting, and the burning of incense. Typically they take place inside the local temple, which is dedicated to several local gods. After setting up a portable altar, the practitioners establish sacred space by hanging up scrolls that represent various gods. Next, ritual implements are set out on the central altar. These items include horns, a sword, an incense burner, a bowl of water, a mirror, a pair of scissors, an audience tablet, and various offerings of tea, wine, and rice. "Daoist ritual covers a vast range of repetitive, symbolic, and transformative actions, including collective rites of offering, sacrifice and thanksgiving, initiation, prayers for rain, exorcisms of disease-bearing demonic forces, requiems for deceased family members and individual rites featuring meditation and visualization."[25] Although some rituals are brief, others can last for several days. Daoist priests are trained to perform a wide range of functions. They can call upon the spirit world and communicate with it, they can cast out demons, they can determine the future, and they can heal the sick.

The Dao is known to humans through a hierarchy of many gods and immortals, and people address them as they would earthly administrators and bureaucrats. Furthermore, the "oral and ritual language used to address them follows the protocol of the Chinese imperial court."[26] Toward the top of the celestial hierarchy are the Celestial Worthy of Primordial Beginning, the Celestial Worthy of Numinous Treasure, and the Celestial Worthy of the Way and Its Virtue, also known as Laojun or Lord Lao, the deified form of Lao-tzu. Under this trio are lower-ranking deities, such as the very popular Jade Emperor, the Yellow Emperor (*Huang-di*), and the Queen Mother of the West. The Jade Emperor is the celestial counterpart to the Chinese emperor and therefore is the most powerful and sovereign of the gods, occupying the highest tier of the Daoist pantheon. He is depicted as sitting on a throne and holding a tablet. His birthday is celebrated on the ninth day of the first month. It is also believed that on the 23rd day of the 12th month the Stove God reports to him on the affairs of every family in China. The Yellow Emperor is believed to be common ancestor of the Chinese people and the founder of the Chinese nation. Conceived of as a warrior, he successfully fought against a series of enemies. After pacifying the world, he and his ministers set about the task of civilizing the people. They are credited for inventing mathematics, the calendar, music, medicine, the writing system, and more. It is believed that the Yellow Emperor's wife raised the first silkworms.

The Heavenly Queen Mother of the West, also known as *Tianhou* or *Mazu*, rules over the Western mountain paradise, where she oversees the orchards where the peaches of immortality grow. This rare and highly prized fruit ripens every 1,000 years, and when eaten can confer considerable longevity. In the *Journey to the West*, attributed to Wu Cheng'en (circa. 1500–1582 C.E.), Monkey eats peaches that were intended for the queen's banquet guests. He is punished by the Buddha, who incarcerates him beneath the Mountain of Five Elements. The Queen Mother of the West's birthday is celebrated on the 23rd day of the third month. Also venerated by many Chinese are the gods of prosperity, luck, and longevity; the god of wealth, the god of war, and the Eight Immortals. From early on, Daoists have been preoccupied with immortality, and to achieve their goal, they practiced breathing techniques, followed special diets, and consumed herbs, minerals, and special elixirs. Accounts of immortals demonstrate that they can fly, stay youthful, and control the body so that they don't feel hunger, heat, or the cold.

Daoist thought and practice have also resulted in the creation of astrology and medical practices. The Chinese observe both lunar and solar calendars. There are 12 months in the lunar calendar; however, an additional month is added every two to three years. "In the solar calendar, 'nodes' or 'breaths,' refer to the 24-hour periods of approximately 15 days into which the year is divided." Years are then divided into cycles, starting with 12 years, each represented by a zodiac animal; and then widening to a 60-year cycle.[27] It is believed that the body is a microcosm of the universe, which means that it operates on the same principles. "According to Chinese medical theory (which is based on Daoism), five of the internal organs . . . correspond to the Five Elements and are yang in nature: the liver is of the nature of yang wood; the kidneys, of yang water; the lungs, of yang metal; the heart, of yang fire; and the spleen, of yang earth. Other internal organs correspond to the five elements and are yin in nature: the gallbladder is . . . of yin wood; the bladder, of yin water; lower intestines, of yin metal; the small intestines, of yin fire; and the stomach of yin earth. The internal organs have mutually enhancing and mutually weakening relations, just as the five elements do."[28] A person's health can be restored in a number of ways, including modifying one's diet, prescribing traditional Chinese herbs, and using acupuncture to unblock one's *chi* or *qi* (vital energy) that flows through meridian lines in the body.

Finally, we need to say a word about Daoist texts. The Daodejing and *Zhuangzi* are undeniably the best known; however, they are far from being the only ones. In fact, the Daoist canon (*Daozang*) runs to an unbelievable 1,500 volumes that include "scriptures, commentaries, hagiographies, cultivation manuals and liturgies. Completed in 1445, it was the result of an intense compilation effort over several decades and continued earlier compilations of Daoist materials that went back as far as the fifth century C.E.; these earlier texts were lost, burned, or otherwise destroyed."[29] Many of these texts only became accessible to the West in the early 20th century.[30] The earliest religious text is the *T'ai P'ing Ching* (*The Scripture of the Ultimate Equilibrium*), in which we find the belief that there are "three Original Energies known as the Ultimate Yang, the Ultimate Yin, and the Harmonious Neuter. These three energies are expressed in the three Embodied Forms of Heaven, Earth and human beings, namely fathers, mothers and children." The text demonstrates that there exists a relationship between nature and humanity.[31] Not part of the Daoist corpus per se, *I Ching* (*Book of Change*), a divination manual that is perhaps 3,000 years old, is important to the religion, especially its principles of feng shui (literally wind-water, but translated to geomancy).

Confucianism

Confucianism, known in East Asia as the Ru School of Chinese Thought,[32] can be traced to Kong Qiu, who was known to his contemporaries as Kongzi or Master Kong. Westerners know this philosopher better by his Latinized name of Confucius. Born in 551 B.C.E., he lived during the tumultuous Axial Age, a time of warfare, instability, uncertainty, and profound societal change. He, like many of his contemporaries, was concerned with finding a way back to peace, stability, and harmony. Because various legends[33] grew around him, separating fact from fiction can be difficult. To learn details of his life, many have turned to Sima Qian's *Records of the Grand Historian*, which contains the "official biography" of Confucius. According to this record, he was born into a lesser aristocratic family in the state of Lu, which is today in Shandong province. His father was a distinguished soldier of an already advanced age, and his mother was the youngest of three sisters. Since Confucius' father died when he was still a child, the boy was raised by his mother under humble circumstances. Despite their financial hardships, she made sure that her son was well educated. When he was 19, Confucius married, had a daughter, and served as a minor government official; he was keeper of stores of grain. In his early 20s, his mother died, and, like the dutiful (and filial) son that he was, he mourned her according to tradition—for three years.[34] It was also in his 20s that he began teaching, rather unusually, anyone who wanted to learn from him—even those of meager means.[35] Of his profession he said, "In teaching there should be no class distinctions."[36]

In his 50s, he returned to government office, and served as the minister of public works and then minister of crime under Duke Ding of Lu. He eventually left that position, and for about 13 years sought an audience with state leaders, urging them to return to the moral ways of the ancient sage kings. He was largely unsuccessful in his attempts. Because of this "failure," he returned home and continued teaching. It is said that he had as many as 3,000 disciples; however, of these only about 72 remained in his inner circle. During his final years, Confucius also reputedly arranged and edited several classic texts. Because he believed that they provided society with a moral template, he felt they should be preserved and taught. In fact, he didn't think of himself as the founder of a tradition but as a transmitter of it. These texts came to be known as the Five Classics: *Shu Ching* (*Book of History*), the *Shih Ching* (*Book of Poetry*), the *Li Chi* (*Book of Rites*), the *I Ching* (*Book of Changes*), and the *Ch'un Ch'iu* (*Spring and Autumn Annals*).[37] He died at 72 years old.

The essence of Confucius' teachings can be found in the Analects or *Lunyu*, which was compiled by his students and was based on what they had remembered of his conversations. Collected into 20 books, the Analects contain discourses on everything from manners and morals to the proper conduct for government and rulers. Confucius believed that when leaders and government led by moral and virtuous example, the result would be a harmonious society. As he said, "If good men ruled the country for 100 years, they could even tame the brutal and abolish capital punishment!" (Analects 13:11). Furthermore, he emphasized the importance of education as a way of creating virtuous men. As he said, "Men are very much the same, it is through practice that they drift apart" (17:2). If a person learned how to act according to one's social duties (Confucius called this *yi*, righteousness); and . . . learn[ed] the rules of propriety (*li*), that is, the rules of conduct and ceremonies laid down in the ancient records; and finally, if one [became] imbued with what is the core Confucian virtue, *ren* (benevolence, or human-heartedness), that is, consideration for others, and [acted] in accordance with what one has learned, then one [would] become what Confucius called a *junzi*, a 'superior man.'"[38] As scholar Xinzhong Yao explains, "At a lower level, a *junzi* is someone whose actions are free from violence, whose bearing is completely sincere and whose speech lacks vulgarity." On a higher level that person "can be entrusted with the destiny of the whole state."[39] For Confucius, nobility shouldn't be based on birth, as had been the case before and during his life; it should be based on learning and self-actualization.

Becoming a *junzi* was so critical to Confucian thought that the word appears in the Analects 107 times.[40] So, how should a "noble man" behave? According to book 1, he is filial toward his parents, fraternal toward his brothers, and trustworthy and loyal to his friends. Book 2 says that he "acts before he speaks, and then speaks according to his action"; he is "broad-minded but not partisan." In book 4, we learn that he "does not, even for the space of a single meal, act contrary to virtue." No matter what, he always follows what is righteous and virtuous. He also "wishes to be slow in his speech and earnest in his conduct." Book 5 outlines four characteristics of a "superior man." He is said to be humble, respectful of his superior, kind in nourishing the people, and just. Book 6 informs us that the *junzi* helps the distressed but never adds to the wealth of the rich. Book 7 explains that he is "satisfied and composed." Unlike a lower man, the *junzi* has neither anxiety nor fear, so says book 12. It also tells us that he never fails reverentially to order his own conduct, is respectful of others, is observant of propriety, and seeks to perfect the admirable qualities of men. Book 13 discusses his understanding of speaking names appropriately, his affable qualities, and his "dignified ease." He's also said to be easy to serve and difficult to please. "If you try to please him in any way which is not accordant with right, he will not be pleased." Book 15 includes several qualities, including the fact that he is "distressed by his want of ability," is dignified and sociable, and doesn't promote a man simply on account of his words. "The object of the superior man is truth. Food is not his object"; he is "anxious lest he should not get truth; he is not anxious lest poverty should come upon him." The *junzi* focused on self-cultivation rather than the external form of conduct, and in the case that he suffered a moral setback, he should accept the blame and correct himself.

Book 16 states that "there are three things which the superior man guards against. In youth . . . he guards against lust. When he is strong and his physical powers are full of vigor, he guards against quarrelsomeness. When he is old . . . he guards against covetousness." The three things of which he stands in awe are the ordinances of heaven, of great men, and the words of sages. Nine additional qualities of a *junzi* are outlined in this book. They include his ability to see clearly and hear distinctly, and his need to have a benign countenance, a respectful demeanor, sincere speech, and a reverently careful way of doing business. It says that when he doubts, he asks questions; when he is angry, he thinks of how it might affect others; and when he sees his own gain, he thinks of righteousness. With regard to his family, the *junzi* maintains a distant reserve toward his son, and when his parents die he mourns them for three years, being mindful that he shouldn't enjoy pleasant food, music, comfort, or ease. Finally, a superior man should not associate with those who engage in unrighteous actions. He should hate those who proclaim the evil of others, who slander their superiors, and are unobservant of propriety. "Without recognizing the ordinance of Heaven, it is impossible to be a superior man." According to scholar A. S. Cua, a *junzi* is a "paradigmatic individual who functions as a guide for practical conduct. . . . [He] provides a standard of inspiration, rather than aspiration—that is, he functions more like a beacon of light than a norm of conduct."[41]

The three utmost qualities of a *junzi* are *ren*, *yi*, and *li*. The most important of the three was *ren*, which has been interpreted to mean a variety of qualities, including benevolence, compassion, altruism, goodness, humanity, love, and kindness. Most importantly, it means being concerned about others and having empathy for them, seeing them as oneself and treating them as such. *Ren* should pervade the *junzi*'s being to such a degree that, as it says in the Analects (15:8), he will not seek to live at the expense of injuring it. In short, he will even sacrifice his life to preserve *ren*. According to scholar James Legge, this suggests that a *junzi* would rather kill himself than abandon *ren*. "No doubt suicide is included in this expression, and Confucius here justifies that act, as in certain cases expressive of high virtue."[42] Being able to distinguish between right and wrong also ties into *yi*.

Li corresponds to ritual decorum, but on a larger scale it dictates how an individual should behave, whether to heaven or to society. It might be said that it delineates "the conventionally accepted style of actions, that is, the form

and possibility of moral achievement within a culture or cultural lifestyle."
Unlike *ren*, it doesn't "define the nature of morality; it defines only the limiting form of execution of moral performance."[43] Being accurate was as important as "understanding the larger moral implications of ritual performance."[44]
Ritual without the sentiment behind it was meaningless. As it says in the
Analects (3:26), "High station filled without indulgent generosity; ceremonies
performed without reverence; mourning conducted without sorrow—where-
with should I contemplate such ways?"

As we've already seen, having filial devotion (*xiao*) was incredibly important to Confucius. He saw the family as a microcosm of society, and he believed that maintaining proper relationships within it had a ripple effect. For
example, when asked why he didn't serve in the government, he replied that
by loving one's parents, brothers, and sisters, one could have a positive effect
on the government. So why was service necessary? (2:21). Three of the five relationships (father-son, husband-wife, elder-younger brother) mentioned by
Confucius take place within the family, while the other two (ruler-subject, and
friend-friend) are "conceived in terms of the family models."[45] All relationships were seen as reciprocal with each side owing something to the other. For
instance, when it came to one's parents Confucius remarked in the Analects
that one should "never disobey. . . . When parents are alive, serve them according to the rules of propriety. When they die, bury them according to the
rules of propriety and sacrifice to them according to the rules of propriety."[46]
One should serve and take care of one's parents, be loyal to them, and have respect and reverence for them. The parents in turn should be sincere, act as
good role models, and "rule" over their children with fairness. And so it goes
for each of the aforementioned relationships. As Confucius said, "A man of
humanity, wishing to establish his own character, also establishes the character of others, and wishing to be prominent himself, also helps others to be
prominent."[47]

Meng Ke, or Mencius (371–289 B.C.E.) as he's known in the West, further
developed Confucius' ideas, such as explaining how important it was to cultivate and nurture these "five constant virtues of humaneness, righteousness,
propriety, wisdom and faithfulness."[48] He also discussed problems not
touched on by Confucius, such as "the way of heaven (*tiandao*), human nature
(*xing*) [and] human destiny (*ming*)."[49] As scholar D. C. Lau explains, "It is not
an exaggeration to say that what is called Confucianism in subsequent times

contains as much of the thought of Mencius as of Confucius."[50] Mencius was born in the state of Zhou and, according to Sima Qian, studied under a disciple of Confucius' grandson. Mencius also lived during a tumultuous time—wars were ever-present—and he worked to change this. He believed that humans were good and moral, and, once developed, that morality could have a ripple effect from the individual to government. Like Confucius, Mencius spent much of his life seeking an audience with rulers. Few paid him much attention, though. Also like Confucius, he retired to a life of teaching and writing his own views, which lead to the creation of *Mencius*, a text that was named after him. Comprised of seven parts, it is a record of conversations between Mencius and rulers, disciples, and adversaries. It also contains his thoughts on such subjects as government and human nature.

How did Mencius expand Confucian thinking? First of all, he addressed the nature of human beings. He stated that even though, like all animals, we are driven by the need for food and sex, we are unique in that we can make moral choices, perform moral actions, and have moral feelings. How do we do these things? By retaining and using our "original heart" or "true heart." When one forgets it, a person becomes attracted to the objects of one's desires. As scholar D. C. Lau explains, "Without the ability to think, a living creature is completely determined by its desires and the desires are totally at the mercy of their respective objects."[51] Mencius believed that no one was devoid of being sensitive to others. His reason for saying this, he explains in book 2A, chapter 6, is that anyone seeing a child about to fall into a well would be moved to compassion. One's motivation wouldn't be to win the parents' favor or to earn societal praise, nor would it even be because the child's scream upset him. Something else would be at work. And "from this it can be seen that whoever is devoid of the heart of compassion is not human, whoever is devoid of the heart of shame is not human, whoever is devoid of the heart of courtesy and modesty is not human, and whoever is devoid of the heart of right and wrong is not human. The heart of compassion is the germ of benevolence (*ren*); the heart of shame, of dutifulness (*yi*); the heart of courtesy and modesty, of observance of rites (*li*); the heart of right and wrong, of wisdom (*zhi*). Man has these four germs just as he has four limbs." As Lau explains, Mencius uses this example because it demonstrates that when a person reacts immediately to such a situation—without reflection—he demonstrates his true nature.[52]

Mencius described human nature as essentially good "in the sense that it was the source and resource for anyone's cultivation and transformation of himself into a person who was moral, trustworthy, 'appreciable,' even great, sagely, or divine."[53] For Mencius, this source of philosophical activity and self-cultivation is *xing*, which is typically translated as heart-mind. Even though everyone possesses it, not everyone cultivates it. And for Mencius, self-cultivation was imperative, because only then can one become a sage. As he says in book 6A, chapter 11, "Humaneness is the human mind. Rightness is the human path. To quit the path and not follow it, to abandon the mind and not know enough to seek it, it is lamentable." Furthermore, he states in book 7A, chapter 1 that "One who has fully developed his mind knows his nature. Knowing his nature, he knows Heaven. By preserving one's mind and nourishing one's nature one has the means to serve Heaven." Mencius didn't understand heaven as a personal god or a physical place. Instead, it was his "ultimate reality; it had an internal order and structure that were to be realized in creative activities—in the formation and transformation of things and people."[54]

Another important Confucian scholar, Xunzi, also known as Hsun Tzu, lived from ca. 310–221 B.C.E. Although he reaffirmed such core Confucian ideas as the importance of education and the possibility of human perfectibility, his ideas on human nature differed considerably from those of Mencius, who concluded that we are basically good. By contrast, the more pessimistic Xunzi stated that humans are inherently bad. How did they come to such divergent beliefs? Scholar D. C. Lau says that it all boils down to their approaches. While Mencius was looking for what was distinctive about human nature, Xunzi was "looking for what forms an inseparable part of it. For this reason, desires do not qualify, for Mencius, as a defining characteristic of the nature of man because they are shared with animal. . . . For Hsun Tzu, on the other hand, only what is instinctive can be counted as nature, and the heart with its varying possibilities disqualifies itself." Therefore, for Mencius morality was unique to humans, and for Hsun Tzu, it was unnatural and "purely artificial behavior."[55]

In chapter 23 of the *Xunzi de*, Xunzi states plainly that the "human nature is evil; its goodness derives from conscious activity. Now it is human nature to be born with a fondness for profit. Indulging this leads to contention and strife, and the sense of modesty and yielding with which one was born disappears." He continues, explaining that when we indulge our feelings of envy and hate, we are led to "banditry and theft." Our fondness for beautiful things leads to licentiousness and chaos. "Hence, following human nature and indulging human emotions will inevitably lead to contention and strife, causing one to rebel against one's proper duty, reduce principle to chaos, and revert to violence." The only way to change this, he explains, is by applying oneself to training and study, concentrating the mind, unifying the will, and pondering and examining things carefully. But this must be done over a long period of time. It's also important to have a teacher who will teach by example and instruct in proper rituals. What's interesting about Xunzi is that his philosophy, especially during the Han Dynasty (206 B.C.E. to 220 C.E.), was more influential than was Mencius'. This, however, would change during the 11th century C.E., when a renaissance of Confucian thought, known as Neo-Confucianism, occurred.

Although the origins of Legalism (*Fajia*) are under debate, by the third and second centuries B.C.E., this "school" of philosophy was already having a profound affect on Chinese society, especially through the writings of Han Feizi (d. 233 B.C.E), who, it is said, was a student of Xunzi. He, too, shared Xunzi's pessimistic belief that human nature was evil, and this is why he advocated strong government and strict laws. We see this stance in chapter 49, "The Five Vermin," of the *Han Feizi*: "The ancient kings allowed law to be supreme and did not give in to their tearful longings. Hence, it is obvious that humaneness cannot be used to achieve order in the state." Later, the author explains how a "young man of bad character" remains unchanged even after his parents yell at him and his teachers show him how to behave otherwise. What does Han Fei say will change him? Fear brought about by the law enforcement, "for people by nature grow proud on love, but they listen to authority."[56]

Rather than focusing on the individual and his concerns, the more utilitarian Legalism placed the state and its interests above all else, believing that a person's only worth was to serve the purposes of the state. Some proponents of Legalism, particularly Shang Yang (d. 338 B.C.E.), who served as prime minister of the state of Qin and who ushered in reforms that paved the way for China's first emperor, Qin Shihuangdi,[57] even outwardly rejected Confucian values, such as *ren* and *yi*, saying that "kindness and humaneness are the mother of transgressions"[58] and that "the six parasites are: rites and music, odes and history, cultivation and goodness, filial devotion and brotherly love, sincerity and trustworthiness, uprightness and integrity, humaneness and rightness, criticism of the army and being ashamed of fighting."[59] Shang Yang "openly advocated war as a means of strengthening the power of the ruler, expanding the state, and making the people strong, disciplined and submissive."[60] As we read in the *Book of Lord Shang* in the section on agriculture and war, the author advocated oppressive totalitarianism as a way to control the masses: "The way to administer a state well is for the law regulating officials to be clear; one does not rely on men to be intelligent and thoughtful. The ruler makes the people single-minded so they will not scheme for selfish profit. . . . The people will love their ruler and obey his commandments, even to death, if they are engaged in farming morning and evening; but they will be of no use if they see that glib-tongued, itinerant scholars succeed in being honored."[61]

As we've seen, the Legalists believed that the way to control the masses wasn't through kindness or compassion but through reward and harsh punishment. The section titled "Rewards and Punishments" in the *Book of Lord Shang* states that anyone who fails to obey the commandments of the ruler, who violates the interdicts of the state, or who rebels against any statutes will be put to death; pardon isn't an option. Turning society upside down was another way to gain control. Again in the *Book of Lord Shang*, in the section titled "Discussing the People," we read that if the state wants to be strong, the poor should be made rich, and the rich made poor.[62] During Qin Shihuangdi's reign, Legalism became the official doctrine of the regime. A severe distaste for intellectualism resulted in severe persecution, especially of Confucianism, and beginning in 213 B.C.E., the emperor issued a decree that enforced the burning of historical, literary, and philosophical works. It is said that in 212 B.C.E, 460 Confucian scholars were buried alive for opposing this decree. Despite it having been persecuted under the Qin Dynasty, Confucianism made a "comeback" when Qin Shihuangdi died and the dynasty was overthrown. During the Han Dynasty (206 B.C.E.–220 C.E.), Confucianism became the official state doctrine in China, and it was introduced to Vietnam, Korea, and Japan.

Since Legalism and Daoism had their proponents, Confucianism had to adapt in order to survive. The result was that "a new form of Confucianism took shape in the flow of eclecticism and inclusiveness. It accepted the cosmic view of the Yin-Yang School[63] and partly adopted the Daoist view of life. It made some use of Legalist policies to strengthen the power of the rulers. . . . It integrated some apocryphal writings to enhance its appeal in a more or less superstitious society." The result was an eclectic form of Confucianism that appealed to every echelon of Han society as well as the rulers.[64] Dong Zhong-shu (179–104 B.C.E.), chief minister to the emperor, was instrumental in bringing Confucian thought to prominence, and he achieved this in several ways. First, he strived to secure exclusive patronage for Confucian texts, especially the *Spring and Autumn Annals*, which he believed regulated "others and the self"; the way it does this was through "humaneness (*ren*) and rightness (*yi*)."[65] Second, he dismissed all non-Confucian scholars from government. And third, he helped to establish institutions that would have a profound influence on his and later ages. The most important of these was the Imperial College at which would-be bureaucrats were trained in Confucian thought, more specifically the Five Classics. When students completed their period of study, they were given civil service examinations. Over time, these exams became more and more rigorous, with only the brightest minds able to pass. Established in 124 B.C.E., this government school proved to be so successful that "in the Latter Han the number [of students] grew to more than 30,000."[66] As the Han Dynasty progressed, "The dogmatism of Confucian learning greatly increased; annotation and interpretation followed strict transmission from master to disciple; and Classical Learning was confined to a very narrow idea in which attention was given exclusively to the minute interpretation of words, sentences and paragraphs. . . . For example, commentaries and interpretations of a five-word text could be as long as 30,000 words."[67] By its end, Classical Learning had become pedantic scholasticism, and many lost interest in Confucianism and turned to Daoism. Some scholars attempted to synthesize the two; Confucian classics were reinterpreted using Daoist language, and the Daoist spirit was inserted to the heart of Confucian learning.[68] The result was called Mysterious Learning or Dark Learning, and it played a critical role in the mutual development and transformation of Confucianism, Daoism, and Buddhism.

For the next 400 years, labeled the Period of Disunion, warfare and geographical expansion were the norm. Buddhism flourished, especially during the Southern and Northern Dynasties (386–581 C.E.), and debates between this religion and Confucianism reached new heights. This doesn't mean that the Chinese didn't embrace both religions, though. For instance, a devoted Buddhist, Emperor Wu of the Liang Dynasty (464–549 C.E.), not only supported Confucian principles of government but he also encouraged his sons to study the Five Classics, the Analects, and another popular Confucian text, the *Classic of Filiality*. Other countries, too, accepted Confucianism during this period. For instance, before, during, and after the Sui Dynasty (589–618 C.E.), the Korean Silla Kingdom established Confucian studies. And in 604 C.E. the Japanese incorporated this philosophical system to its first constitution.

The Tang Dynasty (618–906 C.E.) is known for its vibrant and intellectual culture, so we might assume that Confucianism was instrumental in its development. And, to some degree, this is true. However, the real culprit was Buddhism, which continued to flourish during the Tang. As one scholar has said, between 220 and 960 C.E., "Chinese culture was so closely identified with Buddhism that neighbors like the Japanese and the Koreans embraced the one with the other and thought of the great Tang China . . . as perhaps more of a 'Buddha-land' than the 'land of Confucius.'" The most renowned centers of learning and works of art and architecture belonged to the Buddhists, and "until the close of this period few among the Confucians could dispute the preeminence of the Buddhist philosophers or slow the progress of the Daoist church, officially supported by the Tang imperial house."[69] Although Confucian scholars existed at this time, few people could be thought of as exclusively Confucian. Because it was relegated to certain realms—work, government, and family—when someone wanted to satisfy his or her religious needs, he or she turned to the more popular Buddhism or Daoism.[70] As has frequently been the case with Confucianism, it served well as an ethical system, and its Five Classics continued to be taught to would-be scholars. In fact, during this period the civil service exam was "perfected," and, until 1911, the scholar-official proved to be "of paramount importance as a major link between the government and the people."[71]

The end of the Tang Dynasty grew increasingly violent and unstable with alien invasions and conquests, and palace intrigue. For instance, the highly unstable and immortality-seeking Emperor Wuzong was influenced by his Daoist priests to wage a war on "foreign" faiths. Although Nestorian and Mazdean religions were affected, Buddhism bore the brunt of this attack. According to his "Edict of the Eight Month" of 845 C.E., more than 4,600 temples were destroyed; nearly 27,000 monks and nuns were "returned to lay life" and added to the tax rolls; and more than 40,000 sanctuaries were destroyed, thus releasing millions of acres of land and 150,000 servants to the tax rolls.

As he explained, "If Buddhism is completely abolished now, who will say that the action is not timely? Already more than 100,000 idle and unproductive Buddhist followers have been expelled and countless of their gaudy, useless buildings destroyed."[72]

After nearly 200 years, the anti-Buddhist mind-set hadn't disappeared. In fact, it resurfaced toward the end of the Song Dynasty (960–1279 C.E.) among Neo-Confucians. In their writings, several of them demonstrated just how Confucian ideas were superior to those of Buddhism and Daoism. One scholar in particular, Ouyang Xiu (1007–1070 C.E.) authored the vitriolic "Essay on Fundamentals (*Benlun*)," which in part 2 calls Buddhism "a corruption that eats into and destroys men." The key to defeating it, he says, is to know rites and rightness. Undoubtedly, he's talking about *li* and *yi*, core components of Confucian thought.[73] As Neo-Confucianism took hold, it became more and more rigid with regard to social relationships. Neo-Confucianism was essentially a renaissance of Confucian thinking but with many differences. Stimulated by Buddhist and Daoist teachings, several of the key scholars of this time revisited classical Confucian texts and transformed them so as to "construct a comprehensive and complicated doctrinal system containing an evolutionary cosmology, a humanistic ethics and a rationalistic epistemology."[74] For the most part, Neo-Confucianism was more philosophical in orientation with more emphasis placed on one's spiritual life. Great emphasis was placed on rituals, and the sage became the ideal for all to follow.

By the 13th century, Confucianism was so closely associated with education and the government that even when the Mongols invaded and assumed control of China, thus ushering in the Yuan Dynasty (1279–1368), they employed it for governmental practices and revived the civil service exams.[75] One of the greatest contributors to the development and propagation of Neo-Confucianism during this dynasty was Zhu Xi (1130–1200 C.E.), a prolific writer and editor who was associated with the Rationalistic School (also known as School of Principle). He emphasized reason and intuition, and said that by understanding these and studying the Classical texts, one could overcome one's imperfections. In essence, "to manifest the brightness of human nature and bring Heavenly Principle (*tian li*) within to light, we have to . . . get rid of selfish desires and feeling and let the good nature shine."[76] Although his writings were branded as heretical during his life, this changed after his death. In 1313 C.E., his editions of and commentaries on the Analects of Confucius, *The Great*

Learning (*Ta Hsueh*), *The Doctrine of the Mean* (*Chung Yung*), both of which were excerpted from the *Book of Rites* (*Li Chi*), and the book of *Mencius*, were adopted as the official textbooks for civil service examinations. For the first time, these four books supplanted the Five Classics and remained in use until their abolition in 1905. Zhu Xi's writings dominated Confucian scholarship, and because of this he came to be addressed as Zhu Fuzi, Master Zhu. Only he, Confucius, and Mencius have ever earned that honor.[77] The School of Mind was another important branch of Neo-Confucianism, and its chief proponent was Wang Yangming (1472–1529 C.E.), the most influential thinker after Zhu Xi. He suggested that since the human mind reflects the principle of the universe, we have an innate knowledge of morality—what is right and what is wrong. Rather than investigate that which is external to the mind, the philosopher's duty was simply to look inward. For him, anyone—not just the educated—could become a sage. The simplicity and directness of Wang Yangming's thought is undoubtedly what made it so popular during the Ming Dynasty (1368–1644) and beyond.

During the Ming Dynasty, Confucianism proved a powerful tool. As scholar Edward Farmer writes, "The founders of the Ming firmly believed that they possessed the Mandate of Heaven and that mandate charged them with the task not just to reunify China politically but also to carry out the ethical remaking of its people in the light of the Confucian ideals of antiquity—taking the sage kings as their model. . . . There was also an assumption by the state of an obligation to 'nurture' future scholar-officials by providing the students of China with a public school system, together with Confucian instructors and approved Confucian texts."[78] At the beginning of the dynasty, schools proliferated throughout the country, and the content and form of the civil service exam were simplified. Ming Taizu, who reigned from 1368–1398, was the force behind these changes. Rather than being truly concerned about his people, this autocratic ruler was acting on his fear of opposition. His "reforms" were nothing more than a way to strengthen his own role while weakening that of anyone else's. For instance, he permitted public beatings of officials as a way of showing that they were just servants to the emperor, and he forcibly relocated tens of thousands of wealthy families into poorer areas so they could be watched.

Toward the end of his reign in 1382 C.E., as a way to ensure conformity, he had 12 rules for students cut into stone slabs, which were erected in each school, and at the end of his reign, a 41-point proclamation on conduct was issued. On his *Placard for the Instruction of the People*, we read that the elders of each community will review all minor matters, and officials will deal with serious matters, such as sexual crime, robbery, fraud, and homicide. Any officials or functionaries who violate the order will be sentenced to death; commoners will, with their entire families, be banished. His Article 19 or "Six Instructions" comes directly from the teachings of Zhu Xi, and in part, it says that six times each month, children will lead an elderly, disabled, or blind person through the village, and while ringing a bell, will shout "Be filial to your parents, respect elders and superiors, live in harmony with your neighbors, instruct and discipline children and grandchildren, be content with your occupation, commit no wrongful acts."[79]

It's worth mentioning that even though Confucianism formed the backbone of Ming Taizu's government, he was, in his youth, a Buddhist monk, and several times in the 1340s and 1350s he sought refuge in a Buddhist temple. It might not be surprising then that he issued a statement called *Discussion of the Three Teachings*, which are, of course, Confucianism, Buddhism, and Daoism. After defining what these religions truly mean, rather than how they have been interpreted, he praises them, saying that the "Three Teachings contain things that are abstruse and vital [in substance], yet solidly efficacious when put into practice. Anything that benefits humankind when put into practice is the Way of Heaven." At the end of the statement he lauds the religions again, remarking that all of the teachings are indispensable.[80]

From the Ming until the Qing Dynasty (1644–1911), Confucianism continued to influence Chinese society. During the latter dynasty, the foreign rulers—the Manchus—employed Neo-Confucian ideas in their government and continued the use of the civil service exams. The Qianlong emperor himself was schooled in the Confucian Classics. Sun Yat-sen (1866–1925), the first provisional president of the Republic of China, even championed the idea of making Confucianism the state religion; he was unsuccessful in his efforts. The leader of the Nationalist Party, Chiang Kai-Shek (1887–1975), drew upon Confucian virtues for his campaign of mass education. Despite these examples, an anti-Confucian sentiment was evident by the end the Qing, and some political groups saw it as the cause of all of the country's woes. Mao Zedong, who, under the Communist banner took over the reins of China in 1949, seconded this opinion, and during the Cultural Revolution (1966–1976) set about eradicating the Four Olds: culture, ideas, customs, and habits. As part of this process, a band of Red Guards reportedly damaged Confucius' family home, the temple at his birthplace, and his family cemetery. Furthermore, archives and writings were destroyed, and intellectuals were ridiculed.

Mao Zedong disliked Confucianism for its emphasis on intellectualism, its "superstitious rituals," and its oppression of women and the lower classes. He also blamed it for keeping China in the past rather than moving it into the future and making it competitive with the rest of the world. The Communist attitude toward Confucius is well depicted in the writings of Liu Shaoqi (1900–1969), one of Mao's closest comrades. In his text, *How to Be a Good Communist*, he writes that aside from using the teachings of Confucius for "window-dressing purposes," old-school scholars also used them to "oppress the exploited and make use of righteousness and morality for hoodwinking and suppressing the culturally backward people" as well as "to attempt to secure better government jobs, make money and achieve fame, and reflect credit on their parents."[81] What's interesting about this example is that even though the Communists reviled Confucianism, they rebadged many of its ideas and used them for their own purposes. And the ultimate irony is that in the 21st century, many government officials are arguing that Communist and Confucian ideologies are compatible.[82]

Today, Confucianism is experiencing a resurgence in China and is even being endorsed by the government.[83] President Hu Jintao, for example, has employed the words of Confucius in his speeches. In February 2005, he announced to party officials that "Confucius said, 'harmony is something to be cherished.'" A few months later, he instructed China's party cadres to build a "harmonious society."[84] His "Theory of Three Harmonies" and anticorruption campaign of "Eight Honors and Eight Shames" are also both rooted in the ancient religion. According to an article in the *Washington Post*, many Chinese are growing dissatisfied with their increasingly "materialistic" and "superficial" culture and are seeking solace in the past. "State-supported commemorations of Confucius have become more common, and the number of people studying his works has increased."[85] Some have begun sending their children, who are as young as three, to elementary schools at which they memorize and recite Chinese classics. The Education Ministry has approved more courses in traditional Confucian culture, and at least 18 universities have started offering courses in Confucian studies.[86] In addition, the "government supports 145 nonprofit Confucius Institutes in more than 52 countries and regions" with the goal of "promoting Chinese language and culture."[87] Confucian thought seems to hold something for everyone: The government sees it as a way to legitimize its rule and encourage order; parents believe that it helps their children to maintain a sense of tradition and learn respect and obedience; and the middle class, who are wealthy enough to have free time, see it as a viable form of spirituality. For 2,500 years Confucianism has exerted a profound influence on China, so much so that one might even say that to be Chinese is to be Confucian. As Miao Di, a professor at Communication University of China, remarked, "Maybe 99 percent of Chinese people today never read his writings, but Confucian values are steeped in our culture."[88]

A number of Chinese filmmakers have been openly hostile to Confucianism, usually attacking it for its long-standing patriarchal and repressive stance toward women. But Confucius, himself, doesn't deserve all of the blame. If we look through the Analects, "women feature only rarely . . . and are primarily portrayed as temptations to men—the 'physical beauty' or object of lust that leads men away from . . . morality." The two or three direct references are merely "unflattering."[89] The most oft-quoted reference is found in the Analects (17:25), which reads "of all people, women and servants are particularly hard to manage: if you are too familiar with them, they grow insolent, but if you are too distant they grow resentful."[90] It's true that Confucius lived during a time when "the primary virtues of a young woman were considered to be her filial piety towards parents and parents-in-law, assistance to her husband and education of her children (*xiangfu jiaozi*)."[91] Women were considered to be "lower" than men and, for the most part, were confined to the home, where they were expected to raise children and take care of the household. They also were encouraged to be obedient: first to their fathers, then to their husbands, and then to their grown son.[92] This said, as scholar Xinzhong Yao states, the same could be said of most patriarchal societies; it was certainly true of India. To be fair to Confucius, as Xao again points out, "It was only in a later stage when Confucianism became rigidly dogmatic that all measures against women were associated with Confucian doctrines."[93]

For the most part, in traditional Chinese society, males were sent to school for an education, and females stayed home. A woman's only "education" was learned on the job and involved studying the finer points of caring for her family, including honoring the family's ancestors, obeying and carrying for her parents-in-law, and producing male offspring. Since women of the ruling elite or the imperial family "played a key role in the early education of the young, it was essential for mothers and their female surrogates . . . to achieve mastery of the classical texts and primers that they taught to the young males before the latter went off to school."[94] The education of women in "wifely ways" became particularly important during the Song and Ming Dynasties, and their Confucian studies came in the form of the *Four Books for Women* (*Nu sishu*), which included *Admonitions for Women* (*Nujie*), which was written during the Han Dynasty; the *Classic of Filiality for Women* (*Nu xiaojin*),[95] *Analects for Women* (*Nu lunyu*), both from the Tang Dynasty; and *Instructions for the Inner Quarters* (*Neixun*), which was a product of the Ming Dynasty. These texts, written by women, conformed to the Confucian "hierarchy" of society, with women serving as the yin to men's yang. "Like the earth, which occupies the inferior position below, women are to be subservient, passive and yielding, while men are to be dominant, active and strong like the superior force of Heaven."[96]

One director who, throughout his career, has explored the subject of the subjugation of women under Chinese patriarchy is Zhang Yimou. His early films—*Red Sorghum* (*Hong Gao Liang*, 1987), *Ju Dou* (1990), and *Raise the Red Lantern* (*Da Hong Deng Long Gao Gao Gua*, 1991)—illustrate the restricted and often miserable lives that women have encountered, especially during the early 20th century.

Red Sorghum (*Hong Gao Liang*) (1987)—Directed by Zhang Yimou. Running time: 91 min. Mandarin. China: Unrated. Genre: Drama.

In *Red Sorghum*, a young woman (Gong Li) living in China during the 1920s and 1930s, is arranged to marry an elderly and leprous winemaker. En route, she is ravished in the fields by a servant (Wen Jiang). After the woman's husband dies suddenly, she and this servant, who is now her lover, live together, making sorghum wine. Their happiness is disrupted with the arrival of Japanese soldiers.

Ju Dou (1990)—Directed by Zhang Yimou. Running time: 95 min. Mandarin. China. Unrated. Genre: Drama.

Set during the 1920s, *Ju Dou* also focuses on a beautiful young woman (Gong Li) who is married to an elderly man. An owner of a dyeing workshop, her husband is impotent and extremely violent. One day, while her husband is out of the house, she seduces her nephew. Not long afterward, she learns that she is pregnant. Initially she hides this fact from her husband, but after he is paralyzed in an accident, she tells him. In the end, the son, Tianbi, who has been mentally poisoned by the old man, plots to kill his parents. Of the character, Zhang Yimou has said, "Tianbi the boy is weird because he is the product of an abnormal relationship, which is very twisted and distorted (*niuqu*). As he grows up, all around him is secrecy, so he does not speak. Tianbi calls the old man 'father' because he has to. In those days, his parents would be put to death if it were found out. Even down to the 1920s it was that strict. So you see how horrible this system is."[97] This tragedy was nominated for an Oscar.

Raise the Red Lantern (*Da Hong Deng Long Gao Gao Gua*) (1991)—Directed by Zhang Yimou. Running time: 125 min. Mandarin. China. Unrated. Genre: Drama.

Also nominated for an Oscar, *Raise the Red Lantern* takes place during the 1920s and focuses on Songlian (Gong Li), a 19-year-old former university student who, after her father dies, leaving her family bankrupt, she becomes the fourth "wife" to a much older man. As soon as she moves in, Songlian feels the tension and resentment that swirls in the custom-entrenched household. Because the master gives preferential treatment to whichever woman he desires for the night—red lanterns are hung in front of her doorway, she receives a foot massage, gets to choose the menu item, and has the servants at her beck and call—scheming worthy of Shakespeare ensues. Probably the most tragic film of the three, *Raise the Red Lantern* ends with the murder of Meishan (Caifei He), the man's third wife; the death of Yan'er, his favorite female servant, and mental insanity of the main character. Unaffected by the situation that he has created, the master, in the end, simply adds another female to his home. That a wealthy man had many wives was a long-standing Chinese tradition. As it says in the "Hun yi" chapter of the *Book of Rites*, it wasn't uncommon for the emperor to have, in addition to his empress, many consorts, concubines, mistresses, and paramours.[98] According to *Raise the Red Lantern*, this practice, for the aristocracy was still in place by the 1920s. Women were simply supposed to accept this because they were the subordinates. As scholar Francis L. K. Hsu explains, concubines were either poor girls or girls from wealthier families who had engaged in sexual misconduct.[99]

What's particularly interesting about the dynamic in this household is that even though the master rarely, if ever, visits his first wife, Yuru (Jin Shuyuan), she still holds a prominent position, because only she has produced a son and heir. Realizing that having a child can be her ticket to attention and time with the master, Songlian feigns pregnancy. However, her ruse is soon discovered, and she is punished. *Raise the Red Lantern* clearly demonstrates the powerlessness of women under patriarchy, and the sexual double standards that they were forced to endure.[100] The film also demonstrates how important it was to have a son and the kind of power it brought to the mother. Wealthy men could afford many concubines, but if it was revealed that one of them was barren, she most likely would be ignored. If he already had a male heir, she might retain his favor for a longer period. But eventually, her inability to produce sons would catch up with her. Because concubines were much younger than their husbands, when they died, "the sons of the wife or the other concubines will not pay much attention to her or her needs. When the lineage already has an heir, a concubine has no right to adopt a child. This means that such a person will merely wither on the vine. She has no certain place on any ancestral altar."[101] As scholar Kazuko Ono explains, the foremost aim of the traditional Chinese family was "the perpetuation of the male line of descent, and in order to ensure the purity of that line, female chastity was rigidly enforced on the one hand, and a system of plural wives to facilitate the birth of many sons was widely adopted on the other. (Female children were not counted as heirs—only male children.)"[102]

Under the traditional Chinese system, a woman's life, at any stage, was anything but pleasant. The birth of a daughter was often seen as an unwanted event because the family knew that they would have to produce a dowry for her. In poor areas when food was scarce, girls were sometimes killed. According to *Admonitions for Women*, three days after a girl was born, the "ancients" observed three customs. The first was to place the baby under the bed for three days, thus indicating that "she was lowly and humble and should regard it as a prime duty to submit to others." The second was to give her a spindle with which to play. This was to symbolize how industrious she would need to be in her life. And the third was to announce her birth to the ancestors by an offering. This was to demonstrate her responsibility for the continuation of the ancestral sacrifices.[103] In most areas of China, when the girl was about five or six, her feet were bound, thus making her more "attractive" but unable to walk. When it came time for her marriage, she had little say in the matter. Her parents or a matchmaker selected a partner for her. This marriage wouldn't be based on love but on suitability. After the wedding ceremony, she went to live with her husband's family and was expected to respect and obey her in-laws. If her husband died before she did, she was discouraged from remarriage and encouraged to be chaste until death.[104] During a 1993 interview, Zhang Yimou was asked why he uses female characters to make a statement. He explained that he wants to express a sense of the "Chinese people's oppression and confinement, which has been going on for thousands of years. Women express this more clearly on their bodies (*zai tamen shenshang*) because they bear a heavier burden than men."[105] He also explained that the Cultural Revolution hasn't really changed anything, because China is "still an autocratic system (*zhuanzhi*), a feudal patriarchal system (*fengjian jiazhangzhi*)."[106]

The Wooden Man's Bride (*Wu kui*) (1994)—Directed by Jianxin Huang. Running time: 113 min. Mandarin. China. Unrated. Genre: Drama.

The Wooden Man's Bride is as condemnatory of Confucian patriarchy as Zhang Yimou's "trilogy" is. It focuses on a young woman (Lan Wang), who because of her father's debt, is promised to the son of a wealthy tofu maker. On the way to her future home, her entourage is ambushed by bandits and she is taken captive. Kui (Shih Chang), a local farmer, gets her back and delivers her to the Liu family. Even though the young master has died in a fatal accident, the matriarch of the family, Madam Liu (Yumei Wang), proceeds with the "wedding," marrying her daughter-in-law-to-be to a wooden effigy of her son. Despite the apparent absurdity of the situation, the young widow is expected to honor her wooden "husband," as she would in real life, and, as her mother-in-law has done, preserve her chastity. At the end of the film, Kui, now a bandit, comes back to free the young mistress, who has, because of attempts to escape, been chained in her room and her ankles have been broken. As her punishment, the mother-in-law is forced to hang herself.

Before the film credits begin, the audience learns that the townspeople erected a tombstone to Madame Liu's chastity and that every year, they bow before it. When written for women, funerary inscriptions tended to focus on the deceased person's virtues. In general, the most important of these was her loyalty and duty to her parents-in-law, then it was her subservience to her husband, and finally it was her ability to raise and educate her children.[107] However, considering how much emphasis Chinese society placed on a woman's state of purity, this statement in the film shouldn't seem out of the ordinary. Long before the 20th century, women were told to remain pure and not bring shame to their families by unsightly behavior. In Ban Zhao's *Admonitions for Women*, in the section titled "Womanly Behavior," she warns her readers to guard carefully their chastity and exhibit modesty in every motion.[108] In her *Analects for Women*, Song Ruozhao, too, covered this subject, telling the reader that she should work hard to establish her purity and chastity. "By purity, one keeps one's self undefiled; by chastity, one preserves one's honor." The author states that men and women should be segregated; therefore, if a woman had to venture outside of the home, she should cover her face. And finally, she warns, "Do not be on familiar terms with men outside the family."[109] Although these texts were, by the 20th century, more than 1,000 years old, women were still being held to these standards. "Even in the Republican period, a woman's 'chastity' was still being rewarded. Or, to put it more accurately, precisely because it was the era of the Republic (1912–1949), it was necessary to recognize 'chastity' and 'virtuousness' in order to repair the unraveling ties that might still hold the family system together and to support and maintain the social order." As Lun Xun (1881–1936), a writer and social critic explained, "When the country is about to be subjugated, there is much talk of chastity, and women who take their own lives are highly regarded. For women belong to men, and when a man dies his wife should not remarry."[110]

It's no surprise that all of the aforementioned films are set during the 1920s, because this was during the era of warlordism (1912–1927), a particularly brutal and unruly time in Chinese history that "represented the continuation of feudal rule of China."[111] "It was also an era when kinship, marriage, regional ties, and even school ties remained of paramount importance."[112] Times were starting to change, though, and they had been since 1905 when the civil service examination was abolished, and in 1912 when the monarchy was overthrown. In fact, in the early second decade of the 20th century, many Chinese, seeing the inequities in their society, were calling for an end to Confucianism. After 1915, many Chinese youths increasingly challenged tradition, hoping to replace it with something new and, ultimately, more egalitarian. "In the May Fourth Period (thus named for a student demonstration on May 4, 1919), women emerged as politically assertive, participating in demonstrations, attending schools in much greater numbers, and unbinding their feet."[113] Even more changes lay ahead. In 1950, it seemed that men and women were moving into equal territory when the Marriage Law was announced. It effectively abolished many feudal practices, such as bigamy, concubinage, child betrothal, interference with the remarriage of widows, and the exaction of money or gifts in connection with marriages. It also stated that marriage could be contracted only after the girl had turned 18 and the male 20, and that husbands and wives were to have equal standing in the home and should strive "jointly for the welfare of the family."[114]

The real question is: Did Communism achieve what it set out to do with regard to women? Initially, yes. According to a 2004 article in the *Journal of Population Research*, during the 1950s and the 1970s, when the government actively promoted gender equality, "female infanticide and severe neglect of girls leading to their untimely deaths were reduced to the lowest levels ever seen in China."[115] This changed in the late 1970s, when family planning compulsion increased and the one-child policy was introduced.[116] Today, "China has the most severe shortage of girls compared to boys of any country in the world. . . . Daughters are lost primarily through sex-selective abortion, secondly through excess female infant mortality, and thirdly through neglect or mistreatment of girls up to age three, in cities as well as rural areas."[117] The article continues, explaining that this "abnormal shortage of females" has been in evidence "for centuries or even millennia. . . . Evidence from China's last dynasty, the Qing (1644–1911), indicates a shortage of girls in families from the highest social classes to the lowest. The dearth of girls was caused by female infanticide immediately after birth (drowning, exposure, suffocation, abandonment) or by untimely childhood deaths through selective neglect or maltreatment of girls." The reason these daughters were killed, the author states, was that "a strong Confucian value system . . . honored almost all males over nearly all females. Important religious and ancestral rituals were reserved for males. It is believed, and still is today, that the family lineage can be continued only through sons."[118]

Two additional films that expose the patriarchal attitudes of Confucianism are Zhang Yimou's *Curse of the Golden Flower* (*Man Cheng Jin Dai Huang Jin*

Jia, 2006) and *The King of Masks* (*Bian Lian*, 1996). Because they afford us the opportunity to discuss other religions, we will explore them in depth.

Curse of the Golden Flower (*Man Cheng Jin Dai Huang Jin Jia*) (2006)—
Adapted from a play by Yu Cao. Screenplay and direction by Zhang Yimou. Running time: 114 min. Mandarin. China. Rated R for violence. Genre: Action/Drama.

Summary: Set in 928 C.E., during the Tang Dynasty[119] in China, the film focuses on the layers of intrigue taking place within the Imperial Palace. With the assistance of the Imperial physician, the emperor (Chow Yun Fat) is slowly poisoning his wife (Gong Li). She, in turn, has engaged in illicit relations with her stepson, the crown prince (Liu Ye). Her ardor for him remains strong, but the same can't be said of him. His feelings have cooled because he is having relations with the imperial physician's daughter (Li Man) and they are planning to run away together. Finally, the arrival of Prince Jie (Jay Chou), the empress's faithful son, brings about an imbalance in the house, especially when he learns of his father's diabolical actions. Will he avenge his mother? And which of the three sons—the youngest is Prince Yu (Junjie Qin)—will finally take the throne?

As the film begins, we immediately enter a world of opulence. Gold and silk adorn every inch of the palace, creating a veritable jewelry box in which Emperor Ping (Chow Yun-Fat), Empress Phoenix (Gong Li), and their three children—Crown Prince Wan (Ye Liu), Prince Jie (Jay Chou), and Prince Yu (Junjie Qin)—live. Attending to their every need are thousands of ministers, servants, and soldiers. The source for *Curse of the Golden Flower* is Cao Yu's four-act play, *Lei Yu* (*Thunderstorm*), which is considered a classic of 20th-century drama and is required reading at Beijing's Central Academy of Drama. Written in 1933, it takes place in the home of a wealthy industrialist and offers a 24-hour window into the life of this man's largely dysfunctional family. Zhang Yimou retains the spirit of the play, but he jettisons its 20th-century setting in favor of the late Tang dynasty. As the director explained on the film's DVD featurette titled *Secrets Within*, "There is an old Chinese proverb: 'Gold and jade on the outside, rot and decay on the inside.' It means beneath a beautiful exterior lies a dark and appalling truth. . . . Beneath all that glamour . . . the regime was corrupt. [*Curse of the Golden Flower*] can also be construed as a story about a feudal family. A story of a large family is a reflection of feudalism in China. Chinese culture evolved under extreme male domination. But what I am talking about is ancient China . . . this is no longer the case."

Considered to be the high point of Chinese civilization, the Tang Dynasty (618–907 C.E.) was a golden age of the arts, especially poetry, and, because of military prowess, the country expanded beyond its borders into Japan, Korea, and Vietnam. By the middle of the eighth century, cracks were beginning to appear, brought on by the military defeat in 751 C.E. against Arab forces at Samarkand, increasing economic instability, popular rebellions, and court intrigue. "In its final half century the Tang was an object-lesson in anarchy. Officials, both civil and military, became so cynically corrupt and village peasants so ruthlessly oppressed that the abominable became commonplace."[120] Sandwiched between the Tang and the Song Dynasties (960–1279 C.E.) is a 53-year period known in the north as the Five Dynasties and in the south as the Ten Kingdoms. Characterized by disunity and frequent dynastic change, this period, to the Chinese mind, was "a unique example of the anarchy and moral confusion that inevitably followed the breakdown of the Confucian state."[121] *Curse of the Golden Flower* takes place during this tumultuous period, and it depicts an imperial household governed by Confucian principles, at least on the surface.

Confucianism explains that society is made up of five relationships, and if we want a harmonious and well-ordered society, we must maintain these. Fathers must be role models for their sons; sons must respect and honor their fathers. The same could be said of husbands with their wives, and older brothers with their younger brothers. In *Curse of the Golden Flower* everyone in the imperial household is aware of his or her relationship to others, and for the most part, they act accordingly. The children typically refer to each other by birth position—the youngest son calls the crown prince "First Brother"—and the children typically refer to their parents as "Your Majesty." When the emperor meets Prince Jie after a long absence, the son kneels and says that he is honored by "Father's" personal visit. Even the servants follow the ruler without question. At the emperor's request, the royal physician has altered the recipe of the medicine that is given to the empress. Into the mixture, he has added two ounces of Persian black fungus so that after two months she will lose all of her mental faculties. Also at the emperor's request, the physician's daughter must be the one who serves the concoction. Even though everyone seems to be behaving in a proper and filial manner, there is resentment, hostility, and fear bubbling beneath the surface. Not only is the empress plotting a coup d'état against her husband (she will be assisted by her second son), but the youngest son is also building an army against his father. And in the case of the royal physician, he isn't following the ruler's orders because of devotion or loyalty—even though he says that he would willingly give his life for the ruler—but because he's a social-climbing opportunist who curries the ruler's favor. It pays off for him, too, because toward the end of the film, the ruler promotes him for his "impeccable conduct, loyalty, and honesty." That said, the doctor also knows that if he doesn't do what's asked of him, his "entire clan will be executed."

During one telling scene in the film, the emperor and his wife engage in a power struggle over her refusal to finish her medicine, and he warns her that she had better understand that as long as he is the emperor and she is the empress, they will play their parts to perfection. "The imperial family has to set an example for the entire country," he says. "For the sake of this family, there is much that I am prepared to tolerate, because my concern is to maintain law and order in the home." What the emperor says is in complete accordance with Confucian thought. For Confucius, the family was the paradigm even for the government, and he believed that filial devotion has "bearing on the stability of society as a whole. [Confucius] is convinced that filial devotion practiced within one's family has ramifications in a far wider sphere."[122] We can see how widespread this teaching was when we examine family instruction texts from the Tang Dynasty. In *House Instructions of Mr. Yan* (*Yanshi Jiaxun*), he claims that the three intimate family relationships are the conjugal, parental, and fraternal. Since all other degrees of kinship develop from these, "among human relationships one cannot but take these most seriously." He continues, saying that if disharmony exists between brothers, this will have a trickle-down effect to nephews, cousins, and even servants.[123]

Prior to the Chrysanthemum Festival, the family assembles on a high terrace. When the emperor asks why they do this every year, the youngest son replies, "Father, on the ninth day of the ninth month the sun and the moon unite. It symbolizes the strength and harmony of the family, and we always celebrate on this high terrace." The emperor praises the answer, and then adds, "The terrace is round. The table is square. The law of the heavens dictates the rule of earthly life under the circle; within the square, everyone has his proper placement. This is called natural law. Emperor, courtier, father, son, loyalty, filial piety, ritual and righteousness . . . all relationships obey this law." He's undoubtedly referring to the Mandate of Heaven or "what Heaven ordains" (*tian-ming*), a concept that emerged during the early Zhou period. In this case, heaven refers to the cosmic moral order that impartially guides human destiny. From this concept, it is believed that heaven charged certain good men with rulership. And their offspring might "continue to exercise the Heaven-sanctioned power for as long as they carried out their religious and administrative duties with piety, rightness and wisdom. But if the worth of the ruling family declined, if the rulers turned their backs on the spirits and abandoned the virtuous ways . . . then Heaven might discard them." The Zhou leaders argued that the Shang kings had abandoned wisdom and benevolence for cruelty and degenerate behavior. Heaven punished the Shang by calling upon the Zhou to overthrow them.[124] With its political overtones, the Mandate of Heaven suggested to Confucius that "the ordered process that prevails in the wider world is found to operate in an individual life as well" and that "human beings have a home in the natural order and some assurance of the ultimate significance, and even resonance, of moral action."[125]

In *Curse of the Golden Flower* we encounter several Confucian ideas that, within this context, seem to be incongruous: the importance of filial piety (*xiao*) and one's adherence to humaneness (*ren*). The Analects contribute to this confusion. On the subject of *xiao*, it says that being filial and fraternal are the root of humaneness (1:2) and that being filial means not having discord with one's parents" (2:5). In the Analects (13:18), the Duke of She tells a story about a father who stole a sheep and his son who bore witness against him. This, he says, was the right thing to do. Confucius disagrees, saying it's better for the father to be sheltered by his son. Should we read this to mean that even if the father performs an illegal action, the son should support him because he's their father?[126] This seems to contradict Confucius' own suggestion that people should strive to be in the company of those who are moral and upright. Although *xiao* is an important concept for Confucius, he doesn't focus on it as much as he does *ren*. On this subject, he highlights several key factors. First, the humane person develops himself and then helps others to do the same. As it says in the Analects, "Raise up the upright, put them over the crooked, and you should be able to cause the crooked to become upright"

(12:22). Second, he should recognize himself in others. Third, he should love others, and truly "know" them. As we read in the Analects, "I will not grieve because men do not know me; I will grieve that I do not know men" (1:16). And fourth, a humane person should have these five things: respect, liberality, trustworthiness, earnestness, and kindness (17:6).

Some have criticized *Curse of the Golden Flower* for its tendency to "valorize the rigorous Confucian order, because the bulk of the film's conflict stems from a transgression of wife against husband, and leads to a series of disruptions in a broad portfolio of Confucian relational structures."[127] But we have to ask ourselves: is this the true cause of the film's conflict? Is the blame being laid at the empress's feet? This would seem uncharacteristic for Zhang Yimou, whose films frequently explore patriarchal oppression. His female protagonists are always strong characters who struggle against the system, but ultimately they realize the futility of their actions and they succumb to their tragic fate. Empress Phoenix is no different, and as Zhang Yimou says in the DVD special featurette, *Secrets Within*, "The story represents a time when men dominated society. Women were oppressed. It was a repression of humanity. . . . In a male-dominated society, she is the central victim. Even though she's the empress, she suffers the most. What I want to portray is, first, a female victim. But at the same time, I also describe her rebellion."

To truly understand what the film is saying, we have to examine the character of the father within a Confucian context, more precisely, by seeing if he adheres to Confucius' explanation of *ren*. What does the film reveal about Emperor Ping? According to his first wife, when she knew him he was a lowly captain plotting day and night to become emperor. "You flattered the king of Liang into letting you marry his daughter. You planned meticulously to have my entire family put in prison. Later, I alone managed to escape." With his first wife out of the way, he marries the soon-to-be Empress Phoenix. But instead of telling the truth about his machinations for power, he informs everyone that his first wife is dead, and he makes them worship her as an ancestor. He and his latest wife have been married for about 25 years, and together have had two sons. Whatever their relationship was like in the past, we don't know. What we do know is that it has taken a turn for the worse, because within the past 10 days, he has started poisoning her, hoping to turn her into a cretin. His reason for doing this? We can assume that it's retribution for her affair with his eldest son. "The secret between the two of you has been known to me for some time," he tells his firstborn, who had wounded himself. "Ever since, night after night, I have lain in bed with my eyes wide open. . . . I don't blame you. I know it was she who seduced you." Or he may be poisoning her simply because this is how he deals with people.

For the sake of argument, let's say that the emperor is justified in punishing his wife. She is, after all, an adulteress and has committed incest. Legally defined as "having illicit sexual intercourse (*jian*) with relatives who are of the fourth degree of mourning or closer,"[128] incest (*neiluan*) was listed among the 10 abominations (*shie*). According to the Tang criminal code (*Tanglu*), these were considered to be the most serious of offenses, because they "injure traditional norms and destroy ceremony."[129] By the end of the film, she's also guilty of plotting rebellion (*moufan*). The punishment for breaking this, the first of the 10 abominations, is death. But is the empress morally reprehensible? She is, in many ways, a tragic victim of her circumstance. Her husband didn't choose her for love but saw her as a ladder to success. In fact, at one point, the emperor tells her that if her father wasn't the king of Liang, he would scarcely speak to her with such restraint. Especially during her scenes with her middle son, we see that she is capable of tenderness and maternal love. After he returns from a three-year absence, she is genuinely tearful to see him. She is also a humane person. When she catches the crown prince *in flagrante delicto*, she could, by law, punish the servant girl for seduction and trespassing, which together carry the penalty of 20 lashes, branding of the face, and banishment from the palace. But her love for her stepson and her humanity keeps her from carrying out this punishment. Furthermore, she could be as backhanded as the emperor is and hire an assassin to kill him or she could stab him herself, but she doesn't. "It is not my intention to kill him," she says. Instead, she mounts a military force against him with the intention of forcing him to abdicate. And finally, when the emperor sends his ninja soldiers to kill his first wife, his loyal physician, and his daughter—undoubtedly to remove all traces of his past deceptions—the empress sends a counter force to protect them. The empress has her moral flaws, but she isn't quite the demon that the emperor chooses to portray.

Of course, the emperor is no saint himself, and neither are his sons. From a legal standpoint, the emperor is guilty of depravity, the fifth abomination, which involves preparing, keeping, or giving poison to others in order to harm them. It also entails killing three members of a single household who have not committed a capital crime. At the end of the film, he not only beats his youngest son to death,[130] but he is also responsible for the murder of his first wife, their daughter, and her husband, the physician. Certainly, long ago, he caused the deaths of his first wife's family, whose only crime was to stand in his way. He is, as his first wife says, a coward and a hypocrite. As for the crown prince, he, too, has committed incest not once but twice—first with his mother, and second, unknowingly, with his sister. We should probably fault the father for this last act of incest, for if he had been honest, the firstborn son would have known that this was his sister. The middle son and youngest son would probably be brought up on charges of article seven, which is lack of "filiality" (*buxiao*). The middle son is also guilty of breaking the first article, plotting rebellion. As it says in the legal code, "The king occupies the most honorable position and receives Heaven's precious decrees. Like Heaven and Earth, he acts to shelter and support, thus serving as the father and mother of the masses. As his children, as his subjects, they must be loyal and filial. Should they dare to cherish wickedness and have rebellious hearts, however, they will run counter to Heaven's constancy and violate human principle."[131]

In the end, we should ask ourselves who has brought about this family's downfall. If the ruler is indeed the paradigm for his wife's and children's behavior, and he has behaved in a manner that runs counter to the Dao—he has lied, schemed, murdered, and poisoned; he has delighted in making his wife suffer; and he has put himself above everyone else—then he is ultimately the cause of the tragic consequences, and by extension, he would, if a sequel were to be made, be overthrown and a new regime would take his place. In fact, at the end of the film, his un-*junzi*-like behavior has resulted in the death of all of his heirs and his wife is halfway to insanity. This is hardly a remarkable legacy. As Zhang Yimou says on *Secrets Within*, the emperor "represents all things feudal. As an emperor you will have dual personalities. You are the greatest and strongest, but you will always be the loneliest. You will suffer the greatest defeat. That is his destiny."

Of course, we may be exhibiting a modern sensibility here, being too literal in our interpretation. Confucians at that time probably would have faulted the empress for everything. After all, *House Instructions of Mr. Yan* frequently denigrates the wife with such statements as "A common proverb says, 'Train a wife from her first arrival; teach a son in his infancy.' How true such sayings are,"[132] and "No hen should herald the dawn lest misfortune follow."[133] The emperor, on more than one occasion, faults the empress for causing disruption within the family. And he even blames her when the youngest son kills the oldest one. To be fair, every once in a while we do catch glimpses of the emperor's humanity, particularly when he's interacting with his eldest son. At one point in the film he says, "I never took proper care of you. This has created a distance between us, but you have always been my favorite son." He's even upset when this son is killed. But when it comes to dealing with his wife, he's abhorrent, using everyone around him to control her.

During one power struggle, we see that he isn't above using his children to achieve his own ends. Upon hearing that the empress didn't consume every drop of her medicine, he tells her that "medicine has to be taken in the right measure, at the right time. Everything abides by its own law." He then calls upon his sons to beg her. "Mother, please do not upset Father," says the youngest son, who kneels at her side. "Mother, please take the medicine," says the crown prince. When she continues to defy his wishes, the emperor tells his sons to "remain kneeling until your mother drains the cup" and then adds that "medicine is governed by dosage just as life is governed by its own law. Surely you all know this." The crown prince responds by taking the cup and telling her that she has been taking the medicine for years, so why refuse a small sip? She finally gives in: "I have been taking this medicine for years . . . why refuse now?" With his eyes closed, the emperor stokes his chin and says, "Your mother is sick. If a person is unwell, [she] must be treated. Why is this unusual?" Without any extenuating circumstances, the scene might not be seen as diabolical as it is. But we have to keep in mind that he is poisoning her, and she knows he's poisoning her. Their children, however, don't. And he's using his power over them to make them accomplices in his crime.

We've already determined that the emperor is a bad role model and the empress has too many flaws to be called a good role model, so we might ask ourselves if a *junzi* even exists in *Curse of the Golden Flower*. The youngest son, although he knows ritual (*li*), is unfilial and resentful of his birth position. During the last quarter of the film, he kills his oldest brother, supposedly because of the incestuous affair. He then shouts to his father to "Abdicate immediately and offer me the throne! I know you have never liked me. Who has ever cared about me?" Shocked, the emperor remarks, "He is your older brother." The emotional youngest son screams, "I wanted to kill him. I hate him. I hate you all." The father stabs the boy in the arm, strikes him in the face, and beats him until the boy's body is bloody and lifeless. As he finishes, he laughs. The eldest son may be filial but he's incestuous, lustful, and weak. In a conversation with his father, he even acknowledges that he wouldn't make a good ruler. "I am without talent and do not deserve the throne. Twice in the past, I begged Father to appoint another heir. . . . Father's wish is my wish." As for Jie, early on the emperor admits that he should be the crown prince. He has developed strong military skills, he knows right from wrong, and he is filial. Even when his mother reveals that every day, she has to feign ignorance and swallow his poison without protest, he replies that "A son cannot stand in rebellion against his father! Whatever the circumstances, he is still my father and my emperor." He changes his position, though, when he encounters his father's injustice firsthand, and he sees just how much his mother is suffering. At first, he tries to stop her from drinking the poison, but she refuses. "Your son will help you," he says. "You will never drink this poison again." According to Mencius, "All human beings have a mind that cannot bear to see the sufferings of others. . . . The mind's feeling of pity and compassion is the beginning of humaneness (*ren*) . . . and the mind's sense of right and wrong is the beginning of wisdom."[134]

In the DVD featurette *Secrets Within*, Zhang Yimou explains that he sees the middle son as exhibiting *xiao*, a term he defines as "unconditional love for a parent. If it's the right thing to do, he will sacrifice himself, even if it's impossible." As it has been said, a *junzi* is guided by fellow-feeling—treating others as he would like to be treated—and he does what is right no matter what the consequences. At the end of the film, we see that the middle son truly is a *junzi*. After leading his troops against his father's, Jie is defeated and his officers are killed. The emperor brings the empress and Jie before him. Because the emperor is motivated by power, he thinks that this was the reason for Jie's coup attempt. He even tells his son that after the Chrysanthemum Festival, he was going to remove Wan as crown prince and appoint him as heir. "I told you what I do not give, don't take by force. The imperial flag was a warning," the emperor says. Jie replies that he always knew he could not win: "Kill me or dismember me . . . but I want you to know that I did not rebel for the sake of the crown. I did it for the sake of my mother." Without skipping a beat, the empress is brought another dose of her medicine. It is at this time that we learn that the punishment for rebellion is "to be torn apart by five horses." "Father will spare you, if you do one thing," the emperor says. "From now on, you will serve your mother her medicine." He begins to eat. Jie gets down on his knees and says, "Mother, your son has failed you. Please forgive me," and he grabs a sword and kills himself. His arterial blood sprays into her medicine. Unfazed, the emperor keeps eating. This scene reflects perfectly the situation in *Curse of the Golden Flower*. The empress is still a powerless victim; the middle son, who was guided by compassion, understood what was right and rather than save his own life by becoming corrupt like his father, he kills himself. The emperor continues to be a power-mad individual who is largely devoid of any Confucian virtues.

Curse of the Golden Flower is primarily a Confucian film; however, we can see some Daoist elements. And this is fitting because Daoism flourished during the Tang dynasty. As we've said, the Chinese organize their years into a series of cycles. The most commonly known cycle consists of 12 years. Each year is associated with a different animal of the zodiac, one of the five elements, and either yin or yang forces. For instance, 2008 is the year of the Earth rat, which is associated with yang forces. A 24-hour day is divided into two-hour blocks that are also associated with one of the animals of the zodiac. Because each of the animals is said to have certain characteristics, those translate to the hour they govern. Since the empress in *Curse of the Golden Flower* takes her "medicine" every two hours, the servants who bring it to her announce which animal governs that time. For example, the first time she is served, we hear the following: "Day breaks. The court presides. Peace to all. It is the hour of the Tiger." Although it isn't stated implicitly in the film, we know that this takes place between 3 and 5 a.m. The tiger symbolizes power, passion, and daring, and during its year one can anticipate war, disagreement, and disasters. "Nothing will be done on a small, timid scale. Everything, good and bad, can and will be carried to the extreme . . . if you take a chance . . . understand that the odds are stacked against you."[135] At this point, the tension between the sons, mother, and father is clearly felt.

The next time that they bring her medicine, they say, "Charity seeks no recognition. Virtue seeks no reward. The harvest is abundant. It is the hour of the Rabbit." Again, this isn't implicitly stated, but we know this to take place between 5 and 7 a.m. The rabbit is the "emblem of longevity and is said to derive its essence from the Moon." It's a placid time, when "we should lick our wounds and get some rest after all the battles" that transpired during the time of the Tiger. "We will act with discretion and make reasonable concessions without too much difficulty."[136]

Medicine arrives again with the words: "Law of the nation precept of the home ancient yet unchanged. It is the hour of the Dragon." It's interesting that after the empress takes her medicine, she reveals that she knows about the servant's relationship with the crown prince. This is fitting because the dragon is full of vitality; therefore, during this time one can expect a lot of surprises and violent acts of nature; tempers flame.[137] The dragon is a symbol of the emperor, and this is very much in evidence in *Curse of the Golden Flower*. When Jie returns home, he meets with his father, who is dressed in full armor made of gold. On his helmet and on his shoulders, he sports a giant dragon; Jie's armor is nearly identical, except that his is constructed from silver and his helmet is different.

"Chickens roost. Gentlemen to rest. Streams run clear. It is the hour of the Snake." This means that we are between the hours of 9 and 11 a.m. Typically, the year or hour of the snake is a time for "shrewd dealing, political affairs and coup d'état. People will be more likely to scheme and ponder over matters." Many of the problems that start in the time of the dragon culminate during the time of the Snake.[138] In the film, all of the tension that has been brewing is about to spill over. This is the first time that the Emperor actually gives the medicine to the empress. He does it very purposely, wiping the rim of the cup and cooling it by blowing on it. After she drinks it, he dabs her mouth. "Thank you, Your Majesty," she says, but underneath the words are the seeds of revenge. The film skips over the hours of the horse and sheep, and goes straight to the hour of the Monkey, which takes place between 3 and 5 p.m. It is said that during this time, "we will steam ahead . . . this is definitely not [the time] for the faint-hearted or slow-witted."[139] During this part of the film Jie learns that his mother will mount a rebellion, and he agrees to help her. The final time that we hear the hour announced the servants say: "Heaven, earth and man unite. Fortune and prosperity to all. Midnight. [It is] the hour of the Rat." Indeed, this animal corresponds to the hours between 11 p.m. and 1 a.m., and we skip over the hours of the Rooster, Dog, and Boar to get there. This is a time of plenty, and "all ventures begun at this time will be successful if one prepares well." However, should one speculate indiscriminately and overextend oneself, that person will come to a sad reckoning.[140] The film ends with mixed emotions. It is the beginning of the Chrysanthemum Festival, marked by fireworks displays and music, but the imperial family is in ruins.

Another aspect of Daoism that can be seen in *Curse of the Golden Flower* is the emperor's use of what is called traditional Chinese medicine (TCM). In one sequence, we watch as different herbs are retrieved from several large medicine cabinets. As the camera pans through the room, we also see several large barrels of various ingredients. Once they are selected, they are weighed and then ground with a mortar and pestle. Hot water is added to these to create the empress' drink. The emperor tells his wife that she must take her medicine, otherwise she won't get better. "You have excess bile, poor digestion; yin and yang are out of balance," he says. "This is why you are fractious, listless, and lethargic, capable of nothing but cutting remarks. These are all symptoms of anemia." To reach such a diagnosis, the physician would have used a number of techniques, such as inspecting the empress' complexion, her posture and motion, her tongue, and taking her pulse. Although we don't see most of these techniques, we do see the last one listed. At his eldest son's bedside, the emperor puts his fingers on his son's arm, closes his eyes, and feels his pulse.

Finally, in the film we see ancestor veneration, which is a part of Confucianism, Daoism, and folk traditions. The practice dates as far back as the Shang Dynasty (14th to 11th century B.C.E.). It is believed that when people die, the lines of communication between them and the living continues as if they hadn't died. Typically, the deceased are represented by a photo or a painting and a name plaque that are hung on the wall or placed on a table. Offerings, such as incense and food, are made regularly to the ancestors, and, in the past, people asked them questions regarding the future. Some families have a temple where the names of ancestors go back several generations. In theory, if the ancestors receive proper veneration, they will protect the family; if they don't, the ancestors can take revenge. In *Curse of the Golden Flower*, the emperor's first wife, whom everyone believes is dead, is depicted in a painting that hangs on the wall. In front of the portrait are two red candles, flowers, and three sticks of burning incense. During one scene, the empress goes into the emperor's chamber, and says, "I came to pay respects to the crown prince's birth mother." She lights a long stick of incense before the image. As an official beginning to the Chrysanthemum Festival, the emperor and the empress ring a bell, join hands, and walk through the palace toward an ancestral table that has on it three sticks of incense, two candles, and a set of plaques with names written on them. Honoring these ancestors, the rulers pour water, bow, and, together, write on a scroll the Confucian virtues of loyalty, filial piety, ritual, and righteousness. On this day, the imperial family also honors the first wife by placing berries[141] in their hats and hair. The emperor says that she would always wear them during the Chrysanthemum Festival, and even after it was finished, she would continue to do so for a few days to ward off evil spirits.

On a final note, the Chrysanthemum Festival—also know as Chongyang, Double-Yang, Double Ninth, and Festival of the Nine Imperial Gods—is celebrated in China on the ninth day of the ninth month. Since the Chinese word to signify forever, *jiu jiu*, is pronounced the same as those indicating "double ninth," this was considered to be an auspicious day and thus worthy of a celebration. Why is the chrysanthemum associated with the festival? Not only do they bloom during this time of year but the word for them is *ju*, which is also pronounced similarly to the word for forever. Because chrysanthemums bloom in late autumn and early winter, a time of bitter cold, they have become a symbol of longevity.[142] Furthermore, women used to stick a chrysanthemum in their hair or hang its branches on windows or doors to avoid evil. In the film, 10,000 chrysanthemums are brought to the palace for the festival. In China, the upper limit, with regards to time and size, was 10,000; therefore, it is associated with longevity. The Daodejing talks about the 10,000 things (*wan-wu*) as being produced by the Dao. In Chinese *wan-wu* is a classical term meaning the natural world.[143] Finally, in the film, the emperor is usually shown wearing a dragon, and the empress wears a phoenix. The dragon has long been considers an auspicious symbol of protection and fortune. Long ago, the creature was associated with rain and, thus, good harvests. During the Han Dynasty, it was adopted as the symbol for the emperor.[144] Along with the dragon, unicorn, and tortoise, the phoenix is thought to be one of the four supernatural creatures of China. It is often paired with the dragon to "symbolize a happy and harmonious union," because the bird represents the female essence and the dragon, the male. Just as the dragon represents the emperor, the phoenix represents the empress.[145]

The King of Masks (*Bian Lian*) (1996)—Screenplay by Minglun Wei. Directed by Tian-Ming Wu. Running time: 101 min. Mandarin. China. Unrated. Genre: Drama.

Summary: Wang Bianlian is an aging street performer who enjoys bringing pleasure to his many spectators, but he is remorseful that he has no male heir to whom he can pass on this trade. All of this changes when a father sells the old man his son. Initially this "King of Masks" is delighted, and he affectionately calls his new grandson "Doggie." But an unexpected secret is in store that will test their relationship and challenge established Chinese customs.

Set during the 1930s in Szechuan province, the film focuses on a street performer who practices the ancient art form of mask-making and "change-face" opera. He lives on a boat with a monkey named General and together they travel from town to town, performing for the masses. Within the first five minutes, we hear him lament that he doesn't have a male heir[146] or a grandson. A bit later, he explains to Master Liang, a famous female impersonator of the opera, that although his "skills be meager, only a son may inherit them. It's an ancient rule." When asked if he has a disciple, the old man bows his head. It's a horrible thought, Master Liang asks, but what if you die without an heir? Visibly upset, the King of Masks explains that he will take his secrets to his grave. Before they part, Master Liang tells the old man to get himself an heir.

Not long after this conversation, the old man is walking down an alleyway when several people throw themselves on his mercy. One girl promises that she will cook and clean for him. When he replies, "Oh, dear, I want a boy, not a girl," she grabs his leg and starts crying. The girl's mother chases after him, saying, "You don't have to pay a cent, sir. Just take her, please. If you'll feed her, I'll be content." The old man sadly refuses. Just as he's about to leave, a child's voice shouts, "Grandpa!" He turns around, and sees, staring back at him, a cherubim-faced child with close-cropped hair. He goes for a closer look. The child's father explains that the boy is eight years old, and "if it weren't for the floods, I wouldn't be doing this. Ten dollars and he's yours." "You think I'm the god of wealth," the old man replies and begins to walk away. At half price, the old man finally buys the child. (It's significant that the girls were being given away.) With the child in tow, the deliriously happy man buys "Doggie" a new outfit, some food, and takes him to his boat. Wanting to know more about the child, the old man, who from here on out will be called "Grandpa," asks Doggie from whence he comes and what is his surname. "Father says it's Liu," the child says. The old man is immediately taken aback. That was the child's father? "What father could sell his son dry-eyed? He's a slave trader." The child looks down at his wrist, which is covered in bruises. The old man becomes emotional, wondering how anyone could be so cruel. He comforts the crying child. "You'll be my grandson. No one will strike you now." Grandpa's kindness continues. When the child falls ill, he goes to a doctor to buy medicine, and when he can't afford it, he sells his family heirloom, a sword, for two dollars. After making the medicine for Doggie, he serves it and cradles the child in his arms. Once the child is well, he carries him on his back, and they even take a photo together.

All of this changes when Grandpa discovers that he's "been duped" and Doggie is actually a girl. He shouts at her, calling her a crook. She protests tearfully, saying that she's been sold seven times, and because she's a girl, everyone has abused her. "Only you have treated me well . . . like family," she says. She begs him not to sell her again. He says he won't, but he can't keep her either, and he carelessly tosses her a bag of coins. He pushes the boat away from the shore and begins to sail away. Hysterical, she runs after it and even tries swimming after him. Out of compassion, Grandpa jumps in to save her. But this isn't a moment of reconciliation. He tells her that she can no longer call him Grandpa. Instead, she must call him Boss, because she's his "employee" and will learn to perform gymnastic feats on the street. "Stupid girl," he says.

Over time, his attitude toward her softens, and eventually he says that it doesn't matter if the child is a boy or girl, it gives him an extra pair of hands and company. Later, when he sees that she's prepared a meal for him, he says, "If only you were a boy." Things take a turn for the worse when Doggie accidentally causes a fire, burning Grandpa's boat and destroying many of his masks. His patience has run out, and he abandons her. Dirty, disheveled, and hungry, she is found by a slave owner who grabs her and sells her again. In her new lodgings she finds a young boy who has also been kidnapped. Together, they escape. Thinking of how much her Grandpa would like young Tianci (Heaven Sent), she takes him to his boat and leaves him there. Naturally, Grandpa is overjoyed to find this appropriately named child, especially when he discovers that it does indeed have a "teapot spout." But his joy is shortlived. As the child has been stolen, Grandpa is arrested for kidnapping and put into prison. Wanting to wrap up all of the kidnapping cases, the local magistrate decides to pin them all on Grandpa, thereby clearing the books. Feeling guilty over what she's done, a tearful Doggie visits him in prison, bringing with her his masks. The guard gives them to the old man, saying that he can use them to scare the demons in hell. Realizing that he's broken tradition by not having a male heir, Grandpa tears up the masks. Doggie cries even harder. Comforting her, he says, "In a former life, I must've wronged you badly and now I'm repaying the debt. It was karma." He then tells her to take the monkey with her and "burn spirit money for him in the Ghost Festivals . . . and you'll have done the right thing by me." This last statement crystallizes the central, very Confucian, theme of *King of Masks*, which is "filiality" (*xiao*). According to the aging street performer, sons (or in this case, grandsons) must learn the father's (or grandfather's) trade, work hard, and they will be considered filial. Girls, daughters, or even granddaughters must produce male offspring and honor the ancestors when they die. This film challenges these entrenched gender roles, showing that a filial child is a filial child no matter if it has a "teapot spout" or not. We even hear as much from a prison guard who marvels at Doggie's devotion, saying that she's more filial than he is to his own father. In the end, Grandpa embraces Doggie for who she is and he teaches her the art of "change-face" opera.

Confucian patriarchy seems to be undermined in *King of Masks* through its use of Buddhist stories and symbols, most notably those associated with Kuan Yin. We actually see this bodhisattva of mercy within the first 10 minutes of the film. During a New Year celebration—dragon dancers are performing while fireworks are exploding—a lotus-shaped throne is carried through the streets. On it is a young "woman" sitting cross-legged. Her left hand is in her lap and her right hand is making a blessing gesture. Referred to by everyone as the "Living Bodhisattva," this is actually Master Liang, a female impersonator and beloved opera star, dressed in light-colored, flowing robes and a headdress. Between his eyes, we see a red dot. One of the women standing in the crowd remarks that all one has to do is "touch his lotus throne and a healthy son will be yours." Excited, they all rush over to him. The next time we see an image of Kuan Yin, Grandpa has just left Master Liang, who is now dressed as a man. As Grandpa is walking down the street, he hears someone shouting, "Buy a goddess of mercy. Give birth to a son." He wanders over to the stall and picks up a golden statue. "I want one for the giving of sons," he says. "*She* looks after all those in misery," responds the seller, taking the sculpture from him. He replaces that with another statue, this one holding a child. "This is the one you want," he says. "A son is guaranteed."

Kuan Yin's full name, Kuan Shih Yin, translates to "She who hearkens to the cries of the world," which itself is a translation of the Sanskrit name of her original Indian form, Avalokitesvara. This Bodhisattva of Mercy is first mentioned in the *Sutra of the Lotus Blossom of the Fine Dharma*, more commonly known as the Lotus Sutra. The 25th chapter of this text, titled the Universal Gateway, tells adherents that if they call upon Avalokitesvara, they will be rescued from dangers that include "burning, drowning, being lost at sea, being murdered, being attacked by demons, *being jailed* [my emphasis], falling off a cliff," and more.[147] For millennia, the Chinese, Japanese, and Koreans have worshipped Kuan Yin not only as a bodhisattva ("enlightenment being") but also as a goddess. She is revered by Buddhists and Daoists alike. What's intriguing about Kuan Yin is that while her Indian form is male, her Chinese form is typically female. This process of feminization was gradual, beginning in about the 10th century. By the end of the Ming dynasty (1368–1644 C.E.), her transformation was complete.[148] This is undoubtedly why Kuan Yin is such a critical symbol in *King of Masks*. She is a transformation being, and her human representatives—Master Liang and Doggie—also change from male into female, perhaps indicating the fluidity of gender.

Avalokitesvara has had widespread appeal in East Asia—he's known in Japan as Kannon, in Korea as Kwanse'um, and in Vietnam as Quan'am—and he has spread into Southeast Asia, most notably Cambodia, Java, Burma, Tibet, and Sri Lanka. However, these various "manifestations" of this bodhisattva of compassion can be quite different. For instance, in Japan, Korea, and Vietnam she is the "exemplar of wisdom for meditators and the 'Goddess of Mercy,' who is particularly kind to women, while in Sri Lanka, Tibet and Southeast Asia, Avalokitesvara has been very much identified with royalty."[149] According to the *Surangama Sutra*, popular in China since the Song dynasty, this bodhisattva can assume 32 forms in order to save different types of people. Among these, six are female: a nun, a laywoman, a queen, a princess, a noble lady, and a virgin maiden. In the Lotus Sutra, of the 33 forms, seven are female, one of which is a girl. Appearance here is based on the needs and capacities of those who call on him.[150] A few of the specifically Chinese forms of Kuan Yin include three that are indigenous—the White-robed Kuan Yin, South Sea Kuan Yin, and Fish-basket Kuan Yin—and Kuan Yin as the Venerable Mother. With regard to *King of Masks*, the form that we see from the beginning is the White-robed Kuan Yin (Pai-i Kuan Yin), a fertility goddess who is prayed to as the giver of sons and who is depicted as holding a child. "The desperate need to secure a male heir, the frantic effort to keep the head of the household alive, and the fanatical adherence to the ideal of chaste widowhood . . . began to take on new significance. The cult of Kuan Yin did indeed serve Confucian family values, and in this sense we can speak of a Confucianism of Buddhism."[151]

To understand the popularity of Kuan Yin in China, we must look at a popular saying: "Everybody knows how to chant O-mi-t'o-fo (Amitabha) and every household worships Kuan Yin."[152] She is undeniably the most popular "cult" in China, and scholar Chun-Fang Yu believes that this can be attributed to the fact that she is "regarded as the universal savior by all Chinese, male and female, monastic and lay, the elites and the masses." As Yu is quoted as saying, "The Lotus Sutra says that no matter who invokes her name or for whatever trouble they seek her help, she will grant you wishes. . . . It's unconditional love." In addition, Kuan Yin's worship is purely devotional. No one needs to meditate or become vegetarian to follow her.[153] As we watch the film, we may wonder how a society that places so such emphasis on male lineage could fully embrace a goddess like Kuan Yin. Even Doggie poses a similar question: "What do boys have that I don't?" she asks. "Just a little teapot spout," Grandpa says through laughter. "Does the goddess have a teapot spout?" she asks. "What goddess?" "Bodhisattva [Kuan Yin]," she says and then retrieves the sculpture. "Look, she's got bosoms. Why do you worship her?" Grandpa is speechless.

During the middle of the film, Grandpa takes Doggie to an opera, starring Master Liang in his most famous role of Attaining Nirvana. Here is yet another depiction of Kuan Yin as savior. As Grandpa and Doggie watch the performance, a golden buddha, who wears a giant *mala* around his neck, tells the audience that an "evil leader of this insignificant kingdom has entered the Buddhist hell . . . his soul never to be released." A chorus sings, "Hear the judgment of the law." The evil leader is being pulled about by several Buddhist patriarchs, when we hear a woman's voice. "Be merciful," it says. The princess, as she's called, arrives on the Boat of Kindness. Thunderous applause greets Master Liang, who is dressed as the bodhisattva and who descends to the stage, hanging from a rope. "Oh, patriarchs, the burning of White Sparrow Temple was not my father's intention," she sings. "He fell into a trap set by a wicked minister. Please hear me out in my sincerity and spare the life of my father, the king." A chorus tells her that "the laws of heaven make no exception." "If you will show no compassion," she says, "I shall cut this rope and fall into the pit of death, so that I may share my father's suffering." The father shouts for her to stop. "Princess, you mustn't take your life so lightly," the chorus says. "Let her do as she will," comes another voice. "Father, I haven't been as filial as I could have been," says the princess, who then cuts the rope. Everyone sings, "Amitabha. Buddha of Infinite Qualities" as she rises to stage level again, seated on a lotus. "She's attained Nirvana," shouts a government official in the audience. "Set off the firecrackers." While walking away from the performance, Doggie asks, "If the princess died, how did she come back in the end?" "She turned into a god, like a bodhisattva," Grandpa replies. "She's a good person, then," Doggie asks. "She does good deeds and rescues souls in strife," he replies.

After Grandpa is thrown in prison, and it doesn't seem that the public officials care about justice, Doggie visits the Living Bodhisattva, seeing him as Grandpa's only hope. (When he meets her again, Master Liang is amazed to find that Doggie has "transformed" from a boy into a girl.) Master Liang feeds the bedraggled child and promises to talk to the officials. But in the end, he is told not to interfere. Seeing no other option, and taking a cue from Kuan Yin, Doggie climbs onto the roof of the opera house and ties a rope to her leg. Once the opera is finished, she lowers herself in front of the general, who has been a "guest musician" for the evening. While suspended from her leg, Doggie confesses that she kidnapped Tianci, and if nothing is done to free Grandpa, she'll cut the rope and die. The general doesn't believe her, so she cuts it. The Living Bodhisattva leaps and catches her. Together they roll down the stairs, and both are seriously injured. Carrying the child up to the general, the Living Bodhisattva chastises the general for his heartlessness and walks away. The general stops her, saying, "You live up to your nickname of the Living Bodhisattva. Though merely an actor, you have courage and character . . . she's touched my heart also." The general agrees to help. After he's freed from prison, Grandpa visits Master Liang to thank him. But the opera star admits that he's not the savior here, Doggie is. The old man leaves and seeks out Doggie, who is scrubbing the deck of his boat. Overcome with emotion, he tells her to call him Grandpa.

The story recounted during the pivotal opera scene is a variation on the story of Miao Shan, a princess. As the story goes, this third daughter of King Miao-chuang was a devout Buddhist, so when she reached a marriageable age, she refused a husband. Her father punished her severely for her disobedience. In time, she entered the White Sparrow Nunnery, which her father burned down, killing 500 nuns. For Miao-shan's unfilial behavior, she was executed. After a tour in hell, where she saved many "souls" by preaching to them, Miao-shan was reborn and, on Earth, achieved enlightenment. During this time, her father had taken ill and was told that the only remedy that would save him would be a medicine made from the eyes and hands of someone who hadn't felt anger. Miao-shan kindly gave the requisite body parts. In the end, he was cured, and everyone in her family converted to Buddhism. "Miao-shan was transformed into her true form, that of the Thousand-eyed and Thousand-armed Kuan Yin."[154] As Yu states, Miao-shan, the chaste and filial daughter, is the best-known manifestations of Kuan Yin, and her story was recorded in a variety of ways, including in a novel, a drama, and the opera known as *Great Hsiang-shan (Ta Hsiang-shan)*.[155]

In the *King of Masks*, Grandpa is depicted as a man who has suffered a lot in his life—his wife left him, his only heir died, and he has been imprisoned for a crime he didn't commit, which will likely result in his being put to death. During Doggie's prison visit, we get a sense that his suffering will continue after he dies. As it's understood in China, after a person dies "the material force composing the person dissipates . . . the yin parts of the person—collectively called 'earthly souls' (*po*) move downward, constituting the flesh of the corpse, perhaps returning as a ghost (*gui*) to haunt the living . . . the yang portion—collectively called 'heavenly souls' (*hun*) float upward."[156] Once the *hun* leaves the body, it enters the spirit world. As soon as it passes the boundary line, it sees two roads: one leading to the western world, and the other to the lower world. Typically, one must cross a bridge to get to the Gate of Ghosts, where the person will come before a judge. The deceased must pass 10 judges in all, before he or she can reincarnate. However, if at any stop along the way, this person is found to have committed heinous acts, he or she is tortured according to his or her actions.[157] "Those who pass through purgatory on their way to rebirth and those reborn in hell are without exception hungry and very often naked, and offerings to the ancestors in traditional China always included food and some form of money."[158] An heirless person who dies is unanchored in this world; therefore, he doesn't receive any food, spirit money, or paper clothing that gets showered on ancestors. Many of them come to resent this, and that's why they are considered dangerous. The seventh month of the lunar calendar is called the Ghost Month, a time when the gates of hell are open and ghosts are free to wander as they like. On the 15th day, a festival is held for the deceased. A communal feast is offered, operas are performed, incense is burned, and more. The climax of the festival is "the sending of food, paper clothing, and spirit money to the hungry ghosts. Except for the food, which is distributed later, everything else is burned." (Kuan Yin is also associated with this festival.[159]) And this is why Grandpa asks Doggie to burn spirit money for him at the Ghost Festivals.

It seems significant that the *King of Masks* focuses on a variation of the Miao-shan story. Instead of having the princess offer her body parts to cure her father's illness, she descends to hell to offer her life as a sacrifice. This story is reminiscent of another popular Chinese opera, *Mu-Lien Rescues His Mother.* In it we learn that Mu-Lien's mother has been his mother for 500 years, through many incarnations, but despite encouragement to act otherwise, she continues to be avaricious. Her punishment after death is rebirth as a hungry ghost in *avici* hell. Always the dutiful son, Mu-Lien descends to the underworld to rescue her from her fate. He even offers to trade places with her and suffer the tortures that she alone deserves. The moral of the story is that "no matter how self-sacrificing, children will never fully repay the kindness bestowed on them by parents. Commentators from medieval times to the present have identified filial devotion as the essential teaching of the Ghost Festival."[160] As Yu states, "People could also learn the role of Kuan Yin as savior of beings in hell by watching plays about Mu-Lien."[161]

Because Kuan Yin validates these practices of self-sacrifice to demonstrate filiality, she not only lent legitimacy to this practice but she also upheld the central value system of Confucianism. As Yu states, "Miao-shan's self sacrifice and the cult of *ke-ku* (offering a body part to save the parent) are both connected with the ideology of filial piety. The specific form this . . . took in China must, however, be attributed to the Buddhist idealization of the 'gift of the body' and the related glorification of physical suffering."[162] In *King of Masks*, we see a similar reinforcement of Confucian expectations: that a child must remain filial even if it means her death. Doggie recreates Miao-shan's sacrifice so that she can demonstrate that even though she's a girl, she's worthy of being Grandpa's heir and continue his family traditions. Undoubtedly, this aspect of the story would be understood by a Chinese audience but probably not to a Western one.

Confucian values permeate *King of Masks*, and so do Buddhist myths, and as we'll see, iconography. After Grandpa buys Doggie, they visit the colossal

Buddha of Leshan that is carved out of the side of a mountain in Sichuan Province. On the ground in front of it, the old man bows, while burning several joss sticks of incense. Later, after he refers to Doggie as "stupid girl," they float past the same giant buddha. Standing at 71 meters high, this sculpture is the largest buddha in the world and it looks down on the confluence of three rivers. It was constructed during the eighth century C.E., during the Tang Dynasty. Interestingly enough, the first Buddhist temple in China was built in this area during the first century C.E.

One final example occurs after Grandpa abandons Doggie. He visits a temple where a sculpture of Kuan Yin is housed. He bows before her, and incense sticks glow in front of him. As he's leaving, a voice calls out, "Faithful one. Have you come to pray for an heir?" He returns to find a nun dressed in gray. "Buddha, be merciful," he says. "I just want to ask if in this lifetime I will have an heir to continue the family line." The nun smiles and says, "Guo Ziyi had many children in his home. Dou Yanshan's five sons with glory shone. The Yangs produced eight generals, tigers all. You have one stick of joss in your ancestral hall." He cries, saying how his own son was "trampled." "Don't despair. Luck and misfortune are intertwined. Your fate holds a grandson. You will find him to the north of here, by water." Even though this is clearly Buddhist, it also has some "popular" elements mixed in, especially because the nun serves as a prognosticator. As for the people she refers to, Guo Ziyi (697–781 C.E.) is considered to be one of China's greatest generals and has since been deified in popular religion. "He is generally equated with Fu-hsing, the stellar god of happiness."[163] Dou Yanshan (907–960 C.E.) was a scholar, educator, and an official who lived at Yanshan during the Five Dynasties period. He is epitomized as the ideal parent who raised five outstanding sons, outstanding because they passed the civil service examination with high honors. They came to be known as the "Five Dragons of Yanshan and the Five Osmanthus Flowers." Dou's example was used in the *Three Character Classic*, the primer for beginning readers from the Song dynasty until the 20th century. It read, "Dou Yanshan had an unusual formula. He taught five sons and they all became famous."[164] A variation on this interpretation, which indicates a rhyme scheme, is "Dou Yanshan, Had the right plan, Taught his five sons, Each became a great man."[165] And finally, the Yang family of the Northern Song Dynasty (960–1127 C.E.) is known for its patriotism, loyalty to the emperor, and valor. They also are celebrated by novelists and storytellers, and are the subject of many operas; the 40 extant are still standard repertoire items. The first-generation Yang general Yang Jiye, known to some as Yang the Invincible, and his wife, She Saihua, had seven sons and two daughters. According to historical records, his children followed in his footsteps. In fact, it is said that during one particular battle, when it was realized that outside aid wouldn't reach the area in time, Yang Jiye ordered five of his eldest sons to lead the resistance.[166] The folk opera *The Western Expedition of Twelve Widows* recounts the true tale of the "12 Yang women generals who, having lost their husbands and sons to earlier repulsions of the invading Liao Kingdom . . . commandeered tens of thousands of Song troops to give battle in their dead husbands' stead against the invading Western Xia."[167] Several temples exist in and outside of China in which the family is revered as protective deities.

Confucianism isn't always portrayed in a negative light. Even though China has ushered in a new era of economic prosperity, many are unhappy with its unfortunate and unwelcome consequences, such as the breakdown of the family unit, the devaluation of education, and an overall loss of traditional values. Many also criticize how it has resulted in widespread materialism.[168]

The Road Home (*Wo de fu qin mu qin*) (1999)—Adapted from a novel by Shi Bao, directed by Zhang Yimou. Running time: 89 min. Mandarin. China. Unrated. Genre: Drama/Romance.

In *The Road Home*, director Zhang Yimou looks back with nostalgia to a time when scholars were revered, elders were respected, and the rural community worked together with a purpose. Adapted by Shi Bao from her novel, the film begins with the death of Luo Changyu, an elderly schoolteacher who dies while raising funds for a new local schoolhouse. His son, Luo Yusheng, a businessman, returns home to make funeral arrangements. While consulting his mother on the details, she insists on following traditional burial customs, which means that the body must be carried back, on foot. As she waits for the body's return, she begins weaving a funeral cloth for the casket. Providing a backdrop to this is the genesis of a 40-year love story, detailing how this now-grieving widow met and fell in love with the then-new schoolteacher. As scholar Rey Chow explains, "The road home, then, is the return to the father and the mother, elders and ancestors of a community who are earlier versions of 'us.' More important, it is a return, now possible only in remembrance, to the utopian possibilities of determination, meaningful action, communal purpose, and happiness—the constituents of a sociality that has since . . . become lost."[169]

Happy Times (*Xingfu Shiguang*) (2000)—Directed by Zhang Yimou. Running time: 102 min. Mandarin. China. Unrated. Genre: Drama/Comedy.

In another one of Zhang Yimou's films, *Happy Times* illustrates China's changing values, by contrasting the treatment given to a blind woman by her 40-something stepmother and a group of retirees who barely know her. Whereas the older generation exhibits true empathy and compassion for the girl, and goes to great lengths to help her, the stepmother sees her merely as a financial impediment. In an interview, Zhang Yimou stated that "Money has become very important but in the middle of this wave of commercialization, I have started to feel the importance of real sentiments of the caring among people. Caring is more important than money."[170]

Shower (*Xizao*) (1999)—Directed by Yang Zhang. Running time: 92 min. Mandarin. China. Rated: PG-13 for language and nudity. Genre: Drama/Comedy.

A similar "nostalgic" film, Yang Zhang's *Shower* begins with a big-city executive Da Ming (Quanxin Pu) returning to his boyhood home, where his elderly father and mentally disabled brother run a traditional communal bathhouse. At first, Da Ming fails to see the value in his father's work, and they come to verbal blows. "You don't respect me or what I do," the father says. "You want to do big things and make big money. Go ahead." Over time, though, the eldest son learns to appreciate the languid pace of life and the sense of friendship exhibited by the mainly older clientele who come every day to share stories, food, and drink; play games, such as fighting their crickets; and simply relax with a massage and a soak.

Two particularly poignant stories told during the film highlight the importance of maintaining ritual and family responsibilities. The first story, told by the elderly father, takes place in northwest China, an extremely arid locale where it rains once a year. Despite the scarcity of water, it's a local custom for girls to take a bath the night before their marriage. The family in the story has very little water and barely enough food to survive. This doesn't stop the father and his young son from taking what little food they do have and going from house to house, trading their food so that they have enough water to fill the girl's bathtub. When the father returns, the mother and her son warm the water for the bath of the soon-to-be married girl. The next day, the girl, dressed in traditional red, is put on the back of a horse and led away. Fireworks and horns celebrate her impending marriage. This story demonstrates not only the ritual significance of water but also the family's willingness to make sacrifices for their children.

In the second story, told near the end of the film, we learn of an elderly woman who is taking her granddaughter on a pilgrimage to a holy Tibetan lake, which is said to not only wash the body but also cleanse the soul. It also reputedly cures any matter of ills and ailments. The two walk for many months—the elderly woman is always spinning a prayer wheel—until they can barely walk anymore. The grandchild asks if it won't be too cold to take a bath. The elderly woman replies that the pilgrimage can only be done at certain times, and if they don't do this now, they will have to wait another 12 years, and by that time she will be dead. "Sometimes something so simple as taking a bath can be so difficult," the narrator states. Again, in this story, we see the connection between family and ritual. By the end of the film, Da Ming has learned the meaning of family, community, sacrifice, and ritual, but sadly, development is threatening this older way of life. At the end of October, the entire district is being torn down to make way for a shopping mall. One of the characters laments that in their new community, he won't be able to raise crickets anymore, because the insects can't live in a multistory. Furthermore, he hopes that their new community has a bathhouse. It's so luxurious taking a bath here, he says. And there's so much laughter, says another man.

One popular genre of Chinese film, the *wuxia pian*, or "film of martial chivalry,"[171] focuses on the exploits of a heroic main character, a type of knight errant, who operates by a code of honor that's based in a Confucian moral code. Furthermore, his or her model for correct behavior is "based on a strictly hierarchical system, where individuals know his place and aspire to do his best in the position which fate has allotted him." Because these warriors were mutually interdependent, they were responsible for the actions of the other.[172] The Confucian-educated warrior was righteous and human-hearted, he maintained proper ritual, upheld tradition, and exhibited obedience and respect for his superiors. We will now look at several *wuxia* films and examine how they deal with ideas found in Confucianism, Daoism, and Buddhism.

Crouching Tiger, Hidden Dragon (*Wo Hu Cang Long*) (2000)—Based on the book by Du Lu Wang. Screenplay by Hui-Ling Wang, James Schamus, and Kuo Jung Tsai. Directed by Ang Lee. Running time: 120 min. Mandarin. Rated PG-13 for martial arts violence and some sexuality. Genre: Action/Adventure/Fantasy/Romance.

In the Academy Award–winning film, *Crouching Tiger, Hidden Dragon* (*Wo Hu Cang Long*), the film's protagonists, Master Li Mu Bai (Yun-Fat Chow) and Yu Shu Lien (Michelle Yeoh), live within a *jianghu* community. Literally "river-lakes," this word refers to a group of people who live outside the law but exhibit their own unspoken code of honor. They are "ruled not by state legislation but by moral principle and decorum."[173] Conflict arises in this film when these two characters, who are aware of and act in accordance with their familial and social obligations, come into contact with Jade Fox (Pei-pei Cheng) and her young protégé, Jen Yu (Zhang Ziyi), women who are impulsive, disrespectful, prideful, arrogant, and uncivilized.[174] Yu Shu Lien informs Jen Yu that "fighters have rules, too: friendship, trust, and integrity. Without rules, we wouldn't survive for long." A great warrior and a successful businesswoman, Yu Shu Lien supports traditional Confucian attitudes. Not only has she followed in her father's footsteps by taking over his business, Sun Security—one man tells her that she's a "credit to his memory"—but she also believes that "the most important step in a woman's life" is to get married. Freedom from societal constraints to pursue whomever she loves may appeal to Yu Shu Lien, and she freely admits this, but unlike Jen Yu and Jade Fox, she refuses to step outside societal boundaries, and, in her case, risk dishonoring the memory of her deceased fiancé, Meng, who was a brother by oath to Master Li.

By contrast, the aristocratic Jen Yu dreads her impending marriage to a member of the Gou family. "My marrying [him] will be good for my father's career," she says. To this, Yu Shu Lien states that the girl is "fortunate to marry into such a noble family." But Jen Yu isn't convinced, saying that she wishes she were like the heroes who populate the novels that she reads. In fact, she idealizes the warrior's life, believing that they get to roam free and beat up anyone who gets in their way. The impetuous Jen Yu fails to adhere to Confucian standards and refuses to obey her parents or her elders. When told that her mother wouldn't like to see her consorting with Yu Shu Lien, the young woman replies that she'll socialize with whomever she pleases. Jen Yu is very young and impressionable. If we look at her behavior from a Confucian perspective, we can't put all of the blame on her. She is simply a product of what she's been taught. Since she was 10 years old, she has been raised by the un-*junzi*-like Jade Fox, who assures the girl that "We'll be our own masters. We'll be happy. That's all that matters." With proper role models, such as Yu She Lien or Master Li Mu Bai, who exemplify Confucian values, the girl might have been different. One might say that on a philosophical level, the film demonstrates the tension between Confucian and Daoist perspectives with Master Li Mu Bai and Yu Shu Lien embodying the former tradition and Jade Fox and Jen Yu representing the latter.[175] Can one be filial and be free? The film doesn't seem to think so, because for the most part, the film ends tragically for everyone involved.

In addition to Confucian and Daoist ideology, *Crouching Tiger, Hidden Dragon* contains Buddhist teachings, and the primary mouthpiece for them is Master Li Mu Bai, who at the beginning of the film has returned from "practicing deep meditation" on Wudan Mountain. He says that during his meditation training, "I came to a place of deep silence. I was surrounded by light. Time and space disappeared. I had come to a place my master had never told me about." Yu Shu Lien asks, "You were enlightened?" "No," he says, "I didn't feel the bliss of enlightenment. Instead, I was surrounded by an endless sorrow. I couldn't bear it." He explains that he broke off his training because something was pulling him back, something he couldn't let go of. This, we come to learn, is his love for Yu Shu Lien, but because of prohibitive rules regarding social relationships, the two haven't been able to act on their love.

As we've said, unlike Master Li and Yu Shu Lien, Jen Yu is undisciplined, self-centered, haughty, and materialistic. Master Li even tells her as much. He knows, though, that she is special and even wants to take her on as a disciple, for without proper training and guidance she will become a "poisoned dragon." "Do you think you are a real master?" she asks in a mocking tone. "Like most things, I am nothing," he says. "It's the same for this sword. All of it is simply a state of mind." And here we see evidence of his Ch'an or Zen training. Compare this with an early teaching, attributed to Ma-tsu, a Ch'an patriarch who lived during the Tang Dynasty, "Apart from the mind there is no Buddha, apart from the Buddha there is no mind. Do not cling to good; do not reject evil! If you cling to neither purity nor defilement you come to know the emptiness of the nature of sin. At no moment can you grasp it, since it possesses no self-nature. Therefore, the Three Worlds are only mind."[176] Jen Tu laughs off Master Li's comment, telling him to "stop talking like a monk and just fight." They engage in combat, but throughout he continues to instruct, saying that "real sharpness comes without effort . . . no growth without assistance. No action without reaction. No desire without restraint. Now give yourself up and find yourself again. There is a lesson for you." Zen philosophy lies behind his words, especially the line about giving oneself up to find oneself again. This stripping away of the "self" is at the heart of Zen practice, for it is only when one shatters one's "one-pointed mind" that a new self arises. "This self returns and again sees the things of the world as objects, now as empty objects; it again thinks in differentiated categories and feels attachment, but now with insight into their emptiness."[177] If we look even closer at what he says, we might even recognize Daoist thought, especially in its teaching of yin and yang and the harmony of opposites. It's not surprising, though. Chinese Buddhism was greatly influenced by its encounter with Daoism, and their "interpenetration," as it were, culminated in the Zen movement during the Tang Dynasty.[178]

In spite of Master Li's Buddhist training, we sense that even though he verbally supports its teachings, deep down he may be having second thoughts. He loves Yu Shu Lien but he's been taught the Four Noble Truths and the importance of nonattachment and impermanence. He even acknowledges this during a tender moment with her. After he has held her hand to his face, he remarks that "the things we touch have no permanence. My master would say, there is nothing we can hold on to in this world. Only by letting go can we truly possess what is real." "Not everything is an illusion," she responds. "My hand, wasn't that real?" For most of the film, he's unwavering in his Buddhist thinking, but that changes at the end. Having been struck by a poisoned arrow, Master Li Mu Bai sits in the lotus position, dying. He tells Yu Shu Lien that he has only one breath left. "Use it to meditate," she says. "Free yourself from this world, as you have been taught. Let your soul rise to eternity . . . do not waste [your last breath] for me." "I've already wasted my entire life," he replies. "I want to tell you . . . that I have always loved you." He falls backwards.

She rushes over and kisses him. He continues, "I would rather be a ghost drifting by your side as a condemned soul than enter heaven without you. Because of your love, I will never be a lonely spirit." Despite his many years of Buddhist training, in these last words he eschews the monastic ideal with its emphasis on nonattachment, celibacy, and freedom from family, and acknowledges the importance of the five relationships, including that of husband and wife.

Not only does the film highlight the tension between Daoism and Confucianism, but in this case, it also demonstrates the one that exists between Buddhism and Confucianism. And historically, this is accurate. Neo-Confucianists challenged many core Buddhist teachings, including emptiness, moral relativism, and impermanence. Implicit in these Buddhist doctrines "was a profound questioning of the existence of the 'self' or 'self nature,' which tended to undermine the Confucians' prime concern with the moral person and practical self-cultivation. In response to these challenges, the Neo-Confucians came up with a new doctrine of human nature as integrated with a cosmic infrastructure of principle (*li*) and material-force (*qi*), along with the reaffirmation of the morally responsible and socially responsible self. This culminated in a lofty spirituality of the sage, preserving a stability and serenity of mind even when acting on a social conscience in a troubled world."[179] Furthermore, they taught that the world of human ethics, of "social relations, of history and political endeavor is a real one, an unfolding growth process, and not just a passing dream or nightmare from which men must be awakened to the truth of Emptiness or Nothingness."[180]

It may seem incongruous that Buddhist-trained men and women became great warriors, especially since Buddhism teaches nonviolence, extending even beyond the human realm; and this disconnect is acknowledged by Master Li Mu Bai, himself a Wudan fighter. At the beginning of the film, he wants Yu Shu Lien to take his sword, Green Destiny, to Sir Te. He explains that it's time for him to leave it and the warrior way of life behind him. Acknowledging the violent aspect of his weapon, he says, "It only looks pure because blood washes so easily from its blade." "You use it justly, you're worthy of it," she replies. When Yu Shu Lien finally arrives at Sir Te's home, he's reluctant to accept the weapon, saying that only Master Li Mu Bai should wield it. "It has brought him as much trouble as glory," she replies. Before Master Li can "retire" from his life of fighting, he must avenge the murder of his master, a task he seems reluctant to pursue. When he finally tracks down Jade Fox, she tries to justify her actions, saying that although Master Li's sensei would sleep with her, he wouldn't teach her. Believing that she has a right to this knowledge, she steals the secret manual of Wudan Mountain and teaches herself. Without a teacher, though, she's undisciplined and hasn't internalized the virtues of a warrior, such as justice, compassion, and honor. This is readily apparent when we watch her fight. She employs underhanded techniques, such as hiding a knife in the tip of her shoe, and demanding that her disciple, Jen Yu, "kill them all." According to Buddhist doctrine, he or she who has realized the truth lives fully in the present. The person is also free from "selfish desire, hatred, ignorance, conceit, pride, and all such 'defilements,' he is pure and gentle, full of universal love, compassion, kindness, sympathy, understand and tolerance."[181] He or she has no thought of self and sees beyond such concepts as good and evil, right and wrong. Jade Fox has, obviously, learned nothing by training herself in martial arts techniques. She might be able to fight, but she has failed to internalize the training.

Corrupted by hatred and jealousy, Jade Fox might not be a candidate for "redemption," but this isn't true of Jen Yu, who Master Li says is good at heart. "Even Jade Fox couldn't corrupt her," he says. And we see the truth in this. When Jen Yu returns home after fighting Master Li, Jade Fox tells her that they should run away together, as master and disciple, and rule the world, killing anyone who gets in their way, even Jen Yu's father. "It's the Giang Hu fighter lifestyle . . . kill or be killed," Jade Fox says. In the end, Jen Yu comes to the aid of Master Li and stands against the corrupted worldview of Jade Fox, who tries to polarize gender in the film, making us and Jen Yu believe that traditional ways are "corrupt" and sexist, whereas her gangster lifestyle is more egalitarian. By watching her actions, we realize that everyone in the film has personal responsibility and depending on how he or she acts, consequences follow. The key to creating a harmonious society is studying with a teacher who will teach proper behavior. Those who try to "work outside of the system," as Jade Fox does, only create chaos and disruption. In this, the film firmly supports Confucian and Buddhist values.

House of Flying Daggers (*Shi Mian Mai Fu*) (2004)—Screenplay by Feng Li, Bin Wang, and Zhang Yimou. Directed by Zhang Yimou. Running time: 119 min. Mandarin. Rated PG-13 for sequences of stylized martial arts violence and some sexuality. Genre: Action/Adventure/Fantasy/Romance.

As in *Crouching Tiger* and *Hero*, the main characters in *House of Flying Daggers*—Jin (Takeshi Kaneshiro), Leo (Andy Lau), and Mei (Zhang Ziyi)—adhere to a code of honor, particularly the latter two, who are members of the Robin Hoodesque band of rebels known as the Flying Daggers. They also embody the Confucian ideals of bravery, self-sacrifice, respect, and loyalty. However, Zhang Yimou breaks with *wuxia* tradition by focusing more on the characters' emotions and, particularly, on Jin and Mei's desire to leave behind their socially restricted lives to become a "carefree wind and wander as we please." As the director says in the audio commentary on the DVD, for him the wind represents youth and the desire to seek out freedom and love. One of the main themes of the film is to "go live life like the wind," to be free and independent. This sentiment comes straight from Zhuangzi's writings, whose "central theme may be summed up in a single word: freedom."[182] Furthermore, he "employs the metaphor of a totally free and purposeless journey, using the word *yu* (to wander or a wandering) to designate the way in which the enlightened man wanders through all of creation, enjoying its delights without ever becoming attached to any part of it."[183] In *Flying Daggers*, neither Jin nor Mei ever gets to be "free like the wind," but at least they acknowledge that the way out of their respective, socially restrictive situations is to simply "let go." The next film we will discuss, *Fearless*, is not a *wuxia*; however, it does assert that one must adhere to a code of honor when fighting.

Fearless (*Huo Yuan Jia*) (2006)—Screenplay by Chris Chow, Chi-long To, and Christine To. Directed by Ronny Yu. Running time: 141 min. (Director's cut DVD). Japanese, English, and Mandarin. Rated PG-13 for violence and martial arts action throughout. Genre: Action/Drama.

Fearless gets its title from the Daodejing (2:68), which reads: "One who excels as a warrior does not appear formidable; One who excels in fighting is never roused in anger; One who excels in defeating his enemy does not join the issue; One who excels in employing others humbles himself before them. This is known as the virtue of non-contention; This is known as making use of the efforts of others; This is known as matching the sublimity of heaven." During the course of the film, the protagonist, Huo Yuanjia (Jet Li), must internalize these teachings. In addition to Daoism, the film also contains Confucian elements, such as the importance of maintaining the five relationships (the only one missing is elder-younger brother) and demonstrating what a *junzi* is not. Unlike *Crouching Tiger, Hidden Dragon, Fearless* doesn't suggest that these two systems are anything but complementary; each governs its own realm. Confucianism governs one's relationship with one's family and society, and Daoism "represents the same individual in a private chamber or mountain retreat, often seeking surcease from the cares of official life."[184]

Huo Yuanjia respects his father, who is a *wushu* master, and he's desperate to begin his training. But his father chides him, telling him to practice his calligraphy. The impatient boy doesn't see the merit in this, and he coerces his friend Nong Jinsun (Yong Dong) to do it for him. One day, he and his friend sneak away to see a fight between Huo Yuanjia's father and another man. Rather than strike with a fatal blow, his father holds back and loses the fight. Having avoided his studies, Huo Yuanjia feels shame over this act of "weakness," seeing this as nothing more than a defeat. Angry, he picks a fight with the winning fighter's son. When he returns home, badly beaten, his father tells him to go and copy down the sayings of Confucius. But instead of taking the time to do it properly, internalizing the meaning of the words, he rushes through the task, scribbling them down as fast as he can. His mother visits him and tells him that "*Wushu* is not just winning. The most important part is self-restraint and having discipline. Whatever happens, never forget to be the kind person you are. *Wushu* is to help you be strong so you can help others. It's not for getting even or getting you into trouble. The way to have a good relationship with all people is to understand that, and give kindness to others and treat them with respect and honor." Having not heard what his mother has said, Huo Yuanjia replies that he'll get honor if he's great at *wushu*. "People fearing you and giving you honor are not the same thing," she replies.

As he grows up, Huo Yuanjia's only passion continues to be *wushu*, and he dreams of being the master of all fighters. When his mother tells him that he should get remarried, he says that he's too busy restoring his family's reputation. "I want everyone here and everywhere to know our name." His mother tells him that his biggest enemy is himself and that if he really wants to defeat someone, "that person will be you." Even though he says he understands, he doesn't. And at the family's ancestor altar, he burns incense and candles for his father, saying "Father, you were real fast, but not fast enough. Your heart was too soft. But don't you worry. As long as I live your *wushu* will never be defeated. I swear to it." Because of this obsessive drive for fame, he neglects his daughter and his familial obligations, foolishly accepts unworthy students, and he almost bankrupts his family's estate and Nong Jinsun, his lifelong friend, who keeps covering for him. But the worst of it occurs when he takes the unsubstantiated word of one of his students and, in heat of the moment, fights and kills Master Chin, his "rival." Up until this point, Huo Yuanjia believed that being the champion of the world would bring him happiness, but nothing could be further from the truth. One of Chin's relatives retaliates, killing Huo Yuanjia's mother and daughter. Covered in blood and wanting revenge himself, Huo Yuanjia rushes to Chin's home, sword in hand, and kills the culprit. Rushing toward Chin's wife and daughter, he sees Chin's dead body and hears his wife and daughter huddled in the corner crying. He drops his sword. But the worst is yet to come. He learns that his student was at fault, and he's killed an innocent man. In a daze, Huo Yuanjia boards a ship, undoubtedly determined to get as far away from the situation as possible.

The next time we see him he is stumbling around in a river before he falls in. He nearly drowns, but he's saved by a blind woman named Moon (Betty Sun) and her Grandma (Yun Qu), who nurse him back to health. He spends several morally instructive years in the countryside, gaining a sense of community and learning the value of hard work. He also learns to stop and enjoy the moment, whether by catching dragonflies or feeling the breeze on his face. Old habits die hard, though. The first time he's taken to the fields to plant rice, he thinks of it as a race, and shoves the seedlings in as fast as he can. Moon goes back to replant the young shoots, remarking that "seedlings are alive. They cannot be planted too close together. Too close, they cannot grow properly, like people. We have to learn how to respect each other. We can all live in harmony this way." When he says, "I will remember that," we get a sense that he will. He's finally learning the lessons that he failed to in his youth. When he plants the seedlings, he pays attention to spacing; and when the wind blows, he stops to enjoy it. He's learning balance, and, as the Daodejing (1:19) says, he's manifesting plainness, embracing simplicity, reducing selfishness, and having few desires. In essence, in this small village, Yuanjia learns to live in accordance with the Dao, and he does this by allowing things to happen naturally rather than forcing them. He lives close to nature, letting it be his teacher. Ever since Huo Yuanjia began living in this small community, no one has ever asked him who he is. They simply called him Ox. Furthermore, no one cared from whence he came. They simply accepted him for who he was. As Moon says, "I don't need to know. I only need to know that you're called Ox." For a man who's spent his entire life trying to make a name for himself, he discovers that those who really care about him aren't fixated on who he is, how much money he has, or how much power he has. We are reminded of what his mother said at the beginning of the film, which echoes the Daodejing (2:63): "It is because the sage never attempts to be great that he succeeds in becoming great." It's probably safe to say that without this Daoist interlude, Huo Yuanjia wouldn't have moved into the next phase of his life.

About three-quarters of the way into the film, Grandma announces that it's almost time for everyone to pay their respects to the dead, and Huo Yuanjia takes this opportunity to return home. In China, every year a family makes at least one ceremonial graveyard visit, and this festival, Qingming (literally "Clear and Bright") takes place on the third day of the third month. When Huo Yuanjia arrives home, his servant answers the door, apologizing for the state of the property. "I always hoped that when you returned that everything would be the same, like nothing had changed." "It must have been hard for you," says Huo Yuanjia, for the first time exhibiting human-heartedness. "This is my duty, Master," says the servant. The servant explains that every day, creditors would come and remove items from the house, even foreclosing on it. "Everything you see before you is because of kind charity. Later, I realized the person who did this very kind deed was a good friend, Nong Jinsun," he says. At this point, we see two of the five Confucian relationships exhibited in their ideal state. Even though Huo Yuanjia has been less than the ideal friend or "ruler," Nong Jinsun and Huo Yuanjia's servant have behaved as they should, in a loving, reverential, and loyal manner. This is the proverbial "lightbulb" moment for our protagonist, and Huo Yuanjia tears down his death waivers and begins burning them. His parents wouldn't want to see these, he admits. At his family's gravesite—where he has left food and burns incense—he apologizes to his father for being disobedient. "I finally realize, many years ago, why you held back that last blow," he says. "You are the true champion of Tianjin." To his mother, he says that "Many years ago, you taught me how to be a good person. I was too arrogant to understand. . . . Your son promises to live up to your guidance." And to his daughter, he states that while she was alive, he didn't take good care of her; he wasn't a good father. His apologies don't stop there. He goes to Master Chin's house to pay his respects. Now that he's realized the error of his unfilial and arrogant ways, he decides to make a real difference with his life. Instead of fighting for his own power and glory, he will use his skills for others. And through competition, he will discover himself.

He decides to compete one last time, so that he can restore China's honor, which has been tarnished by Westerners who refer to the Chinese as the "sick men of the East." During the competition Huo Yuanjia easily defeats every opponent. He is increasingly seen as a financial threat to those who have bet against him. To make sure they don't lose anymore money, Huo Yuanjia is poisoned. Although he will surely die—the poison has gone to his heart—he never leaves the ring; he is determined to finish. Furthermore, when one of his disciples seeks revenge, Huo Yuanjia, undoubtedly drawing from his own tragic past, says, "Revenge will only bring us more bloodshed. We must strive to become triumphant." (In this statement, we hear the voice of Buddhism and its stance on nonviolence.) His Japanese opponent, Tanaka, suggests that they end the fight now. But Huo Yuanjia won't do it; "It's no longer about me," he says. During the last round, Huo Yuanjia has the opportunity to use the same move on Tanaka that he used on Master Chin, but he refrains. He has become like his father, a compassionate and honorable man. He dies at peace. In his final moments, he has accomplished what is said in the Daodejing (1:33): "He who knows others is clever; he who knows himself has discernment. He who overcomes others has force; He who overcomes himself is strong; He who knows contentment is rich; He who perseveres is a man of purpose; He who does not lose his station will endure; He who lives out his days has had a long life."

The Forbidden Kingdom (2008)—Screenplay by John Fusco. Directed by Rob Minkoff. Running time: 113 min. English, and Mandarin. Rated PG-13 for sequences of martial arts action and some violence. Genre: Action/Adventure/Fantasy.

Summary: *The Forbidden Kingdom* begins in the bedroom of Jason Tripitikas (Michael Angarano), an American kung fu–crazed teenager. After waking from a dream about a Monkey King (Jet Li) who is fighting off hordes of soldiers with his golden staff, Jason ventures to a pawn shop in Chinatown to obtain some bootleg DVDs. While there, he goes into the backroom and finds a staff similar to the one in his dream. The owner of the shop, Old Hop (Jackie Chan), tells him that long ago, his father obtained the staff, and he is still trying to find its rightful owner. Jason pedals away on his bike only to bump into a group of bullies. The encounter doesn't go well, and eventually Jason is knocked unconscious. He "wakes" up in ancient China—he has gone through the Gateless Gate—where he meets and teams up with Lu Yan (Chan again), a drunken Daoist Immortal; Golden Sparrow (Yifei Liu), an orphan whose heart is set on revenge; and a pacifist Silent Monk (Li again), who is trained in the Shaolin tradition. Together, they journey to Five Elements Mountain, where they hope to free the jovial, staff-wielding Monkey King (Li, again), who has been turned to stone by the evil Jade Warlord (Collin Chou).

Although not an accurate retelling of the story, *The Forbidden Kingdom* does draw upon characters and elements found in the *Journey to the West*. Attributed to Wu Cheng'en, who lived during the 16th century C.E., the tripartite, 100-chapter *Journey to the West* focuses on a monk (in the story, Tripitaka; in reality, Xuanzang) who is joined by three companions: Monkey, Pigsy, and Sandy. Together, they venture westward to retrieve Buddhist sutras. Along the way, they encounter many dangers and foes. Most East Asians know this folk legend; however, despite the existence of a 1943 English language translation by Arthur Waley, known simply as *Monkey*, it is still relatively unknown in the West.[185] Anime aficionados are ahead of the curve as it was the basis for *Saiyuki* (2000), and references to it have been made in everything from *Inu-Yasha* to *Dragonball Z*. A live action, three-hour-long feature film version appeared on TV in 2000, titled *The Lost Empire*. Thomas Gibson of *Dharma & Greg* played the lead.

As far as the story goes, *The Forbidden Kingdom* was made for an audience familiar with kung fu films, therefore, it pays homage more to this cinematic genre than it does to *Journey to the West*. That said, the film retains the spirit of Monkey. The official website of the film (www.forbiddenkingdommovie .com) actually contains a "timeline" of Monkey's life, which one finds in chapters one through seven in *Journey to the West*. It tells us that he was born out of a rock and "seasoned with high heavenly graces and intelligence." In the Land of the Humans, he sought enlightenment from one of the Ten Disciples of Buddha. "Under his tutelage, the pupil learn(ed) the ancient ways quickly from a Daoist Master." It wasn't long before Monkey could dance among the clouds—in the film he is shown riding on a cloud—and fly 108,000 miles in one somersault. Furthermore, Monkey can, at will, transform himself into any creature he wants, from insects to elephants, and even fight enemies within themselves. He is the creator of the kung fu style, known as Monkey. Naturally, his superior skills made him egotistical, and he became boastful and rebellious. Wanting more power, he descended to the sea's bottom, to the palace of the Dragon King of the East, where he found the golden-banded Bo staff, which the gods crafted to measure the depths of the ocean. With the staff in hand and his consummate kung fu skills, Monkey is almost impossible to beat. His exploits find him in Hell, Heaven, and Earth, where he engaged in many battles and angered many beings. For the most part, the website is accurate in its retelling of the Monkey King legend. The film doesn't depict many of Monkey's exploits. It does, however, show him in Heaven, causing problems for the Jade Emperor and his wife, the Queen Mother of the West. For the most part, the website provides expanded information so that the film is in context.

The website also contains details about Jackie Chan's scholar-warrior character, named Lu Yan, known later as the Drunken Master. It explains that as a boy he dedicated himself to WuDang Mountain and Han Zhang Li, an immortal who taught him the martial art ways of a Daoist. After many years, he was invited to take the civil service examinations but he failed. One night, he had a dream about his failed future, and this influenced him to begin cultivating the Dao. If we look to Chinese folklore, this description makes the character sounds a lot like Lu Dongbin or Lu Tungpin, who is one of the Eight Immortals. However, his symbol is a sword, which he uses to slay dragons. (Chan's character doesn't carry a sword.) Lu Dongbin is said to have lived either during the Tang or Song dynasties, and stories tell us that he is a ladies' man and has bouts of drunkenness. If we look at the appearance of Chan's character, he resembles not Lu Dongbin but the Immortal known as Iron-Crutch Li or Tieguali. It is said that he is an unkempt, wooly haired and ill-tempered man who uses a crutch to walk and carries special medicine inside of his bottle gourd. Chan's character does, indeed carry a bottle gourd, but instead of medicine intended for others, the substance is peach alcohol. His character also walks with a crutch, and his hair is wooly and unkempt. We can only assume that the writer of *The Forbidden Kingdom* purposely or erroneously conflated two of the Immortals into one character.

The Forbidden Kingdom isn't going to teach anyone the story of the *Journey to the West*, however, it does expose its viewer to the Monkey King, and it uses the same structure of four people on a journey. To its credit, the film contains some "authentic" sounding Daoist and Buddhist teachings. For instance, Lu Yan remarks that "he who speaks, does not know. He who knows, does not speak." This sounds reminiscent of the first few lines of the *Daodejing*: "The way that can be spoken of is not the constant way; the name that can be named is not the constant name." Daoists and Zen Buddhists believe that words are limiting and cannot adequately convey "truth." This is essentially what Lu Yan is saying that experience is everything. While Lu Yan is training Jason, he hands the teen a cup and starts pouring liquid into it. It isn't long before it overflows. Jason shouts, "The cup's full. Stop. It's full." To this Lu Yan replies, "Exactly. How can you fill your cup if already full? How can you learn kung fu? You already know so much. No Shadow Kick, Buddha Palm. Empty your cup." He means this, of course, literally and figuratively. He's saying to become the uncarved block; to become simple like a child. He is echoing what Yoda, our unofficial Daoist master tells Luke Skywalker, that he must "unlearn what he has learned." Finally, Lu Yan tells Jason to jump. When the teen refuses, the master tells him, "not think, just do." Again, this demonstrates the Daoist and Zen Buddhist belief that too much rational thought gets in the way of real enlightenment. We must leave our thinking minds behind.

Popular Religion

According to scholar Stephen F. Teiser, popular religion can be defined as those aspects of religious life that are shared by most Chinese, whether or not they claim an affiliation with Confucianism, Daoism, or Buddhism. We can find popular religion in the way that people honor their dead—by offering food and burning incense; "conducting funerals, exorcising ghosts, and consulting fortunetellers; belief in the patterned interaction between light and dark; the tendency to construe gods as government officials; the preference for balancing tranquility and movement."[186] One of the best places to find evidence of popular religion is in horror films, and for our discussion, it will be instructive to look briefly at the Hong Kong–made *The Eye* (*Gin Gwai*), the Taiwanese-made *The Heirloom* (*Zhaibian*), and the Singapore-made *The Maid* (2005).

The Eye (*Gin Gwai*) (2002)—Screenplay by Jo Jo Yuet-chun Hui, Danny Pang, and Oxide Pang Chun. Directed by Oxide Pang Chun and Danny Pang. Running time: 99 min. English, Cantonese, Thai, and Mandarin. Rated R for some disturbing images. Genre: Horror.

Summary: *The Eye*[187] focuses on Wong Kar Mun (Angelica Lee), a woman who has been blind, and therefore dependent on her family, for most of her life. A cornea transplant offers her hope of a new life. But even before her vision sharpens, she discovers that she can see more than just the material realm; she can also see ghosts. Realizing that her "gift" is tied to the owner of her corneas, she and her psychologist journey to Thailand, where they learn about a gifted young woman who, after years of being ostracized, paid the ultimate price.

For the most part, *The Eye* derives its ideas of the afterlife from the Buddhist tradition. The ghosts that the protagonist encounters have either been killed violently or have committed suicide; therefore, they are "stuck," so to speak. According to Buddhism, one of the three forms of craving is craving for annihilation as a way to get rid of unpleasant situations. But because of the concept of rebirth, suicide is useless. One is simply reborn, usually in a lower life form or, depending on one's karma, into one of several hell realms. The first one, repetition or *sanjiva* hell, is actually reserved for those who kill. Descriptions of this level[188] don't mention anything about those who self-kill and the term "repetition" isn't necessarily interpreted literally. However, we can see that this hell is the source for *The Eye*. In fact, a Daoist priest even says as much: "Suicide is a dreadful sin. The souls of those who commit it are obliged to repeat their painful deaths every day. To help them break out of this vicious cycle of pain, we need to tackle the cause of his suicide. Only then can his soul leave this world in peace." Because of her suicide, Ling (Chutcha Rujinanon), the originator of the corneas, appears in her room at the same time every day, steps on a chair, and hangs herself. Essentially, in the normal course of events, a person who commits suicide would "remain in an unsettled state after death and neither receive the regular rites nor have hope of becoming socially immortalized through a tomb or a hall tablet . . . because the soul is not in its proper place in the underworld, and can harass the living, making them sick, troubled, and unsuccessful, suicide can be used as an act of aggression against one's kin."[189]

Another ghost that appears to the newly sighted Wong Kar Mun is a baseball-cap-wearing boy who, after losing his report card, kills himself by jumping out of a high-rise window. His punishment is to wander the halls, continually asking if anyone has seen his report card. It is with regard to him that we see the interaction between Buddhism and popular religion. Outside their apartment door, his parents have set out lanterns and candles. Buddhists and Daoists both light lanterns and candles for the dead, and in the folk tradition, a lamp is placed by the deceased person's feet so as to illuminate his or her way through the underworld. In one scene, the ghost is actually shown to be chewing on a candle, remarking that he's hungry. As we've already said, those who pass through purgatory on their way to rebirth and those reborn in hell are without exception hungry and very often naked; therefore, food and some form of money are typically offered to the deceased. On a shelf in their apartment, his parents are burning, in front of his photograph, three joss sticks of incense and two red-bulbed candles.

Later, under the guidance of the Daoist exorcist, Wong's grandmother and her sister sit on the sidewalk in front of their building burning what appears to be his report card, obviously in a bid to resolve the child's conflict, as well as spirit money. After they add these items to the flames, they utter prayers. On the ground next to the brazier, they also have placed several bowls of fruit, including apples and oranges. Burning paper items, usually spirit money, in a red metal can to the deceased is a common popular practice among the Chinese. Because ghosts (*gui*) are "both dangerous and pitiful," people make offerings to them, always "outside of the house, and always outside the back door."[190] Later in the film, Wong's grandmother hires a yellow-robed Daoist "priest," known as a "red hat," to perform an exorcism. "The red-hat priests are an example of the partial fusion of Daoism and popular religion."[191] Using a feng shui compass, he points to various corners of the room and shouts.

The origins of some of the ghosts that appear to Wong Kar Mun are never explained, such as the woman who attacks her while she's practicing her calligraphy. The only thing that the angry spirit says is "Why are you sitting in my chair?" just before she lunges for Wong. We don't know the back story on the elderly man who hovers in the corner of the apartment's elevator. Based on the fact that half of his face is missing, we might assume that his injury and death can be tied to the elevator. In one of the film's most unsettling moments, Wong is sitting in a restaurant when she sees a young woman who is holding a baby. This woman peers through the front window and eventually floats around to the side; Wong notices that the woman has no feet. We watch as the spirit sticks out her long, purple tongue and licks at the strips of meat that are hanging over the stove. One of the restaurant employees, who can also see ghosts, tells Wong that even though the area is being sold for renovation, her boss won't sell because "he seems to be expecting his wife and child to visit." We then see a photograph of the man's wife who is holding a baby.

By contrast, some of the ghosts that Wong can see are being led away by a "shadowy" figure. The first ghost encountered by Wong is that of an elderly woman who occupied the bed next to her in the hospital. Even after death, she moans and says that she's freezing. Toward the end of the film, Wong encounters another fellow patient, Ying Ying, a young girl who has been battling cancer for much of her life. This encounter isn't quite as terrifying for Wong. In fact, before the girl is led away, she remains cheerful and optimistic. After Ying Ying's funeral, which involves the burning of incense and leaving behind food offerings, she doesn't appear again. In general, a person who has died from natural causes or from sickness won't turn into a ghost. About halfway through the film, Wong encounters another ghost. While she's crossing the street, a school-age boy passes through her. He had been the victim of a fatal car accident. The boy's spirit stares down at his own body before the afore-mentioned shadow leads him away.[192]

As explained in the film by an off-screen narrator, the last thought that a person has before he or she dies will "become the eternal consciousness of his soul. Those who die a sudden death have no recollection of the instance of death. Their souls remain in this world as if they're still alive. But there are others who intentionally refuse to leave, mostly due to unresolved problems during their lifetime. These souls can't be consoled while their problems remain. There is only one way to help them, and that is to resolve what they left unsettled." How this is explained in the film is in accordance with Buddhist, especially Tibetan, thought. As Sogyal Rinpoche says, the state of our mind at death is paramount. "If we die in a positive frame of mind, we can improve our next birth, despite our negative karma. And if we are upset and distressed, it may have a detrimental effect, even though we may have lived our lives well. This means that *the lost thought and emotion that we have before we die has an extremely powerful determining effect on our immediate future* [his emphasis]."[193] He continues, saying that ideally, before death, one should give away everything, mentally and physically, so that one is free of attachments.

The Heirloom (*Zhaibian*) (2005)—Screenplay by Dorian Li. Directed by Leste Chen. Running time: 97 min. Mandarin. Rating surrendered; previously rated R for violent images. Genre: Horror.

The Heirloom is about a four-floor mansion that has been in the Yang family for about 70 years. It has sat vacant for the past two decades, because, for some unexplained reason, 15 members of the household committed suicide by hanging themselves at exactly the same time. James, one of two surviving heirs—the other one is in an asylum—returns to Taipei from England to take possession. Shortly thereafter, he and his fiancée, Yo, move in. The real story, though, is what had led the family to its fortune and ultimately its demise. The film starts with a definition: "*Hsiao Guei* (literally "raising child ghosts"): A folk practice prevalent in Chinese societies whereby dead fetuses are worshipped in urns and fed with the blood of their master." It continues, "Child ghosts possess great power to bring their master fortune. Some are so powerful they can even be used to kill. But for such dark arts, a price must be paid." And really, this tells us everything we need to know about what we will encounter in this film.

"Auntie," the woman locked in the asylum, further explains the situation to Yo: "Our ancestors believed that child ghosts bring fortune. So they bought dead babies [on] the black market and then forced family members to feed [them] with blood."[194] (This is done, by the way, in front of the ancestor shrine, with all of the portraits staring down.) "Through this feeding ritual, the child ghost found its master and was controlled by the family. These ghosts obeyed orders and brought prosperity. Sometimes they even helped us eliminate our enemies. Generation after generation, our family made [its] fortune through this dark practice. But finally, there was a price to pay." She reveals that the family's offspring were born either handicapped or terminally ill, with only one or two healthy enough to live. To protect the healthy ones, the unhealthy ones were sent away to asylums or locked inside the house. "Later, to maintain the family fortune . . . the unhealthy children were forced to do the feeding, while the healthy ones inherited the fortune." But the story doesn't end there. The woman who is recounting the tale is a twin. While she was locked in the attic, her sister flourished on the outside. But when the healthy sister got pregnant and had complications during childbirth, the twin's fortunes were switched. Now locked in the attic, the vengeful sister fed all of her blood to the fetus urns so that all 15 members of her family would hang themselves.

After Yo leaves the asylum she returns home, where she climbs into the attic and finds the child ghost urn. Hoping to find a safe place to store it, she and

James take it to a "place for worshipping child spirits," a dead infant temple. Inside, the camera pans over myriad figurines, including a golden buddha and many child sculptures, finally landing on a *yin pa kua* (sometimes also called a *bagwa*) mirror that's placed outside the entranceway. This eight-sided mir-rored device is used for protection because it deflects and dissolves everything in its direct path, good or bad. Most feng shui practitioners advise against us-ing this ritual object indiscriminately.[195] Yo begins looking around the temple, only to be interrupted by a man who tells her that "These spirits don't mean any harm. Some of them were too young to even have a name before they were sent here." "How can we get rid of it?" she says, meaning the urn. "You can't get rid of karma. Some parents bring dead children here thinking it would wipe away their guilt. But in actual fact, the guilt never goes away. After all, it was a human life that was sacrificed." "I would like to keep this here at your temple," James says. "How long have you raised it?" the temple guardian asks. "It's not my doing. It was a long time ago left by the family." "So be it," the man says before he takes the jar. "I'll take this child ghost. . . . Don't worry. Buddha will take care of it."

According to the DVD audio commentary, the filmmakers explain that while preparing for *The Heirloom*, they had encountered an authentic dead in-fant temple but didn't use it as a filming location: "The atmosphere inside . . . was too creepy, just like what you see here. Quite similar. So, after we visited the real temple, we all felt it was too . . . we wouldn't like to stay. And we can't afford to offend the place or touch things here. So one week before the shoot, we decided to build the dead infant temple from scratch." Some of the items that appear in the scene came from the actual temple, including several of the statuettes and dolls. "Of course, we did some rites, to move out the spirits," he continues. "It was still creepy. . . . We collected many things that could be as-sociated with ghosts and urns. We put these things in the room. The desk was full of statuettes, quite scary."

Even though James is trying to outrun his family's past, the power of the ghost is too strong. While he's waiting for his fiancée to perform in a ballet of *Orpheus and Eurydice*—an appropriate choice as Yo has descended into a kind of hell by this point—a voice whispers to James that he's the heir to the Yang family and so must sacrifice all to protect that family. "The ghost's power will help you. Remember, you are the heir. The only heir to the family. Nobody can stop you from what you want. Beware of all those who are not of the Yang family. Its power enables us to help you. Remember, we are of the same family." Suddenly we are back at the temple, and we hear what sounds like shattering glass. The temple guardian sits upright and looks down into the temple. As the camera moves through the building, we catch sight of a shadow hurrying past the front window. It is James who has come to reclaim the fetus jar. When he returns to his ancestral home, we find out that when he was a child, his mother almost escaped from the attic with his help. But she was caught and taken back upstairs, where she tried killing herself. James was sent away. The guilt over his failure to save her is still on James' mind when his fiancée turns up at home. When she reveals that she's pregnant with his child, he knocks her out, carries her to the ancestor shrine room, and hits her repeatedly in the stomach, in an effort to stop the Yang family "curse." But he's unsuccessful. Three days later, Yo wakes up in a hospital bed. She is still pregnant and James Yang is dead. The film ends with her return to the ancestral home.

The Heirloom is obviously a work of fiction; however, it does contain some authentic folk practices and beliefs. For instance, about 45 minutes into the film, Yo is walking in Taipei, when she ventures through the fortunetelling street underground. Here she comes across a fortuneteller who is surrounded by caged birds. He lets one of them out of its small cage, and it picks a card from a stack. "Gain fortune through evil; fall into endless hell," he says, as Yo walks toward him. "Miss, this prophecy is for you." She hurries away. As revealed during the DVD audio commentary, not only is the bird fortuneteller authentic, but as someone in the film crew attests, his predictions are also pretty accurate. Divination practices have a long history in China, dating to the Shang Dynasty (ca. 1554–1045 B.C.E.). During that time, a king or his diviners would pose a question, usually about the harvest or the king's health, while touching a hot poker to a turtle shell or a cattle bone. Afterward, they would inspect the item and read the cracks as either auspicious or inauspicious. Another popular and very ancient tool of divination is the I Ching. Today, people are more likely to go to a diviner for matters concerning marriage or a funeral.

As for the fortuneteller's prophecy, although the person watching The Heirloom doesn't yet know the meaning of this prophecy, the fortuneteller is referring to the Yang family's practice of using fetuses in jars to control their future. The hell of which he speaks is avici, the worst of all possible hells, where suffering is a thousand times more intense than all previous hells and their subdivisions. One can assume that the reason the Yang family ends up here is because they have committed a crime that represents "the highest level of destruction of the foundations of society. . . . These people's minds were inverted and hardened and even at this period the upside-down position of the sinners as they fell into the hells symbolized their reverse views."[196]

If we take a sample of East Asian horror films, more often than not a child younger than 10 is either a ghost or is affected by a ghost. In China, it was believed that if a woman experienced a difficult labor, it was caused by ghosts who were upset with past or present family members. To find out more about the "nature of the ghost," the family would often consult with a "witch."[197] If the child died before he or she was one year old, no ceremony was held. His or her body was simply "rolled into a straw mat and buried in some unused ground outside the town." If this death was followed by the deaths of other children in close succession, life-stealing ghosts were said to be the culprits. Furthermore, the face of the second child who died would be "slapped by shoes, and its body thrown into the lake instead of being buried in the ground." The reason for this? It was believed that ghosts cannot reincarnate if thrown into water; therefore, the only way a person who died by drowning could reincarnate was to get a victim to substitute for him or her. In some cases, instead of hitting the dead child with a shoe, the parent would smear some soot on its face, which was supposed to keep the same ghost from returning to the family, because it would be recognized by the mark on its face. Finally, some families chose to dispose of their children's bodies by hanging them in trees, because of the belief that "any soul whose body does not touch the earth has lost its power of reincarnation."[198]

As scholar Marc L. Moskowitz explains, it isn't uncommon today to find women in Taiwan who are afraid of fetus ghosts (*yingling*), which result from miscarried and aborted fetuses, and in some cases a child who died in infancy.[199] In fact, the author presents six basic scenarios of fetus-ghost hauntings with varying degrees of malevolence. Chapter 5 of his 2001 book, *The Haunting Fetus: Abortion, Sexuality and the Spirit World in Taiwan*, begins with the testimonial of a 39-year-old housewife from Taipei, who explains that several years after having an abortion, she began to get the sense that she was being followed. When she became ill, her parents took her not to a hospital but to a temple. "I didn't see the child in the temple because Buddha protected me when I was there." She returned home after a month, only to feel as if she were being followed again, so she visited a fortuneteller who gave her a talismanic paper. She said that she stuck this to her door and burned incense to the ghost. Furthermore, she set up a memorial plaque for the dead child at the temple. The child didn't appear again.[200] "Feeling anxious but unsure of the reason, ill with no explanation, women often turn to spirit mediums, fortunetellers, and Daoist and Buddhist masters for help."[201] Chapter 10 of Moskowitz's book, which is titled "Blood-Drinking Fetus Demons: Greed, Loathing, and Vengeance through Sorcery in Taiwan," lends credibility to the premise of *The Heirloom*, no matter how far-fetched it seems. In his chapter, he takes the reader into the world of fetus-ghost sorcery, where some practitioners ensnare ghosts to do their bidding.

On a psychological level, *The Heirloom* has a lot to say about Chinese attitudes toward children and ancestors. As someone says in the film's DVD audio commentary, "The core of this movie is the progress from compromise to sacrifice; from individuality to being part of the family. . . . Individuality can be sacrificed for the benefit of the family." And to some degree this has been characteristic of Chinese life throughout the ages. It has always been expected that sons and daughters would get married so that they can carry on the ancestral line. The worst thing that someone could do was to try and destroy the family, which is what James' mother and then James was going to do. This reciprocal relationship between the living and the dead is well established. "The ancestral spirits will help their own descendants whenever they can. They are the spirits upon which the living may depend without any question and to which the living are related, for better or for worse and without any possibility of change. Their behavior in life, as well as in the world of the dead, exerts influence on the fate of the descendants. In turn, their fate is also influenced by the behavior of their descendants. . . . It is clear, then, that the attitude of the living toward the dead and that of the dead toward the living are functionally one."[202]

The Maid (2006)—Written and directed by Kelvin Tong. Running time: 93 min. English, Teochew, Filipino, Tagalog. Rated PG. Genre: Action/Drama.

The film begins with a voiceover: "During the Chinese seventh month, times are good. More paper offerings are burnt for the ancestors. Meat is offered as well, for good luck, for the family. Throughout the whole Chinese seventh month, the Chinese will pay respect to our ancestors. Children are told not to stay out late. Best to be home by 5 p.m. Laundry should be taken in before nightfall. These are customs handed down by the older generation. Once a year during the Chinese seventh month, the gates of hell will open. This is a big occasion for the Chinese. We will first pay respect to our ancestors, then to the wandering spirits, so that they will bless and protect us as well." Images of fire provide a backdrop to the narration. We see papers burning in metal cans, incense being burned, enormous demonic-looking effigies standing in front of a brightly colored paper ship that is eventually engulfed in flames, and large ash heaps smoldering in the streets.

The Maid begins on the eve of the seventh month. Rosa Dimaano, an 18-year-old from the Philippines, arrives in Singapore to work as a maid for Mr. and Mrs. Teo, who run an opera troupe. Because Rosa is Catholic—we later see her reciting the Lord's Prayer—she is unfamiliar with this festival, so Mrs. Teo explains the details. She says that the Hungry Ghost month has just started, which means that the gates of hell have opened and all of the hungry ghosts have come out: "Usually we don't do anything during the seventh month. We don't go swimming, we come back before the sky is dark, and one thing you must remember, if you are walking alone and someone calls your name, you must never turn back." "What will happen if I do turn back?" Rosa asks. Mrs. Teo doesn't respond. Halfway through this explanation, Rosa looks down the street and sees that everyone in the neighborhood is outside, lighting small fires. Later that evening Rosa wakes up to get a glass of water. Outside the front door, we see Mr. and Mrs. Teo consigning papers to a fire, saying, "Calling all spirits. Help yourself to this money. You go your way, and I'll go mine. Please leave me alone." The Hungry Ghost Festival is, as Mrs. Teo explained, a very popular festival that is celebrated primarily in South China, Hong Kong, Taiwan, Singapore, and Malaysia. It is a "hybrid" festival, which means it combines elements from Buddhism, Daoism, and popular or folk religion. Since the dead are returning to visit their relatives after a long time, the living are expected to feed these "hungry ghosts" to ensure good fortune and luck. As we see in the film, people offer prayers, spirit or "hell" money,[203] and food, and they burn incense.

On Rosa's second day in Singapore she meets the Teo's mentally handicapped son, Ah-soon, who gives her a butterfly. Later, while Mrs. Teo is pinning a red dress on Rosa, the woman explains that because she and her husband had a child so late in life, the doctor said there was something wrong with Ah-soon's head. She laments that while other people have children who go to school, grow up, get married, and have babies, her son is still like a "small boy." Still wearing the dress, Rosa is given some lipstick, which she applies. "Now what?" she asks Ah-soon, who laughs and hands her a red cloth to put over her head. Because Rosa is unfamiliar with Chinese customs, she fails to realize what's actually going on: she's being dressed as a traditional Chinese bride.

Rosa wakes up the next morning and sweeps up the ashes that are still in front of the door. Mrs. Teo shouts at her, saying that she can't do this: "This is for the ghosts. You cannot touch. Very bad luck." She dumps the ashes back on the ground, folds her hands together, and she bows repeatedly, saying "So sorry. Sorry. She's not aware. Please forgive her. Please bless and protect my family. She's not aware. Please forgive her. Please don't be mad." As Rosa walks back toward the house, a set of hands grabs her legs and pulls her over. We watch as a dead woman crawls toward her. Later that evening, Rosa hears Mrs. Teo, chanting softly to her son, "Darling, you'll be successful some day. All officials will flatter you. Your family fortunes will grow and you will prosper. When you take part in the imperial examinations everyone near and far will come to congratulate you. The gong sounds once, then twice. Guns will sound throughout the city. Your family fortunes will grow and you will prosper." Mrs. Teo has already admitted her disappointment of having a son who has failed to live up to traditional expectations: one who hasn't been successful in school, gotten married, or produced offspring. By contrast, she recites to him this established "model" of what a filial child should achieve in his life. Emphasized are luck, prosperity, longevity, happiness, and wealth, which are "the five most sought after values in Chinese culture."[204] Even though the civil service examinations were abandoned in 1905, we can assume that they still represent an ideal level of achievement.

About 25 minutes into the film, Rosa is on her way to mail a letter when she comes across a typical community celebration for the seventh month. In one area she sees rows and rows of tables. In front of each chair, there is a place setting of a small bowl holding incense, a spirit tablet, and food and drink, often including a full bottle of a carbonated beverage. Those who will be "dining" here are not human, though. Sitting in a *matshed*, a temporary bamboo-framed structure, yellow-robed priests, who wear black hats, chant liturgies and play instruments. At the entrance, we see sticks of incense burning. These will be kept going day and night. A continual stream of worshippers walks through the area. When Rosa returns home, Mrs. Teo is burning incense in front of an altar. Later that evening, the Teo family and Rosa are leaving for an opera, when they discover that outside their house a young boy who was playing soccer was hit and killed by a car. This street is bad luck, Mrs. Teo says. At the opera, Rosa finds a seat and begins watching the performance. An old man seated a few places down from her leans over and asks her why she is sitting in his wife's seat. Rosa gets up, only to discover that all of the chairs are really empty. Mr. Teo escorts her away, telling her that she can't sit there because the row is reserved for the ghosts. In Singapore and Malaysia, Chinese opera and concerts are often performed at night in the open air for the entertainment of the hungry ghosts. As the film shows, the front row is always left vacant.

Spooked by her experience, Rosa decides to return home. As she crosses the lawn, she sees a bonfire attended to by a circle of specters and then she's hit in the leg by a soccer ball. Its owner, a young boy, asks her if she could help him get his ball. This is, of course, the child who was killed earlier in the evening. We know this because when she returns home, his parents are burning incense for him and have food offered in front of his portrait. When Rosa tells her employers that she's seeing ghosts, Mr. Teo says that it "looks like she has offended something." The next day, Rosa goes outside to send another letter to her family and finds Ah-soon eating the offerings left outside of his house. She corrects him, saying he can't do that, and she takes him to get some food. On their way to a restaurant, she sees a teen-aged boy and girl standing next to each other on the bridge, saying, "Destiny has separated us. May we reunite in the next life." (Are they suicides?) They look straight at Rosa and Ah-soon. Other ghosts are encountered, including a 72-year-old victim of a hit-and-run, but the most mysterious is an ashen-faced woman, about Rosa's age, named Esther Santos. Who is she and why is she always wearing a red dress? A banging noise leads Rosa upstairs to a drum. She grabs a pair of scissors, cuts it open, and finds the mummified remains of Esther. We learn that Ah-soon raped the girl and when she tried to escape, Mr. Teo killed her.

Rosa attempts to leave the house, but she is caught, bound, gagged, and put in the red wedding dress. "Chinese people believe many things," says Mrs. Teo.

"One thing they believe is . . ."—she pulls a red cloth off to reveal side-by-side portraits of Ah-soon and Rosa—"dead men also can marry. Dead men can marry dead women. But the woman, before she dies, must say yes. All my life, [we] have waited for our son to marry." (After Esther died, Ah-soon fell and died. He returns during the Ghost Month, looking for Esther.) Mr. and Mrs. Teo prepare to hang Rosa, after they have tried bribing her with money for taking care of her younger brother. Ah-soon, realizing that his father killed Esther, becomes enraged and throws him into a fire. Esther's spirit, which has been present the entire time, actually saves Rosa, causing the hangman's rope to burn. A truck then hits and kills Mrs. Teo, who was chasing Rosa with a knife.

More than the premise of a horror film, ghost marriages are actually conducted in China. Because it is believed that an unmarried woman is prone to becoming a ghost, parents sometimes marry her "either to an unmarried deceased man, or to a living man who agrees to take her on as a second 'wife.' This allows her to become an ancestor in another family, just as she would have been married. Spirit marriage is quite common in Taiwan today."[205] In a *Times* article from January 26, 2007, we read that three men were arrested in Sha'anxi province, China, for murdering two women. They had "preyed on the superstitions of ill-educated farmers eager to ensure that a dead son was happy in the afterlife. It is not uncommon in rural parts of China for a family to seek out the body of a woman who has died to be buried alongside their son after the performance of a marriage ceremony for the deceased pair."[206] An article from the *Economist* dated July 26, 2007, explained that this practice is indeed an old one. According to legend, "the warload Cao Cao finds a corpse bride for his son who died in 208 CE at the tender age of 13." Mao, of course, disliked anything that smacked of feudal superstition, so he discouraged and suppressed ghost marriages. But with communism on the wane, parts of rural China are "seeing a burgeoning market for female corpses" for ghost marriages. The practice is most common in China's "coal-mining heartland," where "pit accidents kill many men too young to marry. Compensation to the family is spent on giving their son a wife in the afterlife. A black market has sprung up to supply corpse brides. Marriage brokers—usually respectable folk who find brides for village men—account for most of the middlemen. At the bottom of the supply chain come hospital mortuaries, funeral parlors, body snatchers—and now murderers." "Wet" or recently deceased brides can be sold for between $4,000 and $5,300; "dry goods," much older bodies that are dug up, are considerably cheaper.[207]

NOTABLE DIRECTOR: ZHANG YIMOU

Known as one of the Fifth Generation filmmakers, Zhang Yimou was born in 1951 in Xi'an, the People's Republic of China. Because his family's political background was "bad"—his father and two older brothers had been Nationalist officers—his family was a target of oppression, and he remembers witnessing his home being ransacked. He, himself, was sent to the country to be reeducated by peasants, and for three years, "planted seeds, cut tree branches, harvested crops, changed the products of land in food, and learned to cook."[208] As he said in one interview, "There was never hope for us to one day turn things around. So those ten years, from 1966 until 1976, I lived under the shadow of tragedy and hopelessness." He got some relief from photography, which he took up to "battle the emptiness" around him.[209] In 1978, he entered the Beijing Film Academy and studied cinematography. He parlayed those skills into a career, working at the Guangxi Film Studio on such efforts as Chen Kaige's award-winning *Huang Tu Di* (*Yellow Earth*).

Zhang Yimou stepped in front of the camera to act in Wu Tianming's *Old Well* (*Lao Jing*, 1986). His turn as a peasant won him the Best Actor Award at the Tokyo Film Festival. One year later, in 1987, he moved into the director's chair with *Hong Gao Liang* (*Red Sorghum*), which won the Golden Bear at the Berlin Film Festival. As the title suggests, the color red had symbolic meaning on a number of levels. As he explained, "The symbolic meaning of red in China is implicitly understood by everyone; it's recently been used to represent revolution, but how long has this revolution been in China? In China's 5,000 years of cultural transition, the color red has simply represented hot passion, the approach of the sun, burning fire, warm blood. I think that for all humankind, it has a kind of intense feeling. . . . [In the context of this film] it conveys a passionate attitude toward living, an unrestricted vitality of life, an enthusiasm, and an emotionally spirited attitude toward human life."[210] Red continues to be the director's color of choice. Because of some steamy sex scenes in his next major effort, *Ju Dou* (1990) was banned in China. But that didn't affect its success in the United States. Its enthusiastic debut at the New York Film Festival resulted in it being widely shown at art houses across America. *Ju Dou* also received the Luis Buñuel Award at the Cannes Film Festival and garnered an Oscar nomination for Best Foreign Language Film. Zhang Yi-mou cemented his international reputation with his 1991 release, *Raise the Red Lantern*, which received another Oscar nod. Like *Ju Dou*, *Raise the Red Lantern* was banned and never distributed in China. *Red Sorghum*, *Ju Dou*, and *Raise the Red Lantern* are often referred to as a "trilogy" as they are all set during the 1920s and shine a light on harsh patriarchal attitudes in China.

The director changed directions with his next film, *The Story of Qiu Ju* (*Qiu Jud a guansi*, 1992). His favorite muse, Gong Li, was still playing the lead role, but this time her beauty was downplayed. And unlike his previous efforts, this story didn't focus on female repression but on bureaucratic red tape. In the story the main character, a pregnant peasant, feels wronged over an "assault" on her husband, and she seeks justice. When she doesn't receive the results she wants from the local magistrate, she takes her case further and further up the chain of command. As the director explained, "One has to fight to make things happen. In China, in order to solve the most insignificant problem, one has to try 20 times and spend years on it. . . . In this movie I wanted to say that every Chinese person—not only the peasant—has to do the same thing: fight to win the case and discover oneself in the battle to achieve his or her goal."[211] Gong Li, who herself had become an international star, starred in Zhang Yimou's next two films, *To Live* (*Huozhe*, 1994), which follows a family from wealthy landownership to peasantry, from feudal China to Communist China; and *Shanghai Triad* (*Yao a yao yaodao waipo qiao*, 1995), which is set against the backdrop of the Chinese underworld of the 1930s. Both films were banned in China by the state propaganda department, and because *To Live* was shown at the Cannes Film Festival without official permission, the government enacted tougher rules limiting foreign funding for Chinese films, which almost de-railed *Shanghai Triad*. At the time, the director admitted that he felt as if he were "being watched all the time."[212]

A falling out between the director and his favorite leading lady changed the face of Zhang Yimou's films again, and over the next seven years he experi-mented with different themes. *The Road Home* (*Wo de fun qin mu qin*, 1999)[213] and *Not One Less* (*Yi Ge Dou Bu Neng Shao*, 2000) both examine rural life and the people who live within those communities. In the former, the director looks back with nostalgia to a time when schoolteachers were respected and the community pulled together. In the latter, he offers a cinema verité look at the determination of a 13-year-old substitute teacher who will do anything to keep her class intact. *Happy Times* (*Xingfu shiguang*, 2000) reflects the director's concern with the urbanization of China and the country's changing values, especially how materialism affects people's sense of kindness and compassion. This wasn't a new theme for the director but a continuation of one he started in *Shanghai Triad*, five years prior. In fact, when he talked about that film in a 1996 interview, he could just as well have been talking about *Happy Times*: "I think the country will become more and more materialistic. We're heading in that direction. I'm interested in asking the question: As our livelihood improves, how can we maintain our more human side?"

Following in the footsteps of Taiwan-born Ang Lee who had huge success in the West with *Crouching Tiger, Hidden Dragon*,[214] Zhang Yimou also turned to the *wuxia* genre to create his next two films. Told in a series of flashbacks, *Hero* (*Ying xiong*, 2002) focuses on three assassins and Nameless, the one person who foiled their attempts to murder the ruler of Qin, the man who would eventually unite China and become its first emperor. Although for the most part *Hero* enjoyed critical praise and enormous box office success in the West—it, too, received an Oscar nomination—the film was a failure in China. Chinese audiences and many critics didn't appreciate the revisionist way it downplayed Qin Shihuangdi's dictatorial and tyrannical qualities, instead showing him as "the carrier of Chinese culture and the epitome of Chinese heroism."[215] Despite the controversy, according to scholars Chris Berry and Mary Farquhar, "*Hero* is a major turning point for Zhang Yimou. It is his first commercial blockbuster. Like many of his films, it has aroused controversy on the film itself and on the nature of China today. There is, however, a boldness in turning to a story of the founding of the Chinese imperial state and attempting to humanize the King of Qin, despite centuries of bad press. There is a visual grandeur and mysticism in the images that represent China. . . . There is a symbolic and philosophical aspect to the dissertation on the sword that is rare in martial arts movies. There is a continued exploration of the grand themes of transgression, submission, and national character that thread through is work. Finally, there is a timeliness about *Hero*, which debates what China means in the 21st century in terms of heroism, masculinity and the nation as *tianxia*."[216] After making *Hero*, Zhang Yimou admitted that he fell in love with the *wuxia* genre, but for his next film *House of Flying Daggers*, he said that didn't want to make an ordinary martial arts film. "I want to talk about passion, interesting characters . . . my own style of *wuxia* film. This story may be a *wuxia* film, but it is also an evocative and romantic love story, I hope."[217] Set during the Tang Dynasty, *House of Flying Daggers* is named after a large and prestigious underground alliance that steals from the rich and gives to the poor.

In 2005, Zhang Yimou made a smaller more personal film, *Riding Alone for Thousands of Miles* (*Qian li zou dan qi*), a contemporary story that centers on a Japanese father's journey into China's Yunnan province to record a folk-opera star for his ailing son. He returned to epic scale for his next film, *Curse of the Golden Flower*, which also reunited him with Gong Li, after an 11-year "separation." The film's lush costumes, expansive sets, and exquisite color scheme—golds and reds—set a benchmark for cinematic opulence. After *Curse of the Golden Flower*, he contributed the segment "En Regardant le Film" to the 2007 project Chacun son Cinema, also known as *Ce Petit Coup au Coeur Quand la Lumiere s'eteint et que le Film Commence*, a collective film of 33 shorts filmed by as many directors about their feeling about cinema. Just a few other contributors include David Cronenberg, Takeshi Kitano, Jane Campion, Billie August, Chen Kaige, the Coen Brothers, and Lars von Trier. As of this writing, Zhang Yimou doesn't have any projects in the works.

ENDNOTES

1. "World Factbook," *Central Intelligence Agency*, 2008, www.cia.gov/library/publications/the-world-factbook/ (accessed 15 February 2008).

2. Confucianism, Daoism, and Buddhism are often referred to as *sanjiao*, the canonical "three teachings."

3. Julia Ching, *Chinese Religions* (New York: Orbis Books, 1993), 206.

4. Karl Marx, "Contribution to the Critique of Hegel's Philosophy of Right," *baylor.edu*, 1844, www3.baylor.edu/~Scott_Moore/texts/Marx_Contr_Crit.html (accessed 21 February 2008).

5. Party Central Committee, "The Sixteen Points: Guidelines for the Great Proletarian Cultural Revolution," in *Sources of Chinese Tradition: From 1600 through the Twentieth Century*, compiled by Wm. Theodore de Bary and Richard LuFranco (New York: Columbia University Press, 2000), 474.

6. Andrew B. Kipnis, "The Flourishing of Religion in Post-Mao China and the Anthropological Category of Religion," *Australian Journal of Anthropology* 12, no. 1 (2001): 32–46. Available at www.rspas.anu.edu.au/papers/ccc/AK_flourishing_religion.pdf (accessed 21 February 2008).

7. Films to be discussed in this article come primarily from mainland China; however, a few hail from Taiwan and Hong Kong. For instance, Ang Lee was born in Taiwan and Ronny Yu was born in Hong Kong. Because of the generality of this article, Chinese film is being used as an umbrella term, as it has been in other monographs such as Chris Berry, ed., *Chinese Films in Focus:*

25 New Takes (London: British Film Institute, 2003), which includes discussion of Lee; Wong Kar Wai, who although born in Shanghai moved to Hong Kong as a child; King Hu who split his cinematic career between Taiwan and Hong Kong; and even Malaysian-born Ming-Liang Tsai.

8. A debate continues on how to classify Confucianism. A number of people are loath to label it as a religion because Confucius didn't talk "much about a metaphysical world of 'spirits' or a singular notion of the Godhead that is, at once solitary and loving. So, Confucianism has been described by some outsiders as an ethical system based on a this-worldly epistemology." For more on the subject, see Kathleen Nadeau, "Confucianism: Sacred or Secular," *Ateneo de Manila University*, http:eapi.admu.edu.ph/eapr005/nadeau.htm (accessed 5 May 2008).

9. Confucianism and Daoism were just two of the many -isms that flourished during this period, which was known as the era of "Hundred Schools."

10. Daoist scholars, such as Livia Kohn, have challenged this division, even referring to it as problematic. She explains that two Japanese dictionaries suggest dividing Daoism into three strands: philosophy, organized religion, and popular practice. Another way of dividing Daoism is to do it by four phases, including classical, with the dividing line at the Han Dynasty; traditional, traditional organized, which is through the Tang Dynasty, and the present era. Full discussion on this topic can be found in Livia Kohn, ed., *Daoism Handbook* (Leiden: Brill, 2000), xxiv–xxx.

11. Although we will discuss him as if he actually lived, scholars debate this issue. For instance, see Livia Kohn, "The Lao-tzu Myth," in *Lao-tzu and the Tao-te-ching*, ed. Livia Kohn and Michael LaFargue (Albany: State University of New York Press, 1998).

12. A. C. Graham, "The Origins of the Legend of Lao Tan," in *Lao-tzu and the Tao-te-ching*, ed. Livia Kohn and Michael LaFargue, 23.

13. Graham, "The Origins of the Legend of Lao Tan," 24.

14. Vincent Shen, "Daoism (Taoism): Classical (Dao Jia, Tao Chia)," *Encyclopedia of Chinese Philosophy*, ed. Antonio S. Cua (New York: Routledge, 2003), 211.

15. Shen, "Daoism (Taoism)," 209.

16. Shen, "Daoism (Taoism)," 209.

17. Burton Watson, trans., *The Complete Works of Chuang Tzu* (New York: Columbia University Press, 1968), 128. This section comes from chapter 12.

18. Watson, trans., *The Complete Works of Chuang Tzu*, 5–6.

19. Stories about Zhang Daoling claim that he had developed an impressive array of magical skills, including disappearing in front of others, commanding mountain deities, and even being in two places at once.

20. Stephen F. Teiser, "Introduction," *Religions of China in Practice*, ed. Donald S. Lopez Jr. (Princeton, NJ: Princeton University Press, 1996), 10.

21. Livia Kohn, *Daoism and Chinese Culture*, 2nd ed. (Cambridge, MA: Three Pines Press, 2004), 3.

22. Hsiao-Lan Hu and William Cully Allen, *Taoism* (Philadelphia: Chelsea House Publishing, 2005), 74.

23. Hu and Allen, *Taoism*, 74.

24. Hu and Allen, *Taoism*, 29–30.

25. Kenneth Dean, "Daoist Ritual Today," *Daoism Handbook*, ed. Livia Kohn (Leiden: Brill, 2000), 659–60.

26. Jennifer Oldstone-Moore, *Taoism* (New York: Oxford University Press, 2003), 27.

27. Oldstone-Moore, *Taoism*, 75.

28. Hu and Allen, *Taoism*, 81.

29. Kohn, *Daoism and Chinese Culture*, 2.

30. Oldstone-Moore, *Taoism*, 33.

31. Hu and Allen, *Taoism*, 23.

32. Irene Bloom, "Confucius and the Analects," in *Sources of Chinese Tradition from Earliest Times to 1600* (New York: Columbia University Press, 1999), 41. The term *ru*, which evoked a commitment to "learning, refinement, cultural accomplishments, and the practice of rites and music—came to be applied to persons whose notion of virtue had more to do with decorous conduct than with martial prowess. . . . His followers were, from early times, identified as *ru*."

33. Legends describe Confucius' birth as being attended by dragons and/or a unicorn. It is also said that his body bore 49 special marks and that his head was shaped like a mound or hillock.

34. In reality, this was a period of 27 months. Ancient rituals regarding mourning rites were very specific, stating that one should mourn one's father in the first degree for three years. If one's father was still living, one mourned for the mother no more deeply than second degree, for a full year. "This in theory settled the boundary between heaven and earth and rectified the position of male and female (*yang* and *yin*), measuring the affection between parent and child." For more on this subject, see Norman Alan Kutcher, *Mourning in Late Imperial China: Filial Piety and the State* (New York: Cambridge University Press, 1999), 51. Confucius, himself, was asked about mourning rites, and he addresses the subject in book XVII of the Analects, saying that the three-year period is justified because this is how long a child must stay in the arms of his parents. He ends the discussion with a question: "Did Yu enjoy the three years' love of his parents?"

35. In book VII, chapter VII of the Analects, he says that he never refused instruction to anyone, even those who could afford just a bundle of flesh.

36. The Analects, book XV, chapter 38.

37. A sixth classic, the *Book of Music*, has been lost. The *Book of Changes* is a divination manual that predates Confucius. To use it, one poses a question, usually about human affairs, and throws either a series of coins or yarrow sticks. Based on the configuration they form, the person consults *I Ching*, and under one of 64 hexagrams—made up of broken and unbroken lines—he or she finds his or her oracle. The *Book of History* is a collection of statements made by sage rulers and other officials. The *Book of Poetry* contains 305 verses in various genres. Many saw these as representing moral lessons. The *Book of Rites* is an extensive collection of material that contains etiquette for virtually every occasion as well as treatises on a variety of subjects. The *Spring and Autumn Annals* chronicles what happened in the state of Lu, between 722 and 481 B.C.E.

38. Richard Gunde, *Culture and Customs of China* (Westport, CT, Greenwood Press, 2002), 39.

39. Xinzhong Yao, *An Introduction to Confucianism* (New York: Cambridge University Press, 2000), 214.

40. Wing-Tsit Chan, trans. and compil., *A Source Book in Chinese Philosophy* (Princeton, NJ: Princeton University Press, 1963), 15.

41. A. S. Cua, "Junzi (Chun-tzu): The Moral Person," in *Encyclopedia of Chinese Philosophy*, ed. Antonio S. Cua (New York: Routledge, 2003), 335.

42. Confucius, *Confucian Analects: The Great Learning and the Doctrine of the Mean*, trans. James Legge (New York: Dover, 1971), note 8.

43. Cua, "Junzi (Chun-tzu): The Moral Person," 332.

44. Rodney Leon Taylor, *Confucianism: Religions of the World* (New York: Chelsea House Publishing, 2004), 53.

45. Ching, *Chinese Religions*, 58.

46. Chan, trans. and comp., *A Source Book in Chinese Philosophy*, 23.

47. Chan, trans. and comp., *A Source Book in Chinese Philosophy*, 31.

48. Yao, *An Introduction to Confucianism*, 215.

49. Chung-ying Cheng, "Mencius (Mengzi, Meng Tzu)," in *Encyclopedia of Chinese Philosophy*, 441.

50. D. C. Lau, "Introduction," *Mencius* (New York: Penguin Books, 1970), 7.

51. Lau, "Introduction," 15. In general, we don't find dualistic thinking in Eastern thought, and Mencius confirms this. Rather than saying that a person is "evil" for acting on animalistic impulses, Mencius would instead say that he or she simply has his or her priorities wrong.

52. Lau, "Introduction," 18.

53. Chung-ying Cheng, "Mencius (Mengzi, Meng Tzu)," 441.

54. Chung-ying Cheng, "Mencius (Mengzi, Meng Tzu)," 441. Mencius also talked about fate or destiny (*ming*), which he said was imposed from without. However, since the only things that were seen to be fated were death, life, wealth, and position, he suggested that there was no use in pursuing them. Instead, he said, people should spend more time seeking morality and our "original heart."

55. Lau, "Introduction," 21.

56. de Bary and Bloom, comp., *Sources of Chinese Tradition* 200–201.

57. In 221 B.C.E. King Cheng assumed this title, which until this point had been reserved for legendary rulers who had founded civilization. Qin Shihuangdi translates to First August Emperor. Under his rule, he united a nation into what would become China and he began construction of the Great Wall.

58. de Bary and Bloom, comp., "Discussing the People," *Sources of Chinese Tradition*, 195.

59. de Bary and Bloom, comp., "Making Orders Strict," The Book of Lord Shang, *Sources of Chinese Tradition*, 197.

60. de Bary and Bloom, comp., "Legalists and Militarists," in *Sources of Chinese Tradition*, 191.

61. de Bary and Bloom, comp., *Sources of Chinese Tradition*, 194–95.

62. Interestingly enough, Mao Zedong compared himself to Shi Huangdi. And it isn't difficult to see why. Their attitude toward society and government has much in common.

63. The Yin-Yang School taught that there are two pervasive forces in the universe—yin and yang. The former is associated with the female, darkness, wetness, softness, and passivity; the latter with the masculine, light, dryness, hardness, and aggressiveness or the active principle. These

forces oppose yet complement each other; one cannot exist without the other. An imbalance of these forces results in disharmony and chaos. For order to be restored, balance must be attained.

64. Yao, *An Introduction to Confucianism*, 82-83.

65. de Bary and Bloom, comp., *Sources of Chinese Tradition*, 307.

66. B. Watson, "The Codifying of the Confucian Canon," in *Sources of Chinese Tradition*, 312.

67. Yao, *An Introduction to Confucianism*, 87. As a result of the book burnings that took place during the Qin Dynasty, different version of the Confucian Classics existed, leading scholars to produce a variety of understandings, methodologies, and ultimately, schools.

68. Yao, *An Introduction to Confucianism*, 89.

69. de Bary and Bloom, comp., *Sources of Chinese Tradition*, 540.

70. Demonstrating the religious eclecticism of the time was Emperor Taizong (626–649 C.E.) who was educated in the Confucian classics and formed his government based on their teachings. However, he also gave Daoist monks a role in imperial ceremonies and encouraged the translation of Buddhist texts. It was during his reign that these three religions formed the backbone of imperial ideology.

71. *China: A Nation in Transition*, exp. ref. ed., ed. Debra E. Soled (Washington, DC: Congressional Quarterly, 1995), 12.

72. de Bary and Bloom, comp., *Sources of Chinese Tradition*, 586.

73. de Bary and Bloom, comp., *Sources of Chinese Tradition*, 595.

74. Yao, *An Introduction to Confucianism*, 97.

75. In 1260, Kublai Khan ordered an audience with one Confucian scholar. So impressed was he with the man's scholarship that he assigned nearly a dozen Mongol students to study Confucian texts with him. Furthermore, he asked the scholar to learn Mongolian so that he could translate Zhen Dexiu's text *Extended Meaning of the Great Learning* (*Daxue yanyi*).

76. Yao, *An Introduction to Confucianism*, 108.

77. Yao, *An Introduction to Confucianism*, 105–6.

78. Edward Farmer, "Ming Foundations of Late Imperial China," in *Sources of Chinese Tradition*, 780.

79. Ming Taizu, "Article 19," in *Sources of Chinese Tradition*, 790.

80. Ming Taizu, "Discussion of the Three Teachings," in *Sources of Chinese Tradition*, 791–92.

81. Liu Shaoqi, "How to Be a Good Communist," in *Sources of Chinese Tradition*, 430.

82. Maureen Fan, "Confucius Making a Comeback in Money-Driven Modern China," *Washington Post*, 2007, www.washingtonpost.com/wp-dyn/content/article/2007/07/23/AR2007072301859.html (accessed 25 January 2008).

83. Just a few of the articles discussing this revival, include Evan Osnos, "Sage for the Ages Makes a Comeback," *Chicago Tribune*, 2007, www.venturacountystar.com/news/2007/jun/09/a-sage-for-the-ages-makes-a-comeback/ (accessed 21 February 2008); and Chin-Ching Ni, "China Turns to Confucius, with a Modern Twist," *Los Angeles Times*, 2007, www.latimes.com/news/nationworld/world/la-fg-confucius7may07,0,5796389,full.story (accessed 21 February 2008).

84. Daniel A. Bell, "China's Leaders Rediscover Confucianism," *International Herald Tribune*, 2006, www.iht.com/articles/2006/09/14/opinion/edbell.php (accessed 25 January 2008).

85. Maureen Fan, "Confucius Making a Comeback."

86. Jonathan Watts, "Traditional Teachings of Confucius Find Favor as China Looks to Fill Ethical Vacuum in Wake of Market Reforms," *The Guardian*, 2006, www.guardian.co.uk/china/story/0,,1882569,00.html (accessed 25 January 2008).

87. Maureen Fan, "Confucius Making a Comeback."

88. Chin-Ching Ni, "China Turns to Confucius, with a Modern Twist."

89. Edward Slingerland, *Images of Women in Chinese Thought and Culture: Writings from the Pre-Qin Period through the Song Dynasty*, ed. Robin R. Wang (Indianapolis, IN: Hackett, 2003), 62.

90. In his commentary of this passage, Slingerland states that the word *nuzi*, here translated as "women," has been softened by other scholars, and when looking at different translations of this same word, we find that James Legge interprets it as "girls," William Edward Soothill uses the word "maids," and Irene Bloom and Wing-Tsit Chan use "women." Slingerland's final statement on this passage is that, after looking at the Analects as a whole, it probably refers to the "potentially dangerous sexual power" that women possess and their inability to control it; therefore, this is a warning of sorts to men to manage household women with respect, if they want the women to "remain obedient and not overstep their proper roles." For more information, see the rest of the commentary on page 66.

91. Yao, *An Introduction to Confucianism*, 183.

92. Joseph A. Adler, "Daughter/Wife/Mother or Sage/Immortal/Bodhisattva? Women in the Teaching of Chinese Religions," *Kenyon College*, 2006, www2.kenyon.edu/depts/Religion/Fac/Adler/Writings/Women.htm (accessed 21 February 2008) mentions "such views, it is said, led eventually to such misogynistic practices as foot-binding, which began in the Tang Dynasty, and the 'cult of chastity,' which elevated chaste widows to the role of cultural heroes."

93. Yao, *An Introduction to Confucianism*, 183. Contributors to *The Sage and the Second Sex: Confucianism, Ethics and Gender*, ed. Li Chenyang (Chicago: Open Court, 2000), rethink and reevaluate the Confucian view of women, and find that the issues are more complicated than is often supposed. Two of the more interesting examinations of Confucian thought in terms of feminism are Li Chenyang, "The Confucian Concept of Jen and the Feminist Ethics of Care: A Comparative Study," in *The Sage and the Second Sex*, 23–42; and Paul Rakita Goldin, "The View of Women in Early Confucianism," in *The Sage and the Second Sex*, 133–62.

94. Theresa Kelleher, "Women's Education," in *Sources of Chinese Tradition*, 819–20.

95. During the Qing Dynasty, this text was replaced by *A Handy Record of Rules for Women* (*Nüfan jielu*).

96. Theresa Kelleher, "Women's Education," 820.

97. Mayfair Mei-Hui Yang, "Of Gender, State, Censorship, and Overseas Capital: An Interview with Chinese Director Zhang Yimou," in *Zhang Yimou Interviews*, ed. Frances Gateward (Jackson: University Press of Mississippi, 2001), 39.

98. Susan Mann, "Grooming a Daughter for Marriage: Brides and Wives in the Mid-Qing Period," in *Chinese Femininities/Chinese Masculinities: A Reader*, ed. Susan Brownell and Jeffrey N. Wasserstrom (Berkeley: University of California Press, 2002), 100.

99. Francis L. K. Hsu, *Under the Ancestor's Shadow: Kinship, Personality, and Social Mobility in China* (Palo Alto, CA: Stanford University Press, 1971), 256.

100. The master also engages in extramarital dalliances with his servants. When Songlian sulks about it, he brushes her feelings off. However, when the third wife is caught having an affair with the doctor, she is bound and hung. As Songlian learns, two previous women have died in a similar fashion.

101. Hsu, *Under the Ancestor's Shadow*, 257.

102. Kazuko Ono, *Chinese Women in a Century of Revolution (1850–1950)*, ed. Joshua A. Fogel (Palo Alto, CA: Stanford University Press, 1989), 94.

103. Ban Zhao, "Admonitions for Women," in *Sources of Chinese Tradition*, 822.

104. R. Keith Schoppa, *Twentieth-Century China: A History in Documents* (New York: Oxford University Press, 2004), 53–54.

105. Yang, "Of Gender, State, Censorship, and Overseas Capital," 38.

106. Yang, "Of Gender, State, Censorship, and Overseas Capital," 39.

107. Zhu Xi, "Funerary Inscription for Madam You, Lady of Jia'nan," in *Sources of Chinese Tradition*, 837.

108. Ban Zhao, "Admonitions for Women," in *Sources of Chinese Tradition*, 824.

109. Song Ruozhao, "Analects for Women," in *Sources of Chinese Tradition*, 828.

110. Ono, *Chinese Women in a Century of Revolution*, 97–98.

111. Soled, ed., *China: A Nation in Transition*, 42.

112. Soled, ed., *China: A Nation in Transition*, 41.

113. *Twentieth Century China*, 54.

114. Schoppa, *Twentieth Century China*, 143–44.

115. Judith Banister, "Shortage of Girls in China Today," *Journal of Population Research*, 2004, www.jpr.org.au/upload/JPR21-1_Banister.pdf, 19-20 (accessed 27 January 2008).

116. The policy stipulates that each urban-dwelling couple should have only one child, unless one or both spouses are from an ethnic minority or are both only children. The law is more lax for those who live in rural areas. Several years after the birth of their first child, they can try again.

117. Banister, "Shortage of Girls in China Today."

118. Banister, "Shortage of Girls in China Today."

119. Technically, by this date the Tang has ended, and the Five Dynasties and Ten Kingdoms period had been in full swing, starting in 907 and continuing until 960. Characterized by alien invasions and conquests, this was a politically unstable period.

120. John King Fairbank and Merle Goldman, *China: A New History* (Cambridge, MA: Belknap Press of Harvard University Press, 2006), 86.

121. Gungwu Wang, *Divided China: Preparing for Reunification 883–947* (Hackensack, NJ: World Scientific, 2007), 2.

122. de Bary and Bloom, comp., *Sources of Chinese Tradition*, 43.

123. de Bary and Bloom, comp., *Sources of Chinese Tradition*, 544.

124. de Bary and Bloom, comp., *Sources of Chinese Tradition*, 27.

125. de Bary and Bloom, comp., *Sources of Chinese Tradition*, 43–44.

126. For a discussion on whether *xiao* or *ren* takes precedence in Confucian thought, see Alan K. L. Chan, "Does *Xiao* Come Before *Ren*?," in *Filial Piety in Chinese Thought and History*, ed. Alan K. L. Chan and Sor-hoon Tan (London: RoutledgeCurzon, 2004), 154–75.

127. Aynne Kokas, "The Ring of Fire," *Asia Pacific Arts*, 2006, www.asiaarts.ucla.edu/061222/article.asp?parentID=59580 (accessed 28 January 2008).

128. de Bary and Bloom, comp., *Sources of Chinese Tradition*, 552.

129. de Bary and Bloom, comp., *Sources of Chinese Tradition*, 549.

130. In the sections titled "Instructing Children" and "Family Governance" in the *House Instructions of Mr. Yan*, the author explains that corporal punishment—whipping with bamboo—is necessary to "train" the child. He also states that when "a father is kind but the son refractory, when an elder brother is friendly but the younger arrogant, when the husband is just but the wife overbearing, then indeed they are the bad people of the world; they must be controlled by punishments; teaching and guidance will not change them." "Rod and wrath" are recommended. de Bary and Bloom, comp., *Sources of Chinese Tradition*, 545.

131. Ide Bary and Bloom, comp., *Sources of Chinese Tradition*, 550.

132. Ide Bary and Bloom, comp., *Sources of Chinese Tradition*, 543.

133. Ide Bary and Bloom, comp., *Sources of Chinese Tradition*, 545.

134. Ide Bary and Bloom, comp., *Sources of Chinese Tradition*, 129.

135. ITheodora Lau, *The Handbook of Chinese Horoscopes* (New York: Harper & Row, 1979), 67.

136. ILau, *The Handbook of Chinese Horoscopes*, 83.

137. ILau, *The Handbook of Chinese Horoscopes*, 99.

138. ILau, *The Handbook of Chinese Horoscopes*, 117.

139. ILau, *The Handbook of Chinese Horoscopes*, 165.

140. ILau, *The Handbook of Chinese Horoscopes*, 37.

141. We are never told directly from which plant these red berries derive. We do know that the hawthorn, which has red berries and is found in China, has been used to ward off evil spirits, as has mistletoe, which isn't as common in China.

142. Vivien Sung, *Five-Fold Happiness: Chinese Concepts of Luck, Prosperity, Longevity, Happiness and Wealth* (San Francisco: Chronicle Books, 2002), 145.

143. Liu Xiaogan, "The Core Value in Taoism," in *Lao-tzu and the Tao-te-Ching*, 214.

144. Sung, *Five-Fold Happiness*, 53.

145. Sung, *Five-Fold Happiness*, 178–79.

146. We later learn the reason he doesn't have an heir is because his wife ran off 30 years ago. He claims that he was too poor for her. "She left me and our baby boy," he says. "I was mother and father to him. Changed his diapers, watched him grow. When he was 10, he got sick and died. If he were alive today, he'd be 31."

147. Robert Ford Campany, "The Earliest Tales of the Bodhisattva Guanshiyin," in *Religions of China in Practice*, ed. Donald S. Lopez Jr. (Princeton, NJ: Princeton University Press, 1996), 83. It's notable that the Dalai Lama is thought to be the human incarnation of Chenrezig, the Tibetan form of Avalokitesvara.

148. Amy Vames, "The Goddess of Mercy: How Kuan-yin Became a Chinese Deity," *Rutgers University Media Release*, 2001, ur.rutgers.edu/medrel/viewArticle.html?ArticleID=1967 (accessed 31 January 2008).

149. Chun-Fang Yu, *Kuan-Yin: The Chinese Transformation of Avalokitesvara* (New York: Columbia University, 2001), 3.

150. Yu, *Kuan-Yin: The Chinese Transformation of Avalokitesvara*, 294.

151. Yu, *Kuan-Yin: The Chinese Transformation of Avalokitesvara*, 493.

152. Yu, *Kuan-Yin: The Chinese Transformation of Avalokitesvara*, 1.

153. Amy Vames, "The Goddess of Mercy." Yu, *Kuan-Yin: The Chinese Transformation of Avalokitesvara*, is the most comprehensive tome on the subject. Another, more generalized, treatment of the subject is John Blofeld, *Bodhisattva of Compassion: The Mystical Tradition of Kuan* (Boston: Shambhala, 1988).

154. Yu, *Kuan-Yin: The Chinese Transformation of Avalokitesvara*, 293–94.

155. Yu, *Kuan-Yin: The Chinese Transformation of Avalokitesvara*, 298.

156. Stephen F. Teiser, "Introduction: The Spirits of Chinese Religion," 34–35.

157. Hsu, *Under the Ancestor's Shadow*, 144–46.

158. Stephen F. Teiser, *The Ghost Festival in Medieval China* (Princeton, NJ: Princeton University Press, 1988), 199.

159. Joan Law and Barbara E. Ward, *Chinese Festivals in Hong Kong* (Hong Kong: South China Morning Post., 1982), 67–68.

160. Teiser, *The Ghost Festival in Medieval China*, 12–13.

161. Yu, *Kuan-Yin: The Chinese Transformation of Avalokitesvara*, 330.

162. Yu, *Kuan-Yin: The Chinese Transformation of Avalokitesvara*, 345–46.

163. "Kuo Tzu-I," *Encyclopædia Britannica Online*, www.britannica.com/eb/article-9046452 (accessed 13 February 2008).

164. Ann Elizabeth Barrott Wicks, ed., *Children in Chinese Art* (Honolulu: University of Hawaii Press, 2002), 73–74.

165. Craig Clunas, *Pictures and Visuality in Early Modern China* (London: Reaktion Books, 2006), 54.

166. Keith Stevens and Jennifer Welch, "The Yang Family of Generals," *University of Hong Kong Libraries*, sunzi1.lib.hku.hk/hkjo/view/44/4402407.pdf (accessed 31 January 2008).

167. Huo Jianying, "Heroic, Historic, Operatic Yang Generals," *Chinatoday*, 2006, www.chinatoday.com.cn/English/e2006/e200602/2p52.htm (accessed 1 February 2008).

168. For an insightful interview with Ann-Ping Chin of Wesleyan University on these changes, see Mary Pat Fisher, *Living Religions* (Upper Saddle River, NJ: Prentice-Hall, 2005), 203.

169. Rey Chow, *Sentimental Fabulations, Contemporary Chinese Films: Attachment in the Age of Global Visibility* (New York: Columbia University Press, 2007), 71–72. Chow also comments that often Zhang's films are about "poor rural folk or *xiaoshimin* in big cities whose lives are unglamorous and filled with hardships" (151). Examples of women who leave the countryside for a "better life" and then find something much more menacing are *Raise the Red Lantern* and *Shanghai Triad*. In *The Story of Qiu Ju* and *Not One Less*, the rural characters venture to the big city only to find it to be an impersonal and confusing place mired in bureaucratic red tape.

170. Chow, *Sentimental Fabulations, Contemporary Chinese Films*, 156.

171. Mark Pollard, "Wuxia Pian," *Green Cine*, 2005, www.greencine.com/static/primers/wuxia1.jsp (accessed 21 February 2008).

172. Catharina Blomberg, *The Heart of the Warrior: Origins and Religious Background of the Samurai System in Feudal Japan* (Sandgate, Folkestone, Kent, UK: Japan Library, 1994), 20. Ob-

viously *Crouching Tiger* takes place in feudal China, not Japan, but this warrior ideal applies in both scenarios. After all, Confucianism and Ch'an Buddhism, which provided the core teachings of the samurai, were imported to Japan from China.

173. Felicia Chan, "*Crouching Tiger, Hidden Dragon: Cultural Migrancy and Translatability,*" in *Chinese Films in Focus*, 59.

174. It may simply be a coincidence, for I haven't compared Chinese characters, but each of the main characters in the film has one of the Confucian virtues in his or her name. Li means ritual or propriety; Jen is humaneness; Shu is reciprocity. The friend of Li's and soon-to-be recipient of his sword is named Sir Te; in Daoism *te* or *de* translates to virtue; and the bandit who falls in love with Jen is Luo Xiao Hu. *Xiao* is filial piety. The only main character without a Chinese name is Jade Fox, probably because she's the only character without any redeeming qualities in a Confucian or Daoist framework.

175. Scholars Chris Berry and Mary Farquhar concur, saying that *Crouching Tiger* is "as much about generational and gender conflicts as about Confucian values, such as chivalry, filiality and brotherhood." They also find that although Jen Yu should be the villain of the piece, she isn't. Instead she is a "very modern heroine." See *China on Screen: Cinema and Nation* (New York: Columbia University Press, 2006), 72.

176. Heinrich Dumoulin, *Zen Buddhism: A History, India and China* (New York: Macmillan, 1988), 164.

177. Victor Sogen Hori, "The Nature of the Rinzai (Linji) Koan Practice," in *Sitting with Koans*, ed. John Daido Loori (Boston: Wisdom, 2006), 120.

178. Dumoulin, *Zen Buddhism: A History, India and China*, 167.

179. de Bary and Bloom, comp., *Sources of Chinese Tradition*, 668.

180. de Bary and Bloom, comp., *Sources of Chinese Tradition*, 669.

181. Walpola Rahula, *What the Buddha Taught: Revised and Expanded Edition with Texts from Suttas and Dhammapada* (New York: Grove Press, 1974), 43.

182. Watson, trans., *The Complete Works of Chuang Tzu*, 3.

183. Watson, trans., *The Complete Works of Chuang Tzu*, 6.

184. de Bary and Bloom, comp., *Sources of Chinese Tradition*, 77.

185. The story of Monkey is one of three "apparently unrelated tales" found in Gene Luen Yang's award-winning manga/comic book *American Born Chinese*. For more about him and his book, go to www.firstsecondbooks.com/authors/geneYangBlog01.html.

186. Teiser, "The Spirits of Chinese Religion," 21.

187. The film was remade in 2008 as *The Eye*, starring Jessica Alba as the blind woman who sees "dead people." What's interesting about this, and many other Hollywood remakes of Asian horror films, is that when the script crosses cultures, the screenwriter excises its original religious worldview, not realizing that this is what makes the film frightening in the first place. The religious underpinning is what gives cause to the supernatural events. In the case of *The Eye*, the screenwriter replaces popular Chinese religion with Christianity. The result is largely a failure.

188. Daigan Matsunaga and Alicia Matsunaga, *The Buddhist Concept of Hell* (New York: Philosophical Library, 1972).

189. Emily Martin, "Gender and Ideological Differences in Representations of Life and Death," in *Death Ritual in Late Imperial and Modern China*, ed. James L. Watson and Evelyn S. Rawski (Berkeley: University of California Press, 1988), 177.

190. Joseph A. Adler, *Chinese Religious Traditions* (Upper Saddle River, NJ: Lawrence King, 2002), 115.

191. Adler, *Chinese Religious Traditions*, 119.

192. A trivia fact posted for *The Eye* on the Internet Movie Database states that the figure that appears in the film is the Daoist form of the Grim Reaper. "In Daoist belief, there are two Grim Reapers, the white and black '*Wu Chang*.' The Black Reaper is the one that escorts the newly dead to the 'other world' of afterlife." However, this author was unable to substantiate this claim.

193. Sogyal Rinpoche, *The Tibetan Book of Living and Dying* (New York: Harper San Francisco, 1992), 224.

194. Another unusual, by Western standards, film about black market babies and disturbing uses for them is the horror film *Dumplings* (*Gaau ji*, 2004). Directed by Fruit Chan and written by Lilian Lee, the film focuses on an aging actress who wants to rejuvenate her career and her appearance. She's helped by Aunt Mei, a cook famous for her homemade rejuvenation dumplings. Based on an ancient recipe, the dumplings contain human fetuses.

195. Lillian Too, *Total Feng Shui* (San Francisco: Chronicle Books, 2005), 264.

196. Matsunaga and Matsunaga, *The Buddhist Concept of Hell*, 99–100.

197. Hsu, *Under the Ancestors' Shadow*, 201.

198. Hsu, *Under the Ancestors' Shadow*, 205–6.

199. Interestingly enough, and this applies to the film *The Locker*, which is discussed in the next chapter, "Fetus ghosts are almost never thought to remain as fetuses in the afterlife. Instead, they are usually represented as having matured to a physical age range of one to five years old. Usually their mental capabilities reach far beyond this, and they are often thought to be omniscient. Because they lack the maturity to balance this knowledge, this makes them especially dangerous." Marc L. Moskowitz, *The Haunting Fetus: Abortion, Sexuality, and the Spirit World in Taiwan* (Honolulu: University of Hawaii Press, 2001), 49.

200. Moskowitz, *The Haunting Fetus*, 47.

201. Moskowitz, *The Haunting Fetus*, 47.

202. Hsu, *Under the Ancestors' Shadow*, 245.

203. During season three, *The X Files* aired episode 19, titled "Hell Money," which is set in Chinatown, San Francisco. Immigrants play a game of chance, hoping to win big. When they lose, though, they must sacrifice an organ.

204. Sung, *Five-Fold Happiness*, 11.

205. Adler, *Chinese Religious Traditions*, 115.

206. Jane Macartney, "Ghost Brides Are Murdered to Give Dead Bachelors a Wife in the Afterlife," *The Times*, 2007, www.timesonline.co.uk/tol/news/world/asia/article1296184.ece (accessed 12 February 2008).

207. "China's Corpse Brides: Wet Goods and Dry Goods," *Economist*, 2007, www.economist.com/world/asia/displaystory.cfm?story_id=9558423 (accessed 12 February 2008).

208. Michel Ciment, "Asking the Questions: Interview with Zhang Yimou," in *Zhang Yimou Interviews*, 17.

209. Michael Berry, *Speaking in Images: Interviews with Contemporary Chinese Filmmakers* (New York: Columbia University Press, 2005), 112.

210. Jiao Xiongping, "Discussing Red Sorghum," in *Zhang Yimou Interviews*, 6.

211. Ciment, "Asking the Questions," 18.

212. Rone Tempest, "Zhang Still at the Heart of Chinese Filmmaking," *Zhang Yimou Interviews*, 65.

213. Zhang Yimou has a special talent for discovering actresses. Not only did he discover Gong Li, but for *The Road Home*, he gave Zhang Ziyi her first feature film role. Today, both are internationally recognized and revered Chinese actresses.

214. *Crouching Tiger* didn't fare very well in the East, where the audiences criticized the main actors for their pronunciation of Mandarin: Chow Yun Fat speaks Cantonese and Michelle Yeoh is from Malaysia. They also felt that "the characters weren't portrayed according to type." See Chan, "*Crouching Tiger, Hidden Dragon*," 56–64.

215. Chris Berry and Mary Farquhar, *China on Screen: Cinema and Nation* (New York: Columbia University Press, 2006), 167.

216. Berry and Farquhar, *China on Screen*, 168.

217. "House of Flying Daggers," *sonyclassics.com*, 2003, www.sonyclassics.com/houseofflying daggers/_media/presskit.pdf, 9 (accessed 12 February 2008).

5

Religions of Japan

STATISTICS

Japan, which is slightly smaller than the state of California, has an estimated population of nearly 128 million people, of which 98.5% are Japanese. Koreans comprise the largest minority group in Japan, representing about 700,000 people.[1] Approximately 84% of the population observes both Shinto and Buddhism.[2] Between 1% and 2% of the population practices Christianity.[3]

THE BASICS: RELIGIONS OF JAPAN

As in the case of China, Japan has a diverse religious landscape that is characterized by the interaction of several religions, including Shinto, Mahayana Buddhism, Confucianism, popular Daoism, and folk traditions. Mahayana Buddhism arrived in Japan via China and Korea; Emperor Yomei, who reigned from 585 to 587 C.E., was the first ruler to embrace it and Shinto.[4] Confucianism was introduced during the late Yamato Period (300–710 C.E.). Prince Shotoku (574–622 C.E.) studied the Chinese Classics as well as other Chinese philosophical systems, including Daoism and Legalism. Through his efforts, Confucianism and Buddhism became a part of Japanese culture.[5] Between 1600 and 1867 C.E., Confucian ideas dominated Japanese culture and formed the core curriculum in schools.[6] The virtues of uprightness, righteousness, loyalty, sincerity, reciprocity, and benevolence were encouraged, and filial piety became the central principle within the family. Hierarchy within

the society, with an emphasis on the five relationships, and a respect for seniority were stressed.[7] Like Confucianism, Daoism arrived from China by the
sixth century C.E. but it never enjoyed the status of an organized religion. In
fact, its influence "is even more difficult to trace than Confucianism's because
the latter had a more obvious identity in the Analects of Confucius and in
other Confucian (and Neo-Confucian) writings so influential on political and
social systems. By contrast, [Daoist] writings such as the [*Daodejing*] were important in Japan, but they did not come to form a clearly identifiable body of
materials or become the basis for a major school of thought." Daoism in Japan
is more or less "a nebulous set of Chinese beliefs, symbols and practices."[8] As
for folk traditions, they are mainly handed down orally and in the annual
matsuri (festivals); they differ by region.

Of all the religions mentioned, Shinto and Buddhism have probably exerted the largest influence on the country's culture. As scholar Michiko Yusa
states, "The Japanese are 'born Shinto and die Buddhist.' But some Japanese
claim that they 'die Shinto,' because they draw comfort from the thought that
they are joining their ancestors when they die. Be that as it may, for many
Japanese, Shinto and Buddhism complement each other to the point that the
boundary between them is hardly discernible. Most Japanese do not consciously distinguish between Shinto-related and Buddhism-related activities."[9] Noriko Kamachi seconds this, saying that by default all Japanese people
are Buddhist, because in almost everyone's house one will find an ancestral altar (*butsudan*), where they offer daily prayers, burn incense, light candles, and
offer steamed rice.[10]

Shinto comes from the Chinese term *shendao*, which means "the way of
spirits"; in Japanese, the same concept is referred to as *kami no michi* or *kannagara*. As scholar Stuart D. B. Picken explains, it wasn't until the sixth century C.E. that this Japanese religious tradition had a name: "The gradual rise
of Buddhism forced the indigenous cult to distinguish itself from *Butsu-do*,
the way of the Buddha. Hence, the term *Shin-do*, the way of the *kami*, was
coined. . . . Shinto remains a 'way' because unlike Buddhism or Christianity it
has no historical founder. It is the natural expression of the spiritual feelings
of the Japanese people, which grew and evolved with the development of
Japanese history and society."[11] Shinto involves the veneration of spirits or
kami. More than simply deities, *kami* are anything powerful (*ki*) or sacred that
inspires a sense of awe. They can refer to natural phenomenon, such as thun-

der, storms, lightning, and even wind. (The word *kamikaze* means "wind of the gods.") They can be associated with natural landmarks, especially mountains, rocks, bodies of water, and old and oddly shaped trees. Animals, too, are associated with *kami*, particularly foxes, deer, monkeys, pigeons, crows, and wolves. Furthermore, *kami* can be associated with people, including the spirits of ancestors, especially great ancestors, such as "emperors, heroes, wise men and saints; superior human beings in actual human society, such as living emperors, high government officials, feudal lords, etc.; [and] the government itself; that which is above in space or superior in location or rank."[12]

According to sacred texts, there exist 8 million *kami*. Some are benign, some are vengeful, and for the most part they seem to be ethically indifferent. Rather, "their potential derives from contact with the living." The *kami* have two aspects. Because of their affinity with nature, they can be wild, unpolished, and unpredictable; because of their association with humans, they can be calm, civilized, and orderly.[13] Humans and the *kami* are thought to reflect qualities of each other. Humans can become deities, usually after death, but sometimes during life. Since *kami* can exhibit human-like characteristics, such as jealousy and rage, they "need to be treated correctly: honored, propitiated, venerated and thanked in order to maintain a balanced and productive relationship that can benefit the natural order (and hence human beings living in the world) and to direct their energies into creative rather than destructive directions."[14] In short, *kami* are anything "strange, fearful, mysterious, marvelous, uncontrolled, full of power or beyond human comprehension."[15]

Kami can be site specific, thus worshipped on a local level, or they can have national significance and are thus worshipped by the entire nation. In the latter category, we find the sun goddess Amaterasu-omikami, whose grandson, it is said, descended to Earth to become the first emperor. The imperial family traces its lineage back to this goddess, and she is venerated at the Naiku of the Grand Shrines of Ise, which was established in the early fourth century C.E. Every Japanese town has a tutelage shrine (*jinja*); however, the Grand Shrine of Ise has become the most significant. "For many Japanese, a pilgrimage to Ise (known as the Ise *mairi*), at least once in their lives, is a cherished moral obligation."[16]

Although Shinto doesn't have an official scripture, the *Kojiki* (Records of Ancient Matters, written ca. 712 C.E.) and the *Nihonshoki* (Chronicles of Japan, also known as the *Nihongi* written ca. 720 C.E.) are the most important sources for this ancient religion.[17] According to these texts, the first five Heavenly Deities come into existence and become the progenitors of all subsequent *kami*. Two of their more important offspring—Izanagi-no-mikoto (*kami*-who-invites), and his spouse, Izanami-no-mikoto (*kami*-who-is-invited)—created the Japanese archipelago. As the *Nihongi* states, they were standing on the Heavenly Floating Bridge when they took a jeweled spear, put it in the waters below, and stirred. As they lifted the spear, they created the island Ono-goro-jima, which they soon made their home. Not long afterward, the two became intimate and from their union, they produced more islands and additional *kami*. In the *Kojiki*, it says that Izanami died after giving birth to the *kami* of fire. Missing his spouse, Izanagi descended to the underworld, Yomi, to find her. Because she had already eaten the food of the dead, she had begun to decompose. Terrified at the sight of his wife, Izanagi ran away and purified himself in a river. As he washed his left eye, he gave birth to Amaterasu-omikami; from his right eye emerged Tsukiyomi-no-mikoto, the moon *kami*; and from his nose came Susano-o-no-mikoto, the storm *kami*. Having produced these "three noble children," he gave each a mission: Amaterasu was instructed to rule Takama-no-para, the Plain of High Heaven; Tsukiyomi-no-mikoto was told that he must rule the realms of the night; and Susanoo must govern the ocean. Eventually, Ninigi-no-mikoto, Amaterasu's grandson, descended from the heavens to the land of reeds so that he could pacify it and create a civilization. He brought with him three sacred items: a jewel, a mirror, and a sword, objects that are still used in Shinto worship. After several generations, Jimmu Tenno (the later word means Heavenly Ruler) became the first emperor of Japan.

The rivalry between Amaterasu and her impetuous and often offensive brother, Susanoo, is another important aspect of the ancient narratives. After he was expelled for his misbehavior, Susanoo stopped at his sister's for a visit. While there, they engaged in "jewel spitting," which resulted in the birth of more *kami*. Eventually his nature got the better of him, and Susanoo offended his sister to the point that she fled and hid in the Ame-no-Iwato or Heavenly Rock Dwelling, thus plunging the world into darkness. Wanting to restore order, the *kami* come together and tried to figure out what to do. They decided to hang jewels from a *sakaki* branch and place it in front of her cave. Next, one of the *kami* performed a wild and ribald dance, during which this *kami* exposed her breasts and private parts. Those watching laughed, clapped, and shouted, creating such a ruckus that a curious Amaterasu peeked out to see what was happening. Seizing their opportunity, the *kami* took action. One of them placed a polished mirror in front of Amaterasu's face, bewildering her, and another *kami* escorted her from the cave. To make sure that she couldn't return, other *kami* draped a braided rope in front of the door. With light now restored to the world, Susanoo was banished from the High Plain of Heaven and he descended to Izumo, "where he became a hero, slaying the eight-headed, eight-tailed serpent known as Yamata-no-orochi. He also rescued a young woman and acquired the sword known as the Kusanagi, one of the three pieces of imperial regalia."[18]

As scholar Stuart D. B. Picken points out, the stories found in the *Kojiki* and the *Nihongi* continue to exert an influence on Japanese culture, and at no time was this more evident than between 1868 and 1945, when a "narrow interpretation" of them "led to the growth of an ethnocentrism that served the interests of nationalism during the time of Japan's modernization when national self-awareness was necessary. However, it was manipulated and eventually transformed into a doctrine of racial superiority and the basis of a militaristic ideology."[19] During the Meiji Era (1868–1912), Shinto was treated as a state religion, with most of its shrines said to be state institutions and its priests to be state officials. Furthermore, visiting a Shinto shrine was considered to be the patriotic obligation of every citizen.

As a part of national learning (*Kokugaku*), students were taught that the stories in the *Kojiki* and *Nihongi* were actual history, meaning that Japan was created by the gods, the Japanese people were descendants of the gods, and that the emperor was a living *kami*. The emperor was said to be "Heaven-descended, divine and sacred . . . preeminent above his subjects . . . [and] inviolable."[20] Words used in reference to him were *Akitsu mi kami* (divine emperor) and *Arahitogami* (*kami* in human form). For many, "Shinto meant the annual festivals, seasonal celebrations, observances in the home, and the veneration of the *kami*—living within a world blessed by the *kami*."[21] When World War II ended, the Allies demanded the disestablishment of State Shinto (*Kokka Shinto*), which meant that all governmental offices promoting or supporting Shinto were abolished and that all teachers' manuals and textbooks in use were censored and all evidence of Shinto doctrine deleted. In essence, the Japanese had to separate religion from the state. Another condition of surrender was that Emperor Hirohito had to announce publicly that he was not a "manifest god"; he did this on New Year's Day 1946, during a radio address.[22]

State or National Shinto was simply one of six expressions of this religion. According to some scholars, there also exists Imperial Shinto, Sectarian Shinto, Folk or Shamanic Shinto, Dual Shinto, and Shrine Shinto.[23] Imperial Shinto (*Koshitsu Shinto*) corresponds to the various rituals performed throughout the year by the imperial household on imperial grounds. Some of these rituals are agricultural in nature, such as the ones surrounding rice cultivation, and others correspond to cycles of life within the imperial household, such as funerals, weddings, and accession.[24] Sectarian Shinto (*Kyoha Shinto*) includes 13 officially recognized sects or groups that are religious in nature; each has its own historical founder. Shamanic Shinto (*Minkan Shinko*) reflects the oldest expression of Japanese religion, with shamans and shamanesses engaging in faith healing and becoming possessed. Dual Shinto (*Ryobu Shinto*) refers to the "combination of Buddhism and Shinto in which the Buddhas were identified with the *kami*. This melding was encouraged by the Tokugawa Shogunate (1600–1867) and [Shinto] became almost indistinguishable from Buddhism."[25]

As scholar Stuart D. B. Picken states, Shrine Shinto (*Jinja Shinto*) "refers to the shrines and cults that emerged as the historical core of the mainline Shinto tradition; [however,] to completely describe Shrine Shinto as it exists in modern Japan would require a detailed history of every shrine, its buildings, and *kami*."[26] To do this would require thousands of volumes, as by some estimates there are about 80,000 shrines served by Shinto priests and another 120,000 that aren't.[27] In the early stages of Shinto, "shrines" were natural places, such as trees or rocks, usually in an especially beautiful location, that were designated by a straw rope (*shimenawa*). Many of these still exist today. Around the fifth century C.E., shrine buildings began to be constructed in some areas so that the *kami* could descend and be worshipped. (They don't actually reside permanently in these structures but come when called and then leave when they aren't needed.) These structures range from small houses of wood or stone that are placed along the side of the road to much larger, more elaborately planned compounds. "Shrines reflect two deep traits of the Japanese character: the love of purity and the love of newness. The periodic rebuilding of shrines (usually replicating the existing form) expresses the spirit of endless renewal that seems to lie at the root of the culture along with the desire for purity and brightness. The *kami* should not be revered in buildings that are decrepit, dirty and neglected. They should be fresh, clean and well kept."[28]

Even though architectural variations occur, we can cite some general features of a Shinto *jinja*.[29] Marking the entrance to the sacred grounds of a shrine are one or more *torii*, which is a distinctive gateway that consists of two vertical beams topped by one or two horizontal cross beams. These structures can be made from any material, from concrete to porcelain, and can come in various colors, with the most recognizable ones painted red. As scholar D. C. Holtom explains, the original significance of the *torii* wasn't just to serve as a decorative gateway but to ward off evil and contamination.[30] The typical shrine is separated by a fence or wall that is "guarded" by a pair of animals, usually lion-dogs (*koma-inu*) that serve an apotropaic function. One always finds one or more twisted ropes (*shimenawa*) that have zigzag-shaped paper strips hanging down from them, as these mark out a "place, object or person that is sacred, has been purified and freed of pollution."[31] The origins of this ritual object recall the story of Amaterasu, who was prevented from returning to her cave by a twisted rope. Also found within every shrine grounds are standing and hanging lanterns (*toro*)—most have been donated by patrons and are used to light the grounds at night—and a water basin (*temizusha*) at which one must purify (*harai*) oneself.

Two of the most important structures within the compound are the *haiden* ("worship sanctuary") and the *honden* ("chief sanctuary"). When worshippers stand outside the *haiden*, they ring a bell to get the *kami*'s attention. After they have made a monetary gift in the wooden offertory box, they might bow twice and then clap their hands from one to four times. After bowing once more they might recite a short prayer, such as *Saki-Mitama, Kushi-Mitama, Mamori-Tamae, Sakihae-Tamae*, which translates to "God, the spirit of happiness, and to God, the spirit of well-being, we pray for your protection, and we ask for deliverance of happiness and well-being."[32] Implements of worship found inside typically include a purification wand, drums, altars, and offerings of food and drink.[33] The laity doesn't have access to the *honden*, which is where the *kami* "reside." As Holtom explains, the primary function of this area is to "shelter a sacred object called the *shintai* or 'god-body.'" Sometimes explained as a "symbolic representation of the deity," the *shintai* or *goshintai*, which can include locks of human hair, stones, old scrolls, swords, pictures, and more, "is regarded with such awe and reverence that the members of the

priesthood, themselves, are prohibited by law from viewing or handling it except by special permit."[34] Only priests are allowed inside.

Purification (*oharai*) rituals are at the heart of Shinto practice and, as we've
seen, precedents can be found in the *Nihongi* and *Kojiki*. Because the *kami* are
pure, a person must come to them in a similar state. Contact with any number of objects or situations can result in impurity (*tsumi*), and scholar Stuart
D. B. Picken identifies two types, including *Ama-tsu-tsumi* or heavenly impurities, and *Kuni-tsu-tsumi* or earthly impurities. In the latter category, which
concerns us more than does the former, we find such polluting elements as
"death or injury, immodest behavior, the use of magic, certain contagious diseases, damage done by harmful birds, wounds, and other things that may be
beyond human control."[35] To remove these polluting contacts, one must engage in "cleansing" activities. Before worshippers can enter the temple itself,
they must first purify their hands and mouth with running water. It will be
provided at a "purification pavilion," where visitors might also find a wooden
ladle and a trough.[36] A Shinto priest might purify a person or an area by waving a wand of paper streamers (*harai-gushi*) over him, her, or it. Outside the
temple, a person can engage in *misogi harai*, which is the cleansing and purification of the body, mind, and spirit. To immerse oneself in the sea, in a
river, or by standing under a waterfall is called *misogi shuho*. (This act of purification by water is done in imitation of Izanagi, who, after visiting the underworld, removed the pollution of death by washing in a river.) Salt and fire
are also frequently used in purification rituals.

One can simply avoid pollution by not using certain words, such as *kiru*
(cut) during a wedding, or by refraining from performing actions on certain
dates or at certain times.[37] The Japanese refer to certain ages as "challenging"
(*yakudoshi*), which means that they present more physical and emotional difficulties for the person throughout that year. For instance, because of the difficulties associated with the 13th year of one's life, boys and girls receive
special blessings. For men, the major Yaku (*Dai-yaku*) occurs at 42 and for
women it is at 33. Anyone who has reached one of these "inauspicious" ages
can undergo purification rituals and seek blessing and protection on February 21, during a festival called *Toshi-goi-no-matsuri*. Ages that are celebrated
by the Japanese include 61 (*Kanreki*), 70 (*Koki*), 77 (*Kiju*), and 88 (*Beiju*). A
person's 61st year marks the completion of the zodiac cycle; therefore, it
marks the beginning of a new cycle. As for 77, "the kanji character for *ki*

means happiness and is written, using the characters for seven, ten, seven or 77. *Ju* means longevity." And as for 88, which is often referred to as "the rice birthday, it is important because the *kanji* character for rice is written using the characters for eight, ten, and eight."[38]

The Shinto calendar provides adherents with a variety of opportunities to venerate and honor the *kami* at public festivals or in the home. New Year (*Oshogatsu*), which in Japan is a national holiday and a religious event, is undeniably one of the most important times for the Japanese, and preparations begin far in advance. Before the New Year arrives, people usually place an "entrance pine" (*kadomatsu*) in front of their homes. Typically comprised of pine boughs, bamboo stalks, and plum-tree sprigs, this object "welcomes" the *kami*, who will hopefully bring the person or family longevity, which is represented by the pine, and prosperity and strength, which is represented by the bamboo, throughout the year. Since it is believed that during the first three days of the new year, the Seven Lucky Gods (*Shichifukujin*)—Ebisu (god of wealth), Daikokuten (god of marriage), Bishamonten (god of victory), Benzaiten (goddess of wisdom), Jurojin (god of longevity), Fukurokuju (god of long life), and Hotei (god of good fortune)—steer a magic ship (*takarabune*) laden with all manner of treasure (*takara-mono*) into human ports, people, hoping to receive these treasures,[39] often place a picture of a ship under their pillow on New Year's Eve, January 1, or January 2. The first dream of the year (*hatsuyume*) is believed to be prophetic, and if a person keeps the dream to himself or herself, it will come true. Other preparations include cleaning the house (*susuharai*), paying off old debts, and making traditional cold dishes, such as rice cake (*mochi*).

On New Year's Eve, the family usually pays a visit to the local shrine, just before midnight (*hatsumode*) and then throughout the day, and for several days into the New Year. The purpose of this visit is to express gratitude for past blessings, to cleanse the inner self, and to pray for the well-being of one's family and business. Those who choose to stay home make offerings to the *kami* in front of their *kamidana*. Literally translated as "god shelf," this ritual object usually consists of a shelf or cupboard on which one finds a miniature shrine. The New Year is a time to get rid of old religious talismans (*omamori* and *ofuda*, which are amulet boards) and purchase new ones, such as the *hamaya* (or "evil destroying arrow"), which is supposed to drive away bad luck, or a *kumade* (or "rake of prosperity"). Children typically receive money for the New Year, and adults engage in a number of community-based activities.[40] "In rural areas, where the whole celebration was based on the patterns of a rice culture, New Year's festivities used to last until January 15 (*koshogatsu*, literally "Little New Year"), and could continue even beyond that into February." Unfortunately, an increasingly hectic lifestyle has shortened the time of celebration.[41] To "close" the old year, people typically consume a plate of Japanese noodles (*toshi-kosi-soba*).

As in most societies, the Japanese mark the transition from one stage of life to another with ritual. Often, this means making a visit to the local shrine so that one can receive a blessing from the *kami*. Ancient ritual prayers or *norito* are often read and offerings given. Birth (*tanjo*) is the first rite of passage, and the folk belief is that children are officially born when the deity in charge of birth grants them their soul. On the seventh night, children receive their names and are introduced to everyone in the family. Thirty-one days after a boy is born and 33 days after a girl is born, the parents take the child to the shrine for the child's first blessing (*Hatsumairi*) and to introduce him or her to the tutelary *kami*. During the years when children turn three, five, and seven, the parents seek blessings on November 15, a time called *Shichi-go-san*. In Japan, anyone turning 20 years old will celebrate January 15, as this is Coming-of-Age Day (*Seijin-no-hi*). At this age, the individual is thought to be a full member of society and can legally marry.

When a person dies, a bowl of cooked rice is placed by his or her pillow to sustain that person in the spirit world; a sharp-edged weapon is also placed near him or her for protection. The evening before the funeral, the closest family members stay with the body. The next morning, they wash it with warm water, dress the body in white, and place it in a coffin. One week after death (*shonanuka*), a priest gives the deceased a posthumous name, one that will be used in the spirit world. After this, the family members grieve for 49 days. On the final day, "a ceremony is held in honor of the dead person, and from this time the taboos are lifted." Eventually, the deceased person's spirit loses its individuality and becomes one with the ancestral *kami*. Reincarnation may then take place.[42] After a person dies, it is important for the living to maintain his or her gravesite, especially during the *o-bon* festival, when it is believed that the souls of the dead return to Earth to be with their families. The *o-bon* festival takes places in mid-July or August, and during this time a "special altar with offerings to greet the dead souls is set up at the house, and the priest from the *bodaji* is asked to come and read prayers before it. . . . Graveyards and temples are also extremely alive and active, with lanterns and small fires set out to symbolically guide the souls of the dead back to earth, and families visiting the temple to have further memorial prayers offered for the dead and to receive a special Buddhist talisman that will be placed on the grave."[43] At the end of *o-bon*, the souls of the dead return to the underworld. Their way, again, is lit by fires, and in some cases, small boats are constructed to usher them back.[44]

Shinto celebrations also take place whenever the seasons change. For instance, February 3 (*Setsubun*) marks the first day of spring. On this date, "the 'old year' is brought to an end by bean throwing. People celebrate this festival at home and at the local shrine. Its purpose is to expel bad fortune and invoke good fortune."[45] The spring festival (*Haru matsuri*) takes place from the end of March to the end of April. During this time, prayers are offered for a successful harvest and purification rites are performed. The summer festival (*Natsu-matsuri*), which takes place during the month of June, is particularly important because during this month crops "are in the greatest danger of being destroyed by insects, disease, storms and floods."[46] The autumn festival (*Aki-matsuri*), which lasts from September to November, is actually the main festival of the year and thanks are given for the incoming harvest. Since "October is known in Japanese as *kan-na-zuki*, the month when the *kami* are absent . . . September was traditionally a month of strict taboos."[47]

Although many ceremonies take place at a Shinto temple, some transpire off site. For instance, when someone buys a new home, he or she might call a priest to perform a house blessing ceremony (*Iekiyome*) with the intention of bringing "positive, clear energy into the home." Breaking ground for a new business or clearing misfortune from a site might also necessitate a priestly visit. Anyone or anything at the location can be purified or blessed, including the ground, a family, an individual, business partners, equipment, or anything associated with the project. It's important to note that the Shinto *jinsha* serves more than just a religious function. It can act as a community center, where people gather for meetings or for recreational activities, and not too long ago, it united smaller villages with the nation.[48]

Shinto differs from Western religions, especially Christianity and Islam, in a number of significant ways. Because of its ancient origin, Shinto doesn't have a founder. It doesn't talk much about ethics or doctrines. And although it has sacred and revered texts, such as the aforementioned *Kojiki* and *Nihon-shoki*, the 9th-century *Kogoshui* (*Gleanings from Ancient Stories*), the 8th-century collection of verses titled *Manyoshu* (*Collection of a Myriad Leaves*), the

10th-century collection of imperial regulations and penal codes, *Enjishiki*;[49] and the 13th-century collection called the *Shinto Gobusho*,[50] none of these are thought of or treated in the same way that Christians, Jews, or Muslims treat their own religious texts. And unlike Western religions, Shinto isn't as concerned with doctrines or beliefs as it is with rituals and performing them properly. As scholar Ian Reader explains, "Shinto action and ritual largely centre on the development and maintenance of such relationships with the *kami*: purification rituals are performed to eradicate the pollutions of the mundane so as to symbolically bring humans closer to the realms of the *kami*, and rituals of respect, veneration, propitiation and offering seek to gain access to the life-giving powers of the *kami*." The relationship between humans and the *kami* is reciprocal, and this "matrix of reciprocity, of creating obligations, receiving benevolence and responding with gratitude mirrors standard social relationships within Japanese society in general.[51]

Is Shinto a religion? That all depends on how one defines it. The Japanese word for religion, *shukyo*, is a fairly recent concept. And since many see it as implying dogma or doctrine, few would actually label themselves as religious. "Since the vast majority of Japanese people are involved in Shinto rituals and festivals, it seems safe to say that Shinto includes most of the Japanese population in a loose and almost unconscious way. For most people, Shinto is not a deliberate choice or a conscious commitment, but something deeper . . . "joining Shinto" does not need to be a matter of rational choice, because it is of the essence of what it means to be Japanese."[52] Practitioners of Shinto simply follow the will and the way of the *kami* (*kannagara*).[53]

We've seen that Shinto "is so closely allied with the land and the people of Japan that it is impossible to imagine Japan without Shinto, or Shinto without Japan."[54] But this doesn't mean that Shinto is confined to Japan. As its adherents have moved to other nations, they have brought their beliefs with them. And nowhere is this more evident than in Hawaii, and to a lesser degree, Washington state. Hawaii has seven active shrines, including Daijingu Temple of Hawaii, Hawaii Ishizuchi Jinja, Hawaii Kotohira Jinsha–Hawaii Dazaifu Tenmangu, and Izumo Taishakyo Mission of Hawaii, all in Honolulu; Hilo Daijingu in Hilo; Malaea Ebisu Jinja on Maui; and Maui Jinsha Mission in Wailuku. The best known of these is the Izumo Taishakyo Mission, which was founded in 1908 and can be found in downtown Honolulu, at the edge of Chinatown. The design of this wooden A-frame temple was inspired by Shimane Ken's classical Japanese shrine Taisha Machi, and its primary *kami* is Okuninushi-no Mikoto, the creator and dictator of the universe, and the son of Susanoo No Mikoto, Amaterasu's brother. Okuninushi "specializes" in good health, happiness, business success, and harmonious relationships. Every year, about 10,000 people visit the shrine for the New Year holiday weekend. According to its spring newsletter, the shrine offers "typical" ceremonies and rituals, such as weddings, house blessings, and the *Shichigosan* (literally "seven-five-three"); however, it also seems to have adapted to Western traditions by offering a monthly worship service (*Tsukinamisai* or *Tokamatsuri*). Services begin at 7 p.m. on the 10th of each month and consist of blessings and sermons that explain the faith and provide guidance for life. The calendar, too, is peppered with "nonreligious" activities, such as a golf tournament and karaoke, and with quasi-religious activities, such as classes on *ikebana* or flower arrangement, meditation, and calligraphy.

A second Honolulu-based temple, Hawaii Kotohira Jinsha–Hawaii Dazaifu Tenmangu, dates to about 1920 when a "*Gobunrei* (spirit of the deity of the main shrine) from Kotohira-gu in Kagawa-ken, Japan, was brought to Hawaii." Over time, other *Gobunrei* were brought to this location, and today five other shrines are represented at the same site, including Suitengu of Fukuoko-ken, Shirasaki Hachimangu of Yamaguchi-ken, Otaki Jinja of Otake City, Watatsumi Jinja, and Inari Jinja of Kyoto.[55] A third Honolulu-based temple, Daijingu Temple of Hawaii, enshrines Amaterasu. According to an article from 2004, the temple had about 8,000 visitors for New Year observances.[56]

On the mainland, we find the Tsubaki Grand Shrine in America,[57] which was established in 2001 in Granite Falls, Washington, less than an hour from Seattle; at the Shambhala Mountain Center in Red Feather Lakes, Colorado, we find a smaller shrine, the Daitozan Jinja, which was built for Amaterasu-Omikami. Outside the United States, the Bright Woods Spiritual Center in Salt Spring Island, British Columbia, Canada, has a Shinto shrine, the Kinomori Jinja; France has two, including the Mizuya Jinja and Wa Ko Jinja; in Holland, we find the Yamakage Jinja; and, at last count, there were about 10 Shinto temples in Brazil. The case of Brazil is incredibly interesting, because it has the largest Japanese population outside of Japan, with more than 1.5 million calling this country home.[58]

THE FILMS

My Neighbor Totoro (*Tonari no Totoro*) (1988)—Written and directed by Hayao Miyazaki. Running time: 87 min. Japanese. Rated G. Genre: Animated.

Summary: Circa 1955, a father moves his two daughters to the countryside so
that they can be closer to their ailing mother. One day, while exploring, the
youngest girl comes across several furry creatures, called Totoros, that play
music, can fly over the mountains, and increase in size.

The fact that legendary Japanese director Akira Kurosawa included *My
Neighbor Totoro* in his list of the 100 Best Films says something about the quality of Hayao Miyazaki's work. And even though many are marketed to children, his films contain complex themes, three-dimensional characters, and
meticulous and imaginative landscapes that appeal to adults. One of his earliest feature-length films, *My Neighbor Totoro* is a story of childhood, and the
joys and fears that accompany this time of life. At the center of the film are two
sisters, Satsuki Kusakabe, a fourth grader, and her younger sister Mei, who is
four years old. As in most of Miyazaki's films, characters' names are frequently
significant. Both main characters have names that refer to the month of May:
Satsuki literally translates to fifth month of the year, and Mei sounds like the
English word for the same month.[59] Not surprisingly, during the planning
stages of the script, the writer-director conceived of them as one girl, but split
them into two, which might account for their "shared" name.

As the film begins, a university professor, Tatsuo Kusakabe, moves his
daughters to Matsugo village so that they can be closer to their mother, Yasuko,
who has been convalescing in a nearby hospital for about one year. As the family's truck bounces down a bumpy country road, the girls remark how beautiful everything looks. The lush green landscape is dotted with rice paddies, tea
and vegetable fields, and a large green forest. Upon arrival at their country
home, the girls notice an enormous tree that stands at the edge of the forest.
Their father tells them that it's a camphor tree. Known in Japanese as *kusu-no-
ki*, this very fast-growing and long-living evergreen is frequently planted in
Japanese gardens. A camphor tree at Kinomiya Shrine, Atami, Shizuoka Prefecture, known as *Kinomiya-o-kusu* or *go-shin-boku* (which means holy tree) is
estimated to be more than 2,000 years old. "A Shinto god is believed to reside
in that tree, which is endowed with special powers such as making people
healthy and safe from the ills of life and granting the gift of eternal youth and
eternal life." Another tree, growing near the Hana-Kuma Castle, Kobe, was
planted with the hopes of warding off evil spirits.[60] As we will see in *My Neighbor Totoro*, this camphor tree also has "supernatural" associations.

Having explored the yard, the girls begin racing around the house, examining every inch, inside and out. In the kitchen the girls are surprised to find

furry black clumps scurrying around. After these beings disappear, Mei asks, "Were they ghosts?" The girls look at each other and scream. The next room for exploration is the attic, which upon their arrival explodes into a mass of more little black balls. These, too, disappear into a ceiling crack. Covered in soot, the sisters venture downstairs, where they meet "Granny," an elderly neighbor. She informs the girls that they have just seen *Susuwatari*, "soot sprites" that "live in old, empty houses and run all over the place covering everything with dust and dirt." (These "creatures" also make an appearance in *Spirited Away*.) Undoubtedly, the inclusion of these *Susuwatari* gives the film a sense of magic and wonder, which only intensifies as the story continues.

One day, while Satsuki is at school, Mei is outside, playing by herself in the garden, when she finds a trail of acorns. (Oak is apparently a sacred tree in Japan, admired for "its strength and beauty and venerated in Shinto god offerings. Its acorn and leaves have been featured in the insignia of countless powerful lords."[61]) She follows the trail, picking up the nuts one by one. Suddenly, she sees two white triangular shapes poking out of the grass. As she looks on, the ears turn into a knee-high white creature that passes by her. Intrigued, Mei follows it. The original white creature is soon joined by a larger gray one that carries a bag over his shoulder. Still in pursuit, Mei crawls through a vegetation-formed tunnel that terminates at the base of an enormous tree. Stretching around it is a *shimenawa* or a rope with hanging paper streamers. For the viewer, this indicates that Mei is entering sacred space, and the girl literally enters it by falling through a hole and landing in a heavily vegetated area. Her next encounter is with a sleeping brown, furry creature who has a rotund oblong body, upright ears, black whiskers, a rounded tail, and almost catlike features. The curious Mei crawls onto its stomach. When asked who he is, the creature makes a sound, something like Do-do-roo. Mei interprets this to mean its name and from that point on she calls it a Totoro.[62] The tired girl eventually curls up on the creature's stomach and falls asleep.

When Satsuki returns home from school, she discovers that Mei is missing and immediately begins a search. Eventually she finds her younger sister within the tunnel of branches. At first Mei is perplexed: Where is the Totoro? Once her father arrives, she becomes excited, telling him and Satsuki about her encounter. She tries to find the Totoro again. And when she can't, she becomes upset. To comfort her, her father says, "You must have met one of the spirits of the forest. But you can only see them when they want you to. Let's give the forest spirits a proper greeting." That said, the three of them journey to the camphor tree. Mei is surprised to find that the hole has disappeared. "That means the forest spirits don't want to be seen right now. . . . What a magnificent tree. It's been around since a long ago, back in time when trees and people used to be friends and protect one another. Let's give this tree a nice greeting." Standing in front of it, they bow in reverence. The father then says, "Thank you for watching over Mei. Please continue to look after us." In Shinto, large, unusually shaped trees are often thought to be sacred and thus associated with *kami*, and *My Neighbor Totoro* supports this belief. Writer Dani Cavallaro points out something else about this tree ritual that's significant, but which would only be known to those who have access to the Japanese-language version.[63] She states that "Mr. Kusakabe's homage to the Great Tree (*Tsukamori*) utilizes the traditional formula: '*Onegai itashimasu.*'"[64] *Onegai* "comes from the verb *negau*, which literally means 'to pray to (something).'" This entire phrase is used when a person is "feeling really, really humble" . . . "it places you lower on the hierarchy than the person to whom you're speaking."[65] Thus when the father says this, it indicates that he isn't just "going through the motions" for his children's sake but is earnest in his respect for the tree.

The next time that Mei encounters the Totoro is on a dark and rainy night. She and Satsuki take their father's umbrella to a bus stop and wait for him. But he doesn't arrive for a very long time, and Mei falls asleep. Satsuki picks her up and puts her on her back. As they continue to wait, the older girl hears footsteps and then she realizes that someone is standing beside her. When she glances over, she sees a clawed foot. Her eyes widen with terror. She is in the presence of something "awesome." It is Totoro, who has a lotus leaf on his head.[66] Fear soon turns to excitement, and Satsuki offers the drenched creature a blue umbrella, which it accepts. As the raindrops pepper it, the creature becomes playful, and it laughs and jumps. His thunderous movements shake the earth and more rain, shaken from the treetops, pours around them. Totoro lets out a huge roar. Although it may seem to be a stretch, both the lotus and the umbrella are listed among the eight auspicious symbols[67] of Buddhism. A symbol of purity and renunciation, the water lily "represents the blossoming of wholesome activities, which are performed with complete freedom from the faults of cyclic existence."[68] A traditional symbol of royalty and protection, the umbrella or parasol protects a person from the heat of the sun; therefore, "the coolness of its shade symbolizes protection from the painful heat of suffering, desire, obstacles, illnesses and harmful forces." Also, because the umbrella or parasol is "held above the head it naturally symbolizes honor and respect."[69] It's also worth mentioning that near the bus stop is a shrine dedicated to Inari, the *kami* of rice cultivation. His messenger, the fox, is typically found there, dressed in a red bib. In the film, we catch a glimpse of red *torii* and flags behind several large trees.

After they have been waiting in the rain for a while, Satsuki sees a pair of headlamps coming toward them. Is it a bus? Not exactly. It's a bus, but not one made from metal. This one is a live animal: a 12-legged Cat Bus. With its wide eyes and toothy grin, Cat Bus certainly looks like the Cheshire Cat from Lewis Carroll's *Alice's Adventures in Wonderland*. However, cats figure prominently in Japanese legends and many are shape-shifters. In a well-known folk story, *The Boy Who Drew Cats*, a boy named Joji spends every waking minute drawing cats. Even though people try to make him stop, he won't. And it's a good thing, too, because one night one of his creations comes to life and saves him from a monster-sized rat. When Joji realizes what has happened, he presses his palms together and bows to the image on a screen, thanking the "honorable cat" for its kindness. Another ubiquitous image of the cat is the *Maneki Neko*, literally the Beckoning Cat. Business owners put these in front windows or at the entrance of their restaurants or stores. Usually made of ceramic or porcelain, they come in several colors—black is associated with good health, gold with wealth—and typically wear a red kerchief or a bell around their neck.[70] Cats have been popularized in Japanese anime, including Meowth (in Japan, Nyarth) who, in *Pokemon*, is always looking for dropped change. The 2002 popular animated film *The Cat Returns* (*Neko no Danshaku, Baron*) tells the story of a girl who rescues a cat only to find out he's a prince. To thank her for her kindness, she is whisked away to the Kingdom of Cats, where she's supposed to marry him. Miyazaki served as this film's executive producer.

Before Totoro gets into the Cat Bus, he gives the girls a special package wrapped in a bamboo leaf. When they get home and open it, they find that it is filled with acorns. Hoping to "grow a beautiful forest" with the nuts, the girls plant them in the garden. But nothing happens. That is, until one night when three Totoro of varying sizes show up. As the creatures venture toward the garden, they chant. By the time they are performing a ritual, during which they bend and stretch as if coaxing the plants from the ground, the girls have already joined them. Each time they stretch upwards, the sprouts turn into seedlings that turn into trees that grow taller and taller. Finally, the trees merge into one gigantic tree. Exhilarated, the girls shout while the biggest Totoro pulls out a top. Everyone hops on and they fly into the air as the giant furry being roars. "Mei, we're the wind," says Satsuki. When they finish their sky voyage, the Totoro lands at the top of the camphor tree, and everyone plays a tune on an ocarina flute. As writer Dani Cavallaro explains, this "growing scene" is both "ritual and game," demonstrating that "children tend to retain a connection with an 'other' . . . a primordial world that doesn't respect rigid codes and fixed patterns of meaning. . . . The fantastic is posited as a receptacle of energies from which the children can draw at times of uncertainty or grief."[71] Furthermore, the Totoro function as "mediators between nature and the world of childhood—they show the girls how to participate in nature rather than observe as onlookers."[72]

When the girls wake up the next day, they wonder if all they experienced was just a dream. They get their answer when they see new seedlings sprouting in the garden. "It wasn't a dream," they shout, then laugh and jump. The mood turns more somber when the girls learn that their mother's health has suffered a setback. Upset, Mei sets off for the hospital. Being the responsible sister, Satsuki tries to find her. But the longer she searches, the more scared she becomes. Realizing that she needs help, Satsuki seeks out Totoro and asks for assistance. Always one to come to the girls' needs, he lets out a growl and, together, they float to the top of the tree. He howls again, summoning the Cat Bus that traverses the landscape unnoticed. Surprised, Satsuki remarks that "No one else can see it, can they?" Eventually, they find Mei sitting near a long row of stone Jizo statues. One of the most popular bodhisattvas in Japan, Jizo is the Japanese name for Kshitigarbha, who, among other things, is regarded as a protector of travelers and guardian of children and women. These statues can "commonly be seen on a country roadside or at a corner in a village or town. . . . A stone deity such as this was considered sacred and was worshipped in prewar Japan."[73]

The film ends happily. The Cat Bus takes the girls to their mother's hospital and they sit outside in a tree, watching over her. When it's time to depart, they leave behind an ear of corn. Upon arriving in their village, they are greeted warmly by Granny, who in this film serves as a surrogate mother to the girls. It's important to note that many of Miyazaki's films contain an older female character. Often she serves as a nurturer as well as a source of knowledge.

As we see in this case, Granny maintains tradition and grows the corn that will restore their mother to help.

In the end, we are left to wonder: What is Totoro? Is he a *kami* or does he symbolize something else? In the Japanese tradition, he's probably a syncretic being, part *kami* and part bodhisattva. It's said that big Totoro stands nearly seven feet tall and has lived in the forests of Japan for 1,300 years. Medium-sized Totoro is about half that age, and little Totoro is about 100.[74] For much of the film, Totoro behaves *kami*-like: He inspires awe, has control of natural forces (plants and the wind), and is associated with sacred places, including the giant tree. If we look at the iconography associated with him, we also can make a connection between him and Buddhism. We've already mentioned the Buddhist symbols associated with the big Totoro, the lotus and umbrella, so let's look at medium-sized Totoro. The first time that we see him, he is running with a brown sack over his right shoulder. With his rotund frame, he looks a bit like Hotei, which is the Japanese name for Pu-tai, a Chinese monk from the 10th century who wanders around carrying a hempen sack. Also known as the Laughing Buddha, he is, in Japan, the god of good fortune, contentment, and happiness. One of the Seven Lucky Gods (*Shichifukujin*), he is a guardian of children.

My Neighbor Totoro was inspired by Kenji Miyazawa's (1896–1933) *Acorns and Wildcat* (*Donguri to Yameneko*), a children's story about a wildcat that sends a postcard to a nature-loving boy, asking him to come and help settle an argument between some acorns. After we read more about Miyazawa, we can understand the affinity that Miyazaki must have felt with him. Both men wrote stories for children that are populated with humans and animals and that address ecological and ethical concerns. In fact, when we read descriptions of Miyazawa's work, we experience an odd sense of déjà vu. "Kenji felt that all living creatures are brothers and that happiness in the true sense is impossible for the individual to attain unless he seeks the happiness of all other living things as well,"[75] which is written about a Miyazawa story but could just as easily apply to any number of Miyazaki characters, including Nausicaa, Ashitaka, Mei, and Sen.

Kamichu! (2005)—Animated TV series. Written by Hideyuki Kurata and directed by Koji Masunari. Running time: 28 min. per episode. Japanese. Genre: Animated.

What's useful about this four-volume, 16-episode program is how quickly it immerses the viewer in the world of Shinto. For our purposes, the first two episodes of volume 1, *Spite of Youth* and *Please God*, are going to be the most useful. We will also talk briefly about the third episode, *I Didn't Mean It*. *Spite of Youth* introduces us to Yurie Hitotsubashi, an average junior high student, who is best friends with Mitsue Shijou. While the two are eating in their school cafeteria, Yurie explains that sometime during the previous evening she became a god (*kami*). Without skipping a beat, Mitsue gives her friend "an offering." Although the subtitles for *kami* read "god," this really isn't the best translation of the term. As has already been discussed, the word *kami* conveys many ideas, such as the mysterious, spirit, and divinity, which aren't easily encapsulated into the one word "god." Furthermore, that a seemingly ordinary teen-ager can become divine overnight speaks to the mysterious nature of *kami*. In fact, it is never explained why this transformation occurs, and no one really questions that it has happened. Over several episodes, we will see that in spite of her clumsiness and awkwardness, Yurie, indeed, possesses extraordinary powers.

After eating, the two girls, now joined by another classmate named Matsuri Saegusa, go to the rooftop of the school and try to find out what kind of god Yurie might be. Matsuri says that they can do this by seeing what sort of powers she has. Feeling embarrassed by the entire situation, Yurie doesn't make much progress. Before they return to class, the girls meet the calligraphy-loving Kenji, Yurie's classmate and the object of her affections. Matsuri teases Yurie that if she confesses her love, it will ripen. Excited about this idea, Yurie shouts *kami chu*, which means "little deity," but nothing really happens.

After school the girls venture to Matsuri's home, which is the local shrine (*jinja*). They climb hundreds of lantern-lined stairs, eventually arriving at the structure itself, which looks remarkably like the Izumo Taishakyo Mission of Hawaii. In front of the shrine, we see the *Koma-inu* or guardian lion-dogs, the offering box, a *shimenawa* stretched across the entryway, and a large rock decorated with a similar twisted rope/paper streamer. As the "camera" changes position, we see the water purification tank, which stands next to a *shimenawa*-draped tree. "Welcome to Raifuku Shrine," Matsuri announces.

In the next scene, we watch Yurie and Mitsue wash themselves in the purification tank, using a wooden ladle. As the camera pans, we see a stand on which many *ema*, or votive plaques, are attached. After a visitor purchases one of these, he or she can write out his or her wishes. People ask for anything from success in business to doing well on an exam. Once finished, the *ema* are hung on a stand. Yurie and Mitsue next proceed to an area where they pick up a box and shake it. Eventually, a long stick on which they find a number pops out. This number corresponds to a drawer in which the girls find their *omikuji* or fortune.[76] Mitsue's says, "Good luck. Love relationship is slowly moving forward. Go. Go." Yurie's says, "A little luck. Love relationship. Presentment of a storm."

In the next scene, Matsuri introduces the girls to her sister, Miko, who, it is explained, has the ability to feel the power of someone or something. In fact, it is she who communicates with Yashima, the shrine's tutelary *kami*. Still trying to determine what sort of *kami* Yurie might be, the girls perform a ritual. First, they ring the main shrine bell, alerting the *kami* that they are about to begin. Dressed in traditional clothing, Yurie sits on a table in the shrine, while Matsuri bangs a drum and Miko shakes some bells. The music stirs something within her and Yurie rises to her feet. She sneezes. But this is no ordinary sneeze; it's the start of a typhoon dubbed Yurie. Because of their association with the *jinja*, Matsuri and Miko have Shinto-derived names. The older girl's name literally translates to "enshrinement," "elevation," or "deification," but refers to festivals during which practitioners offer prayers, thanks, reports, and praise to the *kami*. A *matsuri* generally involves music, dancing, and feasting. In the case of the younger sister, a *miko* is a shrine maiden. Her role includes performing in ceremonial dances and assisting the priest. Long ago, these women were shamanesses who went into a trance so that they could communicate with the *kami*. As scholar Ichiro Hori explains, there were many wandering shamanesses (*aruki-miko*) in rural areas until the early 12th century. Traveling in groups of five or six, they went from one village to the next, offering services that included "communication with spirits, deities, wraiths, and the dead; divination and fortunetelling through trance; prayers for recovery of the sick; and purification of new buildings, wells, stoves and hearths."[77] Over time, women serving this function within an organized religion all but disappeared. However, they are making a comeback, or so says scholar Haruko Okano, but they are doing it within "new" religious movements.[78]

Realizing that they have to stop this storm, the girls head to the school. Along the way, Yurie begins to see the world as it really is, filled with thousands of *kami*, including ghostlike *chibakaze* (little wind), animated tree leaves, seaweed, daikon, a piece of tofu, a rolling pop can, and various fish. On top of the school's roof, the girls box in an area with a *shimenawa* and Matsuri writes something on the ground. Holding a *harai-gushi* in her hand and standing in the center of the purified area, Yurie asks the typhoon to disappear. Initially, nothing happens, until she sees Kenji being threatened. Wanting to save him, she again says, "*Kamichu.*" At this moment her short-cropped hair grows past her waist,[79] and she rides a *kami* into the eye of the storm, thereby saving her love interest and putting an end to the typhoon. At the end of the segment, Yurie ties her fortune (*omikuji*) to a tree. Fortunes dispensed at a local shrine range from good luck (*daikichi*) to bad luck (*daikyo*), and, in general, once the fortune is read, the person ties it to a tree branch. Trees on shrine grounds are often so covered with these paper slips that, from a distance, it looks as if they are in bloom.

The second episode, *Please God*, continues our story. The girls are in school, and Matsuri is getting increasingly irritated that Yurie isn't being treated with the respect she deserves. She attributes this to the fact that Yurie hasn't done anything "godlike" for them, so she proposes having a *matsuri*. "I want to hold it at least once a year and make it our famous local event," she says. The girls return to the shrine, where the priest is working in the garden. When Miko turns up, Matsuri asks her to open the main shrine so that they can salute Yashima. She wants to make Yurie their exclusive god. At the shrine, Matsuri and Miko clap twice, say "Please come out," and bow. The other girls follow suit. "Please, come out," Matsuri says again. When Yashima doesn't appear, Miko admits that he's been missing for about three months. "It seems like he ran away," the tearful girl reports.

Matsuri and Miko tell their father what happened, and he responds by announcing his retirement as chief priest. He then turns the shrine's operations over to his daughters. Matsuri tells Yurie and Mitsue that the shrine has been declining in attendance, and this has negatively affected her family's finances. "We must work hard to pay off our debt," she adds. As scholar Stuart D. B. Picken explains, the Shinto priesthood traces its origin "to the sacral society that was ancient Japan. The duties are to serve the *kami*, to engage in religious activities based on *Jinja* Shinto, and to administer to shrine business. Many shrines are served by hereditary priests."[80] To become a priest, a person can take courses at Kokugakuin University or Kogakkan University, where he or she will learn to recite liturgies and learn the rituals. Once the program is completed, the person usually finds a shrine and moves up within the ranks. It would be highly uncommon for two young girls to run a shrine as they do in *Kamichu!* Since Shinto shrines aren't state run, the priests do rely on the community to pay for upkeep.

The girls decide to find their runaway *kami*, so Matsuri tells Yurie to copy the characters for "eye power"[81] onto a sheet of paper. When she finishes, the sheet is pinned onto her shirt, and she begins to glow. "It's supposed to change your appearance, too," says Matsuri. It doesn't because Yurie's "handwriting is bad." As has been said, a person can obtain any manner of *omamori* (lucky charms and protective amulets) from a Shinto shrine. In this case, the *kami* herself creates the talisman by drawing a picture of an eye and writing sacred words. Because there is power in the Japanese language (*kotodama*), the film suggests that writing characters incorrectly will hinder the talisman's efficacy. When spoken, sacred words invite the *kami* to visit and, when intoned again, they send the *kami* back. Words, too, have special powers, and if properly pronounced, or in this case written, the results are certain. If not, only some of the effects will be seen.

All four girls, each wearing an eye power charm, walk around the town looking for Yashima. They ask a number of *kami*, including one that looks like a lion, three white cats that look like the traditional *maneki-neko* except that they aren't beckoning to anyone, and more. "I didn't realize the town looked like this," says a dumbfounded Mitsue. We next see a montage of the girls asking more *kami*. At one point, Miko stops in front of a red *kami-dana* and claps twice. A beak-nosed *kami* comes out. Still unable to locate Yashima, the girls rest on a bench near the sea. Suddenly a shining fish emerges from the water, attached to a fishing line. When the fisherman comes to claim his dinner, we see that it is a small fish and a talking shark. Mitsue asks them if they know where the gods convene. Another *kami* tells them to look on top of a nearby mountain.

After climbing to the top, the exhausted girls come upon a small shrine poised on a large rock. Inscribed on it is: Entrance to the Gods' Rest Center. Restricted to Members Only. Since Yurie is the only member present, she approaches the small shrine and is transported inside. In this world of the gods, we see a red *torii* in the middle of a vast body of water. As Yurie walks along a wooden bridge, she hears a voice asking if she needs a ride. The boatman is a raccoon-like creature, probably a *tanuki*. As he ferries her across the water, a long glittering blue eel-like creature swims underneath. They eventually float under the *torii* and find themselves in a world of diverse *kami*, from laser discs to eggplants. When asked how many gods exist, the ferryman says, "About the same amount as things created in the universe." As the camera pans over the landscape, we see cherry trees in bloom, more *torii*, a pagoda, temples, and more. By definition, a pagoda is a four- or eight-cornered Buddhist structure that can be constructed out of myriad materials, from wood to brick. The topmost part consists of a post with a great number of rings. Like a stupa, the pagoda serves as a container for relics or as the tomb of a famous master. The *tanuki* is a favorite subject of Japanese folklore, and ceramic statues of this animal, holding a bottle of sake, wearing a straw hat, and bearing its characteristically large testicles, can be found outside restaurants. Like the fox, the *tanuki* is thought to be a shape-shifter and it frequently changes into either a monk or a teakettle.

In *Kamichu!*, Yurie searches everywhere but still can't locate Yashima. Then, in the distance, she hears the clanging of a shrine bell. She goes to investigate and finds him with a talking *shiba-inu*. During a heart-to-heart talk, Yashima confesses to her that he wants to play in a band: "I saw god Benzaiten's tour this past New Year and was inspired." Yurie returns with Yashima, who possesses Mitsue so that he can apologize to Matsuri. The program finishes with the much-anticipated Yurie Festival. Those in attendance eat, stop at the many booths set up on shrine grounds, socialize, and enjoy performances. A group of men carry Yurie, dressed in a shrine maiden outfit, on a *mikoshi* or portable shrine. Later on, Yashima possesses Mitsue again so he can give a musical performance, and, finally, Yurie is presented at the shrine. Various other *kami* look on. When Yashima says that he saw Benzaiten on tour, he's talking about the goddess of music, beauty, art, and literature who is one of the Seven Lucky Gods of Japan. On New Year's, she and the six deities "go on tour" in a treasure ship. The fact that Yashima is found with a *shiba-inu* isn't too surprising. These ancient dogs have served the Japanese as watchdogs and companions. In December 1936, through the Cultural Properties Act, the breed was designated a "precious natural product of the Japanese nation."[82] And finally, the fact that Yashima has to possess a female in order to communicate is in accordance with Japanese shamanism. As it has been mentioned, these shamanesses were called *miko*, a term that means a mediator between the gods and humans, but is also "used to designate lower orders of priestesses in Shinto shrines and women unconnected with any shrine claiming religious and magical powers." Expanding on that definition, scholar Haruko Okano says that it also applies to women, in general, who were thought to possess charisma.[83]

In episode three, *I Didn't Mean It*, Yurie has started giving advice to her fellow students; most of them ask her about money problems. Wondering why this might be, they call on Yashima, who after he possesses Mitsue, tells them that the poverty god is coming. Hoping to avert this disaster, Yurie and Yashima write up hundreds of good luck amulets. The idea is that by distributing them all over the town, the amulets will purify the city and increase its luck, thereby countering the misfortune spread by the poverty god. A little while later, all four girls and Yashima perform an antipoverty ceremony. "We are not going to be poor. We won't let the people become poor," says Mitsue. "We should have this attitude and act with the deepest of grace." In the town, they have a table-like structure on which we see myriad food offerings as well as two tree sprigs decorated with white paper streamers. One of the girls waves a *harai-gushi* over the table. Dressed in shrine maiden outfits, the girls go throughout the town distributing the good luck amulets. Yurie stops in front of a frog statue, holds up her hand, palm out, closes her eyes, and, after she feels a slight breeze, brings it to life. It promises to keep an eye out for the poverty god. Why might there be a frog in this scene? As Ian Reader explains, the efficacy of the frog derives from a linguistic pun. "The word for frog, *kaeru*, is pronounced the same as the verb *kaeru*, to return. Hence the frog symbolizes both the idea of returning safely (that is, it has a function connected to travel) and returning to health."[84]

Despite the girls' best efforts, the poverty god arrives. Now they must meet it face to face and chase him away. Armed with a bow and arrow, the girls visit the worst hit parts of town, when they meet what seems to be Tama, Yurie's missing cat. In reality, it's the poverty god who has taken over Tama's body. To prevent the god from leaving, Yashima tells Miko to put up divine tags in all directions. During a final confrontation, Yurie learns that the poverty god saved Tama's life and the grateful cat doesn't want the god exorcised. Filled with love for her cat, Yurie decides to "keep" the poverty god and take him back to her house. As she hugs the feline, Yurie's hair, again, grows very long and a great light emanates from her, transforming the town's bad luck to good luck. All of the *kami* rejoice, and the shrine offertory box is filled with money. The girls tie oracles to a tree. By the way, Matsuri's arrow is called a *hamaya*, literally "demon-breaking arrow," which is supposed to ward off misfortune and attract good luck.

Princess Mononoke (*Mononoke-hime*) (1997)—Written and directed by Hayao Miyazaki. Running time: 134 min. Japanese. Rated PG-13 for images of violence and gore. Genre: Animated.

Summary: When an angry spirit-possessed boar goes on a rampage through the countryside, Ashitaka, a young warrior, tries to stop it. Unfortunately, while subduing the beast, he is injured and becomes afflicted with a fatal curse. Hoping to find a cure, he sets out for the forests of the west. Upon his arrival, he finds himself caught between two rival factions. On one side are Lady Eboshi and a ragtag band of humans living in a mining town, and on the other are the forest's animal spirits and San, a girl raised by wolves.

Princess Mononoke is set during the Muromachi period (mid-14th to late 15th century C.E.), an era during which members of the Ashikaga family occupied the position of shogun. Political rivalry between provincial warlords (*daimyo*) and the shogunate came to a head during the Onin War (1467–1477 C.E.), the result of which was warfare and social chaos. Despite these conflicts, because of its economic and artistic developments, the Muromachi period is thought to be the apex of Japanese high culture. Not only was Zen Buddhism an important political force but it also exerted a tremendous influence on the arts and literature. Whatever free time the samurai had, they spent on developing an aesthetic appreciation of landscape painting, the preparation of food, *ikebana* or flower arrangement, Noh theater, poetry, and even the tea ceremony. This period was significant for Miyazaki, because, as he said, it was when "people changed their value system from gods to money," and he demonstrates this in his film.[85]

Mononoke can be translated to "spirit of a thing" and *hime* as "princess," but it's helpful to dig a bit more. As scholar Thomas P. Kasulis explains, "When Shinto discussions focus on spiritual power as internally rather than externally related to materiality, the terms *mi* or *mono* are often used. . . . *Mi* or *mono* do not exist without materiality, nor does materiality exist without them. Neither would be what it is without the other. . . . They suggest that neither spirit nor matter can exist without interdependence."[86] In the film, this human-spirit bond is being forgotten and severed by human greed and economic "development." The biggest offenders are Lady Eboshi and the emperor. He wants someone to kill Shishi Gami, known in translation as the spirit of the forest or the Deer God, cut off its head, and bring it back to him, because he believes it will confer immortality. Eboshi, as we'll see, is the person who gladly fulfills the emperor's command.

In a broad sense, the title *Princess Mononoke* refers to San, "the wild girl whose soul the wolves stole." As Moro, her wolf "mother" explains, when San was a baby, her human parents were caught defiling the forest. Scared, they threw their child at Moro's feet, and the wolf raised the girl as one of her own. Having grown up outside of civilization, San despises everything about humans. A liminal figure, she fights on the side of the *kami* but she isn't fully a *kami*. And although physically she's human, her upbringing means that she isn't fully human. This liminality is what makes her dangerous. Despite its title, the true hero of *Princess Mononoke* is Prince Ashitaka, a compassionate, self-sacrificing, and honorable man who does what's right no matter what the consequences, even if it means his own death. To understand the film, it's necessary to be familiar with Shinto and Buddhism because these religions have been instrumental in shaping the spiritual and moral life of the Japanese. And even though Ashitaka is not a samurai, he follows a similar code, which itself was shaped by the two aforementioned religions as well as Confucianism.

Before the film begins, we read the following over the opening credits: "In ancient times the land lay covered in forest where from ages long past dwelt the spirits of the gods." This leads us to the opening scene, during which a *Tatari Gamai*, an angry and violent god that has taken over a boar, threatens an Emishi village. Covered in wriggling black wormlike structures, it emerges from the trees and scorches everything in its wake. The future ruler of the village, Ashitaka, who is riding his trusted friend Yakul, a red deer, warns everyone that the "Oracle" wants them to return to the village—something is coming. He dismounts his steed and climbs a tower where he and an old man wait, bow and arrow poised. As soon as the being emerges, Ashitaka tries to stop it not only with arrows but also with words. "Quiet your rage, I beg you! O forest god who cannot be named, why do you rampage so?" Even though Ashitaka saves the village, he, himself is "infected" by contact and a mark is burned into his arm. In Shinto, this is the moment of pollution and impurity. When the Oracle arrives on the scene, she brings with her water with which to cleanse the wound. She then approaches the creature, bows to it, and says, "O raging god unknown to us, I bow before you. Where you have fallen we will raise a mound and perform rites. Bear us no hate, and be at peace." But the creature is too filled with rage and hatred, and with its last breath, curses them, saying, "You loathsome rabble! You shall know my hatred and my grief." Immediately, its body rots away, causing an awful smell and leaving behind nothing but an oozing skeleton. Those who experience this event turn away and cover their faces. What we've just encountered sets up the Shinto idea that if people fail to worship the spirits in a way that is pleasing to them, "they will turn malevolent and cause natural disasters and social disharmony. Once malevolent, the deities will not change unless people ritually change their nature."[87] The verity of this will become known as the film progresses.

Trying to figure out what the creature was, the Oracle uses stones for divination purposes. She tells Ashitaka, who is sitting cross-legged in front of her, that the boar-spirit came from far to the west. A poison within him goaded him on, rotting his flesh and drawing evil as he ran, making a monster out of him. Worse news is to come. Are you "steeled to gaze upon your fate?" she asks. "I was prepared the moment I let my arrow fly," he says, recognizing that a warrior should always keep his mind on death. As the *Code of the Samurai* states, "A warrior performs distinguished military feats on the battleground and earns the highest honor only after having accepted the fact that he is going to die. [This way] if he has the misfortune to lose in a duel, when his head is about to be taken by the enemy, on being asked his name . . . he identifies himself clearly and hands over his head with a smile, showing no sign of flinching."[88] The Oracle then reveals that Ashitaka's scar will seep into his bones, resulting in his death. The other men sitting in attendance are outraged, asking if nothing else can be done, especially since Ashitaka sacrificed himself for his village. No one can escape his fate, the Oracle says; "You can, though, rise to meet it." She reveals that an iron ball was found inside the demon, and it was this that caused its agony, shattering its bones and tearing at its entrails. She tells Ashitaka that "calamity has befallen the west" and that he should journey there and see with "eyes unclouded." There may be a way to lift the curse, she adds. Ashitaka, who has remained stoic throughout, cuts his top knot and prepares to journey to the west.

During these first 10 minutes, we have already seen how Buddhist and Shinto elements interact within the film. By having a female Oracle, Miyazaki recalls the ancient tradition in Japan when women were reputedly more important than men in religion and politics. They were seen to have direct contact with deities and could announce the deities' will to everyone else. During certain festivals, deities could even descend upon a group of women, who were selected as mediums. To prepare for these festivals, the women had to practice abstinence and engage in purification rituals.[89] In the case of Ashitaka, he exemplifies not only the Confucian ideal—he is truly a *junzi*—but he is also the quintessential samurai, adhering to the three essential characteristics of loyalty, duty, and valor. As we've said, he is ready at all times for battle, recognizing that he could die at any moment.

It's interesting that the Oracle encourages Ashitaka to see through "unclouded eyes." For a Buddhist, to see clearly means to see the world the way it is—as interconnected and impermanent—but it also means not being attached to the three poisons, which are greed, anger, and ignorance, for these things distort our sight. As the film progresses, it will demonstrate how "blindness" affects most of the characters, leading them to conflict, violence, and death. Ashitaka, by contrast, rises above these human foibles by being compassionate, patient, and clear-sighted. Finally, it's significant that he cuts off his topknot, as this is an act of renunciation; Ashitaka, like any monk, is leaving behind the familiar world. He rides away on Yakul under a quasi *torii*.

The first person Ashitaka comes into contact with is a Buddhist monk, Jiko-bo, who tells him that the "land teems with the twittering of bitter ghosts dead from war; sick or starved and fallen where they stood. A curse, you say? This world is a curse." As far as ghosts are concerned, he may be referring to *goryo*, malevolent spirits of a person who died as the result of violence, a grudge, or unnatural causes. "The spirit most feared by the ancient Japanese was the powerful person who suffered an injustice; the higher the stakes, the more evil he could inflict." War or adverse political events might result in the creation of these ghosts, as the monk in *Princess Mononoke* suggests, and in their anger they might produce natural disasters and social disruption.[90] Ashitaka, who earlier came under attack by a number of samurai and, in defending himself, killed a few men, is lamenting his actions, to which the monk responds, "We all die. Some now, some later." Ashitaka then asks the monk if he recognizes the iron ball that infected the boar; the monk says he doesn't. Instead, he explains that "Far to the west, deep in the mountains, is the forest of the Deer God. There no man may tread. They say the beasts there are giants, as they were in ages past." Naturally, the Deer God lives in the mountains. As we've said, mountains and rivers are particularly sacred for practitioners of Shinto.

When we meet Lady Eboshi, about 20 minutes into the film, it seems that we've met the "villain" of the piece, especially since she's waging a war against the gods. This isn't as bad as her overall disregard for her own people, though. For example, after Moro has attacked Eboshi's entourage, Eboshi tells everyone to get moving. "What about the ones who fell?" someone asks her. She repeats her command and walks away. By contrast, Ashitaka, who is an outsider and thus has no connection to these people, suspends his own journey so that he can help them. As he's fishing bodies out of the river, he catches a glimpse of San, who is sucking the blood out of Moro's shoulder. "Are you ancient gods of the forest of the Deer God?" Ashitaka shouts. "Leave," is San's only reply. Two of the main Shinto taboos are contact with the dead and with blood, so it's significant that San is shown with blood in her mouth, smeared on her face and on her hands. In Shinto "blood, probably as the carrier of life, is a defiling substance when it leaves the body via wounds, disease or even menstruation. Violating such a taboo calls for purification."[91] Purification, as we've seen, can be achieved by washing in water. But even though San is near the river's edge, she doesn't wash. Instead, she remains in a state of defilement, either *kegare* or *tsumi*, and thus remains dangerous, wild, and outside civilization. The word *eboshi*, interestingly enough, refers to the black-lacquered silk headgear worn by a Shinto priest.

Not long after his encounter with San, Ashitaka comes face-to-face with a *kodama*, a harmless, white-bodied tree spirit that is "a sign that the woods are healthy." Ashitaka approaches one, and with reverence, asks if he, Yakul, and his two wounded companions can have passage through their woods. Depicted as small, cheerful, childlike creatures, the *kodama* lead their guests to their "mother," an enormous old tree at the edge of a lake. Walking toward the water's edge, Ashitaka looks around with a sense of awe; he is in the presence of the *kami*. As he fills his bowl with fresh water, he looks down and sees a three-toed track. It belongs to the spirit of the forest, which appears in the distance. Just as Ashitaka looks up, his injured arm begins to throb. He submerges it in the pristine lake, thus calming the source of impurity. According to Dani Cavallaro, the *kodama-do* feature in traditional mythology as spirits of the dead.[92]

Ashitaka emerges from the forest and comes upon Tatara or Iron Town, a place where social hierarchy has, from a Confucian perspective, been turned upside down. Lady Eboshi makes all of the decisions here, but she lets the women, all of them former prostitutes, run everything else. Rather than follow traditional feminine models of being respectful and obedient to their husbands, the women of Iron Town chastise the men for being lazy, stupid, and useless. Furthermore, they are the town's breadwinners. They work the bellows in the ironworks, which pays for the community's food. We get a sense that this unnatural order has serious repercussions. As one man says, the presence of the women "defiles the iron."

During Ashitaka's stay in Iron Town, Lady Eboshi's character continues to develop. As she exhibits both "good" and "bad" characteristics, we realize that she's much more complex than we had previously imagined. On the one hand, she has freed the prostitutes and given them "honest" work. And as an old leper says, she "is the only one who looked upon us as human. Without fear of our disease . . . she washed our rotting flesh, bandaged us." On the other hand, she was the one who gave birth to the boar god's curse. As we learn, the boar wouldn't let the townspeople near the mountains, so Lady Eboshi brought "her guns" and waged war against them. When Ashitaka confronts her with the consequences of her actions, she assumes responsibility, even going so far as to express regret that he must suffer for what she's done. "I fired that shot," she says. "It is me that brainless pig should have cursed. Would your right hand like to kill me?" "To lift the curse, my left would, too," Ashitaka says. "But I fear it would not stop there." In these words Ashitaka reveals that acting in anger only escalates the situation, leading to further devastation.

Whereas Lady Eboshi uses violence to get what she wants, Ashitaka uses it to help others. The first time he takes up arms is to save his village; the second time is to save villagers from marauding samurai. Up until this point, we've never seen him confront or challenge anyone. Not long into his visit, Eboshi asks Ashitaka to follow her. Initially, it seems that her "secret," as she calls it, is her willingness to shelter and rehabilitate the lepers. But, in fact, it's that she's using them to engineer lighter guns that will allow the town's women to "kill monsters and pierce samurai armor." "Beware! Lady Eboshi wants to rule the world," one leper says. And she does. Whatever compassion she seems to possess is tempered by her megalomania and her overall disregard for tradition, the rules, and the gods. "You stole the boar's woods and made a monster of him," Ashitaka says. "Now will you breed new hatreds with those guns?"

If Lady Eboshi were a character in a Disney film, she would conform to dualistic interpretations of human behavior; she would be good or bad without shades of gray. But because she's crafted in the East, where dualism isn't as prevalent, we find a more complex and ethically challenging character. If she isn't inherently sinful or evil, then what can we say about her? In Shinto, "human nature is viewed like a mirror that can cease to reflect light because of dust. Once it is washed or polished, it can once again reflect light as it was originally intended."[93] Buddhists use similar language, saying that her "vision" has become clouded by the three poisons: greed, anger, and ignorance. We know this not only by her actions but also because when she asks Ashitaka what he plans to do, and he replies, "See with eyes unclouded," she laughs hysterically. Lady Eboshi's greedy thoughts are especially revealed when she tells Ashitaka that "Without the ancient gods, the wild ones are mere beasts. . . . With the forest gone and the wolves with it, this will be a land of riches." As for ignorance, she fails to comprehend the interconnectedness of all life, that to harm one person or *kami* is to send a ripple effect throughout the world. We see how limited her vision is when she tells Ashitaka that "the blood of the Deer God will cure disease. It could cure these people and perhaps even lift your curse." Killing the Deer God may indeed save a dozen people, but on a larger scale, killing it will also destroy everything else, a verity we see toward the end of the film. A Buddhist understands that we are made entirely of non-human elements—water, minerals, and plants; therefore, if the environment is destroyed, so are we. "The Diamond Sutra teaches us that it is impossible to distinguish between sentient and non-sentient beings. This is one of many ancient Buddhist texts that teach deep ecology."[94] In terms of Shinto, Eboshi fails to understand that "humanity is descended from the *kami*, not created by them,"[95] so by killing the *kami*, they kill a piece of themselves in the process.

Because we can't fit Eboshi into an absolute category of good or evil, it's equally difficult to label her actions as good and bad. Toward the outcasts—the former prostitutes and lepers—she exhibits compassion and kindness, but only when it suits her. She isn't entirely compassionate, because, as we've said, she refuses to retrieve those who have been injured during the wolf attack and, later, refuses to return to Iron Town when it's under attack. "I've done all I can for the women," she says. "They can defend themselves." If we look at her actions from a Buddhist perspective, we would say that although she's trying to help others, she's going about in the wrong way. The Eightfold Path encourages us to have "right livelihood," which means one that doesn't promote violence, intoxication, or sexual misconduct. It also tells us to exhibit "right thought" and "right action," which means, among other things, being free of harmful thoughts and not engaging in harmful acts. Eboshi could create any number of jobs that would help her subjects, particularly ones that wouldn't lead to destruction, but she doesn't. Her intention is inherently wrong. She admits that she wants to "take over the world," thus demonstrating false belief in an "I," and she believes that she can accomplish her goals through force. She's proud that these new guns can destroy the samurai, whose job it is to maintain law and order, and the gods, which, if honored, result in health, social harmony, and prosperity. In essence, her violent actions will usher in chaos and suffering, a fact that doesn't bother her. For example, when Ashitaka shows her his arm, saying, "Look on this! It is the form of the hate within me! It rots my flesh and summons my death! Do not make the hate grow!" Eboshi ignores him and threatens more violence, saying, "Enough talk of your curse. I'll cut that arm off."

At some point during Ashitaka's stay in Iron Town, San attacks. Her goal is to kill Eboshi, whom she finally engages in a knife battle. As a guardian of peace, Ashitaka tries to stop them, but when neither woman will back down, he knocks them both out, giving Eboshi to her people and throwing San over his shoulders. Angered at his treatment of Eboshi, one of the female ironworkers raises a gun at him and, accidentally, shoots him in his chest. And thus, the cycle of violence continues. But Ashitaka doesn't die. Instead, he walks toward the front gate, still carrying San and leaving behind him pools of blood. In essence, *Princess Mononoke* demonstrates that, as Gandhi said, "An eye for an eye makes the whole world blind."

Ashitaka is one of only a few voices of sanity in this anger-afflicted world. And even though he is under siege by a demon, he maintains his humanity. For instance, the fact that someone injured him critically at Iron Town doesn't prevent him from offering his thanks to them as he leaves. The term *kansha*, or thanksgiving, is widely used by the Japanese, especially in terms of Shinto. People are thankful not only to humans but also to the invisible powers that bless them.[96] Furthermore, when San wakes up outside of Iron Town, she tries to kill Ashitaka, even putting a sword to his throat. But he doesn't return

words of anger or actions of violence; instead, he presents to her a face of loving kindness, telling her that that he wants her to live and that "she's beautiful." His words have a profound effect on San, and she is, in essence,
"neutralized." As Thich Nhat Hanh explains, the best way that one can combat violence is to become nonviolent, "So that when a situation presents itself,
we will not create more suffering. To practice nonviolence, we need gentle-
ness, loving kindness, compassion, joy and equanimity directed to our bodies,
our feelings, and other people."[97]

Nature itself is seen as restorative in *Princess Mononoke*. San knows that the
only way to heal Ashitaka is by calling the Deer God, and she does this by cutting a small tree—several *kodama* appear around the cut stem and stare at it—
and planting it on a sacred island. She then leaves Ashitaka alone. As night
falls, the Deer God, in its Nightwalker guise, appears in the sky and strides
across the landscape. The heads of the *kodama*, who are at the top of the trees,
shake violently the closer it comes. As the transformation takes place, a great
wind begins to violently shake the trees. (The *kodama* seem delighted to ride
the wave of undulating vegetation.) With each hoofed step the Deer God
makes, plants spring up and die; and when it appears over Ashitaka, we see
that it has a golden deer body and a red human-like face topped by antlers.
Under the water, Ashitaka's wound bleeds heavily. It stops, though, as soon as
the Deer God "kisses" it. When Ashitaka wakes up, he's amazed to discover
that his wound is gone; however, he's still cursed.

Because humans and the *kami* have a reciprocal relationship, in *Princess
Mononoke* the world of the *kami* increasingly reflects what's taking place in the
world of the humans. The gods are becoming more aggressive, violent, and
"stupid," which makes sense since "deities seem to be ethically indifferent," de-
riving their potential from contact with the living.[98] For example, the apes,
which come every day to replant the trees to no avail, ask San to give them "the
man" so that they can eat him and absorb his strength. Horrified, San tells
them that this act of cannibalism won't help their situation; it will only transform them into something else. The warmongering boars are the best example of the *kami*'s ever increasing "blindness." They have traveled a long way,
they explain, to kill the humans for the Deer God. But when they learn that
the Deer God has healed Ashitaka, they are enraged, demanding to know why
their own Nago wasn't spared. Moro explains that "the Deer God gives life and
takes it away. Have you boars forgotten even that?" The boars reply, "No! You

begged the Deer God for him. You did not beg for Nago!" Moro explains that Nago "feared death. . . . I, like him, . . . carry within me a poisoned human stone. Nago fled. I remain, and contemplate my death." Tearful to learn this, San begs Moro to see the Deer God. "I have lived long enough, San. The Deer God will take my life." "No, mother! You've protected the Deer God!" The boars chime in, "We are not fooled! Nago was beautiful and strong. Our brother would not run! You wolves ate him." As the situation escalates, Ashitaka says, "Hear me, O wild mountain gods, it was I who killed Nago . . . I came to this land to ask the Deer God to lift this curse. He healed my wound, but the scar remains. I must suffer until the curse destroys me." The attitude that Moro and Ashitaka exhibit toward death is a quintessentially Buddhist one. Since death is inevitable and can strike at any moment, we need to be prepared, usually, as Moro says, by contemplating it. Interestingly enough, the *Code of the Samurai* taught that when one kept death in the mind, one would "fulfill the ways of loyalty and familial duty . . . avoid myriad evils and calamities . . . be physically sound and healthy . . . live a long life." One would also improve one's character and cause one's virtue to grow.[99] When we assume that our stay in this world will last, we become trapped by the three poisons, becoming desirous, wanting what others have, picking fights, and engaging in futile arguments. We see evidence of this throughout *Princess Mononoke*.

Toward the end of the film, Ashitaka asks Moro, "Can't humans and the forest live together in peace? Can't this be stopped?" And then he poses a similar question to Eboshi, "Can't the forest and ironworks live together?" Perhaps, the film says, but not as long as people see through clouded eyes, ones that are blinded by ego, anger, greed, and ignorance. For instance, in her last ignorant bid for power, Eboshi shoots the Deer God while it's walking across the sacred lake; it's trying to reach the dying boar leader, Okkoto. When the first bullet hits, the Deer God begins to sink, but it revives and starts walking again. "Eboshi," shouts Ashitaka, "your enemy is not the Deer God!" The Deer God finally reaches the boar leader and kisses him on the nose. The boar and Moro fall over dead. As the Deer God transforms into the Nightwalker, Eboshi tells everyone to watch closely, because "This is how you kill a god who is also the god of death." Despite Ashitaka's efforts to stop her, Eboshi manages to shoot the Deer God in the neck, thereby severing his head from his body. Immediately, a black jelly-like substance issues from the Deer God's neck wound, killing everything it touches, including the *kodama*, who fall from the trees

like rain. Again, Eboshi is unfazed. After picking up the head, she warns the
survivors not to touch the body: "It'll draw your life into it!" As Eboshi's "punishment," Moro's head comes alive and bites off her arm. As a testament to
Ashitaka's character, in spite of everything that's happened, he helps Eboshi.
After all, he says, he promised the women at Iron Town to bring her back.

Now in a desperate search for its head, the Nightwalker moves across the
landscape, destroying everything in its path. Eventually Ashitaka catches up to
the monk, telling him that he wants to give the head back. "Don't be stupid,"
the monk says. "The sun's coming up. Look . . . a brainless, swollen, life-
sucking god of death. When the sun comes up, he'll vanish. . . . Wanting all between heaven and hell is the human condition." Despite the monk's protests,
Ashitaka and San return the head to the Nightwalker, asking it to "be at peace."
Even with its head attached, the creature still falls to the earth, creating an
enormous wind that blows Iron Town away. The vegetation begins to grow
back. "I didn't know the Deer God made the flowers bloom," says one man,
clearly indicating how much the humans have become distanced from the
natural world. "Even if they grow back, they won't be the Deer God's woods,"
San says. "The Deer God is dead." Ashitaka corrects her: "The Deer God can't
die. He is life itself. Life and death are his to give and take. He's telling us we
should live." In the last frame, we see a *kodama* standing on a sprouting tree
branch. Despite the fact that several characters insist that "life is suffering" and
many characters are shown to be ignorant and violent, overall the film's outlook is positive. This might be because even though the world may be a place
of tragedy and suffering, Shinto is optimistic about the world.

In Hayao Miyazaki's films, especially *Nausicaa, Princess Mononoke, Spirited
Away,* and *Howl's Moving Castle,* self-sacrifice and love are shown to be the
necessary elements that can transform the world. In Shinto, several qualities
are stressed, but the most important is *makoto-no-kokoro.* The first part of this
word means truth, genuineness, or sincerity—being as one truly is. The second part of the term, *kokoro,* means having a "mindful heart." "If the person
is pure, he or she mysteriously mirrors that whole. To be genuinely receptive
to the presence of *kami* and responsive to it, to make full use of the holo-
graphic entry point, people must first be *makoto.* Only then can they recognize how *kami* is part of what they themselves are."[100] If anyone in *Princess
Mononoke* can be said to possess *makoto-no-kokoro,* it's Ashitaka. Not only
does he care deeply for others but he also helps them not because it benefits

him, but because that's who he is without any level of artifice. Furthermore, he stands in awe and reverence of nature and the *kami*, recognizing his responsibility to it. In Shinto, it is believed that human beings are born with the ability to live in harmony with the divine and with nature. Impurity, in its many forms, threatens this harmony; therefore, one must undergo periodic purification. "As the spirit is purified again and again, it can rise to the level of the divine as its spiritual sensitivity is heightened."[101]

Spirited Away (*Sen to Chihiro no Kamikakushi*) (2001)—Written and directed by Hayao Miyazaki. Running time: 125 min. Japanese. Rated PG for some scary moments. Genre: Animated. Won an Oscar for Best Animated Feature.

Summary: While Chihiro, a young girl, and her parents are driving to their new home, her father takes a detour. Lost, the family gets out of the car and finds a tunnel in front of them. Letting their curiosity get the better of them, they wander through it and, when on the other side, find themselves in an open field, dotted with buildings. Soon, tantalizing smells of food draw Chihiro's parents to a series of restaurants, where they find no workers but plenty of food to eat. Unable to resist themselves, her parents begin eating, urging Chihiro to do the same. She refuses, deciding instead to look around. As night falls, the once seemingly benign place begins to change. Shadowy figures emerge from the darkness and head to the bathhouse that looms above. Frightened, Chihiro runs back to find her parents, but they are no longer her parents. And to make matters worse, the trail back to the car is gone. Hope seems lost, until a mysterious young man appears and offers her guidance. Can Chihiro bolster her courage so that she can free herself and her family from this strange and magical landscape?

Spirited Away is undeniably one of Miyazaki's greatest achievements both in Japan and abroad. After its release, it became the highest grossing Japanese film in history, earning $230 million.[102] This highly lauded film garnered no fewer than 35 awards, including the 2003 Academy Award for Best Animated Feature. What's interesting about this is that *Spirited Away* is Miyazaki's most distinctively Japanese film, with most of its action taking place in a bathhouse reserved for the spirits. It's well-noted that Sachiko Kashiwaba's 1995 story *Kirino Mukouno Fushigina Machi* (*The Mysterious*

Town behind the Fog) inspired early drafts of *Spirited Away*.[103] However, as Miyazaki explained, he was also drawing upon a longer Japanese folk tradition: "I would prefer to say that [*Spirited Away*] is rather a direct descendant of *Suzume no Oyado*[104] (*The Sparrows' Inn*—a trap in which sparrows lure people to food and pleasant surroundings) or *Nezumi no Goten* (*The Mouse's Castle*—similar to *The Sparrows' Inn*), which appear in Japanese folk tales. . . . We are often not aware of the rites, designs, and tales of the gods. It is true that 'Kachi-kachi Yama'[105] and 'Momotaro'[106] are no longer persuasive. However, I regret to say that it is a poor idea to push all the traditional things into a small folk-culture world. Surrounded by high technology and its flimsy devices, children are more and more losing their roots. We must inform them of the richness of our traditions."[107] Obviously, a film set in the world of the spirits is useful for exploring Shinto; however, because Miyazaki's film is culturally rich and complex, it also affords us the opportunity to talk about Confucianism and Buddhism.

As the film begins, it introduces us to the film's protagonist, Chihiro, a lazy, whiny 10-year-old who is afraid, sullen, and unappreciative of what she has. Her parents aren't much better, though. Her father is "audacious," "irresponsible," and "overly confident and optimistic";[108] her mother is a "no-nonsense, contemporary woman," who is "realistic and assertive." In fact, she's an unusual female character for Miyazaki in that unlike other women in his films, she's neither nurturing nor maternal. Instead she chides her daughter for being too clingy.[109] Chihiro's parents are more concerned about "things" than people—they probably typify Japan's increasingly materialistic culture—and have a false sense of security in their possessions. For instance, on the way to their new house, Chihiro's father takes a "shortcut" on a dirt road. He's not worried about getting lost or stuck because he has a "four-wheel drive." (The car is a gray Audi.) Later, when they sit down to eat, the parents explain that they will pay later. "Don't worry, you've got Daddy here," he tells Chihiro. "I've got credit cards and cash."

If we view Chihiro's parents from a Confucian standpoint, we would say that they aren't very good role models. They are self-centered, blind to their situation, greedy, impetuous, and disrespectful to the spirits. Furthermore, they don't think of the consequences of their actions. All of these qualities run counter to what Confucius advises in the Analects, book 16, chapter 10: "The superior man has nine wishes. In seeing, he wishes to see clearly. In hearing, he wishes to hear distinctly. In his expression, he wishes to be warm. In his appearance, he wishes to be respectful. In his speech, he wishes to be sincere. In handling affairs, he wishes to be serious. When in doubt, he wishes to ask. When he is angry, he wishes to think of the resultant difficulties. And when he sees an opportunity for gain, he wishes to think of righteousness."

Another character who chooses money and possessions over her child is Yubaba, the large-headed, jewelry-wearing proprietress of the bathhouse Aburaya. She never exhibits *ren* toward her employees and spends much of her time counting her bags of money and jewels. For her, nothing matters but "the bottom line." She is nice to her customers, but only because she can get something from them. If they didn't have money, she wouldn't hesitate to throw them out or refuse them service. Even though she claims to love her enormous and grotesque baby, she never spends any time with him. Instead, she keeps him a veritable prisoner in his pillow-filled chamber, lying to him that if he ventures outside of the room, he'll be exposed to germs that will make him sick. Furthermore, later in the film, the baby and the Yu-Bird, a crow that has Yubaba's head, are transformed into a mouse and a tiny bird. Yubaba's three-headed companions, Kashira, are also transformed, into her baby. Even though she "cares" for all of these beings, Yubaba fails to "recognize" any of them in their transformed state. For instance, Chihiro is carrying the mouse on her shoulder, which repulses Yubaba. "He doesn't look familiar?" Chihiro asks. "Familiar. Don't be stupid," Yubaba replies. Later, Haku tells her that she still hasn't noticed that something precious has been replaced. Angry at his impertinence, she glances at her "baby," who is shoveling candy into its mouth. It is only after the baby turns back into the three heads that she realizes her child is gone. She's as "blind" as Chihiro's parents. All three of them do more damage to their children than good by spoiling them.

One of the themes of *Spirited Away* is how greed begets greed, or how greed corrupts. A Buddhist would interpret this as how clinging invariably leads to suffering. In the case of Chihiro's parents, because of their gluttony, they are transformed into their real selves—pigs. This might not seem too awful until we learn that they are being prepared for slaughter. The most scathing example of greed's corrupting force takes place in the bathhouse. Chihiro allows No Face, a rather unusual and typically silent character, to enter, thinking that he's a customer. Once inside, he begins tantalizing the various workers with gold nuggets. His first victim is Little Green Frog, whom he swallows. Interestingly enough, with the greedy frog inside him, No Face gets his voice. He also develops an insatiable hunger, and he eats everything as soon as it is prepared for him. As long as the money keeps coming, the employees cater to his every need. As the assistant manager sings, "Welcome the rich man. He's hard for you to miss. His butt keeps getting bigger so there's plenty there to kiss. Everyone bow down." Chihiro is the only person unaffected by No Face's riches. When he tries to hand her some gold, she says, "I don't want any. But thanks. . . . I'm sorry but I'm in a really big hurry." She is more concerned with helping her friend, Haku, than filling her pockets. Ironically, at the end of the film the gold turns to dirt, revealing its "true worth."

If Yubaba and Chihiro's parents are "bad" role models, then who are the "good" ones? Haku, Kamaji, and Lin all take Chihiro under their respective "wings" and, by setting proper examples, help Chihiro to transform herself. From the first time we meet Haku, he exhibits *ren*, which embodies loyalty and reciprocity or "not doing unto others what you wouldn't want them to do unto you." As her "master," he watches over and protects her. As a fellow human, he has empathy for her and makes every effort to help her, even though by doing these things he endangers his life. He is, after all, under the control of Yubaba, who doesn't suffer fools or insubordination. For example, he tells Chihiro how she can stay in the spirit world, gives her food so that she doesn't disappear, and, to buoy her spirits, he even takes her to see her parents. He's also loyal, sincere, and upright. And, according to Chihiro herself, he's "a good friend."

Even though Kamaji, the boiler room attendant, seems abrasive when we first meet him, he is capable of human-heartedness. In fact, he gives Chihiro his train tickets, a very rare commodity indeed; he claims that he's been saving them for 40 years. Lin, Chihiro's "boss," is probably the least important role model, because she doesn't fully exhibit Confucian virtues. Her biggest fault is her susceptibility to feelings of greed. When No Name is dispensing gold, she urges Chihiro to come and get some. Remember that, in the Analects (4:16), Confucius said, "The superior man understands righteousness; the inferior man understands profit." Lin may have some faults, but she does teach Chihiro manners, something the girl apparently hadn't learned from her own mother. For example, when Chihiro and Lin leave the boiler room and head for Yubaba's chamber, Lin reminds the girl to say "Yes, ma'am" and "Thank you."

Confucius stressed the need for role models, and in (7:21) of the Analects, he said, "When walking in a party of three, I always have teachers. I can select the good qualities of the one for imitation, and the bad ones of the other and correct them in myself." Thanks to Haku, Kamaji, Lin, and many others, Chihiro, by the end of the film, has gone from being a selfish, lazy, and ill-mannered child to being a veritable *junzi*; she is someone who exhibits loyalty, reciprocity, wisdom, courage, righteousness, filial piety, and faithfulness. The greatest lesson that she learned from Haku is to do what is right, no matter what the consequences, even if it means giving up one's life. In *Spirited Away*, we see her do this at least twice. The first time is when Haku, in his dragon form, has been attacked by paper planes, and he's bleeding profusely. Instead of joining Lin in her pursuit of riches, Chihiro endangers her life to help her wounded friend. After she rescues him from Zeniba, Yubaba's identical sister, Chihiro fears that he's going to bleed to death. Acting selflessly, Chihiro saves him by feeding him half of the River Spirit's gift. Because she was saving this for her parents, hoping it would transform them back to human form, this is the ultimate sacrifice. If that isn't enough, she decides that she will travel to Zeniba's home and try to give back the golden seal that Haku has "stolen" and apologize for him. Upon hearing this, even Kamaji is perplexed. He scratches his head and asks, "You'd go to Zeniba's. . . . It might help but she's one dangerous witch." Undeterred, Chihiro responds with "Haku helped me before. . . . Now I want to help him." At this point in the film, Chihiro doesn't realize how true this statement is. Toward the end of the film she learns that when she was much younger, Haku, then a river spirit, saved her from drowning.

The second time that Chihiro does what's right regardless of the consequences is in the bathhouse. Thinking that he's a customer, Chihiro leaves the door open for No-Face and invites him in. Unfortunately, once inside, he becomes destructive, eating several people and demanding more and more food. He's lonely, he says, and demanding companionship, asks for Sen. Even though she knows that she might be devoured, Chihiro takes responsibility for her actions, and goes to him. "If you want to eat me, eat this first," she says. "I was saving this for my parents, but I think you better have it." She puts the last remaining section of the River Spirit's gift in No-Face's mouth. He doesn't like it, but the pill works its magic, and No-Name is returned to his old self. Harboring no ill feelings toward him, Chihiro lets him tag along on the rest of her journey.

What's particularly interesting about *Spirited Away* is that when Chihiro reaches Zeniba, the old woman gives her a talisman for protection, but she doesn't wave a magic wand to make everything better. Instead, she simply says, "I'm sorry [Yubaba] turned your parents into pigs, but there's nothing I can do. It's just the way things are. You'll have to help your parents and Haku on your own." This echoes what Buddha said in the *Dhammapada* (12.160): "Oneself, indeed, is one's own protector. What other protector could there be? With self-control one gains a protector hard to obtain" and (12.165) "Evil is done by oneself alone; by oneself is one defiled. Evil is avoided by oneself; by oneself alone is one purified. Purity and impurity depend on oneself; no one can purify another." In short, perhaps others can point a person to the door, but essentially, it's up to the individual to walk through.

Confucius taught students irrespective of their class, taking from them whatever payment they could afford. In (17:2) of the Analects, he said that "by nature men are pretty much alike, it is learning and practice that sets them apart." Chihiro would probably agree with these statements, because she treats everyone equally, from her parents to a highly objectionable Stink Spirit. When the latter creature comes into the bathhouse, and everyone is trying his or her best to avoid him, Chihiro puts everything aside to help him. She uses the best herbal tokens to ensure that he gets a good soaking, and when she realizes that he has a "thorn in his side," she doubles her efforts to help him. Her compassion overtakes her self-concern. In this and other examples, we see that not only is Chihiro a model Confucian, but she also embodies the Shinto-inspired characteristic called *makoto*, which embodies truthfulness, pure heartedness, and honesty.[110]

As we've seen in *My Neighbor Totoro*, children are thought to be much more sensitive to the world of the spirits, and this continues in *Spirited Away*. As Chihiro's parents are driving to their new home, they pass by an ancient tree that has an old Shinto *torii* leaning against it and, around its base, are many stone shrines. To the observant viewer, these indicate that the characters are entering sacred space. But instead of recognizing and honoring these Shinto symbols, her parents look beyond them to the residential development above. Chihiro, on the other hand, stares at them wide-eyed, and even asks her mother about the "little houses." A bit later as they are racing down the path, Chihiro notices a stone spirit in the woods. An identical one, which has one face looking forward and one looking backwards, stops their car in front of a "strange building." A plaque on the top of it contains characters for hot water, shops, and bath.[111]

The father, and then Chihiro, get out of the car and stand at the entrance, staring down the long, dark tunnel. When the wind begins to blow—a divine wind, perhaps—we realize that the characters are standing at the border between the sacred and the profane. Naturally, Chihiro's father has no fear and wants to venture inside. Chihiro, on the other hand, recognizes that something isn't right: "It's creepy, Daddy, let's go back," she says, and runs back toward the car. Her parents, however, continue on, telling her to wait in the car. Terrified of the stone guardian standing next to her, she reluctantly joins them. Emerging from the tunnel, they find themselves in a churchlike sanctuary, complete with a font, a stained-glass window,[112] and a vaulted ceiling reminiscent of a Gothic cathedral. Again, this informs us that we are in sacred space. Once outside, a breeze blows across the verdant landscape dotted by houses and more guardian stone spirits. Chihiro's father believes this place to be an abandoned theme park, saying that "they built so many in the early '90s, but they all went down with the economy." Chihiro isn't convinced, and she begs her parents once again to go back. Another large gust of wind hits Chihiro. Her parents ignore it and press forward.

Just as Chihiro's parents are crossing a small brook, her father sniffs the air. They follow it into a dilapidated row of restaurants. Strange signs appear above the surprisingly lopsided buildings that read salt, eyes, lips, cigarettes, meat, and bone. Except for Chihiro, no one seems to be bothered by this "unnatural" atmosphere. The father is too concerned about his stomach; he's starving. He finally finds what he is looking for: a strangely empty al fresco restaurant where mounds of freshly made food[113] await hungry customers. The parents immediately sit down and begin eating, urging Chihiro to do the same. But she refuses, saying, "Let's go! They're gonna be mad at us." After piling three plates with all sorts of meat dishes, her father immediately begins shoveling the food into his mouth with both hands. Chihiro yells at them, but they ignore her.

She leaves them and begins to explore the grounds. Stopping at a vermillion-colored lantern, she looks up to see an enormous bathhouse with smoke billowing from its chimney. "Weird," she says and ventures onto a bridge, where she meets Haku, a boy who yells, "You're not allowed here. Go back! It's almost night! Leave before it gets dark." As if on cue, the lanterns turn on and darkness descends. Now Haku is frantic, and he urges Chihiro to run. He'll distract them, he says. As she rushes back to her parents, we see shadowy figures materialize in the restaurants. When she reaches her mother and father, she realizes that it's too late. Their gluttony, and their violation of consuming food intended for the spirits, has transformed them into pigs. They get their "just desserts," says Yubaba. As her parents continue to act like pigs, they forget what it's like to be human. Buddhism states that as one thinks, one becomes. As it says in the *Dhammapada*, "with dripping drops of water even a water jug is filled. Little by little a fool is filled with evil" (8.121).

Chihiro attempts to return to the car, but the brook has since become a lake. She's trapped, literally *kamikakushi*, which in Japanese folklore means something like "taken away by the spirits" or "spirited away," hence the English translation. Terrified, Chihiro keeps telling herself to wake up: "It's just a dream. Go away, disappear. Disappear." Again, as if on command, her body becomes opaque. At this point, the film begins posing some very Buddhist questions, such as What is the self? Is it stable? As Cavallaro says, this moment (and others) is an "implicit debunking of the liberal humanist faith in the existence of a stable self."[114] "Miyazaki intimates that the notion of a unified identity is no more than a vapid humanist fantasy fuelled by the unwarranted claims of anthropomorphism. Names change; faces and forms change."[115] As the film continues, we learn that no one is really what he or she seems. Haku is the best example of this. At first, he seems threatening; he shouts at Chihiro to go away. Then we see him taking care of her, feeding her, and giving her helpful advice, and he seems to be a compassionate person. Doubt is raised again when other characters refer to his greed, and we learn that he has stolen Zeniba's gold seal. Our opinion changes once again when we discover that Yubaba put a black slug in him to control him. Haku's form also changes throughout the film. Initially, he's a mysterious youth. By the middle of the film, we learn that he can transform himself into a white dragon. And finally, at the end, we discover his true identity. He isn't a boy at all; he is the spirit of the now "extinct" Kohaku River. Reflecting the nonduality present in Asian thought, Miyazaki never presents his characters in black-and-white terms. Overall, Haku might be a "good" character; however, he also has his "dark" side.[116]

Once Chihiro discovers that she's entered the world of the spirits, she is informed that she has to follow certain rules or horrible things will happen. First of all, she has to get a job from Kamaji. If she doesn't, Yubaba will turn her into an animal. The lesson here is that by working, Chihiro will become independent and responsible. Second, if she wants to work, she must sign a contract, giving Yubaba control over her "elaborate" name. The old sorceress does this by taking away three of the four characters that comprise it, leaving behind one. "From now on, you'll be Sen," Yubaba says. Later on, Haku advises Chihiro to remember her name, because if Yubaba steals it, she'll never find her way home. And this is why Haku can't leave, why he's under Yubaba's control. Incidentally, both Sen and the Chi from Chihiro are alternate pronunciations for the same character, meaning 1,000, a number that indicates intensity and power for the Japanese.[117] Hiro, on the other hand, means "fathom" in the nautical sense. As Hayao Miyazaki explains, "In these days, words are thought to be light and unimportant like bubbles, and no more than the reflection of a vacuous reality. It is still true that words can be powerful. The fact is, however, that powerless words are proliferating unnecessarily. To take a name away from a person is an attempt to keep [him or her] under perfect control. Sen shuddered when she realized that she was beginning to forget her own name. And besides, every time she goes to see her parents at the pigpen, she becomes used to seeing her parents as pigs. In the world where Yubaba rules, people must always live among dangers which might swallow them up."[118] If we remember, Shinto is also concerned with language; therefore, it's important that Japanese characters are written precisely and that the prayers are said correctly.

Just what inhabits this film's spirit world? The first ones to emerge from the ferry are "Kasuga" spirits,[119] beings who wear red robes, a black topknot, and a Noh-like mask. Some of the other spirits seen throughout the film are *kawa no kami* (river spirit), *oku sare-sama* (the stink spirit), *oshira-sama* (a daikon radish spirit), *ootori-sama* (bird spirits), *ushioni* (a bull-like spirit), and *kaonashi* (no-face).[120] One being wears a sheet covered with *omamori* and has a bucket on his head. Another one has a straw head that is cinched with a berry-producing plant from which a zigzagged paper streamer hangs. The *susuwatari*, the animated dust sprites from *My Neighbor Totoro*, also make an appearance. They help Kamaji, the spider-like boiler man, fuel the fires. As far as iconography is concerned, it's interesting that the *ootori-sama* look surprisingly like Totoro, for they too have rotund, oblong-shaped bodies and they wear a lotus leaf on their heads. In another scene, when the Ushioni get into an elevator, one is seen to have a white sheet over his mouth. On it is a picture of a *torii*.

With regard to *Spirited Away*, we have talked about Shinto primarily in terms of the presence of spirits, but purification rites are another important aspect of the religion, and what better place is there to remove impurity than in a bathhouse? To understand why this film takes place where it does, we must understand what bathing means to the Japanese. Until the late 1960s, the average person couldn't afford a bath in his or her home. Therefore, to get clean, everyone visited the neighborhood bathhouse (*sento*).[121] Today, even though people might have a bath in their homes, for many, community bathing is still common. Furthermore, "Japanese people . . . will visit hot springs in groups two to three times a year," realizing that together, they can learn more about each other.[122] In general, the Japanese have a different attitude toward bathing than do their Western counterparts. In the West, people take a bath to clean themselves, perhaps to unwind, but with increasingly busy schedules, more and more people take a quick shower. In Japan, getting clean is the primary goal, but there is another dimension to bathing. It's also about "family and community, the washing of each other's backs after bathing; about time to be alone and contemplative—time to watch the moon rise above the garden. . . . The Japanese make bathing a ritual—a prescribed order of rinsing, washing, and soaking that is passed down from one generation to the next, becoming an integral part of the society at large."[123]

There are four steps to bathing Japanese-style. After the person disrobes in the *datsuiba* (changing room), he or she steps into a washing area next to the bathtub. Sitting down on a stool, the individual scoops water from the tub and pours it over himself or herself several times. Once all of the dirt and grime is removed, the person lowers himself or herself into the bath, staying between 3 and 15 minutes, depending on the season. Stepping once again into the washing area and sitting on the stool, the person scrubs the body vigorously, starting with the hair and working downwards. Next, it's time to rinse again, and it's back into the bath to soak. Bathing can take a considerable amount of time, which isn't a concern for the Japanese. After all, they have a disparaging phrase for a short bath—*karasu no gyozui* or raven's bath.[124]

"Entering a bath in Japan is to enter another world. It is a place where one not only cleans the body but also cleanses the mind. Unlike Western bathrooms, Japanese bathing rooms are entirely separate from the toilet—they are independent spaces reserved only for the daily task of taking a bath, cleaning oneself, and relaxing."[125] Another major difference between Western and

Japanese ways of bathing is that in the West, one typically takes a shower or bath in the morning to wake up. In Japan, one takes a bath in the evening as a way to unwind after a long day. And this, undoubtedly, is why the bathhouse comes alive at night in *Spirited Away*. As Yubaba says, this is a place where "eight million gods can rest their weary bones." On a final note, the bathhouse in *Spirited Away* is based on a real place: "an inn at Dogo Hot Springs in Shikoku . . . parts of it are also based on Meguro Gajo-en private park and the Nikko Toshogu shrine."[126]

Hayao Miyazaki has admitted that *Spirited Away* is a film about remembering the past, because "a man without history, or a people that forgot its past will have no choice but to disappear, like a shimmer of light or to lay eggs endlessly as a hen and consumed."[127] However, he evokes the past as a way to move his viewers into the future. One way people can do this is to care about each other and work together as a community. And, again, the bathhouse is a powerful symbol of unity. Nowhere is this more evident in the film than during the purification sequence involving the stink spirit. After Chihiro notices that something is sticking out of the fetid being's side, everyone in the bathhouse comes together. Under the supervision of Yubaba, they throw a rope around the stink spirit, hold on tight, and pull. Those who don't help in the physical act still do their part, by cheering from above and waving Japanese fans. Everyone's efforts pay off, and all of the "detritus of modern life," including everything from a bicycle to a toilet seat, falls out, revealing the true face of their guest. This laughing river spirit is no longer oozing and slimy but wears "the face of the *okina* or old-man type of Noh mask." In a very Shinto-inspired statement, Hayao Miyazaki said of this sequence, "I really believe that the river gods of Japan are existing in that miserable, oppressed state. It is not only humans who are suffering on these Japanese islands."[128] Humans and *kami*, once related, share an important bond that modernity threatens. Perhaps with this film, Hayao Miyazaki hopes to reverse that.

Dreams (*Yume*, 1990)—Written and directed by Akira Kurosawa. Running time: 119 min. Japanese, French, English. Rated PG. Genre: Drama/Fantasy. Nominated for a Golden Globe.

One of Akira Kurosawa's most personal films, *Dreams* is comprised of eight short vignettes, including, in order, "Sunshine through the Rain," "The Peach

Orchard," "The Blizzard," "The Tunnel," "Crows," "Mount Fuji in Red," "The Weeping Demon," and "Village of the Watermills." For our purposes, not all of the segments will be useful; however, we will talk about three of these: the first two and the last one.

"Sunshine through the Rain" begins with a traditionally dressed boy—in a kimono and *obi* and wooden clogs (*geta*)—venturing into the rain. A woman tells him that foxes usually hold their wedding processions during this type of weather, "and they don't like anyone to see them. If you do, they'll be angry." Not listening to her, the boy wanders off into the nearby forest. The wind blows lightly, a frequent indicator that something "mysterious" is about to happen, and the rain continues to fall. Through the fog, we see, just as the woman said, a fox wedding procession. The boy hides behind a tree to watch, but he's soon discovered and he runs away. When he returns home, his mother chides him. She knows that he saw something that he shouldn't have, and therefore she can't let him in. "An angry fox came looking for you. He left this," she says before showing him a knife. "You're supposed to kill yourself. Go quickly and ask their forgiveness. Give the knife back and tell them how sorry you are." Since foxes don't usually forgive people, she tells him that he should be prepared to die. And until they do forgive him, she can't let him in. "But I don't know where they live," he says. "On days like this there are rainbows. Foxes live under the rainbows," she says, and then shuts and locks the door. With the knife in hand, the boy walks through a flower-filled field toward the rainbow. We never find out how the story ends.

Japanese folklore is replete with tales of foxes, and the earliest extant story is found in the *Nihon Ryoiki*, which dates to the eighth century C.E. In this tale, a man asks a woman to marry him. She agrees, and a little while later they have a child. Their peaceful life is later shattered when a barking puppy reveals the woman's true nature: she is a fox in human form.[129] Because his love for his wife is strong, the man asks her to come back every night so they can sleep together. This is why, the story tells us, all foxes bear her name, *Kitsune*, which means "come and sleep."[130] As we also learn from this story, foxes can change their shape, but this is only one of their many supernatural powers. They can also bewitch people, making them think that they see something that isn't there, and possess them. Characteristics found in someone who is fox possessed include the use of abusive language, longing to be outside, uncontrolled spending, crawling on all fours, destructive violence, and spitting. The possessed may also blurt out secrets.[131] Furthermore, "because of its qualities of independence and wildness, the fox is associated with the mystery and fundamental unruliness of nature. Strange happenings in nature are attributed to foxes and badgers: *rain from a sunny sky* [my emphasis], strange lights at night, rocks that emit sulfuric fumes, and even volcanic eruptions. What unites these phenomena is not that they are necessarily bad or violent, but unexpected and uncontrollable."[132] Foxes are seen as messengers of Inari, the protective *kami* of rice cultivation, and at his shrines, one finds a pair of foxes, usually wearing red bibs. Because stories exist in which foxes take revenge for any wrongdoings against them or Inari, people must assume the proper attitude toward them. "Even today, people are loath to move an Inari shrine for fear of the dire consequences."[133] Fried tofu is the most common offering left at Inari shrines, and it is believed that foxes enjoy this food.[134]

The film's second vignette, "The Peach Orchard," takes place during the Doll's Festival. A young, traditionally dressed boy takes a tray of food into his sister, who is joined by five of her friends; all are dressed in kimonos. They are sitting on the floor in front of a red tiered shelf on which are arranged various dolls. The boy asks his sister where her sixth friend has gone, but the girl denies having invited that many girls. Confused, the boy leaves the room, only to see the missing girl, who is dressed in light pink. She runs out of the house, and he follows her through the woods. He finally stops in front of a tiered hill, on which his sister's dolls have come to life. One of the males on the topmost tier announces that they have something to tell the boy, so "listen carefully." "We'll never go to your house again," says a woman. "Why not?" the boy asks. "Because your family cut down all the peach trees in this orchard. [And] Doll Day is for the peach blossoms . . . to celebrate their arrival. We dolls personify the peach tree. We are the spirits of the trees, the life of the blossoms. How can you celebrate with these trees cut down? Those vanished trees are weeping in their sorrow." The boy cries. One of the voices rebukes him: "Don't cry. Tears won't help." Another voice comes to his defense: "This child cried when they cut down our trees. He even tried to stop them." Yet another voice chimes in: "Yes, because he likes peaches." Everyone laughs. "No," the boy shouts. "Peaches can be bought. But where can you buy a whole orchard in bloom? I love this orchard and the peach trees that grew there." The boy cries again. One of the dolls says, "He is a good boy. We will allow him to see our peach orchard in bloom once more." After the dolls perform a slow ritual dance, they turn into trees in full bloom. Eventually, they return to their true nature: branchless trees. Finally, the girl the boy followed becomes a small, flower-filled tree.

This vignette is useful for a number of reasons. First, it exposes us to the iconography of the *Hina Matsuri* or Doll's Festival, which takes place on the third day of the third month. As it shows in the vignette, households display their dolls (*hina ningyou* or *ohina-sama*), dressed in Heian-era (794–1185 C.E.) costumes, on a five- or seven-tiered, red cloth-covered altar. The dolls, typically handed down from mother to daughter, are dedicated to the peach blossoms, which is why this day is also called *Momo no Sekku*, or Festival of the Peach. Offerings of "freshly made rice cakes (*mochi*), either flavored with a wild herb or colored and cut into festive diamond shapes," white sake, steamed buns filled with sweet bean paste, and other pink, white, or green sweet treats are given to the *hina* dolls.[135] The *Hina Matsuri* can be traced to the late 17th century; however, the practice of using dolls for a ritual pur-pose—as objects of exorcism—dates back much earlier. Originally, the dolls, which were constructed of straw, were used in a purification ritual. People transferred their impurities to the dolls, either by breathing on the dolls or by rubbing them on one's body, and then set the dolls adrift on the water.[136] This tradition continues in some parts of Japan. The modern *Hina Matsuri* is as-sociated with establishing good fortune, health, and marriage for one's daugh-ter.

Today, dolls are no longer made of straw or paper but are usually con-structed of wood covered by *gofun*, which comes from ground sea shells. Typ-ical sets consist of 15 brightly dressed dolls. If displayed on a five-tier altar, they are arranged, from top down, in a particular way. On the top shelf, one will always find the emperor and the empress; they are usually seated. The em-peror typically wears a black-lacquered imperial hat, which sports a large *fan-ion* or banner (*usu-bitai*). The empress often wears a colorful, multilayered robe (*juunihitoe*). Behind them is a folding screen (*byoubu*); they may be flanked by lanterns. The second tier of the altar houses the ladies of the court (*sannin-kanjo*). Their purpose is to serve the imperial rulers. On the third tier are found the male court musicians (*gonin-bayashi*). The ministers are next, and they usually flank trays of food. Finally, on the fifth and final tier, we find guards or servants. If there are more than five steps, additional items, such as furniture, dishes, and so forth will occupy these lower areas.[137]

On another level this vignette is really about the nature of the *kami*. Although, in this case, they appear to be dolls come to life, in reality, they are as they say, the "spirits" of the trees, the life of the peach blossoms. If someone cuts down the trees, the *kami* leave. This demonstrates the intimate connection that exists between nature and the *kami*, and sadly, the boy's parents have forgotten this. To some degree, this segment highlights the problem of modernization. We may still practice rituals but the meaning behind them is slowly disappearing. If we cut down all of the trees, what is the purpose of the *Hina Matsuri*? The segment offers hope, though. The boy loved the trees and fought for them. Now that he's experienced the *kami*, will he, as he grows older, replant them? Also, not all of the trees were destroyed—one remains. With this vignette, Akira Kurosawa demonstrates nostalgia for a past when people lived in harmony with nature and respected and honored the *kami*. Perhaps, like Hayao Miyazaki, Kurosawa is trying to inspire people to rekindle that connection.

Village of the Watermills, the film's final vignette, also demonstrates the director's concern for the environment. It begins with a man wandering into a picturesque riverside village that, it is said, has no name. Here he meets a 103-year-old man who is constructing a watermill. The outsider poses to him a number of questions, such as why the villagers don't have such modern conveniences as electricity and tractors. If they had lights, the old man says, we couldn't see the stars. After all, who would want the night to be as bright as day? And what use do they have of tractors? They have horses and cows. The young man asks, What do you used for fuel? Firewood, the man says, "We don't like chopping down trees—enough fall down by themselves. We cut them up and use them as firewood." Charcoal and cow dung are good, too, the old man adds: "We try to live the way man used to. That's the natural way of life. People today have forgotten that they're really just a part of nature. Yet, they destroy the nature on which our lives depend. They always think they can make it better . . . most don't understand nature. They only invent things that in the end make people unhappy. . . . They don't know it, but they're losing nature. They don't see that they're going to perish. The most important things for humans are clean air and clean water, and the trees and grass that produce them."

As we listen to the elderly man's philosophy of life, especially his support of *wu-wei*, we immediately recognize Daoist sentiments. He informs us that he and his fellow villagers live in accordance with nature not against it; they do what comes naturally. They don't cut down trees but pick up ones that fall; they use cow and horse dung, because that's already a ready-made fuel source. As the Daodejing says, "The Dao does nothing, yet through it everything is done,"[138] and that "the sage applies himself to non-action, moves without speaking, creates the 10,000 things without hindrance, lives, but does not possess."[139] Chapter 80 of the Daodejing describes the ideal society as being a small settlement with few inhabitants. Even though they have labor-saving implements, they don't use them. They are content with whatever food and clothes they have. As scholar Benjamin Schwartz explains, this isn't a town from the "primeval past," but is a place where technology exists; people simply don't feel a need to use it. It is rejected. "The whole idea is to reduce to a minimum all the projects of civilization, making it possible for the people to sink back into the simple life, in which they remain so self-sufficiently contented with their essential daily nonaction routines that they require no outside stimulation."[140] The people in *Village of the Watermills* live this ideal by returning to the simplicity of the Dao.

Water is an important symbol in this vignette for a number of reasons. On an aesthetic level, it produces the beautiful flowers that appear on the village's river banks. On a practical level, it feeds and nourishes the people living there. Without water, people will, as the elderly man says, die. Daoism and Shinto teach that we are a part of nature, and that we must live in harmony with it. According to Daoism, "The cosmos is a sacred place, fundamentally interrelated, holy, and complete. Self-creating and self-sustaining, the cosmos evolves and decays in a ceaseless pattern, and all individual manifestations within it are structured according to this pattern."[141] The Daodejing also praises water, saying in chapter 8 that it is "best to be like water; which benefits the 10,000 things and does not compete." Furthermore, chapter 78 says that "Nothing in the world is softer and weaker than water but nothing is superior to it in overcoming the hard and strong; weakness overcomes strength and softness overcomes hardness. Everyone knows this, and no one practices it."[142] How does water overcome hardness? All we have to do is place a rock in the middle of a stream to see how this happens. It may take decades or centuries, but the continual flow of water over its hard substance will cause it to wear away.

This vignette ends with an elderly woman's funeral, but it isn't presented as a solemn occasion. Several villagers carry her coffin, while others, wearing hats with colorful streamers, dance. A brass band plays a joyful tune. Children throw flowers. Eventually the elderly man, now dressed in orange, picks up some bells and some flowers, and joins the procession. Inspired by what he has seen, the outsider, before leaving the village, picks a few flowers and puts them on a stone, where it's said that long ago an outsider died and was buried under the rock. Death isn't feared, because the Daoist sage in the Daodejing meets it with equanimity. "He accepts his destiny to live and his destiny to die. Despite the appreciation of life"—the elderly man in this vignette rejoices that "it's good to be alive. It's exciting"—"The Daodejing at one point even states that 'the reason I have trouble is that I have a body. When I no longer have a body, what trouble have I?'"[143]

On a final note, it's no surprise that the elderly man is vibrant and acts much younger than his 103 years. Or that the recently deceased woman in this story lived to be 99 years old. In Daoism, it is believed that "Human beings have been given a proper 'mandate' (ming) to prosper and live long. . . . There are, however, obstacles which may jeopardize one's natural longevity." For instance, if the "body is destroyed, the 'five spirits' disperse. . . . For this reason, the body must be well taken care of, and the conditions, under which the vital essence may be adversely influenced, must be clearly identified."[144] So how does one achieve longevity? The best way, says Ho-shang-kung, a Daoist writer of commentaries who lived during the second century C.E., is to refrain from avarice and lechery. One should also abide in wu-wei, which this writer defines as "diminishing one's desires." Also important are being natural and humble.[145] If we turn our attention back to the elderly man in Village of the Watermills, we see that he doesn't crave things he doesn't need; he's satisfied with his life. He lives in accordance with nature, waking up when it's light and going to bed when it's dark. Finally, he works when he needs to, but also takes time to celebrate and enjoy life. His understanding of the Dao affords him a long and healthy life.

FOLK TRADITIONS

As we've seen, Shinto explains that the world is filled with 8 million kami. When Buddhism came to Japan in the sixth century C.E., this number increased significantly, resulting in a veritable "rush hour of gods."[146] Add all of this to popular tales of shape-shifting animals, and it's no wonder that Japanese folklore, legends, and myths abound with the exploits of ghosts, goblins, demons, and magical animals. Over the centuries, artists have depicted these beings in pen and ink, on woodblock prints, and in sculpture. Today, cinema has become the perfect medium for bringing these ghoulish stories to a wider audience. And, in fact, supernaturally themed films have proliferated to such an extent in Japan that within the past decade or so, critics have given them their own subgenre, J-Horror.

It may seem unusual for our discussion on religion and film to veer into the realm of horror; however, once we study these films, we begin to realize how much we can learn about Japanese culture, especially "popular" and "folk" religious traditions, from them. As scholars Michiko Iwasaka and Barre Toelken explain, "Folktales, legends, beliefs and the like probably persist because as they develop, they bring together a recognizable constellation of related beliefs and cultural traditions phrased in vivid, concrete detail."[147] These stories offer explanations of the unexplainable, reinforce social norms, and provide comfort. For instance, the "Japanese belief in benevolent gods has increased confidence in the future. Belief in punishing or malevolent powers has restrained people from deviating from the socio-cultural norms. The belief that all human beings can become respected ancestral spirits, and that some can even join the rank of gods, has encouraged the populace to respect their family members and their fellow beings. The belief that gods and ancestral spirits, if neglected and mistreated, may bring adverse and disastrous consequences . . . has cultivated . . . an understanding . . . of the otherwise unexplainable misfortunes of this world."[148] In this section we will discuss two films that venture into folk territory, *The Great Yokai War* and *The Locker.*

The Great Yokai War (*Yokai Daisenso*, 2005)—Based on a novel by Hiroshi Aramata. Screenplay by and directed by Takashi Miike. Running time: 124 min. Japanese. Rated PG-13 for fantasy violence and scary images. Genre: Adventure/Fantasy.

Summary: The vengeance-seeking Lord Kato Yasunori (Etsushi Toyokawa) and his white-haired accomplice Agi (Chiaki Kuriyama) have started a Yokai War and only a 10-year-old boy named Tadashi Ino (Ryunosuke Kamiki) and his sidekicks can stop them. This fantasy adventure aimed at children is populated by scrap-metal robot monsters and goblins from Japanese folklore.

Tadashi seems an unlikely hero. Because his parents are divorced, he and his mother have moved in with his often forgetful grandfather. His older sister lives with their father, and they keep in touch through phone calls. If this weren't bad enough, the scrawny preteen is the frequent target of school bullies. His life changes when he attends a local festival, and he's selected to be the Kirin Rider, which is the "guardian of peace and justice" in a time of darkness. His first task, he's told, is that he must venture to the Tengu Mountain and retrieve the Tengu sword. Not well-versed in mythology, he turns to his grandfather for answers. The elderly man explains that the Tengu is a goblin who grabs children. When he was felled by the Kirin Rider—the guardian spirit of the land—the Tengu swore allegiance to him. Now every year, the Kirin Rider must climb the mountain to get the Tengu sword from the goblin.

Acting upon what he's heard, Tadashi begins his mountainous ascent. After a while he comes upon a giant tree, where he's surprised to find a sign that says Tengu Cave. Scared, the boy runs away and, seeing a school bus, flags it down and climbs aboard. But this is no ordinary bus. Every manner of *yokai* appear on the outside, begging him to help them stop the Great Yokai War, which was started by Lord Kato and his sidekick, Agi. Together, this diabolical twosome are abducting all of the ancient Japanese spirits, throwing them into a cauldron with myriad other discarded objects, and, by using rage as the fuel, are transforming the spirits into machine soldiers in their bid to destroy Tokyo and "bury humanity in darkness." On the bus, Tadashi meets one of the many victims of this Yokai War, a wounded Sune-kosuri, or "sprite that rubs against your shin." When his new ferret-like friend recovers, Tadashi takes it with him on a journey to vanquish the growing menace. Along the way, they are joined by "reinforcements," including Kawahime, the River Princess (Mai Takahashi); Shojo, the red-faced Kirin Herald (Masaomi Kondo); and Kawataro, the River Sprite (Sadao Abe).

In Japan anything that is deemed "weird or grotesque" is referred to as *obake* or *bakemono*, literally "transforming thing," and the *yokai* fall under this designation. Literally, "bewitching apparition," *yokai* are themselves goblins, monsters, and ghouls.[149] The *Great Yokai War* introduces us to many of these traditional creatures, including the Tengu, Kappa, Rokurokubi, Ippon-datara, Shojo, and Kirin. As the film explains, the Tengu is a mountain-dwelling creature that looks like a human being with a long, sausage-like nose. It even dresses in human clothing, wearing the small black cap and pompommed sash of a *yamabushi*, which are mountain-dwelling ascetics. The difference is that the Tengu has wings and birdlike feet. "In literature, he is often depicted as hostile to Buddhism and Buddhist priests, and an abductor of children" because of his shape-shifting abilities.[150] In one collection of tales, translated by Royall Tyler, we find eight Tengu-related stories and in most of them this *yokai* is being mischievous to Buddhist monks, either posing as a Buddha or tricking a hermit with a vision of Amida Buddha. One, however, tells of how a Tengu lodged himself into the "womb of a great lady" so that he could become a monk on Mount Hiei.[151] Over time, this *yokai*'s destructive force was "downgraded to mere mischief, and they were even reputed to protect shrines and temples."[152]

With a shell on its back and a beaklike mouth, the Kappa might resemble a turtle, but it's considerably more malevolent. This scaly river monster is known for "dragging people under the water and then pulling their intestines out through their anuses."[153] On top of the kappa's head is a caplike plate that gives the creature its power. Also characteristic of his appearance are "bushy hair" and webbed toes and feet. Having such a terrifying reputation, it's no wonder that in the *Great Yokai War*, the first time that the young protagonist sees the green creature, he screams and tries to get away.

The Rokurokubi isn't a major character in the film, but it appears during one particularly surreal segment. The young hero wanders into a traditional Japanese house, where he finds a young woman reclining on a mat. At first she seems normal, but she eventually reveals herself to be anything but. As a Rokurokubi, she possesses a rubber-like neck that she weaves back and forth throughout the room. As it's explained, sometimes this condition is "brought about by a curse, and sometimes as a supernatural manifestation of the person's desire. The neck-stretching almost always happens at night . . . and the freed head may wander through the house" engaging in such behavior as "sucking the life energy out of people and animals and licking up the oil of *andon* lamps."[154]

During one fight scene between Tadashi and Agi, she breaks his Tengu sword with her whip. But all hope isn't lost. He just needs to find the furry, red-haired, bearlike Ippon-datara, who happens to be blacksmith to the *yokai*. One of his distinctive physical features is his tubelike body that ends in one very powerful leg. He uses it to fan the fires while he forges the strongest metal imaginable. Another red creature in the film is the Shojo, and he is depicted as having long, moplike hair and carrying a stick with paper streamers from it—a Shinto *harai-gushi*. According to the *Online Encyclopedia of Yokai and Bakemono*, he is also described as a ruddy-colored being with a mane of red hair, but there is no mention of his being the Kirin Herald. Instead, it says that these "drunken sea sprites" hail from China and enjoy drinking sake.[155]

Finally, the Kirin, which we don't see until the end of the film, is a mythical beast that is half deer and half dragon and is said to herald good fortune. It is claimed that the Kirin is so rare that it can only be seen once a millennium, to usher in a new era, or when a great leader is born. According to legends, a Kirin appeared at the birth of Confucius.[156] Interestingly enough, at the end of the film, we see an enormous *yokai matsuri*. As part of the celebration, one of the *yokai* brings a cooler full of the popular beer, Kirin Ichiban, which is made domestically by Anheuser-Busch. An adult journalist who has wandered into the festival opens a can and takes a few gulps. He immediately sees the *yokai*, who were previously invisible to him. The journalist drinks can after can of the beer, so that he can keep seeing the *yokai*, because, as the film tells us, as one gets older, a person loses his ability to see the "spirit world." As scholar Thomas P. Kasulis informs us, alcohol, especially sake, plays an important role in Japanese ritual. "The ancient myths and numerous folktales inform us that the *kami* deities are fond of sake and love parties. . . . [Furthermore] drinking sake does not necessarily mean being intoxicated in the sense of getting falling-down drunk. Alcoholic spirits are, after all, linked with spirituality."[157]

These *yokai* are just a few of the hundred or more that appear in the film. Glancing over crowd scenes, we can see a *bake-neko*, or a catlike creature dressed in a kimono, and a *yuki-onna*, which is an incredibly pale female who shows up when it snows. *Yuki-onna* often trick people so that they can bury their victims in the snow.[158] In another scene, we see an animated one-eyed umbrella that bounces around on its stem and sticks out its tongue. There's also a wall full of eyeballs; a walking water jar; a ceramic-headed effigy; an *abura-sumashi*, which is an "oil presser" that wears a straw cloak and has a purple, potato-shaped head; an *adzuki-arai*, the elusive and obsessive-compulsive adzuki bean washer; a *kamakiri*, which is known for sneaking up on people and cutting their hair; and a *zashiki-warashi*, which is a childlike spirit that inhabits old houses. Most of the iconography associated with these beings is "traditional" as found in Toriyama Sekien's three-volume book, *Hyakki Yako*

(1776), which depicted more than 150 demons and ghosts,[159] and more recently, in the art of cartoonist Shigeru Mizuki. The film also references the *yokai* trilogy—*The Hundred Monsters* (*Yokai Hyaku Monagatari*), *Spook Warfare* (*Yokai Daisenso*), and *Along with Ghosts* (*Tokaido Obake Dochu*)—that was produced in the late 1960s by Daiei Motion Picture Company. In fact, the *Great Yokai War* is a sort of big budget "update" of *Spook Warfare.*[160]

Aside from being a visual introduction to the world of the *yokai*, the film ends in a way that only an Asian film could. All of the *yokai*, who are depicted as rowdy partygoers, descend on Tokyo for a tremendous feast. They dance, shout, and even body surf. Kato is about to transform himself into a hate-filled creature, when some adzuki beans get mixed into the cauldron. The result is that he's defeated, and the Kirin makes his triumphant appearance. Why do the beans have such an effect? Not only are they ingredients in many ceremonial dishes, but as the character says in the film, they are "good for you." After Kato's defeat, one of the *yokai* exclaims that they won the war. Another *yokai* chides him, saying, "Don't be a fool. There is a limit to foolishness. Wars must not happen. . . . They only make you hungry." As if proving this point, right before the credits, we see a grown up Tadashi who, before he rushes off to work, rings a bell and quickly prays at a *kamidana*. As he hurries toward the door, he talks to an off-screen character. In the same room, we see his old friend, the Sune-kosuri, who desperately tries to get his attention. But Tadashi either can't see him or can't be bothered to see him. Sune-kosuri is obviously angry over being ignored, and so it begins—another destructive cycle of rage. This, of course, brings Kato back to life.

Kato became powerful in the first place by drawing upon the suffering and hate felt by discarded objects, from smelly sneakers to bicycles. He explains that humans have earned this resentment, because objects give themselves to us and we just throw things away. "Burn in the demon realm and take vengeance with me," he says to the River Princess, when she was still a straw effigy. Because rage is the emotion that brings about "darkness"—Kato claims that love is a hindrance—the song that plays over the credits is especially poignant. A sampling of the lyrics is: "Lower your fists and laugh it off. Love." Buddhists acknowledge that anger has a corrupting power. The Buddha himself encouraged his disciples to "Give up anger, give up conceit, pass beyond every fetter. There is no suffering for one who possesses nothing, Who doesn't cling to body-and-mind."[161] Anger affects not only the person who feels the emotion, but because of interdependence, it does affect others, as it shows in the film. As the Dalai Lama said, anger and hatred "are extremely powerful emotions [that] can overwhelm our entire mind. . . . While it is true that anger brings extra energy, if we explore the nature of this energy, we discover that it is blind. . . . It can cause an immense amount of destructive, unfortunate behavior. Moreover, if anger increases to the extreme, one becomes like a mad person, acting in ways that are damaging to oneself as they are to others." Compassion and, as the song played during the closing credits states, love are the antidote to anger. The Dalai Lama encourages us to cultivate mindfulness, saying that "The key to a more successful world is the growth of compassion."[162]

Pom Poko (*Heisei tanuki gassen pompoko*, 1994)—Written and directed by Isao Takahata. Running time: 119 min. Japanese. Rated PG for violence, scary images, and thematic elements. Genre: Animation.

Produced by Studio Ghibli, *Pom Poko* is an animated feature about the clash between modern civilization and the natural world, and it is set during Japan's "golden age of economic growth." The narrator tells us that the "demand for housing around Tokyo exploded. Lots of farmland and forest disappeared in waves of uncontrolled development. As Tokyo grew, it gnawed the land in random patterns like a huge insect. Then in 1967, the city fathers hit on a better idea: a plan for a new suburb of Tokyo called Tama New Town. More than 300,000 people would populate an area of 3,000 hectares. Forests would be cleared, hills flattened, valleys filled, farms and fields obliterated, old farmhouses demolished. The Tama Hills would be transformed into an enormous construction site to create a model bedroom town for Tokyo's workers. It was the largest urban development project in history." In the next shot, we see a giant reclining Buddha and three other, much smaller, monk-like beings, overlooking the sprawling city. Mount Fuji is seen poking behind the Buddha. The voice continues: "You've got to hand it to these humans. They're really something. We always thought they were animals just like us, but now we know we are wrong. They must be even more powerful than the gods." The narrator, we discover, is a *tanuki*[163] or raccoon dog.

In response to the encroaching human threat, the *tanuki* community gather at the old and abandoned Manpuku Temple, where a 105-year-old resident,

Master Tsurukame Osho, oversees the meeting. The council elders try to figure out what to do next. As it is becoming more difficult for them to find food and shelter, they decide to fight back. And they do this, by reviving the "neglected art of shape-shifting," which will allow them to study the humans first hand. They also decide to invite renowned masters from Sado and Shikoku islands, where it is said the art form is quite advanced. Eventually, many *tanuki* perfect their shape-shifting skills, allowing them to sabotage the construction sites, but their victories are short-lived. Where will the *tanuki* go when there is no where left to go? And can they learn to live in balance with the modern world?

Using the shape-shifting stories about the *tanuki* as a springboard, *Pom Poko* shows how a creature might go about developing these talents. As the kimono-wearing Granny Oroku explains: "shape-shifting requires the highest degree of mental concentration. It means changing one's very cells in an instant. Truly this is nature's greatest miracle. Lesser forms of transformation can be achieved by such animals as chameleons. But only *tanuki*, foxes, and some old cats can practice real shape-shifting." Ready to demonstrate how this can be done, she begins concentrating. A voice from the audience asks, if she will put a leaf on her head. "That's for beginners!" she replies then transforms into a metal container. Rigorous training ensues, but not everyone is up to the challenge. After all "shape-shifting requires rigorous physical and mental discipline," and unlike foxes, we are told, *tanuki* are inclined to be rather lazy. We can see that they are also ruled by their senses, tending to eat a lot and be rather lusty.

The *tanuki* can transform themselves into just about anything, and we see half a dozen of them becoming statues of Buddhas and bodhisattvas, many of them wearing a red bib or hat; Maneki Neko or the beckoning cat; Daruma dolls (also known as dharma dolls), which are hollow and round wish dolls, usually painted red and without arms or legs, and modeled after Bodhidharma; fox statues; gold fish; the see no evil, hear no evil, speak no evil monkeys; and as ceramic *tanuki*, as are often seen standing outside of restaurants or bars, wearing a straw hat and carrying a sake bottle in one hand and a promissory note in the other. Interestingly enough, in the beginning of *Pom Poko* only the males are taught about shape-shifting. Eventually, though, the women, who have refrained from reproduction and so are without children to rear, too, begin practicing, and many are quite good at it.

Now we arrive at the part in the film that has been fairly controversial in the West.[164] Master Osho calls the males together for a special lecture. While everyone is sitting on a vast red carpet, Master Osho asks "now then, what do you think the carpet you are all sitting on is?" With a wink, he says, "I may as well tell you. It's my testicles! It's exactly eight (*tatami*) mats. And I'll prove it!" At this moment the carpet shrivels back and disappears under his robe. Having learned this additional shape-shifting ability, the males, later in the film, transform their testicles into parachutes and even cannonballs. According to Japanese folklore, *tanukis* do indeed have large testicles, but rather than representing sexuality, these so-called "golden balls" are supposed to bring good fortune.[165]

After the *tanukis* have trained for a while, they transform themselves and venture into the human world to see if they can pass for humans. Tsurukame Osho, of course, is still dressed in a monk's robe and he carries *mala* beads with him. Granny still wears a kimono. The narrator explains that one can identify a shape-shifting *tanuki* by the dark circles under its eyes, which are the result of sheer fatigue. Even expert shape-shifters may have to drink special herbs to replenish their energy "otherwise, out pops the tail, and the next thing you know, they're back to their original form." To graduate from the shape-shifting course, the *tanuki* have to earn money, working in the human world. One transforms himself into a monk carrying a begging bowl and a bell, another "parlayed a discarded *pachinko* ball into big money,"[166] and still another stole from a *jinja* donation box. Because this *tanuki* only obtained a small amount of change, he transformed some "leaves into bills."[167] Granny hits him, saying that shape-shifting shouldn't extend to money-making.

Only one year into their five-year training plan, and one of the *tanuki* named Gonta discovers that much of his childhood home has been ravaged by bulldozers. Furious and grief-stricken he tells the council of elders that they need to take action. Responding in a characteristically Buddhist manner, Master Osho replies that maybe anger is clouding Gonta's judgment. Gonta becomes angry and explains that this isn't the case. He is effective at convincing ten other *tanuki* to join him, but before they leave Granny teaches them how to transform into a fox, which is another well-known shape-shifter. The *tanuki* engage in guerilla-style sabotage of the construction site, and initially their efforts are effective. Everyone cheers. Osho, though, stops them and remarks that they should take a moment to remember "the poor humans who died in this operation." Holding mala beads, they bow their heads as Osho prays. But the moment of solemnity doesn't last, and everyone bursts out laughing and heads outside to celebrate this "auspicious" occasion. Gonta, proud of his accomplishments, shouts that the war has begun, and that they will kill all of the humans, driving them out of Tama Hills. Countering this is another voice, who asks can't they let a few humans remain? After all, they do provide them with *tempura*, corn, donuts, fried chicken, and other delicious foods. With his mouth watering, Gonta concedes. This scene demonstrates the nondualist sensibility that pervades many Asian religions. The solution to one's problems isn't the complete removal of one aspect, but it is to keep things in balance.

The *tanukis* have a television in their abandoned temple, and on it, they see a trio of experts talking about the recent construction problems. A man dressed in a suit suggests that "maybe it was a mistake, moving that Shinto shrine. . . . Maybe all these incidents are revenge from the gods of the shrine." The woman agrees, "It's true that a lot of Jizo statues and shrines have been moved." "Yes, that really worried me. I asked the developers to observe the proper ceremonies before moving them, but . . ." The professor chimes in, saying "these spirit entities are usually associated with a given location. If their abodes are moved, they'll try to return home. If they do, and find everything has changed, they naturally become upset. I have a feeling there's a lot more trouble to come." Hearing this, the *tanukis* go into a nearby woods and shape-shift into two long rows of Jizo statues. (Jizo is one of the most popular bodhisattvas in Japan.)

At another ceremony where an Inari shrine is to be moved, a *tanuki* climbs onto the roof and appears as a fox, the shrine's servant to the gods. The "camera" shows the scene below from the *tanuki's* point of view, revealing a white *torii* at the shrine's entrance, a Shinto priest, and a table of ritual implements on it, including a tree branch. "The fox's eerie cry brought the proceedings to an immediate halt," the narrator states. "The ceremony was canceled, the shrine's relocation put on hold and residents petitioned the authorities to change plans for a road through the area." In the film, the screaming residents are shown throwing themselves down near two fox statues, which are apotropaic in nature, and bowing. Knowing that their efforts are successful, the *tanuki*, in the next attack, appear as glowing lanterns along a desolate country road. As they say, "come this way," one of the lanterns sticks out its tongue.

The DVD chapter titled "Monster Town" contains a quintessential Japanese folk myth. It involves a crying woman whose face is "normal" one minute, and in the next her features disappear. These spirits are known as Nopperabou, and many of the details in the *Pom Poko* encounter conform to the ones found in the short story "Mujina," which Lafcadio Hearn included in his 1904 book *Kwaidan*.[168] In the next DVD chapter, "Shokichi & Okiyo," the *tanuki* continue haunting the construction site, appearing as carbon copies of other people, as children wearing demon masks, and as "gremlins" in the guise of twin girls, who run around, cry and then laugh.

The *tanuki* make some strides, but construction continues, so they set out to find shape-shifting masters. Tamasaburo of Oni Woods—*oni* means demon—is chosen to go to Shikoku, and Bunta of Mizunomi Marsh is selected to travel to Sado. On the next full moon, they set out on their journeys. Seasons pass, and we discover that Tamasaburo has arrived at the Kincho Daimyo Shrine. Outside of it are several *torii*, each with a *shimenawa* stretched across its top, and a *tanuki* statute; inside of the inner chambers of the *jinja*, we see sake, a lantern, a *harai-gushi*, another *tanuki* sculpture, and a *kamidana* on top of a collection box.

After many months of negotiations, Tamasaburo is successful in convincing three shape-shifting masters to return to the Tama Woods. They are the 999-year-old Tazaburo Hage of Yashima; Inugami Gyobu, supreme leader of the raccoons of Matsuyama (his name indicates that he's a dog); and Kincho VI, direct descendent of the first raccoon master of Kincho Shrine. They explain that the people of Shikoku don't anger the *tanuki* because they know there will be dire consequences. "In fact, all three of us are worshipped at every shrine and temple in Shikoku," Inugami says. "The humans revere us." At that moment, they transform—with Inugami holding a sword and being encircled by red flames; Tazaburo has a nimbus behind him and he's making Buddhist *mudras*, and Kincho VI with a sword. As a way to scare the people of Tokyo, the three masters have resolved that they will carry out Operation Goblin, which will require "unprecedented powers of mental concentration." Inugami tells the *tanuki* crowd that they have brought with them a boat, and those who climb aboard it will "reach those blessed shores without fail," indicating, perhaps, that this ship is destined for the Pure Land or Western Paradise. Tazaburo admires the moon, asking everyone to pray on it for success, which they do.

Unless one is pretty familiar with Japanese history, culture, and folklore, the rest of *Pom Poko* has the potential for confusing its audience. It contains folk songs, historical references, and symbols from folk stories and religion. For instance, during Tazaburo's birthday celebration, the crowd asks him to reenact the story of Yoichi the Archer. The ancient *tanuki* quickly transforms into a young archer riding a horse. A 12th-century figure, "Nasu no Yoichi is best known for his exceptional skill at Yashima, a decisive battle between the Minamoto and Taira . . . On horseback, and in full view of both friend and foe, he rode a short distance into the choppy sea and prepared to shoot. He asked the gods to calm the wind and guide his shot. Miraculously, the wind died down and the sea stilled. Nasu no Yoichi raised his bow, took careful aim, and let the arrow fly. It arced toward the Taira ship and sliced through the base of the fan, toppling it into the sea. After a moment's silence the warriors from both sides roared with approval."[169] This scene in the film is an exact replica of these events.

Before beginning Operation Goblin, the three masters lead the *tanuki* in what seems to be a sacred ritual. The *tanuki* jump through a large bonfire only to emerge on the other side "purified." (The fire is in the middle of an area demarcated by poles connected by a rope on which paper streamers hang.) As each one lands, they connect to those in front of them, thus forming a giant dragon. Standing on top of its head is Kincho VI, dressed in priestly garb and waving a *harai-gushi*. Meanwhile, Inugami, who seems to have a scroll in his mouth, conjures a giant toad from his testicles. Smoke issues from the toad's mouth, causing the testicles of several other *tanuki* to grow until they come together and form a huge pumpkin. It's interesting to note that one of the Daoist immortals, Gama, had a large toad as his companion. In one 19th-century description of the toad by the monk Tetsugyu, it is implied that the creature "contains the life-breath which permeates all creatures."[170] Furthermore, it is said that with its "hypnotic eyes and horny skin, the mere presence of a toad has become the harbinger of some unusual happening." In one triptych by Utagawa Kunisada, a cloudlike vapor emerges from what seems to be the toad's mouth.[171]

"Transformation into monsters and goblins has always been a (*tanuki*) strong point," the narrator tells us. "But now, they needed to draw not only on their own latent energy, but also the hidden energy of the cosmos: fire, earth, water, and air." As the *tanuki* continue to work their magic, they dance in a circle and the flames grow higher and more intense. The "spirit" of this sequence is reminiscent of the Kurama Himatsuri,[172] a large, energetic fire festival that takes place in late October in Kyoto. Tall fires are lighted to mark the opening of the festivities, then chanting men march to the sound of drums, while also carrying more than 250 torches, some weighing as much as 176 pounds. The revelers finally converge at the Yuki-jinja.

In *Pom Poko*, the drumming and ecstatic dancing culminates in everyone being transformed into "goblins," that fly away disguised as giant pumpkins connected by vines, as grapes, watermelon, and radishes, as carp or *tanuki* in bubbles, birds, and more. In the sky, we also spy both skeletons of a human and a flying horse, a red-faced Tengu holding a fan, and, as an in-joke perhaps, several of Hayao Miyazaki's characters, including Kiki from *Kiki's Delivery Service*, Porco Rosso from the film of the same name, and even Totoro himself, standing on a top and holding an umbrella. In the distance, we can see the red-skirted Taeko from Takahata's own film *Omohide poro poro*.

The DVD chapter titled "Monster Parade" is appropriately named, as it features wave after wave of characters known to the Japanese, especially through illustrations, such as Utagawa Yoshiiku's *Night Parade of One Hundred Demons*. Before the parade begins, enormous skeletal-looking shadows, perhaps hungry ghosts, are projected onto three high rises, and behind a trio of boys, other buildings turn into what appear to be gravestones. The parade begins with a red-hatted man riding a white (very large) *shiba inu*. He throws powder at the leafless trees, shouting "let the trees burst into full flower." As the powder hits them, they do. Those familiar with Akira Kurosawa's *Dreams* will recognize the next scene—it is a fox wedding. At the front are foxes carrying illuminated lanterns and several attendants. The bride and groom walk hand-in-hand under a red umbrella. Two drummers complete the scene. Next in the parade is a floating lantern that swirls around to reveal a wide-mouthed face. It transforms into an animal skeleton, then the one-eyed, one-legged umbrella with its tongue hanging out. We've already encountered a few of these characters in the *Great Yokai War*. The umbrella soon changes into a red-eyed tiger. Fire comes out of its mouth, creating, perhaps, a red-skinned *oni*, complete with horns, sharp teeth, and claws. He, himself, goes through several transformations, including the bearded and knife-wielding Shoki the Demon Queller.[173] The tiger dissolves into ribbons. In the distance, we hear firecrackers as a diminutive group of women comes through the smoke. Next, it starts to rain, and Raijin, the god of thunder, descends on a cloud. He hits the drums that encircle him before being blown away by his green-skinned counterpart, Fujin, the god of wind.

Other mythological beings appearing in the parade[174] include a Tengu that bounces over four Daruma dolls; a group of fast-running demons and goblins, many of which look as if they were inspired by the upper portion of Utagawa Yoshiiku's handscroll titled *Humorous Record of Japanese History;* several Rokurokubi, the snake-necked female *yokai;* a dragon, even the seven lucky gods appear, throwing money into the crowd. Inugami, who is conjuring the parade, states that "matter is void. Form is emptiness," which is a reference to the Buddhist text, the *Heart Sutra*. But he can't sustain his "magic" any longer and he collapses. Arriving on a cloud is Amida Buddha, the Buddha of Infinite Light, who grabs the dead sage and, we can assume, takes him to the Pure Land. A funeral for the fallen sage follows, and the crowd chants the mantra "Gyahte gyahte hara gyahte," which again comes from the *Heart Sutra*, and in its complete form translates to "Gone. Gone. Gone Beyond. Completely Gone. Beyond Enlightenment."

The *tanuki* believe that this parade has finally helped them accomplish their goals, so they are shocked to discover that no one believes it actually took place. What's worse a greedy entrepreneur of a theme park, called Wonderland, claims that it was his company's doing. Desperate to find out who actually planned the parade, the man begins making phone calls. A mysterious man named Ryutaro shows up, telling him that it was the work of *tanuki*. How does he know? Because, as we learn, he's a shape-shifting fox, who has found a way to adapt to modern living. Saddened by what the *tanuki* have experienced, Ryutaro arrives at the temple, and tells Kincho VI that "there's no future for the raccoons of Tama. They'll die out, just like the foxes." "So that's what happened to the foxes of Tama," Kincho VI replies. "The few of us who could shape-shift have to live like this now," the fox says. "That's the only way to survive in the big city." After listening to the fox's explanation of what must be done, Kincho VI asks what will become of the *tanuki* who can't shape-shift. "They'll have to fend for themselves," he says. "We foxes had to abandon the others, but we had no choice." Meanwhile back at the shrine, the *tanuki* are trying to figure out what to do. Master Osho replies, "I don't think even Buddha could have seen how this would turn out." The end of *Pom Poko* is bittersweet. Defeated, but perhaps not in spirit, the *tanuki* combine all of their energy for one final shape-shift. But not of themselves, the landscape. They transform it to how it used to be before construction began.

Even though *Pom Poko* is a comedy, it reflects the filmmaker's serious concern for the environmental situation in Japan. Granny explains that the Edo period was a golden age for *tanuki*, and painters and writers frequently chronicled their shape-shifting. All of this has changed, though, she says, for in the modern period, raccoon dogs have been hunted for their pelts, which have been used for paintbrushes and toothbrushes. "That's how the humans took revenge for our excesses." We might even say that the film is in the Studio Ghibli tradition of exhibiting *mono no aware* or "sensitivity of things," and demonstrates the filmmaker's appreciation of and yet sadness at the transience of nature. Scholar Yuriko Saito explains that, in Japan, this deeply rooted preoccupation stems from Buddhist teachings on impermanence: "Everything, both nature and man, will sooner or later change through modification, destruction or death." Not only has this lament over transience been the subject of many major literary pieces in Japan, but, as we've seen, many films.[175]

Locker (*Shibuya kaidan*) (2003)—Screenplay by Osamu Fukutani. Directed by Kei Horie. Running time: 71 min. Japanese. Unrated. Genre: Horror.

Summary: Legend has it that if someone uses a certain coin locker in Shibuya, he or she will find love. Six college-aged students take the legend literally and use the locker. But instead of true romance, they find a curse worse than death: ghostly crying, mysterious handprints, and something unearthly that stalks them.

Although not the most academically relevant of films, *Locker*, which was followed by *Locker 2* (*Shibuya kaidan 2*) one year later, begins with a group of friends sitting around a "campfire," telling ghost stories. "Stalkers are scarier than ghosts," they decide and then laugh. While getting some cool beer out of the river, one of the females hears a baby cry. The wind begins to blow. Visibly unnerved, she returns to her friends and tells them what she heard. No one believes her. One of the guys decides not to let this moment pass, though, and he points to a nearby, headless statue. "I've heard that guardian statue is there to pray for aborted fetuses," he says. The female, again, hears a baby cry. Not missing his opportunity, one of other guys produces the sculpture's missing head. Everyone has a scare.

The next day, the friends return home and collect their belongings from a remote locker, staying just long enough to get a group photo. As the girls walk away, they notice tiny handprints on their bags. One of the guys hears a baby cry. As the film progresses, the characters continue to hear the cries of a baby and they start seeing strange things, such as a small body moving under a blanket. "Could it be the ghost of an aborted fetus?" asks one of them. The male who broke the head off of the guardian statue begins to fear for his life, so not taking any chances, he and a few friends return to the campsite to reattach the head. They also burn incense and pray in front of it. Feeling confident that their problems are over, they go to a restaurant to celebrate. The guy who cut the head off even feels confident enough to mock it. But the last laugh is on him. He is killed by an unseen specter. But he's not the only one. One by one each of the friends is murdered. In the end, there are few survivors, and as it is in so many J-Horror films, we learn that the events are caused by a curse—a grudge held by a child who was killed and discarded by her mother.

The *Locker* accomplishes several things. First, it plays upon the deep-seated fears and anxieties that exist within the Japanese psyche regarding children and abortion. And, second, it affirms the efficacy of religious symbols in an increasingly skeptical world. Until 1999, oral contraceptives were illegal in Japan, allowed only for the purposes of irregular cycles or other medical reasons.[176] Therefore, many Japanese have relied on other less reliable methods of birth control, including condoms, withdrawal, and so on. Abortion, on the other hand, didn't carry the same sort of stigma, and Japan was the first industrialized nation after the Second World War where abortion (through the private sector) became the principal method of officially sanctioned birth control.[177] Throughout the 20th century, abortion rates in Japan have fluctuated; however, its highest rate occurred in 1961, when more than 40% of married women of reproductive age reported having experienced an induced abortion.[178] Today, rates have decreased dramatically; however, the numbers are still not low. "Moreover, recent increases in abortion rates among women aged 15–19 and 20–24 is posing a new issue."[179] For example, in 1990, one study showed that pregnancies among adolescents in Japan occur at a rate of about 22 per 1,000, with most of those ending in abortion.[180]

One way that Japanese women have reconciled themselves to having an abortion is by engaging in a religious practice known as *mizuko kuyo*, literally "water-child offering." Practitioners can participate in an informal or formal service. In the former, women may light a candle and offer a prayer at a local temple. She might leave a "handwritten message of apology on a wooden tablet . . . or make an offering of food, drink, flowers, incense or toys. . . . She may purchase her own Jizo statue . . . or toss a few hundred yen into a coin box at a roadside shrine."[181] Jizo is, as we've already discussed, one of the most popular bodhisattvas in Japan. He is seen as the protector of travelers, the guardian of children and women, the guardian of souls in hell, and protector of unborn, aborted, miscarried, and still-born babies. When he is depicted as the Mizuko Jizo, he is usually accompanied by an infant or child, and he may be dressed in a child's sweater, a red bib, or a red hat. One often finds, surrounding the sculptures, the implements of infancy, such as toys, baby shoes, or baby food. In a more formal ceremony, the format of the monthly *mizuko kuyo* might be as follows: "Participants gather at a temple, register, pay a fee, and have their names recorded on small wooden tablets resembling *toba*. A service of approximately one hour is held with chanting of portions of the Lotus Sutra interspersed with repetitions of *namu myoho renge kyo* by the priest and participants, drum beating . . . and a closing monologue by the priest."[182] Although roadside shrines dedicated to children have existed in Japan for a long time, the *mizuko kuyo* only gained "popularity" during the late 1960s to early 1970s. This probably answers the question of why the Jizo statue is in the middle of a "campground" in the *Locker*, but the real question might be, Why does cutting off the sculpture's head release a grudge-filled child against the students? In the 1999 film *Shikoku*, the villagers are upset, and frightened, to learn that someone or something has decapitated a row of Jizo statutes.

We have to consider how children have been viewed in Japan. According to scholars Michiko Iwasaka and Barre Toelken, a child younger than seven was seen as a very powerful, unpredictable, and potentially dangerous entity. In some areas, it is said that these children "belong to the *kami*." The spirits of young children are often described as "fresh-young-leaves' spirits," thus affirming their enhanced power. "Originally the idea seems to have been that a fetus (dead or alive) retains its primordial vitality; since it is not yet under the control of societal norms, it can constitute a threat to [the] living."[183] The authors list three categories of legends associated with the liminal fetus. In one of these, a memorial stone is erected for children who have been drowned, murdered, or aborted, and it weeps until someone holds a proper ceremony, including the reading of sutras, for the deceased. "Usually, the area around such stones is considered very dangerous."[184] We might write off these beliefs as "archaic," but they still exist. As writer Peggy Orenstein states, temples dedicated solely to the *mizuko kuyo* stressed the "malevolent potential of the fetus: whether miscarried or aborted, it could become angry over being sent back. If not properly placated, it could seek revenge."[185]

At the end of the *Locker*, we learn that the child who is responsible for the deaths was unwanted by her mother. In fact, her mother went so far as to stab herself in the stomach and then shut the dead infant in the locker. We can assume that this child became angry over being rejected, thus setting a grudge into motion. After all, it is believed that if someone dies angry, his *yurei*, or ghost, "has the power to seek revenge on anything and anyone in the vicinity for as long as seven generations."[186] The *Locker* is far from unique when it comes to murdered children wreaking havoc on the lives of the living. Just a few of the Asian films in this vein include *Dark Water* (*Honogurai mizu no soko kara*, 2002), *The Grudge* (*Ju-On*, 2000), *Silk* (*Guisi*, 2006), *Reincarnation* (*Rinne*, 2005), and *Acacia* (2003).

Finally, the students depicted in the *Locker* are modern, educated people who don't pay much attention to "superstitions," which is why several of them conspire to cut the head off a guardian statue. They do this as a prank, expecting no consequences. The film, though, reaffirms that the ritual object is powerful, for when it is disfigured or dismembered, it no longer serves a protective role. The vengeful ghost or *goryo* is now free to seek its revenge. What's particularly interesting is that once the students realize what they've done, they return to the "scene of the crime," so to speak, find the head, glue it on, and recite prayers. Thinking they've escaped their fate, they celebrate. But what they've done has had no effect. So, what does this tell the viewer? Obviously, the film is made for entertainment purposes; however, it's bound to tap into some of the viewers' unconscious, deep-seated fears about the spirit world. The film reminds them that unless the dead are treated with respect and are given the proper ceremonies, they become dangerous. And it also warns them what can happen when religious symbols are defaced or disrespected. In short, the film supports traditional religious beliefs.

NOTABLE DIRECTORS

Hayao Miyazaki

Hayao Miyazaki was born in 1941 in Tokyo. During World War II, his father served as director of Miyazaki Airplane, which was owned by Miyazaki's uncle. They made rudders for Zero fighter planes. Miyazaki's mother has been described as strict and intellectual.[187] In his youth, his family moved around, and he attended three different grade schools. After graduating from high school, he attended Gakushuin University, where he earned degrees in political science and economics. In 1963, he landed his first job at Toei Douga (Toei Animation), and over the next decade or so, he was employed at a number of animation companies, where he performed every job from key animation to director.

In 1984, he wrote and directed *Nausicaa of the Valley of Wind* (*Kaze no tani no Nausicaa*), which was based on his original *manga* serialized in *Animage* magazine. At the center of the film is a brave, intelligent, and self-sacrificing princess who exhibits kindness and compassion toward all sentient beings. In many ways, Nausicaa would become a template for many of his future heroines. Themes characteristic of Miyazaki's oeuvre, such as "the fate of the ecosystem, phantoms of war, evils of totalitarianism, and the vicissitudes of self-development," also make an appearance in this film.[188] The success of *Nausicaa* led to the establishment, in 1985, of Studio Ghibli. A string of successful feature films followed, including *Castle in the Sky* (*Tenku no shiro Rapyuta*, 1986), *My Neighbor Totoro* (*Tonari no Totoro*, 1988), *Kiki's Delivery Service* (*Majo no takkyubin*, 1989), and *Porco Rosso* (*Kurenai no buta*, 1992). Miyazaki gained international success and critical acclaim with his next film, *Princess Mononoke* (*Mononoke-hime*, 1997). Not only did it win the award of the Japanese Academy for Best Film but it also became the highest-grossing domestic film in Japan's history, earning about $150 million.

He broke his own box office record four years later with the release of *Spirited Away* (*Sen to Chihiro no kamikakushi*). The accolades came from all over the globe with wins at the Berlin International Film Festival, Film Critics Circle of Australia Awards, and Hong Kong Film Awards. In his own country he won the award of the Japanese Academy for Best Film, and in the United States, he garnered an Oscar for Best Animated Feature. After helming a few short animated films, he made another feature, *Howl's Moving Castle* (*Hauru no ugoku shiro*, 2004), for which he received an Oscar nomination. Several shorts followed. At the time of this writing, his first feature length film in four years is in postproduction. The film, *Ponyo on a Cliff* (*Gake no ue no Ponyo*, 2008), centers on a five-year-old boy and his relationship with a goldfish princess who longs to become human. Its tentative U.S. release date is in 2009.

Akira Kurosawa

Akira Kurosawa was born in 1910 in Tokyo. The youngest of seven children, he displayed an early talent for art and, through art classes, developed into a talented painter. When he was about 20 years old, he parlayed his artistic acumen into the film industry. His started as an assistant director to Kajiro Yamamato, and after just five years, was already writing scripts and directing entire sequences for the director. In 1943, he got the chance to helm his own film, *Judo Saga* (*Sanshiro Sugata*), which is about a young man who wants to learn the martial art of judo. Throughout the 1940s, Kurosawa worked regularly, making one to two films a year. Highlights during this period include the 1948 release *Drunken Angel* (*Yoidore Tenshi*), which marked his first collaboration with actor Toshiro Mifune, and the 1949 release *Stray Dog* (*Nora Inu*), a film about a rookie police officer (Mifune) who "loses" his revolver while riding the bus. *Stray Dog* deals with such ethical concerns as justice and personal responsibility. Kurosawa gained international acclaim with his next film, *Rashomon* (1950). Set during the 11th century, it weaves a story of rape and murder. The twist is, it's told from four different perspectives. This portrait of human greed and fallibility won the Golden Lion at the Venice Film Festival Kurosawa returned to the modern-day setting for *Ikuru* (1952), a film about a pencil-pushing bureaucrat (Takashi Shimura) whose life changes when he's diagnosed with a terminal illness. After some intense self-reflection, the man decides to find meaning in his life, and he does this by making a difference in his community.

Between 1954 and 1985, Kurosawa helmed nearly 10 samurai epics. What's interesting is that once we peel back the historical veneer from his most lauded stories—*Throne of Blood* (*Kumonosu jo*, 1957) and *Ran* (1985)—we discover not a Japanese source but a Western one, more specifically William Shakespeare. The former was inspired by *Macbeth*, and the latter by *King Lear*. The East-West exchange went both ways, though. *Seven Samurai* (*Shichi-nin no Samurai*, 1954) was remade by John Sturges as *The Magnificent Seven* (1960). Kurosawa's *Yojimbo* inspired Clint Eastwood's "no name" persona, which could be found in Sergio Leone's *A Fistful of Dollars* (1964). *Hidden Fortress* (1958) inspired George Lucas' *Star Wars* epic (1977). Kurosawa's final three films include the very personal *Dreams* (1990), *Rhapsody in August* (*Hachi-gatsu no kyoshikyoku*, 1991), and *Madadayo* (1993). He died from a stroke in 1998.

Critics and filmmakers alike continue to rank Kurosawa and his films among the world's best. For example, in 1992, *Sight & Sound* asked 101 directors to come up with a Top 58 list. *The Seven Samurai* was in a four-way tie for sixth place, and *Rashomon* was in a three-way tie for tenth.[189] When Oscar-award-winning director Alexander Payne selected his Top 10 films, works that have influenced him or were personal favorites, his no. 1 choice was *Seven Samurai*. Of the film he said that it "is an achievement like climbing Mount Everest. My vote for best movie ever made. It's the film that most made me want to become a filmmaker."[190] What has made Kurosawa such a revered auteur? As Peter Grilli, president of the Japan Society of Boston, stated, "Although the materials from which Kurosawa fashioned his films are Japanese—his stories and their settings, his actors and their language—his fundamental messages are for everyone, everywhere. If one looks beyond the cultural patterns on the surfaces of his films, beneath the costumes that identify his actors as Japanese, the themes that lie within are neither arcane nor esoteric: man's struggle for fulfillment and self-perfection, the illusions of reality that disguise truth, conflicts of good and evil. What other subjects can there be for an artist whose real subject is mankind? In film after film, Kurosawa returned to these themes, shifting the premises slightly, altering historical periods, changing the costumes of his actors but never their souls."[191]

ENDNOTES

1. Noriko Kamachi, *Culture and Customs of Japan* (Westport, CT: Greenwood Publishing Group, 1999), 4.

2. Information found under each country at the "CIA World Factbook," *Central Intelligence Agency*, 2008, www.cia.gov/library/publications/the-world-factbook/index.html (accessed 17 February 2008).

3. Kamachi, *Culture and Customs of Japan*, 29.

4. Michiko Yusa, *Religions of the World: Japanese Religious Traditions* (Upper Saddle River, NJ: Lawrence King, 2002), 34–35.

5. Yusa, *Religions of the World*, 36.

6. H. Byron Earhart, *Religions of Japan: Many Traditions within One Sacred Way* (San Francisco: Harper & Row, 1984), 19.

7. Kamachi, *Culture and Customs of Japan*, 27–28.

8. H. Byron Earhart, *Religion in the Japanese Experience: Sources and Interpretations*, 2nd ed. (Belmont, CA: Wadsworth, 1997), 120.

9. Yusa, *Religions of the World*, 17.

10. Kamachi, *Culture and Customs of Japan*, 38.

11. Stuart D. B. Picken, *Essentials of Shinto: An Analytical Guide to Principal Teachings* (Westport, CT: Greenwood Press, 1994), xxii.

12. D. C. Holtom, "The Meaning of Kami," in *Religion in the Japanese Experience*, 11.

13. Herbert Plutschow, *Matsuri: The Festivals of Japan* (Surrey: Japan Library, 1996), 20–21.

14. Ian Reader, *Religion in Contemporary Japan* (Honolulu: University of Hawaii Press, 1991), 27.

15. Holtom, "The Meaning of Kami," 9.

16. Yusa, *Religions of the World*, 25.

17. The *Kojiki* is the oldest surviving text in Japanese; the *Nihonshoki* is written in classical Chinese with poetic sections in archaic Japanese.

18. Stuart D. B. Picken, *The A to Z of Shinto* (Lanham, MD: Scarecrow Press, 2006), 212.

19. Picken, *Essentials of Shinto*, 68.

20. Picken, *Essentials of Shinto*, 77.

21. Earhart, *Religion in the Japanese Experience*, 38.

22. To read a copy of this document, "Abolition of State Shinto" and "The Imperial Rescript of January 1, 1946," see Earhart, *Religion in the Japanese Experience*, 39–44.

23. George Williams, *Religions of the World: Shinto* (Philadelphia: Chelsea House, 2005), 17.

24. For descriptions on the specifics of these rituals, see Picken, *Essentials of Shinto*, 75–89.

25. Williams, *Religions of the World*, 21.

26. Picken, *Essentials of Shinto*, 93.

27. Williams, *Religions of the World*, 20.

28. Picken, *Essentials of Shinto*, 129.

29. Picken, *Essentials of Shinto*, explains that there are approximately 16 main styles of architecture and more than 20 types of *torii* associated with different *kami* and locations.

30. Holtom, "Shinto Places of Worship," 21.

31. Picken, *Essentials of Shinto*, 164. The author explains that the zigzag-shaped paper strips that hang on the ropes are "symbolic offerings to the *kami*."

32. These instructions and short prayer are posted on the door of the Izumo Taishakyo Mission of Hawaii on the island of O'ahu.

33. Williams, *Religions of the World*, 84.

34. Holtom, "Shinto Places of Worship," 22.

35. Picken, *Essentials of Shinto*, 171.

36. Many that this author saw in Hawaii were concrete "sinks" with a drain and a row of spigots. Usually, a roll of paper towels was nearby, as was a trash can.

37. Picken, *Essentials of Shinto*, 172.

38. "Gokito-Private Ceremonies," *Hawaii Kotohira Jinsha—Hawaii Dazaifu Tenmangu*, www.e-shrine.org/privateceremonies.html (accessed 17 February 2008).

39. These treasures include a hat of invisibility, an inexhaustible purse, the sacred keys to a treasure shed, scrolls of wisdom and life, a magic mallet, a lucky raincoat, a robe of fairy feathers, and a bag of fortune.

40. Williams, *Religions of the World*, 106.

41. Williams, *Religions of the World*, 105.

42. Hitoshi Miyake, "Rites of Passage," in *Religion in the Japanese Experience*, 127–28.

43. Reader, *Religion in Contemporary Japan*, 99.

44. Reader, *Religion in Contemporary Japan*, 100.

45. Williams, *Religions of the World*, 107.

46. Williams, *Religions of the World*, 108.

47. Williams, *Religions of the World*, 109.

48. Reader, *Religion in Contemporary Japan*, 60.

49. As Donald L. Philippi explains in the introduction, especially pages 1 and 2, to his *Norito: A Translation of the Ancient Japanese Ritual Prayers*, the "*Engi-shiki* rituals are as a rule extremely repetitive . . . (They) are cast in antique language of the most flowery sort. Sentences are long and loosely connected; the grammatical relationship of parts is difficult to determine; the meaning of many words is unclear; and everywhere semantic clarity is sacrificed to sonority." Furthermore, he said there is evidence that the rituals were supposed to be recited in accordance to a "special musical technique." Rather than being important for their literary value, *norito* are, he said, more interesting as examples of "ancient Japanese ritual, as a mirror of the religious concepts and the stately ritual language of the ancient Japanese." By the way, *norito*, when broken into its component parts, essentially means "magic by means of words."

50. Williams, *Religions of the World*, 52–53.

51. Reader, *Religion in Contemporary Japan*, 27.

52. Williams, *Religions of the World*, 6.

53. Picken, *The A to Z of Shinto*, 109.

54. Williams, *Religions of the World*, 4.

55. *Hawaii Kotohira Jinsha-Hawaii Dazaifu Tenmangu*, www.e-shrine.org/home.html. (accessed 28 January 2008).

56. Leila Fujimori, "Traditions Preserved at Shinto Temple," *Star Bulletin*, 2004. starbulletin.com/2004/01/05/news/story7.html (accessed 27 January 2008).

57. *Tsubaki Shrine*, www.tsubakishrine.com (accessed 29 January 2008).

58. The result of the Japanese living in South and Central America has been a rise in new religious movements (NRMs). "Most of the more than 30 Japanese NRMs in Brazil are Buddhist in content and Shinto in ritual. . . . Shinto-based groups that date back to the 1920s and 1930s are also to be found . . . in the Amazon region of Brazil. These groups tend to be highly inclusive in terms of their content and have fused core Shinto beliefs and practices with African, Catholic and Amerindian beliefs and rituals to provide a form of ecstatic religion known as *batuque*." Peter Bernard Clarke, *New Religions in Global Perspective: A Study of Religious Change in the Global Perspective* (New York: Routledge, 2006), 230.

59. Dani Cavallaro, *The Anime Art of Hayao Miyazaki* (Jefferson, NC: McFarland, 2006), 72.

60. Ran Levy-Yamamori and Gerard Taaffe, *Garden Plants of Japan* (Portland, OR: Timber Press, 2004), 79.

61. Robert O. Kinsey, "21st Century Netsuke," *netsukeonline.org*, www.netsukeonline.org/htm/kinsey_lecture.html (accessed 27 January 2008).

62. According to two notes on imdb.com, Totoro is a mispronunciation of *Tororu*, which means troll in Japanese. Apparently in a Japanese-language version of the film, excised from the

English-language version, when Mei first tells Satsuki that she saw a Totoro, the latter asks, "Do you mean troll from the storybook?" At the end of the film, we also can see the mother in bed with the daughters reading a book that has a goat crossing a bridge, under which is a Totoro-esque creature.

63. When released on video, the film was dubbed in English only.

64. Cavallaro, *The Anime Art of Hayao Miyazaki*, 72.

65. J. Akiyama, "Meaning of Onegai Shimasu," *aikiweb.com*, www.aikiweb.com/language/onegai.html (accessed 28 January 2008).

66. Interestingly enough, sometimes the *tanuki*, a similarly rotund creature, is depicted with a lotus leaf over its head.

67. All eight are a white parasol, a pair of golden fishes, a treasure vase, a lotus, a right-spiraling white conch, an endless knot, a victorious banner, and a golden wheel. According to tradition, the Vedic gods gave these to the Buddha when he attained enlightenment.

68. Robert Beer, *The Handbook of Tibetan Buddhist Symbols* (Boston: Shambhala, 2003), 7.

69. Beer, *The Handbook of Tibetan Buddhist Symbols*, 3–4.

70. Vivien Sung, *Five-Fold Happiness: Chinese Concepts of Luck, Prosperity, Longevity, Happiness and Wealth* (San Francisco: Chronicle Books, 2002), 249. This cat has successfully been exported to China where it is also incredibly popular.

71. Cavallaro, *The Anime Art of Hayao Miyazaki*, 69.

72. Cavallaro, *The Anime Art of Hayao Miyazaki*, 70.

73. Yoshimitsu Khan, *Japanese Moral Education Past and* Present (Cranbury, NJ: Associated University Presses, 1997), 154.

74. Hayao Miyazaki, *My Neighbor Totoro: Picture Book*, trans. Naoko Amemiya (San Francisco: VIZ Media, 2005), 3.

75. "Who Is Kenji Miyazawa?" *kenji-world.com*, 2002, www.kenji-world.net/english/who/who.html (accessed 28 January 2008).

76. In Hawaii, most of the shrines visited by this author had an automated *omikuji* dispenser. All a person had to do was put in a quarter and out popped a piece of paper about the size of a stick of gum. Unfold that piece of paper to reveal one's fortune.

77. Ichiro Hori, *Folk Religion in Japan: Continuity and Change*, ed. Joseph Kitagawa and Alan L. Miller (Chicago: University of Chicago Press, 1968), 202–3.

78. Haruko Okano, "Summary: Woman and the Shinto Religion," in *Religion in the Japanese Experience*, ed. H. Byron Earhart (Belmont, CA: Wadsworth, 1997), 37–38.

79. Why does Yurie's hair grow when her powers are "activated"? This could stem from two traditions regarding long hair. During the Heian period (794–1191 C.E.), the standard of beauty dictated that aristocratic women possessed extremely long hair—longer than one's own body. In modern Japanese horror films, female ghosts usually have long, jet black hair that often obscures their eyes. This always has the effect of absolutely terrifying their "victims." See, for instance, *Ringu*, *Tomie*, and *Ju-On*. In *Phone*, a Korean horror film, when a murdered woman is found within a wall, her hair has grown substantially. The premise of *Ekusute*, a Japanese horror film from 2007, is that hair extensions attack the women who wear them.

80. Picken, *Essentials of Shinto*, 187.

81. Interestingly enough, "eye power" signs are also prevalent in *Spirited Away*.

82. "Shiba Inu History," *American Kennel Club*, www.akc.org/breeds/shiba_inu/history.cfm (accessed 30 January 2008).

83. Okano, "Summary: Woman and the Shinto Religion," 35.

84. Reader, *Religion in Contemporary Japan*, 178.

85. Susan Napier, *Anime from Akira to Howl's Moving Castle, Updated Edition: Experiencing Contemporary Japanese Animation* (New York: Palgrave Macmillan, 2005), 237.

86. Thomas P. Kasulis, *Shinto: The Way Home* (Honolulu: University of Hawaii Press, 2004), 14–15.

87. Plutschow, *Matsuri: The Festivals of Japan*, 20.

88. Thomas Cleary, *Code of the Samurai: A Modern Translation of the Bushido Shoshinsu* (Boston: Tuttle, 1999), 60.

89. Plutschow, *Matsuri: The Festivals of Japan*, 42.

90. Plutschow, *Matsuri: The Festivals of Japan*, 73–74.

91. Kasulis, *Shinto: The Way Home*, 48.

92. Cavallaro, *The Anime Art of Hayao Miyazaki*, 122.

93. Picken, *Essentials of Shinto*, 350.

94. Thich Nhat Hanh, *For a Future to Be Possible: Commentaries on the Five Wonderful Precepts* (Berkeley, CA: Parallax Press, 1993), 14.

95. Picken, *Essentials of Shinto*, 63.

96. Picken, *Essentials of Shinto*, 346–47.

97. Hanh, *For a Future to Be Possible*, 17.

98. Plutschow, *Matsuri: The Festivals of Japan*, 20.

99. Cleary, *Code of the Samurai*, 3.

100. Kasulis, *Shinto: The Way Home*, 24.

101. Picken, *Essentials of Shinto*, 346.

102. Cavallaro, *The Anime Art of Hayao Miyazaki*, 135.

103. Cavallaro, *The Anime Art of Hayao Miyazaki*, 137. The author notes other "influences," including *Pinocchio*, *The Odyssey* (the porcine metamorphosis), and *Alice in Wonderland*.

104. A version of this story titled 'The Sparrows' Gifts' can be found in Royall Tyler, *Japanese Tales* (New York: Pantheon Books in 1987), 4–6.

105. The story, sometimes translated to *Kachi-Kachi Mountain*, tells how an old man and woman were tricked by a *tanuki*, a shape-shifting badger-like creature, and then the couple is avenged by a rabbit. A scanned copy of a translation from 1885 can be found at "Kachi-Kachi Yama," baxleystamsp.com, www.baxleystamps.com/litho/hasegawa/kachi.shtml (accessed 17 February 2008).

106. Momotaro is Peach Boy, named thus because he was born out of a giant peach. Once he's old enough, about 15 years old, he tells his adopted parents that he must go to Ogre Island, where he will fight the monsters there and bring back their treasure. He is joined in his journey by a spotted dog, a monkey, and a pheasant. This and many other popular tales can be found popularized in such books as Florence Sakade, *Japanese Children's Favorite Stories* (North Clarendon, VT: Tuttle, 2003).

107. Hayao Miyazaki, "Chihiro's Mysterious Town: The Aim of this Film," *The Art of Miyazaki's Spirited Away* (San Francisco: VIZ, 2004), 16.

108. Miyazaki, *The Art of Miyazaki's Spirited Away*, 56.

109. Miyazaki, *The Art of Miyazaki's Spirited Away*, 57.

110. Kamachi, *Culture and Customs of Japan*, 27.

111. Thanks to Reiko Take-Loukota, instructor of Japanese at the University of Nebraska at Omaha, for helping with these translations.

112. Interestingly enough, the sectioned circle with the color motif of red, blue, green, and yellow is similar to the one found in Miyazaki's 2004 feature film *Howl's Moving Castle* (*Hauru no Ugoku Shiro*), only this time it's green, pink, blue, and black.

113. For a film that's Japanese, the food displayed is uncharacteristic of this country's cuisine. On Chinese-style plates one finds what looks to be fried rice, sweet and sour chicken, and a fish head complete with eyes and sharp teeth. When the mother begins to eat, even she wonders what she's eating.

114. Cavallaro, *The Anime Art of Hayao Miyazaki*, 137.

115. Cavallaro, *The Anime Art of Hayao Miyazaki*, 163.

116. In this regard, Haku is very similar to Howl in *Howl's Moving Castle*. Initially, the blond character seems vain, shallow, and foppish, but over time we see his alternate side, as a fanged black bird who engages in warfare.

117. Michiko Iwasaka and Barre Toelken, *Ghosts and the Japanese: Cultural Experience in Japanese Death Legends* (Logan: Utah State University Press, 1994), 63.

118. Miyazaki, *The Art of Miyazaki's Spirited Away*, 16.

119. As indicated in Miyazaki, *The Art of Miyazaki's Spirited Away*, 81. Kasuga Taisha (Shrine) dates to the early eighth century C.E. in Nara. *Kami* housed here include Kashima Jingu (the Fujiwara clan deity) and three other *kami*. The shrine has associations with Shinto and Buddhism. Sacred deer, thought to be messengers of the Kasuga deities, still roam Nara Park. The best-known aspect of the shrine is the fact that over the centuries, worshippers have donated thousands of stone lanterns that line the way. Furthermore, Noh drama was developed by a priest of this shrine and his son. For more, see June Kinoshita and Nicholas Palevsky, *Gateway to Japan* (New York: Kodansha International, 1988), 577.

120. Cavallaro, *The Anime Art of Hayao Miyazaki*, 138.

121. Kamachi, *Culture and Customs of Japan*, 99.

122. Bruce Smith and Yoshiko Yamamoto, *The Japanese Bath* (Salt Lake City: Gibbs Smith, 2001), 64. In *My Neighbor Totoro*, there is also a bath scene, during which the father and his young daughters share a bath. Although this may seem strange to Westerners, it is still common for preteens to take a bath with their parents. The reason for this is that the Japanese usually have only one bathing facility, but more so, it's also the common nature of a communal bath.

123. Smith and Yamamoto, *The Japanese Bath*, 51.

124. Smith and Yamamoto, *The Japanese Bath*, 51–52.

125. Smith and Yamamoto, *The Japanese Bath*, 12–13.

126. Miyazaki, *The Art of Miyazaki's Spirited Away*, 96.

127. Miyazaki, *The Art of Miyazaki's Spirited Away*, 16.

128. Napier, *Anime from Akira to Howl's Moving Castle*, 184–85.

129. Shape-shifting foxes also can be found in Chinese lore, as is evidenced in the 1991 Hong Kong film *Fox Legend* (*Ling Hu*), which is about a beautiful yet cursed fox spirit known as Snow Lady.

130. Karen A. Smyers, *The Fox and the Jewel: Shared and Private Meanings in Contemporary Japanese Inari Worship* (Honolulu: University of Hawaii Press, 1999), 72.

131. Smyers, *The Fox and the Jewel*, 178.

132. Smyers, *The Fox and the Jewel*, 98.

133. Smyers, *The Fox and the Jewel*, 105.

134. Smyers, *The Fox and the Jewel*, 95.

135. For more information on Hina Dolls, go to "All about Japanese Hina Dolls," *Kyoto National Museum*, 2007, www.kyohaku.go.jp/eng/dictio/data/senshoku/index.htm (accessed 31 January 2008).

136. Kamachi, *Culture and Customs of Japan*, 143.

137. A more detailed description of these dolls can be found online at Rinkya–Japan Auction & Shopping Service. "Hina Ningyou: The 'Doll' in 'Doll Festival,'" *rinkya.com*, 2004, www.rinkya .com/newsletter/01132004.php (accessed 26 January 2008).

138. This comes from the first two lines of no. 37, as found in James Fieser and John Powers, eds., *Scriptures of the World's Religions* (Boston: McGraw Hill, 2004), 185.

139. This comes from no. 2, as found in Fieser and Powers, eds., *Scriptures of the World's Religions*, 182.

140. Benjamin Schwartz, "The Thought of the *Tao-te-Ching*," in *Lao-tzu and the Tao-te-ching*, ed. Livia Kohn and Michael LaFargue (Albany: State University of New York Press, 1998), 206.

141. Jennifer Oldstone-Moore, *Taoism* (New York: Oxford University Press, 2003), 63.

142. Fieser and Powers, eds., *Scriptures of the World's Religions*, 183, 186.

143. Schwartz, "The Thought of the *Tao-te-Ching*," 199.

144. Alan K. L. Chan, "A Tale of Two Commentaries: Ho-shang-kun and Wang Pi on the Lao-tzu," in *Lao-tzu and the Tao-te-ching*, 95.

145. Chan, "A Tale of Two Commentaries," in *Lao-tzu and the Tao-te-ching*, 96–97.

146. Akira Y. Yamamoto, "Introduction," in *Japanese Ghosts & Demons: Art of the Supernatural*, ed. Stephen Addiss (New York: George Braziller, 1985), 9.

147. Iwasaka and Toelken, *Ghosts and the Japanese*, 44.

148. Yamamoto, "Introduction," 10.

149. Tim Screech, "Japanese Ghosts," *Mangajin*, www.mangajin.com/mangajin/samplemj/ ghosts/ghosts.htm (accessed 30 January 2008).

150. Picken, *The A to Z of Shinto*, 221.

151. Tales 33, 34, 35, 118, 119, 120, 123, and 126 all have a *tengu* connection. It is in 33 that he has a change of heart so he can become a monk. Tyler, *Japanese Tales*.

152. "Tengu," *The Obakemono Project*, www.obakemono.com/obake/tengu (accessed 28 January 2008).

153. Screech, "Japanese Ghosts."

154. "Rokuro-kubi," *The Obakemono Project*, www.obakemono.com/obake/rokurokubi (accessed 28 January 2008).

155. "Shōjō," *The Obakemono Project*, www.obakemono.com/obake/shojo (accessed 28 January 2008).

156. "Kirin," *The Obakemono Project*, www.obakemono.com/obake/kirin (accessed 28 January 2008).

157. Kasulis, *Shinto: The Way Home*, 56.

158. "Yuki-onna," *The Obakemono Project*, www.obakemono.com/obake/yukionna (accessed 28 January 2008).

159. Midori Deguchi, "One Hundred Demons and One Hundred Supernatural Tales," in *Japanese Ghosts & Demons*, ed. Stephen Addiss (New York: George Braziller, 1985), 15.

160. Keith Aiken, "The Great Yokai War," *SciFi Japan*, 2006, www.scifijapan.com/articles/2006/10/18/the-great-yokai-war (accessed 30 January 2008).

161. Gil Fronsdal, *The Dhammapada: A New Translation of the Buddhist Classic with Annotations* (Boston: Shambhala, 2006), 59. This comes from the first few lines of chapter 17.

162. Tenzin Gyatso, "Compassion and the Individual," *dalailama.com*, www.dalailama.com/page.166.htm (accessed 31 January 2008).

163. Another film that has this animal at its center is *Princess Raccoon* (*Operetta tanuki goten*, 2005), a musical about Amechiyo (Jo Odagiri), a banished prince who, on the forbidden grounds at the foot of Mt. Kaiasu, meets *Tanukihime* (Zhang Ziyi), a royal *tanuki* in human form. They fall in love, but because "no man should love a *tanuki*," all sorts of problems arise.

164. An article on the website for Turner Classic Movies (http://www.tcm.com/thismonth/article.jsp?cid=114171&mainArticleId=114160) explains that "despite the fact that *Pom Poko* was the highest grossing film in Japan in 1994, and was even submitted by Japan to the Academy of Arts and Sciences as their Oscar contender . . . it never found a U.S. distributor until recent years. Part of the reason may be due to the film's peculiar but oddly endearing protagonists. . . . In Japanese folklore, these woodland creatures are considered harbingers of good fortune with a mischievous side . . . the male tanuki also possess a special talent—the ability to alter the size of their testicles. . . . This little detail was highly amusing to Japanese audiences, particularly children, but probably prevented it from getting a theatrical release here because of conservative parental groups." If one does a search online, searching for comments on Pom Poko, invariably one finds comments, usually disgusted ones, about its depiction of male genitalia and female breasts. Cracked.com actually ranked *Pom Poko* at number one on its "10 Best Animated Movies for (Traumatizing) Kids." The reason? The *tanuki*s use of "their magical testicles." (See the http://www.cracked.com/article_15070_10-best-animated-movies-traumatizing-kids.html.)

165. For more on this and other questions regarding Pom Poko, see the question and answer section at http://www.nausicaa.net/miyazaki/pompoko/faq.html.

166. Pachinko is a meeting of pinball and a slot machine in one upright device. One can play the game in any number of pachinko parlors, which are typically very noisy, light filled, and crowded. Gambling is forbidden in Japan, however, the parlors have found a way to sidestep this issue. If one wins one ball or more, the player can take his winnings to the parlor's "gift shop" and exchange the balls for money or other gift items.

167. One website explains that in the video game *Super Mario Brothers*, whenever Mario obtains a leaf, he grows pointed ears and a raccoon-like tail. This establishes the connection between leaves and tanukis. See http://www.nausicaa.net/miyazaki/pompoko/faq.html.

168. It can be found online at http://www.trussel.com/hearn/mujina.htm. (accessed 11 June 2008).

169. Hideharu Onuma with Dan and Jackie DeProspero, *The Essence and Practice of Japanese Archery* (NY: Kodansha International, 1993), 14-15.

170. Janet Carpenter, "Sennin: The Immortals of Taoism," in *Japanese Ghosts & Demons: Art of the Supernatural*, ed. Stephen Addiss (New York: George Braziller, 1985), 59.

171. Fumiko Y. Yamamoto and Akira Y. Yamamoto, "Two and a Half Worlds: Humans, Animals, and In-between," in *Japanese Ghosts & Demons: Art of the Supernatural*, ed. Stephen Addiss (New York: George Braziller, 1985), 174.

172. The 1985 Japanese drama, *Himatsuri*, also deals with the clash between traditional culture and modernization. Tatsuo, a womanizing woodsman, who is fond of hunting in the mountains, comes into conflict with an outsider who wants to build a marine park in the largely pristine area. The annual fire festival leads Tatsuo to commit an act of violence.

173. Matthew Welch talks about this folk mythological person, who was imported from China, in chapter five of *Japanese Ghosts & Demons: Art of the Supernatural*.

174. At the end of Satoshi Kon's 2006 animated film *Paprika*, there is a similar parade scene in which one sees everything from Daruma dolls to Maneki Neko.

175. Yuriko Saito, "The Japanese Appreciation of Nature," in *Worldviews, Religion, and the Environment: A Global Anthology*, ed. Richard C. Foltz (Belmont, CA: Wadworth, 2003), 257. In the West, a few animated films that decry and lament the destruction of habitat are *Watership Down* (1978), *The Secret of NIMH* (1982), *FernGully: The Last Rainforest* (1992), and *Over the Hedge* (2006).

176. "Abortion Policy in Japan," United Nations report, www.un.org/esa/population/publications/abortion/doc/japan.doc (accessed 30 January 2008).

177. Stanford University News Service, "Djerassi on Birth Control in Japan—Abortion 'Yes,' Pill, 'No,'" *United Nations report*, www.un.org/esa/population/publications/abortion/doc/japan .doc (accessed 30 January 2008).

178. Ryuzaburo Sato, "Contraceptive Use and Induced Abortion in Japan—How Is It So Unique among the Developed Countries?" *National Institute of Population and Social Security Research* (2005), 3. Available at iussp2005.princeton.edu/download.aspx?submissionId=51736 (accessed 30 January 2008).

179. Ryuzaburo Sato, "Contraceptive Use and Induced Abortion in Japan," 8.

180. "Abortion Policy in Japan," *United Nations report*.

181. Peggy Orenstein, "Mourning My Miscarriage: In Japan, I Find a Culture Willing to Acknowledge My Loss," *New York Times Magazine*, 2002, www.peggyorenstein.com/articles/2002 _mourning_miscarriage.html (accessed 30 January 2008).

182. Elaine Martin, "Rethinking the Practice of *Mizuko Kuyo* in Contemporary Japan: Interviews with Practitioners at a Buddhist Temple in Tokyo," bama.ua.edu/~emartin/publications/mkarticl.htm (accessed 30 January 2008).

183. Iwasaka and Toelken, *Ghosts and the Japanese*, 70.

184. Iwasaka and Toelken, *Ghosts and the Japanese*, 71.

185. Peggy Orenstein, "Mourning My Miscarriage."

186. Iwasaka and Toelken, *Ghosts and the Japanese*, 86.

187. Steven Feldman, "Hayao Miyazaki Biography," *nausicaa.net*, 1994, www.nausicaa.net/miyazaki/miyazaki/miyazaki_biography.txt (accessed 30 January 2008).

188. Cavallaro, *The Anime Art of Hayao Miyazaki*, 7.

189. The other films vying for sixth place were *The Godfather* (1972), *Vertigo* (1958), and *Modern Times* (1936); for tenth place, it was *Godfather II* (1974) and *The Passion of Joan of Arc* (1928). The results can be found online at http://www.geocities.com/Athens/Oracle/7207/polls10.htm#_ftn1. For the most part, Kurosawa's popularity in the West was never matched in his native Japan. In fact, he had a difficult time during the latter part of his career securing funding for his films.

190. Bob Fischbach, "Payne's Choices for Film Streams Lean to Classics," *Omaha World Herald*, 2007, www.omaha.com/index.php?u_page=2620&u_sid=10070942 (accessed 30 January 2008). Payne chose the films for a series to be shown at Film Steams, a nonprofit art house movie theater in Omaha, Nebraska.

191. Peter Grilli, "Akira Kurosawa: A Giant among Filmmakers and among Men," *PBS: Great Performances*, www.pbs.org/wnet/gperf/shows/kurosawa/essay1.html (accessed 30 January 2008).

6

Multiple Interpretations

When we examine the teachings of world religions, we find that many share a similar outlook. For instance, Buddhism, Christianity, Islam, Judaism, Sikhism, Hinduism, and even Confucianism see self-sacrifice, love, mercy, humility, honesty, benevolence, generosity, and the cultivation of morality, which includes not stealing or killing, as virtues. As for vices, most religions list avarice, egotism, envy, lust, and anger. No religion advocates killing, sexual misconduct, lying, or stealing. Because certain ideas seem to transcend culture—probably because they support a harmonious society—we can refer to these as "universally held" values.

As Carl Jung and, later, Joseph Campbell pointed out, many religions also share character types, such as the wise old man, the hero on a journey, and the trickster. Of the hero, Campbell said that he or she "has found or done something beyond the normal range of achievement and experience" and "has given his or her life to something bigger than oneself." The deed that the hero performs is either physical (acting courageously in battle or saving a life) or spiritual (the hero learns "to experience the supernormal range of human spiritual life and then comes back with a message").[1] Religious heroes frequently have a remarkable birth, have the ability to perform miracles or receive magical aid, clash with an adversary, and, in the end, emerge victorious. A short list of heroic figures from different world religions includes Jason, Hercules, Perseus, and Odysseus from Greek myth; Moses and King David from Judaism; Marduk from Babylonian myth; Jesus of Nazareth from Christianity; Siddhartha Gautama from Buddhism; Krishna from Hinduism; Huangdi or the Yellow Emperor from Chinese myth; Momotaro or Peach Boy from Japanese myth; and Mithras from Persia.

Heroes can act as saviors in two ways: They can literally save other beings from danger or destruction, or they can bring about salvation, which can be liberation from ignorance or illusion (e.g., Buddhism and Hinduism) or deliverance from the power and effects of sin (e.g., Christianity). Sometimes these salvific figures die and are subsequently "reborn," either literally or figuratively. Western literature and film are replete with these sacrificial heroes, and representations range from Neo in *The Matrix* to E.T. in *E.T.: The Extraterrestrial*. In the East, too, we find saviors,[2] especially in anime and the films of Hayao Miyazaki, more specifically *Princess Mononoke* and *Nausicaa*. In Mahayana Buddhism, we find saviors in the guise of bodhisattvas. Two of special note are Kuan Yin, who in certain legends is depicted as Miao-shan, a young woman who goes to hell, where she transforms it into a paradise, and is then reborn on an island where she protects seafarers from storms,[3] and Jizo, a Japanese divinity who is depicted as a monk and who eases the suffering and shortens the sentence of those serving time in hell.[4]

When viewing many of these characters from a Christian perspective, writers tend to affix to them the label of "Christ figure." But the question remains: What makes these characters particularly "Christ-like"? As one person asked of a Christian blogger, is the person a Christ-figure because the author intends him to be? Do his words have to come from scripture? Does the film have to have biblical allusions or names? Must there be a kingdom of heaven or hell?[5] The blogger responded with 10 points, including that Christ figures are "always fighting for a cause bigger than themselves, battling an evil power, tested in their faith, talks about truth, helps if they die and come back to life, often have dual identities, rise from obscurity, misunderstood, and does things other say can't be done."[6] As the conversation continued, the original poster admitted that these characteristics are vague enough to apply to anyone from Moses, the Hebrew prophet, to modern-day superheroes. Detractors to those who liberally affix the label "Christ figure" to cinematic characters would point to the example of Superman who, since his origin in 1938, has been linked to Jesus. One might ask how this Christological reading reconciles with the fact that Jerry Siegel and Joe Shuster, the creators of Superman, were Jewish, citing inspiration in the biblical stories of Moses and, from Jewish folk-lore, of the golem, which is an artificial human endowed with life.[7]

Furthermore, being Christ-like isn't as cut and dried as it seems. Several religious leaders, including Thich Nhat Hanh and the Dalai Lama, have noted the similarities between the teachings of Jesus and the Buddha. And one book, *Jesus and Buddha: The Parallel Sayings*, takes things even further, by comparing the teachers' sayings side-by-side. As Jack Kornfield says in the book's introduction, "Over and over again in the New Testament and ancient Buddhist scriptures, we discover that the lives, deeds and teachings of Jesus and Buddha are strikingly similar. . . . The correlations among these ancient texts are almost eerie. As will become immediately evident in the collections of parallel sayings that follow, Jesus' and Buddha's later teachings are as alike as their early biographies. Whether speaking of love, material wealth, temptation or salvation, they were two masters with one message."[8]

It is possible to label a film as Christian, Buddhist, Shinto, Jewish, or Muslim, and some films overwhelmingly represent one tradition over the others. No one would deny that *The Passion of the Christ* or *Jesus Christ Superstar* are Christian films, that *The Mahabharata* is Hindu, *The Message* (also known as *Mohammed, Messenger of God*) is Muslim, *The Chosen* or *Yentl* is Jewish, or that *Little Buddha* or *Kundun* is Buddhist. These are implicitly religious films. But what happens when we look at films such as *Bruce Almighty* or its "sequel" *Evan Almighty*? In the former film, we see our main character walking on water and performing miracles, reminiscent of Jesus, but he also parts a bowl of tomato soup, which is reminiscent of Moses' parting of the Rea Sea from the Hebrew Bible. Furthermore, God is, at one point, referred to as Yahweh,[9] which is more closely associated with Judaism than Christianity. The latter film is a modern take on the story of Noah and his ark, which is found in the Hebrew Bible. So does that make the film Jewish or, since Christians also use this text, Christian? The fact that the director is Tom Shadyac, "a professing Catholic who reads Augustine and Merton," seems to make our categorization easier.[10]

The greatest challenge for a scholar is figuring out what do with films that seem to be spiritual in nature, meaning that they contain those "universally held" values, but don't overtly belong to a specific religious tradition. For instance, how should we categorize *The Matrix* or *Star Wars*, films that borrow liberally from Eastern and Western traditions but fail to present a consistent religious worldview? For many decades, *Star Wars* was discussed primarily in Christian terms, but this is changing. Writers are still penning titles such as *Star Wars Jesus—A Spiritual Commentary on the Reality of the Force* and *The Gospel According to Star Wars: Faith, Hope and the Force*; however, within the past five years, we've also seen books such as *The Tao of Star Wars* and *The Dharma of Star Wars* that are uncovering the films' Eastern roots.

THE LORD OF THE RINGS TRILOGY

As we've seen, if a film isn't placed in an overtly religious context, meaning it isn't about a specific religious figure or about priests, rabbis, nuns, or monks, then classifying it can be tricky. To demonstrate how we might interpret a film from different perspectives, in this chapter we will examine *The Lord of the Rings* (*LOTR*) trilogy, first from a Christian (Roman Catholic) and then from a Buddhist perspective.

The Lord of the Rings trilogy (2001–2003)—Based on the novels of J. R. R. Tolkien. Directed by Peter Jackson. Total running time of extended edition: 682 min. English. Rated PG-13 for epic battle sequences and some scary images. Genre: Action/Adventure/Fantasy. Won 17 Academy Awards. The trilogy consists of *The Fellowship of the Ring* (2001), running time 208 min.; *The Two Towers* (2002), running time 223 min.; and *LOTR: The Return of the King* (2003), running time 251 min.

Summary: *The Lord of the Rings* trilogy contains a plethora of characters and back stories; however, the main thread concerns a young Hobbit named Frodo Baggins (Elijah Wood), who inherits a ring from his cousin Bilbo (Ian Holm). But this is no ordinary piece of jewelry. It is the One Ruling Ring, an instrument of absolute power that could allow its creator, Sauron, the dark Lord of Mordor, to control Middle-earth and enslave its peoples. Knowing that power like this must not remain in the world, Gandalf the Grey (Ian McKellen), a wizard, encourages Frodo to take the ring back from whence it came. Accompanying him is a diverse Fellowship of Middle-earth inhabitants that consist of three of his most loyal Hobbit friends (Sean Astin, Billy Boyd, and Dominic Monaghan), two humans (Viggo Mortensen and Sean Bean), Gandalf, a dwarf (John Rhys-Davies), and an elf (Orlando Bloom). Together they will make their way toward the Cracks of Mount Doom, where the ring must be destroyed. This perilous voyage will lead the heroes through Sauron's territory, where they will engage in battle with such formidable foes as an evil wizard Saruman (Christopher Lee) and a litany of diabolical forces, including Orcs, Uruk-hai, and Nazgul (Ringwraiths). External forces aren't all they must combat, though, for the ring has a way of corrupting anyone it touches, filling him or her with greed, lust for power, and the murderous impulse to see that the other two desires are fulfilled.

Christianity

J. R. R. Tolkien was a committed Catholic,[11] and as he has admitted, one can gain an understanding of his faith through his writings. His most famous tome, of course, was *The Lord of the Rings* trilogy, which he confirmed was a "fundamentally religious and Catholic work; unconsciously so at first, but consciously in the revision."[12] Most scholars have interpreted his works through the lens of Christianity, and it isn't difficult to see why.[13] The story is a classic example of good vs. evil, with goodness symbolized by light and represented by the valiant inhabitants of Middle-earth, and the bad symbolized by darkness and shadows and represented by Sauron's repulsive and evil hordes on the other. As in the Christian New Testament, the *LOTR* trilogy also ends with an apocalyptic battle and with the reign of a messiah-like figure. Furthermore, while many of the heroic characters embody Christian values and seem to be modeled on biblical figures, the evil characters seem to mirror the faults of the Bible's devil and his demons. It's important to note that Tolkien may have thought of these characters in this light, but, as he said in his letter to a Jesuit friend, he had not "put in or cut out, practically all references to anything like 'religion,' to cults or practices in the imaginary world. For the religious element is *absorbed into the story and the symbolism*" [my emphasis].[14]

Acting as a kind of trinity of goodness, the three main heroes[15]—Frodo, Gandalf, and Aragorn—can be interpreted in several ways. On the one hand, they all possess Christ-like qualities, and in specific situations seem to represent a type of Jesus, either as the suffering servant, as the warrior of the apocalypse, or as the messiah; but on the other hand, when viewed from a wider perspective, each serves a biblical function either as a prophet, an angel, or a theocratic king/messiah. In *The Fellowship of the Ring*, everyone at the Council of Elrond is told: "You have been summoned here to answer the threat of

Mordor. Middle-earth stands upon the brink of destruction, none can escape it. You will unite or you will fall. Each race is bound to this fate; this one doom." The cause of this consternation is Sauron, who since he lost his One Ruling Ring to Isildur, long ago, has been looking for it. For 538 years, the ring has been hidden, and up until this point, very few have even seen it. Trying to decide what to do about it, the Council of Elrond asks Frodo to take it out of his pocket and set it down. When he does, he sighs heavily, as if a great weight has been lifted. Spying the ring, Boromir[16] (Sean Bean) rises and moves toward it, his hand outstretched. Already the ring is working its spell on him. The ring "is a gift," he says, his eyes glazed over. "A gift to the foes of Mordor. Why not use this ring? . . . Give Gondor the weapon of the enemy. Let us use it against him." Gandalf stops Boromir, explaining that "the ring is altogether evil" and that it cannot be wielded by anyone, because it "answers to Sauron alone." Almost immediately, everyone begins to fight over the ring, except for Frodo, who watches the bickering men reflected from the gold band. Realizing that no one else can carry the ring, he steps forward and sacrifices himself to be the Ringbearer. Once he claims this burden, which is his destiny, the other men step up to pledge their arms.

Frodo Baggins seems the unlikeliest of heroes: He's diminutive in statute, and he's sensitive and intelligent in personality. But inside of him one finds a well of strength and a nobility of spirit that are put to the test. Frodo's destiny as the "deliverer" of Middle-earth isn't immediately revealed to the audience,[17] and in fact, Frodo doesn't even know of his destiny until Gandalf tells him of it. In the novel, Gandalf says that it wasn't by chance that the One Ring fell into the hands of Frodo's relative: "There was something else at work, beyond any design of the Ring-maker. I can put it no plainer than by saying that Bilbo was *meant* to find the ring, and *not* by its maker. In which case, you also were *meant* to have it. And that may be an encouraging thought."[18] Later, Frodo questions him, "Why did it come to me? Why was I chosen?" Gandalf responds that "Such questions cannot be answered. You may be sure that it was not for any merit that others do not possess: not for power or wisdom, at any rate. But you have been chosen, and you must therefore use such strength and heart and wits as you have."[19] Galadriel, "the last remaining of the Great among the High Elves,"[20] reiterates to the Hobbit that "this task was appointed to you."

Who actually "chose" Frodo for this task or when he was chosen for it is never explained in the cinematic trilogy; however, Tolkien did create an extensive mythology in his books.[21] It probably doesn't matter who chose Frodo, the fact remains that he was chosen; therefore, in this capacity he is a prophet, which is defined as "an authorized spokesman of divinity. In religious phenomenology the following were marks of a prophet: a consciousness of having been chosen and called by God; awareness of having a message from God, and with this message a mission to make it known in the name of God and his word."[22] Furthermore, prophets are inspired by God and can see future events in dreams or visions. And finally, prophets are unable to resist their mission or mandate from God, because of their sense of obligation or moral commitment to the call.[23] Frodo may not have a message to deliver, but, like Moses, he has a task to complete, to free his follow Hobbits—and everyone else in Middle-earth—from the impending bondage of Sauron and his One Ring. Like a prophet, he, too, has nightmares that reveal the future, and an intuitive sense of things to come. And, even though Gollum shows Frodo a ghastly mirror of his possible future, Frodo is compelled to be the Ringbearer; he is determined to fulfill his task. As Gandalf tells him, carrying the ring is a heavy burden, "So heavy that none could lay it on another. I do not lay it on you. But if you take it freely, I will say that your choice is right."[24]

This leads us to how Frodo is Christ-like. Taking up the One Ring is like taking up the cross, for both lead to anguish and physical and mental suffering. Throughout the three films, the ring intoxicates its wearer;[25] it tempts him by whispering the Black Speech of Mordor, and it drives him to the brink of madness. What's worse, the longer a person possesses it, the more bestial or dehumanized that person becomes. One only needs to see how Smeagol transforms from one of the typical River-folk to the salamander-like being called Gollum to understand this.[26] The One Ring also makes a person forget who he is. For example, in the Land of Shadow, at the end of *The Return of the King*, Frodo seems to be near death—his breathing is raspy, he's weak, and he's hallucinating—and he's also losing everything that makes him, him. Sam asks him if he remembers the Shire, Frodo responds that he can't recall the "taste of food, the feel of water, the sound of wind, no memory of tree or grass or flower, no image of moon or star are left to me. . . . I am naked in the dark, Sam, and there is no veil between me and the wheel of fire. I begin to see it even with my waking eyes, and all else fades." As Frodo gets closer to Mount Doom, the ring becomes unbearably heavy; "It's such a weight to carry," Frodo says. In fact, the ring proves to be so heavy that Sam, in *The Return of the King*, ends up carrying Frodo over his shoulders, saying, "I can't carry it for you . . . but I can carry you."

What's more, the ring's power manages to be even too great for this kindhearted Hobbit, who at the moment of throwing it into the volcano hesitates: "What are you waiting for?" Sam asks. "Just let it go." Frodo looks at the ring then back at Sam. "The ring is mine," he says, then puts it on his finger with a slight smile.[27] Temptation is a constant companion for Frodo, and in this, one is reminded of Jesus' own temptation in the desert, when, in Matthew 4:8–10, "The devil took him to a very high *mountain* [my emphasis], and showed him all the kingdoms of the world and the glory of them and he said to him: 'All these I will give you, if you will fall down and worship me.'" The daily struggle to overcome these temptations drains Frodo emotionally and physically, much as Jesus is wearied by his task, as is evidenced in Mark 14:32, when Jesus is praying in the Garden of Gethsemane, and again in Mark 15:34, when, on the cross, he cries out "*Eloi, Eloi, lama sabachthani?*" ("My God, My God, why hast thou forsaken me?"). Lending additional support that Frodo is a "suffering Christ" is a scene at the end of *The Return of the King*, during which Sam cradles a very weak Frodo in what looks like a Pietà.

As one can see, Frodo truly is a suffering servant, and in this sense, he is like Jesus in the Gospel of Mark, which more than any of the other Gospels, depicts his physical and psychological pain. In describing Jesus' Passion, Mark also stresses Jesus' vulnerability to evil, by showing how he falls into the power of his enemies.[28] In *The Return of the King*, when the Mouth of Sauron comes out of the Black Gate to meet Aragorn, Gandalf, Legolas, and Gimli and tells them, "Know that [Frodo] suffered greatly at the hand of his host. Who knew that one so small could endure so much pain? And he did, Gandalf, he did." Most of Frodo's torment is psychological; however, he does bear several physical reminders of his undertaking. In *The Fellowship of the Ring*, he is stabbed in the shoulder by a Ringwraith. The wound nearly kills him, and even after several years, Frodo tells Sam that it still hasn't healed.[29] Furthermore, in *The Return of the King*, as Frodo and Sam move closer to Mount Doom, the audience can see that the chain on which the ring hangs is burning into Frodo's neck, and when he is in the lair of the spider Shelob, she paralyzes him. In all,

Frodo suffers more than anyone else in the trilogy. But what's most commendable is that he suffers all of these torments willingly. As it says in Matthew 10:22, "The man who preserves up to the end is the man who will be saved." Frodo's motives aren't selfish, though, as Elijah Wood explained in an interview that Frodo is "essentially giving away his soul to save Middle-earth."[30] Again, this echoes the Markian idea that Jesus was born to suffer, but for a greater salvific purpose. While talking about Frodo in a letter from 1963, Tolkien states that some people "seem to be placed in sacrificial positions: situations or tasks that for perfection of solution demand powers beyond their utmost limits. . . . Frodo undertook his quest out of love—to save the world he knew from disaster at his own expense, if he could; and also in complete humility, acknowledging that he was wholly inadequate to the task."[31]

Frodo isn't the only one asked to "save the world." Everyone in the Fellowship is charged with this task, and even though they know that suffering, pain, and death await them, they continue. They are like Jesus' 12 disciples, who when called to service they follow without much thought of themselves. As it says in Mark 1:17–19, "And [Jesus] said to them, 'Follow me and I will make you fishers of men.' And immediately they left their nets and followed him." And also, in Mark 8:34–38, Jesus says, "Anyone who wishes to be a follower of mine must leave self behind; he must take up his cross and come with me. For whoever would save his life will lose it; and whoever loses his life for my sake and the gospel's will save it. For what does it profit a man to gain the whole world and forfeit his life?" As Wood explained, everyone in the LOTR plays an important role in defeating the evil forces. "No person can complete a task on their own. They cannot do it without the help of their friends. And that's not only true for Frodo and Sam. As they head up the mountaintop to destroy this ring, Aragorn and Gimli and Legolas and Gandalf are charging the Black Gate to draw Sauron's eye away and give them an opportunity. That's real friendship, real teamwork. There's something so beautiful about risking your life for the good of everyone."[32]

Gandalf is another character who possesses Christ-like characteristics. In The Fellowship of the Ring, Gandalf the Grey sacrifices himself while battling the Balrog, an ancient demon. He then returns, in The Two Towers, resurrected as Gandalf the White. In the film, he first appears to Aragorn, Gimli, and Legolas as a blinding white light, his face barely perceptible. Once the men recognize who he is, Legolas kneels before him. Gandalf then speaks, "I am Saruman as he should have been." In the book, he is described as having "hair as white as snow in the sunshine" and wearing a "gleaming white robe. . . . The eyes under his deep brows were bright, piercing as the rays of the sun."[33] Gandalf's new appearance might remind the viewer of several passages from the New Testament. The first occur in the Book of Acts, especially Acts 9:1–19, 22:5–16, and 26:12–18, when Saul, later named Paul, is on the road to Damascus, and a light from heaven, "brighter than the sun, shining round me and those who journeyed with me. And when we had all fallen to the ground, I heard a voice." The shining being was, of course, Jesus. This powerful event caused Saul to convert to Christianity and become its most important champion.

The second account occurs in the Book of Revelation 7:13, which reads, "Then one of the elders addressed me, saying, 'Who are these, clothed in white robes, and whence have they come?' . . . And he said to me, 'These are they who have come out of the great tribulation; they have washed their robes and made them white in the blood of the Lamb.'" Of the change in his character, Ian McKellen said, "When he goes back in *The Two Towers*, it's clear what has to be done. And what's needed is not the old academic . . . who is keeping an eye on things . . . [but] a commander, a military point of view, a man of action. . . . He's going to be in the thick of it, helping lead the troops to victory in a series of mighty battles."[34] This shift in demeanor and purpose mirrors Jesus' own transformation between the Gospels and the Book of Revelation. In the Gospels, Jesus is a wise teacher who acts as a shepherd, watching over his disciples, but when he returns in the Book of Revelation, he is "no longer Mark's suffering servant or John's embodiment of divine Wisdom. Revelation's Jesus is the Messiah of popular expectations; a conquering warrior-king who slays his enemies and proves beyond all doubt his right to universal rule . . . the Jesus of Revelation comes not to forgive sinners and instruct them in higher righteousness but to inflict a wrathful punishment upon his opponents."[35]

The parallels between Gandalf the White and the Jesus of the apocalypse continue with the imagery evoked in Revelation 19:11–16, with the image of a man, dressed in a white robe dipped in blood and with a sharp sword issuing from his mouth, who comes charging on a white horse to "smite the nations." During the final battle in *The Return of the King*, Gandalf rides a majestic white horse, Shadowfax, the king of the horses, onto the battlefield and carries a long white staff in his hand, which he uses with punitive force. Another hint that Gandalf represents a Christ-like figure is the fact that, like Jesus, he is known to "speak in riddles," as Aragorn says after the wizard returns as Gandalf the White. In the Gospels, especially Mark, Jesus taught with the aid of parables, many of which weren't understood by those around him.

In his letters, Tolkien spoke at length about Gandalf, and in one dated from 1954, he explains that Gandalf is an "incarnate 'angel,' . . . an emissary from the Lords of the West, sent to Middle-earth."[36] And in another dated 1956, he says that Gandalf's function "as a 'wizard' (Istari) is . . . to assist the rational creatures of Middle-earth to resist Sauron, a power too great for them unaided."[37] Which angel he might have been thinking about is unclear; however, it's likely that it was St. Michael the Archangel, who is known as the "prince of the presence, angel of repentance, righteousness, mercy and sanctification."[38] According to the *New Advent Catholic Encyclopedia*, Christian tradition gives to St. Michael four offices: to fight against Satan; to rescue the souls of the faithful from the power of the enemy, especially at the hour of death; to be the champion of God's people (he was the patron of the order of knights during the Middle Ages); and to call away from earth and bring men's souls to judgment. Furthermore, St. Michael was known for giving victory in war to his clients.[39] In the Dead Sea Scrolls, Michael is called the "Prince of Light," and leads the angels of light in battle against the legions of the angels of darkness, the latter under the command of the demon Belial, who is equated with Satan.[40] The parallels between Tolkien's creation and the Bible are uncanny, as even on *The Lord of the Rings* site, the heroes are called "the Forces of Light" and the villains are "the Forces of Darkness." Another possible choice for Gandalf would be the Archangel Gabriel who is known as the "angel of the annunciation, resurrection, mercy, vengeance, death and revelation."[41] In rabbinic literature, he is the prince of justice; Origin calls him the angel of war.[42] Michael and Gabriel are the only angels mentioned by name in the Hebrew Bible, and stories about them become easily confused as to which one did what.

Gandalf serves many of the aforementioned angelic functions, especially once he becomes Gandalf the White. In fact, one could say that Gandalf orchestrates most of the events that occur in the story, from telling Frodo about the ring and "announcing" to the Hobbit his destiny to conducting the defense of Minas Tirith and even leading the heroes to the Black Gate. Furthermore, he is always fighting beside the heroes in their quest for victory against the dark hordes. Furthermore, Gandalf is the only character in the trilogy who knows of Aragorn's true lineage and of his destiny to be the future king. Gandalf is, in every sense of the word, a guardian angel, whose role it is to "lead us, if we wish it, to the Kingdom of Heaven."[43] This heaven, in the *LOTR*, is perhaps more in line with the Jewish concept of a time when a messiah or king, from the line of David, crushes his foes and purifies the holy land, thus establishing a kind of theocracy.

Even though Revelation 19:11–16 claims that this horseman, who is followed by the armies of heaven, has come to rule the nations with a rod of iron and "on his robe and on his thigh, he has a name inscribed, King of kings and Lord of lords," this doesn't apply to Gandalf the White; his task isn't to rule the land. That privilege belongs to Aragorn (Viggo Mortensen), who, like no one else in the trilogy, embodies wisdom, bravery, and "divine" kingship. Again this concept of a hidden king who is descended from a special bloodline reminds one of the Jewish concept of the *moshiach* or messiah, a secular ruler who comes to gather the exiles, restore the religious courts of justice, put an end to wickedness, reward the righteous, and most importantly, restore the line of King David.[44] This actually transpires at the end of *The Return of the King*—the Free Peoples have been reunited, and a king who traces his lineage back to Isildur has returned to the throne after a 1,000-year absence. It is said in the book that during his 120-year reign, he extended the borders of the kingdom and reestablished long-absent peace, justice, and prosperity.[45]

In *The Return of the King*, Aragorn also demonstrates a Christ-like ability to "raise the dead." Outnumbered against Sauron's soldiers, Aragorn decides that he will seek help from the legions of dead, men who had sworn allegiance to his ancestor but who were corrupted by Sauron and thus betrayed the king and the alliance of men and elves. As Legolas explains, "They swore an oath but they fled; now they are cursed, never to rest until they fulfill their pledge." Aragorn, Legolas, and Gimli take the Path of the Dead into the Haunted Mountain of Dwimorberg, where the spirits and remains of these men dwell. Upon meeting them, the King of the Dead tells them that the "dead do not suffer the living to pass." A fearless Aragorn replies, "You will suffer me." He then summons them to fulfill their oath. "None but the king of Gondor may command me," the King of the Dead says, and then tries to engage Aragorn in battle. But Aragorn holds his ground, and again commands them to "Fight for us and regain your honor. Fight for me and I will release you from this living death." After realizing that Aragorn holds the reforged sword of his ancestor, they acquiesce. This scene recalls Jesus' descent into "hell," a place that is the equivalent of death or dwelling place of the dead. "In the Jewish-Christian tradition, the descent of Christ into Hades has a salvific character, for with it comes the liberation of the just of the Old Testament. Thus they begin to benefit from the fruits of the redemption."[46] Aragorn, like Jesus, can offer the dead "redemption" if they will only follow and fight for him. Once they have fulfilled their oath and have dispatched many of Sauron's soldiers, Aragorn, who proves himself to be a trustworthy man of his word, tells them to "go in peace" and they disappear. Finally, like Jesus, Aragorn has an uncanny ability to heal the sick. In the book version of *The Return of the King*, he heals Faramir, Boromir's younger brother, after he falls under the Black Breath of the Nazgul. In the book and only in the special extended edition of the DVD,[47] he also cures Eowyn, after she kills the Nazgul-lord.

Several of the other characters in the trilogy possess ideal Christian characteristics, including humility, kindness, and absolute loyalty; however, no one embodies these better than Samwise[48] Gamgee (Sean Astin), who really is the heart of the film. In an interview with *MovieWeb*, Astin said of his character, "Sam is the best kind of friend. Through thick or thin, he is always there. I found myself gravitating toward that quality in my portrayal, toward this idea of an earnest, loyal, decent fellow."[49] As the film progresses and Frodo becomes psychologically weakened, Sam does everything he can to help him, including carrying him. For the most part, Sam is largely unaffected by the encroaching darkness around him, and he maintains an optimistic attitude. For example, unlike Frodo, who wonders "what are we holding on to," Sam somehow, even in the midst of despair, finds meaning in their quest, and responds that "There is some good in this world . . . and it's worth fighting for." At another point, he says: "By rights we shouldn't even be here. But we are. It's like in the great stories, Mr. Frodo. The ones that really mattered. Full of darkness and danger, they were. And sometimes you didn't want to know the end. Because how could the end be happy? How could the world go back to the way it was when so much bad had happened? But in the end, it's only a passing thing, this shadow. Even darkness must pass. A new day will come. And when the sun shines it will shine out the clearer. Those were the stories that stayed with you. That meant something, even if you were too small to understand why. But I think, Mr. Frodo, I do understand. I know now. Folk in those stories had lots of chances of turning back only they didn't. They kept going. Because they were holding on to something." Many things drive Samwise forward, particularly friendship, loyalty, and duty. Even when they are in the Land of Shadow and their situation seems lost, Sam looks up in the sky and says, "Look Frodo, there's light up there, beauty that no shadow can touch."

In *The Return of the King*, we see Sam's purity, courage, and commitment put to the test, and he emerges largely unscathed.[50] When Frodo is taken hostage by the Orcs,[51] Sam picks up the One Ruling Ring for safekeeping. The two eventually meet up again in the Tower of Cirith Ungol ("path of the spider"), where Frodo tells him that the Orcs have taken everything, including the ring. Cheerfully, Sam tells him that he has it, and begins to offer it back to its owner. In the film version, Sam hesitates for a second, listening to the seductive whispers, but eventually he relinquishes it. In the book, he doesn't even hesitate, and when Frodo verbally assaults him, demanding that he return the ring, Sam ends up on his knees, sobbing.[52]

As Astin explains, Sam has a loving servant/master relationship with Frodo that only deepens as the trilogy advances. Perhaps we can take a leap and say that if Frodo is Christ-like, then Sam's relationship to him demonstrates the ideal relationship that Christians should have to God/Jesus; they, too, should remain steadfast and loyal no matter what happens, even when they are staring despair in the face. Another option is that Sam represents Jesus's disciple Peter, who had certain preeminence among the 12 and who, when the Passion was imminent, he, more than the others, protested his loyalty (even if he betrayed Jesus by denying him three times as predicted).[53] Producer Barrie M. Osborne echoes this idea, saying that "Sam is the rock; he will not give up on his friend." Whether Sam shows Christians the path of self-sacrifice and loyal service or he simply represents Peter, the "rock of the church," he remains, as Christopher Lee says, the heroic ordinary man: "It is Sam who was chosen by Gandalf; it is Sam who supports Frodo; it is Sam who distrusts Gollum . . . he is, for me, the hero of the stories."[54]

In the *LOTR* trilogy, good is balanced equally by evil, and we see a kind of diabolical trinity in Sauron, Saruman, and the One Ruling Ring. Although none of this is revealed in the films, it's interesting to note that like Gandalf and Saruman, Sauron was born a Maia, which is supposed to be the purest of the spiritual beings. But sometime during the First Age, he fell under the spell of Melkor, also known as Morgoth ("dark enemy") and he turned to the "dark side," waging war and corrupting as many men as he could. During the Second Age, he began building the fortress called Barad-dur, literally "dark tower," and began forging the Rings of Power with which he hoped to enslave the world. After much warfare, the ring was taken from him by Isildur. Finally, in the Third Age, Sauron began his fervent search for the missing ring. Now formless, he appears only as a giant, lidless eye wreathed in flame. Under his control are legions of demons and "slaves," such as the Nazgul (Ringwraiths), who were originally men but were corrupted by the rings that they were given by Sauron. In the stories about him, one also learns that he is deceitful, assumes pleasing shapes to trick people, and is full of pride.[55]

To find a Christian parallel to Sauron, one need only examine the figure of Satan, whose name literally means "adversary." In the Hebrew Bible, Satan is "God's faithful servant" who "patrols the earth to examine the lives of men so as to be their accuser before God."[56] A change comes about in the Wisdom literature, where he is linked to the serpent that tempted Eve in the Garden of Eden. An even greater change occurs in the New Testament, where "Satan is the prince of demons and the prince of this world which is subjected to his power. The coming of the kingdom of God, which is definitive salvation brings with the destruction of the kingdom of Satan."[57] In the *LOTR* trilogy, Sauron is painted as the powerful adversary of everything that is good in Middle-earth, and it is only through his defeat that peace can reign. As Tolkien explains, although he didn't believe that absolute evil existed, for him "Sauron represents as near an approach to the wholly evil will as possible. He had gone the way of all tyrants: beginning well . . . but he went further than human tyrants in pride and the lust of domination."[58] Throughout the films, Sauron is called many names, including "faithless and accursed," and Gandalf even says that his diabolical plan involves "covering the land with a second darkness." This idea of man's hidden adversary who is waiting in the shadows and biding his time while also building his army of demons is reminiscent of how Christians envision the apocalypse.

If we look at Sauron in light of the Christian Bible, especially the Book of Revelation and other apocalyptic texts, one might even say that he is an Antichrist, a being who is called "'a man of lawlessness,' sustained by Satan, who will oppose whatever bears the name of God." As explained in the *New World Dictionary-Concordance to the New American Bible*, the apocalyptic authors never make it clear who exactly will rise against God, and this same vagueness colors the Gospel accounts. They simply tell us that the term refers to those who "deny that Jesus is the Christ."[59] Sauron is largely fearless; however, like Satan, he has a weakness, and that's the messiah, the Christ. And in the case of *LOTR*, that threat comes in the guise of Aragorn. As Gandalf says, "Sauron will suffer no rival. From the summit of Barad-dur his eye watches ceaselessly. But he is not so mighty yet that he is above fear. Doubt ever gnaws at him. The rumor has reached him. The heir of Numenor still lives. Sauron fears you, Aragorn. He fears what you may become. And so he will strike hard and fast at the world of Men."

Like Gandalf, Saruman the White is one the five Istari or wizards who were sent to Middle-earth to unite and counsel the Free Peoples in their struggles against Sauron. Even though these beings were forbidden to dominate anyone or to match Sauron's power with power, Saruman disobeyed this command.[60] At one point in *The Two Towers* he states that "We have only to remove those who oppose us," and later he tells his henchmen that "a new power is rising. Its victory is at hand. This night the land will be stained with the blood of Rohan. March to Helm's Deep. Leave none alive." Like Sauron before him, Saruman's downfall is that he lets his pride and lust for power overcome his wisdom. Not only did he become the chief adversary of the freedom-loving people of Rohan, but by dark means he also bred a vast army of Uruk-hai warriors to conquer their lands and destroy them. As Saruman says in *The Two Towers*, "Together, my lord Sauron, we shall rule this Middle-earth. The old world will burn in the fires of industry. Forests will fall. A new order will rise. We will drive the machine of war with the sword and the spear and the iron fist of the Orc."

Again, returning to Christian myth, we find that Saruman is not unlike Lucifer, whose name means "morning star," and whose identity has become fused with that of Satan. In Isaiah 14:12–20, we learn that Lucifer's "fall" was also a result of pride: "How you are fallen from heaven, O Day Star, son of Dawn! How you are cut down to the ground, you who laid the nations low! You said in your heart, 'I will ascend to heaven; above the stars of God I will set my throne on high. . . . I will make myself like the Most High.'" His punishment is to be "cast out, away from your sepulcher, like a loathed untimely birth, clothed with the slain, those pierced by the sword." Saruman suffers a worse punishment. In *The Return of the King*, he is locked in the tower[61] of Orthanc, in Isengard, which he has transformed from a vegetative place to one of stones and machinery. Gandalf promises to spare his life in exchange for information, but a prideful Saruman's scoffs at him, saying, "Save your pity and your mercy. I have no need of it." He then tries to set Gandalf on fire. Gandalf responds by breaking Saruman's staff (a wizard's power is in his staff). Eventually, Saruman is stabbed in the back by his own "agent of evil," Grima Wormtongue.

The One Ruling Ring is the final foe to the free peoples of Middle-earth. The mythology of this ring is contained in a story that dates to the Second Age of Middle-earth, when 19 Great Rings, each bestowing long life and magical powers to the wearers, were created. As the Ring-spell reads, three rings were for the Elvin kings; seven for the Dwarf lords; nine for mortal men; "and one for the Dark Lord [Sauron] on his dark throne. In the land of Mordor where the shadows lie. One Ring to rule them all, One Ring to find them, One Ring to bring them all and in the darkness bind them."[62] As Gandalf explains, this one ring wields tremendous power, and if it falls back into Sauron's hands, he will be rendered invincible. The ring holds great allure, because of what it can do for its wearer. It prevents or slows the aging process—Bilbo lives much longer than most Hobbits and ages considerably once he gives away the ring. It renders its wearer invisible while making the invisible world visible; Frodo can see the Ringwraiths in their true form when he puts on the ring. And it enhances the natural powers of the possessor, a motive, Tolkien said, that was easily corruptible into evil.[63] Even though these may sound harmless, the ring poses incredible dangers to anyone who possesses it, because it will literally take her or him over; and in the case of Gollum, it will "devour them."[64]

The ring is so dangerous that not even a person filled with goodness can take hold of it, and that includes Gandalf and Galadriel. For example, in *The Fellowship of the Ring*, Frodo tries to give it to Gandalf, who recoils, saying, "Don't tempt me, Frodo. I dare not take it even to keep it safe. I would use the ring in a desire to do good but through me it would wield too great a power." When it is offered to Galadriel, she responds, "I do not deny that my heart has greatly desired this." Then her fair countenance changes to a dark being that says, "In the place of a Dark Lord you would have a Queen. Not dark but beautiful and terrible as the morning. Treacherous as the sea. Stronger than the foundations of the earth. All shall love me and despair." Ultimately she rejects the ring, stating that she will "diminish, and go into the West and remain Galadriel." As Gandalf and then Elrond, a half-elf, says at the Council of Elrond: "We cannot use [the ring]. . . . You have only one choice. The ring must be destroyed, taken deep into Mordor and cast back into the fiery chasm from whence it came."

This One Ruling Ring doesn't seem to have a Christian parallel per se, at least not in an identifiable personage, but what it does seem to represent is original sin. As *The Catechism of the Catholic Church* explains, man, who was "tempted by the devil, let his trust in the Creator die in his heart and, abusing his freedom, disobeyed God's command. All subsequent sin would be disobedience toward God and lack of trust in his goodness." Furthermore, "in this sin man *preferred* himself to God and by that very act scorned him. *He chose himself over and against God* [my emphasis]. . . . Man was destined to be fully 'divinized' by God in glory. Seduced by the devil, he wanted to 'be like God,' but 'without God, before God, and not in accordance with God.'"[65] St. Augustine elaborates on Adam's transgression in *City of God*, saying that "to abandon God and to exist in oneself, that is to please oneself, is not immediately to lose all being; but it is to come nearer to nothingness. That is why the proud . . . are called 'self-pleasers.'"[66] The original evil is that "man regards himself as his own light, and turns away from the light which would make man himself a light if he would set his heart on it."[67] Undoubtedly, Tolkien was influenced by Augustinian thinking, because he, too, believed in the power of evil, and more specifically, in its ability to corrupt us. Looking at his trilogy, we see that all of the characters who give in to the power of the One Ring—Sauron, Saruman, Boromir, and Gollum—place self-interest above all else; those who reject it— Sam, Gandalf, Galadriel, Elrond, and for most of the film, Frodo—don't. The latter characters favor humility, a quality that Augustine says is "highly prized in the City of God."[68]

Sauron and Saruman both desire to become like the Christian God, and even engage in God-like behavior but with a diabolical twist. For instance, Saruman takes his Eden-like surroundings in Rohan ("horse land") and transforms it into a literal hell on Earth, complete with fire belching from the ground and demons toiling in dark caverns. Furthermore, like God, he begins creating his own race of "men." These Uruk-hai were considered to be superior to Orcs, which were themselves corrupted elves, because "they were almost as tall as men, had straight, strong legs, and did not weaken in sunlight." Physically, they were black and slanty-eyed.[69] In Sauron and Saruman's quest for power, they end up destroying themselves and everything around them.

Many other *LOTR* characters become "evil" or spiritually "lost," because they either choose self-interest (or self-exaltation, as Augustine would say) over the greater good or they choose the material realm over the spiritual one. As Augustine says, they succumb to one of the various sins, most notably pride and lust. (Depending on the circumstances, lust also can give rise to anger, greed, obstinacy, vanity, and "lust for domination."[70]) In the *LOTR*, Sauron was able to ensnare nine kings by appealing to their sense of pride and greed. He gave each a Ring of Power that was supposed to confer long life and endless power. These "gifts," though, came with a heavy price. The kings were transformed into the immortal Nazgul or Ringwraiths, whose principal task it was to "lead Sauron's armies and cow his enemies."[71] No longer resembling human beings, they "were invisible to normal eyes and could be seen only by their black clothing."[72] And instead of voices, they emitted extremely loud, piercing cries. The only way someone can see their true selves is to wear the One Ruling Ring, and when one does, what he or she sees is terrifying. The Nazgul are shown to be "writhing, tormented beings, all of tattered gray and white they are, their expressions distorted by the greed and grief of their condition, their crowns a mockery of the honor and rule they have lost."[73] Although no names are listed for these creatures, it is suggested that "Gothmog was possibly the name of the second highest Nazgul,"[74] and the mightiest is called the Witch King of Angmar.

Sauron's chief servants, the "Orcs were bred in mockery of elves, and, like elves, they were fierce warriors and did not die naturally . . . they tended to be short, squat and bow-legged with long arms, dark faces, squinty eyes and long fangs. . . . They hated all things of beauty and loved to kill and destroy."[75] Compare this to the description of elves, which are considered to be the fairest of earthly creatures. They stand about six feet and are graceful. They don't sleep, but "rest their minds in waking dreams or by looking at beautiful things."[76] In this juxtaposition, Tolkien suggests that when a person gives into "evil," he or she becomes perverted and grotesque.

Boromir is another character who falls under the spell of the ring. As was previously mentioned, the minute he sees it he seems to be intoxicated by it and he tries to take it for himself. Gandalf stops him, but eventually the lure of "Isildur's bane," as he calls the ring, proves too strong, and in *The Fellowship of the Ring*, he waits for his opportunity to take it for himself. In the DVD and book chapter titled "The Breaking of the Fellowship," Boromir sees Frodo, alone in the forest, and he begins making conversation. "The Ring. It is not a strange fate that we should suffer so much fear and doubt for so small a thing. . . . Could I not have a sight of it again?" In the book it says that at this moment, Frodo's heart went suddenly cold, and "he caught the strange gleam in Boromir's eyes, yet his face was still kind and friendly." The conversation turns to the use of the ring, and Frodo reminds him that "what is done with it turns to evil." Boromir boasts that "true-hearted men will not be corrupted. We of Minas Tirith have been staunch through long years of trial. We do not desire the power of wizard-lords, only strength to defend ourselves, strength in a just cause." As he continues to talk, his choice of words becomes all too familiar— "we" and "our" become "I" and "me." "The ring would give me power of Command. How I would drive the hosts of Mordor, and all men would flock to my banner," Boromir expounds. The book continues, "Almost he seemed to have forgotten Frodo, while his talk dwelt on walls and weapons . . . and he drew up plans for great alliances and glorious victories to be . . . and [he] became himself a mighty king, benevolent and wise."[77] We hear in those words the seal of Boromir's fate. After Frodo rejects his request to "borrow the ring," Boromir becomes angry and lunges at the Hobbit. Frodo puts on the ring (becomes invisible) and gets away. Later, Samwise explains to Faramir, Boromir's brother, what happened: "Do you want to know why your brother died? He tried to take the ring from Frodo, after swearing an oath to protect him! He tried to kill him! The ring drove your brother mad." Like so many before him, Boromir begins with a vision of helping others and ends with one of himself exalted and powerful. As Augustine says, "The beginning of all sin is pride."[78]

Some have listed Gollum as evil,[79] but as Gandalf says in *The Fellowship of the Ring*, he deserves more of our pity than our hatred, or as Christians might say, "Love the sinner but hate the sin." Why should he be pitied? In the book, when Gandalf is explaining the history of the One Ring and how it affected Gollum, he reminds Frodo that "even Gollum was not wholly ruined. . . . There was a little corner in his mind that was still his own, and light came through it, as through a chink in the dark."[80] Audiences see a dramatization of Smeagol's "fall"[81] as *LOTR: The Return of the King* opens. Smeagol and his cousin Deagol are out fishing. When Deagol catches a fish, he gets pulled under the water, and there, at the bottom of the lake is the ring, partially hidden in the dirt. He brings it to the top, and while he's "gloating over" it, Smeagol comes up behind him. The minute his eyes catch the glint of metal, his voice changes to Gollum's as he says, "Give us that, Deagol, my love." When Deagol refuses, they get into a fight and Smeagol strangles his cousin to death. In the book, Gandalf explains that "No one ever found out what had become of Deagol; he was murdered far from home, and his body was cunningly hidden."[82]

Smeagol learned how to use the powers of the ring, and he "used it to find out secrets, and he put his knowledge to crooked and malicious uses."[83] Over time, he is shunned, cursed, and exiled. "He wandered in loneliness, weeping a bit for the hardness of the world. . . . He caught fish . . . and ate them raw. One day . . . he was bending over a pool [and] he felt a burning on the back of his head, and a dazzling light from the water pained his wet eyes."[84] Gandalf reveals that the sun caused the burning, and that he must now travel by night. Later, the reader will learn that Orcs are also weakened by the sun. The idea that the villains of the story are more or less allergic to light is in keeping with a long-standing tradition that light represents purity and goodness, and therefore will repel "evil," while the dark is the dwelling place of all malevolent beings.[85]

What's particularly interesting about the Smeagol and Deagol story is how similar it is to that of Cain and his brother Abel. Found in Genesis 4, the men bring an offering to God; Cain brings the "fruit of the ground" and Abel brings the "firstlings of his flock and of their fat portions." God accepts Abel's offering and rejects Cain's, which leaves him angry.[86] God responds to him: "If you do well, will you not be accepted? And if you do not do well, sin is crouching at the doors; its desire is for you, but you must master it" (Genesis 6–7). In the explanation given by the *New Advent Catholic Encyclopedia*, "Sin here is represented under the figure of a wild beast crouching at the door of the heart ready to pounce upon its victim. Cain is able to resist temptation, but he does not."[87] Cain does the worst thing imaginable and murders his brother in a field. When God returns, inquiring where Abel is, Cain lies, saying that he doesn't know, and then utters, "Am I my brother's keeper?" "And the Lord said, 'What have you done? The voice of your brother's blood is crying to me from the ground' (Genesis 10). God then puts a curse upon Cain, telling him that he will be a fugitive and a wanderer on the Earth. Cain replies, "Behold, thou hast driven me this day away from the ground; and *from thy face I shall be hidden* [my emphasis] . . . and whoever finds me will slay me" (Genesis 4:14). But God responds that no one "shall ever kill Cain, not in vengeance" (Genesis 15). Like Cain, Gollum kills in anger or greed and then hides the body. Once he's found out, he too is shunned and exiled. And even though many characters, including Sam and Frodo, who come across Gollum think about killing him, they don't or can't. Perhaps, Gollum's "mark" for his crime is for others to pity him and spare him his life, thus leaving him to a much worse fate, which is to ruminate incessantly over the horrors he has committed and pine for a ring that he can never possess.

In the *LOTR*, we don't see any God or gods who pass judgment on Gollum, or any other character for that matter, but he suffers for his "sins" all the same. His addiction to the ring transforms him, physically, into an ashen-colored "creature" that crawls around on all fours. It's as if the ring causes him to devolve into something that's more animal than man: "They cursed us and drove us away. And we wept, precious, to be so alone. And we forgot the taste of bread. . . . The sound of the trees. We even forgot our own name." In his madness, he is subjected to repeated tauntings by his "evil side," which calls him a liar, a thief, and a murderer. As it says in the novel, the ring "was eating up his mind . . . and the torments had become almost unbearable. All the 'great secrets' under the mountains had turned out to be just empty night: there was nothing more to find out, nothing worth doing, only nasty furtive eating and resentful remembering. He was altogether wretched. He hated the dark, and he hated light more; he hated everything, and the Ring most of all."[88] As one can see, like Frodo, Gollum suffers more in his mind than in his body. Augustine explains that these kinds of torments or "so-called pains of the flesh are really pains of the soul, experienced in the flesh and from the flesh. The flesh can surely feel no desire by itself, apart from the soul. . . . Bodily pain is really nothing but a distress of the soul arising from the body."[89]

Christianity teaches us that redemption is possible for all, and Frodo seems to believe in this. In *The Two Towers*, he asks Sam why he's always calling Gollum names and running him down. Sam replies that "there's naught left in him but lies and deceit. It's the ring he wants; it's all he cares about." Frodo refuses to believe this, saying, "I want to help him . . . because I have to believe he can come back." Sam reminds him that Gollum can't be saved. Frodo obviously sees himself in Gollum, and at one point says that "This creature is bound to me and I to him." He wants to save Gollum because if that's possible, then he knows that there might also be hope for him. But in the end, Gollum continues to place the ring, his precious, above everything else. He follows the Hobbits to Mount Doom, and once he sees the ring, he wrestles with Frodo, bites off his finger, and gets his prize. But he loses his balance and falls into Mount Doom, thus saving Middle-earth and freeing Frodo from the ring's spell.

One might wonder how such an "evil" being can, in the end, "redeem" himself, and how such an avaricious act can accomplish something so good. Gandalf tells Frodo that "I have not much hope that Gollum can be cured before he dies, but there is a chance of it. And he is bound up with the fate of the ring. My heart tells me that he has some part to play yet, for good or ill, before the end; and when that comes, the pity of Bilbo may rule the fate of many—yours not least."[90] Following Tolkien's logic, because Gollum's nature would make him susceptible to the ring's power, some "force" put his lies and treachery for something good: to remove Sauron's control from Middle-earth and to restore the rightful heir to the throne of Gondor. As Augustine explains, God is "completely just in his employment of evil choices in his design, so that whereas such evil choices make a wrong use of good natures, *God turns evil choices to good use* [my emphasis]. . . . In the very creation of the Devil, though by God's goodness he was made in a state of good, God had already, in virtue of his foreknowledge, laid plans for making good use of him even in his evil state."[91] Tolkien agrees with this, explaining that "salvation" in the *LOTR* was dependent on several factors. First, others had to have taken pity on and had forgiveness for Gollum, thus sparing his life. Second, "by grace," that last betrayal happened at a precise moment when the "final evil deed was the most beneficial thing anyone could have done for Frodo."[92]

Of Gollum, Tolkien said that he "was pitiable, but he ended in persistent wickedness, and the fact that this worked good was no credit to him. His marvelous courage and endurance . . . being devoted to evil was portentous but not honorable. . . . We have to face the fact that there are persons who yield to temptation, reject their chances of nobility or salvation, and appear to be 'damnable.'"[93] He continues, saying that the ring was too strong for Smeagol, but he never would have had to endure it had he not been the mean person that he was prior to receiving it. One might say that in this instance, Gollum might very well be the *LOTR*'s answer to Judas Iscariot, who, "tradition is almost unanimous in giving avarice as the motivation for his betrayal."[94] According to Christianity, all apparently morally evil acts serve a purpose. As the *Catechism of the Catholic Church* says, even the rejection and murder of Jesus "brought the greatest of goods: the glorification of Christ and our redemption."[95]

Finally, as was previously mentioned, those who reject the ring do so because they place others higher than themselves and live in a spirit of humility.
The best example is, of course, Samwise. But another is Faramir, Boromir's
virtuous younger brother and second son to Denethor II, the steward of Gondor. Because Faramir was gentle in nature—he didn't care for battle for its
own sake—and he seemed to prefer Gandalf over his father, who treated him
with disdain.[96] Faramir is particularly wounded by this, especially because he
knows his brother's true nature. During an exchange about the One Ruling
Ring, Denethor tells his son that he should have brought it back to the citadel,
where it could be hidden: "Boromir would have remembered his father's need;
he would have brought me a kingly gift." Faramir responds, "Boromir would
not have brought back the ring. He would have stretched out his hand to it . .
. and kept it for his own." Sadly, this is exactly what Boromir planned to do. In
The Return of the King, Faramir is ready to sacrifice himself on the battlefield
against Sauron's evil horde. Gandalf tries to stop him, but Faramir says,
"Where does my allegiance lie if not here? This is the city of the men of Numenor. I would gladly give my life to defend her beauty, her memory, . . . her
wisdom." In a chilling sequence, we watch as Faramir and his fellow warriors
are cut down by their foes, while an arrogant and uncaring Denethor greedily
devours a meal, letting juices roll down his chin. Faramir actually comes back
from the battlefield alive, but Denethor, in his madness, tries to burn him and
himself on a funeral pyre. Thankfully, Gandalf and Pippin, a Hobbit, save
Faramir.[97] What made Denethor act this way? He, too, was undermined and
driven insane by greed. Even though he knew that the crown of Gondor was
supposed to be given to the heir of Isildur, he was loath to give up his political position as steward.

One final note before we move on to Buddhism. As has been shown,
Tolkien drew on his Christian faith to conceive of the *LOTR*, and he even admitted that it represents a "monotheistic world of 'natural theology.'" However, he rejected the idea that the Third Age, during which the *LOTR* takes
place, was a "Christian world."[98] This may seem difficult to believe, especially as the events at the end of *The Return of the King* are remarkably similar to those found in the Book of Revelation. For example, in addition to
some examples already given, we find in Revelation 19:17–18 that "an angel
standing in the sun, and with a loud voice called to all of the birds that fly
in midheaven, 'Come, gather for the great supper of God, to eat the flesh of

kings, the flesh of captains, the flesh of mighty men." In *The Return of the King*, giant eagles swoop in to kill the flying beasts that are ridden by the Ringwraiths. Furthermore, Gandalf, who it was suggested might be an angel, uses eagles to rescue Frodo and Sam from the lava pouring out of Mount Doom. In Christianity, not only is the eagle a symbol of the "soaring spirit" but it also has connections to the "Resurrection and of the Christian spirit. The eagle is [also] the attribute of St. John the Evangelist, whose gospel begins with a statement of the divine nature of Christ."[99] Furthermore, the eagle is used "to represent the new life begun at the baptismal font and with the Christian soul strengthened by grace. . . . The eagle is said to have the ability to soar until it is lost to sight, and still retain its ability to gaze into the blazing mid-day sun. For this reason, it has come to symbolize Christ." Finally, it also symbolizes those who are just, or stands for courage, faith, and contemplation.[100]

The eagle makes an earlier appearance in *The Fellowship of the Ring*, when Gandalf is captured by Saruman and held on the pinnacle of Orthanc, the tower of Isengard. There a moth visits him, and Gandalf quietly speaks to it in another language. Later, the moth returns, bringing with it an eagle, and together they free Gandalf from Saruman's captivity and torture. This event is split between the DVD chapters "The Caverns of Isengard" and "Rivendell." In the book, the same event is recounted during "The Council of Elrond" chapter. The text never says anything about a moth, just that Gandalf spoke with "a messenger" that brought "Gwaihir the Windlord, swiftest of the Great Eagles," to his rescue.[101] Although there is no mention of a moth as being associated with Jesus, the butterfly is a symbol of the Resurrection. "It is a symbol of eternal life, of metamorphosis . . . soaring toward heaven in a new and beautiful form."[102]

Other glaring similarities can be found between the book of Revelation and *LOTR*. In Revelation 20:7–10 we learn that Satan will be bound in a bottomless pit for 1,000 years then "released to deceive the nations, to gather them for battle; their number is like the sand of the sea. And they marched up over the broad earth and surrounded the camp of the saints." But the devil won't prevail, because he will be "thrown into the lake of fire and sulfur" (Rev. 20:11). After this, a new heaven and earth will come to pass, and a loud voice will say, "Behold, the dwelling of God is with men. He will dwell with them and they shall be his people" (Rev. 21:1–3).

First, when *LOTR* begins, it has been 1,000 years since the incident between Isildur and Sauron, and it is only at this point that Sauron begins bringing together people from every corner of the world to fight on his side against the inhabitants of Middle-earth. Second, when Aragorn and his army face Sauron's soldiers, they are eventually outnumbered and encircled by them. Third, when Sauron is defeated, Barad-dur crumbles and most of his minions are killed by the collapsing earth; Mount Doom, which is a volcano, erupts, spilling lava and belching sulfur into the air. And finally, a new "kingdom" is established under Aragorn, who when crowned by Gandalf is called King Elessar. As Galadriel says at the very end of *The Return of the King*, "The power of the three rings is now ended. The time has come for the dominion of men."

Buddhism

What seems to be the central problem in the *LOTR*? From a Roman Catholic perspective, one could fault "original sin"; after all, St. Augustine asserted that we are born sinners, tainted from Adam and Eve's first act of disobedience. Also, because of pride, certain individuals simply place themselves before God, and when they do this, they try to build a kingdom on Earth with themselves at the center. What humans should do is be obedient to God, serving his will, and "building a kingdom of heaven or Kingdom of God," as it is suggested in the Gospels, particularly in Matthew. This Kingdom of God means "the ruling of God in our hearts; it means those principles which separate us off from the kingdom of the world and the devil; it means the benign sway of grace."[103] Although Buddhism recognizes many of the same problems that Christianity does, such as the corrupting power of greed, pride, and anger, it interprets these in a different way. While Christians look to a higher power for answers, Buddhists don't because they don't believe in an almighty creator. This shifts responsibility for what happens in *LOTR* from an external corrupting being, such as the devil or original sin, to the individual. As the Buddha said, "Your own self is your master; who else could be? With yourself well controlled, you gain a master very hard to find."[104]

Many of the characters in *LOTR* are suffering, but the ones who seem to suffer the most are Frodo and Gollum. Frodo, who is the "suffering servant," actually sacrifices himself for the greater good, and because of this he would be held up as an ideal. After all, Jesus of Nazareth is said to have endured being mocked, beaten, nailed to a cross, and then left to die. And Christians would say that Gollum suffers because he chooses self over God—the material world and all of its allure over self-denial. Buddhists, again, would arrive at neither of these interpretations, because they understand suffering in a different way. Buddhists acknowledge that suffering is a part of life, and list it, along with impermanence and no-self, as the three marks of existence. As the Buddha said, all created things are transitory, are involved in sorrow, and are without self: "Those who realize [these] are freed from suffering. This is the path that leads to pure wisdom."[105] Even though suffering is acknowledged as a part of life, Buddhism doesn't embrace it or ask its followers to "suffer more." Its goal is to actually extinguish suffering by no longer grasping at impermanence. And we do this by following the Eightfold Path. Furthermore, if we think of "suffering" in terms of physical pain, Buddhism would say that it isn't "noble" to suffer. When Siddhartha Gautama was on the path to enlightenment, he practiced asceticism, living on very little food and water and eschewing any amount of comfort. He almost died from doing this. His conclusion was that these extreme methods weren't getting him any closer to his goal than was living a life of hedonism. Based on his experience, he told his followers to follow the Middle Way.

If we look at Gollum, we see that he suffers mental and physical anguish whether or not he's in possession of his precious. To borrow a phrase from *The Matrix*, the One Ruling Ring is like a "splinter in his mind, driving him mad." Anyone who has encountered the ring[106] looks into it and sees power. When it tempts Boromir, he sees himself as a great warrior commanding all of the forces against Mordor. Galadriel sees herself as beautiful and strong but also fearful and terrible. The ring also bestows upon its wearer "special powers," including invisibility, acute hearing and sight, and the ability to understand unknown languages. Perhaps the most alluring is the ring's promise of youth and immortality, for it slows down aging and decay. According to Galadriel in *The Two Towers*, "the ring brought to Gollum unnatural long life. For 500 years it poisoned his mind." In the same film, Gandalf says that "for 60 years, the ring lay quiet in Bilbo's keeping, prolonging his life, delaying old age." To most mortal beings, these seem like the most important gifts in the world. Who wouldn't "sell their soul" for power, youth, and immortality?

For the most part, Buddhists don't find these "gifts" to be appealing, because they recognize them as nothing more than illusions. No one can wield power forever—nations rise and they fall; and no one can live forever—all of us, eventually, return to dust. Even if we could live forever, in the same uncorrupted form, Buddhists know that over time we would become "bored" by the sameness of it all. Why? Because, as the Buddha discovered, we are always seeking something other than we find. If we're sitting for too long, we want to stand. When we stand too long, we want to sit. We tire of our clothes, our possessions, and even our lives. One writer suggests that, from a Buddhist perspective, the ring, which is a symbol of binding and circularity, represents *samsara*: "It is the quintessential description of our existential dilemma, being bound by the endless repetitions of rebirth."[107] As the First Noble Truth tells us, life is characterized by suffering, whether we understand that as "imperfection," "impermanence," "emptiness," or "insubstantiality."[108] Clinging to these ideas of power and immortality as if they were permanent is the real source of suffering in the *LOTR*. If Gollum came to understand this, the ring would no longer have an effect on him.

So, why does Frodo suffer? To some degree, he is seduced by the gifts promised by the ring. However, he and the other Hobbits also suffer because of their attachment to their village and their way of life. Leaving behind the comforts of home to make a long, arduous journey to fulfill a seemingly impossible goal weighs on Frodo. He just wants to be back at the Shire with all of his friends, where they can dance, sing, drink, and laugh. His attachment to home and hearth, and the belief that this Hobbit way of life will always remain the same, is a real source of his suffering. In fact, in *The Return of the King*, Sam uses memories of the Shire to spirit Frodo forward, saying, "Do you remember the Shire, Mr. Frodo? It'll be spring soon, and the orchards will be in blossom. And the birds will be nesting in the hazel thicket. And they'll be sowing the summer barley in the lower fields . . . and eating the first of the strawberries with cream. Do you remember the taste of strawberries?" The Hobbits aren't alone. Other characters in the *LOTR* are tormented by visions of how things used to be. Denethor is so attached to Boromir that after his son dies, he slips even deeper into madness. He even admits to his only living son, Faramir, that he wishes the brothers could have exchanged places.

In the cases of Gollum and Frodo, neither realizes that life is characterized by suffering, impermanence, and no-self. In essence, Buddhism claims that there is nothing to cling to; everything is *shunyata* or empty. And as Thich Nhat Hanh explains, "We are empty of a separate, independent self. We cannot be by ourselves alone. We can only inter-be with everything else in the cos-

mos. . . . Our happiness and suffering are the happiness and suffering of others. When we act based on non-self, our actions will be in accord with reality,
and we will know what to do and what not to do."[109]

According to Mahayana Buddhism, another problem in the *LOTR* is that
characters desperately cling to concepts of good and evil, and based on this dualistic worldview, they engage in wrong action, more specifically killing Orcs,
Uruk-hai, and other inhabitants of Middle-earth. What's perhaps more disturbing, from a Buddhist perspective, is the fact that in *The Two Towers* and in
The Return of the King, Legolas and Gimli make a game out of battle, seeing
who can kill the most. During the Battle of Helm's Deep, Gimli learns that
Legolas is "ahead," and remarks, "I'll have no pointy-ear outscoring me!" Seeing the world in black and white almost always results in conflict. When the
Venerable Mahakaccana, one of the Buddha's most eminent disciples, was
asked about this, he explained that one of the causes for conflict is "lust for
views," which results in "greed, obsession and cleaving to views."[110] Mahayana
Buddhism claims that we need to go beyond duality and beyond subject-ob-
ject.[111] As I-hsuan, a ninth-century Ch'an Buddhist, said, we must see good and
evil as the same. "Followers of the Way, with a clear eye destroy both Buddha
and demon. If you love the sacred and hate the profane, you will continue
floating and sinking in the sea of birth and death. . . . Once you realize that all
things are not produced, the mind, too, is like an illusion and, without a speck
of dust, is at all times pure."[112] The only *LOTR* character who expresses a sentiment even close to a Buddhist one is Faramir, who, in *The Return of the King*,
muses, "The enemy? His sense of duty was no less than yours, I deem. You wonder what his name is, where he comes from, and if he really was evil in his
heart. What lies or threats led him on this long march from home, and would
he not rather have stayed there . . . in peace? War will make corpses of us all."

As professor David Loy explains, the dualism of good vs. evil is attractive
because it is a simple way of looking at the world. Not only does it tend to pre-
clude further thought, but it also keeps us from "looking deeper." Once the
good and evil labels have been applied, we, representing the "good side," only
have one thing left to do, and that is to fight. But this isn't the case in Buddhism; "Evil, like everything else, has no essence or substance of its own; it is
a product of impermanent causes and conditions."[113] "Sin" doesn't exist as a
concept in Buddhism; instead, practitioners believe that people do the wrong
things because of false views, ignorance, and lack of wisdom. "These do not

flaw human nature . . . but only obscure the enlightened mind like clouds obscuring the moon."[114]

According to Mahayana Buddhism, we can get beyond dualism by seeing things as they really are and developing compassion for our so-called foes. Saruman is cast as a "bad guy" in *LOTR*, but he's really no different than Gandalf. They are both extraordinarily powerful wizards who were supposed to unite and counsel the Free Peoples of Middle-earth. In fact, it is said that at first, Saruman was a "true friend to Rohan."[115] Could this be the same man who, in *The Two Towers*, said, "Together, my lord Sauron, we shall rule this Middle-earth. The old world will burn in the fires of industry. Forests will fall. A new order will rise. We will drive the machine of war with the sword and the spear and the iron fist of the Orc." Yes, this is just like Boromir, who started on the side of the "good guys" but ended up trying to take the ring from Frodo and kill him—after swearing an oath to protect him. And it's just like Smeagol who was transformed into Gollum. All people engage in unwholesome behavior, not because their nature is sinful or evil, but "because they are complicated: sometimes selfish and greedy, and sometimes just so narrowly focused on what they are doing that they do not see the wider implications of their actions."[116]

Buddhists wouldn't fault the ring for the situation in *LOTR* because if it had some kind of magical mind control, why were some people able to reject it? The blame rests solely on the shoulders of those who grasped at the intangible thinking it was tangible; clutched for power when it, too, is empty; and longed for immortality, when they knew they would die. Because they didn't see the world as it truly is, they lacked right understanding. Without purification of the mind and heart and the growth of unselfish attitudes, they failed to exhibit right thought. By encouraging malice and hatred, they didn't practice right speech. Many characters lied, stole, and killed, so they also abandoned right action. None prevented unwholesome thoughts and actions from arising, so they failed to have right effort. All of them looked to the future rather than focusing on the present, so all failed to maintain right mindfulness. And finally, no one had trained his or her mind to resist their delusions of grandeur, so no one exhibited right concentration.

During Siddhartha's second watch of the night, he saw beings pass away and, based on their actions, be reborn into one of six realms. Those who "behaved wrongly by body, speech and mind, who reviled the noble ones, held wrong views, and undertook actions based on wrong views, with the breakup of the body, after death, they were reborn in a state of misery, in a bad destination, in the lower world, in hell."[117] Those who did the opposite were reborn in a good destination, in a heavenly realm. Buddha also saw that the "three poisons"—greed, hatred, and ignorance or delusion—drive the Wheel of Life. Also known as the "three unwholesome roots," these represent behavior that is "spiritually detrimental to the agent, morally reprehensible, and potentially productive of an unfortunate rebirth and painful results."[118] It is also stated that from these three arise a plethora of secondary "defilements," such as anger, hostility, envy, selfishness, arrogance, pride, presumption, and laziness.[119] On the flip side, the Buddha recognized that there were wholesome roots—nongreed, nonhatred, and nondelusion—which translate to generosity, loving-kindness, and wisdom.

The point of discussing the "three poisons" is to show that the Buddha didn't place good on one side and evil on the other, and then say they would fight it out. Instead, he said that human beings make choices and from those choices consequences will result. Since Buddhists can't find justice in death, they aren't supposed to mete out violence for violence. Instead, one breaks the bonds of the "three poisons" by transforming them into something benign. Greed is changed into generosity, hatred into loving-kindness, and ignorance into wisdom,[120] for it is believed the true moral action isn't possible without wisdom. The ideal way of putting belief into action is to follow the dharma, listen to the spiritual masters, always being aware of one's motives, and testing "theoretical teaching in one's own experience."[121]

Even though Tolkien wrote *LOTR* from a Roman Catholic perspective, this isn't to say that we can't find any Buddhist elements in it. Mahayana Buddhism encourages practitioners to develop the Four Immeasurable Minds—love, compassion, joy, and equanimity—and during the film we see some characters who have developed some of these qualities. Like most of us, Samwise isn't an ideal person. He engages in wrong speech when interacting with Gollum, calling him Stinker and, at one point, saying, "Miserable little maggot. I'll stove your head in." He engages in wrong action when he kills some Orcs. He fails to have clarity of mind, because he is often troubled, worried, exhausted, afraid, sad, and frustrated. He is frequently distracted by his growling stomach and thoughts of feeding it, and he's fixated on the Shire and all of the pleasures it holds. But this doesn't make him a contemptible character. As the films and the novels develop, we see that he is a loyal companion, a loving friend, and a generous person. Referring to a scene from the *The Return of the*

King novel, Jorge J. E. Gracia writes, "His loving nature is revealed when Sam realizes the power of the seed-box Lady Galadriel had given him at Lothlorien. Instead of keeping it for his garden, as even Frodo suggests, he uses it for the restoration of the whole Shire to its former splendor after it had been devastated by Saruman and his minions. His thought is always on others."[122]

Samwise truly cares for Frodo, and he's attentive and insightful enough to know when his "master" needs food, encouragement, rest, or comfort. His love seems to be unconditional, because even when Frodo snaps at him, Sam never returns a face of anger, instead faulting the ring and Frodo's lack of sleep and food. Even if Sam resists extending compassion to Gollum, he doesn't hold it back from Frodo. He truly wants to lighten his master's suffering. He knows, as Thich Nhat Hanh says, "the other person is suffering," so he sits close, looking and listening deeply so as to touch his pain. He knows when to offer a compassionate word, action, or thought to ease Frodo's pain and to bring him joy.[123] When it comes to joy, Sam is usually in good spirits, delighting in even the simplest of things. As Frodo tells him, "Nothing dampens your spirits, Sam."

When we look at equanimity, few if any of the characters possess the ability to "shed all discrimination and prejudice, and remove all boundaries between ourselves and others."[124] Most view the world and their situation in dualistic terms. Even Aragorn, the "hero" of the epic, tells the other soldiers to "show no mercy . . . for you shall receive none!" To be fair, though, he does, on many occasions show mercy and encourages others to follow his lead. For instance, when Theoden threatens to kill Wormtongue, Aragorn says, "No my lord. Let him go. Enough blood has been spilt on his account."

In *The Two Towers*, we see that Sam has a more balanced perspective on the situation than most, remarking that "It's only a passing thing, this shadow. Even darkness must pass. A new day will come. And when the sun shines it will shine out the clearer." Another aspect of equanimity is having the ability to let go, and this extends to relationships. Although Christians might praise Sam for his devotion to Frodo, Buddhists might see it as possessive; he is as attached to Frodo as he is to the Shire. At one point in *The Return of the King*, thinking that Frodo has died, Sam panics, saying, "Oh no! Frodo! Mr. Frodo, wake up. . . . Don't leave me here alone. Don't go where I can't follow."

One final characteristic that Sam possesses is humility. During a conversation with Frodo in *The Two Towers*, Sam says maybe one day Frodo's adventures with the ring will be put into song. "You've left out one of the chief characters—Samwise the Brave. I want to hear more about Sam. Frodo wouldn't have got far without Sam," Frodo replies. The humble Sam responds, "Now, Mr. Frodo, you shouldn't make fun. I was being serious." In *The Return of the King*, Sam is tempted by the ring. And in the novel, he receives a vision of himself as "Samwise the Strong, Hero of the Age." But Sam knows he is a gardener and not a warrior, and he rejects the ring. "His refusal to use the Ring for his own glory stems from the hobbit's deep-seated humility together with his love for Frodo."[125] For the most part, Sam isn't alone in being humble; his fellow Hobbits—Merry, Pippin, and Frodo—are also unassuming and mild-mannered. The best example of Frodo's humility takes place during the Council of Elrond. Everyone in the Fellowship is arguing about who will take the ring, except for Frodo and his friends. Finally, very quietly, Frodo steps forth and offers himself as Ringbearer. At first, few even know he's there, so he raises his voice and repeats himself. As soon as he does this, everyone offers their arms for protection. Aragorn, too, shows humility. Even though he's the heir to the throne of Gondor, the great and long-prophesized king, he submits himself to Frodo's protection, pledging at the Council of Elrond, "If by my life or death I can protect you, I will." After Boromir has tried to attack Frodo, Aragorn sends the Hobbit on his way. Aragorn's parting words are "I would have gone with you to the end, into the very fires of Mordor." He never once demands special treatment, and, in fact, he's reluctant for much of the film to reveal that he is the king. When he is crowned, he, again, puts others first by saying, "This day does not belong to one man but to all. Let us together rebuild this world that we may share in the days of peace."

Like Sam, Frodo, too, has faults, but he exhibits admirable qualities. For instance, he does what no one else will: he extends compassion to the most loathed character in *LOTR*, Gollum. In *The Fellowship of the Ring*, he can't understand why Bilbo would have spared Gollum's life, but by *The Two Towers*, he has a change of heart, saying, "Maybe he does deserve to die, but now that I see him I do pity him." Twice, Frodo asks Faramir to spare Gollum's life, once during their initial meeting, and second, at the Forbidden Pool.[126] In another scene, Sam is being particularly mean to Gollum, and Frodo asks why he's calling him names and running him down all of the time. Sam responds, "Because . . . because that's what he is, Mr. Frodo. There's naught left in him but lies and deceit. It's the ring he wants; it's all he cares about." But Frodo won't accept that: "You have no idea what it did to him . . . what it's still doing to him. I want to help him, Sam. . . . Because I have to believe he can come back." Some may argue that

Frodo only wants Gollum to "come back" for selfish reasons, because if Gollum can be "saved" then hopefully so can Frodo. This might be partially true, but Frodo also increasingly treats Gollum with enough kindness so that a real transformation, albeit a temporary one, occurs. In *The Two Towers*, Smeagol emerges and argues with Gollum, saying "Master looks after us now. We don't need you anymore. . . . Leave now and never come back." When Gollum falls silent, Smeagol is triumphant that he is free. But ultimately, he returns to his old ways, plotting to kill Frodo and Sam, and, since the latter is "always watching," Gollum plans to "stab out his eyes and make him crawl."

Because death is inevitable, Buddhists are encouraged to be mindful of it. In fact, it is said that Milarepa, one of Tibet's greatest saints, was so concerned about death that he didn't even take time out of meditating to mend his tattered clothes: "If I were to die this evening, it would be wiser to meditate than to do this useless sewing."[127] We find a kind of Buddhist sensibility in a scene from *The Return of the King* that involves Pippin and Gandalf. The Hobbit remarks sadly that he didn't think the battle would end this way. And Gandalf replies that the "journey doesn't end here. Death is just another path. One that we all must take." Most of the characters claim to "not fear death." They live when they live and are prepared to die when that time comes. For example, in *The Return of the King*, Gimli says, "Certainty of death, small chance of success. . . . What are we waiting for?" Faramir, too, is ready to die in battle, saying to Gandalf, "Where does my allegiance lie if not here? This is the city of the men of Numenor. I would gladly give my life to defend her beauty, her memory, . . . her wisdom."

Finally, we can see karma at work in *LOTR*. Gollum's life of treachery, craving, murderous actions, and maliciousness catches up to him in the end. Unable to walk away from the ring, he follows Frodo to Mount Doom, where he pounces on the Hobbit. After struggling with Frodo and biting off his finger, he regains the ring. Gollum is triumphant, but his victory is short-lived. Stumbling backwards, he falls into the Crack of Doom and, along with the ring, is incinerated. Christians might say that this is proof of divine providence; Buddhists would say that eventually one's willful actions—good of bad—bear fruit. No deity planned this or orchestrated it. Gollum was responsible, and if one reviews his choices, one after another, one would see that every unwholesome and selfish choice lead to more disastrous consequences. As the *Dhammapada* says, "When the evil has matured, the evildoer will meet with misfortune . . .

like fine dust thrown against the wind, evil comes back to the fool who harms a person who is innocent, pure and unblemished."[128] And "the unwise who rely on evil views ... produce fruit that destroys themselves."[129]

The same could be said of any of the other characters, especially Saruman and Sauron, who seek their own happiness by causing the suffering of others. For example, Saruman befriended the people of Rohan and then turned against them. This once-wise counselor also turned on Gandalf, imprisoning him in the tower and beating him. As Treebeard, the Ent or tree-herd encountered by Merry and Pippin, says in *The Two Towers* novel, Saruman used to talk with him: "He was polite in those days, always asking my leave ... and always eager to listen." However, the Ent discovered that Saruman wasn't acting out of general concern for others, he was simply gathering information for his plans of taking over Middle-earth. Saruman's unwholesome thoughts soon become unwholesome actions. "He has taken up with foul folk, with the Orcs. Worse than that: he has been doing something to them, something dangerous."[130] Furthermore, in Saruman's pursuit of industry, he orders his minions to cut down all of the trees, which have stood for centuries in peace. One section from the *Dhammapada* explains Saruman's situation: "Bad conduct is corruption in a person ... evil traits corrupt people in both this world and the next. More corrupt than these is ignorance, the greatest corruption."[131]

ENDNOTES

1. Joseph Campbell with Bill Moyers, *The Power of Myth*, ed. Betty Sue Flowers (New York: Doubleday, 1988), 123.

2. In her chapter titled "saviors," Anne Birrell, *Chinese Mythology: An Introduction*, (Baltimore: Johns Hopkins University Press, 1993), 67–87, writes that the term *savior* "belongs by convention to Christian religion with the meaning of a mesocosmic figure, the Christ, who, although innocent, offers himself in sacrifice to redeem humanity. Although this soteriological dimension is absent from Chinese mythical accounts, the concept of deliverance from evil or harm, usually in its physical manifestation rather than the spiritual, is inherent in many Chinese myths. Although the word *savior* is avoided by Western mythologists in general because of its Christological aspect, it is used here in its neutral meaning of 'deliverer or rescuer,' with an altruistic and divine coloration in the term."

3. See the entry on Kuan-yin in Michael H. Kohn, *The Shambhala Dictionary of Buddhism and Zen* (Boston: Shambhala, 1991).

4. See the entry on Kshitigarbha in Kohn, *The Shambhala Dictionary of Buddhism and Zen*.

5. The discussion follows the blog posting by Greg Arthur, "Superman as Jesus and Other Christ Figures in Film," *Holiness Reeducation*, 2006, holinessreeducation.com/2006/07/04/superman

-as-jesus-and-other-christ-figures-in-film (accessed 12 February 2008). The response is by Dave on July 5, 2006, at 4:33 a.m.

6. See response by Greg Arthur posted July 5, 2006, at 12:58 p.m., "Superman as Jesus and Other Christ Figures in Film."

7. "Superman: Gay Icon? Christ Figure? New Film Ignites Talk of What, Who Man of Steel Represents," *CBS News*, 2006, www.cbsnews.com/stories/2006/06/14/entertainment/main 1711570.shtml (accessed 12 February 2008).

8. Jack Kornfield, "Introduction," in *Jesus and Buddha: The Parallel Sayings*, ed. Marcus J. Borg (Berkeley, CA: Ulysses Press, 2004), 3–4.

9. "Jehovah (Yahweh)," *The New Advent Catholic Encyclopedia*, www.newadvent.org/cathen/ 08329a.htm (accessed 12 February 2008).

10. Eric David, "From Ace to the Almighty," *Christianity Today*, 2006, www.christianitytoday .com/movies/commentaries/fof_shadyac.html (accessed 12 February 2008).

11. In a letter to Deborah Webster, dated 25 October 1958, he writes, "I am a Christian (which can be deduced from my stories) and in fact a Roman Catholic. The latter 'fact' perhaps cannot be deduced; though one critic (by letter) asserted that the . . . character of Galadriel as directly described . . . [was] clearly related to Catholic devotion to Mary." And in another to Michael Tolkien, dated 1 November 1963, he writes, "I fell in love with the Blessed Sacrament from the beginning—and by the mercy of God never have fallen out again." J. R. R. Tolkien, *The Letters of J. R. R. Tolkien*, ed. Humphrey Carpenter and Christopher Tolkien (Boston: Houghton Mifflin, 2000).

12. Tolkien, *The Letters of J. R. R. Tolkien*, ed. Carpenter and Tolkien, 172.

13. One contrary opinion belongs to Tom Shippey, who said that he finds it difficult to find any evidence of Christianity or Catholicism in the author's works, stating that "one could say that Middle-earth is a sort of Limbo, in which the characters, like unbaptized innocents or the pagan philosophers of Dante, are counted as neither heathen nor Christian but something in between." Tom Shippey, *Tolkien: Author of the Century* (Boston: Houghton Mifflin, 2002).

14. Tolkien, *The Letters of J. R. R. Tolkien*, ed. Carpenter and Tolkien, 172.

15. In his article "Archetypes on Screen: Odysseus, St. Paul, Christ and the American Cinematic Hero and Anti-Hero," John Fitch III explains that in our traditional notions of a hero he or she "delivers salvation, enacts positive change and brings relief from suffering or oppression." The hero usually possesses the positive traits of "emotional, physical and moral strength as well as charity and fortitude." All of these characteristics fit Frodo, Gandalf, and Aragon, and working together and with the rest of the Fellowship, they attain all of the aforementioned objectives. John Fitch III, "Archetypes on Screen: Odysseus, St. Paul, Christ and the American Cinematic Hero and Anti-Hero," *Journal of Religion and Film*, 2005, http://www.unomaha.edu/~jrf/Vol9 No1/FitchArchetypes.htm (accessed 12 February 2008).

16. Boromir is a human, and as Elrond says in *The Fellowship of the Ring*, "Men are weak. The Blood of Numenor is all but spent, its pride and dignity forgotten. It is because of Men the Ring survives. I was there, Gandalf. I was there three thousand years ago. I was there the day the strength of Men failed."

17. Compare this to the Gospel of Mark, in which Jesus knows his destiny but tells others to keep quiet about who he is. As Stephen L. Harris writes in *Understanding the Bible*, "Mark's repeated emphasis on Jesus' hidden identity is known as the 'messianic secret.'" Stephen L. Harris, *Understanding the Bible* (Palo Alto, CA: Mayfield, 1985), 286.

18. J. R. R. Tolkien, *The Lord of the Rings: One Volume Edition* (New York: HarperCollins, 1994), 54–55.

19. Tolkien, *The Lord of the Rings: One Volume Edition*, 60.

20. Tolkien, *The Letters of J. R. R. Tolkien*, ed. Carpenter and Tolkien, 180.

21. In a letter Mr. Hastings, who was the manager of the Newman Bookshop in Oxford, dated September 1954, he responds to the question "Whose authority decides these things?" with "The immediate 'authorities are the Valar (the Powers or Authorities): the 'gods.' But they are only created spirits—of high angelic order . . . with their attendant lesser angels" (193–94). In a letter to Mrs. Eileen Elgar, dated September 1963, he explained that "Frodo was an instrument of Providence." Tolkien, *The Letters of J. R. R. Tolkien*, ed. Carpenter and Tolkien, 325.

22. *The New World Dictionary-Concordance to the New American Bible* (Charlotte, NC: C. D. Stampley, 1970), 549.

23. *The New World Dictionary-Concordance to the New American Bible.*, 552–53.

24. Tolkien, *The Lord of the Rings: One Volume Edition*, 264.

25. As Wood said in an interview with *Hollywood Jesus*, "The best way we found to dramatize what Frodo was going through in terms of the Ring, was simply an addict." "Carrying the Ring: An Interview with Elijah Wood," *Hollywood Jesus*, 2004, www.hollywoodjesus.com/lord_of_the _rings_interview_07.htm (accessed 12 February 2008).

26. For instance, in *The Two Towers*, Gollum catches some rabbits and brings them to Frodo and Sam to eat. Instead of cooking them, though, Gollum begins tearing them apart and eating them raw. Sam grabs them and puts them in a stew. Rather than responding favorably to this preparation, Gollum keeps telling Sam that he's ruining the food. When Sam says that he would like some nice potatoes to put in the dish, Gollum asks him what "taters" are. This scene demonstrates how Gollum has become carnivorous and has forgotten even basic foods.

27. In his letters, Tolkien is adamant that Frodo "failed as a hero." "I do not think that Frodo's was a *moral* failure. At the last moment the pressure of the Ring would reach its maximum—impossible, I should have said, for any one to resist, certainly after long possession." Tolkien, *The Letters of J. R. R. Tolkien*, ed. Carpenter and Tolkien, 326.

28. Harris, *Understanding the Bible*, 290. Frodo doesn't undergo the same kinds of overt cruelty that Jesus must endure, including being spat on and mocked. Frodo is affected psychologically by his enemies, by being tempted and drained emotionally. He is, in *The Return of the King*, captured by Orcs, tricked by Gollum, and attacked by a giant spider.

29. At the end of *The Return of the King*, Frodo, who is still affected by his wound, and a very aged Bilbo Baggins join Gandalf and the elves, most notably Galadriel and Elrond, on their ship bound for Valinor, also known as the Undying or Deathless Lands and the Isles of the West. This scene is very similar to the end of Sir Thomas Malory's *Morte d'Arthur* in which a mortally wounded King Arthur is taken to a barge that is bound for the western Isle of Avalon, where his

wounds will be healed. Legend claims that Arthur is still living in Avalon with the fairest of spirits and will return one day.

30. "Frodo Lives: Elijah Wood Reflects on a Journey for the Ages," *lordoftherings.net*, www.lordoftherings.net/legend/interviews/elijahwood (accessed 12 February 2008).

31. Tolkien, *The Letters of J. R. R. Tolkien*, ed. Carpenter and Tolkien, 327.

32. "Frodo Lives: Elijah Wood Reflects on a Journey for the Ages."

33. Tolkien, *The Lord of the Rings: One Volume Edition*, 483–84.

34. "White Light: Ian McKellen on the Rebirth and Revitalization of Gandalf," *lordoftherings.net*, www.lordoftherings.net/index_editorials_gandalf.html (accessed 12 February 2008).

35. Harris, *Understanding the Bible*, 395.

36. Tolkien, *The Letters of J. R. R. Tolkien*, ed. Carpenter and Tolkien, 202.

37. Tolkien, *The Letters of J. R. R. Tolkien*, ed. Carpenter and Tolkien, 237.

37. Gustav A. Davidson, *Dictionary of Angels* (New York: Free Press 1967), 193.

38. "St. Michael the Archangel," *The New Advent Catholic Encyclopedia*, www.newadvent.org/cathen/10275b.htm (accessed 12 February 2008).

40. Davidson, *Dictionary of Angels*, 194. The Dead Sea Scrolls were discovered between 1947 and 1956; Tolkien wrote *The Lord of the Rings* trilogy, in fits and starts, 1937 to 1949, so it's unlikely that the Dead Sea Scrolls had any impact on Tolkien's depiction or idea of Gandalf, especially since the wizard appears in *The Hobbit*, which was written much earlier.

41. Davidson, *Dictionary of Angels*, 117.

42. Davidson, *Dictionary of Angels*, 119.

43. "Guardian Angel," *The New Advent Catholic Encyclopedia*, www.newadvent.org/cathen/07049c.htm (accessed 12 February 2008).

44. Like Aragorn's ancestor Isildur, Jesus' ancestor King David wasn't without his human faults and frailties. Instead of destroying the ring when he had the chance, Isildur retained it, bringing havoc into the world. King David committed any number of atrocities, including letting lust overcome him so that he committed adultery with Bathsheba and then, to cover up his crime, he asks that her husband Uriah the Hittite be set in the "forefront of the hardest fighting" and then left to die (2 Samuel 11:14–15). This story of David's lust and "murder" of Uriah is reminiscent of King Arthur's father, Uther, who while he's magically transformed to resemble Igraine's husband, he seduces and impregnates her. Accounts differ from one author to another, but this one is found in Geoffrey of Monmouth's and Thomas Malory's versions.

45. Robert Foster, *Tolkien's World from A to Z: The Complete Guide to Middle-Earth* (New York: Ballantine Books, 1978), 21.

46. *The New World Dictionary-Concordance to the New American Bible*, 130.

47. The chapter in the book and on the special extended edition is called "The Houses of Healing."

48. In his letters, Tolkien explained the name Samwise was Old English for "half wit." Tolkien, *The Letters of J. R. R. Tolkien*, ed. Carpenter and Tolkien, 83.

49. "Interview: Sean Astin as 'Samwise the Brave,'" *movieweb.com*, 2003, www.movieweb.com/news/45/2245.php (accessed 12 February 2008).

50. Sam isn't always kind and compassionate, though. He has a tendency to be cruel toward Gollum, calling him "Stinker." In his letters, Tolkien said that Sam's treatment of Gollum was reminiscent of that between Ariel and Caliban in Shakespeare's *The Tempest.*

51. Tolkien said that the word *Orc* derives from the Old English word for "demon." See Tolkien, *The Letters of J. R. R. Tolkien,* ed. Carpenter and Tolkien, 177–78.

52. Tolkien, *The Lord of the Rings: One Volume Edition,* 891.

53. *The New World Dictionary-Concordance to the New American Bible,* 526.

54. All of the statements come from an exclusive video. "Sam," *lordoftherings.net,* www.lordoftherings.net/legend/characters/detail.html?sam (accessed 12 February 2008).

55. See his discussion of Sauron in his letter to Naomi Mitchison, dated 25 April 1954, in Tolkien, *The Letters of J. R. R. Tolkien,* ed. Carpenter and Tolkien, 173–81.

56. *The New World Dictionary-Concordance to the New American Bible,* 603. See, for instance, his role in the Book of Job.

57. *The New World Dictionary-Concordance to the New American Bible,* 604.

58. Tolkien, *The Letters of J. R. R. Tolkien,* ed. Carpenter and Tolkien, 243.

59. *The New World Dictionary-Concordance to the New American Bible,* 28.

60. Foster, *Tolkien's World from A to Z,* 433–34.

61. It isn't a coincidence that the pride-filled Sauron and Saruman carry out their diabolical plans in towers. Genesis 11 also tells of a famous tower in Shinar—the Tower of Babel—which was constructed to ensure that the peoples' names would be remembered, "lest they get scattered." "And the Lord came down to see the city and tower . . . and said 'Behold, they are one people and they have all one language; and this is only the beginning of what they will do; and nothing that they propose to do will now be impossible for them.'" So God confused their language and scattered them across the Earth, and "they left off building the city." As it says in the *New World Dictionary-Concordance to the New American Bible,* this story is frequently understood as God passing judgment on those who were motivated by a "Promethean desire for unity, fame and security."

62. Tolkien, *The Lord of the Rings: One Volume Edition,* 49.

63. Tolkien, *The Letters of J. R. R. Tolkien,* ed. Carpenter and Tolkien, 152.

64. Tolkien, *The Lord of the Rings: One Volume Edition,* 54.

65. U.S. Catholic Church, *Catechism of the Catholic Church with Modifications from the Editio Typica* (New York: Doubleday, 1995), 112.

66. St. Augustine, *City of God,* trans. Henry Bettenson (New York: Penguin Classics, 1984), 572.

67. St. Augustine, *City of God,* 573.

68. St. Augustine, *City of God,* 573.

69. Foster, *Tolkien's World from A to Z,* 513. In the books, Sauron is said to be the one who creates the Orcs and Uruk-hai.

70. St. Augustine, *City of God,* 576–77.

71. Foster, *Tolkien's World from A to Z,* 358–59.

72. Foster, *Tolkien's World from A to Z,* 359.

73. Jude Fisher, *The Lord of the Rings: Complete Visual Companion* (Boston: Houghton Mifflin, 2004), no page listed, but found in the section called "The Shadow: Nazgul."

74. Foster, *Tolkien's World from A to Z*, 360. Perhaps it's coincidental, but the name is reminiscent of Gog, "the sovereign prince of the Meshech and Tubal of the land of Magog, which in some future time would attempt an invasion of Israel only to be annihilated by God" (Ezekiel 38–39). Another reference occurs in Revelation 20:7–8, a part of which reads: "Satan will be loosed from his prison and will come out to deceive the nations which are at the four corners of the earth, that is, Gog and Magog, to gather them for battle."

75. Foster, *Tolkien's World from A to Z*, 387–88.

76. Foster, *Tolkien's World from A to Z*, 147.

77. Tolkien, *The Lord of the Rings: One Volume Edition*, 388-89.

78. St. Augustine, *City of God*, 477.

79. Even *The Lord of the Rings* website lists him under the "Forces of Darkness." Also listed there are Saruman, Sauron, Shelob the giant spider, Witch King, the Lord of the Nazgul, and Wormtongue, a servant to Saruman.

80. Tolkien, *The Lord of the Rings: One Volume Edition*, 53.

81. In his letters, Tolkien speaks of a repeated cycle of characters who suffer a moral fall. First it was Melkor, then Sauron, then the Elves, and so on. See especially, his extensive undated letter to Milton Waldman of Collins, which appears in Tolkien, *The Letters of J. R. R. Tolkien*, ed. Carpenter and Tolkien, 143–61.

82. Tolkien, *The Lord of the Rings: One Volume Edition*, 52.

83. Tolkien, *The Lord of the Rings: One Volume Edition*, 52.

84. Tolkien, *The Lord of the Rings: One Volume Edition*, 52–53.

85. Vampires are just one of the undead beings who can be dispatched with sunlight. In numerous films about Dracula, he begins burning, eventually evaporating into dust, when he is exposed to the sun. In *Blade II* (2002), the heroes of the film figure out that they can use ultraviolet light to kill a new race of vampires, called the Reapers.

86. This sort of rivalry between brothers will be repeated in the story of Jacob and Esau in Genesis 27. This time it is Isaac who favors Jacob over his older brother Esau. But unlike Cain, even though Esau "hates" Jacob and even thinks about killing him, his plot is stopped by Rebekah, their mother, who tells Jacob to run away for a while. In the film version of *LOTR*, we also see a rivalry between brothers—Boromir and Faramir—that is perpetuated by their father, Denethor II, the steward of Gondor, who prefers his eldest son.

87. "Cain," *The New Advent Catholic Encyclopedia*, www.newadvent.org/cathen/03142b.htm (accessed 12 February 2008).

88. Tolkien, *The Lord of the Rings: One Volume Edition*, 54.

89. St. Augustine, *City of God*, 576.

90. Tolkien, *The Lord of the Rings: One Volume Edition*, 58. This seems to suggest the concept of predestination or fate, which runs counter to the concept of free will, but Tolkien is always careful to temper these kinds of statements with "even the wise cannot see all ends." For more on this discussion, see Thomas Hibbs, "Providence and the Dramatic Unity of *The Lord of the Rings*" and Scott A. Davison, "Tolkien and the Nature of Evil," both of which appear in *The Lord of the*

Rings and Philosophy: One Book to Rule Them All, ed. Gregory Bassham and Eric Bronson (Chicago: Open Court 2003).

91. St. Augustine, *City of God*, 448–49.

92. Tolkien, *The Letters of J. R. R. Tolkien*, ed. Carpenter and Tolkien, 234.

93. Tolkien, *The Letters of J. R. R. Tolkien*, ed. Carpenter and Tolkien, 234.

94. *The New World Dictionary-Concordance to the New American Bible*, 336. Judas was paid 30 shekels of silver for pointing out Jesus so that the authorities could arrest him and put him on trial for sedition.

95. U.S. Catholic Church, *Catechism of the Catholic Church*, 93.

96. Foster, *Tolkien's World from A to Z*, 173.

97. Faramir is presented a bit differently in the book than he is in the screenplay. In the book, he rejects the ring outright; in the film, he vacillates. Furthermore, we learn more about Faramir in the special extended edition of the film, which includes new and extended scenes.

98. Tolkien, *The Letters of J. R. R. Tolkien*, ed. Carpenter and Tolkien, 220.

99. Gertrude Grace Sill, *A Handbook of Symbols in Christian Art* (New York: Collier Books, 1975), 20. In Louis Charbonneau-Lassay's *The Bestiary of Christ*, he suggests that not only is the eagle associated with Christ, but it has also been associated with his adversary. Although in the context of the *LOTR*, this other interpretation doesn't fit the circumstance. Gandalf is never associated with anything "evil." For more on this, see Louis Charbonneau-Lassay, *The Bestiary of Christ* (New York: Arkana, 1992), 30–32.

100. George Ferguson, *Signs and Symbols in Christian Art* (New York: Oxford University Press, 1954), 17. In his letters, Tolkien talks briefly about the inclusion of eagles in his fiction, and at one point says, "The eagles are a dangerous machine. I have used them sparingly, and that is the absolute limit of their credibility or usefulness" (see page 271 of his *Letters*). Interestingly enough, Tolkien's patron saint was St. John the Evangelist (see page 397 of his *Letters*).

101. Tolkien, *The Lord of the Rings: One Volume Edition*, 254-55.

102. Sill, *A Handbook of Symbols in Christian Art*, 18.

103. "Kingdom of God," *The New Advent Catholic Encyclopedia*, www.newadvent.org/cathen/08646a.htm (accessed 12 February 2008).

104. *The Dhammapada*, trans. Eknath Easwaran (Tomales, CA: Blue Mountain Center for Meditation, 1999), 121.

105. *The Dhammapada*, trans. Easwaran, 162–63.

106. The ring doesn't affect everyone the same way, though. Some characters can reject its "allure" while others seem to be possessed by it. So why does it have such a hold on Gollum, Boromir, Saruman, and Sauron? A Buddhist would say that they simply doesn't see clearly, they don't have right view, meaning that they don't recognize the verity of the Four Noble Truths, dependent origination, and the three marks of impermanence, suffering, and nonself. Those who reject the ring do.

107. "A Buddhist Reading of J. R. R. Tolkien: Middle Path and Middle Earth," *arrowriver.ca*, www.arrowriver.ca/dhamma/tolkien.html (accessed 12 February 2008).

108. Walpola Rahula, *What the Buddha Taught* (New York: Grove Press, 1974), 17.

109. Thich Nhat Hanh, *The Heart of the Buddha's Teaching: Transforming Suffering into Peace, Joy and Liberation* (New York: Broadway Books, 1999), 146–47.

110. *Numerical Discourses of the Buddha: An Anthology of Suttas from the Anguttara Nikaya*, trans. and ed. Nyanaponika Thera and Bhikku Bodhi (Walnut Creek, CA: Altamira Press, 1999), 43.

111. Theravada Buddhism does not support this belief, and Bhikkhu Bodhi, an American Buddhist monk ordained in Sri Lanka, has written on the subject, saying that the "teaching of the Buddha as found in the Pali Canon does not endorse a philosophy of non-dualism of any variety, nor, I would add, can a non-dualistic perspective be found lying implicit within the Buddha's discourses. At the same time, however, I would not maintain that the Pali Suttas propose dualism, the positing of duality as a metaphysical hypothesis aimed at intellectual assent." Bhikkhu Bodhi, "Dhamma and Non-Duality," *vipassana.com*, www.vipassana.com/resources/bodhi/dhamma_and_nonduality.php (accessed 12 February 2008).

112. William Theodore de Bary, ed., *Buddhist Tradition in India, China and Japan* (New York: Vintage, 1972), 226.

113. David R. Loy, "The Nonduality of Good and Evil: Buddhist Reflections on the New Holy War," *The Pacific Rim Report No. 25*, 2002, www.pacificrim.usfca.edu/research/pacrimreport/pacrimreport25.html (accessed 12 February 2008).

114. Peggy Morgan, "Buddhism," *Ethical Issues in Six Religious Traditions*, ed. Peggy Morgan and Clive Lawton (Edinburgh, Scotland: Edinburgh University Press, 2004), 79.

115. Foster, *Tolkien's World from A to Z*, 433.

116. David R. Loy, "The Nonduality of Good and Evil."

117. Bhikkhu Bodhi, ed., *In the Buddha's Words: An Anthology of Discourses from the Pali Canon* (Somerville, MA: Wisdom Publications, 2005), 66.

118. Bodhi, ed., *In the Buddha's Words*, 146.

119. Bodhi, ed., *In the Buddha's Words*, 146.

120. David R. Loy, "The Nonduality of Good and Evil."

121. Morgan, "Buddhism," 58.

122. Jorge J. E. Gracia, "The Quests of Sam and Gollum for the Happy Life," in *The Lord of the Rings and Philosophy*, 66.

123. Hanh, *The Heart of the Buddha's Teaching*, 172–73.

124. Hanh, *The Heart of the Buddha's Teaching*, 174.

125. Douglas K. Blount, "Uberhobbits: Tolkien, Nietzsche, and the Will to Power," in *The Lord of the Rings and Philosophy*, 97.

126. Blount, "Uberhobbits," 96.

127. John Powers, *Introduction to Tibetan Buddhism* (Ithaca, NY: Snow Lion, 1995), 284.

128. Gil Fronsdal, *The Dhammapada: A New Translation of the Buddhist Classic with Annotations* (Boston: Shambhala, 2006), 32–33.

129. Fronsdal, *The Dhammapada*, 43.

130. Tolkien, *The Lord of the Rings: One Volume Edition*, 462.

131. Fronsdal, *The Dhammapada*, 63.

7

Hybrid Films

Even though many films have been viewed through the lens of only one religious tradition, it is possible to gain additional insight when we broaden our perspective and apply other approaches. In the case of *The Lord of the Rings* trilogy, we discovered that although J. R. R. Tolkien was clearly writing from a Christian perspective, we can find Buddhist elements if we look for them.[1] One scholar has even managed to find Daoist elements.[2] Several films, ones that we will call "hybrids," demand a bit more work. It isn't possible to view them through just one or more religious lenses, because they don't seem to offer a consistent worldview. In most cases, the screenwriter has borrowed liberally from not one but from a variety of religious traditions, which means that we might find Buddhist, Christian, and even Hindu concepts intermingling. Because of this, to fully understand these films, we must examine all of the religious ideas contained therein. Films especially from East Asia typically contain Confucian, Buddhist, and even folk elements, because this tendency reflects the nature of religion in those countries; many religions simply coexist in the culture. Add Shinto to that list for films, and especially to anime, coming from Japan.

Box office giant *Star Wars* is just one of the movies that we have singled out in this chapter for discussion. Although comprised of six films, three of which were made nearly 20 years after the first three, writer-director George Lucas insists that the *Star Wars* saga is actually one film and should be viewed that way. If we follow his advice, we get to witness the development of a vibrant and complex mythology. The remaining two films to be discussed in this chapter are *What Dreams May Come*, *Fight Club*, and *Kung Fu Panda*.

Star Wars (1977–2005)—Written and directed by George Lucas. Total running time: 802 min. English. Rated PG for sci-fi violence and brief mild language. Genre: Science-fiction/action. Included in this series are (chronologically by release date) *Star Wars: Episode IV—A New Hope* (1977), 125 min.; *Star Wars: Episode V—The Empire Strikes Back* (1980), 127 min.; *Star Wars: Episode VI—Return of the Jedi* (1983), 135 min.; *Star Wars: Episode I—The Phantom Menace* (1999), 133 min.; *Star Wars: Episode II—Attack of the Clones* 142 min.; and *Stars Wars: Episode III—Revenge of the Sith* (2005), 140 min.

Like *The Lord of the Rings*, *Star Wars* is a seemingly classic tale of good vs. evil with the Jedi Knights and the Rebel Alliance on one side, and the Sith Lords and the corrupt empire on the other. It deals with issues of moral responsibility, destiny, the bonds of love and friendship, and human frailty. In *Star Wars: The Annotated Screenplays*, Lucas explained that from the beginning he knew that he would be writing a "space opera, a fantasy film, a mythological piece, a fairy tale."[3] And as many writers have pointed out, Lucas drew upon a diverse mythological palette that includes the Bible, the tales of King Arthur and the Knights of the Round Table, Robin Hood, Greek myth, Flash Gordon, Buck Rogers, Westerns—especially John Ford's *The Searchers* (1956), Carlos Castaneda's *The Teachings of Don Juan: A Yaqui Way of Knowledge*, and even Bruno Bettelheim's *The Uses of Enchantment: The Meaning and Importance of Fairy Tales*. Japanese filmmaker Akira Kurosawa was another strong influence, especially his film *Hidden Fortress* (1958), which Lucas claims he had seen while a student at University of Southern California. But Joseph Campbell's book *The Hero of a Thousand Faces* has overshadowed all other influences. As Lucas is quoted as saying, "I spent about a year reading lots of fairy tales—and that's when [the script] starts to move away from Kurosawa and toward Joe Campbell. About the time I was doing the third draft, I read *The Hero with a Thousand Faces* and I started to realize I was following those rules unconsciously. So I said, I'll make it fit more into that classic mold."[4]

Campbell was greatly influenced by Jung's concept of the archetype, and he incorporated many of them into his own writings.[5] Lucas discovered these archetypes through Campbell, and he employed them in *Star Wars*.[6] Upon close inspection many are apparent. Luke Skywalker (Mark Hamill) is the hero on a journey who must rescue the maiden, Princess Leia (Carrie Fisher), and fight against the shadow, which is often represented by a dragon, a snake, or a monster. In this case, Luke's shadow is his father, Darth Vader (David Prowse). Interestingly enough, Luke is replaying the journey that his own father, Anakin Skywalker, took before he accepted the dark side. Anakin (Hayden Christensen) had to safeguard and rescue Queen Amidala (Natalie Portman) and fight the shadow that is embodied in Senator Palpatine (Ian McDiarmond), also known as the Emperor and Darth Sidious.

According to Jung, the shadow represents the dark side of the ego, and it is a repository for all of the qualities that we shun, including cruelty, lust for power, greed, and thoughts of murder. The shadow is the alter ego of the hero, his doppelgänger. The goal of the hero is to recognize and face the shadow, thus diminishing its power. In *The Empire Strikes Back*, as part of his Jedi training, Luke must enter a cave, where he encounters what appears to be Darth Vader. But when Luke "defeats" this dark Sith, the front part of his helmet falls away, revealing that Luke has really just confronted and overcome himself. As Jung said in *Archetypes of the Collective Unconscious*, "Whoever looks into the mirror or the water will see first of all his own face. Whoever goes to himself, risks a confrontation with himself. The mirror does not flatter, it faithfully shows whatever looks into it; namely the face we never show to the world. . . . But if we are able to see our own shadow and can bear knowing about it, then a small part of the problem has already been solved."[7] The heroes in *Star Wars* are aided in their quest by two wise old men (Obi-Wan Kenobi and Yoda). The trickster—a clown who causes problems for the hero—appears in the "earlier" films, in the guise of Jar Jar Binks. And finally, the loyal animal archetypes can be found in Chewbacca and perhaps even C-3PO and R2-D2.[8] Lucas was actually so interested in Campbell's writings that he befriended the scholar and invited him to watch the *Star Wars* trilogy with him. "Campbell reveled in the ancient themes and motifs of mythology unfolding on the wide screen in powerful contemporary images," wrote Bill Moyers, who was present during one of the screenings. Campbell also "grew

animated as he talked about how Lucas had 'put the newest and most powerful spin' on the classic story of the hero."[9]

After the release of *Star Wars*, practitioners from most religious traditions
tried to find parallels between the film's message and their own. However,
Christian interpretations have been the most numerous, with writers seeing
the Jedi Knights as Crusaders from the Middle Ages; the Force as God; "Luke's
development as analogous to a serious Christian's progression as a follower of
Jesus";[10] Darth Maul, with his red face and horns, as Satan; and pride as the
cause of Anakin's "fall." Author and Christian theologian John C. McDowell
adds to this list: "Vader's and Sidious's temptations echo Satan's temptations
of Adam and Christ; the *Millennium Falcon*'s emergence from the space slug's
belly alludes to Jonah's emergence from the belly of the fish; Obi-Wan's guiding presence to Luke sounds a little like the Holy Spirit's presence; Anakin's
name may be a reference to the . . . Anakites who descended from the . . .
Nephalim warriors, the latter significantly being the fruit of the union between the 'sons of God . . . [and] the daughters of humans' and whose name
significantly means 'fallen ones' (Genesis 6:4); and finally there is, of course,
the virgin birth image used of Anakin." He also states that "the cultivation of
the virtues of knowledge and peace as opposed to ignorance, greed, and aggression is also vital to a life of Christian integrity."[11] Christians find it significant that in the last three films, the hero is named Luke,[12] which is seen as
referring to Jesus' disciple and the "author" of the third Gospel.[13] Luke's twin
sister's name, Leia (Carrie Fisher), could be a variant of Leah, which is from
Hebrew, meaning "cow." In Genesis 29, this matriarch of Israel is said to have
been Jacob's first wife and the sister of Rachel. Leah and Jacob, who would
later be named Israel, had seven sons. Finally, Christians focus on the film's
dualistic viewpoint, pointing out that that both Han Solo (Harrison Ford) and
Anakin Skywalker undergo a resurrection, and that at the end of the films
Darth Vader is redeemed.

Increasingly scholars are uncovering the film's Eastern roots, and examining the character names in the *Star Wars* universe proves to be revelatory. Luke
Skywalker's[14] surname might sound as if it comes from an American Indian
tradition; however, as one poster who was responding to a blog on *The Vaishnava Voice* noted, Skywalker is the English translation of the Sanskrit word
dakini.[15] A *dakini* is a female demon in Indian folk belief. In Tibetan the word
becomes *khadroma*, which, when broken down, *kha* means "celestial space,"

dro, means *walking* [my emphasis]; and *ma* indicates the feminine. Therefore, in Tibetan Buddhism, this same female being "moves on the highest level of reality."[16] As one writer explains, "The *dakini* is a manifestation of the energy of enlightened awareness in the stream of consciousness of the individual male practitioner, which awakens the consciousness to the spiritual path, thus playing the role of the archetypal figure the Swiss psychologist C. G. Jung designated as the *anima*."[17] This connection between Skywalker and the Sanskrit term might seem to be a stretch, until you consider that in *Willow*, a 1988 film for which Lucas and Bob Dolman contributed the screenplay, the baby Elora Danan is said to belong to the species Daikini. Danan is, by the way, seen as a "child of prophecy, the daughter of the Sun and Moon, and future empress of all kingdoms." She is the powerful child who is prophesized to appear and unite the people.[18] In *Star Wars*, too, Luke Skywalker plays an important part in the prophecy that a "chosen one" will restore balance to the Force. As Lucas said, the second and third drafts of his screenplay began with the quote: "And in time of greatest despair there shall come a savior and he shall be known as: The Son of the Sun."[19]

Queen Padme Amidala (Natalie Portman) is Luke Skywalker's mother and the wife of Anakin. Her first name comes from the Sanskrit word *padma*, the lotus flower that is a symbol of purity and lucidity. Many Hindu deities and Buddhist figures sit on a lotus, including Brahma, Lakshmi, Buddha, and Maitreya. It is said that after Siddhartha was born, he walked, and in those places where he had stepped, lotus plants grew. Her surname Amidala seems to recall the Sanskrit word Amitabha, also known as Amida, the "Buddha of Measureless Light." He is thought to reside in Sukhavati, which is the Pure Land or Western Paradise, and is frequently depicted as seated in the middle of a lotus blossom. The veneration of Amitabha demonstrates a sharp change in Buddhist thinking. Instead of being one's own refuge, Mahayanists believe that they can call upon a number of savior beings, including Amitabha, for help. One of the most important texts for these Buddhists is the *Amitabha-sutra* or *Sutra of the Buddha Amitabha*. It is believed that if a person "hears Amitabha Buddha spoken and holds the name . . . with one heart unconfused, when this person approaches the end of life, before him will appear Amitabha Buddha and all the assembly of Holy Ones. When the end comes, his heart is without inversion; in Amitabha Buddha's Land of Ultimate Bliss he will attain rebirth."[20] As a character, Queen Amidala is brave, loyal, and selfless. Even when her life is threatened, she never shirks from duty, believing that her subjects must come first. And when her reign ended, instead of indulging in her private life, she sought a position in the Senate so that she could present a rational and reasonable perspective. Always a champion of peace and diplomacy, Padme is ruled by her compassion for others.

Other Sanskrit or Vedic derived words can be found throughout the *Star Wars* epic. Two female Jedi masters are named Shaak Ti and Depa Billaba. The first character has black eyes, a red and white face, and sports, on her head, white hornlike protrusions called montrals that "sense space ultrasonically."[21] It is said that she was "one of the most cunning warriors" in the Jedi order. Her name echoes back to *shakti*, which means "the power." Examples of *shakti*, which is the dynamic energy of a Hindu god personified as his female consort, include Kali, Durga, Parvati, Sarasvati, Lakshmi, and more. The second character is played by an Indian actress, Dipika O'Neill Joti, and a transliteration of her character's name, which is Deepa Ballabha, means "the master of the light."[22] Her character also sports two dots on her face; one between her eyes and the other one on her forehead just slightly above the place where her eyebrows meet. This dot was coined a "mark of illumination," and is very similar to the *bindi* worn by Hindu women. It is suggested that the name for Jar Jar Binks' amphibious race, the Gungans, is connected to the word Ganga, the name of the River Ganges. It is believed that Ganga is the daughter of the mountain god, Himavan, and sister to Parvati, Shiva's wife. A character mentioned, but never seen, in the *Star Wars* films is Padme's predecessor, King Veruna.[23] In the Vedic pantheon, Varuna "was king of the universe and of the starry sky, the bringer of rain, until Indra, the Thunder-god, took that boon-giving function away from him."[24]

A Jedi apprentice is called a Padawan, which is the combination of two Sanskrit words with *Pada* meaning foot and *wan* or *van* meaning forest. In Hinduism, the third stage of life for a twice-born male is the *vanaprastya* or the stage of the forest-dweller, during which, once a person reaches retirement age, he leaves his possessions with his children, and he and his wife retire to the forest as hermits. Although not full renunciation, the forest-dweller reduces his pursuit of material goods and physical pleasures. Leaving one's home for a life of wandering in the forest continued in the Buddhist tradition. In fact, scholar Reginald A. Ray demonstrates that the Mahayana text, the *Mahaprajnaparamita Sastra*, elevates the ideal of the "forest-dwelling" bodhisattva, explaining that "although the Bodhisattva is physically secluded from others, his mind never abandons them. In his solitary retreat, he practices meditation and gains true wisdom in order to save others. . . . Through the power of his meditative states, he avails himself of wisdom; when he has obtained the power of the superknowledges, he returns among beings and becomes, among them, father, mother, husband or son, master, servant, school master, god, man, or even animal; and he guides them by all manner of teachings and salvific methods."[25] We know by watching *Star Wars: Episode IV—A New Hope* that Obi-Wan Kenobi (Sir Alec Guinness) retires to a cave, also common for an ascetic in the Buddhist tradition; Yoda lives in a quasi cave surrounded by trees.

As for Yoda, Steven J. Rosen wonders if his name might refer to the Sanskrit word *yoga*, which means "to yoke." During Luke's training with Yoda, the diminutive being advocates using certain postures—at one point Luke is performing a one-handed handstand with Yoda perched on his foot—to train and subdue the mind and to overcome his fear. In the Bhagavad-Gita, Krishna tells Arjuna that "even for the man of discernment who strives, the harassing senses forcibly seize the mind. Restraining all the senses, one should sit, yogically disciplined, focused . . . for if one's senses are under control one's mentality is ground."[26] Rosen also says that "Yoda's name is closely linked to the Sanskrit *yuddha*, which means war. Accordingly, this character teaches a chivalrous form of warfare, imbued with ethics and spirituality."

Furthermore, after making some comparisons, Rosen wonders if perhaps Lucas[27] might have been inspired by the *Ramayana*, which also features a princess who is kidnapped and must be saved by a hero who is assisted by various beings, including the half-human/half-monkey Hanuman,[28] or even the Bhagavad-Gita, in which we find a guru-disciple relationship, an emphasis on overcoming desire and anger; and the idea of a "force" pervading the universe.[29] Furthermore, we can read chapter 16 of the Bhagavad-Gita, and apply what it says to just about any of the "bad guys" in *Star Wars*, including everyone from Emperor Palpatine to Anakin once he nears his transformation to Darth Vader. "Demonic men" are "subject to insatiable desire, filled with intoxicating hypocrisy and pride . . . having fastened onto false views through delusion, they follow the polluting rules of conduct." The chapter continues by saying that because these people are tangled in the web of delusion, are obsessed with the gratification of desires, and are depend on egotism, violence, and pride, they are hurled into demonic wombs. "Desire, anger, and greed: that is the destruction of the self, the triple gate of hell."[30]

In *Star Wars: Episode V—The Empire Strikes Back*, Luke must fly to the Dagobah System so that he can begin his Jedi training with Yoda.[31] Dagoba is the Sinhalese word for the more commonly known Sanskrit term *stupa*. Originally memorial monuments over the mortal remains of the historical Buddha and other saints, stupas are symbolic reminders of various events in the Buddha's life. The word *Dagoba* was "originally Dhatugarbha, literally 'womb of objects,' i.e. a repository of the Buddha's relics around which a stupa, later a temple was built and around which a *vihara* (Buddhist monastery) arose. Dagoba later became *pagoda*."[32] Interestingly enough, stupas are traditionally bell-shaped and are topped by a long, narrow spire. When we see Yoda's abode, it looks uncannily like a stupa.

Two minor characters in the *Star Wars* pantheon have Adi in their names; one is a Jedi master known as Ki-Adi Mundi. In Hinduism, an Adi is "a demon who can take the shape of a bird or a snake";[33] however, the word also means the original, essential, and the first, and is used in the term "Adi-Buddha." Sikhs refer to their sacred text as the Adi Granth Sahib. One character who was supposed to appear in *Star Wars: Episode II—Attack of the Clones* but was cut from the film was named Pooja. Usually spelled *puja*, this word indicates worship of the gods in the form of prayer, offerings, and sacrifices. Anakin's mother's name is Shmi, which sounds as if it might come from the name of the Hindu goddess Lakshmi, whose name is often shortened to Sri. Lakshmi means "mark or sign," and as the consort of Vishnu, she is the universal mother, the goddess of prosperity, fertility, and success. She is usually depicted as standing or seated on a lotus flower. Because of Shmi Skywalker's selfless devotion to her son, she is able to give him a brighter future. One of the Wookie chieftains is named MeruMeru. Mount Meru has two associations. One is a volcanic cone in northern Tanzania, and the other, in Hindu, Buddhist, and Jain mythology, is believed to be the center of the universe, the axis of the world. Its foothills are the Himalayas, and it is thought to be the abode of the gods. The diabolical cyborg Darth Grievous is said to be from the Kaleesh species. This word sounds a bit like Kalash, who are a small group of non-Muslim people living in the Hindu Kush Mountains in northern Pakistan. The Sanskrit word *Kalasha* also means water pot, pitcher, or jar, and it refers to a pot of water used during temple rites that is topped with mango

leaves and a husked coconut. This represents the deity during special ceremonies.

Count Dooku (Christopher Lee), a fallen Jedi Master who is now a powerful Sith Lord, is also known as Darth Tyranus. Dooku is Japanese for poison;[34]
however, his name also sounds very much like *dukkha*, which, in Buddhism,
means suffering. He certainly brings suffering to the galaxy through his attachment to greed, hatred, and ignorance. Two characters bear the last name
of Fett, including Jango (Temuera Morrison), a bounty hunter, assassin, and
mercenary, and his "son," Boba, who when he grows up, also becomes a
bounty hunter; his prize being Han Solo. In the context of Buddhism, again,
Fett could refer to "fetter," which is the translation of Siddhartha's son, Rahula.
In one version of the Buddha's story, it is said that when he learned that his
son had been born, he responded "a fetter has arisen." In *Star Wars: Episode
II—Attack of the Clones*, we learn the back story of Jango and Boba. Apparently, a Jedi named Sifo-Dyas commissioned the mysterious Kaminoans to
create for him a clone army. Jango agrees to be the genetic source of the clones
with the stipulation that, in addition to his large fee, he will be given an unal-
tered clone of himself so that he can raise it as his son. Although not addressed
in the films, in the *Star Wars* expanded universe, it is suggested that Jango
wanted to raise a son because when his own parents were murdered he became an orphan. Jango's desire for a family leads to the creation of what is essentially a morally "neutral" army.

Bred to be docile and trained to take orders, these foot soldiers serve whoever is in charge without question. To follow this chain of thought, we could
say that Jango's desire for progeny and wealth undoubtedly leads to much suffering in the galaxy and helps to create an imbalance in the Force. In many
ways, the clone army is used by the Sith as the Trojan horse was used by the
Greeks. Even though the Jedi are supposed to be keepers of the peace, they accept this "gift" without much question, never bothering themselves with the
fact that inside these white suits are human beings, who are being bred as dis-
posable objects during times of conflict. If we look at this within a Buddhist
context, can we say that Order 66, which causes the clone army to turn against
and assassinate all of their Jedi leaders, is a kind of karmic response to a series
of "wrongs" on the part of the Jedi? Before we leave behind the Kaminoans,
we can find several Sanskrit terms associated with them. It is said that they live
beyond the Outer Rim, just south of the Rishi Maze. Rishis were the ancient

priests or sages to whom the Vedic hymns were revealed. These seven "seers" are associated with the Big Dipper. As for the Jedi who commissioned the clone army, his last name, Dyas, when spelled Dyaus, means sky or heaven. He is the Vedic sky god.

Finally, the person responding to the *Vaishnava Voice* blog pointed out that Sanskrit isn't limited to character names. Several songs played during the first three episodes are written in the ancient language. *Duel of the Fates*, which is featured in *Star Wars: Episode I—The Phantom Menace* during the battle between Obi-Wan Kenobi, Qui-Gon Jinn, and Darth Maul, is actually from a Celtic poem, *Cad Goddeu (Battle of the Trees)*, that has been transcribed into Sanskrit. The words used in the poem apparently correspond to the lines "under the tongue root a fight most dread, and another raging behind, in the head."[35] The song titled "The High Council Meeting and Qui-Gon's Funeral" also features Sanskrit lyrics, which are loosely translated to mean "sweet sleep [dream] go acquire self-control [and] overcome death."[36]

Names and places that have an East Asian connection aren't as numerous as those having a Sanskrit or Vedic one; however, their significance to the sextet is perhaps more important. For instance, the word *Jedi* derives from the Japanese term *jidai geki*, which is a "period film" that retells old legends, recreates epic historical events, and keeps the spirit of the samurai alive. *Geki* literally means theater and these films and television series have roots in Japan's Kubuki and Noh theater. In general, the *jidai geki* refers to movies set before 1868, when Japan's modern era began.[37] Director Akira Kurosawa has made some of the most popular films of this type, including *Ran* (1985), *Yojimbo* (1961), *The Seven Samurai* (1954), and *Hidden Fortress*, a film that Lucas said inspired elements in *Star Wars*. Jedi masters Qui-Gon Jinn (Liam Neeson) and Obi-Wan Kenobi (Sir Alec Guinness and Ewan McGregor) have names that come from East Asian traditions, and both of these characters are instrumental in the development of the *Star Wars* mythology. Not only do Jedi Knights represent a "more civilized time" but they also educate Anakin Skywalker and Luke in the ways of the Force, thus imparting them with a strict moral code.

The name Qui-Gon indicates the Chinese, and specifically Daoist, concept of *qigong*, sometimes written as *ch'i-kung*. "Everything that ever existed, at all times, is made of *qi*, including inanimate matter, humans and animals, the sky, ideas and emotions, demons and ghosts, the undifferentiated state of wholeness, and the world when it is teeming with different beings." Also referred to as "vital energy," *qi* is connected to human thoughts and feelings and the physical body.[38] Gong means the "skill of working with or cultivating self-discipline and achievement. The art of *qigong* consists primarily of meditation, relaxation, physical movement, mind-body integration, and breathing exercises. . . . When the practitioners achieve a sufficient skill level (master), they can direct or emit external *qi* for the purpose of healing others."[39] *Qi*, when written in Romanized Japanese, becomes *ki*, which is the first name of Ki-Adi Mundi.[40]

When speaking about Obi-Wan Kenobi, not only did Joseph Campbell point out that the character had a "Japanese-sounding name . . . but also the look and demeanor of the Japanese sword master, a venerable teacher of the art and spirituality of swordplay."[41] Part of Obi-Wan Kenobi's name seems to refer to the everyday costume worn by a samurai ("those who serve"), specifically the kimono.[42] Traditionally this costume would be made from silk, and it would be held together by an *obi* belt. The samurai's sword, typically the long *katana*, was normally pushed through this belt. Obi-Wan's last name seems to derive from this fighting tradition, because as we see in the term *kendo*, which in Japanese means "the way of the sword," *ken* means sword. As for the principles of weaponry, the first thing that a samurai learned was swordsmanship, then "lancing, riding, archery, shooting, and any other martial arts."[43] These warriors also became scholars and physicians. Some taught Confucian classics; others went into the religious orders, especially the Rinzai order of Zen Buddhism.[44] The samurai were supposed to live according to the *bushido* code, which stressed filial piety, modesty, courtesy, frugality, patience, tolerance, valor, loyalty, and duty.[45] Furthermore, they were to avoid useless talk, personal luxury, and sexual feelings. A samurai was also encouraged to keep death in mind at all times, because "if people comfort their minds with the assumption that they will live a long time, something might happen, because they think they will have forever . . . and they may fail" in their duties to their employers and family.[46]

The training for a Jedi is similar to that of a samurai or Zen monk. After being detected as having a high "midi-chlorian" count in their bloodstream, a prospective Jedi began training in infancy. At this point all connections to one's family were severed. In the initial stages of training, one Jedi master trains a group of hopefuls. We see this in *Attack of the Clones*, which shows Yoda instructing a group of "younglings." As these children mature, a Padawan

is paired with a single master, who will continue his or her one-on-one training. Although combat is not the Jedi's first impulse—as Mace Windu says of
the Jedi, "We are keepers of the peace not soldiers"—when he or she does
fight that person uses a lightsaber, a weapon that Obi-Wan Kenobi says is "el-
egant." "The Jedi use the lightsaber as a symbol of their dedication to combat
in defense, not attack, and of their philosophical concern for finely tuned
mind and body skills. Ambassadors, mediators and counselors, Jedi are warriors only as a last resort."[47] For further evidence of the connection between
the Jedi and the samurai: "Lucas expressed his interest in feudal Japan to artist
Ralph McQuarrie when he asked him to come up with the first renderings of
the *Star Wars* look and even offered images of samurai warriors for inspiration."

What about the *wan* in Obi-Wan? It could simply mean "arm" as it does in
Japanese, or if from Chinese, the surname Wan means 10,000, which, has been
associated with longevity, "the most highly esteemed value of the five-fold
happinesses. . . . Expressions of the desire for longevity can be traced back as
far as the Shang and Zhou dynasties (1600–256 B.C.E.), with phrases such as
wan shou (ten thousand lives) and *junzi wan nian*, meaning nobility and
10,000 years."[48] As it says in the Daodejing, the Dao "gave birth to the One, the
One to the Two; the Dao produced the Three and the Three the 10,000 beings." Throughout the centuries, the Chinese have also used 10,000 to indicate
a kind of "upper limit," indicating whatever is or should be plentiful. We see
this especially in the writings of Zhuangzi. He writes that "if we calculate the
number of things that exist, the count certainly does not stop at 10,000. Yes we
set a limit and speak of the '10,000 things' because we select a number that is
large and agree to apply it to them."[49]

Other characters and places have East Asian names, such as Han Solo, the
antiheroic gunslinger in the last three films. His first name could refer to the
Chinese dynasty that lasted from 206 B.C.E. to 220 C.E., for it was during
this period that poetry, literature, and philosophy flourished, especially
Confucianism, which formed the basis of conduct. Also during this time,
Buddhism was introduced to China and philosophical Daoism was taking
shape.[50] Han could have a Japanese origin, for in Zen monasteries, a *han* is
a wooden board on which a rhythm is beaten three times a day. "Often the
following verse appears on the *han*: Heed, monks! Be mindful in practice.

Time flies like an arrow; It does not wait for you."[51] His surname Solo is largely just indicative of his nature. He is, at least in the early stages, a loner who cares only about himself.

Minor characters in *Star Wars: Episode II—Attack of the Clones* are named Hermione Bagwa, a waitress at Dexter's Diner; Lama Su, the prime minister of Kamino; Tuan We, the administrative aid to the Kamino prime minister; Saesee Tiin, a member of the Jedi Council, and Ryoo Naberrie, niece of Padme Amidala. A *bagwa*, also called *Pa Kua*, is an "eight-sided pictogram that contains the symbols, directions and numbers required for basic feng shui analysis." There exist two types of *bagwa*, yin and yang. The latter is used for analyzing the feng shui of houses, apartments, and buildings.[52] Feng shui masters believe that the *bagwa* is paramount for deflecting negative *qi* and encouraging the flow of positive *qi*, for health, wealth, and happiness.

The title *lama*, in the name Lama Su, comes from Tibetan Buddhism, means "superior one," and indicates a spiritual teacher. Tuan We sounds surprising like the fourth century C.E. Chinese Buddhist monk-scholar, Tao-an, who was originally surnamed Wei. During his early life, he engaged in intensive studies of meditation (*dhyana*) texts and the *Prajnaparamita*. Throughout his life, he studied, wrote commentaries, and organized Buddhist scriptures into catalogs, which meant that he had to literally examine each sutra himself. Tao-an also helped to organize a cult of Maitreya, and with eight of his disciples sat before an image of the Buddha, praying to be reborn in the Tushita heaven, which is the abode of the future Buddha. Of him, one scholar wrote, "Tao-an was therefore the pivotal figure in all the main developments within Buddhism during his age. It was because of this that he was acclaimed as one of the most eminent of Chinese Buddhist monks."[53] Quite a few East Asian words are, not surprisingly, associated with the martial arts. Ryoo, in Japanese *ryu*, means "style" or "school," usually referring to a martial arts style. Sifo-Dyas' first name, when spelled Sifu, is a Chinese term for teacher or father. In martial arts, it is used as a term of respect for a skilled kung-fu teacher. The Jedi Knights have seven lightsaber styles, one of which is *Ataru*. To the Jedi, this is the fourth form, a fast-paced, aggressive style. In Japanese, this term has multiple meanings, including "to be successful," "to face," "to lie (in the direction of)," "to undertake," "to be hit," and more. In southern England, there exists an Ataru Shotokan Karate Club.[54] The surname of Saesee Tiin, one of the

12 members of the Jedi High Council, is often translated as "teen" in Japanese. A personality trait that might refer to his namesake is his tendency to "travel at extremely high speeds."

Even though Padme Amidala's name has a Sanskrit origin, her makeup and costumes, especially in *Star Wars: Episode I—The Phantom Menace*, are reminiscent of East Asian traditions. For example, several of her hairstyles and her beauty spots were inspired by ancient Mongolian styles, and her white face paint is like that worn by the Japanese geisha, Mongolians, actors in *Kubuki* theater, and Chinese opera. In China, women also painted a red beauty spot on their cheeks. In *The Phantom Menace*, Queen Amidala wears nearly a dozen outfits in all, but only a few of them are of interest. The queen's Throne Room Gown, which is red with a black faux fur hem, was inspired by Chinese imperial court styles. Ever since prehistoric times in China, red has been seen as a life-giving color and has long been associated with wealth. For instance, during the New Year celebration, children often receive money in a red envelope with the hope of ensuring their good health. Her Palpatine Office Outfit I, which she wears before she appears before the Galactic Senate, is essentially a Japanese kimono with long Mongolian-style sleeves. On her head she wears an elaborate "Shiraya" fan headdress that is decorated with "Veda pearl beading."[55] To complement her Episode I Senate Gown, which she wore while begging the Senate to help her people, she sports a Mongolian-influenced headdress that almost looks like a set of horns capped by red and gold cylinders. And finally, her Celebration Gown, which is white, has a jeweled collar that was inspired by a Japanese parasol.[56]

Other characters have Japanese- or Asian-inspired clothing. In *Attack of the Clones*, Jango Fett hires female assassin Zam Wesell to kill Queen Amidala. Actually a changeling, she is dressed in purple and has a veil over her face, looking remarkably like a Ninja warrior. Although each Jedi Knight is dressed a bit differently, all wear a variation of the Japanese kimono. As costume designer John Mollo said, "George [Lucas] wanted [Obi-Wan] to look part monk and part Samurai warrior."[57] Even Darth Maul [Ray Park], the red-faced Sith warrior, wore a "black, layered, kimono-style underrobe," and his cloak was "inspired by a photograph of a Tibetan lama taken about 1940."[58] Darth Vader's mask and helmet, too, came from Japan. During the feudal period, warriors wore a *kabuto* or Japanese helmet, which usually had a bowl-like crown that flared at the back of the neck. As for his mask, that was modeled on the *mempo* or mask of iron, steel or lacquered leather that samurai warriors of the upper ranks usually wore to protect their faces.[59] Of *Episode IV—A New Hope*, Mark Hamill remarked that he felt it "was a very Japanese movie. Darth Vader's costume and his duel with Ben Kenobi are very Samurai."[60] What interesting is that, as an homage to Kurosawa, Lucas had even considered making the entire film in Japanese with subtitles, and casting Japanese actors in several key roles. "This was actually when I was looking for Ben Kenobi," Lucas said. "I was going to use Toshiro Mifune; we even made a preliminary inquiry. If I'd gotten Mifune, I would've also used a Japanese princess."[61]

Hundreds of species and cultures make up the Jedi, so it's a bit difficult to generalize about their appearance. However, the human members do sport a very distinctive hairstyle. While in training, Padawans keep their hair very short with the exception of a single, long braid. When they pass their trials, thus being elevated to knighthood, their braid is cut off with a lightsaber. Several Jedi masters are completely bald, such as Mace Windu and Yoda. Some have long hair and facial hair, such as Qui-Gon, and a few others, such as Oppo Rancisis, Yaddle, and Even Piell, wear their hair in a "Jedi topknot." The topknot has long been associated, particularly in Eastern traditions, with religion. Shiva, a figure of renunciation, is often depicted with his matted hair tied in a topknot; the river Ganga sprouted from it. In Japan, the samurai pulled their hair into a *chomage* or topknot.

The eclecticism of Lucas's vision can also be seen when we look at a few other words found in his films. In the *Star Wars* universe, Naboo is a provincial planet that is populated with art-loving and highly refined humans and the indigenous Gungans. When written as Nabu, the word refers to the Babylonian god of wisdom. A dangerous and shifty podracer from *Star Wars: Episode 1—The Phantom Menace* is named Sebulba. When written Xibalba, this is the name for the Mayan underworld. Qui-Gon's last name Jinn means "hidden" or "concealed" in Arabic. In Islam, "jinn are ambiguous creatures, somewhat like human beings and somewhat like angels."[62] One similarity between humans and jinn is that both can choose between good and evil; one difference is that humans are made from clay and *jinn* come from fire. (Angels are made from light.) One of the doomed Jedi, a cerulean blue woman, is Aayla Secura. Her first name is Arabic for sublime. Her last name, obviously of Latin origin, is from *securus*, which means safe, secure, without care. In *Revenge of the Sith*, Anakin fights Obi-Wan on the volcanic planet of Mustafar.

This word recalls the Arabic name Mustafa, which means "chosen one" and is one of Muhammad's names. The home world of Mace Windu (Samuel L. Jackson), a Jedi Master, is Haruun Kal. If spelled Haroun or Harun, this word means "lofty or exalted" and is the Arabic form of Aaron. Tatooine, Luke Skywalker's home planet, is a real place in Tunisia where one finds a "fabulous series of old grain stores." The filmmakers were going to use it as a street in Mos Eisley, but didn't get to. Lucas "integrated that name into the work-in-progress fourth draft."[63] Queen Apailana (Keisha Castle-Hughes) is ruler of Naboo in *Revenge of the Sith*. Apparently, her name was originally spelled Apairana, which is an "ancient house of the Maori people." The actress who plays the role is herself a Maori from New Zealand.[64]

What's particularly interesting about Lucas's ubiquitous use of East Asian and Indian terminology is that he generally employs it for the films' chief "good guys," the Jedi Knights[65] and the heroine of the first three films, Queen Amidala. The only "good" primary characters who don't have names from these traditions are Anakin and his son and daughter. Until the last film, though, Anakin isn't a "good guy" at all, not in a black and white, and certainly not in a Jedi, sense. He's unpredictable, reckless, disrespectful, undisciplined, selfish, violent, lustful, prideful, and impatient. Furthermore, throughout much of the films, the Jedi Knights are divided on how to view Anakin. Qui-Gon believes strongly that he is the Chosen One, but others, including Mace Windu and Obi-Wan have their doubts. The latter believes he is too old and too emotionally attached to become a Jedi. Most of the names of the "bad guys" have either a Latin origin, such as Bib Fortuna, a servant of Jabba the Hut, or are self-describing terms, such as Greedo, a greedy character; General Grievous, a ruthless hunter of the Jedi, or Elan Sleazebaggano, a guy who tries to sell Obi-Wan "death sticks." Senator Palpatine's (Ian McDiarmid), the cause of all corruption in the Star Wars universe, name sounds like a mixture of palpitate and palatine, conjuring up an image of a man of royal privilege who causes terror. In his Sith form, he is called Darth Sidious, which undoubtedly comes from the Latin derived insidious. His name is appropriate, because he is as harmful as he is enticing, seductive, and treacherous. Darth Maul, Qui-Gon Jinn's killer, also couldn't have a more appropriate name, as the original Latin means to grind and as a noun the word means a "heavy hammer used for driving wedges."

Many assume that the vision of *Star Wars* is predominantly Judeo-Christian, because while growing up, Lucas was raised Methodist—although he apparently "loathed the religion's self-serving piety and especially resented Sunday School, which was worse than regular school in his eyes"[66]—and even visited his housekeeper's German Lutheran congregation, which he apparently found to be more "interesting and different."[67] The truth of the matter is that Lucas doesn't seem to subscribe to any one religious system: "From an early age, Lucas had been interested in the fact that all over the world, religions and peoples had created different ideas of God and the spirit. 'The Force of others is what all basic religions are based on, especially the Eastern ones, which is essentially that there is a force, God, whatever you want to call it."[68]

Several elements in the films do seem to have a Judeo-Christian influence, such as Luke's and Leia's names, Anakin's "virgin birth," and the concept of a "chosen one." However, if we survey other world mythologies, we see that stories of heroes resulting from a virgin birth and being seen as the Chosen One aren't particularly unique to this tradition. As far as the virgin birth is concerned, many ancient, especially Greco-Roman, deities were said to be the result of "virgin births." Mithra, the ancient Persian god of light, was born on December 25 from a rock and was attended in some versions by shepherds. King Sargon of Babylonia was born of a virgin, hidden in a basket, put in the river, and found by a lowborn person. Hercules and Dionysis were the products of sexual union between the god Zeus and their mothers. It is said that Siddhartha was born after appearing to his mother as a white elephant.

For further proof of the Judeo-Christian influence, writers point to the film's theme of redemption, something particularly associated with Christianity; the battle between good and evil, represented by the Jedi and Sith; and the diabolical "temptation" of Anakin. With regards to the idea of temptation, in Siddhartha's "biography," he, too, was tempted by a demon named Mara. Obi-Wan Kenobi's hermetic desert life in *Episode V—A New Hope* seems similar to that of St. Anthony. The difference, of course, is that Obi-Wan wasn't in the desert for spiritual reasons. He was in exile after the empire's massacre of the Jedi, and only lived on Tatooine, so that he could watch over Luke Skywalker, who was being reared by Anakin's family. One place name that seems to come directly from the Hebrew Bible is the ringed planet Geonosis, which is in the outer rim territories. Here one finds large factories for the production of droids and weapons. The inhabitants, insect-like creatures, seem to enjoy watching gladiatorial fighting, as Anakin, Obi-Wan, and Amidala are taken captive, put in the ring, and are forced to fight to the death for everyone's amusement. Geonosis, which sounds a lot like Genesis, has served as a "hide-out" for Count Dooku and Jango Fett.

So what about the film's "good vs. evil" theme? If we view the films as they were released in the theaters, watching just *Episodes IV* through *VI*, the good and evil theme is much more pronounced. Darth Vader really does emerge as the black-clad pinnacle of evil. As Lucas said about the character, he "became such an icon in the first film (*Episode IV*) that that icon of evil took over everything, more than I intended." However, if one watches them as Lucas intended, *Episodes I* through *VI*, then, as the writer-director says on the DVD featurette *The Chosen One*, which is included with *Star Wars: Episode III—Revenge of the Sith*, Vader is revealed "to be this pathetic character at the end of the movie. . . . By adding [*Episodes I, II,* and *III*] people begin to see the tragedy of Darth Vader as it was originally intended to be. The person that you thought was the villain is really the victim, and that the story is really about the villain trying to regain his humanity. It becomes really the story of Darth Vader's redemption." As Lucas later explains in the documentary "no one who is evil thinks they are evil; they always think they are doing good even though they're not. [*Episode III*] is a matter of how a person who is good turns to becoming evil."

Lucas is adamant that "Anakin is the Chosen One; even when he's Darth Vader." So how does this fit within the Judeo-Christian mythos? Usually when we think of chosen ones, we think of Jesus, Moses, Abraham, David, and Jacob. None of them embraced the "dark side of the force." They were heroic because they rejected "evil" and followed God. When Emperor Palpatine tempts Anakin with promises of power and longevity, Anakin struggles with himself, but ultimately he rejects the Jedi and chooses the path of the Sith. However, that's far too simplistic of an explanation of what really happens. From the beginning, even when Anakin was a child, the Jedi Knights, especially Mace Windu, a Jedi who is on par with Yoda, are ambivalent about whether or not he could be the Chosen One. And even throughout his training, Anakin exhibits un-Jedi-like behavior that should have gotten him expelled from the order. For instance, in *Attack of the Clones*, someone is trying to assassinate Padme, so Anakin is assigned to protect her. When he has a "vision" that his mother is suffering, he leaves Padme behind to return to Tatooine. After finding his mother as a Tusken Raiders' captive, he is overcome with rage and slaughters them—men, women, and children. He justifies this by saying that they are "animals." Anakin also manipulates the Jedi rules anytime it suits his purposes. Early in *Episode II* he says that "being around Padme is intoxicating." Obi-Wan cautions him to remember his commitment to the Jedi. Despite this, Anakin persists in pursuing Padme, who also dissuades him from a romantic relationship by asking, "Isn't it forbidden for a Jedi to love?" Anakin replies, "Attachment is forbidden. Possession is forbidden. Compassion, which I would define as unconditional love, is central to a Jedi's life, so you might say we are encouraged to love."

Anakin is blind to the way things are—seeing situations as he wants to see them—and he's blind to his own faults. To see how deluded he is, we only need to watch *Episode III*, especially the scene during which he and Palpatine discuss the natures of the Jedi and the Sith. Palpatine mentions that "All who gain power are afraid to lose it. Even the Jedi." Anakin counters with "The Jedi use their power for good." Palpatine says that good is a point of view: "The Sith and the Jedi are similar in almost every way, including their quest for greater power." Anakin: "The Sith rely on their passion for their strength. They think inward, only about themselves. . . . The Jedi are selfless, they only care about others." What's tragic about what Anakin says is that even though he understands the Jedi perspective, he doesn't internalize it. He actually thinks and behaves more like a Sith. With these few examples, we can see that the seeds of the Sith have been in Anakin from the beginning. And these personal flaws are magnified when he joins Emperor Palpatine. As the newly named Darth Vader, he is told to go to the Jedi Temple, where a massacre of the innocents, so to speak, ensues. He then flies off to kill all of the members of the Separatist Council. When we try to reconcile these elements with the Judeo-Christian tradition, perhaps our only option is to see Darth Vader as Lucifer, the angel who fell because of pride. Pride is certainly one of Anakin's flaws. In *Revenge of the Sith*, he boasts to Count Dooku that his powers have doubled since they had both met. Dooku responds, "Twice the pride, double the fall." But, again, seeing Anakin/Darth Vader—the Chosen One—as Lucifer is problematic. Who then are Luke and Leia?

To say that the film is about good vs. evil seems overly simplistic. Our "hero" Anakin isn't good or evil, he simply makes bad choices, and those bad choices have karmic consequences. As author Matthew Bortolin writes, "Vader becomes trapped by the dark side; every evil act he commits takes him deeper into the dark side and makes it harder and harder for him to break the karmic chain of his malefactions until evil seems his only choice." As Obi-Wan Kenobi says about Vader, he "was seduced by the Dark Side of the Force. He ceased to be Anakin Skywalker and became Darth Vader. When that happened, the good man . . . was destroyed." As the *Dhammapada* reminds us, "As rust corrupts the very iron that formed it, so transgressions lead their doer to states of woe. . . . Bad conduct is corruption in a person . . . evil traits corrupt people in both this world and the next. More corrupt than these is ignorance, the greatest corruption."[69]

Buddhism doesn't claim, though, that once a person makes a wrong decision that he or she is "doomed." Vader has for many years gone down the "wrong path"; however, he is still capable of doing selfless, compassionate actions. As Luke tells Leia in *Return of the Jedi*, "There is good in [Darth Vader]. I've felt it. He won't turn me over to the emperor. I can save him. I can turn him back to the good side." Before Amidala dies in *Revenge of the Sith*, her words—"I know there's good in him"—are nearly identical to Luke's. What Vader must do is to let go of his hate and develop compassion. The emperor knows that hatred makes a Jedi weak, and he encourages Anakin and Luke to give into their aggressive feelings. To Luke in *Episode VI*, he says, "The hate is swelling in you now. Take your Jedi weapon. Use it. I am unarmed. Strike me down with it. Give in to your anger. With each passing moment you make yourself more my servant." He even claims that Luke's compassion will be his undoing, but quite the opposite happens. Luke's compassion for his father ends up "saving" Vader and the galaxy.

Unlike the monotheistic traditions, Eastern religions don't see in black-and-white terms. And, for the most part, neither do the Jedi. In *Revenge of the Sith*, Anakin says, "If you are against me, you're my enemy." Obi-Wan replies, "Only a Sith deals in absolutes." In *The Return of the Jedi*, Luke asks Obi-Wan why he lied to him about his father. Obi-Wan replies, "What I told you was true . . . from a certain point of view. . . . Luke, you're going to find out that many of the truths that we cling to depend greatly on our own point of view." In Buddhism, seeing the world in dualistic terms stems from wrong understanding and wrong view. As Zen master Shunryu Suzuki explained, our body and mind are both two and one, plural and singular: "Our usual understanding of life is dualistic: you and I; this and that; good and bad. . . . These discriminations are themselves the awareness of the universal existence. 'You' means to be aware of the universe in the form of you; 'I' means to be aware of it in the form of I. You and I are just swinging doors. . . . This moment the swinging door is opening in one direction, and the next moment the door is swinging in the opposite direction. Moment after moment each one of us repeats this activity." In the end, he says, good and bad are only in one's mind.[70] And in the "big mind" there is no difference between heaven and earth, man and woman, teacher and disciple; everything has the same value, everything is Buddha.[71]

Buddhism teaches that there are two kinds of truth—relative and worldly. The first kind interests us here, because we can apply it to Anakin. He claims that he's suffering, but why? He doesn't feel that he has enough power, he is sad that his mother is dead, he longs to be with Padme even though he's not supposed to, he's not moving fast enough along the career track to Jedi Master, and so on. Can we really say that Anakin is suffering, when these sources of his pain are subjective? Suffering depends largely on the way a person perceives his or her situation; therefore, it is relative truth. After all, another person in Anakin's situation might not suffer from any of these situations. As Palpatine rightly suggests, good and evil, too, are relative concepts. Most religions say that killing is wrong; however, adherents justify killing based on their perception of a situation. If an audience watching *Star Wars* saw the Jedi Knights kill Darth Vader and the emperor, they would rejoice, because they wouldn't see killing in this situation as "bad." But should the emperor kill Yoda or Luke Skywalker, the audience would be outraged, demanding justice. Both sides kill, which is prohibited by religion, and yet one side is "justified" in its actions and the other is not.

Daoism is in accordance with Buddhism in its rejection of absolutes and dualism. As it says in chapter 20 of the Daodejing, between yes and no what is the difference? Between good and evil, how great is the distance?[72] With equal measure of white and dark, the yin-yang symbol embodies the perfect state of being. In this symbol, too, light is found in darkness, and darkness is found in light. *Star Wars* supports this. Many of the Sith Lords were once Jedi Knights, and there exists a master-student chain between the "good" and "evil" characters. For instance, Yoda trained Count Dooku who trained Qui-Gon who trained Obi-Wan who trained Anakin. What's particularly interesting about this is that despite their best efforts, good characters still produced evil students and evil teachers produced good students. Furthermore, *Star Wars* doesn't advocate the slaughter of the Sith Lords; in fact, the overall message of the films isn't to go to war but to reach agreement through diplomatic relations. (As Queen Amidala states, war is a failure to listen.) Because this isn't possible, chaos ensues. According to Daoism, chaos arises in the universe when too much yang overshadows yin or too much yin overpowers yang. In essence, it is the result of disharmony and imbalance—not the presence of evil.

The prophecy in *Star Wars* states that the Chosen One will bring "balance to the Force," which is very Daoist. A few times the Jedi Knights expand this prophecy, saying that it actually says that the Chosen One will destroy the Sith and bring balance to the Force. At the end of *Revenge of the Sith*, Obi-Wan says to Anakin that he was "supposed to destroy the Sith not join them" and that he was supposed "to bring peace [to the galaxy] not leave it in darkness." But even this seemingly black-and-white dualism is offset by other ambivalent remarks that have already been discussed. In *Return of the Jedi*, Darth Vader picks up Darth Sidious and throws him over a railing, essentially killing him. Vader, too, dies. But does this mean that the Sith have all been destroyed?

Apparently, the Sith order was started nearly 2,000 years ago by a "renegade Jedi who sought to use the Force to gain control." The Sith fought each other for power until only Darth Bane remained. "To prevent internecine strife, Bane remade the Sith as an order that would endure in only two individuals at a time."[73] When we examine the films, though, this isn't true. Darth Sidious had Count Dooku as his apprentice whose own apprentice was Darth Maul. Obi-Wan kills Maul; Anakin kills Dooku. Sidious then takes Anakin, later Darth Vader, as his apprentice. Vader then kills Sidious. Even though this appears to wipe out all of the Sith, it seems highly unlikely that others aren't in hiding or on other planets. In fact, Palpatine's statement that "once more the Sith will rule the galaxy" suggests that history has witnessed a back-and-forth power struggle between the Jedi and the Sith. This again accords with many Eastern traditions that talk about a period of peace followed by degeneration and eventually destruction, only to begin again. Zhuangzi perfectly summarizes the Daoist way of seeing things: "Life is the companion of death, death is the beginning of life. Who understands their workings? Man's life is a coming together of breath. If it comes together, there is life; if it scatters, there is death. And if life and death are companions to each other, then what is there for us to be anxious about? The 10,000 things are really one. We look on some as beautiful, because they are rare or unearthly; we look on others as ugly because they are foul and rotten. But the foul and rotten may turn into the rare and unearthly (and vice versa). So, it is said, you have only to comprehend the one breath that is the world. The sage never ceases to value oneness."[74]

Despite his Jedi training, Anakin, as Yoda and Buddhists would say, fails to live in the present; he grasps at impermanent things, such as ego, love, life, and power; and he is hindered by the three poisons, greed, anger, and ignorance. He also fails to realize that suffering is a part of life. To get an idea of what Anakin should have learned during his training, we need to look at *The Empire Strikes Back*. When Luke arrives on Dagobah, he finds a swampy planet, teeming with snakes, bats, and lizards, and a small figure living in a dome-shaped abode. Expecting Yoda to be someone much bigger, more masterful— a great warrior—Luke is shocked to learn that his wizened and cheerful host is none other than the revered Jedi Master. Yoda, an ancestor of the shaman and yogi, is "master of both the powers of nature and of those found deep within himself, although this mastery is often hidden behind a simple, naïve façade."[75]

On Dagobah, Luke has entered the "sacred grove," where he will learn about the "Force." Of the Force, Yoda says, "life creates it, makes it grow. Its energy surrounds us and binds us. . . . You must feel the Force around you; here, between you, me, the tree, the rock, everywhere, yes. Even between the land and the ship." Yoda explains that "A Jedi's strength flows from the Force." Of it, Obi-Wan Kenobi says that "It gives a Jedi his power. It's an energy field created by all living things. It surrounds us and penetrates us. It binds the galaxy together." On the *Millennium Falcon*, Obi-Wan tells Luke that "A Jedi can feel the Force flowing through him." Luke: "You mean it controls your actions?" Obi-Wan: "Partially, but it also obeys your commands." What Yoda and Obi-Wan are describing could very well be what the Daoists call the Dao ("the way"). In chapter 25 of the Daodejing we learn that the Dao was born before heaven and earth, it is silent and void, and it is the mother of the world.[76] Chapter 34 tells us that the Dao is "broad, reaching left as well as right. The myriad creatures depend on it for life."[77] As a text from the third century C.E. explains, "The great Dao embraces Heaven and Earth, nourishes all lives, governs the myriad workings (of the world). Formless, imageless . . . it gives birth to the myriad species."[78]

In the writings of Zhuangzi, the author is asked where the Dao exists. He responds that "There's no place it doesn't exist." Perhaps irritated by this, the other man presses him, telling him to be more specific. Just as Yoda gave his short list of interconnected beings, Zhuangzi explains "It is in the ant. It is in the . . . grass. It is in the tiles and shard. It is in the piss and shit. . . . You must not expect to find the Way in any particular place—there is no thing that escapes its presence."[79] The Dao in its tangible form on Earth is cosmic energy or *qi*, which is the vital power of the Dao at work in the world. "It is a continuously changing, forever flowing force, an energy that can appear and disappear, can be strong and weak, can be controlled and overwhelming."[80] In Chinese thought, the universe itself is sacred, and by extension so is the human body, which is a microcosm of the cosmos. *Qi*, or vital energy, comes from the Dao, and all things, from rocks to spirits, are comprised of *qi*. Furthermore, it flows through channels or meridians in the Earth, giving life and energy to all creatures. Humans can assess and manipulate *qi* that is found in the material realm through feng shui; they can do the same with the *qi* found in their bodies through meditation, visualization exercises, and by eating certain foods.

Yoda teaches Luke to always be "in the present," to be serious, controlled, patient, self-sacrificing, even-minded, and compassionate. He is also cautioned to be aware of the dark side's allies, "anger, fear, and aggression." When Luke asks him if the dark side is stronger, Yoda says, "No. Quicker, easier, more seductive." Luke: "But how am I to know the good side from the bad?" Yoda: "You will know . . . when you are calm, at peace, passive. A Jedi uses the Force for knowledge and defense, never for attack." Luke's training on developing the mind, being peaceful, and living in the present is undeniably Buddhist. As Suzuki says, "When we do something with a quiet, simple clear mind, we have no notion or shadows, and our activity is strong and straightforward."[81] Furthermore, what Yoda says during *Revenge of the Sith* could have come straight from the Buddha's mouth.[82] When Anakin is agonizing over his premonitions of "pain, suffering, death," Yoda says, "The fear of loss is a path to the dark side. Death is a natural part of life. . . . Mourn them do not. Miss them do not." At another time, he says that a person should "rejoice for those around you who transform into the Force." In his writings, Suzuki also talks about death, explaining that "we die and we do not die"[83] and that "our life and death are the same thing. When we realize this fact we have no fear of death and we have no actual difficulty in our life."[84]

Anakin is unable to understand that death and life are the same thing, and he clings to everyone around him, even though Yoda cautions that "attachment leads to jealousy. The shadow of greed that is. Train yourself to let go . . . of everything you fear to lose." During another part of the film, Yoda states that "Fear is the path to the dark side. Fear leads to anger. Anger leads to hate. Hate leads to suffering." When the Buddha arrived in the town of Kalamas named Kesaputta, he announced that "A person who is greedy, hating and deluded, overpowered by greed, hatred and delusion, his thoughts controlled by them, will destroy life, take what is not given, engage in sexual misconduct and tell lies; he will also prompt others to do likewise. Will that conduce to his harm and suffering for a long time?" Those listening to him responded, "Yes, Lord."[85] This same sentiment can be found in the chapter titled "Craving," in the *Dhammapada*: "The craving of a person who lives negligently spreads like a creeping vine. Such a person leaps ever onward, like a monkey seeking fruit in the forest. Sorrow grows . . . for anyone overcome by this miserable craving and clinging to the world. . . . The person of wrong views is carried away on the currents of lustful intent. . . . Let go of the past, let go of the future, let go of the present. Gone beyond becoming, with the mind released in every way."[86] As author Matthew Bortolin says, "Greed is not itself 'bad' because some authority says so, or because of some moral decree in some doctrine. Greed is 'bad' because it is based on a wrong view of the self."[87] It is also based on the discrimination and separation between one person and another, which in itself stems from ignorance, because, as the Buddha taught, everything in the universe is interdependent not independent.

As part of Luke's Jedi training, he is engaging in myriad physical exercises, but he doesn't seem to be concentrating on what he's doing. Rather, he keeps asking Yoda one question after another. Finally, Yoda ends the training and tells him to "Clear your mind of questions." At this moment, Luke demonstrates that although his body might be in shape; his mind is not. He exhibits what Buddhists call "monkey mind." Rather than being calm and focused, it jumps from one thing to the next. At another part in the film, Yoda even chastises Luke for having an uncontrolled mind, remarking that "All his life he has looked away . . . to the future, to the horizon. Never his mind on where he was.

What he was doing." We find this same teaching in the *Dhammapada*'s chapter on "Mind," which reads, "The mind, hard to control, flighty—alighting where it wishes—one does well to tame. The disciplined mind brings happiness."[88]

In *Star Wars: Episode I—The Phantom Menace*, Qui-Gon says to Anakin something about mind that's particularly Buddhist: "Remember. Your focus determines your reality." This means that if one is greedy, selfish, vengeful, or lustful, one's thoughts will produce actions that follow. This also means that if a person believes that the world is unfair and everyone is "against him," whether this is true or not, this is how that person will perceive the world. Suzuki, too, said that nothing comes from outside the mind: "When you think something comes from outside, it means only that something appears in your mind. . . . You yourself make the waves of your mind."[89] One final, particularly Buddhist moment comes in *The Empire Strikes Back*, when Luke tells Yoda that he will try, and Yoda responds that he must "Do or do not. There is not try." This sounds very similar to what Suzuki says: "Even though it is impossible, we have to do it because our true nature wants us to. Whether it is possible or not is not the point. We do it."[90]

To say that everything taught to a Jedi comes from Buddhism is misleading. One can also see a lot of Daoism in the films. Let's start with Yoda himself, who resembles what Daoists refer to as an immortal or a perfected being. These individuals possess unshakable equanimity in all situations, they don't hasten after gain, don't take pride in their achievements, don't worry about their ventures, and don't despair in failure. "They are calm and uninvolved, yet take action in just the way that is best for any given situation. . . . They are compassionate and understanding, compliant and gentle, helpful and upright. They seem to do the most outstanding feats with ease and no particular effort, full in control of themselves."[91] These sages create harmony, become models for others, are humble, and are a "free passageway for the cosmic energy of the Dao to flow from the root of creation to the benefit of all."[92] To get a sense of Yoda's sagelike personality, one only needs to watch him in the first three episodes, particularly in *Attack of the Clones* and *Revenge of the Sith*. For instance, no matter how bad a situation seems to get, he always remains clearminded and calm, choosing to meditate on a problem rather than rushing to action. This is the very principle of *wu-wei*. But nonaction doesn't mean doing nothing, it means cultivating the mind, which is to cultivate the Dao. "The more he remains in non-action, the more the Dao that is concentrated in him can freely radiate and thereby create harmony and openness for all."[93]

It is said that immortals prefer to live far from the world, withdrawing into the mountains or living in caves. Yoda, who lives in a cavelike dwelling, seems to be the only humanoid on Dagobah. According to Daoism, immortals are masters of the rain, fire, and the wind, like the *wu* sorcerers, and can pass through fire without burning and through water without getting wet. Several Sith lords, Jedis who have embraced the Dark Side, can command lightning and "shoot" it from their hands. Examples are Senator Palpatine and Count Dooku. Immortals can "move up on clouds," know the future, and are masters of time and space. Jedi masters can sense things, knowing of events that might come to pass—often they say that the future is uncertain—and can control the weak-minded. During the famous fight scene between Yoda and Count Dooku, the diminutive Jedi does a variety of flips and turns while flying through the air. In one scene in *Attack of the Clones*, he is shown levitating while sitting in the lotus position. In *Attack of the Clones*, Anakin demonstrates his mental abilities by causing a ball to float in the air. Immortals often have long ears and square pupils. Yoda has long, elfin ears. As healers, immortals practice breathing and gymnastic exercises.[94]

Luke's training consists of climbing ropes and doing flips through the swamp. By performing certain actions, eating certain foods, and using breathing techniques, practitioners of Daoism also believed that they could extend their lives, to ultimately become immortal. As it says in the *Nei Ching*, "Those who follow the Dao achieve the formula of perpetual youth and maintain a youthful body."[95] At Yoda's death, he is said to be 900 years old. Emperor Palpatine claims that Darth Plagueis the Wise could use the Force to influence the mid-chlorians to create life and keep the ones he cared about from dying. In the fourth-century text, *Shenxian Zhuan* (*Biographies of Spirit Immortals*), it says that an immortal could lift a ton without any trouble. In *The Empire Strikes Back*, Yoda easily "lifts" Luke's X-wing fighter and moves it; during his numerous fight sequences, especially one between him and Count Dooku, he prevents part of a building from falling on and killing Anakin and Obi-Wan Kenobi. Finally, immortals or Daoist sages are often said to be cheerful, sometimes to the point of seeming eccentric. Even though Yoda is often serious, he does have his moments when he giggles, thus demonstrating his lighter side.

While Yoda is talking about the "Force," he tells Luke that "Luminous beings are we, not this crude matter." This is in accordance with Daoism. In the
Taiping Jing Shengjun Bizhia (*Secret Instructions of the Holy Lord on the Scriptures of Great Peace*), a Daoist text from the second century C.E., we read that
"human beings originally come from the energy of primordial chaos. This energy brings forth essence, which in turn gives birth to spirit. Spirit brings forth
light. People are also based on the energy of yin and yang. As this energy revolves it brings forth essence. Essence in turn revolves and becomes spirit.
Spirit revolves and light is born."[96] The commentary to another Daoist text,
The Xuanzhu Xinjing Zhu (*Mysterious Pearly Mirror of the Mind*), which dates
to the ninth century, explains that attaining "The Prime of the One" is a rather
lengthy process. One must be "firm even in hardship and live in solitary serenity. As one darkens the mind and refines the body, naturally the spirit becomes
more intense and the body more open. Eventually bones and flesh are blended
with the dark mystery; they transform to pure primordiality. Shaking off the
old body like a cicada sheds its skin, you can be in several places at the same
time." With enough practice, one's mind becomes "merged with the Cosmic
Chaos, free from the body of the self." As it explains further, eventually one
can simply erase one's trace on Earth, leaving behind "a staff instead of a
corpse."[97] When one is still an ordinary body or mind, a person is limited;
when one sheds the body, one can leave being and nonbeing and fly all over
the void. This sounds remarkably like what happens after Darth Vader strikes
down Obi-Wan Kenobi in *A New Hope*. Vader's red lightsaber hits the old Jedi
master, and all that's left behind are his cloak and light saber. His body has disappeared, but he's still present. We can hear him as he tells Luke to run for the
Millennium Falcon.

As Luke prepares to leave the Dagobah system in *The Empire Strikes Back*,
Obi-Wan appears to him as a luminous being. He looks as he did in life and
he can speak. The only difference is that he can materialize at will and he emanates a blue light. According to Daoist thought, "The physical cosmic body is
part of creation; it merges with the spirit to realize the Dao. The cosmic body
belongs to the universal, yet it can only be nourished through concentration
and visualization of the spirits residing in it." The personal body is an imaginary self built through discriminating consciousness, passions, and desires.
Since it is the source of sorrow and afflictions, it must be abandoned for the
cosmic body. "Only in a state of no-self, free from constructed identity, can the

Dao and the spirit flourish." When the body turns to dust, the spirit immortal ascends to heaven.[98] Other Jedi Knights who can appear in this luminous form are Qui-Gon, Yoda, and Anakin. It is said in *Star Wars: Revenge of the Sith—The Visual Dictionary* that Qui-Gon tutored the exiled Yoda on "how to survive death with one's consciousness intact. In time, Yoda tells Obi-Wan of this, and that he, too, will begin training with Qui-Gon."[99]

Many of the films' lines could be understood from a Daoist perspective. Everyone in the *Star Wars* universe had given up on Darth Vader. Even his teacher, Obi-Wan, tried to convince Luke that his father couldn't be saved, saying, "He is more machine now than man; twisted and evil." But Luke won't be dissuaded, even if it means his own life, he will try. This is in accordance with the Daodejing, chapter 27, which reads, "Therefore the sage always excels in saving people, and so abandons no one."[100] When Yoda tells Luke to "unlearn what you have learned," we see this reflected in chapter 20 of the Daodejing, which reads, "Exterminate learning and there will no longer be worries. Between yea and nay, how much difference is there? Between good and evil, how great the distance." The section continues with the speaker praising the fact that he has nothing, his heart is foolish; and he is dim, confused, dull, and ignorant: "I alone am muddled, calm like the sea; Like a high wind that never ceases." The author seems to reject all that he has been taught, seeing instead the truth that everything is an aspect of the one Dao. This sentiment is repeated in the writing of Zhuangzi, who says, "Only when there is no pondering and no cognition will you get to know the Way"[101] and "Smash up your limbs and body! Drive out your perception and understanding! Cast off your physical form! Get rid of all wisdom! Thus you can join the great pervasion of all!"[102] Zen Buddhism, too, is in accordance. Suzuki wrote that the most important thing is for a person to "forget all gaining ideas, all dualistic ideas. In other words, just practice *zazen*. . . . Do not think about anything."[103] He also said that Buddhism shouldn't be about gathering many pieces of information. Instead one should clear the mind. For when one's mind is clear, "true knowledge is already yours."[104]

The Jedi Knights are described as guardians of peace and justice, and they only use their weapons as a last resort. Chapter 31 of the Daodejing says that "Arms are instruments of ill omen, not the instruments of the gentlemen. When one is compelled to use them, it is best to do so without relish. There is no glory in victory. . . . When victorious in war, one should observe the rites

of mourning." Yoda says essentially the same thing in *Star Wars: Episode II—
Attack of the Clones*. Obi-Wan says, "I have to admit that without the clones, it
would have not been a victory." Yoda: "Victory? Victory, you say? Master Obi-
Wan, not victory. The shroud of the dark side has fallen. Begun the Clone War
has." Responding to Luke's statement that he's looking for a great warrior,
Yoda says, "Wars not make one great." As Daoism adapted to Buddhism, it developed a set of 10 precepts for its adherents. The first three are not to harbor
hatred or jealousy, maintain a kind heart and do not kill, and maintain purity
and be withdrawing in one's social interactions. Elaborating on the second
precept, it states that one should have pity for and support all living beings, be
compassionate and loving, and to reach out to bring universal *redemption* (my
emphasis) to all.[105] The *Sanyuan pin* (*Precepts of the Three Primes*) tells students and laypersons that it is a sin to pick a fight, to kill living beings, and to
give rise to evil thoughts. Daoism praises many of the same qualities that Buddhism does, such as being emotionally detached, nonviolent, and free of
greed. Daoism also asserts that the sage should live in harmony with the
world, treat everyone the same, and be selfless, generous, and compassionate.
Along with restraint and unimportance, compassion is one of the three treasures of Daoism.

When Luke is trying to raise his X-wing fighter out of the swamp, he fails,
saying, "I can't. It's too big." Yoda chastises him, saying, "Size matters not. Look
at me. Judge me by my size, do you?" To illuminate this exchange, we will look
at the writings of Zhuangzi. In chapter 17, the Lord of the River is talking to
Jo of the North Sea, and the former asks the latter how we come to have the
distinctions of noble and mean, great and small. The latter responds that from
the point of view of the Way, things have no nobility or meanness, because
each regards itself as noble and other things as mean. He explains that even
though we have designations of big and small, useful and not useful, functional and not functional, all of these are dependent on circumstance and perspective. "Embrace the 10,000 things universally—how could there be one you
should give special support to? This is called being without bent. When the
10,000 things are unified and equal, then which is short and which is long?"[106]
In essence, people get caught up in distinction, when all is really one. Yoda
demonstrates that it doesn't take a large person to move the X-wing fighter,
because it isn't about physical strength, it's about mental clarity and
"strength." Once Yoda has done what Luke couldn't, he exclaims, "I can't be-

lieve it." To this Yoda responds, "This is why you fail." Buddhism can shed light on this later statement. As Suzuki says, "A mind full of preconceived ideas, subjective intentions or habits isn't open to things as they are."[107]

Finally, let us again return to this prophecy that the "Chosen One will bring balance to the Force." Daoism teaches us that everything in the universe is comprised of either yin or yang forces, dark and light, wet and dry, passive and active, feminine and masculine. Even though these seem incompatible, for one to exist, we must have the other. "There is neither pure brightness nor pure darkness; neither pure good nor pure evil; neither pure yin nor pure yang." These elements stand for the contradicting and opposing elements that contain, supplement, and balance each other.[108] All processes are marked by change, making it inevitable that at one time yin will predominate and then yang will; however, the goal of human beings is to seek a harmonious balance between the two. Sleep (yin) should be balanced by wakefulness (yang); salty foods (yin) by bitter ones (yang). If one overpowers the other, then on a physical level, sickness and death can result.[109] In the *Star Wars* universe, it's possible that the Sith, which is more active, is represented by yang; and the Jedi, which is more passive, is represented by yin. When yang is predominant, states are organized, power is distributed among rulers and their aides, armies go to war, and soldiers kill each other.

What Dreams May Come (1998)—Based on a novel by Richard Matheson. Directed by Vincent Ward. Running time: 113 min. English. Rated PG-13 for thematic elements involving death, some disturbing images, and language. Genre: Drama/fantasy.

Summary: Physician Chris Nielsen (Robin Williams) and his wife, Annie (Annabella Sciorra), are the perfect couple. After they meet in Switzerland, they fall in love and start building a life together. But everything takes a turn for the worse when their two children die in a car crash. Four years later, tragedy strikes again. Following a pileup in an interstate tunnel, Chris rushes to attend to the injured. He, too, quickly becomes a victim when a car flies through the air, fatally wounding him. After his death, he ascends to a paradise-like place, where he meets a friendly spirit (Cuba Gooding Jr.) who is assigned to help him adapt to his new state of being. Chris believes that, one day, Annie will join him in heaven, but his optimism is hampered when he learns that, overcome by depression and guilt, she has committed suicide and has been consigned to a kind of hell. Not willing to let his soul mate remain there, Chris vows to rescue her, even if that means navigating the treacherous terrain of the underworld.

A Gallup Poll survey conducted May 10–13, 2007, discovered that 81% of Americans believe in heaven and 69% believe in hell,[110] and, on the surface, *What Dreams May Come* seems to tap into Judeo-Christian concepts of the afterlife. But does it? The Hebrew Bible actually says very little about what happens to a person's soul following death. "Generally speaking, most biblical writers either ignore the subject or adopt the prevailing Mesopotamian view that all the dead, good and bad alike, descend permanently into a gloomy subterranean realm where they lead an impoverished and shadowy postmortem existence."[111] This place was known as Sheol, but other names were also used, such as *kever* (the grave), *bor* or *shachat* (the pit), and *avadon* (the wasteland).[112] Little discussion of Sheol exists in preexilic literature, and what we find in later writings, especially Psalms, Isaiah, Job, and Ecclesiastes, refers to it as a dark place where the deceased have no thought, strength, or even consciousness.[113] In the Book of Isaiah 14:10–11 we read that the dead greet new arrivals with the words: "So you have been stricken as we were, you have become like us! Your pomp is brought down to Sheol, and the strains of your lutes! Worms are to be your bed, maggots your blanket."[114]

During the Hellenistic period, after the fourth century B.C.E., Jewish thought underwent a major change, particularly with regard to ideas concerning death and the afterlife. Some literature, such as the Book of Daniel, talk about a future time of bodily resurrection and judgment; others, such as the Testament of Abraham (second century C.E.), talk about an immediate judgment of the soul following death, wherein the "righteous receive salvation" and the "wicked are given over to fiery torments."[115] What happened after death proved contentious between the Sadducees, the noble-born priests, and the Pharisees, a sect that developed into rabbinic Judaism, especially during the Second Temple period (third century B.C.E. to 70 C.E.). The former sect didn't believe in the afterlife, while the latter did. Since the Pharisaic sect produced normative Judaism, many Jews today believe that actions in this life will have an effect in the world to come (*olam ha-ba*).

During the first century B.C.E., rabbinic sages taught that the spirit maintains a connection with the body for about a year, after which the relationship is severed. Mourners traditionally say the Kaddish for a loved one for 11 months following his or her death, because the Talmud states that the "truly evil spend a full year after their deaths undergoing the tortures of *Gehenim*, the closest thing Jews have to Hell."[116] According to rabbinic tradition, the righteous receive their reward in the afterlife in the celestial Garden of Eden, which is a place beyond time where the righteous live in an ecstatic intimacy with God. The wicked suffer in Gehenna or *Gehinnom*,[117] a first-century-C.E. term that indicates the place where sinners are punished, especially by fire, after death. "In the Mishnah and later rabbinic texts, the name Gehenna has superseded the older term for the underworld (Sheol). Gehenna is also the ordinary term in the Qur'an for the place of ultimate punishment."[118]

For more elaborate forays into heaven and hell, one can read the apocalyptic, pseudepigraphical Ethiopic Book of Enoch, or First Enoch, and the Slavonic Enoch, or Second Enoch. In First Enoch, which dates to about 200 B.C.E. to 200 C.E., the narrator sees that after the final judgment, the righteous go to heaven, while the wicked go to Sheol, which is characterized by darkness and fire. As it says in 56:8, "In those days Sheol shall open its jaws, and they shall be swallowed up therein. And their destruction shall be at an end; Sheol shall devour the sinners in the presence of the elect."[119] As the *New Advent Catholic Encyclopedia* states, "This is one of the earliest mentions of Sheol as a hell of torment, preceding portions of the book having described the place of retribution for the wicked as Tartarus and Geennom."[120] Second Enoch also depicts hell as a terrible place rife with all manner of tortures, including "cruel darkness, dim gloom" and the only light source seems like a murky fire. Everywhere one looks there is fire, frost, and ice. Even the angels are "fearful and merciless, bearing sharp weapons and merciless tortures."[121]

To clarify matters, when the Hebrew Bible was translated into Greek, the word *Sheol* became known as Hades, which, by this time, had its own mythology. For instance, it was believed that the virtuous went to a paradise known as Elysium, and the wicked went to Tartarus, a place of punishment. Because of philosophers such as Plato and Pythagoras, the Greeks made a direct connection between one's behavior in this life and one's "fate" in the next. When mentioned in the Hebrew Bible, particularly in Jeremiah, 2 Kings, and 2 Chronicles, Gehenna was associated with an actual geographical location—a ravine near Jerusalem—and was seen as the place where "humans were sacrificed and burned as offerings to false gods, a practice that Israelite prophets vehemently condemned." Over time, it became, especially in 1 Enoch, as a place of suffering for the wicked. [122]

Because of its central image of the death and resurrection of Jesus, early Christianity focused more on the afterlife than had Judaism. In the Gospels we find references to a blissful eternity spent with God; however, this doesn't necessarily correspond to a literal place. For images of a heavenly realm, we have to look to the Book of Revelation, in which we find descriptions of the "throne of God and the Lamb, with living creatures and elders, angelic hosts and multitudes of the redeemed, drawn from every nation, bringing homage and praise. Popular conceptions of heaven have been derived largely from the imagery of this book."[123] The *Catechism of the Catholic Church* explains that "Those who die in God's grace and friendship and are perfectly purified live forever with Christ. They are like God forever, for they 'see him as he is,' face to face.'" It also states that "this perfect life with the Most Holy Trinity—this communion of life and love with the Trinity, with the Virgin Mary, the angels and all the blessed—is called 'heaven,'" which is "the ultimate end and fulfillment of the deepest human longings, the state of supreme, definitive happiness."[124] Heaven is the "blessed community of all who are perfectly incorporated into Christ."[125]

As for a discussion of hell in the New Testament, the best evidence exists in the Book of Matthew, especially 5:22, 29–30; 10:28; 23:15, 3, the only Gospel to attach "eschatological warnings to the parables Mark attributed to Jesus,"[126] and, of course, the Book of Revelation, which describes the fate of the righteous and the damned, particularly in chapters 19 through 21. In 19:17–18, we read that an angel calls to all of the birds, telling them to "Come, gather for the great supper of God, to eat the flesh of kings." In 19:20–21, the beast and the false prophet are captured and thrown "alive into the lake of fire that burns with sulfur. And the rest were killed by the sword of the rider on the horse, the sword that came from his mouth; and all the birds were gorged with their flesh." In Revelation 20:1–3, an angel comes down from heaven, holding keys to the bottomless pit, and grabs Satan, binds him for 1,000 years, and throws him into the pit. Once he's released, he is thrown into the lake of fire and sulfur, where he, the beast, and false prophet were and will be forever tormented day and night. And in 20:13, we read that after the final judgment, "anyone whose name was not found written in the book of life was thrown into the lake of fire."

The Bible isn't the only source for Judeo-Christian concepts of the afterlife, though. As scholar Stephen L. Harris explains, other sources include Mesopotamian and Egyptian lore, noncanonical Jewish and Christian writings, Dante's *Divine Comedy*, and Milton's *Paradise Lost and Regained*.[127] In fact, many Christians adhere to popular sentiments that haven't necessarily been integrated to Protestant and Catholic theological systems, such as the idea that they will be reunited with loved ones. Furthermore, scholars find a sharp division between two types of Christians: those who feel comfortable with a detailed afterlife in the style of a "modern heaven" with its continuation of family, work, and progress, and the others who have a more theocentric image of heaven, complete with beatific vision, heavenly light, and robed angels singing praises. The first group may look to descriptions found in near-death experiences—either in "fact" or fiction—for evidence and explanation of the afterlife. The second group rejects our ability to know what happens next or simply denies the possibility of an afterlife.[128]

As we can see, *What Dreams May Come* doesn't follow canonical concepts of the afterlife. Instead, it draws upon "popular" imagery found in art and literature and then mixes those with everything from Greek myth to Buddhist thought. Immediately after dying, Chris becomes an astral body, remaining near his grieving wife and watching his own funeral. He even relives certain key moments from his life; it's as if snippets of his life are "flashing before his eyes." He travels to an Eden-like landscape that is as vibrant and colorful as an impressionist painting that has come, quite literally, to life. Here he is reunited with his children, a former colleague named Albert, and even his family dog. After he is greeted by his Dalmatian, Chris says, "I screwed up, I'm in dog heaven. Maybe I'm not in your heaven, girl. Maybe you are in mine." On his descent to hell, Chris encounters a monochromatic, sometimes sulfuric landscape that seems ripped from the pages of Dante's *Divine Comedy*, or at least as conceived of by engraver Gustave Dore. When Chris and his party ferry across a lake, the dead grasp frantically at their boat. In another location, Chris must walk across a gray landscape that is dotted with the upturned faces of the dead. This image comes directly from Dante's *Inferno*, which in Canto XXXII, lines 19–21 reads: "Look how thou steppest! Take heed thou do not trample with thy feet the heads of the tired, miserable brothers."[129] Undeniably director Vincent Ward, an artist himself, drew heavily upon imagery found in Western art, envisioned by artists as diverse as Hieronymus Bosch, Caspar David Friedrich, Claude Monet, and Dore.

Even if *What Dreams May Come* feels visually familiar to Westerners, its theology won't. The aforementioned Gallup Poll found that 86% of Americans believe in God, and yet in this film a personal deity is mentioned just once. While surveying heaven, Chris asks his spiritual guide, at this point known as "Albert," "Where's God in all this?" Albert replies, "Somewhere up there, shouting down that he loves us and wondering why we can't hear him. You think?" The inclusion of these last two words is interesting, because they change what seems to be a statement into a query. It's almost as if Albert is saying what Chris expects to hear and then asks him if he's in accordance. This is significant, because the audience learns that everything that Chris encounters is a product of his mind; if he thinks it, it will happen. As Albert explains, only "thought is real; physical is the illusion." Everything from the cliff tops to the grass beneath Chris' feet comes from his imagination, and it animates on his command.

The fact that God is mentioned only briefly and then is never brought up again has upset a number of Christian reviewers. As David Cownie, a "proto-presbyter" at the Orthodox Christian Information Center, writes, "What is truly sad about this film is that an attempt is made to portray heaven and hell without any significant reference to God."[130] Furthermore, even though 75% of Americans believe in angels and 70% in the devil, neither angels nor the devil is shown in *What Dreams May Come*. Heaven, or paradise, is surprisingly free of winged creatures dressed all in white and sporting a glowing nimbus; and hell is noticeably devoid of red, horned creatures stabbing the damned with pitchforks.

What Dreams May Come didn't fare well at the box office, and, although critics praised the film's aesthetics, their response to the storyline was largely lukewarm. Some have even labeled it "New Agey."[131] What seems to be the problem with *What Dreams May Come* is that it fails to present a consistent religious viewpoint, and for some that proves unnerving. The film seems to be inspired by the Greek story of Orpheus and Eurydice; however, even when elements are similar, including the fact that in both stories the male leads descend to the underworld to rescue his deceased wife, the finer points are changed. For instance, a snakebite kills Eurydice; Annie kills herself. In the Greek myth, a distraught Orpheus descends to the underworld, all the way playing his lyre. He appears before the throne of Hades and Persephone and sings to them of his woe. It is said that his music was so enchanting that Hades gave in to Orpheus' request and allowed Eurydice to leave with him. The only stipulation was that Orpheus must never look back during their ascent. But he couldn't help himself, and when he glanced back, Eurydice returned to the underworld. In one account, an inconsolable Orpheus meets his end when the Thracian Maenads tear him from limb to limb. Now dead, he finds himself in Hades, where he is reunited with his wife. None of these moments occur in *What Dreams May Come.*

The Greeks believed that Hades and his wife, Persephone, ruled the underworld, and depending on which account one reads, to get there, the souls of the deceased had to cross either the River Acheron (the river of woe) or the River Styx (the river of hate). The other underground rivers include Cocytus (river of lamentation), Lethe (river of oblivion), and Phlegethon (the river of fire). To get safe passage across the river, one had to pay the old ferryman Charon a coin. If the deceased didn't have the price of passage, he or she was forced to wander the banks of the river for 100 years. Once on land, the deceased encountered the three-headed Cerberus, who guarded the gate through which the person had to pass. Before this could happen, though, the beast needed to be mollified with a cake of honey. According to the *Aeneid*, once one passed this beast the first sound that he or she heard was the wailing of young children and those who had perished under false charges. The next group he or she encountered were those "who had died by their own hand, hating life and seeking refuge in death."[132]

Where the deceased went next depended on what sort of person he or she was. The average person went to the "realm of shadows," where one lacked strength and "full command of [his or her] faculties. . . . Loss of personality at death is also implied."[133] This was a dull place where the sun never shined. For some, such as King Menalos, their final destination was the Elysian Fields, which were described by Homer in *The Odyssey* as a kind of paradise. Here no one would ever die and everyone nourished himself or herself on ambrosia and nectar, the food of the gods.

Finally, those who had offended the gods could expect to find themselves thrown into Tartarus or Tartaros, which was the deepest part of Hades. In book 6 of the *Aeneid*, we learn that its gate was made of adamantine, a metal that neither the gods nor men could break through, and that an iron tower stood by the gate from which an avenging Fury kept guard. "From hence are heard the groans of ghosts, the pains of sounding lashes and of dragging chains."[134] Within Tartarus, one finds some famous and not-so-famous guests. The latter includes the Titans, who warred against the gods; Tantalus, who abused his godlike privileges; Sisyphus, who was cursed to forever roll a boulder up a hill; and Ixion, who because he tried to seduce Hera was fastened to a ceaselessly revolving wheel. As far as imagery is concerned, *What Dreams May Come* acknowledges these Greek mythological "roots" several times. For instance, when Chris enters "hell," we see shipwrecks on fire. On the side of one of them is written the word Cerberus. Also while Chris is walking across a floor comprised of mud and human heads, one of them calls to him, claiming to be his father. This seems reminiscent of the scene in the *Aeneid* when Aeneas sees his father in the underworld and when he reaches out to embrace him, his father encloses an unsubstantial image.

To get to the heart of *What Dreams May Come*, the viewer must go beyond the film's visuals and listen to what the characters are saying. When we do this, we realize how closely the screenplay reflects concepts from several Eastern traditions, particularly Hinduism and Buddhism. "For Hindus, the plot bears a striking resemblance to the 'Final Test' at the end of the . . . *Mahabharata*. As the righteous King Yudhisthira enters heaven, he learns that his brothers and wife are not there." He asks Indra, God of heaven, where they are, and is then led, just as was Chris, into the deepest regions of the Naraka Loka. Finding his family suffering there, he selflessly decides to stay with them rather than return to heaven, just as did Chris, because his "presence gives them comfort." The author continues, explaining that once Yudhisthira makes this sacrifice, he and his family are allowed to enter heaven.[135]

The similarities may seem striking; however, Richard Matheson, the author of *What Dreams May Come*, has never acknowledged a direct Hindu influence on his work. Matheson was raised a Christian Scientist—a faith he has referred to as "a good religion"—but left it to create his own belief system, which he said, "does not adhere to what has been described as 'Churchianity.'" He did this by reading "countless books on parapsychology, metaphysics," with his favorite being Harold Waldwin Percival's *Thinking and Destiny*.[136] This book has been so influential on him that in 1993 Matheson wrote *The Path: A New Look at Reality*, a fictional work about an everyman who encounters a mysterious stranger who imparts to him 10 lessons about the true reality of the soul." In the section titled "To the Reader," Matheson writes, "I have prepared *The Path* ... to introduce readers to these concepts in Percival's book which are the easiest to comprehend. These are taken directly from *Thinking and Destiny*, most of the statements in this book being in Percival's own words."[137] Some of the subjects covered in *The Path* include "Why are you reborn?" "What is your karma?" and "What is your true self?"

Percival himself was a staunch member of the Theosophical Society, which was founded in the late 19th century by Madame H. P. Blavatsky and Colonel H. S. Olcott. Since its beginning, Theosophy has been strongly influenced by Eastern thought. For instance, in 1879, the founders established their headquarters in India, and when they arrived in Sri Lanka they "appeared to embrace Buddhism by publicly taking the refuges and precepts."[138] Theosophists understand karma in very much the same way that practitioners of Eastern religious traditions do, as the "justice of the universe [that] goes hand-in-hand with reincarnation." Furthermore, Theosophy teaches that "the spirit is reincarnated into another body to learn new lessons."[139] With Theosophical influences, it isn't too surprising that *What Dreams May Come* sounds Hindu.

Many ideas in the film also sound undeniably Buddhist. While Chris is in paradise, he attempts to understand what has happened to him. He has died and yet he still exists. But what is *he*? He and his spirit guide have a metaphysical exchange on the subject, with the latter asking, "What do you mean by you anyway? Are you your arm or your leg? If you lost all of your limbs, wouldn't you still be you? So what is 'the me'?" Chris: "My brain, I suppose." Spirit guide: "Your brain. Your brain is a body part. Like your fingernail or your heart. Why is that the part that's you?" Chris: "Because I'm sort of a voice in my head. The part of me that thinks and feels, that is aware that I exist at all." Spirit guide: "Your brain is meat. It rots and disappears. Do you really think that's all there was to you? You're in your house, but you aren't your house. We see what we choose to see. Thought is real. Physical is the illusion. Ironic, huh?" Later in the film, the Tracker (Max Von Sydow) remarks that even though he still wears glasses, his eyes are "a figment of his imagination." We can find these same sentiments in Zen Buddhism. As Shunryu Suzuki says, "Nothing comes from outside your mind. . . . The true understanding is that the mind includes everything; when you think something comes from outside it means only that something appears in your mind. . . . You yourself make the waves of your mind."[140]

This concept of "you are what you think" permeates *What Dreams May Come.* For instance, after Annie kills herself, she ends up in a hell-like realm, but not because she's being punished. As the spirit guide explains to Chris, "There are no judges or crimes here; everybody is equal. That's just the way it is." He explains further that "What you call hell is for those who don't know they're dead; they can't realize what they've done. Too self-absorbed in life, suicides go to hell for a different reason. Each of us has an instinct that there is a natural order to our journey, and Annie's violated that. She won't realize . . . accept what she's done. Everybody's hell is different. It's not all fire and pain. The real hell is your life gone wrong." Annie's hell is actually a crumbling house populated with spiders and strange creaking noises. Nothing that she experiences is real, though. As the Tracker tells Chris, "The whole place is an illusion. Suicides can get pretty tortured, pretty committed to punishing themselves."

Several Christian reviewers recoiled at this idea of a morally "neutral" universe, primarily because Christianity teaches that since we do not own our lives, we have no right to terminate them—and this is why they perceive suicide to be wrong. The official teaching of the Catholic Church is that "Suicide contradicts the natural inclination of the human being to preserve and perpetuate his life. It is gravely contrary to the just love of self. . . . Suicide is contrary to love for the living God." Whether or not it is seen as "contrary to moral law," one must determine if the suicide was "voluntary" or not. And in the latter category we find people suffering from psychological disturbances, anguish, or grave fear of hardship, suffering, or torture. Christians should not despair of the eternal salvation of suicides, though, for "by ways known to him alone, God can provide the opportunity for salutary repentance. The Church prays for persons who have taken their own lives."[141] At the other spectrum, many evangelical Christian churches teach that suicides go to hell or more specifically "to the lake of fire."

When we survey world religions, we find that all respond differently to the issue of suicide. Because a human life is thought to be sacred, Jewish law opposes suicide. In fact, "One who commits suicide is abhorred by Judaism as one who has denied the life given him by God." Furthermore, a suicide cannot be buried in a Jewish cemetery with full funeral rites.[142] They are, instead, buried near the outer limits of the cemetery, "at least six feet from other Jewish dead."[143] Hindu literature contains several stories of women who, because of grief or despair of being in a hopeless situation, committed suicide, especially by self-immolation. For the most part, they are not condemned for their actions. In fact, quite the opposite happens. Seeing *sati* as an ideal, some believe that those who make this ultimate sacrifice "become instantly a goddess (*devi*)" who will then be "worshipped as a symbol of the ideal female."[144] Most Buddhists believe in karma and rebirth; therefore, they explain that committing suicide will have karmic repercussions. However, the individual's volition and state of mind at death are important factors. For instance, in Japan, stories tell of "brave" samurai who committed suicide. "'To die *isagi-yoku*' is one of the thoughts very dear to the Japanese heart. In some deaths, if this characteristic is present, crimes committed by the offenders are judged even charitably. *Isagi-yoku* means 'leaving no regrets,' 'with a clear conscience,' 'like a brave man,' 'with no reluctance,' 'in full possession of mind' . . . the Japanese hate to see death met irresolutely and lingeringly; they desire to be blown away like the cherries before the wind."[145]

Looking at all of these traditions, we find that *What Dreams May Come* seems to reflect Buddhist ideas more than anything else. Annie is "trapped" in hell for a number of reasons. First of all, she is unable to "let go" of her attachment to her loved ones, believing that without them, she can't live. Second, and perhaps most importantly, she can't forgive herself for the death of her children and her husband. Even though she wasn't driving the car when her children were killed, she believes that had she been, her children would still be alive. Psychologically, she punishes herself on Earth and in the afterlife. And once someone is in the midst of delusion, such as Annie, there is no end to it. Their delusion consumes them and it becomes their reality. "When you start to wander about in some delusion . . . then your surroundings are not real anymore, and your mind is not real anymore."[146]

Tibetan Buddhism can illuminate Annie's situation. It, too, teaches that all that we can know is our own mind, and that it is by the power of our mind that we create our world and, eventually, our subsequent worlds. Depending on one's actions, after one dies, a person is born into one of six realms. These can be thought of as "real" or as states of the mind. As monk and scholar Trungpa Rinpoche explained, the realms are strategies for maintaining "ego's games in the face of awakening. They arise from the poisons [greed, hatred, and ignorance], and when we allow one of these . . . to build up and take over our lives, we find ourselves in the particular realm associated with it. . . . All the realms are based on grasping and holding on, not allowing ourselves to let go into spaciousness."[147] As has been expounded upon in other chapters, the six realms include heaven and a hell realm, which itself is comprised of eight hot and eight cold hells. In the first level of the hot hells, people fight against each other, seeing everyone as an enemy.

And this is exactly what we find in *What Dreams May Come*. Chris, his spirit guide, and the Tracker travel to hell in a boat with a red sail. Almost immediately they encounter rain, lightning, and large waves. As they get closer, they find their boat surrounded by the dead who eventually tip it over. The three journeymen wash up on shore, where they encounter shipwrecks. Fire, explosions, and smoke choke the air. Just as they are about to enter through hell's gate, they come face-to-face with myriad dead people shouting and brandishing their weapons. This is the embodiment of anger, aggression, and rage. But before they engage the hordes, Chris stops, realizing that Annie isn't in there. After saying good-bye to his spirit guide, Chris and the Tracker step onto an elevator that's "going up." They stop at a "floor" where humans are buried up to their faces. As Chris navigates through them, many express regret about their earthly lives. The ground eventually gives way, and Chris falls into an inverted cathedral, where, at what would be the very top of the arch, we see Annie's house. Only this one is dilapidated. The Tracker tells Chris that he can tell Annie good-bye, but he only has three minutes. Any more time and he could lose his mind; "once her reality becomes yours, there is no way back."

In the *Bardo Thodol*, those who "freeze" others out of their lives end up in the cold hells, a place where the depressed, despairing, and self-hating go. "As though locked in a pillar of ice, we are unable to communicate or respond to others. Since there is no sense of relationship, there are no external tormentors here; it is a world of self-enclosed isolation. . . . [Here] we are surrounded by walls of ice, and our own reflections haunt us and our own voices echo back at us."[148] This description corresponds well to *What Dreams May Come*. As Chris walks into the front room of their dilapidated home, he calls out and his voice echoes. Once he sees Annie, he approaches her, but she doesn't recognize him. She's scared and confused, telling him that there isn't any electricity, gas, or water pressure. Everything is dark, wet, and disintegrating. Interestingly enough, once Chris decides to remain with Annie, he remarks how cold it is. As has been said, this world isn't real; it's only a product of Annie's mind. It's just as Chris says: "Good people end up in hell, because they can't forgive themselves" and "What's true in our minds is true, whether some people know it or not." As scholar Francesca Fremantle writes about this realm, "Hell beings are imprisoned in their pain because they are convinced that it is real; the burning or the freezing has become their whole existence."[149]

At this point, it's worth mentioning a series of very short, very rapid frames that occur in the film at about 1 hour, 38 minutes, and 47 seconds. These are only perceptible to the at-home viewer who has the ability to freeze-frame the DVD. At first, we quickly see an image of Chris under the water. This is followed by blackness, which gives way to bright light and then two very quick shots of an arm with what looks like an IV tube taped down to it. At 1 hour, 38 minutes, and 50 seconds, we see an extreme close-up of Chris' face alternating with more white light. Two seconds later, his eyes open. A few seconds after that, he wakes up to find himself back in "heaven." After watching this sequence, we begin to wonder if Chris actually undertook this spiritual journey or if, as in *Jacob's Ladder*, we were watching emanations of his mind in the after-death or dying state? If we reexamine the film with this in mind, we can find support for this latter hypothesis.

Throughout the film, Chris relives the more joyful and painful moments of his life. The most poignant times are when he failed to connect with those around him. For instance, we learn that instead of letting his son be himself, Chris pressured him into meeting his expectations. The Tracker even asks Chris if he was proud of his children. Naturally, Chris responds in the affirmative. Knowing he's being lied to, the Tracker replies, "Well, that's an easy bullshit answer" and he asks again. Clearly annoyed, Chris replies, through his teeth, "I said, 'of course.'" Having seen him interact with his son, we know that this isn't true. Chris also failed to connect with his daughter, who in the afterlife assumes the guise of a "beautiful" air hostess she saw on a flight to Singapore.[150] Because in life Chris didn't know the people around him—his son, daughter, or his mentor—when he dies he doesn't recognize them; he has to learn to really see them. After revealing that he's actually Albert, the Tracker explains, "You know why we chose to look so different? The old baggage—the old roles of authority, who's the teacher, who's the father—gets in the way of who we really are to each other." The lesson here, from a Buddhist perspective, is that when we listen to others, we should "give up all preconceived ideas and subjective opinions." Usually when we listen to others, we hear it as an echo of ourselves; "You are actually listening to your own opinion. If it agrees with your opinion, you may accept it, but if it does not you will reject it or you may not even really hear it."[151] Chris' greatest failure was pulling away from Annie after their children died. Feeling alienated and alone, Annie slashes her wrists and ends up in a mental hospital. Chris' journey to the underworld is as much for him as it is for her. In fact, we could see this journey in symbolic terms. When he was alive, he thought only of himself; he was self-absorbed. After death, he learns to be self-sacrificing. Rather than spending an eternity in heaven without Annie, he decides to remain in hell with her, even though it means slowly forgetting everything and going mad. Once he chooses to remain with her, he wakes up in paradise.

Both Hinduism and Buddhism teach us that we live innumerable lives, and *What Dreams May Come* supports the idea of reincarnation; however, what it says about it is more a reflection of the author's interpretation than that of the aforementioned religions. According to Hinduism and Buddhism, *samsara* is a fact of life, and we are essentially ensnared and enslaved by it. In *What Dreams May Come*, *samsara* is more benign. As Chris learns, he will be reborn only if he wants to be; it's voluntary. At the end of the film, Chris is reunited with Annie, who asks him, "What about going back and being reborn? Make different choices? Try again?" In the film's alternative ending, which is included on the DVD, we get a very different slant on reincarnation. It is said that because Annie committed suicide, she has to go back for atonement. But everything will work out fine. She will be born to a family in Jaffra, Sri Lanka, and in her teens she will contract an illness that causes sleep deprivation. Not wanting to leave her behind, Chris chooses to be reborn. He will then travel to Sri Lanka, where he will meet, fall in love with, and marry "Annie" who will eventually die in his arms. The catch is, he will have to spend 40 years after her death mourning her. Happily, they both decide that this is a great idea and they seal their decision with a kiss. In the last minutes, we see both of them being born—one in Philadelphia, the other in Sri Lanka. In the version shown in theaters, the film ends with them meeting as children.

Buddhism and Hinduism aren't the only religions that mention reincarnation or transmigration of souls, though. Judaism, more specifically Kabbalah, also discusses it, which in Hebrew is known as *gilgul*. As scholar Gershom Scholem states, there is no definite proof of the existence of this doctrine during the Second Temple period nor is there direct mention in the Talmud. By contrast, "transmigration is taken for granted in the Kabbalah from its literary expression in the *Sefer ha-Behir* (late 12th century)" and the idea grew and developed from there, becoming one of the major doctrines of Kabbalah.[152] Some writers discussed *gilgul* in terms of punishment, serving "as a rational excuse for the apparent absence of injustice in the world and as an answer to the problem of suffering of the righteous and the prospering of the wicked."[153] It was also seen as a way for those who committed offenses against procreation and sexual transgressions to seek atonement or restitution. According to the Spanish Kabbalah, to atone for one's sins, a soul transmigrates "three more times after entering its original body." However, like those who take the bodhisattva vow in Mahayana Buddhism, it is also believed that the "righteous transmigrate endlessly for the benefit of the universe."[154] In this description, we see some similarities to what Annie does in *What Dreams May Come*. Because she killed herself, she decides "to take responsibility for what she has done," so she freely decides to come back in another body.

Finally, the film explains that Chris and Annie are "soul mates," which Chris' spirit guide explains is "an extremely rare condition"; and that it's "like twined souls tuned into each other . . . apparently even in death." This is similar to what Plato wrote in his *Symposium*—that Zeus decided to humble human pride by cutting men into two, and after the division, the two parts desired the other half, "came together, and throwing their arms about one another, entwined in mutual embraces, longing to grow into one, they were on the point of dying from hunger and self-neglect, because they did not like to do anything apart, and when one of the halves died and the other survived, the survivor sought another mate, man or woman as we call them, being the sections of entire men or women and clung to that . . . so ancient is the desire of one another which is implanted in us, reuniting our original nature, making one of two, and healing the state of man."[155]

It's doubtful that Matheson was referencing Plato, though. The idea of having a soul mate has been embraced and expounded upon by a number of "New Age" writers. For example, in 1984 Richard Bach wrote *The Bridge across Forever: A Love Story* in which he recounts his own "modern-day fairy tale" with actress Leslie Parrish. Bach has defined a soul mate as "someone who shares our deepest longings, our sense of direction. When we're two balloons, and together our direction is up, chances are we've found the right person. Our soul mate is the one who makes life come to life." A decade later, Thomas Moore wrote the *New York Times* best seller, *Soul Mates: Honoring the Mysteries of Love and Relationships*, and in it defines a soul mate as "someone to whom we feel profoundly connected." Over the years, this concept has become so mainstream that even Oprah Winfrey has a soul mates primer on her website. Weighing in on the issue are the codirector of the National Marriage Project, a psychic, a father, and a rabbi. Father Charles Kraus of St. Charles Borromeo Church, Brooklyn, explains that the Catholic Church teaches of "a complete holy marital union. The relationship develops in God's presence, transmitting total trust, committing to each other in life, and continuing the abiding love of God and each other in heaven." Rabbi Miriam Ancis of Havurat-Shalom synagogue, Brooklyn, explains that if a marriage works out then it was *b'shert* or meant to be. "That's the extent of romantic destiny in Judaism."[156] This isn't entirely true, though, at least not in Kabbalah. According to Rabbi David A. Cooper, the *Zohar*, which is the central text of Kabbalah, also talks of soul mates. It says that "before God sends souls into the world, they are formed into male and female pairs. Then they are placed in the hands of an emissary named Night, who has charge of conception. The pair is separated, and each person is born in his or her time. The *Zohar* goes on to say that these souls are rejoined by God at the right time into one body and one soul."[157]

In the novel version of *What Dreams May Come*, Matheson addresses the reader, explaining that even though the characters and their relationship are fictional, every other detail in the story comes from his research. And, if we turn to the back of the book, we find a six-page bibliography. Reading through these entries is eye-opening, because only a few would be considered "scholarly" or even scientific. Just a few of the titles are *Your Psychic Powers and Immortality*, *Love in the Afterlife*, and *The Way of Life: A Guide to the Etheric World*. A number are published by the Theosophical Publishing House, another comes from the Psychic Press, and one even comes from the Rosicrucian Fellowship. What's intriguing, though, is the inclusion of W. Y. Evans-Wentz's *The Tibetan Book of the Dead*; Raymond Moody's *Life after Life*, the 1975 best seller that is based on "more than 100 case studies of people who experienced 'clinical death' and were subsequently revived"; and Yogi Ramacharaka's *The Life beyond Death*. In the latter book we read that there are cases "in which a strong desire of the dying person has caused him to project his astral body into the presence of someone near to him, immediately after death." He also talks about a dying person who becomes "psychically conscious of a nearness to loved ones who have passed on before."[158] We find the very same phenomenon occurring in *What Dreams May Come.*

Furthermore, Matheson includes the Noel Langley book *Edgar Cayce on Reincarnation.* Cayce was an American born in the late 19th century who claimed to have psychic abilities. As far as reincarnation is concerned, he stated that we are spiritual beings who are having a material experience with the purpose of learning valuable lessons. He also believed that when a soul *chose* to be born, it could select its gender and the circumstances of its birth. And finally, Cayce talked about soul mates as "twin souls" or "two souls sharing a common purpose or ideal."[159] Both of these explanations are similar to those found in *What Dreams May Come.* This bibliography indicates that with the exception of the *Tibetan Book of the Dead,* Matheson developed his ideas on the afterlife not from mainstream religions but from a variety of "New Age" sources that range from psychics to members of the Theosophical Society.

Fight Club (1999)—Based on the novel by Chuck Palahniuk. Directed by David Fincher. Running time: 139 min. English. Rated R for disturbing and graphic depiction of violent antisocial behavior, sexuality, and language. Genre: Action/Drama/Thriller. Nominated for an Academy Award for Best Effects, Sound Effects Editing.

Summary: The film's nameless narrator (Edward Norton), who also goes by Jack's (insert the corresponding body part), spends his days working as a recall coordinator for a major automobile company, and at night, lies awake for hours. He can't sleep and nothing seems to help. That is until he begins attending therapeutic group sessions for people who are suffering from any manner of disease, from testicular cancer to brain disorders. At one of these, he spots another "faker" named Marla Singer (Helena Bonham Carter), who threatens everything he has. And then one day, on a plane, he finds himself seated next to a soap salesman (Brad Pitt), and his life takes an unexpected tailspin into chaos. After the narrator's apartment blows up, he becomes roommates with Tyler. Eventually they share more than lodging; they also share a dream of reclaiming their manhood, and they do this by channeling their primal male aggression into a shocking new form of therapy called Fight

Club. Their concept catches on and underground "fight clubs" form in every town. But everything gets out of hand, and, by the end, the narrator's world is quite literally poised for annihilation.

Fight Club has been called antisocial, fascist, anarchist, nihilistic, and even Marxist. For this chapter, we will be adding Daoist, Confucian, and Zen Buddhist to that list, because the film contains ideas that are in accordance with religious worldviews from these three traditions. Even though Daoism and Confucianism coexist in many Asian countries, they have very different perspectives on the role of the individual, society, and education. Like the yin-yang symbol that is central to these religions, they can be understood as representing complementary yet contradictory elements. Whereas Daoism represents yin—the feminine, passive, yielding, weak, soft, and solitary perspective, Confucianism represents yang—the masculine, active, hard, decisive, and social perspective. The goal for any practitioner of these religions is to achieve balance between what may seem to be two extremes.

We can extend the yin-yang imagery to *Fight Club*, in which we find two extreme sides of one man's personality as exemplified by Tyler Durden and "Jack." Tyler is a blond-haired, handsome, ultramasculine, active, and dynamic force. He wears vibrant reds, has spiked hair, and exudes confidence; every man wants to be him. Jack, the brunette who is "appealing in a dry sort of way," is the passive corporate drone who spends his days leafing through catalogs and trying to satisfy a kind of maternal "nesting instinct." This hypochondriac dresses in muted earth tones, suffers from insomnia and melancholia, and speaks in a monotone; no one wants to be Jack. On the surface, Tyler seems to be the embodiment of yang; Jack, yin. But the script contains an interesting twist. Tyler champions a Daoist worldview, and Jack lives a miserable and unsatisfying Confucian one. So how does this play out? Initially, the film supports Tyler's message of being spontaneous and natural and "letting the chips fall where they may." But by the end, it shifts its perspective, depicting Tyler as an increasingly dangerous, chaos-creating fanatic who must be destroyed. The only one who can do this is a new Jack, who by this point has moved to the middle of both extremes. In the end, he shoots Tyler and embraces an external yin, as embodied in Marla, the dark (Gothic), largely passive female. Balance and harmony are, perhaps, achieved within and without.

So what about Tyler's philosophy seems particularly Daoist? First of all, he advocates getting back to basics, and this means casting off the artificial construct of society and everything that goes along with it, including a 9-to-5 job, a condominium with all the trimmings, echelon-appropriate clothes and accessories, and even socially approved manners and behavior. He also champions a life of spontaneity. Known in the Daodejing as *tzu-jan*, this is the "cardinal and central value of Daoism."[160] If we read the Daodejing, we gain insight into what creates political and social disorder. It states that in the beginning was the Dao, the original "Way" and humans lived in accordance with it. But over time, the Dao weakened and declined, and moral codes and social norms arose, causing humans to lose their natural sense of spontaneity. To remedy this situation, humans are encouraged to return to a simple, natural life. As chapter 19 of the Daodejing states, one should "give up learning and be free from fear, give up sageliness and discard wisdom. . . . Manifest plainness and embrace simplicity, reduce selfishness and have few desires." Tyler embodies these very principles, and when he's about to crash a car—with Jack and several of his Project Mayhem disciples on board—he reminds Jack that he must forget everything he knows, everything he thinks he knows. (If we go back to *Star Wars*, he sounds a lot like Yoda who also tells Luke "to unlearn what he's learned.") Daoism tells us that once people are at one with the Dao, they "act from their innermost being; they no longer deliberate or think about their actions. Free from all choice, they reflect the situation with perfect clarity and duly respond in the only possible and perfectly appropriate way."[161]

Zhuangzi, who is, after Lao-tzu, the second most important Daoist sage, said that part of the problem is that people "place a distance between themselves and their experiences by giving names to things. They perceive them as good or bad, desirable or undesirable."[162] For most of the film, *Fight Club* avoids labeling anything as good or bad, normal or deviant. It simply presents characters and situations in a matter-of-fact way. In many ways, *Fight Club* itself gives the viewer a very real, in-your-face kind of experience and then lets the audience member interpret it as he or she sees fit. And this is undoubtedly why reactions have varied so widely. Just compare Alexander Walker of the *London Evening Standard*'s statement that the film "is an inadmissible assault on personal decency. And on society itself" to *Rolling Stone*'s review, "How good is *Fight Club*? It's so fired up with explosive ideas and killing humor that the guardians of morality are yelling, 'Danger—keep out!' That's how good."

Fight Club indicates that because we are alienated from our lives, we are genuinely unhappy. Jack is a perfect example of the man who seems to have it all but is left wanting. He is the embodiment of capitalism, believing that "meaning" can be found in the consumption of consumer goods. As he says, "Like everyone else, I had become a slave to the IKEA nesting instinct." Like a Confucian, Jack is very conscious of labeling everything with its proper name, because this gives him a sense of security. For him, everything must be in its place and be clearly defined and delineated. Confucians believe that society experiences problems when traditional social structures break down, because these are the means for promoting order. Therefore, they stress one's strict adherence to the observance of rules (*li*) that govern social behavior, such as having respect for those in positions of power. Furthermore, Confucian thinkers, especially Mencius, expanded *li* to include respectfulness (*gong*), reverence or seriousness (*jing*), politely declining (*ci*), and yielding to others (*rang*). *Gong* means that one should pay close attention to one's "appearance, posture, speech and attire." Confucius himself encouraged his followers to wear the proper clothing, fold them in a specific way, and stand with good posture. In the Analects (10:6–7), we see that Confucius was quite specific about what a sage should and should not wear. For instance, he shouldn't wear purple, mauve, red, or crimson, and when fasting he should always wear a spotless suit of linen cloth. As for Mencius, his qualities inform human behavior: *Jing* tells the person to be cautious, serious, and devoted. *Ci* translates to declining something good or an honor. And *rang* means to defer one's honor to someone else. When examined together, these encourage the person to lower his or her status while elevating his or her superior's.[163]

Initially, Jack has a very Confucian attitude. He goes to work, dressed in his peer-approved corporate attire—dress shirt, tie, and muted colored suit—and when in the office he works very diligently in his cubicle or at the copy machines. When his boss tells him to do something—prioritize or deprioritize some task—he does it without question. In fact, he seems to perform his job despite his misgivings and guilt. In one scene he explains to a stranger seated next to him on the plane how his company calculates the "bottom line" on whether or not to recall a vehicle. As this is a kind of confession, one can only assume that he's uncomfortable about what he does. He even states, in voiceover, that every time the plane banked too sharply on takeoff or landing, he prayed for a crash or a midair collision—anything. For some reason, though, he continues to work for this employer, probably because he's mired in complacency, afraid of change and the unknown. It is only after he meets

Tyler that he becomes increasingly insubordinate in attitude and slovenly in appearance. In the DVD chapter titled "Jack's Smirking Revenge," his boss rattles off Jack's flaws, including his constant absenteeism and unpresentable appearance. An indifferent Jack usurps his boss's apparent control by reciting a list of the company's unethical standards. He then offers his silence on these matters in exchange for his continued paycheck. When his boss calls security, Jack beats himself up, throwing himself through glass tables and shelves and smashes himself in his face. And this is how Fight Club got corporate sponsorship, Jack says.

Tyler, on the other hand, is just the opposite of Jack. He even tells him to "fuck off with your sofa units and Strinne green stripe patterns, I say never be complete, I say stop being perfect, I say . . . let's evolve, let the chips fall where they may." Unlike Jack, he invites chaos and uncertainty into his life. We see him picking fights with total strangers, splicing pornographic frames into family films, "tainting" food that is destined for wealthy patrons, and stealing human fat from the dumpsters of liposuction clinics so that he can make soap, which he then resells to rich women. Unlike Jack, Tyler doesn't believe in accumulating "things," because as he tells Jack, "the things you own, they end up owning you." And he sees the destruction of everything Jack owns as a positive situation. His philosophy is that "it's only after we've lost everything that we're free to do anything."

We can see Tyler as a Daoist sage-king, whom the Daodejing depicts as the "savior" of humankind. As in the case of Confucius, the author of the Daodejing doesn't believe that the masses can save themselves, especially when they have been exposed to "the seductions of civilization and the oppressions inflicted by civilization." Instead, it states that only the Daoist sage can "put an end to the artificial projects of civilization and allow the majority of people to return to a state of nonaction."[164] How this person was supposed to gain control is never explained in the text, however; it is assumed that his charisma and his embodiment of the Dao would draw others to him. "The sage of the Daodejing empties the people's minds in order to make them instruments of the ruler's policies, which are themselves aimed at maximizing his goals of . . . power." His policy then, is "nothing more than a more subtle brand of imperialism."[165]

As it states in chapter 36 of the Daodejing, to weaken something, one must allow it to grow strong; and to do away with something, one has to set it up.

In *Fight Club*, Tyler follows this directive. He isn't really concerned with the acquisition of power for power's sake. He simply wants to free the masses from control, allowing them to be spontaneous and unburdened. Like Daoists, Tyler believes in "freeing human beings from the preconceptions that separate them from their natural state of existence," so as to restore "natural human functioning."[166] It's important to note that even though he trains his Space Monkeys to engage in guerilla activities, he doesn't advocate killing people or even blowing up occupied buildings. Instead, they use high-powered magnets to wipe video store tapes, they smash satellite dishes to free people from their TV sets, and they feed pigeons on top of a car dealership's roof so they will defecate all over the cars. His "war" isn't against the masses but against the financial institutions and the corporations that keep everyone mentally and financially enslaved. Once everything is "reset," Tyler's job is done and Jack can "kill" him. Even though many see the Daodejing as a text dealing with esoteric, otherworldly concerns, it can and has also been seen as a text that deals with this world and how it should be run. It seems to advocate yin qualities, and a natural or "uncivilized" society that borders on social anarchy, and yet it "thinks that this society needs to be brought about by the deliberate activity of that most 'unnatural' of civilized institutions, a king or emperor."[167] And in *Fight Club*, Tyler Durden is that ruler.

Since *wu-wei* is mentioned in 10 chapters of the Daodejing we must do our best to understand this concept, especially with regard to *Fight Club*. Translated as "actionless action," *wu-wei* is the preferred mode of behavior by Daoist sages. Contrast this to *yu-wei*, which means taking action by "making prohibitions, establishing law and order, making sharp weapons, learning cunning and skill, pursuing goals, and seeking to satisfy desires—all of which only lead to poverty, trouble, viciousness and crime."[168] Chapter 63 of the Daodejing lists all the unconventional ways in which change can occur. We can act without acting, do without doing, and prepare for what is difficult while it is still easy. Furthermore, if one wants to accomplish a task, one should remain humble and passive. Often scholars use the example of a stream and a rock to explain *wu-wei*. Water does what it does—it flows—so when one throws a rock into the middle of a stream, without doing anything contrary to its nature, it will, over time, wear away that rock. What is natural? According to scholar Liu Xiaogan, "If one's existence is forced or interfered with, one is not in naturalness; on the other hand, if someone forces or inter-

feres with the existence of another, he also ruins that other person's naturalness. The concept of naturalness thus postulates the independence and sub-
jectivity of each individual although it claims also to foster harmony in
general."[169] Balance and harmony should result without conflict or strife.

So what does all of this mean in reference to Tyler Durden and Project
Mayhem? It's difficult to make an assessment, because Tyler isn't an independent entity. As we learn at the conclusion of the film, Tyler and Jack are one
and the same person. Is Jack acting in a way that's unnatural to himself? Did
he come to this state in a "steady, continuous, and predictable" way? We have
no way of knowing, because we don't know enough about Jack's background.
Maybe this is a natural progression of who he is. And as for Project Mayhem,
neither Jack nor Tyler forces anyone to join Fight Club or carry out the various "homework assignments." Everyone is a willing participant. The real question is: are they creating strife? Certainly, but to what end? Are they, in fact,
ushering in a natural progression of societal development? Are they following
the Dao itself, leading society, which has gone astray, back to its natural state?
As Xiaogan says, "The key definition of naturalness is the first criterion of *tzu-
jan*, the inner impulse or cause. The more an action comes from internal
sources, the more natural it comes."[170] Furthermore, what makes an action
not natural is any semblance of artificiality, forced effort, falseness, affectation,
reluctance, abruptness, and competition. Again, in the case of *Fight Club*,
none of these exist. Everyone, except Jack at the very end, believes wholeheartedly in what he or she is doing, and they do everything willingly in allegiance to Tyler.

As it has been mentioned, we don't know that Jack and Tyler are the same
person until the end of *Fight Club*; however, hints of this can be found
throughout the film. For instance, early on, right before Jack encounters Tyler,
he wonders "if you wake up at a different time and in a different place, could
you wake up as a different person." Later, he asks "Have I slept? I'm not sure if
Tyler is my bad dream? Or if I'm Tyler's?" This sounds very similar to a story
that Zhuangzi tells about a man named Zhuang Zhou who dreamt—"and then
he was a butterfly . . . the butterfly did not know about Zhou. Suddenly it
awoke—and then it was fully and completely Zhou. One does not know
whether there is a Zhou becoming a butterfly in a dream or whether there is a
butterfly becoming a Zhou in a dream. There is a Zhou and there is a butterfly,
so there is necessarily a distinction between them. This is called the changing

of things." In this allegory, scholar Hans-Georg Moeller explains that there exists a "kind of autonomy for Zhuang Zhou and the butterfly." In fact, it indicates that there are three phases, "first Zhuang Zhou awake, then the butterfly in the dream, and then, strictly speaking, another Zhuang Zhou after the dream," with all three stages being equally real.[171]

Are we supposed to understand *Fight Club* in this way? Jack has his own "life" as does Tyler. As much as we know, they are mutually ignorant of each other until the end of the film, and even then there is some doubt as to who Tyler Durden really is. Could we say that in the beginning there is Jack, in the middle there is Tyler, and in the end there exists a kind of Jack Durden? Since the end of the film is open-ended, it's uncertain what the future brings for our protagonist. Tyler is dead, but his Space Monkey disciples still exist, inhabiting every city in the world; and even though Jack prevented one of Tyler's strategically placed bombs from detonating, 10 more go off, taking out the economic centers of the Western world. As Tyler says, it's "one step closer to global equilibrium." Despite Jack's best efforts, chaos triumphs, which, according to Daoism, may not such an unfavorable outcome. When Zhuangzi writes about the age of Perfect Virtue in chapter 9, he says that "men live the same as birds and beasts. . . . Who then knows anything about 'gentleman' or 'petty man'? Dull and unwitting, men have no wisdom; thus their virtue does not depart from them. Dull and unwitting, they have no desire; this is called uncarved simplicity. In uncarved simplicity the people attain their true nature."[172] In chapter 80 of the Daodejing, we find a description of an ideal community. It is small with few inhabitants, and even though "labor-saving implements"—boats, carts, arms, and weapons—exist, no one uses them. People are content with their food, clothing, and dwellings. "The whole idea is to reduce to a minimum all the projects of civilization, making it possible for people to sink back into the simple life, in which they remain so self-sufficiently contented."[173]

To understand other aspects of *Fight Club*, we can look at Buddhism, specifically Ch'an or, as it's known in Japan, Zen. Zen emphasizes the mind-to-mind transmission of teachings from teacher to student. Disciples aren't given texts to read and memorize, because Zen de-emphasizes one's dependence on words. Instead, one engages in various practices with the goal of gaining direct insight into the mind and, ultimately, Buddha nature. Through direct experience, one encounters *shunyata*, emptiness or void, which is the reality of all things. Both Daoism and Buddhism encourage adherents to go beyond language and refrain from attempting to define or label their experiences. In very much the same way, Tyler has listed the first two rules of Fight Club as "You don't talk about Fight Club." Is this because he wants it to remain secret? This is doubtful, because from the first fist fight between Tyler and Jack, which takes place in the parking lot of a bar, the number of "devotees" increases and Tyler doesn't turn anyone away. The reason "one doesn't talk about Fight Club" is because it isn't about words, it's about sweat, blood, adrenaline, and pain. To intellectualize the experience diminishes it, reduces it to a "thing."

Furthermore, words can't articulate the feeling of straining sinews, aching joints, and smashed noses. It's like trying to explain what nirvana is. The Buddha refrained from talking about it, because nirvana is a way of seeing the world that has to be experienced. This holds true for Fight Club. One doesn't talk about it, because one has to experience it. As D. T. Suzuki explains, "Personal experience . . . is everything in Zen. No ideas are intelligible to those who have no backing of experience."[174] During one particularly brutal fight, Jack even says that "Fight Club wasn't about winning or losing. It wasn't about *words*."[175] Once Project Mayhem starts, Jack wants to know more, but Tyler won't tell him anything because, as he says, Jack is "asking questions that don't have answers." This is in accordance with Zen that deals "with facts and not their logical, verbal, prejudiced and lame representations." Furthermore, it recognizes that facts are facts and words are words and nothing else. "Zen thinks we are too much of slaves to words and logic. So long as we remain thus fettered we are miserable and go through untold suffering. But if we want to see something really worth knowing, that is conducive to our spiritual happiness."[176]

Rational thinking and intellectualism are foes to enlightenment. Therefore, the sensei employs a number of methods to help his or her disciples break down these rational thought patterns. Some, especially practitioners of Rinzai Zen, use koans, mental puzzles that often seem nonsensical, such as "What is the sound of one hand clapping?" Others use physical force, such as shouts and beatings, to achieve the same end. In the *Sodoshu* account of Lin-chi, the ninth-century Rinzai master, we learn that his enlightenment was precipitated by a sharp blow by his master's staff. Later, when he was about to be beat again, Lin-chi grabbed his master's staff and began hitting his master. "Ta-yu was overjoyed to see that the disciple had reached enlightenment."[177] When Lin-chi, himself, became a teacher he used threatening shouts and blows from his staff to "shock the disciples out of their hesitating doubts."[178] Zen Buddhism teaches that one should allow the mind to operate "freely, spontaneously and naturally. It was in accordance with this emphasis on freedom and spontaneity that the Ch'an master I-hsuan called upon his disciples to 'kill everything that stands in your way. If you should meet the Buddha, kill the Buddha. If you should meet the Patriarchs, kill the Patriarchs. If you should meet the *arhats* on your way, kill them too.'"[179]

In *Fight Club* Tyler acts as Jack's sensei, and his Zen-like motto could be summed up as "Self-improvement is masturbation . . . self-destruction is the answer." Like Lin-chi, Tyler uses mental and physical "shock therapy" to wake Jack up. He delivers a karate chop to his identity, telling him that "You're not your job. You're not how much money you have in the bank. You're not the car you drive. You're not the contents of your wallet. You're not your fucking khakis. You're the all-singing, all-dancing crap of the world." And then he pummels Jack into, what the screenplay calls, an "endorphin-induced [state of] serenity."[180] As Jack explains, "You weren't alive anywhere like you were there. . . . After Fight Club, everything else in your life gets the volume turned down . . . we all started seeing things differently. Wherever we went." Zen strongly emphasizes the attainment of freedom from all unnatural encumbrances, and it wants to open the "mental eye" so that one can look into the very reason of existence.

Once Project Mayhem has begun, Tyler takes a gun out of Jack's backpack and proceeds—much to Jack's horror—to a convenience store so they can offer up a "human sacrifice." Once they encounter the store clerk, Raymond, Tyler shoves the gun barrel into the man's temple and tells him that his parents are going to have to get his dental records because "there won't be much left" of his face. But Tyler doesn't kill him. Instead, he puts the gun between the man's eyes, and tells Raymond to go back to school and pursue his earlier interest in veterinary science. If he doesn't do it, he'll be dead. Jack tells Tyler that what he did was wrong, but Tyler is unapologetic. His shock tactics are only a means to an end. If putting a gun to someone's head will make that person appreciate life and try to do something with it, rather than waste his time in a convenience store, than so be it. As Jack says, Tyler had a plan: "No fear. No distractions. The ability to let that which does not matter truly slide."

In the beginning of the film, Jack is the embodiment of "civilization" and consumerism. When he refers to his articles of clothes, he always prefaces them with the brand name. They aren't shirts and shoes, but C.K. shoes and D.K.N.Y shoes. As he explains, "I would flip through catalogs and wonder: 'What kind of dining set defines me as a person?' . . . I had it all. Even the glass dishes with tiny bubbles and imperfections, proof they were crafted by the honest, simple, hard-working indigenous peoples of . . . wherever." And then, his world is shattered, quite literally, by a bomb that destroys everything that he owns. His only option, he believes, is to call up Tyler and live with him. Under Tyler's tutelage, Jack embraces an entirely new life. Instead of renting an expensive place uptown, he squats in a dilapidated three-story house in a relatively uninhabited part of town. And rather than maintaining a structured day-to-day existence, he does whatever comes naturally; he learns to live spontaneously. "I should have been haggling with my insurance company," he says in a voiceover. "I should have been looking for a new condo . . . I should have been upset about my nice, neat, flaming little shit. But I wasn't." Like Daoism, Zen teaches that life should be lived freely. "As soon as there are signs of elaboration, a man is doomed; he is no more a free being. You are not living as you ought to live, you are suffering under the tyranny of circumstances; you are feeling a constraint of some sort, and you lose your independence. . . . Zen wants to live from within. Not to be bound by rules, but to be creating one's own rules."[181]

Fight Club teaches its audience two key Buddhist concepts: that life is suffering, and that life is characterized by impermanence When Jack visits his doctor at the beginning of the film, he explains that he can't sleep so he wants some drugs. "I'm in pain," he says. "You want to see pain," the intern replies, "swing by the First Methodist Tuesday nights. See the guys with testicular cancer. That's pain." And he's right. One man, who breaks down into sobs, shares that his wife abandoned him to start a family with another man. Bob, a man who has large breasts, tells Jack that he's bankrupt, divorced, and has been abandoned by his own children. Jack becomes addicted to these stories of heart-wrenching woe, because "every evening I died and every evening I was born again. Resurrected." As soon as the illusion wears off, though, especially when he's in the presence of Marla, another faker, he's unable to sleep. Eventually, the only antidote for him isn't to die vicariously through other people but to engage in fighting and be taken to the brink of death itself. By being beaten to a pulp, he comes alive.

Buddhist monks learn to appreciate their lives by meditating on their own deaths. Some even carry with them photographs of dead bodies in various states of decomposition, the purpose of which is to "simply hold in your mind, very clearly, that when you look at a [living] person, you're seeing only the external aspect of that physical person. We just sort of live in denial of the fact that we have all these organs and bones and liquids and fluids."[182] Like a Zen master, Tyler constantly reminds his disciples of life's impermanence. At one point, he pours lye onto Jack's hand, and as it is eating into his flesh, he delivers the lesson that "without sacrifice, without death, we would have nothing." Then, when Jack is trying to forget the pain, work through it with guided meditation, Tyler tells him to stop it: "This is your pain—your burning hand. It's right here. Look at it." Again trying to avoid the experience, Jack mumbles that he "understands." But Tyler knows he doesn't and he slaps him, saying that what he's feeling is premature enlightenment. "This is the greatest moment of your life and you're off somewhere, missing it." Finally, Tyler offers him a way to stop the pain, but first, Jack has to give up; he has to know that some day he's going to die. And until he knows that, he will be useless. No matter which branch of Buddhism we examine, all concur that meditation on the inevitability of death is critical, for not only does it keep us from clinging to worldly things but it also keeps us from wasting one moment of our human lives. As Judith L. Lief writes, "Cultivating an awareness of death is at the same time cultivating an awareness of life. We are reconnecting with the experience of actually living a life."[183] Rather than thinking about death, though, Tyler goes further, trying to gain a direct experience of death. After he crashes his car, he tells the survivors that they've just had a "near-life experience."

Later in the film, we hear Tyler's words coming out of the mouth of one of his disciples, "You are not a beautiful and unique snowflake. You are the same decaying organic matter as everything else. We are all part of the same compost heap." Death is inevitable; however, Jack and most of society's members deny this fact by anesthetizing themselves by consuming and overconsuming. As Jack says, after his home has blown up, "That condo was my life, okay? I loved every stick of furniture in that place. That was not just a bunch of stuff that got destroyed, it was *me!*" Even when we see Jack acting as a recall coordinator, we get a shocking, matter-of-fact example of life's impermanence. As he examines a smashed car, we learn that "the teen-ager's braces around the backseat ashtray would make a good 'anti-smoking' ad," and that "the father must've been huge. See how the fat burnt into the driver's seat with his polyester shirt?" The idea is that one day we're here, and the next we're "modern art" in a car crash. Once Project Mayhem has commenced, several men replace the airplane safety cards with ones on which passengers are screaming and flailing about in terror. This, again, reminds them that every minute could be our last.

Buddhism has an ascetic side to it, and so does *Fight Club*. Once Fight Club has caught on, Tyler begins recruiting students for Project Mayhem. As he says to Jack, "If the applicant is young, tell him he's too young. Old, too old. Fat, too fat. If the applicant then waits for three days without food, shelter, or encouragement, he may then enter and begin his training." Compared to some stories that come from the Buddhist tradition, Tyler's initiation ritual seems pretty tame. For instance, it is said that a man named Hui-k'o was particularly eager to study with Bodhidharma, and he begged him day and night to become his disciple. But the sixth-century Ch'an master ignored him, leading the would-be disciple to take more extreme measures. One night, while standing motionless in the snow, Hui-k'o asked again. Bodhidharma replied that he would only take him on when the heavens snowed red. Not willing to give up, the young man pulled out a knife and chopped off his left arm, turning the snow red with his blood. He then offered his arm to Bodhidharma as a gesture of his commitment. Bodhidharma accepted him as a student.

An even more extreme case of Buddhist initiation rituals involves the modern-day "marathon monks of Mount Hiei." To become a monk at this mountain monastery, one must practice a term of 100, 700, and 1,000 days of chanting and visiting stations of worship. To become an abbot, one must endure a grueling 100-day term of "circling the mountain" on foot, dressed only in a white shroud, handmade straw sandals, and raincoat. Each day begins at midnight, when the monk consumes a small meal. He starts his daily 18-mile run at around 1:30 and must be finished and back at the monastery seven or eight hours later. "These 100 days are very difficult. Their feet and legs begin to throb and often get cuts and infections. Being so cold in Japan, they often get frostbite and very sick. . . . They also experience many problems such as pains in their back and hips, diarrhea and hemorrhoids." If a person completes the 100-day term, he can petition to undergo a 1,000-day term that will take seven years to complete. Interestingly enough, should a person engage in this run, after day 700, he must survive nine days without food, water, sleep, or rest. Anyone who starts any of these marathons and can't finish must commit suicide, either by hanging or disembowelment.[184]

Finally, *Fight Club* is peppered with other Buddhist elements and ideas. After Jack learns that Tyler is engaging in carnal relations with Marla, we hear Jack say, in voiceover, that he "became the calm, little center of the world. I was the Zen master." He demonstrates this by writing haiku and faxing them around the office. After his boss notices that he's wearing a shirt stained with blood, he tells Jack to go home and get himself together. As he's leaving, we hear Jack's voiceover that says, "I got right in everyone's hostile little face. Yes, these are bruises from fighting. I'm comfortable with them. I am enlightened." In the novel, we find a similar line but in a different context. Jack and Tyler are making soap when Jack explains that he's enlightened, "you know, only Buddha-style behavior . . . the Diamond Sutra and the *Blue Cliff Record*. Hari Rama, you know, Krishna, Krishna. You know enlightened." Tyler introduces a dose of reality, saying, "Sticking fingers up your butt does not make you a chicken."[185] It's interesting that Jack would mention the Diamond Sutra, as it "shows that all phenomenal appearances are not ultimate reality but rather illusions, projections of one's own mind."[186] Could this be a knowing wink by the author with regard to the supposed duality of Jack and Tyler? *The Blue Cliff Record* is a translation of *Pi Yen Lu*, a collection of 100 Zen koans, which are accompanied by commentaries and verses from the teachings of Chinese Ch'an masters. And the mantra "Hari Rama, Krishna, Krishna" comes from the Hindu tradition, but probably reflects Jack's exposure to the "Hari Krishnas" or, more specifically, followers belonging to the International Society for Krishna Consciousness. Devotees of Krishna traditionally chant the name of their deity in this way.

Another Buddhist concept mentioned in *Fight Club* is that of karma, which Tyler refers to when he says that "We are defined by the choices we make." More specific evidence of karma can be found on the film's official website, www.foxmovies.com/fightclub, where we read Tyler's words of wisdom that say, "The next time you feel like complaining to your chaplain about how miserable your life is, be thankful you are not cursed with the three terrible karmas—beauty, riches, and fame." Obviously this doesn't come directly from Buddhism, but he is expressing a Buddhist sentiment. Why wouldn't a person want beauty, riches, or fame? Because all of these further ensnare us in the world of *maya* or illusion. Like sparkling jewels, they distract us from the realities of suffering, death, and decay. The world of things also distracts us from the reality of our situation. As Tyler explains, "Advertising has us chasing cars and clothes, working jobs we hate so we can buy shit we don't need. . . . We've all been raised on television to believe that one day we'd all be millionaires, and movie gods, and rock stars. But we won't. And we're slowly learning that fact. And we're very, very pissed off."

Kung Fu Panda (2008)—Screenplay by Jonathan Aibel and Glenn Berger. Directed by Mark Osborne and John Stevenson. Running time: 92 min. English. Rated PG for martial arts action. Genre: Animation.

Summary: Po (voiced by Jack Black), a panda, idolizes the Furious Five— Tigress (Angelina Jolie), Monkey (Jackie Chan), Crane (David Cross), Viper (Lucy Liu), and Mantis (Seth Rogen)—all consummate kung fu masters, and he dreams of one day becoming a master himself. But destiny has played him another card. He is, instead, the son of Mr. Ping (James Hong), a noodle-making duck who hopes that one day Po will have the "noodle-making dream" so that he can reveal to him the secret ingredient in his Secret Ingredient Soup. As Mr. Ping says early on: "We are noodle folk. Broth runs through our veins." A dutiful son, Po denies his own ambitions. That is, until he learns that the time has come for Oogway (Randall Duk Kim), a very wise and very ancient Galapagos turtle, to choose the prophesized Dragon Warrior; a being who will bring peace to the land and to Master Shifu (Dustin Hoffman), a hot-headed red panda.

Up the mountain, Po climbs only to find that he's too late. The gates are locked, and despite his many efforts, he can't get inside. Spying a mound of fireworks, he straps them to a chair and, after some difficulty, shoots himself into the Jade Palace arena. He lands, much to everyone's surprise, in front of Oogway's pointing finger. Thus, he is named the legendary Dragon Warrior. No one is more surprised than Po, who doesn't even know kung fu. Flabbergasted, Master Shifu says, "you were about to point at Tigress and that thing fell in front of her." But Oogway won't change his mind. Shifu reluctantly begins training the soft-bodied panda, but he's determined to make him quit; after all, it was "just an accident." Meanwhile, another prophecy is coming true inside of the maximum security Chor Ghom Prison, which was, 20 years ago, carved out of the most inaccessible peak of the snow-blasted Tavan Bogd

Mountains in Outer Mongolia. Tai Lung (Ian McShane), a very dangerous former student of Master Shifu, breaks free and heads back to Peaceful Valley, determined to claim the title of Dragon Warrior and obtain the secrets of the Dragon Scroll. Will Po prove himself to be the town's savior or will he be unable to stop Tai Lung, who is hell bent on unleashing his vengeance and leaving behind a path of destruction?

Few would probably imagine that an animated comedy from DreamWorks can teach us about Buddhism and Daoism, but it does. On the film's official site (www.kungfupanda.com), director John Stevenson explained that the theme of the film is to "'Be your own hero,' which means "don't look outside of yourself for the answer. Don't expect someone else to make things right. You are empowered to achieve anything you want, if you set your mind to it." The Buddha couldn't have said it better himself. In the *Dhammapada*, we read "raise yourself by your own efforts . . . thus self-reliant and vigilant you will live in joy. Be your own master and protector. Train your mind as a merchant trains his horse." Furthermore, it is said that before he died, the Buddha told his disciples that they should be a refuge unto themselves; rely on themselves and nothing else. "Hold fast to the dharma as your lamp, hold fast to the dharma as your refuge, and you shall surely reach nirvana, the highest good and the highest goal."

Stevenson admitted that while growing up during the 1970s, he was a fan of the David Carradine TV show *Kung Fu* and kung fu films, in general, as were apparently, many of the other people working on *Kung Fu Panda*: "We definitely didn't want to do a parody. . . . We all wanted to respect and honor those movies." Co-director Mark Osborne explained that "typically, in the past in a kung fu movie, you see a human imitating an animal doing those fighting styles, but this is the first time anyone's ever actually seen these animals executing the fighting styles from which they derive their names." So, as the official site explains, Tigress embodies Tiger style, which should be strong, firm and aggressive, using "speed, agility and power to shatter opponents' defenses." Crane's movements are natural, graceful, effortless, fluid, and balanced; Monkey is acrobatic, playful, comical, unpredictable, and energetic. "Monkey is the only one of the Five to fight with an apparatus, mainly a staff—a well-known weapon of the Shaolin temple monks." To ensure that they were creating real kung fu, the artistic team had marathon viewing sessions of kung fu films and even invited Eric Chen, a *wushu* instructor, to lead them in a class. Having 18-year martial arts veteran Rodolphe Guenonden serve as kung fu choreographer only added another level of authenticity to the project.

Because the kung fu genre has typically been filmed in CinemaScope, the creative team used the same wide-screen format for *Kung Fu Panda*. And to make sure that they were being "true to Chinese culture," the creative team spent many months studying Chinese art, especially pottery; the Chinese landscape—they were influenced by the look of the Li River Valley and city of Guilin—and its architecture. They watched such films as *Hero* and *Crouching Tiger, Hidden Dragon*, so as to "absorb as many Eastern influences as possible." Not only did they draw upon Chinese mythology, but they also employed color symbolism, including gold, which is the color of the emperor; red, for good luck and fortune; and green, for life and spring. Often all three of these colors can be found together in Chinese art. For example, "of the three gods of good fortune, the one who confers high office and riches wears a red robe; the one beside him, dressed in green, blesses a family with children, while the third, who gives long life, is dressed in yellow or white."[187] Number symbolism also exists in *Kung Fu Panda*. The number five, for instance, is "one of the most important numbers in Chinese number mysticism. Being uneven, it is a 'male' number. It is associated with the Five Directions, five odours, and the five tastes." We find frequent mention of the number five in Chinese thought, from the Daodejing to the Confucian Classics.[188] The number 1,000 is mentioned frequently in *Kung Fu Panda*. For instance, it is said that after 1,000 years, the Dragon Warrior will bring peace to the land. Not surprisingly, in Chinese thought this number indicates longevity. According to legend, a white bat that hangs with its head downwards is 1,000 years old. If a person catches this animal, dries it, and eats it, he or she will have a long life.[189]

What seems particularly Zen Buddhist about *Kung Fu Panda*? First of all, since it focuses on martial arts, we see master-student relationships in the film. Oogway, whose name undoubtedly derives from *gui*, the Mandarin word for "turtle,"[190] is the teacher of Master Shifu, whose own name is the Mandarin word for "master," "teacher," or "father." Shifu is, in turn, the "sensei" of the Furious Five, and he served in the same capacity for Tai Lung. Zen Buddhism stresses the importance of finding a teacher, but cautions the student in his or her choice. The 14th-century Japanese Zen master Bassui Tokusho explained how to distinguish between a teacher of false views and a true teacher. "The true teacher is one who has seen into his own nature. One who gives sermons while not having seen into his own nature is a false teacher. Though he may have studied the teachings . . . kept the five precepts, sat in meditation for long periods without feeling sleepy, practiced the Way during the six periods, been in the desireless state of purity, and gathered as many followers as the sands of the Ganges, if he has not been properly certified he should not be trusted. If, for example, he has received the seal of transmission from someone, that person's qualifications should be carefully checked."[191] Bassui goes on to say that a good teacher combines understanding and practice and has no lingering delusions of good and bad, right and wrong. "If you want to distinguish between a truly superior person and a false one, there are three kinds of lingering delusions. They are . . . opinion, emotion, and speech. With lingering delusions of opinion, one can't separate himself from the domain of the thinking mind and hence falls into the poisonous ocean. With lingering delusions of emotion, one always looks at things from the standpoint of the intellect. . . . With lingering delusions of speech, one loses sight of the wondering teaching of the true nature of things and becomes blinded to its true activity."[192]

Using what Zen Master Bassui has said, let's examine the characters of Oogway and Master Shifu in terms of "good" and "bad" teachers. According to the *Legend of the Legendary Warrior*, a six-part animated comic book on the film's official site, we learn that Oogway journeyed from his home in the Galapagos Islands almost 1,000 years ago, before settling down in China. He was walking in the bamboo forest, when at the top of a lonely mountain peak, he discovered a pool. "Moved by the beauty of nature and the plight of the oppressed, he stared at his reflection in the pool and wept." In very Daoist language, the narrator continues, telling us that Oogway felt the universe in motion around him. He could hear a butterfly's wings; he could see light in the darkest cave. By focusing, he achieved harmony and peace. This insight, we learn, formed the basis of kung fu. The Jade Palace was built to honor Oogway, and it is here that he trained a multitude of students. At some point, we don't know when, the enlightened Oogway took on Shifu as a student, and, he's still acting as the red panda's much needed advisor. If we compare the two characters' personalities, we find that Oogway is the consummate Zen master, while Shifu, well, he has a long way to go. Oogway is patient and serene, as is evidenced in an early scene. Shifu comes into Oogway's room and finds him meditating, up-side down, balanced on his staff. After he rights himself, the old sage walks slowly over to what look like thousands of candles, and he takes his time to blow out each one. The impatient, Shifu, becomes irritated, and with a sweeping gesture, extinguishes them all at once. This scene is particularly revealing as to what sort of mind each master possesses.

Oogway focuses on the present moment and keeps his thoughts unclouded by emotion. Later in the film, when Po is thinking about leaving the Jade Palace, Oogway tells him that he is "too concerned with what was and what will be. . . . Yesterday's history, tomorrow is a mystery, today is a gift." These "lyrics" might have come from country singer T. Graham Brown's song *The Present*; however, Taisen Deshimaru, a 20th-century Zen master who died in 1982, said nearly the same thing when talking about impermanence: "What is happening here and now is what matters. Don't think about the past or the future, but concentrate on here and now. When you urinate, just urinate; when you sleep, just sleep; when you eat, practice zazen, walk, make love, exactly the same. Concentrate on the present act and nothing else. If you are not happy here and now, you never will be."[193] Shifu, on the other hand, suffers from "grasshopper" mind, and he allows his emotions to disrupt his serenity. In one scene, he's trying to meditate. Sitting cross-legged, he has his eyes closed, and he's saying to himself "inner peace, inner peace." A flapping sound breaks the silence. Not surprisingly, Shifu becomes irritated and tells the bird to be quiet. As it says in the *Dhammapada*, a trained mind brings health and happiness, and a wise person will direct his thoughts, subtle and elusive, wherever he chooses. Shifu is neither happy nor mentally well. He lets the past control his present, and he agonizes about the future.

Another telling moment occurs when Oogway says, without any percepti-ble fear or concern, that he's had a vision, and in it Tai Lung returns to Peace-ful Valley. Shifu is horror stricken, remarking that it isn't possible. "Nothing is impossible," Oogway replies. Shifu then commands Zeng, a duck, to fly to Chor Ghom prison and have them double the guards and double their weapons. "One often meets his destiny on the road he takes to avoid it," Oog-way says. Too caught up in his emotions, Shifu ignores this statement, and says that they can't just be idle and do nothing, thereby allowing Tai Lung to waltz in and start destroying everything. And yet, because Shifu acts out of fear and ignorance, he sets Tai Lung's escape in motion. Not long after Zheng arrives, one feather falls from his body, providing the snow leopard with a "key" to his escape.

Most of those around Shifu are affected by the diminutive teacher's anxiety but not Oogway. Near the mid-point of the film, Shifu comes upon the old master as he's doing T'ai Chi, and he tells Oogway that he has bad news. The turtle replies, "there is just news not good or bad." Shifu explains that Tai Lung has escaped from the prison, and for a moment Oogway seems to change his tune. But his serenity returns, and he counsels Shifu to "Let go of the illusion of control." He drives home his point, by saying that no one can make a peach tree blossom or bear fruit before its time. Undeterred and argumentative, Shifu counters with the fact that he can control when and where to plant the peach seed. "But that seed will always become a peach tree (not an apple or something else)," Oogway says. "You have to be willing to guide it, nurture it and believe in it."

Oogway believes in destiny, and if a slovenly, out-of-shape panda is supposed to be the Dragon Warrior, then he accepts this, uttering "very interesting." Shifu is just the opposite, and he does everything he can to convince Oogway that he's made a mistake, claiming that it was an accident. Oogway calmly explains, "There are no accidents." In this instance, we see that Oogway doesn't judge; therefore, he is free from the delusions of opinion and emotion. Shifu, himself, is attached to the outcome of the martial arts competition and believes that Tigress is the prophesized Dragon Warrior. When he is proven wrong, he becomes furious, insulting, and manipulative. All of these indicate that he's enmeshed in the delusions of opinion, emotion, and speech. And because of this, he fails to be kind and compassionate to Po, therefore, failing to practice right speech or right action. Oogway can see Shifu's faults, but he never outright corrects him. Instead, he guides his student with aphorisms and analogies. For example, after Shifu has told Zheng to double the guards so that Tai Lung doesn't escape, Oogway says "your mind is like this water. When it becomes agitated, it becomes difficult to see. But when you allow it to settle, the answer becomes clear."

As he's a Zen master, we can assume that Shifu has studied the four seals of the dharma—that all compounded things are impermanent, all emotions are painful, all phenomena are empty, and nirvana is beyond extremes—however, he doesn't seem to understand or internalize them, especially the second and third seals. And this is why Tai Lung turned out as he did. His teacher conveyed false teachings, and as a Confucian might say, he wasn't a good "role model." It's interesting to look at Tai Lung as a "process." We learn from a flashback that Shifu found the leopard as an infant. We can probably assume that Shifu gave him his name, which, interestingly, translates to "Great Dragon." So from day one, instead of teaching his student about impermanence and no-self, Shifu was filling his head with "big dreams" of a destiny of "greatness." He undoubtedly repeats his mistakes with Tigress. When she isn't named Dragon Warrior, she doesn't accept the news with grace and dignity, but she insults Po and tells him that he "doesn't belong." Crane, too, admits that he has suffered crushing disappointment from the news. Why would they react this way? Because instead of teaching them about no-self, Shifu built up their "egos." And even though Shifu makes such statements as "humility is the mark of a true hero," and "obeying your master is not weakness," he acts contrary to these, therefore, who is going to listen to a master who "talks the talk but doesn't walk the walk"?

Unlike Shifu, Oogway recognized early on that Tai Lung was not Dragon Warrior material. He knew that the leopard was too deluded by the three poisons—greed, anger, and ignorance—and he refused to give him the Dragon scroll, which would have conferred the "secret of limitless power." Oogway was right, because Tai Lung reacts to this rebuke not by using it as an opportunity for improvement but by becoming a destructive force of nature. Because Shifu's mind is also clouded by the three poisons, he is unable stop his marauding student. It takes the serene, clear-headed Oogway to do the job.

Finally, we learn a lot about Oogway and Shifu when we look at their martial arts styles. Through his insight of "harmony and peace" the turtle develops a non-violent way of immobilizing his opponents, simply by activating several acupressure points. He also practices the slow and methodical art of T'ai Chi Chuan. Shifu, on the other hand, is much faster and more merciless, which, again, explains Tai Lung and Tigress' fighting styles. As it says on the film's official site, the 900-year-old training hall is refined, expanded, and modified to "reflect the wishes and training philosophy of its martial arts instructor." The present one, with its spiked "Field of Fiery Death," "Gauntlet of (Spiked) Wooden Warriors," "Seven Talon Rings," and its "Seven Swinging Clubs of Instant Oblivion," of which the site says "to be struck in the stomach is to be rendered instantly unconscious . . . to be struck by its long metal spikes is to have instant agonizing death," reflects much about Shifu. And particularly telling is the fact that the present hall is the most "dangerous, difficult and terrifying place of training in the entire history of China." While sparring, Shifu tells Po that he should make his opponent suffer. This statement reflects, again, the master's deluded mind. No martial arts code of ethics would advocate such behavior, as most stress the need for a "warrior" to be respectful, humble, truthful, brave, benevolent, compassionate, sincere, and loyal.

In the end, we would conclude that gentle Oogway is the "true" master; and hot-headed Shifu is the "false" one. But since we are speaking in Buddhist terms, we want to avoid such dualistic judgment, allowing for a transformation of character. And by the end of the film, partly because of Po's influence, Shifu does change. He becomes more mindful, jovial, and peaceful. But, perhaps, more importantly, he realizes that his wrong thoughts and actions helped to create Tai Lung's wrong thoughts and actions, and he takes responsibility for his contribution to the current situation. During their final battle, he admits to Tai Lung "it was my pride that blinded me. *I couldn't see* [my emphasis] . . . what I was turning you into. I'm sorry." This demonstrates a step in the right direction for Shifu. As for Tai Lung, he rejects the apology; this act of "contrition." He's still too blinded by his anger to forgive, which is sad for him, because, as the Dalai Lama says, forgiveness is an important step for a Buddhist to take. It "is something like an end result, or a product, of patience and tolerance. When one is truly patient and tolerant, then forgiveness comes naturally."[194] Tolerance and patience, His Holiness has explained, are the tools for overcoming anger and hatred. "And in order to practice sincerely and to develop patience, you need someone who willingly hurts you. Thus, these people give us real opportunities to practice these things. They are testing our inner strength in a way that even our guru cannot."[195]

Daoism can help to further our understanding of *Kung Fu Panda*, and especially to shed light on the character of Po, which, appropriately, is Mandarin for "slope." As actor Jack Black said of his character, "Po is like a big kid." And he's right. Po is simple, enthusiastic, energetic, spontaneous, willing to try anything and not afraid to look like a fool in doing it. He's also trusting, generous, impulsive, and silly. He is the Daoist's uncarved block (*pu*); the paradigmatic infant. Liu I-Ming, the 18th-century Daoist adept and Buddhist scholar, explained that an infant cannot be harmed because it is mindless. "The reason people cannot attain the Way is always because they have minds. Having a mind means having an ego, which means seeing others as others and self as self . . . true seekers of the Way make haste to otherthrow egoism and abandon selfish behavior. In their lives and response to the world, they regard themselves and others impartially, and regard all classes as equal. Dealing with things as they arise, true seekers respond to them but do not take them in; they pass by and do not linger. They handle all sorts of situations without minding."[196] Po is mindless in many ways. He is always humble and self-effacing before others. Even though he's the Dragon Warrior, he never boasts of the fact; he's never arrogant or full of himself. He never judges anyone, because he's too busy being awestruck by their "awesomeness." And even when others verbally attack him, saying he's too fat or lazy to be great, he turns the other cheek, never returning insults. When he's undergoing martial arts training, and he's getting pummeled, he simply gets to his feet, and cheerfully prepares for another round. Even when he's "fighting" Tai Lung, he maintains a sense of playfulness. He doesn't seem to be attached to results or harming others. In fact, what he's doing isn't as much fighting as falling, crashing, etc., and somehow his accidents result in success.

Finally, we can learn a lot about Po by studying his reaction to the "blank" Dragon Scroll. Unlike Shifu, he isn't angry at finding what is essentially a piece of reflective paper in the tube, but he is disheartened. Without the "secret" knowledge, he believes he will never be able to defeat Tai Lung. Po returns home, and finding his father, they begin talking about the future. It is at that moment that Ping reveals to Po that Secret Ingredient Soup, in fact, has no secret ingredient. Almost immediately, a lightbulb goes off in Po's mind. The mystery of the Dragon Scroll is revealed. The Dragon Scroll could be likened to a *koan*, only instead of being an enigmatic utterance; it's a visual puzzle in much the same vein as the Buddha holding up a flower to an assembly of monks on Vulture Peak.[197] Just as Mahakasyapa was the only disciple who smiled in response to the Buddha's message, Po is the only one capable of understanding the scroll's message that the secret to limitless power is "you." Why? Because he didn't approach the scroll with his rational mind—as Shifu and, later, Tai Lung did—but he "thought" with his unconscious. His response was instant; like a flash. It was kensho.

At the end of the film, Po is fighting with Tai Lung and the leopard obtains the Dragon Scroll. Seeing that it's blank, Tai Lung becomes upset. Looking at his face reflected back at him, he says "it's nothing!" Unlike any kung fu master the audience will have ever encountered, Po isn't even worried that his opponent has been privy to the "secret of limitless power." He simply replies, "I didn't get it the first time either" then he proceeds to give him the answer to the riddle. "It's just you." Again, Tai Lung fails to understand. Po's willingness to share the message of the Dragon Scroll—he shows it to Shifu, the Furious Five, and Tai Lung, his "enemy"—demonstrates not only his generosity but, more importantly, his lack of ego. The secret to limitless power isn't just Po, just one person, but it's everyone, working together for a common goal. That's what brings peace to the Valley.

On the surface this "believe in yourself" message may seem akin to New Age philosophy, and, in fact, many reviewers were perhaps openly critical of it, because of this association. For instance, Manohla Dargis of the *New York Times* lamented that yet another animated feature had the message; to believe. Furthermore, he said, rather dismissively, that "the screenplay . . . is ho-hum without being insulting, a grab bag of gentle jokes, sage lectures, helpful lessons and kicky fights. To make something special, you just have to believe it's special." Contrary to what some might think, *Kung Fu Panda*'s message is rooted in something other than a "self-help of the week" sentiment. In his commentary to the *Dhammapada*, scholar Eknath Easwaran reminds us that "'Our life is shaped by our mind, for we become what we think.' This is the essence of the Buddha's universe and the whole theme of the *Dhammapada*. If we can get hold of the thinking process, we can actually redo our personality, remake ourselves. Destructive ways of thinking can be rechanneled, constructive channels can be deepened, all through right effort and meditation. 'As irrigators lead water to their fields, as archers make their arrows straight, as carpenters carve wood, the wise shape their lives.'"[198] We find a similar idea expressed by Zen master Takuan Soho (1573–1645) in his essay "The Clear Sound of Jewels": "Consider the core of the mind to be a wagon, with willpower to be carried about in it. Push it to a place where there can be failure, and there will be failure. Push it to a place where there can be success, and there will be success."[199]

Just as the Dragon Scroll couldn't be solved rationally, so Po cannot learn martial arts in the traditional way. And, initially, this frustrates the logical Shifu who has expected his students to conform to his techniques. Eventually, though, the master learns that to achieve his goals, he must be the one who adapts to his unconventional student, turning what he sees as Po's perceived weaknesses into his strengths. Observing that when Po focuses on kung fu, he "stinks," Shifu centers the panda's training on food, for this is when he's truly mindless. Just as Shifu imagines, Po quickly excels when a bowl of steamed dumplings enters the equation. "You are free to eat," Shifu says. "Am I?" Po asks, knowing that the minute he advances toward the dish, it will taken from him and a chopstick fight will ensue. "Are you?" Shifu queries. In this exchange, we see a sort of verbal jockeying that's character-istic of the *koan* tradition. It's also reminiscent of the exchange between King Milinda and the monk Nagasena. Milinda begins: "I'm going to ask you a question. Can you answer it?" "Please ask your question." "I've already asked it." "I've already answered it." "What did you answer?" "What did you ask?" "I asked nothing." "I answered nothing." Where does Shifu have a breakthrough when it comes to training Po? At the pool of sacred tears, the place where Oogway "achieved harmony and peace," and "unraveled the mysteries of yin and yang."

Also sacred to Oogway is the Peach Tree of Heavenly Wisdom. As it says on the official site, "the peach is a symbol of longevity and renewal. Its wood wards off evil and its petals have medicinal properties." Oogway's staff is also carved from peach wood. When Oogway's "time has come," about midway through the film, he becomes a luminous being, and he dissolves into the peach blos-soms, floating away with them. But even though this great sage is no longer present physically, he acts as a guiding presence throughout the film. In fact, when Shifu picks up Oogway's staff and summons the Dragon Scroll, a collec-tion of peach blossoms on the surface of the Moon Pool swirl upwards and re-lease it. According to Chinese legend, peaches are indeed symbols of immortality, and peach wood is believed to keep demons away. Peaches aren't the only Daoist symbol in *Kung Fu Panda*. On Oogway's back, we see a stylized yin-yang. Tortoises themselves have always been an "enigmatic and highly sym-bolic creature. The saying 'it conceals the secrets of heaven and earth' is still current in China." Legends say that the first emperor rewarded the tortoise with a 10,000-year lifespan, therefore, the creature has been long been considered a symbol of longevity and immortality.[200] Finally, in one scene that is played for laughs, we see Mantis using acupuncture, incorrectly, on Po.

ENDNOTES

1. David R. Loy's *The Dharma of Dragons and Daemons: Buddhist Themes in Modern Fantasy* has a section on *The Lord of the Rings*. *Publishers Weekly* review says that the author finds "Frodo's quest is one of renunciation, and the story is fundamentally a lesson of nonattach-ment." This short tome by Wisdom Publications was published in 2004.

2. Jennifer L. McMahon and B. Steve Csaki, "Talking Trees and Walking Mountains: Buddhist and Taoist Themes," in *The Lord of the Rings and Philosophy: One Book to Rule Them All*, ed. Gregory Bassham and Eric Bronson (Chicago: Open Court, 2003).

3. Laurent Bouzereau, *Star Wars: The Annotated Screenplays* (New York: Ballantine Books, 1997), 5–6.

4. J. W. Rinzler, *The Making of Star Wars: Based on the Lost Interviews from the Official Lucasfilm Archives* (New York: Ballantine Books, 2007), 46–47.

5. Joseph Campbell, *The Hero with a Thousand Faces* (Princeton, NJ: Princeton University Press, 1973), 17–19.

6. George Lucas is interviewed on *Joseph Campbell—The Hero's Journey* (1997) and *Joseph Campbell and the Power of Myth* (1988), both of which are available on DVD.

7. C. G. Jung, *The Basic Writings*, ed. Violet Staub de Laszlo (New York: Modern Library, 1959), 304.

8. If you do a survey of the Top 10 highest-grossing Hollywood films of all time—*Titanic*, *Star Wars*, *Shrek 2*, *E.T: The Extra-Terrestrial*, *Star Wars: Episode I—The Phantom Menace*, *Pirates of the Caribbean: Dead Man's Chest*, *Spider-Man*, *Star Wars Episode III—Revenge of the Sith*, *The Lord of the Rings: The Return of the King*, and *Spider-Man 2*—you discover that Lucas was certainly onto something. With perhaps the exception of *Titanic*, *E.T.*, and *Pirates*, the other films conform to Jung's theory of universal archetypes. All of these films are about a hero on a journey who must confront and defeat the shadow. (Of the *Spider-Man* films, the third one contains the most blatant example of a hero battling his "dark side.") The film that has most in common with the *Star Wars* saga is *The Lord of the Rings* trilogy, which also has a number of heroes (Frodo, Sam and various Hobbits, Legolas, and Aragorn), a wise old man (Gandalf), the shadow (Saruman, Sauron, and the Orcs), various maidens (Arwen and Galadriel), and a trickster (Gollum). Also conforming to this formula are the Harry Potter films, *The Chronicles of Narnia: The Lion, the Witch and the Wardrobe*, and the *Matrix* films, which all rank in the Top 40. A number of screenwriting books have drawn upon Campbell's ideas, including the very popular *The Writer's Journey: Mythic Structure for Writers* by Christopher Vogler. Another text, *Myth & the Movies: Discovering the Myth Structure of 50 Unforgettable Films* by Stuart Voytilla, shows concrete examples of how these films have used Campbell's myth structure.

9. Joseph Campbell with Bill Moyers, *The Power of Myth*, ed. Betty Sue Flowers (New York: Doubleday, 1988), xiv.

10. Stan Guthrie, "Dick Staub on the Star Wars Myth," *Christianity Today*, 2005, http://ctlibrary.com/34605 (accessed 11 February 2008).

11. John McDowell, *The Gospel According to Star Wars: Faith, Hope and the Force* (Louisville, KY: Westminster Knox Press, 2007), 21.

12. Luke, could, of course, simply be a variant of George Lucas' own last name.

13. Unlike the Pauline letters, which actually bear this author's name, the Gospels are anonymous. Even though the ancient church attributed the third gospel to Luke, most modern commentators are skeptical about the validity of this attribution. See the entry, "Luke, The Gospel According to," in The *Oxford Companion to the Bible*, ed. Bruce M. Metzger and Michael D. Coogan (New York: Oxford University Press, 1993), 469–74.

14. In early drafts, the 16-year-old main character of *Star Wars* was named Annikin Starkiller. His father was named Kane and his 10-year-old brother was named Deak. Laurent Bouzereau, *Star Wars: The Annotated Screenplays* (New York: Del Rey, 1997), 7.

15. The responder named Shiva posted the response on 16 August 2007. Shiva, "Sanskrit and *The Matrix*," *The Vaishnava Voice*, 2007, deshika.wordpress.com/2007/08/15/sanskrit-and-the -matrix (accessed 11 February 2008).

16. See the entry "Dakini" in Michael H. Kohn, *The Shambhala Dictionary of Buddhism and Zen* (Boston: Shambhala, 1991), 50.

17. John Myrdhin Reynolds, "Wisdom Dakinis, Passionate and Wrathful," *Vajranatha*, 2008, http://www.vajranatha.com/teaching/Dakinis.htm (accessed 11 February 2008). Interestingly enough, in Steven A. Galipeau, *The Journey of Luke Skywalker: An Analysis of Modern Myth and Symbol* (Peru, IL: Open Court, 2001), the Jungian analyst discusses the development of the anima and animus, especially with regard to Luke Skywalker's quest for the self.

18. From the "Elora Danan," *Star Wars: Databank*, www.starwars.com/databank/updates/ 401/character/eloradanan (accessed 11 February 2008). In this script, Lucas recycles some of his ideas from *Star Wars*, as well as comingles Eastern and Western mythology. When Queen Baymorda hears about a child who will unite the kingdom, she orders her guards to capture all pregnant women (sounds like King Herod's edict to kill all firstborn sons). Saved by a midwife, the infant Elora is put on a makeshift raft and sent down a river. Willow and his family find the baby and take her in. When brought before the "High Aldwin," Elora is seen to have great potential; however, he isn't able to hear her "voice" through the Force. Willow is ordered to take her to find another guardian. At the end of the film, the young girl, now a princess, is surrounded by the "dark side." Elora's being sent down a river and discovered seems to echo the story of Moses; however, this motif can also be found in the story of Sargon, who was a long-reigning Akkadian king.

19. Bouzereau, *Star Wars: The Annotated Screenplays*, 6.

20. From "The Amitabha Sutra," trans. Ronald Epstein, 1998, online.sfsu.edu/~rone/Buddhism/ amitabha.htm#translation (accessed 11 February 2008).

21. David West Reynolds, James Luceno, and Ryder Windham, *Star Wars: The Complete Visual Dictionary* (New York: DK, 2006), 127.

22. Kripamoya Das, "Sanskrit and *The Matrix*," *The Vaishnava Voice*, 2008, deshika.wordpress .com/2007/08/15/sanskrit-and-the-matrix (accessed 11 February 2008).

23. Das, "Sanskrit and *The Matrix*."

24. Jan Knappert, *Indian Mythology* (London: Diamond Books, 1991), 258.

25. Reginald A. Ray, *Buddhist Saints in India: A Study in Buddhist Values and Orientations* (New York: Oxford University Press, 1994), 251–52.

26. *The Bhagavad Gita*, trans. W. J. Johnson (New York: Oxford University Press, 1994), 11–12. Buddhism and Hinduism have much in common when it comes to being mindful. The primary difference is the object of focus. For Hindus, and especially in the Bhagavad-Gita, Arjuna is told to meditate on Krishna, who reveals himself to be the supreme lord. In Buddhism, one may meditate on a mantra, an object, light, and so forth. For the most part, Buddhism, particularly Theravada, is nontheistic. Gods exist but aren't the object of devotion because they, too, are stuck in *samsara*.

27. Lucas has repeatedly said that Akira Kurosawa's *The Hidden Fortress* (1958) was a strong influence. The story is about a princess who escapes an enemy clan with her commander. They are assisted by two "bumbling" farmers. See Bouzereau, *Star Wars: The Annotated Screenplays*, 9.

28. Steven J. Rosen, "Yoda and Yoga," *Beliefnet*, www.beliefnet.com/story/166/story_16672_1 .html (accessed 11 February 2008). The author equates Hanuman with Chewbacca, who is also apelike.

29. Rosen, "Yoda and Yoga."

30. *The Bhagavad Gita*, trans. W. J. Johnson, 67–68.

31. Under the entry for Yoda at Wookieepedia.com, the author states that the name may also be connected to the Hebrew *yodea*, which means "he knows" or "one who knows." See "Yoda," *Wookieepedia*, starwars.wikia.com/wiki/Yoda.

32. Knappert, *Indian Mythology*, 69.

33. Knappert, *Indian Mythology*, 30.

34. Trisha Biggar, *Dressing a Galaxy: The Costumes of Star Wars* (New York: Harry N. Abrams, 2005), 36.

35. For lyrics and a bit more explanation, go to the entry "Duel of the Fates" on Wookieepedia, which can be found at http://starwars.wikia.com/wiki/Duel_of_the_Fates.

36. The lyrics are *Madhurah svehpna, go rahdomah svehpna. Madhurah svehpna, go rahdomah svehpna, maritu, madhurah, svehpna*. Das, "Sanskrit and *The Matrix*."

37. Tom Mes and Jasper Sharp, *The Midnight Eye Guide to New Japanese Film* (Berkeley, CA: Stone Bridge Press, 2005) mention several *jidai geki* films.

38. Stephen F. Teiser, "The Spirits of Chinese Religion," in *Religions of China in Practice*, ed. Donald S. Lopez Jr. (Princeton, NJ: Princeton University Press, 1996), 32.

39. *Qigong Institute*, www.qigonginstitute.org/main_page/main_page.php (accessed 11 November 2007).

40. When all of the words in his name are translated, with *mundi* being Latin for world, it reads something like "first breath of the world."

41. Mary Henderson, *Star Wars: The Magic of Myth* (New York: Bantam Spectra, 1997), 189.

42. Does the name for the planet Kamino, home of the Kaminoans, refer to kimono or is it just a play on the Chevy El Camino? Lucas, after all, had a penchant for cars when he was a teenager and even paid homage to classic cars in his 1973 film *American Graffiti*.

43. *Code of the Samurai: A Modern Translation of the Bushido Shoshinshu of Taira Shigesuke*, trans. Thomas Cleary (Boston: Tuttle, 1999), 11.

44. *Code of the Samurai*, xv.

45. The seven folds in a samurai's *hakama*, skirtlike pants, are said to be symbolic of *yuki*, valor; *jin*, benevolence; *gi*, righteousness; *rei*, civility; *makoto*, honesty; *chugi*, fidelity; and *meiyo*, dignity.

46. *Code of the Samurai*, 3.

47. David West Reynolds, *Star Wars Episode I: The Visual Dictionary* (New York: DK Publishing, 1999), 8.

48. Vivien Sung, *Five-Fold Happiness: Chinese Concepts of Luck, Prosperity, Longevity, Happiness and Wealth* (San Francisco: Chronicle Books, 2002), 94–95.

49. *The Complete Works of Chuang Tzu*, trans. Burton Watson (New York: Columbia University Press, 1968), 291.

50. See chapter 2 titled "Introduction and Early Development: Han Dynasty," in Kenneth Ch'en, *Buddhism in China* (Princeton NJ: Princeton University Press, 1973), 21–53.

51. Kohn, *The Shambhala Dictionary of Buddhism and Zen*, 82.

52. Lillian Too, *Total Feng Shui: Bring Health, Wealth and Happiness into Your Life* (San Francisco: Chronicle Books, 2005), 263.

53. Ch'en, *Buddhism in China*, 103. Ch'en devotes pages 94–103 to Tao-an.

54. *Ataru Shotokan Karate Club*, www.ataru-karate.co.uk/index.htm (accessed 11 February 2008).

55. This is obviously another reference to the Vedic tradition, with the Vedas being the sacred "revealed" texts of the Aryans.

56. For more explanation about the costumes, see Biggar, *Dressing a Galaxy*. To see the costumes online, see *Dressing a Galaxy: The Costumes of Star Wars from the FIDM Museum & Galleries*, starwars.fidm.edu/introduction/welcome.shtm?section=introduction&subsection=start welcome (accessed 11 February 2008), and especially *The Padawan's Guide to Star Wars Costumes*, www.padawansguide.com (accessed 11 February 2008).

57. Biggar, *Dressing a Galaxy*, 13.

58. Biggar, *Dressing a Galaxy*, 35.

59. Henderson, *Star Wars: The Magic of Myth*, 189.

60. Biggar, *Dressing a Galaxy*, 9.

61. Rinzler, *The Making of Star Wars*, 69.

62. Sachiko Murata and William C. Chittick, *The Vision of Islam* (New York: Paragon House, 1994), 98.

63. Rinzler, *The Making of Star Wars*, 87. The author also claims that when writing the initial treatment for what would become *Star Wars*, Lucas used a sort of stream-of-consciousness approach to coming up with many of the character and place names. In fact, on page 172, a sidebar titled "Musical Names" discusses many of the characters. For instance, for Obi-Wan Kenobi, he writes, "I picked Ben because it was a very easy name; Kenobi was a combination of a lot of words I put together. The name came out of thin air."

64. See the entry on the queen at "Apailana," *Wookieepedia*, http://starwars.wikia.com/wiki/Apailana.

65. It's fitting that the Jedi Order has its headquarters on Coruscant, which means "shining" and "glittering."

66. Dave Pollock, *Skywalking: The Life and Films of George Lucas* (New York: Harmony Books, 1983), 20.

67. Pollock, *Skywalking: The Life and Films of George Lucas*, 20. One website claims that Lucas lists his religion as "Buddhist Methodist," and that his friend, Gary Kurtz, introduced him to Eastern religions. See "The Religious Affiliation of Director George Lucas," *adherents.com*, 2005, www.adherents.com/people/pl/George_Lucas.html (accessed 11 February 2008).

68. Rinzler, *The Making of Star Wars*, 18.

69. *The Dhammapada*, trans. Gil Fronsdal (Boston: Shambhala, 2005), 63.

70. Shunryu Suzuki, *Zen Mind, Beginner's Mind*, ed. Trudy Dixon (New York: Weatherhill, 1972), 25–26.

71. Suzuki, *Zen Mind, Beginner's Mind*, 40.

72. Lao Tzu, *Tao Te Ching*, trans. D. C. Lau (London: Penguin Classics, 1963), 24.

73. Reynolds, *Star Wars Episode I*, 44.

74. *The Complete Works of Chuang Tzu*, trans. Burton Watson, 235–36. Notice the similarity between what the Buddhists say and what the Daoists say.

75. Henderson, *Star Wars: The Magic of Myth*, 68.

76. Lao Tzu, *Tao Te Ching*, trans. D. C. Lau, 30.

77. Lao Tzu, *Tao Te Ching*, trans. D. C. Lau, 39.

78. Isabelle Robinet, *Taoism: Growth of a Religion*, trans. Phyllis Brooks (Stanford, CA: Stanford University Press, 1997), 67.

79. *The Complete Works of Chuang Tzu*, trans. Watson, 241.

80. Livia Kohn, *The Taoist Experience: An Anthology* (Albany: State University of New York Press, 1993), 133.

81. Suzuki, *Zen Mind, Beginner's Mind*, 58.

82. Apparently Irvin Kershner, the director of *Star Wars: Episode V—The Empire Strikes Back*, has Buddhist leanings and wanted to give Yoda and the scenes on Dagobah more of a Zen feel.

83. Suzuki, *Zen Mind, Beginner's Mind*, 21.

84. Suzuki, *Zen Mind, Beginner's Mind*, 90.

85. *Numerical Discourses of the Buddha: An Anthology of Suttas from the Anguttara Nikaya*, trans. and ed. Nyanaponika Thera and Bhikkhu Bodhi (London: Altamira, 1999), 65.

86. *The Dhammapada*, trans. Fronsdal, 87–91.

87. Matthew Bortolin, *The Dharma of Star Wars* (Boston: Wisdom, 2005), 113.

88. *The Dhammapada*, trans. Fronsdal, 9.

89. Suzuki, *Zen Mind, Beginner's Mind*, 30–31.

90. Suzuki, *Zen Mind, Beginner's Mind*, 41–42.

91. Kohn, *The Taoist Experience*, 279.

92. Kohn, *The Taoist Experience*, 280.

93. Kohn, *The Taoist Experience*, 280.

94. Isabelle Robinet, *Taoism: Growth of a Religion*, 49.

95. *Huang Ti Nei Ching Su Wen: The Yellow Emperor's Classic of Internal Medicine*, trans. Ilza Veith (Berkeley: University of California Press, 1972), 12.

96. Kohn, *The Taoist Experience*, 194.

97. Kohn, *The Taoist Experience*, 216–17.

98. Livia Kohn, *Early Chinese Mysticism: Philosophy and Soteriology in the Taoist Tradition* (Princeton, NJ: Princeton University Press, 1992), 170.

99. James Luceno, *Star Wars: Revenge of the Sith—The Visual Dictionary* (New York: DK, 2005), 35.

100. Lao Tzu, *Tao Te Ching*, trans. Lau, 32.

101. *The Complete Works of Chuang Tzu*, trans. Watson, 234.

102. Kohn, *The Taoist Experience*, 218.

103. Suzuki, *Zen Mind, Beginner's Mind*, 45.

104. Suzuki, *Zen Mind, Beginner's Mind*, 80.

105. Livia Kohn, *The Taoist Experience*, 98.

106. *The Complete Works of Chuang Tzu*, trans. Watson, 182.

107. Suzuki, *Zen Mind, Beginner's Mind*, 90.

108. Hsiao-Lan Hu and William Cully Allen, *Taoism* (Philadelphia: Chelsea House, 2005), 30–31.

109. Stephen F. Teiser, "The Spirits of Chinese Religion," in *Religions of China in Practice*, ed. Donald S. Loopez Jr. (Princeton, NJ: Princeton University Press, 1996), 33–34.

110. Frank Newport, "Americans' More Likely to Believe in God Than the Devil; Heaven More Than Hell," *Gallup News Service*, www.gallup.com/poll/27877/Americans-More-Likely-Believe -God-Than-Devil-Heaven-More-Than-Hell.aspx (accessed 11 February 2008).

111. Stephen L. Harris, *Understanding the Bible*, 7th ed. (New York: McGraw Hill, 2007), 51.

112. David S. Ariel, *What Do Jews Believe? The Spiritual Foundations of Judaism* (New York: Schocken Books, 1995), 73.

113. Wayne T. Pitard, "Afterlife and Immortality: Ancient Israel," in *The Oxford Companion to the Bible*, 16.

114. *Sacred Writings Judaism: The Tanakh, The New JPS Translation*, ed. Jaroslav Pelikan (New York: Quality Paperback Club, 1992), 646.

115. Sidnie Ann White, "Afterlife and Immortality: Second Temple Judaism and Early Christianity," in *The Oxford Companion to the Bible*, 17.

116. George Robinson, *Essential Judaism: A Complete Guide to Beliefs, Customs and Rituals* (New York: Pocket Books, 2000), 191.

117. Ariel, *What Do Jews Believe*, 74–75.

118. Bo Reicke, "Gehenna," in *The Oxford Companion to the Bible*, 243.

119. "The Book of Enoch," *Wesley Center Online*, 1995, wesley.nnu.edu/biblical_studies/ noncanon/ot/pseudo/enoch.htm (accessed 11 February 2008).

120. "The Book of Henoch (Ethiopic)," New Advent, www.newadvent.org/cathen/01602a .htm (accessed 11 February 2008).

121. Alice K. Turner, *The History of Hell* (New York: Harcourt Brace, 1993), 44.

122. Harris, *Understanding the Bible*, 388.

123. Thomas Francis Glasson, "Heaven," in *The Oxford Companion to the Bible*, 270.

124. U.S. Catholic Church, *Catechism of the Catholic Church with Modifications from the Editio Typica* (New York: Doubleday, 1995), 289.

125. U.S. Catholic Church, *Catechism of the Catholic Church*, 290.

126. Turner, *The History of Hell*, 54.

127. Harris, *Understanding the Bible*, 388.

128. Colleen McDannell and Bernhard Lang, *Heaven: A History* (New York: Vintage Books, 1990), 308.

129. *Dante's Divine Comedy: Hell, Purgatory, Paradise*, trans. Henry W. Longfellow (Edison, NJ: Chartwell Books, 2006), 147.

130. David Cownie, "Movie Review: What Dreams May Come," *Orthodox Christian Information Center*, www.orthodoxinfo.com/death/dreams_movie.aspx (accessed 11 February 2008).

131. A number of films have earned this label, even when they present ideas found in mainstream Asian religions. This undoubtedly reflects ignorance on the part of the Western viewer. He or she may simply not know what people from other religious backgrounds believe. The easiest assumption then is to refer to the film's philosophical or religious worldview as "New Agey." Writers Sydney Coale and Archana Dongre found this to be true, and say so in their article, "Did They Get It?" for *Hinduism Today*. They found that in the United States, *What Dreams May Come* seems to appeal most to the "spiritually-minded 'Generation X.'" As far as Hindus, for whom many of the film's concepts should seem familiar, Dongre could find very few who had seen it or were going to see it. One felt it was too boring; another thought it was "making fun" of Hinduism. For more, see Archana Dongre, "Movie Making's High-Tech, High Budget Film Teaches a Well-Researched Lesson in Metaphysics," *Hinduism Today*, 1999, http://www.hinduismtoday.com/archives/1999/2/1999-2-08.shtml (accessed 11 February 2008).

132. As recounted in Thomas Bulfinch's *Mythology: The Age of Fable, The Age of Chivalry, Legends of Charlemagne* (New York: Modern Library), 215.

133. Robert Garland, *The Greek Way of Death* (Ithaca, NY: Cornell University Press, 2001), 1.

134. Virgil, *Aeneid*, trans. John Dryden, Harvard Classics, Vol. 13 (New York: P. F. Collier, 1909). Available at www.ilt.columbia.edu/academic/digitexts/vergil/aeneid/book06.html (accessed 11 February 2008).

135. Dongre, "Movie Making's High-Tech, High Budget Film."

136. Ed Gorman, "Richard Matheson—Part Two—The Interview," *Filmfax*, 2006, edgorman-rambles.blogspot.com/2006/03/richard-matheson-part-two-interview.html (accessed 11 February 2008).

137. Richard Matheson, *The Path: A New Look at Reality* (New York: Tor Books, 1993), 11.

138. Peter Harvey, *An Introduction to Buddhism: Teachings, History and Practices* (New York: Cambridge University Press, 1990), 290–91.

139. Stewart Hawkins, "Theosophy," *virginia.edu*, 1998, etext.lib.virginia.edu/relmove/nrms/theosophy.html (accessed 17 February 2008).

140. Suzuki, *Zen Mind, Beginner's Mind*, 30–31.

141. U.S. Catholic Church, *Catechism of the Catholic Church*, 609.

142. Robinson, *Essential Judaism*, 185.

143. Alfred J. Kolatch, *The Jewish Book of Why* (New York: Penguin Compass, 2000), 54.

144. Werner Menski, "Hinduism," in *Ethical Issues in Six Religious Traditions*, ed. Peggy Morgan and Clive Lawton (Edinburgh: Edinburgh University Press, 2004), 34.

145. Daisetz T. Suzuki, *Zen and Japanese Culture* (New York: Bollingen Foundation, 1959), 84.

146. Suzuki, *Zen Mind, Beginner's Mind*, 78.

147. Francesca Fremantle, *Luminous Emptiness: Understanding the Tibetan Book of the Dead* (Boston: Shambhala, 2003), 144.

148. Fremantle, *Luminous Emptiness*, 147.

149. Fremantle, *Luminous Emptiness*, 149.

150. At this point, we catch a glimpse of another Eastern religion—Daoism. On his daughter's name tag is a yin-yang symbol.

151. Suzuki, *Zen Mind, Beginner's Mind*, 83–84.

152. Gershom Scholem, *Kabbalah* (New York: Meridian, 1978), 345.

153. Scholem, *Kabbalah*, 345.

154. Scholem, *Kabbalah*, 346.

155. Plato, "Symposium," *Internet Classics Archive*, classics.mit.edu/Plato/symposium.html (accessed 11 February 2008).

156. "Soul Mates: A Primer," *oprah.com*, 2002, www.oprah.com/relationships/relationships _content.jhtml?contentId=con_20020916_soulmates.xml&section=Couplehood&subsection =Dating (accessed 17 February 2008).

157. Rabbi David A. Cooper, *God Is a Verb: Kabbalah and the Practice of Mystical Judaism* (New York: Riverhead Books, 1997), 107.

158. Yogi Ramacharaka (pseud.), *Life beyond Death* (Whitefish, MT: Kessinger, 2003), 45. The text was originally published in 1912.

159. "Soulmates," *edgarcayce.org*, www.edgarcayce.org/about_ec/cayce_on/soulmates/index .html (accessed 11 February 2008). Kevin J. Todeschi explains more about Cayce's ideas in *Edgar Cayce on Soul Mates*.

160. Liu Xiaogan, "Naturalness (*Tzu-jan*), and the Core Value in Taoism: Its Ancient Meaning and Its Significance Today," in *Lao-tzu and the Tao-te-Ching*, ed. Livia Kohn and Michael La-Fargue (Albany: State University of New York Press, 1998), 211.

161. Livia Kohn, *Early Chinese Mysticism*, 53.

162. Livia Kohn, *Early Chinese Mysticism*, 55.

163. Kwong-loi Shun, "Moral Philosophy," in *The Encyclopedia of Chinese Philosophy*, ed. Antonio S. Cua (New York: Routledge, 2003), 471.

164. Benjamin Schwartz, "The Thought of the *Tao-te-Ching*," in *Lao-tzu and the Tao-te-Ching*, 204.

165. Schwartz, "The Thought of the *Tao-te-Ching*," 207.

166. Shun, "Moral Philosophy," 473.

167. Schwartz, "The Thought of the *Tao-te-Ching*," 209.

168. Xiaogan, "Naturalness (*Tzu-jan*), and the Core Value in Taoism," 219.

169. Xiaogan, "Naturalness (*Tzu-jan*), and the Core Value in Taoism," 221.

170. Xiaogan, "Naturalness (*Tzu-jan*), and the Core Value in Taoism," 225.

171. Hans-Georg Moeller, *Daoism Explained: From the Dream of the Butterfly to the Fishnet Allegory* (Chicago: Open Court, 2004), 48–49.

172. *The Complete Works of Chuang Tzu*, trans. Watson, 105.

173. Schwartz, "The Thought of the *Tao-te-Ching*," 205–6.

174. D. T. Suzuki, *An Introduction to Zen Buddhism* (New York: Grove Press, 1964), 33.

175. It is important to note that the screenplay makes repeated references to redemption, being saved, God, and so on. During this fight sequence, Jack says that the "hysterical shouting was in tongues, like at a Pentecostal church." So does this mean that the film is Christian or can be

interpreted from this religious perspective? Tyler Durden could be seen as a kind of messianic figure (or a false prophet or a cult leader) who has come to "liberate" the disenfranchised male masses from ennui and their consumer-centered lives. He does this by offering them blood sacrifice as a way to be "reborn." But a monotheistic God isn't really present.

176. Suzuki, *An Introduction to Zen Buddhism*, 61.

177. Heinrich Dumoulin, *Zen Buddhism: A History*. Vol. 1: *India and China*, trans. James W. Heisig and Paul Knitter (New York: Macmillan, 1988), 184.

178. Dumoulin, *Zen Buddhism: A History*, 192.

179. Kenneth Ch'en, *Buddhism in China*, 358.

180. Jim Uhls, "Fight Club," *hundland.com*, 1998, www.hundland.com/scripts/Fight-Club _third.htm (accessed 11 February 2008).

181. Suzuki, *An Introduction to Zen Buddhism*, 64.

182. Richard S. Ehrlich, "Tsunami: Thousands of Cremations a Grim Task," *Scoop*, 2005, www .scoop.co.nz/stories/HL0501/S00019.htm (accessed 11 February 2008).

183. Judith L. Lief, *Making Friends with Death: A Buddhist Guide to Encountering Mortality* (Boston: Shambhala, 2001), 6.

184. Holly A. Schmid, "The Spiritual Athlete's Path to Enlightenment," *Ultra Marathon Running*, 1996, www.lehigh.edu/~dmd1/holly.html (accessed 11 February 2008). One can find out more by reading John Stevens' *The Marathon Monks of Mount Hiei*, published by Rider in 1989 or by watching Christopher J. Hayden's 2002 documentary with the same title. Another good source is Kenji Hall, "Buddhist Monk Completes Seven-Year Run," *Salon.com*, 2003, dir.salon .com/story/mwt/wire/2003/09/19/monk_run/index.html (accessed 11 February 2008).

185. Chuck Palahniuk, *Fight Club* (New York: W. W. Norton, 1996), 69.

186. Kohn, *The Shambhala Dictionary of Buddhism and Zen*, 57.

187. Wolfram Eberhard, *A Dictionary of Chinese Symbols: Hidden Symbols in Chinese Life and Thought* (New York: Routledge & Kegan Paul, 1983), 248.

188. Eberhard, *A Dictionary of Chinese Symbols*, 108. The author goes on to explain the prolific use of the number, mentioning the five precepts of Buddhism, five Classics, Five Dynasties, Five Moral Qualities, Five gifts, Five Permutations of Being, Five Thunders, and Five Bushels of Rice.

189. Eberhard, *A Dictionary of Chinese Symbols*, 32.

190. According to Eberhard, the word *wu-gui*, which sounds much closer to our sage's name, translates to "black tortoise," which is a pimp. See page 296.

191. Bassui Tokusho, *Mud and Water: The Collected Teachings of Zen Master Bassui*, trans. Arthur Braverman (Somerville, MA: Wisdom Publications, 2002), 63.

192. Tokusho, *Mud and Water: The Collected Teachings of Zen Master Bassui*, 64–65.

193. *Questions to a Zen Master: Taisen Deshimaru*, trans. Nancy Amphoux (New York: E.P. Dutton, 1985), 82.

194. The Dalai Lama, *Healing Anger: The Power of Patience from a Buddhist Perspective* (Ithaca, NY: Snow Lion Publications, 1997), 64.

195. The Dalai Lama, *The World of Tibetan Buddhism: An Overview of Its Philosophy and Practice* (Somerville, MA: Wisdom Publications, 1995), 82.

196. Liu I-Ming, *Awakening to the Tao*, trans. Thomas Cleary (Boston: Shambhala, 2006), 72–73.

197. For more on this *koan*, see Albert Welter's "Mahakasyapa's Smile: Silent Transmission and the Kung-an (Koan) Tradition" in *The Koan: Texts and Contexts in Zen Buddhism*, which was published in 2000 through Oxford University Press.

198. *The Dhammapada*, trans. Eknath Easwaran (Tomales, CA: Nilgiri Press, 1999), 72.

199. Takuan Soho, "The Clear Sound of Jewels," in *The Unfettered Mind: Writings from a Zen Master to a Master Swordsman*, trans. William Scott Wilson (New York: Kodansha International, 2002), 82.

200. Eberhard, *A Dictionary of Chinese Symbols*, 294–295.

Bibliography

'Abdu'l-Bahá, "'Abdu'l-Bahá on Science and Religion." *Bahá'í International Community*, info .bahai.org/article-1-5-3-1.html (accessed 11 February 2008).

"Abortion Policy in Japan." *United Nations Report.* www.un.org/esa/population/publications/ abortion/doc/japan.doc (accessed 30 January 2008).

"About the production." *zeitgeistfilms.com.* 2003, www.zeitgeistfilms.com/films/travellersand magicians/presskit.pdf (accessed 17 February 2008).

Adler, Joseph A. *Chinese Religious Traditions.* Upper Saddle River, NJ: Lawrence King, 2002.

Adler, Joseph A. "Daughter/Wife/Mother or Sage/Immortal/Bodhisattva? Women in the Teach-ing of Chinese Religions." *Kenyon College.* 2006, www2.kenyon.edu/depts/Religion/Fac/Adler/ Writings/Women.htm (accessed 21 February 2008).

Aiken, Keith. "The Great Yokai War." *SciFi Japan.* 2006, www.scifijapan.com/articles/2006/10/18/ the-great-yokai-war (accessed 30 January 2008).

Akiyama, J. "Meaning of Onegai Shimasu." *aikiweb.com,* www.aikiweb.com/language/onegai .html (accessed 28 January 2008).

"All about Japanese Hina Dolls." *Kyoto National Museum.* 2007, www.kyohaku.go.jp/eng/dictio/ data/senshoku/index.htm (accessed 31 January 2008).

American Religious Identification Survey. *City University of New York.* 2001, www.gc.cuny.edu/ faculty/research_briefs/aris/key_findings.htm (accessed 14 February 2008).

"The Amitabha Sutra." Translated by Ronald Epstein, 1998, online.sfsu.edu/~rone/Buddhism/ amitabha.htm#Translation (accessed 11 February 2008).

"Apailana." *Wookieepedia,* http://starwars.wikia.com/wiki/Apailana (accessed 10 February 2008).

"Aparna Sen Makes a Statement Again." *India Today.* 2002, www.rediff.com/entertai/2002/jul/ 27aparna.htm (accessed 10 February 2008).

Ariel, David S. *What Do Jews Believe? The Spiritual Foundations of Judaism.* New York: Schocken Books, 1995.

Arthur, Greg. "Superman as Jesus and Other Christ Figures in Film." *Holiness Reeducation.* 2006, holinessreeducation.com/2006/07/04/superman-as-jesus-and-other-christ-figures-in-film (accessed 12 February 2008).

Ataru Shotokan Karate Club. www.ataru-karate.co.uk/index.htm (accessed 11 February 2008).

Bahr, Ann Marie B. *Religions of the World: Indigenous Religions.* Philadelphia: Chelsea House, 2005.

Banister, Judith. "Shortage of Girls in China Today." *Journal of Population Research.* 2004, www .jpr.org.au/upload/JPR21-1_Banister.pdf (accessed 27 January 2008).

"Baptism." *New Advent Catholic Encyclopedia.* www.newadvent.org/cathen/02258b.htm#III (accessed 10 February 2008).

Beer, Robert. *The Handbook of Tibetan Buddhist Symbols.* Boston: Shambhala, 2003.

Bell, Daniel A. "China's Leaders Rediscover Confucianism." *International Herald Tribune.* 2006, www.iht.com/articles/2006/09/14/opinion/edbell.php (accessed 25 January 2008).

Benson, Sheila. "Eroticism of Kama Sutra Goes Beyond Mere Titillation." *Orlando Sentinel,* 1992, www.mirabaifilms.com/wordpress/?page_id=22 (accessed 10 February 2008).

Berry, Chris, ed. *Chinese Films in Focus: 25 New Takes.* London: British Film Institute. 2003.

Berry, Chris, and Mary Ann Farquhar. *China on Screen: Cinema and Nation.* New York: Columbia University Press, 2006.

Berry, Michael. *Speaking in Images: Interviews with Contemporary Chinese Filmmakers.* New York: Columbia University Press, 2005.

The Bhagavad Gita. Translated by W. J. Johnson. New York: Oxford University Press, 1994.

Biggar, Trisha. *Dressing a Galaxy: The Costumes of Star Wars.* New York: Harry N. Abrams, 2005.

Bilhartz, Terry D. *Sacred Words: A Source Book on the Great Religions of the World.* New York: McGraw Hill, 2006.

Birrell, Anne. *Chinese Mythology: An Introduction.* Baltimore: Johns Hopkins University Press, 1993.

Blofeld, John. *Bodhisattva of Compassion: The Mystical Tradition of Kuan Yin.* Boston: Shambhala, 1988.

Blomberg, Catharina. *The Heart of the Warrior: Origins and Religious Background of the Samurai System in Feudal Japan.* Sandgate, Folkestone, Kent, UK: Japan Library, 1994.

Bloom, Irene. "Confucius and the Analects." In *Sources of Chinese Tradition from Earliest Times to 1600.* Compiled by Wm. Theodore de Bary and Irene Bloom. New York: Columbia University Press, 1999.

Blount, Douglas K. "Uberhobbits: Tolkien, Nietzsche, and the Will to Power." In *The Lord of the Rings and Philosophy: One Book to Rule Them All,* edited by Gregory Bassham and Eric Bronson. Chicago: Open Court, 2003.

Bocking, Brian. "Japanese Religions." In *Worldviews, Religion, and the Environment: A Global Anthology.* Edited by Richard C. Foltz. Belmont, CA: Wadsworth/Thomson, 2003.

Bodhi, Bhikkhu. "Dhamma and Non-Duality." *vipassana.com.* www.vipassana.com/resources/bodhi/dhamma_and_nonduality.php (accessed 12 February 2008).

Bodhi, Bhikku, ed. *In the Buddha's Words: An Anthology of Discourses from the Pali Canon.* Boston, MA: Wisdom, 2005.

Boggs, Joseph M., and Dennis W. Petrie. *The Art of Watching Films.* New York: McGraw-Hill. 2008.

Bombay Sarvodaya Mandal. www.mkgandhi.org/religionmk.htm (accessed 10 February 2008).

"The Book of Enoch." *Wesley Center Online,* 1995, wesley.nnu.edu/biblical_studies/noncanon/ot/pseudo/enoch.htm (accessed 11 February 2008).

"The Book of Henoch (Ethiopic)." *New Advent.* www.newadvent.org/cathen/01602a.htm (accessed 11 February 2008).

Bortolin, Matthew. *The Dharma of Star Wars.* Boston: Wisdom, 2005.

Bouzereau, Laurent. *Star Wars: The Annotated Screenplays.* New York: Ballantine Books, 1997.

Bowan, Peter. "Standing on Ceremony: Mira Nair Returns to India for Monsoon Wedding." *Filmmaker Magazine.* 2001. www.mirabaifilms.com/wordpress/?page_id=26 (accessed 10 February 2008).

Box Office Mojo. "Water." 2006, www.boxofficemojo.com/movies/?id=water06.htm (accessed 10 February 2008).

Boyce, Mary. *Zoroastrians: Their Religious Beliefs and Practices* (New York: Routledge. 2001).

Brun, Ole. "Feng Shui and the Chinese Perception of Nature." In *Worldviews, Religion and the Environment: A Global Anthology.* Edited by Richard C. Foltz. Belmont, CA: Wadsworth/Thomson, 2003.

Buck, William. *Ramayana.* Berkeley: University of California Press, 2000.

"A Buddhist Reading of J. R. R. Tolkien: Middle Path and Middle Earth." *arrowriver.ca,* www.arrowriver.ca/dhamma/tolkien.html (accessed 12 February 2008).

The Buddhist Tradition in India, China and Japan. edited by William Theodore de Bary. New York: Vintage, 1972.

Bulfinch, Thomas. *Mythology: The Age of Fable, the Age of Chivalry, Legends of Charlemagne.* New York: Modern Library, no date.

Burns, John F. "Once Widowed in India, Twice Scorned." *New York Times,* 1998, www2.soe.umd.umich.edu/rpkettel/NY_Times_article.pdf (accessed 10 February 2008).

"Cain." *The New Advent Catholic Encyclopedia.* www.newadvent.org/cathen/03142b.htm (accessed 12 February 2008).

Campany, Robert Ford. "The Earliest Tales of the Bodhisattva Guanshiyin." In *Religions of China in Practice.* Edited by Donald S. Lopez Jr. Princeton, NJ: Princeton University Press, 1996.

Campbell, Joseph. *The Hero with a Thousand Faces.* Princeton: NJ: Princeton University Press, 1973.

Campbell, Joseph, with Bill Moyers. *The Power of Myth*. Edited by Betty Sue Flowers. New York: Doubleday, 1988.

Janet Carpenter. "Sennin: The Immortals of Taoism." In *Japanese Ghosts & Demons: Art of the Supernatural*. Edited by Stephen Addiss. New York: George Braziller, 1985.

"Carrying the Ring: An Interview with Elijah Wood." *Hollywood Jesus*. 2004, www.hollywoodjesus .com/lord_of_the_rings_interview_07.htm (accessed 12 February 2008).

Cavallaro, Dani. *The Anime Art of Hayao Miyazaki*. Jefferson, NC: McFarland, 2006.

Chan, Alan K. L. "Does *Xiao* Come before *Ren*?" In *Filial Piety in Chinese Thought and History*. Edited by Alan K. L. Chan and Sor-hoon Tan. London: RoutledgeCurzon, 2004.

Chan, Alan K. L. "A Tale of Two Commentaries: Ho-shang-kun and Wang Pi on the Lao-tzu." In *Lao-tzu and the Tao-te-ching*. Edited by Livia Kohn and Michael LaFargue. Albany: State University of New York Press, 1998.

Chan, Felicia. "*Crouching Tiger, Hidden Dragon*: Cultural Migrancy and Translatability." In *Chinese Films in Focus: 25 New Takes*. Edited by Chris Berry. London: British Film Institute, 2003.

Ch'en, Kenneth. *Buddhism in China: A Historical Survey*. Princeton, NJ: Princeton University Press, 1964.

Cheng, Chung-ying. "Mencius (Mengzi, Meng Tzu)." In *Encyclopedia of Chinese Philosophy*. Edited by Antonio S. Cua. New York: Routledge, 2003.

China: A Nation in Transition, exp. ref. ed. Edited by Debra E. Soled. Washington, DC: Congressional Quarterly, 1995.

"China's Corpse Brides: Wet Goods and Dry Goods." *The Economist*. 2007, www.economist .com/world/asia/displaystory.cfm?story_id=9558423 (accessed 12 February 2008).

Ching, Julia. *Chinese Religions*. New York: Orbis Books, 1993.

Choezom, Tsering. "Outline of the Tibetan horoscope." *tibet.com*, 1996, www.tibet.com/Med _Astro/astro2.html (accessed 15 February 2008).

Chow, Rey. *Sentimental Fabulations, Contemporary Chinese Films: Attachment in the Age of Global Visibility*. New York: Columbia University Press, 2007.

Chryssavgis, John. "The World of the Icon and Creation: An Orthodox Perspective on Ecology and Pneumatology." In *Worldviews, Religion, and the Environment: A Global Anthology*. Edited by Richard C. Foltz. Belmont, CA: Wadsworth/Thomson, 2003.

Ciment, Michel. "Asking the Questions: Interview with Zhang Yimou." In *Zhang Yimou Interviews*. Edited by Frances Gateward. Jackson: University Press of Mississippi, 2001.

Clarke, Peter Bernard. *New Religions in Global Perspective: A Study of Religious Change in the Global Perspective*. New York: Routledge, 2006.

Cleary, Thomas. *Code of the Samurai: A Modern Translation of the Bushido Shoshinsu*. Boston: Tuttle, 1999.

Clunas, Craig. *Pictures and Visuality in Early Modern China*. London: Reaktion Books, 2006.

Code of the Samurai: A Modern Translation of the Bushido Shoshinshu of Taira Shigesuke. Translated by Thomas Cleary. Boston: Tuttle, 1999.

The Complete Works of Chuang Tzu. Translated by Burton Watson. New York: Columbia University Press, 1968.

Confucius. *Confucian Analects: The Great Learning and the Doctrine of the Mean.* Translated by James Legge. New York: Dover, 1971.

Cooper, Rabbi David A. *God Is a Verb: Kabbalah and the Practice of Mystical Judaism.* New York: Riverhead Books, 1997.

Corless, Roger J. *The Vision of Buddhism: The Space under the Tree.* New York: Paragon House, 1989.

Cownie, David. "Movie Review: What Dreams May Come." *Orthodox Christian Information Center* . www.orthodoxinfo.com/death/dreams_movie.aspx (accessed 11 February 2008).

Cua, Antonio S. "Junzi (Chun-tzu): The Moral Person." In *Encyclopedia of Chinese Philosophy.* Edited by Antonio S. Cua. New York: Routledge, 2003.

Dalai Lama. *Healing Anger: The Power of Patience from a Buddhist Perspective.* Ithaca, NY: Snow Lion Publications, 1997.

Dalai Lama. *The World of Tibetan Buddhism: An Overview of Its Philosophy and Practice.* Boston: Wisdom Publications, 1995.

Dante's Divine Comedy: Hell, Purgatory, Paradise. Translated by Henry W. Longfellow. Edison, NJ: Chartwell Books, 2006.

Das, Kripamoya. "Sanskrit and *The Matrix*." *The Vaishnava Voice.* 2008, deshika.wordpress.com/ 2007/08/15/sanskrit-and-the-matrix (accessed 11 February 2008).

Davaa, Byambasuren. "Director's Notes." *caveoftheyellowdog.co.uk,* www.caveoftheyellowdog.co.uk (accessed 17 February 2008).

David, Eric. "From Ace to the Almighty." *Christianity Today.* 2006, www.christianitytoday .com/movies/commentaries/fof_shadyac.html (accessed 12 February 2008).

Davidson, Gustav A. *Dictionary of Angels.* New York: Free Press, 1967.

Davis, Richard H. "Religions of India in Practice." In *Asian Religions in Practice: An Introduction.* Edited by Donald S. Lopez Jr., 8–55. Princeton, NJ: Princeton University Press, 1996.

de Bary, William Theodore. *The Buddhist Tradition in India, China and Japan.* New York: Vintage, 1972.

Dean, Kenneth. "Daoist Ritual Today." *Daoism Handbook.* Edited by Livia Kohn. Leiden: Brill, 2000.

"Deepa Mehta Inks Deal with Amitabh." *Hindustan Times.* 2007, www.hindustantimes.com/Story Page/StoryPage.aspx?id=15bc1940-da4b-4400-808d-607b9a04a9a9&&Headline=Big+B +signs+Deepa+Mehta+film (accessed 10 February 2008).

"Deepa Mehta's Signs Big B for Exclusion." *Indiafm.com.* 2007, www.indiafm.com/news/2007/ 02/19/8920/index.html (accessed 10 February 2008).

Deguchi, Midori. "One Hundred Demons and One Hundred Supernatural Tales." In *Japanese Ghosts & Demons*, edited by Stephen Addiss. New York: George Braziller, 1985.

"Demographics." *UNESCO Parsi Zoroastrian Project*. www.unescoparzor.com/project/demographics.htm (accessed 10 February 2008).

The Dhammapada. Translated by Eknath Easwaran. Tomales, CA: Nilgiri Press, 1999.

The Dhammapada. Translated by Gil Fronsdal. Boston: Shambhala, 2005.

Dharma, Venerable Karuna. "Daughters of the Buddha." *Tricycle* (Winter 2006): 51.

"Dietary Law." *Encyclopedia Brittanica*. www.britannica.com/eb/article-66416/dietary-law#538310.hook (accessed 10 February 2008).

"Discussing the People." In *Sources of Chinese Tradition: From Earliest Times to 1600*. Compiled by Wm. Theodore de Bary and Irene Bloom. New York: Columbia University Press, 1999.

Dongre, Archana. "Movie Making's High-Tech, High Budget Film Teaches a Well-Researched Lesson in Metaphysics." *Hinduism Today*, 1999, http://www.hinduismtoday.com/archives/1999/2/1999-2-08.shtml (accessed 11 February 2008).

Donin, Rabbi Hayim Halevy. *To Be a Jew: A Guide to Jewish Observance in Contemporary Life*. New York: Basic Books, 1972.

Dorji, Kunzang. "A (Bhutanese) Dog's Life." *Lonely Planet: Bhutan*. Oakland, CA: Lonely Planet Publications, 1998.

Dumoulin, Heinrich. *Zen Buddhism: A History*. Vol. 1: *India and China*. Translated by James W. Heisig and Paul Knitter. New York: Macmillan, 1988.

Dupont, Joan. "Mira Nair Peels Back Layers of Punjabi Society." *International Herald Tribune*. 2001, www.mirabaifilms.com/wordpress/?page_id=32 (accessed 10 February 2008).

Earhart, H. Byron. *Religion in the Japanese Experience: Sources and Interpretations*. Belmont, CA: Wadsworth, 1997.

Earhart, H. Byron. *Religions of Japan: Many Traditions within One Sacred Way*. San Francisco: Harper & Row, 1984.

Eberhard, Wolfram. *A Dictionary of Chinese Symbols: Hidden Symbols in Chinese Life and Thought*. New York: Routledge, 1988.

Ehrlich, Richard S. "Tsunami: Thousands of Cremations a Grim Task." *Scoop*. 2005, www.scoop.co.nz/stories/HL0501/S00019.htm (accessed 11 February 2008).

"Elora Danan." *Star Wars: Databank*, www.starwars.com/databank/updates/401/character/eloradanan (accessed 11 Feb 2008).

Epstien, Dan. "The Mouse That Roared." *ugo.com*, www.ugo.com/channels/filmTv/features/brucejoelrubin (accessed 17 February 2008).

Fairbank, John King, and Merle Goldman. *China: A New History*. Cambridge, MA: Belknap Press of Harvard University Press, 2006.

Fan, Maureen. "Confucius Making a Comeback in Money-Driven Modern China." *Washington Post*. 2007, www.washingtonpost.com/wp-dyn/content/article/2007/07/23/AR2007072301859 .html (accessed 25 January 2008).

Farmer, Edward. "Ming Foundations of Late Imperial China." In *Sources of Chinese Tradition: From Earliest Times to 1600*. Compiled by Wm. Theodore de Bary and Irene Bloom. New York: Columbia University Press, 1999.

Feldman, Steven. "Hayao Miyazaki Biography." *nausicaa.net*. 1994, www.nausicaa.net/miyazaki/ miyazaki/miyazaki_biography.txt (accessed 30 January 2008).

Ferguson, George. *Signs and Symbols in Christian Art*. New York: Oxford University Press, 1954.

Fieser, James, and John Powers. *Scriptures of the World's Religions*. Boston: McGraw Hill, 2004.

Fischbach, Bob. "Payne's Choices for Film Streams Lean to Classics." *Omaha World Herald*. 2007, www.omaha.com/index.php?u_page=2620&u_sid=10070942 (accessed 30 January 2008).

Fischer, Norman. "Revealing a World of Bliss." *Tricycle: The Buddhist Review* (Winter 2006): 72.

Fisher, Jude. *The Lord of the Rings: Complete Visual Companion*. Boston: Houghton Mifflin, 2004.

Fisher, Mary Pat . *Living Religions*. Upper Saddle River, NJ: Prentice-Hall, 2005.

Fitch, John, III. "Odysseus, St. Paul, Christ and the American Cinematic Hero and Anti-Hero." *Journal of Religion and Film*. 2005, http://www.unomaha.edu/~jrf/Vol9No1/FitchArchetypes .htm (accessed 12 February 2008).

Foltz, Richard C., ed. "Genesis 1—The Most Misunderstood Part of the Bible." In *Worldviews, Religion and the Environment: A Global Anthology*. Belmont, CA: Wadsworth/Thomson, 2003.

Foster, Robert. *Tolkien's World from A to Z: The Complete Guide to Middle-Earth*. New York: Ballantine Books, 1978.

Fremantle, Francesca. *Luminous Emptiness: Understanding the Tibetan Book of the Dead*. Boston: Shambhala, 2003.

"Frodo Lives: Elijah Wood Reflects on a Journey for the Ages." *lordofthe rings.net*, www.lordof therings.net/legend/interviews/elijahwood (accessed 12 February 2008).

"From Birth to Exile." *dalailama.com*. www.dalailama.com/page.4.htm (accessed 15 February 2008).

Fronsdal, Gil. *The Dhammapada: A New Translation of the Buddhist Classic with Annotations*. Boston: Shambhala, 2006.

Fujimori, Leila. "Traditions Preserved at Shinto Temple." *Star Bulletin*. 2004, starbulletin.com/ 2004/01/05/news/story7.html (accessed 27 January 2008).

Galipeau, Steven A. *The Journey of Luke Skywalker: An Analysis of Modern Myth and Symbol*. Peru, IL: Open Court, 2001.

Gandhi, Mohandas K. *The Story of My Experiments with Truth*. New York: Dover, 1983.

Garland, Robert. *The Greek Way of Death*. Ithaca, NY: Cornell University Press, 2001.

Gerstenfeld, Manfred. "Jewish Environmental Studies: A New Field." *Jerusalem Center for Public Affairs*. April 2001, http://www.jcpa.org/art/jep1.htm (accessed 11 February 2008).

Glasson, Thomas Francis. "Heaven." In *The Oxford Companion to the Bible.* Edited by Bruce M. Metzger and Michael D. Coogan. New York: Oxford University Press, 1993.

"*Gokito*—Private Ceremonies." *Hawaii Kotohira Jinsha – Hawaii Dazaifu Tenmangu.* www .e-shrine.org/privateceremonies.html (accessed 17 February 2008).

Gokulsing, K. Moti, and Wimal Dissanayake. *Indian Popular Cinema: A Narrative of Cultural Change.* Stoke on Trent, UK: Trentham Books, 1998.

Gore, Al. *Earth in the Balance: Ecology and the Human Spirit.* Boston, MA: Houghton Mifflin, 1992.

Gorman, Ed. "Richard Matheson—Part Two—The Interview." *Filmfax.* 2006, edgormanrambles .blogspot.com/2006/03/richard-matheson-part-two-interview.html (accessed 11 February 2008).

Gracia, Jorge J. E. "The Quests of Sam and Gollum for the Happy Life." In *The Lord of the Rings and Philosophy: One Book to Rule Them All.* Edited by Gregory Bassham and Eric Bronson. Chicago: Open Court, 2003.

Graham, A. C. "The Origins of the Legend of Lao Tan." In *Lao-tzu and the Tao-te-ching.* Edited by Livia Kohn and Michael LaFargue. Albany: State University of New York Press, 1998.

Grilli, Peter. "Akira Kurosawa: A Giant among Filmmakers and among Men." *PBS: Great Performances.* www.pbs.org/wnet/gperf/shows/kurosawa/essay1.html (accessed 30 January 2008).

Gross, Rita M. "Toward a Buddhist Environmental Ethic." In *Worldviews, Religion and the Environment: A Global Anthology.* Edited by Richard C. Foltz. Belmont, CA: Wadsworth/Thomson, 2003.

"Guardian Angel." *The New Advent Catholic Encyclopedia.* www.newadvent.org/cathen/07049c .htm (accessed 12 February 2008).

Gunde, Richard. *Culture and Customs of China.* Westport, CT: Greenwood Press, 2002.

Guthrie, Stan. "Dick Staub on the Star Wars Myth." *Christianity Today.* 2005, http://ctlibrary .com/34605 (accessed 11 February 2008).

Gutschow, Kim. *Being a Buddhist Nun: The Struggle for Enlightenment in the Himalayas.* Cambridge, MA: Harvard University Press, 2004.

Gyatso, Tenzin. "Compassion and the Individual." *dalailama.com,* www.dalailama.com/page.166 .htm (accessed 31 January 2008).

Hall, Kenji. "Buddhist Monk Completes Seven-Year Run." *Salon.com.* 2003, dir.salon.com/story/ mwt/wire/2003/09/19/monk_run/index.html (accessed 11 February 2008).

Halpern, Baruch. *David's Secret Demons: Messiah, Murderer, Traitor, King.* Bible in Its World. Grand Rapids, MI: Wm. B. Eerdmans, 2003.

Hanh, Thich Nhat. *For a Future to Be Possible: Commentaries on the Five Wonderful Precepts.* Berkeley, CA: Parallax Press, 1993.

Hanh, Thich Nhat. *The Heart of the Buddha's Teaching: Transforming Suffering into Peace, Joy and Liberation.* New York: Broadway Books, 1999.

Hanh, Thich Nhat. "What Happens When You Die?" *plumvillage.org.* 2007, www.plumvillage
.org/dharmatalks/html/whathappenswhenyoudie.html (accessed 15 February 2008).

Harris, Stephen L. *Understanding the Bible.* 3rd ed. London: Mayfield, 1985.

Harris, Stephen L. *Understanding the Bible.* 7th ed. Boston: McGraw Hill, 2007.

Harvey, Peter. *An Introduction to Buddhism: Teachings, History and Practices.* Cambridge: Cambridge University Press, 2002.

Hawaii Kotohira Jinsha - Hawaii Dazaifu Tenmangu. www.e-shrine.org/home.html (accessed 28 January 2008).

Hawkins, Stewart. "Theosophy." *virginia.edu.* 1998, etext.lib.virginia.edu/relmove/nrms/theosophy
.html (accessed 17 February 2008).

Henderson, Mary. *Star Wars: The Magic of Myth.* New York: Bantam Spectra, 1997.

"Hindu Leader Says Lesbian Film Should Be about Moslem Family." *South Asian Woman's Network.* 1999, www.sawnet.org/news/fire.html#2 (accessed 10 February 2008).

"Hindus-Muslim Violence Imperials India." *Time Magazine.* 2002, www.time.com/time/world/
article/0,8599,213670,00.html (accessed 10 February 2008).

Hirst, Jacqueline Suthren. "Myth and History." In Themes and Issues in Hinduism. Edited by Paul Bowen. London: Cassell, 1998.

The History of the Buddha's Relic Shrine. A translation of the *Sinhala Thupavamsa.* Translated by Stephen C. Berkwitz. Atlanta, GA: American Academy of Religion, 2006.

Holtom, D. C. "The Meaning of *Kami.*" In *Religion in the Japanese Experience: Sources and Interpretations.* Edited by H. Byron Earhart. Belmont, CA: Wadsworth, 1997.

Hooker, Richard. "Bhagavad Gita Krishna's Answer." *Washington State University,* 1996, www
.wsu.edu/~dee/ancindia/gita2.htm (accessed 10 February 2008).

Hori, Ichiro. *Folk Religion in Japan: Continuity and Change.* Edited by Joseph Kitagawa and Alan L. Miller. Chicago: University of Chicago Press, 1968.

Hori, Victor Sogen. "The Nature of the *Rinzai (Linji)* Koan Practice." In *Sitting with Koans.* Edited by John Daido Loori. Boston: Wisdom, 2006.

"House of Flying Daggers." *sonyclassics.com.* 2003, www.sonyclassics.com/houseofflyingdaggers/
_media/presskit.pdf (accessed 12 February 2008).

"How to Perform the Daily Prayers." *Al-Islam.org.* al-islam.org/nutshell/files/prayers.pdf (accessed 10 February 2008).

Hsiao-Lan, Hu, and William Cully Allen. *Taoism.* Philadelphia: Chelsea House, 2005.

Hsu, Francis L. K. *Under the Ancestor's Shadow: Kinship, Personality, and Social Mobility in China.* Palo Alto, CA: Stanford University Press, 1971.

Huang Ti Nei Ching Su Wen: The Yellow Emperor's Classic of Internal Medicine. Translated by Ilza Veith. Berkeley: University of California Press, 1972.

"India—Politics by Other Means: Attacks against Christians in India." *Human Rights Watch* 11, no. 6(C). Available at www.hrw.org/reports/pdfs/i/india/india999.pdf (accessed 10 February 2008).

"India's Unwanted: 30 Million Widows." *International Herald Tribune.* 2005, www.iht.com/articles/2005/01/30/news/India.php (accessed 10 February 2008).

"Indian in Western Hearts." *buzzle.com.* 2005, www.buzzle.com/editorials/3-31-2005-67849.asp (accessed 10 February 2008).

"The Instruction to the Kalamas." *Buddhistinformation.com.* www.buddhistinformation.com/the_kalama_sutra.htm (accessed 10 January 2008).

"Interview: Sean Astin as 'Samwise the Brave.'" *movieweb.com.* 2003, www.movieweb.com/news/45/2245.php (accessed 12 February 2008).

"Introduction: Beyond Lynn White, Jr." *counterbalance.net.* www.counterbalance.net/enviro/intro-frame.html (accessed 10 February 2008).

"Introduction: The Nature of Japanese Religion." In *Religion in the Japanese Experience: Sources and Interpretations.* Edited by H. Byron Earhart. Belmont, CA: Wadsworth, 1997.

Iwasaka, Michiko, and Barre Toelken. *Ghosts and the Japanese: Cultural Experience in Japanese Death Legends.* Logan: Utah State University Press, 1994.

"Jacob's Ladder." *imdb.com.* www.imdb.com/title/tt0099871/ (accessed 17 February 2008).

Jaishankar, K., and Debarati Haldar. "Religious Identity of the Perpetrators and Victims of Communal Violence in Post-Independence India." *ERCES Online Quarterly.* 2004, www.erces.com/journal/articles/archives/v02/v_02_04.htm (accessed 17 February 2008).

"Jehovah (Yahweh)." *The New Advent Catholic Encyclopedia.* www.newadvent.org/cathen/08329a.htm (accessed 12 February 2008).

Jianying, Huo. "Heroic, Historic, Operatic Yang Generals." *Chinatoday.* 2006, www.chinatoday.com.cn/English/e2006/e200602/2p52.htm (accessed 1 February 2008).

Jung, C. G. *The Basic Writings of C. G. Jung.* Edited by Violet Staub de Laszlo. New York: Modern Library, 1959.

Jung, C. G. "The Psychology of the Child Archetype." In *Psyche & Symbol: A Selection from the Writings of C. G. Jung.* Edited by Violet S. de Laszlo. New York: Anchor, 1958.

"Kachi-Kachi Yama." *baxleystamsp.com.* www.baxleystamps.com/litho/hasegawa/kachi.shtml (accessed 17 February 2008).

"The Kalachakra Mandala." *tibet.com.* 1997, www.tibet.com/Buddhism/kala1.html (accessed 17 February 2008).

Kamachi, Noriko. *Culture and Customs of Japan.* Westport, CT: Greenwood, 1999.

Karnow, Stanley. *Mao and China: A Legacy of Turmoil.* New York: Penguin Books, 1990.

Kasulis, Thomas P. *Shinto: The Way Home.* Honolulu: University of Hawaii Press, 2004.

"Katas or Silk Scarves." *tibet.com.* 1998, www.tibet.com/Buddhism/katas.html (accessed 17 February 2008).

Kelleher, Theresa. "Women's Education." In *Sources of Chinese Tradition: From Earliest Times to 1600.* Compiled by Compiled by Wm. Theodore de Bary and Irene Bloom. New York: Columbia University Press, 1999.

Khan, Yoshimitsu. *Japanese Moral Education Past and* Present. Cranbury, NJ: Associated University Presses, 1997.

Khyentse, Dzongsar Jamyang. *What Makes You Not a Buddhist.* Boston, MA: Shambhala, 2007.

"Kingdom of God." *The New Advent Catholic Encyclopedia.* www.newadvent.org/cathen/08646a .htm (accessed 12 February 2008).

Kinsey, Robert O. "21st Century Netsuke." *netsukeonline.org.* www.netsukeonline.org/htm/kinsey _lecture.html (accessed 27 January 2008).

Kipnis, Andrew B. "The Flourishing of Religion in Post-Mao China and the Anthropological Category of Religion." *Australian Journal of Anthropology* 12 (no. 1, 2001): 32–46. Also available at rspas.anu.edu.au/papers/ccc/AK_flourishing_religion.pdf (accessed 21 February 2008).

"Kirin." *The Obakemono Project.* www.obakemono.com/obake/kirin (accessed 28 January 2008).

Klostermaier, Klaus K. *A Concise Encyclopedia of Hinduism.* Oxford: One World, 1998.

Klostermaier, Klaus K. *Hinduism: A Short History.* Oxford: One World, 2000.

Klostermaier, Klaus K. *A Survey of Hinduism.* Albany: State University of New York Press, 1994.

Knappert, January. *An Encyclopedia of Myth and Legend: Indian Mythology.* London: Diamond Books, 1995.

Kohn, Livia. *Daoism and Chinese Culture.* Cambridge, MA: Three Pines Press, 2004.

Kohn, Livia. *Early Chinese Mysticism: Philosophy and Soteriology in the Taoist Tradition.* Princeton, NJ: Princeton University Press, 1992.

Kohn, Livia. "The Lao-tzu Myth." In *Lao-tzu and the Tao-te-ching.* Edited by Livia Kohn and Michael LaFargue. Albany: State University of New York Press, 1998.

Kohn, Livia. *The Taoist Experience: An Anthology.* Albany: State University of New York Press, 1993.

Kohn, Michael H. *The Shambhala Dictionary of Buddhism and Zen.* Boston: Shambhala, 1991.

Kokas, Aynne. "The Ring of Fire." *Asia Pacific Arts.* 2006, www.asiaarts.ucla.edu/061222/article .asp?parentID=59580 (accessed 28 January 2008).

Kolatch, Alfred J. *The Jewish Book of Why.* New York: Penguin Compass, 2000.

Kornfield, Jack. "Introduction." *Jesus and Buddha: The Parallel Sayings.* Edited by Marcus J. Borg. Berkeley, CA: Ulysses Press, 2004.

Kshetra, Dharma. "The Matsya Purana." www.dharmakshetra.com/avatars/Matsya%20Purans .html (accessed 10 February 2008).

Kumar, Rajesh. "Mira Nair Returns to Her Kolkata Chromosomes with 'Namesake.'" *KolkataScoop.* 2005, www.mirabaifilms.com/wordpress/?page_id=48 (accessed 10 February 2008).

"Kuo Tzu-I." *Encyclopedia Britannica Online.* www.britannica.com/eb/article-9046452 (accessed 13 February 2008).

"The Kusti Ritual." *Avesta-Zoroastrian Archives.* www.avesta.org/ritual/ritualk.htm (accessed 10 February 2008).

Kutcher, Norman Alan. *Mourning in Late Imperial China: Filial Piety and the State.* New York: Cambridge University Press, 1999.

Lau, D. C. "Introduction." *Mencius.* New York: Penguin Books, 1970.

Lau, Theodora. *The Handbook of Chinese Horoscopes.* New York: Harper & Row, 1979.

Law, Joan, and Barbara E. Ward. *Chinese Festivals in Hong Kong.* Hong Kong: South China Morning Post, 1982.

The Laws of Manu. Translated by Wendy Doniger and Brian K. Smith. New York: Penguin Books, 1991.

"Legalists and Militarists." In *Sources of Chinese Tradition: From Earliest Times to 1600.* Compiled by Wm. Theodore de Bary and Irene Bloom. New York: Columbia University Press, 1999.

"Legend of Bagger Vance." *Hinduism Today.* 2001, www.hinduismtoday.com/archives/2001/3-4/16_bagger_vance.shtml (accessed 10 February 2008).

Levy-Yamamori, Ran, and Gerard Taaffe. *Garden Plants of Japan.* Portland, OR: Timber Press, 2004.

Lief, Judith L. *Making Friends with Death: A Buddhist Guide to Encountering Mortality.* Boston: Shambhala, 2001.

Liu I-Ming. *Awakening to the Tao.* Translated by Thomas Cleary. Boston: Shambhala, 2006.

Logan, Pamela. "Witness to a Tibetan Sky-Burial: A Field Report for the China Exploration and Research Society." *caltech.edu.* 1997, alumnus.caltech.edu/~pamlogan/skybury.htm (accessed 17 February 2008).

Lopez, Donald S., Jr. "Exorcising Demons with a Buddhist Sutra." In *Religions of Tibet in Practice.* Edited by Donald S. Lopez Jr. Princeton, NJ: Princeton University Press, 1997.

Lopez, Donald S., Jr., ed. *Religions of Tibet in Practice.* Princeton, NJ: Princeton University Press, 1997.

Loy, David R. "The Nonduality of Good and Evil: Buddhist Reflections on the New Holy War." *The Pacific Rim Report No. 25.* 2002, www.pacificrim.usfca.edu/research/pacrimreport/pacrimreport25.html (accessed 12 February 2008).

Luceno, James. *Star Wars: Revenge of the Sith—The Visual Dictionary.* New York: DK, 2005.

"Luke, The Gospel According to." In The *Oxford Companion to the Bible,* edited by Bruce M. Metzger and Michael D. Coogan. New York: Oxford University Press, 1993.

Lyons, Elizabeth, Heather Peters, Ch'eng-mei Chang, and Gregory L. Possehl. *Buddhism: History and Diversity of a Great Tradition.* Philadelphia: University of Pennsylvania Museum, 1985.

Macartney, Jane. "Ghost Brides Are Murdered to Give Dead Bachelors a Wife in the Afterlife." *The Times.* 2007, www.timesonline.co.uk/tol/news/world/asia/article1296184.ece (accessed 12 February 2008).

Mackenzie, Vicki. "Jeweled Demise." *Tricycle* (Spring 2007): 74–77, 118–19.

Major, Andrea, ed. *Sati: A Historical Anthology.* Oxford: Oxford University Press, 2007.

"Making Orders Strict." The Book of Lord Shang. *Sources of Chinese Tradition: From Earliest Times to 1600.* Compiled by Wm. Theodore de Bary and Irene Bloom. New York: Columbia University Press, 1999.

Mann, Susan. "Grooming a Daughter for Marriage: Brides and Wives in the Mid-Qing Period." In *Chinese Femininities/Chinese Masculinities: A Reader.* Edited by Susan Brownell and Jeffrey N. Wasserstrom. Berkeley: University of California Press, 2002.

"Many Stories in India Are Just Crying Out to Be Made." *Cinema India-International.* 1988, www.mirabaifilms.com/wordpress/?page_id=17 (accessed 10 February 2008).

Martin, Elaine. "Rethinking the Practice of *Mizuko Kuyo* in Contemporary Japan: Interviews with Practitioners at a Buddhist Temple in Tokyo." *University of Alabama.* bama.ua.edu/~emartin/publications/mkarticl.htm (accessed 30 January 2008).

Martin, Emily. "Gender and Ideological Differences in Representations of Life and Death." In *Death Ritual in Late Imperial and Modern China.* Edited by James L. Watson and Evelyn S. Rawski. Berkeley: University of California Press, 1988.

Marx, Karl. "Contribution to the Critique of Hegel's Philosophy of Right." *baylor.edu.* 1www3.baylor.edu/~Scott_Moore/texts/Marx_Contr_Crit.html (accessed 21 February 2008). Originally published 1844.

"Matakabhatta Jataka." *accesstoinsight.org.* www.accesstoinsight.org/lib/authors/kawasaki/bl135.html#jat018 (accessed 15 February 2008).

Matheson, Richard. *The Path: A New Look at Reality.* New York: Tor Books, 1993.

Matsunaga, Daigan, and Alicia Matsunaga. *The Buddhist Concept of Hell.* New York: Philosophical Library, 1972.

McBrien, Richard P. *Catholicism.* New York: HarperCollins, 1994.

McDannell, Colleen, and Bernhard Lang. *Heaven: A History.* New York: Vintage Books, 1990.

"McDonald's Supersizes Hindu Endowment." *Hinduism Today.* www.hinduismtoday.com/press_releases/mcdonalds (accessed 10 February 2008).

McDowell, John. *The Gospel According to Star Wars: Faith, Hope and the Force.* Louisville, KY: Westminster Knox Press, 2007.

McLeod, Hew. *Sikhism.* New York: Penguin, 1997.

McMahon, Jennifer L., and B. Steve Csaki. "Talking Trees and Walking Mountains: Buddhist and Taoist Themes." In *The Lord of the Rings and Philosophy: One Book to Rule Them All.* Edited by Gregory Bassham and Eric Bronson. Chicago: Open Court, 2003.

Mehta, Deepa. "What's Wrong with My Film? Why Are People Making Such a Big Fuss: Deepa Mehta Defends Her Film, *Fire.*" *Rediff.com.* 1998, www.rediff.com/entertai/1998/dec/10fire.htm (accessed 10 February 2008).

Menski, Werner. "Hinduism." In *Ethical Issues in Six Religious Traditions.* Edited by Peggy Morgan and Clive Lawton. Edinburgh: Edinburgh University Press, 2004.

Mes, Tom, and Jasper Sharp. *The Midnight Eye Guide to New Japanese Film*. Berkeley, CA: Stone Bridge Press, 2005.

Miyake, Hitoshi. "Rites of Passage." In *Religion in the Japanese Experience: Sources and Interpretations*. 2nd ed. Edited by H. Byron Earhart. Belmont, CA: Wadsworth, 1997.

Miyazaki, Hayao. "Chihiro's Mysterious Town: The Aim of This Film." In *The Art of Miyazaki's Spirited Away*. San Francisco: VIZ, 2004.

Miyazaki, Hayao. *My Neighbor Totoro: Picture Book*. Translated by Naoko Amemiya. San Francisco: VIZ Media, 2005.

Moeller, Hans-Georg. *Daoism Explained: From the Dream of the Butterfly to the Fishnet Allegory*. Chicago: Open Court, 2004.

Morgan, Peggy. "Buddhism." In *Ethical Issues in Six Religious Traditions*. Edited by Peggy Morgan and Clive Lawton. Edinburgh, Scotland: Edinburgh University Press, 2004.

Moskowitz, Marc L. *The Haunting Fetus: Abortion, Sexuality, and the Spirit World in Taiwan*. Honolulu: University of Hawaii Press, 2001.

Mukherjea, Ananya. "indo-chic." www.makezine.org/indo.html (accessed 10 February 2008).

Murata, Sachiko, and William C. Chittick. *The Vision of Islam*. New York: Paragon House, 1994.

Nadeau, Kathleen. "Confucianism: Sacred or Secular." *Ateneo de Manila University*. eapi.admu.edu.ph/eapr005/nadeau.htm (accessed 5 May 2008).

Napier, Susan. *Anime from Akira to Howl's Moving Castle, Updated Edition: Experiencing Contemporary Japanese Animation*. New York: Palgrave Macmillan, 2005.

Narayan, R. K. *The Ramayana: A Shortened Modern Prose Version of the Indian Epic*. New York: Penguin Books, 1972.

Nasr, Seyyed Hossein. *Islam: Religion, History, and Civilization*. San Francisco: Harper San Francisco, 2003.

"Nechung—The State Oracle of Tibet." *tibet.com*. 1997, www.tibet.com/Buddhism/nechung_hh.html (accessed 15 February 2008).

Nesbitt, Eleanor. "Sikhism." In *Ethical Issues in Six Religious Traditions*. Edited by Peggy Morgan and Clive Lawton. Edinburgh, Scotland: Edinburgh University Press, 1996.

"New Mehta Film about Kamagata Maru Incident." *Canadian Broadcasting Corporation*. 2006, www.cbc.ca/news/story/2006/10/24/exclusion-mehta.html (accessed 10 February 2008).

The New World Dictionary-Concordance to the New American Bible. Charlotte, NC: C. D. Stampley, 1970.

Newport, Frank. "Americans More Likely to Believe in God Than the Devil; Heaven More than Hell." *Gallup News Service*, www.gallup.com/poll/27877/Americans-More-Likely-Believe-God-Than-Devil-Heaven-More-Than-Hell.aspx (accessed 11 February 2008).

Ni, Chin-Ching. "China Turns to Confucius, with a Modern Twist." *Los Angeles Times*. 2007, www.latimes.com/news/nationworld/world/la-fg-confucius7may07,0,5796389,full.story (accessed 21 February 2008)

Nigosian, S. A. *The Zoroastrian Faith: Tradition and Modern Research.* Montréal: McGill-Queen's University Press, 1993.

Nihongi. Translated by W. G. Aston. Rutland, VT: Tuttle, 1972.

Norbu, Khyentse. "Comments from Writer-Director Khyentse Norbu." *zeitgeistfilms.com.* 2003, www.zeitgeistfilms.com/films/travellersandmagicians/presskit.pdf (accessed 17 February 2008).

Norget, Kristin. *Religion and Culture: An Anthropological Focus.* Upper Saddle River, NJ: Prentice Hall, 2007.

Numerical Discourses of the Buddha: An Anthology of Suttas from the Anguttara Nikaya. Translated and edited by Nyanaponika Thera and Bhikku Bodhi. Walnut Creek, CA: Altamira Press, 1999.

Obst, Lynda. "Valentine to Science: Interview with Carl Sagan." *Interview Magazine.* 1996, findarticles.com/p/articles/mi_m1285/is_n2_v26/ai_18082728/pg_1 (accessed 11 February 2008).

Office of the Registrar General. *Census of India.* 2001, www.censusindiamaps.net/page/Religion _WhizMap1/housemap.htm (accessed 10 February 2008).

Okano, Haruko. "Summary: Woman and the Shinto Religion." In *Religion in the Japanese Experience: Sources and Interpretations.* Edited by H. Byron Earhart. Belmont, CA: Wadsworth, 1997.

Oldstone-Moore, Jennifer. *Taoism.* New York: Oxford University Press, 2003.

Ono, Kazuko. *Chinese Women in a Century of Revolution (1850–1950).* Edited by Joshua A. Fogel. Palo Alto, CA: Stanford University Press, 1989.

Onuma, Hideharu with Dan and Jackie DeProspero. *The Essence and Practice of Japanese Archery.* New York: Kodansha International, 1993.

Orenstein, Peggy. "Mourning My Miscarriage: In Japan, I Find a Culture Willing to Acknowledge My Loss." *New York Times Magazine.* 2002, www.peggyorenstein.com/articles/2002_mourning _miscarriage.html (accessed 30 January 2008).

Osnos, Evan. "Sage for the Ages Makes a Comeback." *Chicago Tribune.* 2007, www.venturacounty star.com/news/2007/jun/09/a-sage-for-the-ages-makes-a-comeback/ (accessed 21 February 2008).

"Our Knowledge of God and Nature: Physics, Philosophy and Theology." *L'Osservatore Romano,* 1988, clavius.as.arizona.edu/vo/R1024/ppt-Message.html (accessed 11 February 2008).

The Oxford Companion to the Bible. Edited by Bruce M. Metzger and Michael D. Coogan. New York: Oxford University Press, 1993.

Oxtoby, William G., and Alan F. Segal, eds. *A Concise Introduction to World Religions* (New York: Oxford University Press, 2007).

The Padawan's Guide to Star Wars Costumes. www.padawansguide.com (accessed 11 February 2008).

Pagels, Elaine. *Beyond Belief: The Secret Gospel of Thomas.* New York: Vintage, 2004.

Paine, Jeffrey. *Re-enchantment: Tibetan Buddhism Comes to the West.* New York: W. W. Norton, 2004.

Palahniuk, Chuck. *Fight Club.* New York: W. W. Norton, 1996.

Pals, Daniel L. *Eight Theories of Religion.* New York: Oxford University Press, 2006.

Party Central Committee. "The Sixteen Points: Guidelines for the Great Proletarian Cultural Revolution." In *Sources of Chinese Tradition: From 1600 through the Twentieth Century.* Compiled by Wm. Theodore de Bary and Richard LuFranco. New York: Columbia University Press, 2000.

Pelikan, Jaroslav, ed. *Judaism: The Tanakh.* Vol. 1 of Sacred Writings. Philadelphia, PA: Jewish Publication Society, 1985.

Pelikan, Jaroslav, ed. *Judaism: The Tanakh, The New JPS Translation. Sacred Writings.* New York: Quality Paperback Club, 1992.

Philippi, Donald L. *Norito: A Translation of the Ancient Japanese Ritual Prayers.* Princeton, NJ: Princeton University Press, 1990.

Phillips, Richard. "If People Want to Separate, They Should Understand What It Would Really Mean." *The World Socialist Web Site.* 1999, www.wsws.org/articles/1999/aug1999/meh-a06 .shtml (accessed 10 February 2008).

Picken, Stuart D. B. *The A to Z of Shinto.* Lanham, MD: Scarecrow Press, 2006.

Picken, Stuart D. B. *Essentials of Shinto: An Analytical Guide to Principal Teachings.* Westport, CT: Greenwood Press, 1994.

Pitard, Wayne T. "Afterlife and Immortality: Ancient Israel." In *The Oxford Companion to the Bible.* Edited by Bruce M. Metzger and Michael D. Coogan. New York: Oxford University Press, 1993.

Plato. "Symposium." *Internet Classics Archive.* classics.mit.edu/Plato/symposium.html (accessed 11 February 2008).

Plutschow, Herbert. *Matsuri: The Festivals of Japan.* Surrey, UK: Japan Library, 1996.

Pollard, Mark. "Wuxia Pian." *Green Cine.* 2005, www.greencine.com/static/primers/wuxia1.jsp (accessed 21 February 2008).

Pollock, Dave. *Skywalking: The Life and Films of George Lucas.* New York: Harmony Books, 1983.

"Position and Purpose of Prayer in Islam." *Kingdom of Saudi Arabia's Ministry of Islamic Affairs, Endowments, Da'wah and Guidance.* www.al-islam.com/articles/articles-e.asp?fname=Alislam _R30_E (accessed 10 February 2008).

Powers, John. *Introduction to Tibetan Buddhism.* Ithaca, NY: Snow Lion, 1995.

Prebish, Charles S., and Kenneth K. Tanaka, eds. *The Faces of Buddhism in America.* Berkeley: University of California Press, 1998.

"Production Notes." *Mongrel Media.* 2005, water.mahiram.com/production.html (accessed 10 February 2008).

"Production Notes." *the-cup.com.* www.the-cup.com/cup_aboutproduction.html (accessed 17 February 2008).

Questions to a Zen Master: Taisen Deshimaru. Translated by Nancy Amphoux. New York: E.P. Dutton, 1985.

Qigong Institute. www.qigonginstitute.org/main_page/main_page.php (accessed 11 November 2007).

Rahula, Walpola. *What the Buddha Taught: Revised and Expanded Edition with Texts from Suttas and Dhammapada.* New York: Grove Press, 1974.

Ramacharaka, Yogi. *Life beyond Death.* Whitefish, MT: Kessinger, 2003.

Rambachan, Anantanand. "Human Nature and Destiny." In *Themes and Issues in Hinduism.* Edited by Paul Bowen. London: Cassell, 1998.

Ray, Reginald A. *Buddhist Saints in India: A Study in Buddhist Values and Orientations.* New York: Oxford University Press, 1994.

Reader, Ian. *Religion in Contemporary Japan.* Honolulu: University of Hawaii Press, 1991.

Reicke, Bo. "Gehenna." In *The Oxford Companion to the Bible.* Edited by Bruce M. Metzger and Michael D. Coogan. New York: Oxford University Press, 1993.

"Religion and Ethics—Islam." *British Broadcasting Corporation.* 2006, www.bbc.co.uk/religion/religions/islam/practices/salat.shtml (accessed 10 February 2008).

"Religion and National Identity." *tibet.com.* 1996, www.tibet.com/WhitePaper/white7.html (accessed 17 February 2008).

"The Religious Affiliation of Director George Lucas." *adherents.com.* 2005, www.adherents.com/people/pl/George_Lucas.html (accessed 11 February 2008).

"Religious Emblems." *Sikhism.* www.sikhs.org/khanda.htm (accessed 10 February 2008).

"The Revelation to John." In *The New Oxford Annotated Bible, Revised Standard Version.* New York: Oxford University Press, 1973.

Reynolds, David West. *Star Wars Episode I: The Visual Dictionary.* New York: DK, 1999.

Reynolds, David West, James Luceno, and Ryder Windham. *Star Wars: The Complete Visual Dictionary.* New York: DK, 2006.

Reynolds, John Myrdhin. "Wisdom Dakinis, Passionate and Wrathful." *Vajranatha.* 2008, http://www.vajranatha.com/teaching/Dakinis.htm (accessed 11 February 2008).

Rinehart, Robin, ed. *Contemporary Hinduism: Ritual, Culture and Practice.* Santa Barbara, CA: ABC-CLIO, 2004.

Rinkya—Japan Auction & Shopping Service. "Hina Ningyou: The 'Doll' in 'Doll Festival.'" *rinkya.com.* 2004, www.rinkya.com/newsletter/01132004.php (accessed 26 January 2008).

Rinpoche, Sogyal. *The Tibetan Book of Living and Dying.* Edited by Patrick Gaffney and Andrew Harvey. San Francisco: Harper San Francisco, 1992.

Rinzler, J. W. *The Making of Star Wars: Based on the Lost Interviews from the Official Lucasfilm Archives.* New York: Ballantine Books, 2007.

Robinet, Isabelle. *Taoism: Growth of a Religion*. Translated by Phyllis Brooks. Palo Also, CA: Stanford University Press, 1997.

Robinson, George. *Essential Judaism: A Complete Guide to Beliefs, Customs and Rituals*. New York: Pocket Books, 2000.

"Rokuro-kubi." *The Obakemono Project*. www.obakemono.com/obake/rokurokubi (accessed 28 January 2008).

Rosen, Steven J. *Gita on the Green: The Mystical Tradition behind Bagger Vance*. New York: Continuum International, 2000.

Rosen, Steven J. "Yoda and Yoga." *Beliefnet*. www.beliefnet.com/story/166/story_16672_1.html (accessed 11 February 2008).

Rosenberg, Joel. "Bible: Biblical Narrative." In *Back to the Sources: Reading the Classic Jewish Texts*. Edited by Barry W. Holtz. New York: Simon & Schuster, 1984.

Rosenbush, Marc. "Profound Questions." *zenmovie.com*. www.zenmovie.com/questions.html (accessed 17 February 2008).

Rubin, Bruce Joel. "Jacob's Ladder." *dailyscript.com*. www.dailyscript.com/scripts/JacobsLadder.html (accessed 17 February 2008).

Rubin, Bruce Joel. *Jacob's Ladder*. New York: Applause Theatre Book, 1990.

Ruozhao, Song. "Analects for Women." In *Sources of Chinese Tradition: From Earliest Times to 1600*. Compiled by Wm. Theodore de Bary and Irene Bloom. New York: Columbia University Press, 1999.

Saito, Yuriko. "The Japanese Appreciation of Nature." In *Worldviews, Religion, and the Environment: A Global Anthology*. Edited by Richard C. Foltz. Belmont, CA: Wadsworth, 2003.

Sakade, Florence. *Japanese Children's Favorite Stories*. North Clarendon, VT: Tuttle, 2003.

"Salah: The Muslim Prayer." *University of Buffalo Muslim Student Association*. wings.buffalo.edu/sa/muslim/library/salah/index.html (accessed 10 February 2008).

"Sam." *lordoftherings.net*. www.lordoftherings.net/legend/characters/detail.html?sam (accessed 12 February 2008).

Sangh, Rashtriya Swayamsevak. 2003, www.rss.org/New_RSS/Mission_Vision/Why_RSS.jsp (accessed 10 February 2008).

Sardar, Ziauddin. "Haunted by the Politics of Hate." *New Statesman*. 2006, www.newstatesman.com/200601300022 (accessed 10 February 2008).

Sato, Ryuzaburo. "Contraceptive Use and Induced Abortion in Japan—How Is It So Unique among the Developed Countries?" *National Institute of Population and Social Security Research*. 2005, iussp2005.princeton.edu/download.aspx?submissionId=51736 (accessed 30 January 2008).

Schmid, Holly A. "The Spiritual Athlete's Path to Enlightenment." *Ultra Marathon Running*, 1996, www.lehigh.edu/~dmd1/holly.html (accessed 11 February 2008).

Scholem, Gershom. *Kabbalah*. New York: Meridian, 1978.

Schoppa, R. Keith. *Twentieth-Century China: A History in Documents*. New York: Oxford University Press, 2004.

Schwartz, Benjamin. "The Thought of the *Tao-te-Ching*." In *Lao-tzu and the Tao-te-Ching*. Edited by Livia Kohn and Michael LaFargue. Albany: State University of New York Press, 1998.

Screech, Tim. "Japanese Ghosts." *Mangajin*. www.mangajin.com/mangajin/samplemj/ghosts/ghosts.htm (accessed 30 January 2008).

Seiler, Andy. "You'll Soon Know Mo' about Nemo." *USA Today*. 2003, www.usatoday.com/life/movies/news/2003-06-03-mo-dvd_x.htm (accessed 10 February 2008).

Sekida, Katsuki, trans. *Two Zen Classics: The Gateless Gate and The Blue Cliff Records*. Boston: Shambhala. 2005.

Shaoqi, Liu. "How to Be a Good Communist." In *Sources of Chinese Tradition: From 1600 through the Twentieth Century*. Compiled by Wm. Theodore de Bary and Richard LuFranco. New York: Columbia University Press, 2000.

Shen, Vincent. "Daoism (Taoism): Classical (Dao Jia, Tao Chia)." In *Encyclopedia of Chinese Philosophy*. Edited by Antonio S. Cua. New York: Routledge, 2003.

"Shiba Inu History." *American Kennel Club*. www.akc.org/breeds/shiba_inu/history.cfm (accessed 30 January 2008).

Shippey, Tom. *Tolkien: Author of the Century*. Boston: Houghton Mifflin, 2002.

Shiva, "Sanskrit and *The Matrix*." *The Vaishnava Voice*. 2007, deshika.wordpress.com/2007/08/15/sanskrit-and-the-matrix (accessed 11 February 2008).

"Shōjō." *The Obakemono Project*. www.obakemono.com/obake/shojo (accessed 28 January 2008).

Shun, Kwong-loi. "Moral Philosophy." In *The Encyclopedia of Chinese Philosophy*. Edited by Antonio S. Cua. New York: Routledge, 2003.

"Silent Waters Press Kit." First Run Features. 2003, www.firstrunfeatures.com/shopsite_sc/store/html/presskits/silent_waters_press_kit/silent_waters_press_kit.pdf (accessed 10 February 2008).

Sill, Gertrude Grace. *A Handbook of Symbols in Christian Art*. New York: Collier Books, 1975.

Siu, Wang-Ngai, and Peter Lovrick. *Chinese Opera: Images and Stories*. Seattle: University of Washington Press, 1997.

Slingerland, Edward. *Images of Women in Chinese Thought and Culture: Writings from the Pre-Qin Period through the Song Dynasty*. Edited by Robin R. Wang. Indianapolis, IN: Hackett, 2003.

Sluyter, Dean. *Cinema Nirvana: Enlightenment Lessons from the Movies*. New York: Three Rivers Press, 2005.

Smart, Ninian. *Worldviews: Cross-cultural Explorations of Human Beliefs*. New York: Charles Scribner's Sons, 1983.

Smith, Bruce, and Yoshiko Yamamoto. *The Japanese Bath*. Salt Lake City: Gibbs Smith, 2001.

Smyers, Karen A. *The Fox and the Jewel: Shared and Private Meanings in Contemporary Japanese Inari Worship*. Honolulu: University of Hawaii Press, 1999.

"The Social Construction of 'Self' and Womanhood in a Hindu Village of Bangladesh." *Journal of World Anthropology*. 2007, wings.buffalo.edu/research/anthrogis/JWA/V3N1/Jahan-art.pdf (accessed 10 February 2008).

Sood, Sushma. "Domestic Violence: Towards a New Theoretical Approach." 1994, www.aic.gov .au/publications/proceedings/27/sood.pdf (accessed 10 February 2008).

"Soul Mates: A Primer." *oprah.com*. 2002, www.oprah.com/relationships/relationships_content .jhtml?contentId=con_20020916_soulmates.xml&section=Couplehood&subsection=Dating (accessed 17 February 2008).

"Soulmates." *edgarcayce.org*. www.edgarcayce.org/about_ec/cayce_on/soulmates/index.html (accessed 11 February 2008).

A Source Book in Chinese Philosophy. Translated and compiled by Wing-Tsit Chan. Princeton, NJ: Princeton University Press, 1963.

Sources of Chinese Tradition: From Earliest Times to 1600. Vol. I. Compiled by Wm. Theodore de Bary and Irene Bloom. New York: Columbia University Press, 1999.

Sragow, Michael. "King of Comedy." *Salon.com*. 2000, dir.salon.com/story/ent/col/srag/2000/11/ 02/ramis/index2.html (accessed 17 February 2008).

St. Augustine. *City of God*. Translated by Henry Bettenson. New York: Penguin Classics, 1984.

"St. Michael the Archangel." *The New Advent Catholic Encyclopedia*, www.newadvent.org/cathen/ 10275b.htm (accessed 12 February 2008).

Stanford University News Service, "Djerassi on Birth Control in Japan—Abortion 'Yes,' Pill, 'No.'" www.un.org/esa/population/publications/abortion/doc/japan.doc (accessed 30 January 2008).

Stevens, Keith, and Jennifer Welch. "The Yang Family of Generals." *University of Hong Kong Libraries*. sunzi1.lib.hku.hk/hkjo/view/44/4402407.pdf (accessed 31 January 2008).

Stone, Brad. "Alan Moore Interview." *The Comic Wire*. 2001, www.comicbookresources.com/ news/newsitem.cgi?id=554 (accessed 10 February 2008).

"The Story of the Weeping Camel." *german-cinema.de*. www.german-cinema.de/app/film archive/film_view.php?film_id=1035 (accessed 17 February 2008).

Strand, Clark. "Worry Beads." *Tricycle: The Buddhist Review* (Winter 2006): 38.

Strong, John S. *The Experience of Buddhism: Sources and Interpretations*. Belmont, CA: Wadsworth/Thomson Learning, 2002.

Strong, John S. *Relics of the Buddha*. Princeton, NJ: Princeton University Press, 2004.

Sugirtharajah, Sharada. "Women in Hinduism." In *Themes and Issues in Hinduism*. Edited by Paul Bowen. London: Cassell, 1998.

Sung, Vivien. *Five-Fold Happiness: Chinese Concepts of Luck, Prosperity, Longevity, Happiness and Wealth*. San Francisco, CA: Chronicle Books, 2002.

"Superman: Gay Icon? Christ Figure? New Film Ignites Talk of What, Who Man of Steel Represents." *CBS News*. 2006, www.cbsnews.com/stories/2006/06/14/entertainment/main1711570.shtml (accessed 12 February 2008).

Suzuki, D. T. *An Introduction to Zen Buddhism*. New York: Grove Press, 1964.

Suzuki, Daisetz T. *Zen and Japanese Culture*. New York: Bollingen Foundation, 1959.

Suzuki, Shunryu. *Zen Mind, Beginner's Mind*. Edited by Trudy Dixon. New York: Weatherhill, 1972.

Taizu, Ming. "Article 19." In *Sources of Chinese Tradition: From Earliest Times to 1600*. Compiled by Wm. Theodore de Bary and Irene Bloom. New York: Columbia University Press, 1999.

Taizu, Ming. "Discussion of the Three Teachings." In *Sources of Chinese Tradition: From Earliest Times to 1600*. Compiled by Wm. Theodore de Bary and Irene Bloom. New York: Columbia University Press, 1999.

Takuan Soho. "The Clear Sound of Jewels." In *The Unfettered Mind: Writings from a Zen Master to a Master Swordsman*. Translated by William Scott Wilson. New York: Kodansha International, 2002.

Taraporevala, Sooni. "Parsis—The Zoroastrians of India: A Photographic Journey." Woodstock, NY: Overlook, 2004.

Taylor, Rodney Leon. *Confucianism: Religions of the World*. New York: Chelsea House, 2004.

Teiser, Stephen F. *The Ghost Festival in Medieval China*. Princeton, NJ: Princeton University Press, 1988.

Teiser, Stephen F. "Introduction." In *Religions of China in Practice*. Edited by Donald S. Lopez Jr. Princeton, NJ: Princeton University Press, 1996.

Tempest, Rone. "Zhang Still at the Heart of Chinese Filmmaking." In *Zhang Yimou Interviews*. Edited by Frances Gateward. Jackson: University Press of Mississippi, 2001.

"Tengu." *The Obakemono Project*. www.obakemono.com/obake/tengu (accessed 28 January 2008).

Thera, Ñanamoli, trans. "Adittapariyaya Sutta." *accesstoinsight.org*, 1993, www.accesstoinsight.org/tipitaka/sn/sn35/sn35.028.nymo.html (accessed 15 February 2008).

Tokusho, Bassui. *Mud and Water: The Collected Teachings of Zen Master Bassui*, trans. Arthur Braverman. Somerville, MA: Wisdom Publications, 2002.

Tolkien, J. R. R. *The Letters of J. R. R. Tolkien*. Edited by Humphrey Carpenter and Christopher Tolkien. Boston: Houghton Mifflin, 2000.

Tolkien, J. R. R. *The Lord of the Rings: One Volume Edition*. New York: HarperCollins, 1994.

Too, Lillian. *Total Feng Shui: Bring Health, Wealth and Happiness into Your Life*. San Francisco: Chronicle Books, 2005.

Troster, Rabbi Lawrence. "From Apologetics to New Spirituality: Trends in Jewish Environmental Theology." *Coalition on the Environment and Jewish Life*. 2004, www.coejl.org/scholarship/jetheology.pdf (accessed 11 February 2008).

Tsubaki Shrine. www.tsubakishrine.com (accessed 29 January 2008).

Turner, Alice K. *The History of Hell.* New York: Harcourt Brace, 1993.

Tyler, Royall. *Japanese Tales.* New York: Pantheon Books, 1987.

Tzu, Lao. *Tao Te Ching.* Translated by D. C. Lau. London: Penguin Classics, 1963.

U.S. Catholic Church. *Catechism of the Catholic Church with Modifications from the Editio Typica.* New York: Doubleday, 1995.

"Uganda: The Return." *PBS.org.* 2007, www.pbs.org/frontlineworld/rough/2007/05/uganda_the_retuint.html (accessed 10 February 2008).

Uhls, Jim. "Fight Club." *hundland.com.* 1998, www.hundland.com/scripts/Fight-Club_third.htm (accessed 11 February 2008).

The Upanishads. Translated by Eknath Easwaran. Tomales, CA: Nilgiri Press, 2000.

"Uphold Tradition of Tolerance, says Narayanan." *Hindu.* 2002, www.hinduonnet.com/thehindu/2002/07/25/stories/2002072504370100.htm (accessed 10 February 2008).

Vames, Amy. "The Goddess of Mercy: How Kuan-yin Became a Chinese Deity." *Rutgers University Media Release.* 2001, ur.rutgers.edu/medrel/viewArticle.html?ArticleID=1967 (accessed 31 January 2008).

Verhoeven, Martin J. "Buddhism and Science: Probing the Boundaries of Faith and Reason." *Religion East and West* 1 (June 2001): 77–97.

Virgil's Aeneid. Translated by John Dryden. Harvard Classics, vol. 13. New York: P. F. Collier & Son, 1909. Also available at www.ilt.columbia.edu/academic/digitexts/vergil/aeneid/book06.html (accessed 11 February 2008).

Vreeland, Nicholas, ed. *An Open Heart: Practicing Compassion in Everyday Life.* New York: Little Brown, 2001.

Wagner, Kim A. *Thuggee: Banditry and the British in Early Nineteenth-Century India.* New York: Palgrave Macmillan, 2007.

Waley, Arthur. "Did Buddha Die of Eating Pork? With a Note on a Buddha's Image." *Melanges Chinois et Bouddhiques.* 1932, ccbs.ntu.edu.tw/fulltext/jr-mel/waley.htm (accessed 15 February 2008).

Walter, Tony, and Helen Waterhouse. "A Very Private Belief: Reincarnation in Contemporary England." *Sociology of Religion* (Summer 1999). Also available at findarticles.com/p/articles/mi_m0SOR/is_2_60/ai_55208520 (accessed 17 February 2008).

Wang, Gungwu. *Divided China: Preparing for Reunification.* Hackensack, NJ: World Scientific, 2007.

Wasson, R. Gordon, and Wendy Doniger O'Flaherty. "The Last Meal of the Buddha." *Journal of the American Oriental Society* 102, no. 4 (October 1982).

"Water." *Fox Searchlight.* 2006, http://www.foxsearchlight.com/water (accessed 10 February 2008).

Watts, Jonathan. "Traditional Teachings of Confucius Find Favor as China Looks to Fill Ethical Vacuum in Wake of Market Reforms." *The Guardian.* 2006, www.guardian.co.uk/china/story/0,,1882569,00.html (accessed 25 January 2008).

Wenger, Michael. "The Making of a Zen Mystery." *Buddhadharma: The Practitioner's Quarterly* (Winter 2006): 94.

"What Is the Bahá'í Attitude towards Science and Technological Progress?" *Bahá'í International Community*. www.bahai.org/faq/social_action/science (accessed 11 February 2008).

"White Light: Ian McKellen on the Rebirth and Revitalization of Gandalf." *lordofthe rings.net*. www.lordoftherings.net/index_editorials_gandalf.html (accessed 12 February 2008).

"White Rainbow, Emancipation of Widows." *Screen India*. 2004, www.screenindia.com/fullstory .php?content_id=7398 (accessed 10 February 2008).

White, Sidnie Ann. "Afterlife and Immortality: Second Temple Judaism and Early Christianity." In *The Oxford Companion to the Bible*. Edited by Bruce M. Metzger and Michael D. Coogan. New York: Oxford University Press, 1993.

"Who Is Kenji Miyazawa?" *kenji-world.com*. 2002, www.kenji-world.net/english/who/who.html (accessed 28 January 2008).

Wicks, Ann Elizabeth Barrott, ed. *Children in Chinese Art*. Honolulu: University of Hawaii Press, 2002.

Williams, George. *Religions of the World: Shinto*. Philadelphia: Chelsea House, 2005.

"World Factbook." *Central Intelligence Agency*. 2008, www.cia.gov/library/publications/the -world-factbook/ (accessed 14 February 2008).

"The World's Successful Diasporas." *World Business*. 2007, www.worldbusinesslive.com/ Entrepreneurship/Article/648273/the-worlds-successful-diasporas (accessed 10 February 2008).

Xi, Zhu. "Funerary Inscription for Madam You, Lady of Jia'nan." In *Sources of Chinese Tradition: From Earliest Times to 1600*. Compiled by Wm. Theodore de Bary and Irene Bloom. New York: Columbia University Press, 1999.

Xiaogan, Liu. "The Core Value in Taoism." In *Lao-tzu and the Tao-te-Ching*. Edited by Livia Kohn and Michael LaFargue. Albany: State University of New York Press, 1998.

Xiaogan, Liu. "Naturalness (*Tzu-jan*), and the Core Value in Taoism: Its Ancient Meaning and Its Significance Today." In *Lao-tzu and the Tao-te-Ching*. Edited by Livia Kohn and Michael La-Fargue. Albany: State University of New York Press, 1998.

Xiongping, Jiao. "Discussing Red Sorghum." In *Zhang Yimou Interviews*. Edited by Frances Gateward. Jackson: University Press of Mississippi, 2001.

Yamamoto, Akira Y. "Introduction." *Japanese Ghosts & Demons: Art of the Supernatural*. Edited by Stephen Addiss. New York: George Braziller, 1985.

Yamamoto, Fumiko Y., and Akira Y. Yamamoto. "Two and a Half Worlds: Humans, Animals, and In-between." *Japanese Ghosts & Demons: Art of the Supernatural*. Edited by Stephen Addiss. New York: George Braziller, 1985.

Yang, Mayfair Mei-Hui. "Of Gender, State, Censorship, and Overseas Capital: An Interview with Chinese Director Zhang Yimou." In *Zhang Yimou Interviews*. Edited by Frances Gateward. Jackson: University Press of Mississippi, 2001.

Yao, Xinzhong. *An Introduction to Confucianism.* New York: Cambridge University Press, 2000.

Yu, Chun-Fang. *Kuan-Yin: The Chinese Transformation of Avalokitesvara.* New York: Columbia University, 2001.

"Yuki-onna." *The Obakemono Project.* www.obakemono.com/obake/yukionna (accessed 28 January 2008).

Zhao, Ban. "Admonitions for Women." In *Sources of Chinese Tradition: From Earliest Times to 1600.* Compiled by Wm. Theodore de Bary and Irene Bloom. New York: Columbia University Press, 1999.

Zimmer, Heinrich. Edited by Joseph Campbell. Princeton, NJ: Princeton University Press, 1972.

Index

About the Author

Julien R. Fielding is a part-time lecturer at the University of Nebraska at Omaha, where she teaches Introduction to World Religions in the Department of Philosophy and Religion. She has a bachelor's degree in art history from the University of Nebraska at Omaha and a master's degree in religious studies from the University of Kansas at Lawrence.

Fielding's main research interest is religion and film, and she has had several articles published in the *Journal of Religion and Film*. She also has contributed three entries—a profile on Robert Bresson, religion in European cinema, and religion in Chinese films—for a soon-to-be published encyclopedia on religion and film, and book reviews for the *Journal of Religion and Popular Culture*. She is contributing two essays for a *Companion to Religion and Film*. The topics are indigenous religions in film and redemption in film. She has an infrequent podcast on religion and film at her website, www.jrfielding.com.

Additional interests include East Asian religions, particularly in China and Japan; representation of indigenous people in film; popular and folk religion in film; heretical thought; and representations of good and evil in religion, particularly images of devils, angels, heaven, and hell.